VOLCANIC

VOLCANIC

Vesuvius in the Age of
Revolutions

JOHN BREWER

YALE UNIVERSITY PRESS
NEW HAVEN AND LONDON

Endpapers: Map of Vesuvius from John Auldjo, *Sketches of Vesuvius with a short account of its principal eruptions, from the commencement of the Christian era to the present time*, Naples, 1832.

Published with assistance from the Annie Burr Lewis Fund.

Copyright © 2023 John Brewer

All rights reserved. This book may not be reproduced in whole or in part, in any form (beyond that copying permitted by Sections 107 and 108 of the U.S. Copyright Law and except by reviewers for the public press) without written permission from the publishers.

All reasonable efforts have been made to provide accurate sources for all images that appear in this book. Any discrepancies or omissions will be rectified in future editions.

For information about this and other Yale University Press publications, please contact:
U.S. Office: sales.press@yale.edu   yalebooks.com
Europe Office: sales@yaleup.co.uk   yalebooks.co.uk

Set in Adobe Caslon Pro by IDSUK (DataConnection) Ltd
Printed in Great Britain by TJ Books, Padstow, Cornwall

Library of Congress Control Number: 2023941190

ISBN 978-0-300-27266-6

A catalogue record for this book is available from the British Library.

10 9 8 7 6 5 4 3 2 1

In Memoriam
Claire L'Enfant and Andrew Wheatcroft

CONTENTS

ILLUSTRATIONS

Plates

1. Giacomo Lenghi, *Calesso di Resina*, 1820. © Victoria & Albert Museum, London.
2. Elizabeth Campbell, *The Hermitage on Vesuvius*, c. 1820. Author's collection.
3. Henry Tresham, *The Ascent of Vesuvius*, 1785–90. Yale Center for British Art, Paul Mellon Collection.
4. Visitors' Book, December 1826–October 1828. Houghton Library, Harvard University, MS Ital 139.
5. Entry and annotation for 28 April 1828, Visitors' Book, 1826–8. Houghton Library, Harvard University, MS Ital 139.
6. Penry Williams, *Festa of the Madonna dell'Arco at Naples*, 1836. Artepics / Alamy.
7. Franz Ludwig Catel, *Gulf of Naples with Fruit Merchant*, 1822. © bpk / Nationalgalerie, SMB / Andres Kilger.
8. August Kopisch, *The Crater of Vesuvius with the Eruption of 1828*, 1828. akg-images.
9. Lava medal of Salvatore Madonna from Vesuvius. Collezione Vesuviana donazione Mariano Carati c/o Museo dell'Osservatorio Vesuviano (Ercolano – Napoli).

Figures

PREFACE AND
ACKNOWLEDGEMENTS

This book has been (too) long in preparation, a time during which I have incurred many debts, made new friends and learned a great deal. The list of acknowledgements is a long one, and I ask the forbearance of anyone who has been overlooked. I've benefited from the comments and criticism of many who have read the manuscript either in part or whole. Malcolm Baker, Dehn Gilmore, Michael Goulden, Michael Hutter and Frank Trentmann were all kind enough to comment on the entire manuscript in one of its several iterations. Andrew Joncus brought his professional (and fierce) editing skills to bear on my text, though, as he knows, I did not always follow his suggestions. Ian Kumekawa's timely intervention made me reshape the text. Paola Bertucci, Bill Brewer, Lorenzo Brewer, Nicholas Cavanagh, Hal Cook, Pietro Corsi, Peter Hansen, Matthew Hunter, Myles Jackson, Kevin James, Fredrik Albritton Jonsson, Rosaly Lopes, Renaud Morieux, Sophus Reinert, Simon Schaffer, Silvia Sebastiani and Stella Tillyard all read and commented on parts of the manuscript.

I have been fortunate in the research assistance I've had in Paris from José Beltran and in Naples from Angelo Odore and especially Eleonora Meo, who helped put together materials from the Monticelli archive. In Copenhagen Dan Andersen followed up on the Danish connection; Janine Maegraith's skills of decipherment were essential for work on German materials, and Bérengère Pinaud and Francesca Antonelli on French and Italian sources. They have all saved me from many errors. At Harvard Jeremy Guillette and Gabriel Pizzorno helped me analyse the Visitors' Book data. Michael Heafford very helpfully identified some of the figures in the Vesuvius Visitors' Book.

Drafts and versions of parts of this project have been presented at Caltech, the Huntington Library and at the University of Southern California (USC). I'd especially like to thank all my colleagues for their support at Caltech, the staff and researchers at the Huntington, especially Roy Ritchie and Steve Hindle, and Peter Mancall at USC. More recently, I had the pleasure of speaking at the University of California Riverside celebration for the retirement of Malcolm Baker. I gave papers that outlined the project in its infancy in Japan (I would especially like to thank Toshio Kusamitsu, Satomi Ohashi, Chikashi Sakashita and Majima Shinobu for their help and hospitality) and in Taiwan, where Kui-Ying Huang was a wonderful host. Closer to home, I have spoken about this project in lectures and seminars at the European University Institute in Florence, the Swedish Academy in Rome, the British School in Rome, the history department of the University of Bologna, the École des Hautes Études in Paris, the History and Philosophy of Science Department in Cambridge, the Cambridge University eighteenth-century seminar, the Oxford University eighteenth-century seminar, the Courtauld Institute, the University of York, the Paul Mellon Centre in London, the Dutch working group for Italian Studies, the Harvard eighteenth-century seminar, the Harvard book history seminar and the history department, Yale University, and at the virtual workshop on Visitors' Books organised by Kevin James. I'm especially grateful to the participants in that event for their help in thinking through how to understand a largely undervalued historical source.

I have had the pleasure of holding visiting positions at the History Department of the University of Pittsburgh, hosted by the indefatigable Holger Hoock; at the École des Hautes Etudes en Science Sociale, where Jacques Revel and Silvia Sebastiani guided me through the French academic corridors of power; and at the Institute for Advanced Study at the University of Durham, which enabled me to renew acquaintance with Ludmilla Jordanova and Nicole Reinhardt and to discuss the sublime (and much else) with the engaging philosopher David Macarthur. I was a visiting fellow in the History, Literature and Cultural Studies Programme at Radboud University in Nijmegen, enjoying feedback from many scholars, including Helleke van den Braber, Jan Hein Furnée, Nathalie Haan, Olivier Hesker, Marian Janssen, Dries Lyna and Floris Meens, as well as Eric Moormann who shared his comprehensive knowledge of Pompeii. A fellowship at the Bogliasco Foundation in Italy, in the company of dancers, composers and writers of drama and fiction, stimulated my thoughts on Vesuvius as performance and spectacle.

Over the years I have benefited from the advice and guidance of scholars in fields with which I had only begun to feel familiar, notably Melissa Calaresu, John Davis and Lucy Riall on Naples, Pietro Corsi, Corinna Guerra and Simon Schaffer on science and geology.

I would especially like to thank those friends and colleagues whose support and conversation have sustained me over the years: Malcolm Baker and Jesse Carillo, Nicholas Cavanaugh, Joanna Innes, Andrew and Berta Joncus, Simon Schaffer, John Styles, Frank Trentmann and John Wyver in Britain; Iain Chambers, Davide Lombardo, Roberta Sassatelli and Flaminia Gennari Santori in Italy; Malcolm Baker (that man pops up everywhere), Dehn Gilmore, Steve Hindle, Peter Stallybrass and Cindy Weinstein in California; Ann Blair, Deirdre Lynch and Sophus Reinert in Cambridge, Massachusetts.

I'd like to add special thanks to Sabrina Hameister, my assistant at Caltech, who has worked with and for me since I arrived there in 2002. She has had the happy knack of remembering and reminding me of what I have to do, has organised many workshops and meetings, and has always been extraordinarily helpful, whatever the problem. Few combine such kindness with such efficiency.

I am grateful to the Provost of Caltech, and to the Division of Humanities and Social Sciences for their financial support.

Earlier versions of material in Chapter 1 have appeared in 'Visitors' Books and Travel Narratives: The Case of Romantic Vesuvius', *Studies in Travel Writing* 25, 3 (2023). Chapter 2 on guides includes much of the analysis in 'Visiting Vesuvius: Guides, Local Knowledge, Sublime Tourism and Science, 1760–1890', *Journal of Modern History* 93 (March 2021). Material on John Moore in Chapter 3 appeared in 'Between Distance and Sympathy: Dr John Moore's Philosophical Travel Writing', *Modern Intellectual History* 11, 3 (2014). I first sketched out the career of Teodoro Monticelli in 'Scientific Networks, Vesuvius and Politics: The Case of Teodoro Monticelli in Naples, 1790–1845', *Incontri* 34, 1 (2019). I'd like to thank the editors and readers of those articles for their support and critical commentary.

I would like to thank all at Yale University Press in London who have worked on this book, especially Heather McCallum and Katie Urquhart. Thanks also to Eve Leckey for her exemplary copyediting.

Anja Goeing deserves special thanks for her love, forbearance and guidance in living with this project and its obsessed author during its entire gestation.

This book is dedicated to two editors who sadly died while it was being written. Claire L'Enfant and Andrew Wheatcroft together edited and published six of my books. Though their careers often overlapped, they were radically different characters. Claire, whom I first met at a party in Cambridge in 1973, was a person of remarkable modesty considering her exceptional talents, quiet, shrewd in her deliberations, with an eagle eye for any nonsense. She loved publishing (she seemed to have read everything), and was an outstanding critic, a loyal friend and a gracious host. Andrew, whom I also met in Cambridge, but in the late 1960s, was a rebel, a dreamer and schemer, a bit of a bull in a china shop.

He lived a life of chaotic improvisation, though this did not prevent him from being a highly effective publisher, a firm friend, able to act with great swiftness when needed. His colourful life was also a constant source of anecdote, whether about Scotland, the Persian Gulf or China. The times I spent with Claire and Nick in Great Percy Street, and with Andrew and Janet in Lincolnshire and Scotland, are some of my most cherished memories. This book, which they both in their different ways encouraged, is for them.

INTRODUCTION

The epoch is the epoch of movement.

Friedrich Schlegel[1]

Keep moving! Steam, or Gas, or Stage,
Hold, cabin, steerage, hencoop's cage —
Tour, Journey, Voyage, Lounge, Ride, Walk,
Skim, Sketch, Excursion, Travel-talk —
For move you must! 'Tis now the rage,
The law and fashion of the Age.

Samuel Taylor Coleridge, 'The Delinquent Travellers', 1825

This book began, as so many projects do, almost by accident, the result of a serendipitous encounter. I was browsing through the holdings of the Houghton Library at Harvard while writing an essay on the Grand Tour for an exhibition that was held at the Ashmolean Museum in Oxford and at the Yale Center for British Art in New Haven. There I came across a manuscript, MS Ital 139, which claimed to be the Visitors' Book to Vesuvius and was in some way associated with the distinguished Longfellow family of New England. When I examined its contents I was astonished at what it revealed. Signature and comment upon signature opened up a world in which people of all nationalities and persuasions, and from all walks of life, expressed their feelings when confronted with one of the most powerful forces of nature. It also brought to light a complex social world of amity and hostility that encompassed visitors of different nationalities and the local guides who assisted them. I have to confess that as I scanned its pages I experienced a sense of relief. Here was a different and rich collection of experiences to set against what I had come to see as the stifling and repetitive Grand Tour story of north European gentlemen enacting a cosmopolitan nationalism rooted in antiquity, boys clutching their copies of Cicero, Virgil and Ovid, while spending, collecting, drinking and fornicating their way down the Italian peninsula. Granted, the Visitors' Book chiefly covered the third decade of the nineteenth century, when the Grand Tour was supposed to have been eclipsed by a more demotic (perhaps bourgeois) type of travel, and it described responses to a site of natural history rather than of antiquity. But it opened up the possibility of writing a more multidimensional history, one that was not dominated by a single point of view. Not that I was ever wedded to the notion that the Visitors' Book was some sort of ur-source that trumped other historical documents. On the contrary, I hoped that the insights it made possible might animate not just overlooked historical actors but other and different sorts of archive, especially those that were produced by Neapolitans themselves. What it promised was a more expansive vision of the Bay of Naples, Italy and Vesuvius in the ages of Enlightenment and Romanticism.

The result is *Volcanic*, a study of the famous Neapolitan volcano in the period between the mid-eighteenth and mid-nineteenth centuries that treats Vesuvius, dominating the Bay of Naples, not as a fixed place but as a crossroads, a site of exchange and transit that was constantly changing. The volcano was a meeting point of people, ideas and aspirations, an object of scientific inquiry and a symbol and metaphor used to express a rich variety of emotions and political views.

Never experienced, understood, imagined or represented in quite the same way or from a single perspective, Vesuvius should be seen as a fabulously rich human resource as well as, or perhaps because it was, an ungovernable force of nature. A site some kilometres south-east of the city of Naples where nature and culture confronted one another and often melded, its material environment of rock, craters, fumaroles, clinker, lava and crystals changed constantly, not just because of its seismic activity, but because of human activity linked to the volcano. These exchanges between man and nature operated on different scales and registers. They might be enacted in its immediate vicinity – by humble Neapolitans, guides and visitors of every rank and nationality on the slopes of the fiery mountain, or among the indigenous population of Europe's third-largest city. But they also occurred at a distance: in the laboratories of scientific academies and the drawing rooms of literary salons, on the stages of theatres and opera houses, on the shelves of natural history museums and collections, on the walls of art galleries, and on summer evenings at outdoor pleasure gardens.

Central to an understanding of this story are the processes of mediation discussed throughout my account: the numerous ways in which the volcano was projected to a public through personal correspondence, travel writings, journalism, literary and scientific studies, collections of rocks, lava and crystals, a vast array of graphic images, theatrical performance and via such technological novelties as the panorama and diorama. We can imagine this as an explosive dispersal in which versions and parts of the volcano were scattered through Europe and into the New World, but we can also see the volcano as a site of intensification, where different forces and values congealed.

What happened on Vesuvius was never purely local. What makes a place distinctive, what gives it a locus and identity, are the pathways that lead to and from it, and the people and goods that flow along them. In the anthropologist James Clifford's formulation, routes

create roots.[2] These pathways were not only geographical and topographical, taken by the sail- and steamships that reached Naples
from foreign ports, or the footpaths, mule tracks, roads and then railways that connected the volcano to Naples and a larger world. They
were created through texts, objects, images and people that moved
back and forth between Vesuvius and its vast hinterland. Much of
this book, though focused on one place, is therefore about the nature
and effects of movement. It is itself a journey in which we travel from
the slopes of the volcano, through the networks of science and into
the cities of Europe and the New World. The fascination with
Vesuvius and the experience it offered was fed by an urban culture of
spectacle that used a wide range of technologies to create a virtual
reality that simulated the experience of confronting the volcano.

It is a major claim of this book that the volcano and the classical
cities it buried during the eruption of 79 CE should be understood as
part of a highly contentious history that was both local – about
Neapolitan society, politics, science and religion – and international –
about the politics of European regimes, the history of the earth, and the
place of science in society. The optics here therefore involve closeness
and distance: we move back and forth between the volcano and a larger
world, tracing the connections and links between the two. In Part I, a
detailed account of who came to Vesuvius, what they were doing there
and how they understood their experiences on the mountain, I use a
microhistory of Vesuvian visitors to challenge prevailing views about
the history of travel and tourism, complicating the connection between
voluntary or leisure travel and other forms of human migration. Visitors
to Vesuvius were never isolated from the turbulence of an era dominated
by European warfare, conflicting political ideologies and the displacement and movement of peoples. Aristocratic Neapolitans, Swiss mercenaries, English entrepreneurs, Austrian and German soldiers, French
traders and writers, Italian, English and Danish geologists, American
politicians and literati, Russian and German architects and painters,
along with a bevy of tourists, local guides and tradesmen, all found their

way to the slopes of the volcano. The mountain bubbled and seethed not just with lava, but with men and women whose passions, interests and aims were as disparate as their origins. The volcano was an end point – no one climbed Vesuvius to get somewhere else – but it was also often one stopping place in a journey towards some larger end. Using the Visitors' Book to the volcano, analysing the 2,300 travellers who signed and commented in its pages, *Volcanic* reconstructs and charts the changing seismic and social dynamics on the mountain, and the meanings attached by travellers to their sublime confrontation with nature.

A concatenation of circumstances prompted the Romantic preoccupation with the volcano. During these years Vesuvius was persistently active, but rarely very dangerous, making it an ideal object of what I call 'sublime tourism'. More generally, the Bay of Naples, Vesuvius and its surroundings were an ideal site for the Romantic preoccupation with the self and nature, with the ways in which different environments affected feelings and encouraged the exploration of emotions. This is usually treated as a personal phenomenon, but the case of Vesuvius points in another direction, one that repeatedly connects being in nature not just to individual exultation but to the importance of shared emotions and friendship, a subject examined in Part II. These were particularly pressing issues in a period of political turmoil when the much-travelled were repeatedly confronted with problems of closeness and distance – the issue of how to maintain attachments when far away from home and how to form friendships with strangers who were much closer to hand.

The pyrotechnics of political revolution and global warfare made volcanic activity the perfect metaphor or analogy for the dynamics of the geopolitical world, fuelling revolutionary enthusiasm and conservative trepidation. As we see in Part III, contemporary eruptions were construed as manifestations of destructive but regenerative power, justifications of violent revolutions as 'natural'. The Enlightenment view that volcanic action was at heart beneficial, even if it brought short-term misfortune, was taken up by radical proponents of revolution, who argued that wholescale insurrection was not just a political and social necessity but a normal transformative process. The destruction of property and the killing of persons was deemed a regrettable if inevitable loss as 'nature' took its course. The question of whether geological change was inherently gradual or abrupt, incremental or sudden and precipitous, became more than a matter of natural history. Geology, and especially vulcanism, was therefore never without its politics. The pursuit of volcanic sciences could be a dangerous business. The dashing Frenchman Déodat de Dolomieu and the gregarious Neapolitan Teodoro Monticelli, two of the most important vulcanologists of the late eighteenth and early nineteenth centuries, spent years incarcerated by the Neapolitan monarchy.

In the eighteenth century, enlightened scholars became more and more interested in the role of fire and heat in changing the earth. As we see in Part IV, the local scientific investigation of Vesuvius and its pyrotechnic activities was increasingly linked to geological debates in the academies and scientific societies of Europe and the New World. Neapolitan knowledge about the volcano was disseminated as well as informed by transcontinental networks of knowledge, orchestrated by figures such as Monticelli. His enormous correspondence is only the most conspicuous (though previously overlooked) instance of the part played by local Neapolitan figures in promoting knowledge of the volcano. The work of such internationally recognised figures such as Dolomieu, Sir William Hamilton, Alexander von Humboldt, Humphry Davy and Charles Lyell would not have been possible without their active support.

In using the term 'Romantic Vesuvius', I am trying to capture the many ways in which Vesuvius and its surroundings were understood and the ways in which they changed between the mid-eighteenth and mid-nineteenth centuries. The unpredictable activity of the volcano; the vagaries of European and Neapolitan politics; the movement, both forced and voluntary, of different peoples; the shifting state of vulcanological, historical and archaeological knowledge; changing tastes; the developing technologies and economies of representation: they all have their distinctive and different chronologies, though they often intersect, albeit differently at different times.

The history of the philosophical investigation of Vesuvius reverts to the 1631 eruption, the most destructive since antiquity, which sparked some of the first extended inquiries into its workings. But the arc of my study begins in the 1740s – shortly after the Kingdom of Naples acquired its independence from Spanish suzerainty, when royal excavations of the 'buried cities' (Herculaneum and Pompeii) began in earnest, and when the classics of Enlightenment literature, such as Buffon's *Natural History* and Diderot and d'Alembert's *Encyclopédie* (with its influential entries on volcanoes, Vesuvius and more generally on the mineral world) first appeared.[3] And it stretches to the 1840s – when Naples hosted the Seventh Congress of Italian Scientists and opened the scientific observatory on the slopes of the volcano, and when the revolt in Naples against the absolute monarch was put down by Swiss mercenaries whose favourite recreation was to climb the volcano.

The fulcrum of this study lies in the 1820s. The opening year of that decade saw the brief establishment of a constitutional regime in Naples; two years later it witnessed the most violent eruption of Vesuvius in the nineteenth century. The decade also saw the rapid proliferation of stories and spectacles about the eruption of 79 CE and the buried cities, published and staged in major European cities. The science of Vesuvius was notably enriched by the publication of the *Prodromo della mineralogia vesuviana*, a remarkable, comprehensive catalogue of Vesuvian rocks and crystals, and by the visits to the volcano of the famous savants Alexander von Humboldt, Scipione Breislak, Alexandre Brongniart, Humphry Davy, Charles Babbage and Charles Lyell. At the same time, Vesuvian tourism was consolidated in the hands of a small group of humbly-born families living on its slopes. Equally importantly, the Visitors' Book to Vesuvius, an invaluable source with its signatures and comments, survives for the period between late 1826 and the end of 1828, providing a uniquely detailed account of activity on the volcano.[4]

The landscape of Romantic Vesuvius underwent many changes. There was a growing disjunction between Neapolitans on the volcano and the larger public and scientific community. Vesuvius's guides, who linked local information to scientific knowledge, and international visitors to the local economy, were gradually marginalised or replaced by new technologies – modern roads, the railway, the seismograph. Thanks to the comforts of organised tourism, the trip up the slopes of Vesuvius lost its romantic adventurousness; instruments replaced local people as guides to scientific investigation. The revolutionary idea of the volcano as a *natural* force came to be opposed and largely superseded by a *historical* view of Vesuvius, based on the evolving excavation and story of the fate of the antique cities – Herculaneum, Stabia and, above all, Pompeii – during the massive Vesuvian eruption of 79 CE. Vesuvius was construed as a destroyer of the wicked but also as a conservator of spiritual values, giving rise to a plethora of conservative, moralising stories and images of human catastrophe of which Edward Bulwer-Lytton's *The Last Days of Pompeii* (1834) is perhaps the most famous example. This Vesuvian story has been handed down to us as *the* story of Vesuvius but, as I show in Part VI, it was far from politically innocent.

What visitors to Vesuvius and Naples wrote, depicted and inscribed, what rocks and lava, images and engravings they collected and dispersed throughout much of Europe, not only placed Vesuvius and the buried cities at the heart of contemporary debates about politics, science and taste, but helped shape a virtual Naples, untethered from its Neapolitan surroundings, dispersed and displayed in panoramas, dioramas and exhibition spaces, and re-enacted in public pleasure gardens, as well as scientific lecture rooms and the stage. This commodified nature, the subject of Chapter 13, professed no politics; it became a celebration of the human power to manipulate nature, feeding into a nineteenth-century myth of environmental control whose hubris continues to haunt us.

I use 'Romantic Vesuvius' as a chronological and descriptive term, a generic label rather than one that sees the volcano in this period as a product of 'Romanticism'. Romantic Vesuvius was full of tensions and contradictions: dispassionate observation and a highly aestheticised and emotional view of nature; anti-academic art and neo-classicism; competing versions of the history of the earth and of classical antiquity; conflicting views of politics and nationhood. It is the contradictions that should command our attention, not the exercise of separating them out and tossing them into neat boxes.

The cult of Vesuvius and the buried cities was complex, its contours multifaceted, its meaning bitterly contested, its makers not only Vesuvius itself but the geologists, archaeologists, savants, clergymen, guides, visitors, artists, literary figures, travel writers, merchants, politicians and humble *contadini* (peasants) who lived, either literally or metaphorically, in its shadow, and struggled to understand the relations of nature and culture, history, religion and science. Though it would be absurd to suggest that the volcano and its remains – both geological and human – were an exclusive obsession of an age preoccupied (and with very good reason) with time, history, loss, mortality and the unpredictability of both human society and the natural order of things, there are good historical reasons, both local and far afield, why Vesuvius and its victims should feature so prominently in such Romantic narratives.

Like several of my earlier works, *Volcanic: Vesuvius in the Age of Revolutions* combines archival research with a critical synthesis of existing scholarship. It draws on the techniques of science studies, art history, literary studies, political and social history, biography and microhistory. Given its breadth it inevitably mines a rich vein of published research in such fields as the history and literature of travel, the history of geology, the history of Naples, and the history of antiquity in the eighteenth and nineteenth centuries. Without such studies this book would not have been possible. But at the heart of the book lies not only the volcano itself, but the rich Neapolitan sources that enable us to see the international importance of what Neapolitans affectionately referred to as '*il nostro Vesuvio*'.

PROLOGUE
The Journey to Vesuvius

In the late eighteenth and early nineteenth centuries, travellers agreed that no visit to Naples was complete without a trip to Vesuvius.[1] But how to get there, how to reach what the French doctor Charles Flandin called 'this wonder ... the glory of Naples'?[2] For the wealthy the journey was quite simple: take your private carriage if not from the old city then from the wealthy seafront suburbs of Chiaia or Mergellina, from the nearby village of Vomero, or from one of the growing number of hotels at Santa Lucia – like the Crocelle, the Vittoria, the Grand Bretagne and Hotel Roma – and travel the 10 kilometres south-eastwards on the coastal road towards the volcano. But the cheapest option (and easiest until the opening of the railway to Portici in 1839) was to pay for a seat on a *corricolo* or *calesso* (the terms for the type of carriage are virtually interchangeable) (Plate 1). Like much that happened in Naples, the journey was exhilarating, mildly terrifying and part of local legend. The vehicle itself was, in the words of the French painter and engraver Antoine Castellan, 'a sort of shell-shaped cabriolet, uncovered, extremely light, and dragged by an improbably small horse, but which is full of ardour and speed.'[3] To one observer, 'The horse's head, the harness, and the live freight within, bedizened with gilding, and ribbons, and flowers of all imaginable

colours', made it look 'like a runaway flower-pot'.[4] Originally intended for one or two passengers, and with only two wheels, its load, as
Alexandre Dumas explained in his travelogue titled after 'this fantas-
tical machine', was often more cumbrous. His picaresque account is
worth quoting in full:

> First, almost invariably, a fat monk is seated in the middle, forming
> the centre of this coil of human beings. On one of his knees is
> some blooming nurse from Aversa or Neptuno, on the other,
> some handsome peasant woman from Bauci or Procida. On either
> side of him, between the wheels and the body of the vehicle, stand
> the husbands of these ladies. Behind the monk, on tip-toe, is the
> driver, holding, in his left hand, the reins, and, in his right, the
> long whip, with which he keeps the horse at an equal rate of
> speed. Behind the latter, after the manner of footmen, are two or
> three *lazzaroni*, who get up and down, go away and are succeeded
> by others, without ever being asked to pay for their ride. On the
> shafts are seated two boys; supernumerary *ciceroni* of Herculaneum
> and Pompeii, or guides to the antiquities of Cumae or Baiae,
> picked up on the road from Torre del Greco, or Pozzuoli. Finally,
> suspended under the axle of the carriage, in a sort of coarse rope
> net-work, with large meshes, which jolts up and down and swings
> in every direction, stirs a shapeless mass, which cries, laughs, sings,
> screams, shouts and bellows, and which it is impossible to see
> distinctly amidst the clouds of dust raised by the horse's feet. This
> mass consists of three or four children who belong, no one knows
> to whom; who go, no one knows where; who live, no one knows
> upon what; who are there, no one knows how; and who remain
> there, no one knows why.[5]

This tumultuous scene was often rendered graphically. Indeed Dumas's
description may well have been taken from a local print. Neapolitan
art publishers, most notably the firm of Gatti and Dura, produced

numerous lithographs and aquatints of the *calesso* or *corricolo* crammed with passengers en route to Resina (modern-day Herculaneum), where the ascent of the volcano began.

Thus the conveyance, which even an official (and exceptionally enthusiastic) guide to Naples admitted was 'more convenient and fast than secure'. Now the route. Leaving the city in a southerly direction, the traveller crossed the wide, five-arched bridge over the river Sebito, the Ponte della Maddalena, with its eighteenth-century statues of San Giovanni Nepomuceno (the protector of those in risk of drowning) and San Gennaro, the patron saint of the city, with his 'potent arm' upraised towards Vesuvius, as if to forbid (as he was often believed to have done) the volcano's destructive power from reaching Naples. Passing what was once a royal granary, the road followed the shoreline through densely populated villages, though the travellers' view of the sea was largely obscured by the many opulent villas and their splendid gardens that lapped the shore and stretched down the coast and beyond to Torre del Greco. These were the summer homes and residences built by royal courtiers, the Neapolitan aristocracy, who followed the Kings and Queens of Naples whose summer residence after 1742 was the nearby Palace at Portici. The road running southward to Salerno passed through the main courtyard of the palace and then entered the town of Resina, the home of the guides to Vesuvius. Most visitors headed to the Piazza della Fontana, turning into a courtyard surrounded by two buildings and a stable, the property of the head guide, who for most of this period was a member of the Madonna or Cozzolino families.

By the 1820s, this journey had acquired a fixed and well-known itinerary, described in many guidebooks and travel memoirs, its defining moment the scene at Resina when travellers from Naples entered the courtyard and were engulfed by what a visiting Knight of Malta called the 'dependents of the Kingdom of Vesuvius'.[6] Visitors had to haggle with a small army of importunate men, women and young children who spilled out into the square, bargaining for donkeys (with colourful names like 'Macaroni', 'Rostbif' and 'Lacryma Christi') and guides to take them up the mountain, or for *chaises à porteurs*, chairs suspended between poles that were used to carry the frail, the elderly, the indolent and any woman who did not want to attempt the hike on foot. The scene was variously described as 'a merry-go-round', 'a cried fair' and 'a battle', the noise as 'uproarious' and 'exceeding in . . . hubbub the uproar and buzz which a thousand hives of bees . . . might be supposed to make'.[7] In the late 1820s the teenage Genevan Catherine-Valérie Boissier depicted the commotion as an exhilarating piece of theatre, with one of the guides, waving a thick bludgeon, seizing the reins of her family's carriage, stammering in bad French, 'Let's go . . . let's go to Vesuvius', while others cried out '*Io* . . . beautiful guide! . . . guide *comfortable!*', while another slapped the saddle of his ass, calling out, 'Tonight he's yours'. Her account relishes the enormity of it all: 'The multitude was growing; the donkeys, the beggars, the women without noses, the children in rags, the scabies, the ringworm, the lepers.'[8] Abject and importunate poverty was ubiquitous. It was this scene that many years earlier, in the winter of 1818–19, had terrified the poet Percy Bysshe Shelley, confirming his view of modern Italians as 'degraded, disgusting & odious'.[9] Lady Blessington, Irish beauty, friend of Byron and author of *The Idler in Italy*, who lived in Naples between 1823 and 1826, took a more distanced view, comparing the spectacle to a canvas by such great genre painters as William Hogarth or James Wilkie. Arriving in a party of eight travellers, she found herself and her companions with:

sixteen asses, attended by twice as many men and boys, followed by their mothers, wives, sisters, daughters . . . vociferating loudly the most hyperbolical commendations of theirs, and the most unqualified abuse of the animals of their competitors. The dresses of this animated group were composed of the gaudiest colours, and were sufficiently tattered to satisfy the most ardent admirer of the picturesque.[10]

Blessington's tongue-in-cheek tone alerts us to the possibility, not admitted by many visitors (who, like Shelley, often seem to have been genuinely frightened by the scene) that the theatre in the courtyard and piazza was, in the words of Marianne Talbot, a young English woman resident of Naples, 'the usual scene of noise, scramble, and quarrel',[11] a performance enacted for the visitors' benefit, one the guides knew fitted into many travellers' preconceptions of Neapolitan plebeian ways.

Once the bargaining was complete (though as we shall see, it usually persisted up the mountain), the visitors, most mounted on asses, some stalwarts on foot, and others tossed about on their *chaises à porteurs*, headed uphill, through the town and along a street that soon reached fields and lanes full of rich vegetation. As the Danish dancer and choreographer August Bournonville told his daughter, 'Chestnuts, figs, mulberries, apricot trees and, above all, vines that produce the superb Lacryma Christi, grow here with matchless luxuriance, while fences are adorned with cactus and flowering plants.' The trees 'generally extend their boughs over the pathway, making in many places a shady avenue'. Or, as one prosaic Englishman remarked (probably erroneously), the land was so fertile that it rented for £10 an acre.[12]

But as the travellers reached the lower slopes of the volcano, the landscape began to change; the rich volcanic soil and the abundant fruits it nurtured were increasingly intersected with swathes of lava, the remnants of earlier eruptions, cutting through the fertile fields. The visitor contemplated layer after layer of dark, twisted whorls, whose history, neatly attached to the dates of previous volcanic outbursts, was told by the guides. It reminded the visitor that what they saw was a landscape always in flux.

The greater the ascent, the bleaker and darker the landscape became. Jean-Marie Roland de la Platière, in an often-cited description from the 1770s, made the change clear: 'No more vegetation: everything on the contrary announced the destruction and reversal of nature. One looked back from time to time, to catch one's breath: what a spectacle! The richest, most abundant, most magnificent that there is in the world.'[13] This transition from fecundity to barrenness, from light to dark and from life to death, was most famously expressed by Madame de Staël in her bestselling novel and travelogue, *Corinne, ou l'Italie* (1807):

> The country at the foot of Vesuvius is the most fertile and best cultivated of the kingdom most favoured by heaven in all Europe. The celebrated Lacryma Christi vine flourishes beside land totally devastated by lava, as if nature here made a last effort and resolved to perish in her richest array. As you ascend you turn to gaze on Naples and on the fair land around it – the sea sparkles in the sun as if strewn with jewels; but all the splendours of creation are extinguished by degrees as you enter the region of ashes and of smoke, that announces your approach to the volcano. The iron waves of other years have traced their large black furrows in the soil. At a certain height birds are no longer seen, farther on plants become very scarce, then even insects find no nourishment. At last all life disappears, you enter the realm of death and the slain earth's dust alone slips beneath your unassured feet.[14]

The boldness of de Staël's contrast is overdrawn but was not forgotten. Half a century later, and after much repetition, it was echoed in the reaction of Selina Bunbury, the prolific Anglo-Irish evangelical author, describing her return from the summit: 'What a contrast was this [rich land] to the upper region of the mountain! A scene of perfect desolation! . . . There is no vegetation – no sign of life.'[15]

But before the visitor approached the crater, they usually paused at the hermitage of San Salvatore, seen by travellers as a place of rest and a beauty spot on their journey to the summit of the volcano (Plate 2). The hermitage had been built high up on the mountain in the 1650s, 600 metres above sea level, by fugitives from the plague who erected San Salvatore on a site close to where an earlier and smaller hermitage had been largely destroyed in the terrible Vesuvian eruption of 1631.[16] It occupied 'one spot ... which always seems to have escaped destruction ... a long shoulder stretching out from the foot of the crater, and which seems itself like a little mountain planted on the side of Vesuvius.' Made up of 'strata above strata of ashes, [at the] very extremity of the green knoll is placed a neat, white-washed building, surrounded with trees, the famous Hermitage of Mount Vesuvius.' August Bournonville described his first sighting of the building: 'After an hour's climb we reached the famous hermitage, which is shaded by mighty chestnut and oak trees ... [it] looks like a well-built farmhouse.' It was surrounded by 'a dozen little shrines ... erected in imitation of Mount Calvary'.[17] Galignani's *Guide* of 1824 described the hermitage as:

> a neat plain white building of two stories, having a parapet front, in a small arch of which a bell is suspended. It is divided into three parts; at one end, a pair of folding doors open into the chapel; the centre is the habitation of two or three friars, and a sort of yard gate at the other end, having a small room over it, leads into the offices of the building. Its inhabitants are never without the society from among the neighbouring peasantry, who cultivate the celebrated vineyards of Somma in the vicinity.[18]

To other visitors it was 'the halfway house to heaven' and the 'casa bianca'.

Its chapel was where, as one correspondent put it, 'at certain seasons, religious processions from Naples and the neighbouring villages climb to the hermitage to celebrate the anniversaries of some of their saints.' The building also contained a comfortable parlour where a Visitors' Book that travellers were invited to sign was kept on a desk, and whose sofas, as guests complained, were infested with bugs. There were also a number of rooms that could accommodate visitors overnight, affording privacy to a French couple on their honeymoon and accommodating groups like the English party of Captain Cator, Mrs Cator and Miss Basset who slept at the hermitage on 4–5 March 1828 before waking very early 'to see the sun rise'.[19]

When the German playwright Kotzebue visited what he called 'the friendly Hermitage' in 1805 he found the walls covered in decorations:

An expert artist had been there some time before; and had sketched with charcoal, over the chimney piece, the good-natured face of the host, as large as life. He had probably been in the company with Lucien Bonaparte [Napoleon's older brother], for the latter with his wife, and several other French faces, were drawn round about in great medallions on the walls.[20]

A generation later such decoration had gone. Harriet Morton, an English Protestant evangelical with a hypersensitivity to all things superstitious or Catholic – for her much the same thing – observed that the hermit's possessions included two crucifixes, a print of 'La Santa Maria', and a book entitled *L'amico fidele*.[21] Visual renderings of the exterior of the hermitage and its surroundings – watercolours, lithographs and engravings – were almost always depicted as 'picturesque', giving it the appearance of a rural cottage or farm.[22] Its fame was such that when the leading painter of the local Posillipo School, Giacinto Gigante, gave lessons to the children of the royal family, he chose the hermitage and its site as one of the subjects they should study and copy.

Visitors arriving at the hermitage often rested their asses, sometimes changed guides, and prepared themselves for the final part of the journey – a walk of about an hour to the foot of the cinder cone of the volcano, followed by its strenuous ascent. The hermits welcomed them, offering food and drink. There was no fixed tariff, they were treated as gifts, but the hermits expected and, if necessary demanded, a good reward; they were essentially innkeepers. This was certainly the view of Madame de Staël, who dismissively wrote in her journal: 'the hermit is nothing more than an inn-keeper'.[23] The American writer James Fenimore Cooper concurred: 'One who has the appearance of a monk lives there, and administered to our wants, for which consolation we punctually paid. His whole manner was that of an official of the bar, rather than of the altar.'[24] The German painter August Kopisch took a dimmer view, calling the hermit 'a pious robber', who sold Lacryma Christi by the bottle at prices that varied by the hour.[25] A French visitor described the hermitage as *'une guinguette'* or a country café. When visitors first arrived, they were usually served glasses of Lacryma Christi, the famous wine made from grapes harvested on the slopes of Vesuvius. Sometimes they were served food (Stendhal, who described the wine as undrinkable, ate an omelette), provided at what Alexandre Dumas later described as exorbitant prices, and they could, if space permitted, then nap in one of the hermitage's rooms before setting off for the volcano's crater in the early hours of the morning, returning after sunrise to eat breakfast. Visitors were advised to travel at night. An Italian guidebook of 1790 recommended waiting until the heat of the day had passed, arriving at the summit after sunset; the air was cooler and the lava and fire of Vesuvius were more spectacular in the dark.

English visitors, many of whom had a strong aversion to Italian food – they hated the oil and garlic – usually brought their own cold collation up the mountain, but most visitors, especially the Italians, relished the meals and drink.[26] One German's terse comment written in the Visitors' Book for 26 November 1827 reveals his priorities – 'I came, I drank, I saw, I drank' (*'veni, bibi, vedi, bibi'*) – and a year later a party of three Italians managed to consume twelve bottles of wine. The hermits were especially busy providing meals for parties of Italians celebrating saints' days in September and October. No other nationality dwelt so lovingly – or critically – upon the hermit's food. To one party the hermit served 'an excellent timpano [baked pasta pie], a sausage sauce, roast veal and most excellent frittata'. Another group of ten from Naples praised the hermit's food to the skies: they ate, they recorded, a 'priceless' roast of veal, sausage, while the 'usual frittata' was 'beyond value'. The side dishes included 'excellent' salad, salami, olives and *caciocavallo* (a Neapolitan cheese). 'The appetite', the entry concludes, 'makes you grateful for any dish ever made by the Hermit.'[27] One can not only taste the food but hear the banter and playfulness of these Neapolitan entries in the Visitors' Book, the cheerful familiarity and collective gusto.

During the autumn season the hermitage was busy; when an eruption occurred it was often crowded, with visitors spilling out onto the surrounding grounds. During the eruption of 1822, the largest of the nineteenth century, the two hermits hired three helpers to cope with the trade: 'A great number were assembled within, and guides, *lazzaroni*, servants and soldiers, were lounging around.' Outside, Austrian soldiers, part of the army of occupation, 'assembled in groups, some standing, some sitting, and some stretched on the ground and wrapped in their cloaks'. An English visitor recalled that 'At the Hermitage [there] was a confusion of tongues, which every language in Europe aided, calling and shouting for refreshment'.[28]

The hermits who welcomed visitors – by the early nineteenth century they were so busy that at least two were regularly in residence – were shadowy and shady characters, though many visitors seem to have thought of them as men of God if not members of a religious order. The Irish novelist and travel writer Lady Morgan described the two hermits in 1820 as Franciscan monks.[29]

The first recorded hermit, an Italian from Alessandria in the region of Piedmont, was in residence in 1667. On their visits to Vesuvius in the 1760s, two French travellers, the astronomer Joseph-Jérôme Lalande and the painter and engraver Jean-Claude Richard, Abbé de Saint-Non, identified the hermit as Father Claude Veleine or Velene from Amiens, a former soldier who had got himself into trouble and was forced into vagrancy. Another French traveller, Pierre

Brussel, though he enjoyed Father Claude's food and wine, dismissed him as a wretch and a liar. Veleine died in 1773.[30]

In the 1790s, when there were already two hermits, the younger one was described as tall with a flushed complexion and a black beard, assuming the air 'more of the sinner than the penitent'. The Scottish army officer Captain David Sutherland found the older hermit perplexing. He wrote:

> Father Pietro, the hermit received us with great hospitality; and although turned eighty, he is by no means insensible to those charms of society which are consistent with the gravity of his order. He seemed a person of liberal education, spoke with great judgment of the ancients, and was well informed of the state of Europe at the time of his retirement.

However, 'In the course of the conversation, he mentioned his having been in England, which led us to inquire in what capacity. Conceive our surprise, when this venerable sage told us he had been a French hairdresser.'[31] A few years earlier he had reminded the writer and friend of Dr Johnson, Hester Piozzi, the former Mrs Thrale, that he had dressed her hair in London.

There was always a whiff of scandal or oddity about the hermits. Lady Holland, who ascended Vesuvius in 1793, recorded that 'We all wrote our names at the Hermitage, a retreat inhabited by a man clothed in a holy garb, but whom report says is not sanctified in his deeds; many rendezvous are kept in his neat trim cell, and but for his paying he would be expelled from his nominal solitude.' Lord Holland identified this hermit as Alexandre Sauveur, a teacher of Italian, who had retired to Vesuvius from Berlin when his illicit (and unrequited) passion for one of his pupils, a German princess, had been discovered.[32] Stendhal reported that the hermit of the first decade of the nineteenth century was regarded as a converted bandit, though it is unclear whether this was intended literally, or merely as a comment on the inflated prices he charged for food and drink. There was a persistent rumour that the tall, handsome young hermit and former soldier who greeted Chateaubriand on one of his visits to Vesuvius and who often flirted with women visitors had murdered his predecessor to secure his post. The wife of a British Peninsula War veteran, Harriet Dennison, visiting the hermitage in 1816, refused the hermit's offers of drink – 'we had heard much of his propensity to cheat' – and was amused 'by seeing him sit down at his desk, and pretend to be very busy writing about the Mountain, saying he had to send an account of its health every day to Naples, when on inspection we found he had not written a single word'.[33] Her (incorrect) implication was that he was illiterate. A similar ambiguity surrounded the hermits of the 1820s, one of whom hailed from Corsica. A Frenchman from Dijon praised this 'simple and virtuous hermit' who offered him a drink and fed him, but another entry commented, in the sort of linguistic pastiche that was not uncommon in the Visitors' Book, that 'the monk das is her is a gode mann but what leads a debauche live'.[34]

But we must take our leave of the hermitage and proceed on our climb. The way from its door to the summit followed a pathway along a ridge which could always be navigated on foot and sometimes on the back of an ass. Yet, as visitors made their way across more lava fields, the route grew more hazardous and difficult until it reached the foot of the volcano's cone. This last part of the journey, wading through ash, cinders and clinker that gave way at every footstep, was, as one climber complained, an 'inexhaustible fatigue'. Even the fittest and strongest found the ascent hard: 'A more fatiguing task mortal man never undertook', commented one young American sailor.[35] The reaction of the English traveller and author Henry Swinburne was typical: 'Before that day I had mounted some very exalted points of the Alps, and clambered up the highest peaks of the Pyrenees, without feeling such oppressive weariness and exhaustion of spirits and strength as I experienced on Vesuvius.'[36] The briefest pause led the climber to slip backwards, making the ascent like climbing 'a sandhill',

21

while the sulphurous fumes made it hard to breathe: 'The wind, the smoke, and the steepness of the slopes, interrupt the breathing in a very uncomfortable manner', complained the boyhood friend and cousin of Stendhal, Romain Colomb, during his ascent in 1828.[37]

It was at this juncture that the guides came into their own, wrapping belts around their charges and dragging them forcefully to the summit (Plate 3). As the *New Guide* of 1826 explained, guides 'who are generally strong and active, then present to the travellers girdles, which are attached to their own backs, and in this way proceed towards the summit'. 'Travellers,' it warned, 'would be in imminent danger of falling, were they not to take the necessary precaution of thus fastening themselves to the girdles of their conductors.'[38] It was also possible, though at much greater expense, to be carried on a sedan chair, accompanied by a crew of eight men, 'a means practiced by many people, especially by ladies, for whom indeed the walking up would be too painful'. The Duke of Buckingham, who ascended the volcano on 22 March 1828 at the height of an eruption, and who was famously obese, known as the '*gros marquis*' and much worse besides, had to be carried up the cone of the mountain in such a *chaise à porteur* by a twelve-man team of guides, who changed every ten minutes. Years later, the chief guide Salvatore Madonna told Charles Greville, that from carrying the Duke 'his shoulder was afterwards swelled up nearly to his head'.[39]

A visitor's experience at the summit varied, of course, with the state of the volcano. At times Vesuvius was virtually silent (though on such occasions travellers were much less numerous), often it threw out occasional explosions, and sometimes it was in full eruption. Paradoxically, the greater the volcano's activities and the greater the danger, the larger the number at the summit. When the young German Romantic poet Wilhelm Waiblinger arrived at the cone during the eruption of spring 1828, he found '30–40 people who had ascended to enjoy the spectacle'; on a busy day on the volcano the numbers were even greater.[40]

Most of these spectators responded with a mixture of fear, apprehension and awe. The reaction of one American, Abraham Reeves Jackson, was typical: 'The broken ground; the smoke; the sense of suffocation of the sulphur; the fear of falling through the crevices in the yawning ground; and the magnificent kaleidoscope of beautiful colors brought before the view on every side – what words can paint the gloom, and grandeur, and beauty of the scene!'[41] The volcano's powers were utterly absorbing. As the Duke of Buckingham put it, 'The effect of the scene was at first so awful as to take away all feeling but that of dread, and all recollection save that of the scene before our eyes.' The constant barrage of sound – 'no thunder, no mortal forge ever produced noise so appalling', the periodic explosions sending rocks into the air, the smell, and the 'shaking of the whole mountain so incessant and obvious' filled the Duke – and many others – with a stupefaction that he found difficult to control.[42]

As the artist David Wilkie explained in a letter to his brother, purportedly written on the lip of the crater in March 1826, the experience affected all the senses. 'This extraordinary phenomenon is now before me', he writes, 'and in the midst of every inconvenience and a crowd of people, I must still write to say that it surpasses all expectation.' Searching for an analogy, he writes, 'It is like looking down an immense mortar, or the interior of a deep draw-kiln for burning lime.'[43] Its grandeur is conveyed not just by sight, but sound and smell. 'It resounds to the hallo of our guides with a remarkable and sonorous echo; to the ear it occasionally gives a hissing sound from the gallery of rubbish; while the smell is regaled with the sublime effluvia of burning brimstone.'[44]

The conditions at the top of the volcano changed constantly; circumstances were often less threatening and less spectacular. But even when relatively quiescent, the heart of the volcano amazed its visitors. The brilliance and variety of the colours in the crater, all the more vivid when compared with the surrounding lava, and all the more unexpected by many travellers, made an especially strong impression. Young James Forbes, the aspiring Scottish scientist, admired 'deep beds of yellow sulphur varying in colour from the deepest red orange . . . to the palest colours where alum predominated' and contrasted 'white depositions of great size' with 'black and purple porphory', and 'green colour glittering through with micaceous particles' with the 'deep brown *brescia* on volcanic ashes'.[45] Others marvelled at 'fantastic shapes into which lava is moulded in oozing out from the crevices and mouths of its natural furnace'.[46] Above all the bottom of the crater, whose depth was constantly shifting, 'the burning gulf, viewless and fathomless'[47] as one English visitor described it, excited thoughts not just of the forces of nature, but of their scope and immense power when compared with the human condition. The Frenchman J.M.L. Borel, visiting in the spring of 1824 when the volcano was comparatively quiet, felt his own fragility and that of all human life:

> In the midst of these enormous masses and their sublime deformities, [man] discovers that he is really an atom! The agents of destruction that growl around him seem made only to form storms and to launch lightning. Convulsive efforts took place in the mysterious bosom of Vesuvius, while we were on its flank, separated from an abyss of fire and flame only by shifting light ash.[48]

Peering into a crater that had 'often vomited death and desolation' prompted thoughts on the vanity of human wishes and on the brief and transitory nature of human life. On their way to the summit, travellers had stumbled across the layers of Vesuvian lava, whose strata told a very old story that extended far back before human history. Many of those who went on to record their experiences showed that they were mindful of 'deep time', of a history of the earth that dwarfed the timescale of man's presence on earth. Equally importantly, they were mindful that natural and historical changes involved destruction. The young Maximilian, brother of the Austrian emperor Franz Joseph

I, and the ill-fated future Emperor of Mexico, was a nineteen-year-old lieutenant in the Austrian navy when he climbed Vesuvius in 1851 in the company of his shipmates. The crater astonished him: 'I was overpowered by the inconceivably mysterious spell of the subterranean working', prompting him to reflect that 'it is the language of nature that frightens the conscience of man, and which convinces him of his vanity.'

Maximilian felt himself transported 'to a time, when the foot of a race of sinners had not yet made an impression on earth, filled with the germs of life, when the soft mess of clay was not yet animated by the breath of the Most High'. Vesuvius, he concluded, 'is a remnant of chaos. Thus the past speaks to us, through the spirit of fire; and also gives us a warning of the future. As God created, so He will destroy'.[49] His views were shared by Marianne Talbot, a genteel woman in her late thirties who lived in Naples between 1829 and 1832. Prompted by a re-reading of de Staël's comments on the volcano in *Corinne*, she wrote in her journal:

> All the greatness & splendour of the world are not comprised in the powers of Man, & we feel its [Vesuvius's] powers conducted by laws that we can't penetrate, mysteries we can't penetrate; matters we know nothing of, protect or menace our existence. Vesuvius is the descent into Hell, certainly poetically so, & a little wd convince us of its really being so, as the Sailors & the lower people think it.[50]

Such sentiments were obviously informed by the knowledge, made all the more vivid after the 1760s when the excavation of more victims made clearer the death toll of the eruption of 79 CE, that the volcano's effect on human life could be devastating. Up until then the eruption had been seen chiefly as destructive of a material environment – the bricks, mortar and artifacts of the buried cities. Like Herculaneum and Pompeii, Vesuvius was a ruin whose remnants revealed a history, but it was also, more dauntingly, itself an agent of change, not just in the past, but in the present and the future.

One final act by visitors on the top of the volcano reinforced this view. An ideal trip to the summit occurred at night and was not fully complete without a dawn view of its surroundings, a moment of awakening, of admiration of contemporary civility and cultivation that was clearly understood as antithetical to the horror and darkness of the volcano. As Henry Matthews put it, 'The look down into the great crater at the summit, is frightfully grand; and when you turn away from the contemplation of this fearful abyss, you are presented with the most forcible contrast, in the rich and luxuriant prospect of Naples, and the surrounding country; where all is soft and smiling as far as the eye can see.'[51] The French jurist Charles Dupaty had expressed similar sentiments in his graphic account of his ascent a generation earlier: 'When I had contemplated this darkness and this splendour, this frightful, sterile, abandoned nature, and this laughing, animated, fruitful nature, the empire of death and that of life, I threw myself through the clouds, and I continued to climb.'[52] This was very much a scripted moment, recommended in travel guides and dutifully recorded in diaries, letters and travel literature. It was the occasion to relish what one Frenchman called a 'striking contrast' ('*contraste frappant*')[53] between the pellucid beauties of man – cities and cultivated land – and the darkness of a terrifying and sublime nature. As Nathaniel Parker Willis, the American writer and publisher who visited Naples in the early 1830s, remarked, 'I can compare standing on the top of Vesuvius and looking down upon the bay and city of Naples, to nothing but mounting a peak in the infernal regions overlooking paradise.'[54] Willis was probably plagiarising, among others, Chateaubriand, who pithily described the view as '*le Paradis vu de l'Enfer*'.

The contrast was not quite that clear-cut and simple. As Jane Graham, the recent bride of Patrick Home, the laird of Wedderburn, had realised as she surveyed the view from the summit of Vesuvius in the spring of 1772: 'From the top there is the most heavenly prospect of the Campagna Felice, but one is struck with horror to see what beautys what fertile plains Vesuvius has yet to destroy when one sees in the heart of these rich Meddows streams of antient Lava – upon the whole it is more dreadful than pleasing to see.'[55] A French visitor a quarter of a century later had the same reaction. The landscape, he felt, 'offers all the riches of vegetation and all the horrors of annihilation!' Though he delighted in 'a veritable garden where the produce of all the auspicious seasons merge', his eye was 'often saddened by those more or less black lavas' that had so upset Jane Graham. He saw them as a sort of violation. 'They seem,' he said, 'to resemble a bottle of ink spilt on the dress fabric of flowers of a young wife.' This was more than tarnishing; it was destruction. 'Hell's fluid,' he concluded, 'has spared nothing wherever it has been able to penetrate, and what it has left intact, and as if with regret, only serves to make people more bitterly regret what it invades and defiles.'[56]

Reaching the summit of Vesuvius was therefore not merely a thrilling and hazardous adventure, but also an occasion for reflection on the nature of human existence, the vicissitudes of everyday life, the history of the earth, and the complex mixture of the destructive and creative forces of nature. It would, of course, be foolish to think of this as a universal response. I very much doubt if such thoughts were on the minds of the four young French boys who celebrated their arrival by pissing into the crater on a cool winter's day in 1827.[57] The journey had its ribald moments and its distractions – cooking eggs in the hot crevices of the volcano; the picnics and drinking; making impressions of coins and medals, pressed into the lava; the jokes and banter that to have been a regular part of the journey. But these seem to have been responses to the trepidation and dread that so many visitors felt, and which so many accounts of the ascent describe as the source of their reflections.

The descent was much quicker than the climb and altogether much less sombre. 'The famous gliding through the ashes . . . the feeling is so agreeable' was a sort of catharsis, a release from the terror and gloom of the crater and the dark thoughts they provoked. What made the ascent so arduous – the shifting unstable ash – cushioned the descending traveller. Bounding and leaping, it was easy and exhilarating to plunge down the side of the mountain, and back to safer climes. The experience was, one traveller remarked, 'laughably ludicrous'.[58] 'One was so glad,' wrote Maximilian, 'to be once again allowed to be a child with one's heart, and on a legitimate occasion, and to give unrestrained vent to merriment.'[59] Almost without exception, returning visitors found this stage of their journey pleasurable and reassuring.

The rest of the trip often included a further visit to the hermitage for refreshment and rest – the Visitors' Book was more usually signed as travellers returned from the summit – and back in Resina visitors would pay off their guides, gather their souvenirs of crystal and rock, and return to the city of Naples. Many displayed their wounds proudly – showing off the cuts and bruises suffered when they tripped or fell, displaying boots and clothes that were often shredded, singed and scorched by the hot sharp lava.

Visitors to Naples saw Vesuvius as one of its chief attractions. The volcano and its surroundings were forces of nature, an accessible wonder that enabled visitors to explore a full gamut of emotions, to revel in the experience of what I call 'sublime tourism'. Different parts of the journey prompted different feelings, a shifting topography of emotion: seriousness in the face of the cruel crater, childish joy at the descent and successful escape from the cone, pleasure at the contemplation of the Neapolitan landscape which was 'soft', 'smiling', 'laughing' and which invited travellers to share in its pleasures. The powers of nature absorbed visitors, the changing surroundings producing sharp contrasts in mood. Immersed in the challenging task of the climb and enthralled by the richness of their surroundings, some visitors began to reflect on the larger significance of this wonder of nature.

Before the mid-eighteenth century, visitors to the volcano were infrequent, limited to savants like Athanasius Kircher and John Evelyn, travellers like Joseph Addison, and local hunters and foragers. Mountains and volcanoes were regarded with suspicion and fear, as places generally to be avoided; they were certainly not subject to the aesthetic praise and positive emotional excitement they enjoyed in the Romantic era. Along with aesthetics went politics. The cataclysmic events – the wars, revolutions and regime changes – that rocked Europe in the late eighteenth and early nineteenth centuries raised in their sharpest form questions that haunted not just the Kingdom of Naples but much of the rest of Europe: about human history and its relation to what was widely recognised as a much more profound history of the earth, and about the nature of change in both the human and natural environment – was it gradual and incremental or cata-strophic, or was it fuelled by creative or destructive impulses? Like the Bay of Naples, which was littered with the ruins and detritus of natural and human history, Vesuvius and its relics constituted the rich but profoundly puzzling ('mysterious' was the most frequently used term) vestiges of a past whose interpretation seemed vital, but which revealed little more than an inscrutable future. If its surface effects were palpable, its deeper meaning remained largely unfathomable, a puzzle to natural philosophers, historians and antiquaries and a source of persistent anxiety and debate among the public at large.

Part I
On the Volcano

1
CLOSE AT HAND
The Visitors' Book and Vesuvius

What connexion can there have been between many people in the numerous histories of this world, who, from opposite sides of great gulfs, have, nevertheless, been very curiously brought together!

Charles Dickens, *Bleak House*, 1853

W ho, then, were the travellers who undertook this thrilling and thought-provoking journey up and down the volcano? This question usually prompts a vague and general response related to the history of tourism. It is assumed that Vesuvius should be seen as an item on a tourist itinerary, which indeed it was, and that all visitors were tourists, which indeed they were not. We know this because of the fortuitous survival of a remarkable document, a visitors' book to the volcano from the 1820s.[1] The book has special qualities as a historical source. The scientific paper or newspaper article, the travel diary, narrative or fiction, gouaches and oil paintings, political tracts and sermons all help the historian to understand what Vesuvius meant and represented to different historical actors. But all these materials operated at a distance, even when they depended for their authority on the presence of the artist, savant or author on the mountain. Rather different in character is the Visitors' Book to the volcano. Neither printed nor circulated, it remained in a specific location, the hermitage of San Salvatore on the slopes of Vesuvius itself. It did not travel, its only movement occurring when it was passed from hand to hand among visitors.

How many such books there were, we do not know – there are occasional references to them from the 1770s to the 1840s – but one surviving book, covering the period from December 1826 to October 1828, reveals an extraordinary wealth of information.[2] On the one hand it is full of stories about the experience of climbing the volcano: the often violent emotions fuelled by its visual spectacle and by a sense of imminent danger; the feelings, both hostile and friendly, towards fellow travellers and guides. It brims with anecdotes whose immediacy conveys a powerful sense of 'being there'. Its focus is not on the detailed appearance of Vesuvius – unnecessary to any reader of the book, who had only to poke their head out of the hermitage's door to see 'the real thing'. Rather its comments bring *responses* to the volcano and to its visitors to the fore. The book, even more than the slopes of Vesuvius itself, was a site of sociability in which visitors with radically different backgrounds and experience interacted with one another and with the volcano.

Within its pages, covering 638 days of entries, there are over 2,300 signatures, and a myriad of points of view. Some are quite prolix – sentimental, argumentative, celebratory or philosophical – but most confine themselves to a signature and some sort of personal identification (rank, nationality, profession, occupation or place of residence). The contrast with the optic of the single author narrator, the default position of the travel writer, is both stark and, as we shall see, revealing. It is not that the picture it conveys is more 'real' than the account of an individual author, but that it opens up different perspectives, enabling us to reconstruct a general picture of activity on the mountain, one that includes the contribution of those who either through choice or necessity did not produce their own extended account of the experience.

The surviving album betrays its frequent use (Plate 4). A large, leather-bound volume, it is in poor condition: many of its more than 110 folios have been cut out or bear the signs of excisions. The binding is cheap and serviceable, but the paper is of quite a high quality and has survived remarkably well. It contents are written chiefly in four languages – English, Italian, French and German – but there are also entries in Latin, Portuguese, Spanish, Greek, Russian and Polish. The entries are often written in an execrable script, there are many errors of vocabulary and orthography (lots of entries were obviously not written in a mother tongue), and the text is interleaved with squiggles, interpolated comments, and the occasional diagram and drawing. It is a pastiche of commentary produced under far from ideal circumstances: more than one entry was written while sitting on a mule, and many were scribbled by visitors intoxicated by the wines served by one of the two hermits resident there. An entry and subsequent annotation from 28 April 1828 (Plate 5) reveal a typical occasion of its creation:

Good Friar you ask me to write in your book But will you think of me when in it you look, Vesuvius we found in excessive good nature and I thought to leap into the Crater. John Williams, Fred Reeves and Richard Caghill have brought him quite safe to the foot of the hill. Written in haste on the back of a Mule So I pray all ye Poets don't think me a Fool.

Another hand adds the annotation: 'I wish that the Poet had told us the name of the stupid Mule, which could be so tame as to allow so much writing to be made "on his backside".'[3]

Visitors' books

Visitors' books, sometimes called albums and, by the French, *livres d'or*, were to be found at many sites around eighteenth- and nineteenth-century Europe, especially in chapels, convents, hermitages and hospitals in remote and mountainous regions. They were sufficiently numerous for John Scott, the radical journalist and much-admired travel writer, to use 'the various albums, &c. all along the roads', to flesh out his account of the different nationalities (and quiddities) of European travellers in his *Sketches of France, Switzerland and Italy*, published in 1821.[4] In the Hospice du Grand-Saint-Bernard in the Swiss Alps, at the Monastery in Saint Pierre-de-Chartreuse in the mountains north of Grenoble, as well as at much humbler dwellings, such as the hermitage at the top of Lo Capo at Santa Maria del Soccorso on the island of Capri, as indeed in the hermitage of San Salvatore on Vesuvius, members of religious orders and hermits offered shelter and sustenance to travellers, asking them in return to record their visit in an album or book.

Writing in 1811, the first historian of the album, the Parisian journalist and satirist Victor-Joseph Étienne de Jouy, traced its origins back to the graffiti of the ancients, and patriotically praised his fellow countrymen for the 'gay, spiritual and original things that the French have left [on the walls of inns] over thirty years in their frequent travels on the roads of Italy and Germany'. But, as a man with literary pretensions, Étienne de Jouy saw the apogee of the album in pre-Revolutionary visitors' books such as that kept at the Chartreuse, where the magnificent scenery had inspired men of learning and taste to pen finely turned comments and noble sentiments. (Famously, in 1741, the English poet Thomas Gray had written a Latin poem, the so-called Alcaic Ode, celebrating the sublime nature of the monastery's surroundings; the verse had been destroyed along with the album during the French Revolution, but survived as a copy.) Étienne de Jouy's story of what he called the *'album vulgaire'* was a tale of progressive 'degeneration', the decline of elevated comment by noble male travellers in such books, and its replacement by the cliché and rank sentiment in which run-of-the-mill tourists, above all, he claimed, women, were prone to record their experiences.[5]

The downgrading of the album from a repository of literary gems (always a fanciful construction) to a more pedestrian record book of travels – a list of names – had its deleterious effects, not least in diminishing the book's chances of survival. No longer a cultural fetish, or a celebration of great men, it became ephemeral, another instance of the innumerable paper products that were likely to be destroyed, pulped and recycled, or simply disposed of. Not even the literary fame of the albums at the Chartreuse could save them from the depredations of the French Revolution; they were destroyed along with other monastic records in October 1792. Less august records also did not survive. On his visit to the Vesuvian hermitage in 1805, the prolific German dramatist August von Kotzebue, looking at the hermit's album, was disappointed to discover 'that the volumes already filled are no longer in extant [sic], but have been disposed of. There is but one full, and a second which is just begun.'[6] Even when they survived, many such books often succumbed to the nineteenth-century obsession with the autographs of important figures, which meant that they were often mutilated, signatures and sometimes comments excised, pages ripped out to leave only the long litany of the obscure and the also-ran. We are just fortunate that what was later taken from the hermitage was not a single page but the entire book.

It is therefore not surprising that few such books survive. It needed both a strong institutional presence and the ability or good fortune to avoid the depredations of war and revolution to ensure survival. A series of visitors' books for the Hospice of Saint-Bernard covering the entire nineteenth century remains in its library, their preservation probably ensured by the value of the hospice to travellers, the assiduity of its monks, its remoteness, and its presence in a neutral country.

The Vesuvius Visitors' Book

The surviving Visitors' Book to Vesuvius owes its preservation to its removal to the Harvard University Library. Even as early as the

1820s there were several American visitors to Vesuvius (the book records fifty-six in all, including one, Joseph Elden, who had climbed the volcano on four occasions), most of them well-educated young men from New England and New York. The exact story of the journey of the Visitors' Book to New England remains obscure, but the signature of Henry Wadsworth Longfellow, poet, professor, Italophile and translator of Dante, along with four other patrician Americans, in the entry for 17 February 1828, suggests that another American, probably a Harvard graduate, obtained the book, either by theft or purchase or – least probably – as a gift sometime after 1848, the last date at which the book was annotated, and later presented it to the college library. (It is even possible that Longfellow's son, Ernest, an artist who visited Naples in 1868 and painted Vesuvius, may have obtained it,[7] as the book was probably bequeathed as part of a gift to the library from the Longfellow family.) Certainly, the Harvard Library catalogue sees the presence of Longfellow as vital – his is the only signature identified in its entry, where he is also categorised as the manuscript's 'author/creator'. It is as if the librarians wanted to align the book with those earlier albums of literary gems from famous authors, like that at the Chartreuse.

Sadly, however, Longfellow was at his most succinct; he merely added 'U. S. of America' to his name. Though he wrote lyrically to his brother Stephen a few days later about the Bay of Naples, describing its scenery as having 'those rich combinations – which were they found everywhere, would make the world we live in, too much like Paradise',[8] his contribution to the Vesuvian album was a mere signature, to which he added, like most American visitors to the volcano, his nationality. Like most other contributors to the book, he made his mark but did little more. Étienne de Jouy identified such signatures as signs of pride and exaltation, intended simply to record the presence of the signatory at 'places which one doesn't reach without danger or without some special purpose'.[9] Hence the delight, or more accurately 'gloire' expressed in the Vesuvian book by a much-travelled Knight of

Malta, Louis Jérôme de Goujon de Thuisy, when he became the very first visitor to reach the crater after the terrible eruption of 1794; and hence, more modestly, the sentiment of Joseph Rustichelli from Alessandria (Piedmont), who in October 1828 wrote in the album in French that he hoped that one day someone would see in the book that he had been there.[10] Such signatures were like those de Jouy described scratched on the vertiginous spire of Strasbourg cathedral or, indeed, the tags attached today to the seismic equipment on the edge of the crater of Vesuvius. Markers, forms of identification, signs of achievement, but of no literary merit.

The album was not a literary throwback, much less a polished record of an extended journey, but rather a large collection of comments, interjections and thoughts made on the spur of the moment (even when planned beforehand). It had precisely those qualities that troubled de Jouy – it was a 'mélange, pot-pourri, confusion, galimatias, macédoine',[11] written in a profusion of languages, whose promiscuousness was of the sort that excited de Jouy's mockery and apprehension. It lacked a single authorial voice; indeed it had 2,300 authors, the number of entries made in so many different hands and expressed in many different tongues. It lacked both coherence and distinction.

Ephemeral, anecdotal, inconsequential: such books have long been disparaged or dismissed, even though they were often scrutinised by travellers with avidity. By the early nineteenth century, reading and signing the Vesuvian Visitors' Book was scripted into the experience of visiting Vesuvius; it had become, in the words of one visitor, 'the received custom', repeatedly referred to in guidebooks and many travel narratives. Lady Blessington describes how, after her ascent of the volcano with a large party in the spring of 1824, she and friends were served a 'homely repast' at the hermitage. 'During our dessert of apples', she recorded, 'we amused ourselves with reading the albums of the hermitage, in which the visitors are requested to write their names, with any observation that Vesuvius, or the hermitage, may have suggested.'[12] Henry Coxe in his *Picture of Italy* (1815) explained that 'At the hermitage, an *album* book being kept, it is usual for everyone who wanders thus far, to insert his name, at least, or any remark he may choose to make', though he added that 'these memorandums have been described as a mass of the most disjointed disparities that the mind of man can possible conceive.'[13]

Why then were visitors so drawn to what critics called the 'vagrant genius' of this 'Catalogue of Adventurers'? This curiosity about the entries in the album was sometimes fuelled by the search for the signatures of particular persons – more usually friends and acquaintances than literary lions, though Stendhal was delighted to discover the signatures of Madame de Staël and August Schlegel.[14] Thus the Scottish banker Sir James Forbes and his wife, browsing what they called the hermit's register, were pleased to find 'many of our Acquaintances recorded who had been there in former years'.[15] A young Belgian from Liège, who had signed the Visitors' Book with thirteen friends on 1 April 1828, was delighted to look back at their signatures when he returned to the volcano ten months later. For both signatories and readers the book embodied a shared experience, linking them together through their presence on the mountain.

But it was the comments, quips and anecdotes, what Betsey Fremantle, the no-nonsense wife of the commander-in-chief of the British Mediterranean fleet, called 'very silly remarks, and more silly verses',[16] that really attracted the reader's interest and opprobrium. Most readers of the albums had two objections to the entries – pretentiousness and banality – both of which were identified by Kotzebue. Somewhat ironically, in view of his reputation as a melodramatic playwright, he complained that 'Many of the writers had been seized with a troublesome sensibility, and these were the most intolerable: they had expectorated the whole of their sensations on "the grand prospect" and "the monstrous volcano". One had even maintained that the flames had contemplated him with gaiety.' This hyperbole was only matched, in his view, by the trite comment and low humour of many entries. 'Others had recorded sorry jests and disgusting witticisms: one, for example, related that a sly chambermaid Lisetta had fallen from her ass in the journey; – it is a wonder that he did not describe her posture.'[17] (Jokes about asses and about backsides were common in the book.) As a French commentator wrote in the album in August 1828, it was 'a singular property of Vesuvius to inspire more vulgar comments than any other mountain in the world – just look over the book'. Small wonder that Chateaubriand in 1804 concluded that 'In this book I didn't find a thought that deserved to be recorded', and that the high-minded philologist Karl Morgenstern (who coined the term *Bildungsroman*) dismissed the book as 'full of trash and jokes and unworthy of a second thought'.[18] The English gentleman William Webb, examining the book in 1822, felt that the only true sentiment among the 'trash' that he read was the remark that 'Where God and nature speak in fullness, it becomes man to be silent.'[19] Fortunately many did not follow this injunction.

If readers expected, as some certainly did, to find deep insight into the experience of visiting the mountain, or illumination into the volcano's workings in the Visitors' Books, then they would certainly have been disappointed. The default mode of the entries was picaresque rather than epic. Many were flippant and foolish, as is so often the case with books inviting comments. The constant complaint of critics was that the numerous entries were 'anecdotal'.

This disparagement deserves closer scrutiny, for the anecdote is a distinctive literary form. As Joel Fineman in a brilliant essay on the history of the anecdote argues,

> The anecdote is the literary form that uniquely *lets history happen* by virtue of the way it introduces an opening into the teleological, and therefore timeless narration of beginning, middle, and end. The anecdote produces the effect of the real, the occurrence of contingency, by establishing an event as an event within and yet without the framing context of historical successivity, i.e. it does so only in so far as its narration both comprises and refracts the narration it reports.[20]

Another way to look at it is to say that the anecdote is the least literary of forms – often of course taking spoken form, often expressed through performance – one that embraces the here and now. For Fineman the compact integrity of the anecdote has always meant that it will inevitably impede 'the progress of more comprehensive historical narratives and [prompt] ... new surrounding sequences.'[21] If we reflect on the criticisms made of the Visitors' Book we can see that their hostility is towards the sort of remarks – humorous, inconsequential, expostulatory – that precisely puncture a more authorised narrative. And these anecdotes do so by introducing a sort of earthiness and everydayness that I think were seen as both threatening to dominant narrators and as more 'real'.

In other words, the Visitors' Book enables us to construct a fuller, more particular and more embodied account of the ascent of Vesuvius, at the same time encouraging us to disaggregate visitors/travellers/ tourists and reveal the heterogeneous nature of their journeys. This makes the document of limited value in constructing a narrative of the history of tourism as part of modernity. 'To mainstream historians', as the literary critics Catherine Gallagher and Stephen Greenblatt remark, 'anecdotes are no-account items: tolerable perhaps, as rhetorical embellishments, illustrations, or moments of relief from analytical generalization, but methodologically nugatory'.[22] I would put it more strongly. Whereas some anecdotes – in the case of the Visitors' Book, remarks about sublimity – can be fitted easily into a grand narrative, rendered tame and domestic, harnessed to pull along the chariot of progress – others cannot. They threaten to interrupt, punctuate or divert the journey's path, which is why they so often are thrown aside. But we do so at our peril, losing, in my view, more than we gain.

The Visitors' Book reveals the vicissitudes and pleasures of the journey up the volcano, often drawn in vivid personal detail: the feelings provoked by the wonders of nature, the joys of a shared experience, and the vexed and complex relations with guides and fellow travellers. The trip – in the words of the Italian geologist Spallanzani, 'rather an excursion than a journey'[23] – undertaken for whatever motive was almost never an isolated experience and almost always a sociable one. On the slopes of Vesuvius and in the pages of the Visitors' Book, society, in its broadest sense, met cheek and jowl with living nature and reacted in a variety of different ways.

The crowded and often disorderly pages of the Visitors' Book memorialised those who came together to the volcano. Its signatories left a lasting record of their transitory presence, attempting to make enduring the fleeting moments they spent in the presence of powerful forces over which they had no control. In certain respects its pages resembled those of one of the Romantic age's most fashionable accessories, a personal album. A visitors' book was more public, less domestic than an album, though a 'personal' album was also meant to connect its owner to others. Both were a pastiche of comment from several different hands; both were about memorialising a particular event or person, and both were about public sharing. They began their lives as books of blank pages – *album* in Latin means a white writing tablet – empty spaces that needed to be filled with sentiments and feelings, the busy white noise of human life. For both, in their different ways, were about an anxiety, absence, emptiness and loss. The books were the material remains of fragile and vulnerable relationships. Their signatories expressed apprehension of their loss through separation (notably through death); the act of signing such books expressed the hope that such inscriptions could achieve an immortality denied to their authors.[24]

The personal album may have grown out of the diary or the commonplace book, but it was quite distinct. It was not a daily or periodic record (here it differed from the visitors' book), nor was it intended to cull and collect words of wisdom. Its pages were far more miscellaneous and personal, an expression of the self, though one that was defined through friendship(s), of which the album was their repository. As one home-made title page put it: 'For Scraps to love and friendship dear / In various forms are treasured here'. These books of blank pages often with fancy bindings were produced by commercial stationers, who also printed visitors' books. Their owners filled them with verses, sketches, proverbs, jokes and epigrams, songs and sonnets, some lifted from the literary canon (Goethe, Byron and Sir Walter Scott), others entered by friends, and most expressing the thoughts and anecdotes that revealed their owner's character and sentiments. The books were interactive, passed round and shown to friends as expressions of amity. The request to someone to sign one, to write verses or draw a sketch, was a strong gesture of friendship.

Many albums contained verses or reflections on the nature of friendship – a favourite was a 'recipe' for friendship purportedly from the *Natural History*, of the ancient philosopher the elder Pliny, who had died, of course, as a result of the eruption of Vesuvius in 79 CE. Made up of equal parts of 'sincerity, frankness, disinterestedness, pity and tenderness', lubricated by two emollient oils, 'perpetual kind wishes' and 'serenity of temper', it was perfumed by the 'desire of pleasing' and its potency 'increased in its weight and value the longer you have kept it'.[25] The personal album was meant to assuage its owner's fear of loss: loss of a friend through absence or death, and loss of the memory of friendship that the album's entries were supposed to make perpetual. The themes of exile, broken ties, dispersal, separation, departure and death were ubiquitous.[26]

The Visitors' Book at the hermitage, often referred to as an 'album', was a more public version of this concern to memorialise a visitor's presence and their affections. But it differed from the personal album in two important respects. It was not the property of an individual but was rather part of a site or institution; it was fixed and embedded, immobile and sedentary, part of the material environment where it was located. It had a home. The signatories travelled but it did not. The Visitors' Book derived its significance from being there, one of the reasons why, despite the occasional copy and transcription, such books did not find their way into print. Their inscription was an act that tied the author to a place (and usually a time), giving the signatory a sense of 'hereness' or location. Signing was declarative. The importance of presence was demonstrated by the anger and disappointment travellers expressed if they did not find their signatures when they returned.

When in September 1827 Monsieur Henry from Berne returned to Vesuvius with his wife and son, twenty-two years after his previous ascent, he had eagerly anticipated the pleasure of showing his wife his old entry in the Visitors' Book. But he was bitterly disappointed that he was unable to share his past experiences with his family; the relevant pages were missing.[27] The Scottish geologist David James Forbes, who returned to Vesuvius in December 1843, and thumbed his way through the old Visitors' Books, was luckier. He soon found what he was searching for: an entry dated 28 March 1827, signed by himself, his brother and his banker father. 'All this time has passed as a watch in the night', he commented, dwelling on the journeys he had undertaken as a teenager up the volcano.[28] Forbes wanted to recall what had been a decisive moment in his youth, an experience that had powerfully shaped his future as a geologist and educator.

This sense that the album at the hermitage was not just a record of presence but a testament to the feelings inspired by Vesuvius is clear in the comments of Kennett Dixon, who made six ascents of the volcano. He wrote to declare his attachment not to an individual but to Vesuvius itself:

As in the cold sepulchral stone
some name arrests the passer by;
Thus when thou viewest this page alone
May mine attract thy pensive eye
& when by thee this name is read
Perchance in some succeeding year,
Thou'll think of me, as on the dead
And think my heart is buried here. K.D.[29]

Dixon wants a certain immortality, while recognising the inevitability of his own demise. His sentiments resemble those written in numerous personal albums. And just as the owners of private albums sought to enhance their sentiments by including the work of such writers as Goethe and Byron, so visitors to the hermitage drew on the literary canon. No verse was more apt than Goethe's lines from *Wilhelm Meister's Apprenticeship*, painstakingly inscribed by a visitor in German 'Fraktur' (German black-letter script). In the first of a series of songs that Mignon, the Italian child kidnapped and taken from her home-land, sings to Wilhelm Meister after he has promised never to leave her, she asks if he is familiar with the Mediterranean south:

> Knowest thou where the lemon blossom grows,
> And under dark foliage the golden orange glows?[30]

The verses mark a shift in the relations between Meister and Mignon, a bond of perpetual friendship between two itinerants who have met on the road, one that is cemented by a request to share in a nostalgic longing for home.

It is notable that the harshest critics of the album were literary figures and travel writers, authors of extended individual narratives who saw little literary value in a collection of anecdotes. By the early nineteenth century the visitors' book as a literary failure had become a commonplace, found in travel accounts and even in the book itself. Such criticism established a difference among visitors, one akin to that between travellers (legitimate visitors) and tourists (the vulgar, the ignorant and the parvenu), an enduring distinction that first emerged in the Romantic era.[31] But the serial ordinariness of the entries in visitors' books, the very feature that excited de Jouy's disparagement of the album '*en sense vulgaire*' (the language makes the class bias clear), has today become its strength and virtue. In a pioneering paper, two Italian masters of the historical craft, Carlo Ginzburg and Carlo Poni, pointed out the central importance of *names* to the processes of historical reconstruction and analysis: 'The thread of Ariadne,' they wrote, 'that leads the researcher through the archival labyrinth is the same thread that distinguishes one individual from another in all societies known to us: the name.' Names enable us to trace connections, follow paths through time and space, place people in their milieu, understand their patterns of sociability. 'The lines that converge upon and diverge from the name, creating a kind of closely woven web,' they conclude, 'provide for the observer a graphic image of the network of social relationships into which the individual is inserted.'[32] Ginzburg and Poni wrote before the astonishing proliferation of the World Wide Web made such researches much simpler. The tracing of names and connections, once the task of the itinerant scholar, moving from archive to archive, can now be accomplished seated before a computer terminal.

So the hermit's album is not merely a conventional historical source, in which we can find anecdotal evidence of the attitudes, conduct and sentiments expressed by those on the volcano; it can also be used as a database and as a finding aid. The size of its sample enables us to lend a certain precision to the many generalisations that have been made about visitors, often on the slenderest of evidence.[33] As we will see, we can build up a picture of the disparate places from which visitors came – including more than 160 towns and cities – the varied social groups and occupations, from princes to artisans, that they belonged to, as well as their age and gender composition, their nationalities and languages. What is immediately apparent is not only the social diversity and geographical extent of the visitors, but how difficult (and unhelpful) it is to distinguish tourists – people travelling of their own free will – from those who found themselves in Naples because of the powerful forces of war, commerce, politics and religion.

Visitors to the volcano

Though the Visitors' Book is a cornucopia, its abundance does not mean that it is complete. It has been easiest to learn the place of

47

origin of visitors as, apart from a name, this is the most common form of identification. Placing travellers socially has been much more difficult. Persons of rank and title usually indicate their status. So too do some members of the professions and trades. But a large swathe of visitors offer no such description, occupying a place beneath nobility but above vulgar employment. Even with the tracing of many names, it has not been possible to identify the occupations of more than about 20 per cent of visitors. And, as we shall see, we need to be wary of any assumption that the signatories of the Visitors' Book account for the total number of people on the volcano. There were many who did not wish to sign the book or were prevented by their status from doing so.

Many travellers simply omitted to sign the book. They complained of being importuned by the hermit, just as the hermit complained of their failure to write in the book. Evidence from within the book itself makes clear that many visitors remained unrecorded. Thus on 24 April 1827, on a particularly foggy day, Mr Edward Fish 'Fell into the Crater and was dragged out in Ropes by Tomasso [his Italian guide], and 7 others.' His companions were less helpful. As he complained: 'My company of 26 from such fright all bolted.' Fish, though English, lived in the Strada Vittoria in Naples and worked as a saddler and harness maker, supplementing his income by renting out a number of apartments in the fashionable district of Chiaia.[34] He was a frequent visitor to Vesuvius (four separate trips are recorded in the hermit's album), and he usually climbed the volcano in the company of other British tradesmen and merchants, 'Natives of Albion', but on this occasion, none of these (doubtless shamefaced) colleagues chose to sign the Visitors' Book.[35]

From other sources we learn of visitors who were also unrecorded by the hermit. Thomas Uwins, an English artist who lived in Naples between 1825 and 1831, wrote a vivid description to his brother on 24 March 1828 of peering down into the crater during the eruption of that year: 'The sight was too beautiful to be terrific; but you are sometimes called back to a sense of danger by the fiery stone falling near and rolling down the side of the mountain, or by the ashy mound on which you stand being shaken to its base by the tremendous thunderings from beneath.'[36] But, like other residents of Naples, he did not see fit to sign his name in the hermit's album.

If some visitors were under-reported, others, such as servants, were almost completely invisible by virtue of their rank. The British artist William Bewick recorded that he ascended Vesuvius on 26 August 1828 in a large party that consisted of Roman, English and Neapolitan aristocrats. Almost all of these illustrious travellers signed the book. But they were accompanied by an entourage of 'seven menservants and a lady's maid', none of whom appear as signatories.[37] This was typical: the servant class is almost completely absent from the hermit's album. There are a total of ten signatures covering the entire period, even though we know from Bewick's account (and from many others) that genteel travellers almost invariably travelled with at least one and often several servants. The servants that did manage to sign – 'Henry' of Lübeck, attending two Americans and a Cambridge graduate; Joseph Ames, servant to the Jerningham family from Norfolk; Vincenzo del Peschio, 'garçon de M. Fargasse'; Raffaele Tirotti, servant to a Swiss soldier; and the valet de chambre of the Comte d'Ursel – somehow muscled their way into the book, overwriting their employers' entries, squeezing their names in, or adding them separately elsewhere on the page[38] – sure signs that they were not seen as members of the party and therefore not entitled to record their presence.

Similarly, guides and attendants, with the exception of the head guide Salvatore Madonna, are almost never mentioned in the album. A rare instance of such recognition was when Catherine Casle from Lyon recorded that 'her porter was called Macaron',[39] though this was clearly a nickname. Yet, as we know, almost every visitor employed at least one – often two or more – men or boys to help them reach the summit.

A few signatories might well conceal what was often a large party. One of the three gendarmes assigned to protect visitors to the summit in 1828 – there had been bandits on the mountain during the 1820s – remarked on the entourage of thirty guides that accompanied a party of two women and one man. When the libertine and profligate Long-Wellesley, the nephew of the Duke of Wellington, was contesting his wife's exclusion of him from her will, he denied that his adulterous relationship with Eleanor Bligh, the wife of Captain Bligh, had first been consummated on the slopes of Vesuvius in 1822, on the grounds that they never had any privacy.[40] His party included a Russian princess and her niece, the Blighs, the Honourable Colonel Stanhope, two other Englishmen and himself, eight travellers who 'together with guides, servants, peasants &c amounting altogether to 50 persons'. Wellesley had a strong incentive to inflate the numbers, but there can be no doubt that the signatures in the hermit's book constitute a significant under-estimate of the number of people on the volcano, and largely exclude those who made the visitors' journey possible. We probably need at the very least to treble the number of 2,300 signatories in the period between December 1826 and October 1828 to begin to get a sense of how many people were present on the mountain.

The Visitors' Book enables us to see travellers in the aggregate, to discern patterns, some more complete than others, and to identify the presence of groups that need explanation. It also sometimes provides us with clues that enable us to flesh out a much fuller narrative. Many visitors survive only as a signature (often virtually illegible), some give their place of origin, while a few wrote at length about themselves, the volcano and their fellow travellers. So most of these figures are shadowy, almost invisible, their traces too faint to reveal to us their purposes as travellers, either to Naples or to the volcano. The details gleaned from the Visitors' Book, rich as they are, are tantalising. Why were Edward Rastawiecki, the aristocratic Polish art historian, George Burrows, the future president of the Royal College of Physicians in

London, Joseph Mülner, a Viennese jeweller, and Vernon Childe, an American who hosted a salon in Paris, all in Naples? Why did they choose to climb the volcano? We will probably never know. The same is true of the father and son Charles Henri and Eugène Frosmont, from La Louvière (in modern Belgium), who made three ascents together in 1828. Nor do we know the motives for ascending Vesuvius of Eduard Läpple, the journeyman comb-maker from Berlin, the Piedmontese engineer Gio Battista Cesa, and Amalia Klentz from Lübeck (though a clue lies in her later investment in Neapolitan steamships). Among many, many others Nicolai Krivtsov, the diplomat and friend of Pushkin, Michele Palazzolo, a poet from Palermo, John Hagendorn, the Baltic merchant and consul, the carriage-maker Antonio Calba from Milan, and Palmer Esten, a judge from Bermuda, all left their traces in the Visitors' Book. But we have no explanation or story to explain their presence.[41]

Yet others are much more vivid: at best they leave an indelible mark, at worst sufficient remains that enable us to trace their lives and place their travelling to Naples and Vesuvius within a personal narrative or larger story. The picture is inevitably skewed. It is easier to trace the wealthy, genteel and literate than to recover the lives of the humble; the nature of record-keeping and the scope of online data means that we are more able to bring British and French visitors to life than the Germans and Italians who signed the hermit's album.

We can think of the signature in the Visitors' Book as the visible extrusion of a continuous, concealed thread – the Italian *filo rosso* (red thread) – that runs both back from its point of entry and forward into the future life of the signatory. Taken altogether, the threads make up the fabric of the visitors' experiences, giving them a certain synchronic shape and pattern that we can trace and explain. But every bit as important is to follow the individual thread both back and forward through time. Often, as I have indicated, the thread is broken, lost or invisible, but sometimes it is not: the more we pull on such threads, the more they reveal.

51

Take one example: on 13 January 1827 Bertrand Martial signed the Visitors' Book with the entry *'Bertrand Martial vicaire général du Kentucky Amérique'*. At first sight this appears as a joke: pseudonyms and false titles are not unusual in the book, and who was the Francophone who dubbed himself 'vicar general of Kentucky'? Martial, however, did not write in jest. He was born in Bordeaux in 1770, was a priest who went as a missionary to New Orleans in 1818 (he arrived in May of that year sailing with five Sisters of the Sacred Heart), where he quickly established himself as a much-loved priest and energetic educator, founding a new boarding school for boys in the city, which housed more than seventy pupils. In 1824, he moved his school to Bardstown, Kentucky, the centre of a Catholic diocese established by Pope Pious VII in 1808. The town was already an important Catholic centre, whose educational institutions included a boys' school founded in 1819, a girls' school established by the Sisters of Charity of Nazareth in 1814, and a seminary, St Thomas's, opened in 1812. Resources both material and financial constrained these very successful Catholic educational initiatives – even local Protestants were eager to send their children to the schools – and in 1827 the Bishop, Bénédict Joseph Flaget, sent Martial as his envoy back to Europe to raise money and recruits. His first stop was in Naples where, in addition to ascending Vesuvius, he tried to recruit the local archbishop, Cardinal Ruffo Scilla, and a number of aristocrats to help persuade Francis I, King of the Two Sicilies, to establish a Society for the Propagation of the Faith. The scheme foundered – the king was not interested in Catholics in North America – and Martial was forced to travel on to Rome and to apply directly to the Holy See. There he procured a grant of 2,000 scudi from Pope Leo XII, together with devotional books and some relics. Armed with his spoils, he returned to Bardstown in February 1828. He later moved back to New Orleans, only to die in the cholera epidemic of 1834.[42]

Martial was one of more than fifty clerics who signed the Visitors' Book, ranging from local Catholic priests with their parishioners, to

Protestants from Paris, Edinburgh and all over Britain, and important members of the Catholic hierarchy from Rome, like the future Cardinal Nicholas Wiseman and his friend, the vicar apostolic from the Western district of England, Peter Augustine Baines. There were many different reasons for their presence on Vesuvius. The Neapolitan priests were at the hermitage to celebrate Mass and saints' days, something of an annual ritual for many of them. One Capuchin seminarian from Naples, Giuseppe Perrone, proudly recorded his sixth ascent of the volcano in October 1827. Wiseman and Baines were there to celebrate the completion of the former's thesis and to strategise about the British parliament's Catholic Emancipation Bill. Some Anglican clergy were present as members of genteel families such as the Fortescues of Writtle Lodge near Chelmsford in Essex; others, such as the Reverend Wilson, accompanied patrician travellers like the passionate amateur geologist the Duke of Buckingham, as their chaplain. The twenty-five-year-old Adolphe Monod, a Parisian Protestant, though he travelled to Naples for his health, had become one of two ministers in the recently founded German-French Evangelical Community in Naples. George Kendrick, erudite classicist and Unitarian from Maidstone in Kent, was in pursuit of his antiquarian interests.[43]

Bertrand Martial's experience was in no way typical of other clerical travellers. His 'Grand Tour' – Bordeaux, New Orleans, Bardstown, Naples, Rome, Bardstown and New Orleans – was quite unlike the journeys undertaken (and with very different purposes) by other clergymen, though its transcontinental itinerary was matched by many other Vesuvian visitors. When we look up close, we see the detail. Proximity brings particularity and variety: the very different motives for climbing the volcano, the distinctive ways that people behaved on its slopes and when confronting its crater, the disparate views they had of their experience. Its appeal – like any sort of intimacy – is that it humanises experience, conveying the rich idiosyncrasies that are lost if we speak simply of 'travellers', 'visitors' or 'tourists' – general categories that flatten out and make uniform a variety of individuals.

A sceptic might then ask what visitors did have in common, other than a wonder of nature that would 'naturally' attract the curious onlooker. What can the journey from Naples of less than a day, often undertaken for pleasure, tell us about anything more than the nature of human inquisitiveness? Can the trip be more than a small side eddy in the great flow of events that marked the early nineteenth century, a peripheral distraction from the epic business of war, revolutions and economic progress? For most visitors, Vesuvius was a diversion as a destination, a brilliantly illuminated cul-de-sac; at best it seems to resemble an exotic lay-by from which to contemplate the frantic traffic of modernity. The volcano was a place apart, a zone of intensity in which its natural heat, volatility and hazardousness provoked powerful emotions and strong feelings both towards Vesuvius itself – awe and admiration, elation, fear and trembling, courage and cowardice, shock and stupefaction – and towards fellow travellers who expressed sentiments of melancholy, longing and loss, nostalgia and homesickness, feelings of friendship and hostility, love and lust.

Yet, paradoxically, as a fixed point the Visitors' Book is an ideal vehicle (albeit a stationary one) to trace and examine travel and movement. Movement, as geographers repeatedly remind us, creates place, or, as in Clifford's formulation mentioned earlier, routes create roots.[44] Roots also create routes. The people identified in the Book can be tracked and traced, their journeys and itineraries followed and placed in the context of their particular lives. These travels were sometimes short – a trip from the city of Naples; but they could also be lengthy, begun, like Martial's journey, in the American Midwest, or, like the Estonian Baron Strandman (b. 1799), from St Petersburg (where he taught at the Imperial University), or, again, like the Dane Carl Striber who travelled from Calcutta.[45] Some journeys also ended far afield: the amiable, handsome con artist and nephew of the Mayor of New York, Cornelius Bradford (1805–30), fleeing from his creditors, vanished from the slopes of Vesuvius and ended his journey and his life in the Holy Land.[46] So too did the English botanist

William Arnold Bromfield (1801–51), who died pursuing plants and seeds in Damascus. (Bromfield's Middle Eastern collections were donated to Kew Gardens.)[47] The Augsburg artist Johann Moritz Rugendas (1802–58) climbed Vesuvius during a European journey that punctuated two long trips to Central and South America, which were to make him the most famous painter of Latin American life in the first half of the nineteenth century.[48]

For some visitors, the climb up the volcano was also part of a lifetime of travel, one journey or a part of a journey that was sometimes purely voluntary, often part of a career or job, or even overtly coerced. Vesuvius turns out to be not so much a lay-by as a crossing point, an intersection where people on many different journeys met. At one level they all shared the experience of the volcano – the drudgery and danger of the ascent, the thrill of proximity to unstoppable natural power, the joint pleasure of admiring the sublime horror of Vesuvius and the beauty of the Bay of Naples. On another, their experiences were extraordinarily varied. They brought very different backgrounds, attitudes, aims and identities to the volcano, and many of them expressed these in the hermit's book. It was hard, though not impossible, for an individual or group to climb Vesuvius and largely ignore everyone else (not least because it inevitably provoked the hostility of the Neapolitan guides). More often than not visitors' experiences were not just shared, but connected, entangling them with strangers, people of other nationalities, faiths, politics, languages and occupations. The Visitors' Book therefore affords us exceptional insight into these relationships, both hostile and amicable, and into the identities and allegiances they both reflected and consolidated.

As we will see, many of those on Vesuvius had lived lives that were mobile, rootless and sometimes traumatic. Though the end of the massive upheaval of the Napoleonic Wars was more than a decade distant, its effects were still very much present. Mass mobilisation had moved soldiers and sailors far from home, scattering them across the globe. The toxic mix of nationalism, religion, and reactionary and radical ideologies had spread civil war, civilian massacres, banditry and exile. The Peace of Paris and the Holy Alliance, intended to do away with Napoleonism and most forms of constitutionalism, and to reconsolidate the powers of the *ancien régime*, helped foster identities and allegiances that were at once ferocious and confused. This was a period in which private individuals, subjects and citizens, carried with them a public history of which they had necessarily and often forcibly been a part; some, like the French officer Count Ferdinand de la Ville-sur-Illon, who lost an arm at the Battle of Alexandria, but who nevertheless made it to the summit of Vesuvius in June 1828, even carried its physical scars.[49]

What do the more than 2,300 entries in the book reveal? The very first impression is of numerousness, a plethora of names and nationalities. Britons were the largest group, followed by the Italians, French and Germans, while the Swiss were represented in numbers that were disproportionate to their population (Chart 1). The travellers came from more than 160 destinations (Maps 1 and 2), as far north and east as the chilly Baltic cities of Riga, Tallinn and St Petersburg, as far south and west as New Orleans in the United States, the Caribbean Islands and Rio de Janeiro. Most of the visitors who identified their place of residence or origin came from major cities. By far and away the greatest number (more than twice any other city) were from Naples itself. (It was a cliché of many foreign visitors that Neapolitans showed no interest in their volcano; such a view was a nonsense.) Naples was followed by Paris, Milan, New York, London, Frankfurt, Lyon, Bologna, Rome, Vienna, Lausanne, Berlin and a raft of other towns. Two Swiss cities were especially prominent, Lausanne and Neuchatel, but this is attributable, like the disproportionate number of Swiss in general, to the presence in Naples of Swiss mercenaries employed by the monarch, Francis I. Yet every bit as important as the major cities was the extraordinary diversity of the places that visitors proudly entered into the book. The roll call is a long one (Table 1) that included twenty-seven British towns, thirty-one Italian cities,

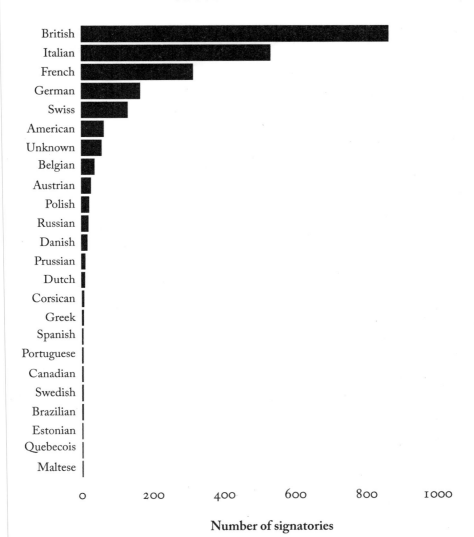

Chart 1. Nationality of signatories in the Visitors' Book.
Source: MS Ital 139, Houghton Library, Harvard University.

thirty-two in the German-speaking lands, twenty-three French towns, as well as sites in Switzerland, the Low Countries, the Baltic and eastern Europe. Visitors came from sixteen sites in the Americas, both North and South, as well as from the Caribbean.

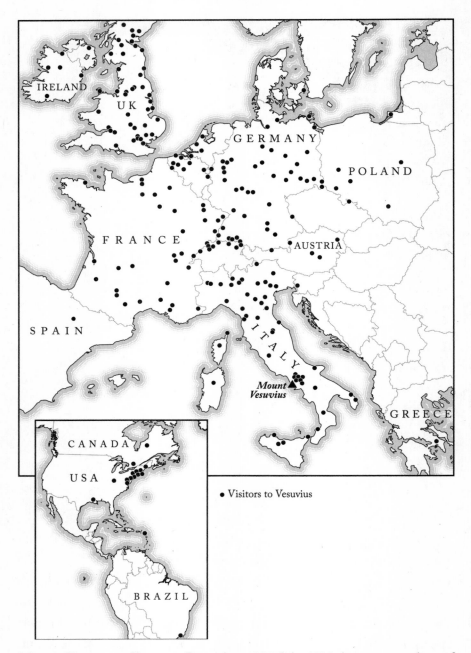

Map 1. Visitors to Vesuvius, December 1826–July 1828, by town or place of residence.

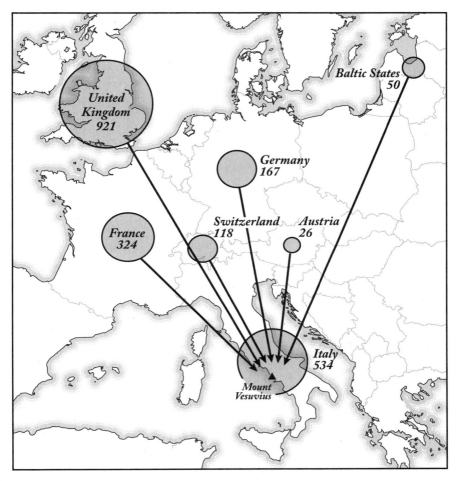

Map 2. Regional distribution of visitors to Vesuvius, including numbers from the major cities.

The remarkable diversity in the geographical origins of Vesuvian visitors is matched by a similar social diversity: princes and aristocrats, members of the professions – soldiers, clergymen, diplomats, doctors, architects, artists and lawyers – bankers, merchants, tradesmen and shopkeepers, and even the occasional artisan, recorded their visit to the hermitage and the volcano. Though very prominent and more easily identified than many other visitors to Vesuvius, we should not

Table 1. Places of residence or origin of visitors to Vesuvius, 1826–8.

Italy	Naples, Milan, Rome, Turin, Bologna, Salò, Parma, Padua, Verona, Ferrara, Venice, Vicenza, Trieste, Lecce, Palermo, Florence, Perugia, Carrara, Genoa, Pisa, Livorno, Faenza, Cosenza, Foggia, Otranto, Campobasso, Avellino, Cappa, Pesaro, Casoria, Brienza	31
France	Paris, Lyon, Dijon, Toulouse, Troyes, Lille, Limoux, Bordeaux, Montélimar, Épinal, Dreux, Soissons, Béziers, Douai, Louviers, Mulhouse, Nancy, Nice, Villefranche, Arles, Rouen, Marseille, Chambéry	23
German-speaking lands	Berlin, Frankfurt, Breslau, Kassel, Lubeck, Hamburg, Karlsruhe, Nuremberg, Bonn, Freiburg, Munich, Reichenberg, Hanover, Dresden, Erfurt, Stuttgart, Mainz, Leipzig, Regensburg, Braunschweig, Elberfeld, Magdeburg, Königsberg, Koblenz, Augsburg, Anklam, Donauworth, Glogau, Mayen, Cologne, Vienna, Graz	32
Americas	New York, Boston, Philadelphia, Hartford (CT), Albany and Poughkeepsie (NY), Keene (NH), Brunswick (ME), Catahoula (LA), Natchez (MS), Quebec, Montreal, the Bahamas, Guadeloupe, Martinique, Rio de Janeiro	16
Great Britain and Ireland	London, Edinburgh, Dublin, Cork, Oxford, Cambridge, York, Hull, Darlington, Derby, Wakefield, Sunderland, Halifax, Liverpool, Newcastle upon Tyne, Whitehaven, Wolverhampton, Manchester, Stockport, Norwich, Bristol, Chichester, Chelmsford, Buckingham, Howick, Glasgow, Lanark	27
Switzerland	Lausanne, Neuchatel, Fribourg, Uri, Baer, St Gallen, Geneva, Zurich, Appenzell, Solothurn, Morges, Thurgau, Walensee	13
Low Countries	Liège, Antwerp, Ghent, Amsterdam, Rotterdam, Brussels, Bruges, Mons, Tilburg, Aachen, Stavelot	11
Baltics	Stockholm, Copenhagen, St Petersburg, Stralsund, Virtsu, Tallinn	6
Eastern Europe	Tambov, Moscow, Liebau/Lubaszka, Warsaw, Krakow	5

exaggerate the number of aristocrats on the mountain. Only about 7 per cent were knights or members of the European nobility – the French represent the greatest number of aristocratic visitors – though if we included members of noble and genteel families the figure would be much higher. The largest single occupational category was the military – inflated no doubt because of the presence of so many Swiss mercenaries, but also a symptom of the extraordinary degree of militarisation of Europe in the early nineteenth century. There were four times as many military men as those of any other occupation. Ministers of religion and doctors and surgeons were the most numerous members of the professions, their numbers slightly exceeding those of merchants, traders, manufacturers and artisans.

Most visitors to the volcano were in their twenties and thirties, born after the French Revolution (Chart 2). Where I have been able to learn their ages, more than half of the travellers were born between 1790 and 1810. Nevertheless, the volcano was climbed by old and young alike. The oldest ascendants of Vesuvius, those in their sixties and seventies, were typically aristocratic, retired military men and their wives, usually travelling with old comrades or with their children and grandchildren. They were among the grandest visitors to the volcano. On 10 December 1827, for example, the seventy-year-old General Sir George Nugent, former Governor of Jamaica and commander-in-chief of British troops in India, together with his American wife, Maria, an accomplished diarist, climbed Vesuvius in the company of two of their children, and a group of military friends. Nugent had fought in the Americas, Europe, the Caribbean and India, postings that enabled his wife to write perceptively on slavery and sexual exploitation on two continents. He was one of several men born in the 1750s who made it up the mountain, including the secretary of the Academy of Sciences in Naples, Teodoro Monticelli; a Scottish lawyer and politician, Sir James Suttie; a distinguished German general, Ludwig Graf Yorck von Wartenburg; and Admiral Richard Hussey Bickerton, who had been Horatio Nelson's second-in-command in the Mediterranean.[50]

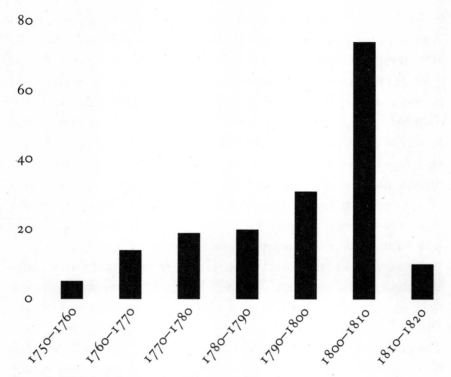

Chart 2. Birthdates by decade of visitors to Vesuvius.
Source: MS Ital 139, Houghton Library, Harvard University.

The old were complemented by the young. The Russian Princess Obolensky recorded taking her two daughters to the crater, accompanied only by an experienced guide. A schoolteacher from Strasbourg also travelled with his ten-year-old pupil to the summit. The youngest children to ascend the volcano were the eight-year-old French aristocrat Eugène de Saint-Julien, and Martha Kemp 'aged nine years and three months', an English girl who lived in Naples and who first ascended Vesuvius with her extremely disgruntled mother ('for the first and last time') on 15 June 1827. Children were usually found among extended family parties such as that organised by the Neapolitan professor Javier Bonamici in November 1827, or by the Swiss banker, diplomat and art collector James-Alexandre Comte de Pourtalès, who took his two teenage daughters up the volcano with two other teenage friends, Caroline and Peppine de Préville, together with their aunt. This latter group had many connections to the Kingdom of the Two Sicilies. Pourtalès was married to the daughter of a Neapolitan banker, and the Préville girls were both born in Palermo, where their father, Dominique de Gros-Préville, was an admiral in the Neapolitan navy.[51]

These children were often the object of comment in the hermit's album. They were portrayed as timid and fearful, not sharing the sublime thrill of their parents and elders, but genuinely frightened by their surroundings, and reluctant to make the trip to the summit. When not timorous, like Professor Bonamici's son who was delighted that the weather prevented the family from travelling to the summit, they were described as mischievous, like the four young French boys already mentioned, who pissed 'boldly' and 'pleasantly' into its crater, or the four teenagers (again French) who wrote their names in the Visitors' Book using the Greek alphabet.[52] Whether fearful or foolish, their youth was seen as preventing them from enjoying the sublime pleasures of the mountain that were central to most adults' experience.

Women and the volcano

At first glance the volcano appears a male environment, chiefly populated by soldiers and guides, all of whom were men. Clambering across the lava and scrambling through the ashes seemed unlikely to promote female decorum. Physical danger was for the male sex. Yet there were plenty of women on the mountain, at least one for every five men recorded in the Visitors' Book – a figure that is almost certainly an underestimate of their numbers. In groups and families a male usually signed the book, and might omit female members of the party. One irate French wife, Marie Bruyère, wrote her signature separately in the book after her husband's entry because, as she indignantly explained, she was not *la fougère*, 'a decorative fern' – what in English we would probably call a wallflower. Anna Wilbraham, a passionate and intrepid amateur geologist, an acquaintance of Alexander von Humboldt, Charles Lyell and Ugo Foscolo, worked on Vesuvius in the spring of both 1827 and 1828, spending nights on the mountain alone with her Neapolitan male assistant making drawings of the crater. She never stopped to sign the book on those expeditions, but when she climbed Vesuvius with her two sisters and a group of visiting English friends – very much a social rather than geological outing – her name was recorded in her party of eight.[53]

Conventional male wisdom about women on the volcano tended to follow the views of the Northumberland philhellenist Sir Charles Monck, who asked himself, 'How women ever do it I cannot imagine.'[54] The young poet and novelist Wilhelm Waiblinger, reporting in April 1828 on a minor eruption for the German newspaper *Morgenblatt*, was shocked to see three English women climbing towards the erupting crater: 'Who,' he demanded, 'wouldn't want to see in this a rather unfeminine audaciousness than courage? Because, not to mention propriety, in case of an unforeseen sudden event a man could if needed descend in three minutes, but how could a woman with inhibiting clothing and inferior strength?'[55] About the same time, a young Neapolitan royal guard, Matteo Petola, assigned to protect visitors from robbers and bandits on the slopes of Vesuvius, approached three women near the summit, incredulously asking why they had chosen to visit such a dangerous place; he found the idea unimaginable.[56]

Most women ascending Vesuvius travelled in couples with their male partners or companions, or with larger groups that included children, chiefly composed either of Italians or 'English'. It was rare, but not unheard of, for women to climb the volcano unaccompanied by the opposite sex. The geologist Sir James Hall, returning to the hermitage from the summit, was pleasantly surprised to be 'joined [by] a party of very agreeable ladies that had been to see the lava and rode along with them down to Portici'.[57] On 17 December 1827 a group of five women, including two Italians, a French and an English woman, all travelled together. Such a mix of nationalities was unusual;

the normal pattern was that of Mrs Graham and the two Miss Grahams, mother and daughters, an English family that ascended Vesuvius together in April 1828.[58]

It was often assumed that women would end their journey at the hermitage, not the summit, or by the 'crucifix planted on an eminence overlooking the deep and wide hollow which separates Mount Vesuvius from the adjoining Mount Somma'. 'This is the spot', wrote the Scottish banker Sir William Forbes, 'at which Ladies with some few exceptions usually stop in their peregrination, when in daylight there is a most glorious view of the Bay & City, & when the eruptions are on that side a good site of the Lava.'[59]

For many male commentators, the presence of women on the volcano was bound up with the assumption that climbing Vesuvius had become less dangerous. In his successful guidebook Joseph Forsyth played down the perils and difficulties, writing:

The idea of danger attending this journey ought to be done away with by the consideration that *Mrs Piozzi*, and another lady with a child of four years of age, ascended it as high as the extremity of the Crater. In 1796, Madame Lebrun made a similar visit attended by two children, and the charming description of her journey ought to be read by every visitor. In 1801, eight Frenchmen descended into the Crater; and we agree with the opinion of a traveler in 1803, and M. Chateaubriand in 1806, that this enterprise is not dangerous.[60]

'Vesuvius,' Forsyth claimed, 'is now an exhausted subject. Its fire and smoke, its glory and terrors, are vanished for the present.' He cited as proof that 'Ladies, as I read in the Hermit's Album, go down to the bottom of the crater.'[61]

Such insistence on the ease of the journey up Vesuvius assumed that undertaking a hazardous climb was a breach of female decorum and fragility. But women seem to have taken pride in their boldness and intrepidity, and in their accounts made certain that their readers understood the real risks they were taking. They took considerable satisfaction in demonstrating that they were capable of matching the men in physical stamina and courage. The first of several ascents of Madame Vigée-Lebrun in 1790 was not at all like the journey that Forsyth described in his guide. Vigée-Lebrun and her companions were greeted by a 'terrible storm ... like a deluge', whose thunder matched the noise of the volcano, and threatened them with lightning. The bad weather prevented them from seeing the crater, and Vigée-Lebrun returned to Naples 'in a state that excited pity', her dress nothing more than a tissue of ashes. But a few days later, on a more clement day, she reached the summit at sunset. Though she confessed to being a little afraid, she found so much to admire in her surroundings that she overcame her apprehension.[62]

Vigée-Lebrun was, of course, a flamboyant character, who claimed that not only did she love Vesuvius, but Vesuvius loved her, 'because he fêted and received me in the most grandiose manner.' Not many women visitors compared the eruption of the volcano with a lover's orgasm. But more modest women visitors were equally intrepid. In 1803 Catherine Wilmot, the daughter of an Irish army officer, described in a letter to her barrister brother how she had climbed Vesuvius with some male companions and one other woman; by the time she reached the summit 'my foot was bleeding through my boot, tho' I had a pair of strong ones made for the occasion.' At first their party decided that 'the Ladies, who were Mrs Derby, a beautiful little American, and myself, should sit contemplating the view, while the gentlemen descended into the Crater.' But the women quickly changed their minds: 'We were suddenly fired with a spirit of enterprise, and resolved to go on too.' Though the task was, in her words, 'perilous beyond description', they made it to the bottom where they 'were obliged to rest from their fatigues', while Mrs Derby insouciantly employed herself 'writing a little letter to her friends in America, descriptive of surrounding scenery'. On her return to Naples, Wilmot found it hard to persuade her Neapolitan friends of her triumphant journey, 'until convinced by my bleeding foot', which they took as evidence that 'nothing in the world was so incomprehensible as the incongruous character of an English woman!'[63]

Wilmot's triumphalist tone is found in other accounts of female ascents. Harriet Morton, an English evangelical of modest means, describes in her oddly titled travel narrative, *Protestant Vigils*, how she and her sister climbed Vesuvius with their boon companion, Catherine Puckle. Puckle raced to the summit ahead of their guide and was soon joined by the two sisters; all three shook hands, congratulating themselves on their intrepidity. For the next few hours they scrambled round the perilous perimeter 'appalled and literally trembling', and ate eggs cooked in the lava. Morton does not deny their fears but portrays the women as courageous and independent.[64]

This sort of behaviour was sometimes acknowledged on the volcano. In October 1827 Scipion Fougasse, a prosperous Lyonnais, a frequent visitor to Naples and a passionate lover of the kingdom ('This splendid country of Naples which had become for me a second homeland'), author of *Histoire de la question Italienne*, and a close friend of the composer Giuseppe Verdi, took his family – his wife, two girls and a boy – up Vesuvius. They were accompanied by other French travellers, at a time when 'Vesuvius was quiescent, and its profound slumber allowed viewers to fathom the depths of the abyss/ crater or even to descend into it, if their heart told them so.' But, when the Fougasse family reached the lip of the crater and stared down into its 'horrible depths', they lost their nerve. Their guides urged them to stay put, but a young girl from Marseilles, about 'fifteen or sixteen years old', plunged down into the crater, and then pulled out her handkerchief to wave from the bottom to her companions strung out along the lip. Fougasse, the girl's brother and another Frenchman swept down after her 'heedless of the consequences of their foolhardiness'. What they found at the bottom was what

Fougasse called 'truly a hell, with its burning atmosphere, its subter-ranean rumblings, its rain of fire, its burning dirt', making up a 'vast valley of lava, where a multitude of little volcanoes boiled in a state of eruption', reminding him of 'tents of a camp', spread out across a valley.[65]

The bravery – or folly – of the young woman from Marseille reminded Fougasse of a previous visit to Vesuvius, during the spec-tacularly violent eruption of 1822, which lasted more than two weeks and blew ninety-three metres off the summit. Accompanied by French and Neapolitan friends, Fougasse struggled through a sea of local villagers fleeing the eruption and watched as many abandoned their efforts to reach the volcano, turning back towards Naples. But again, as later in 1827, it was women who led the way. The family of the British envoy William Richard Hamilton (not to be confused with his more famous predecessor, Sir William Hamilton), including his wife and daughter and several young women, refused to turn back, despite the envoy's pleading, telling him that witnessing such a spectacle far outweighed the dangers they confronted. Following 'the courageous daughters of Albion', Fougasse joined them when they stopped to shelter under an overhang where they were protected from the falling debris. There,

> We were able to enjoy at our ease, during the rest of the night, the most sublime and most moving spectacle that has ever been given to man to contemplate . . . rivers of fire . . . gigantic rocks launched into the air . . . huge blocks suddenly detaching from the crater and rolling their flaming masses almost to the sea . . . the most magnificent spectacle you could have had before your eyes during four hours that passed like four minutes.

The women, who persistently refused Hamilton's pleas to return to Naples, fuelled Fougasse's determination not to show fear 'because it would be shameful to show the least apprehension next to these young and beautiful women who faced peril with a sang-froid and courage that was truly heroic.'[66]

Lady Morgan took a similar view of the young women she encountered on the slopes of Vesuvius, praising their 'laudable curiosity and an energy of character that belongs alone to British women, seemingly superior to fatigue, reckless alike of the sun that sullied their bloom, and the lava that burnt their chaussure, and excoriated their feet.'[67] Even the Vesuvian guides flattered their English clients by dwelling on the intrepidity of English women. The former soldier turned antiquarian scholar W.T.P. Shortt recorded that:

> My Cicerone [the head guide, Salvatore Madonna] had been four times on the volcano in company with the Princess of Wales (late Queen of England) and many other persons of distinction, and spoke of the English with great satisfaction. The English ladies, our fair country-women, who travel these regions in spite of banditti and privation, and have even been known to dance quadrilles in the sacred arena of the Coliseum, with all that spirit peculiar to their nation, he said were famed for ascending the mountain with more alacrity than the French; and that more visitors came from our island than any other part of the globe.[68]

Salvatore Madonna was skilled at telling his clients what they wanted to hear. Doubtless there were intrepid women of nationalities other than the British, and timid and fearful women (but also men) who turned back from the volcano, or who did not revel in its overweening power. One woman from Quebec, Madame de Léry de Chaussegros, made her views clear, stating like others, 'for the first and last time'.[69] But we need to bear in mind that the slopes of the volcano were not like the drawing rooms of genteel society. They were an environment without the gendered rules of decorum, and for at least some women that was a part of their attraction.

Families

As the presence of women attests, travel up the volcano was almost invariably an event to be savoured with family and friends. It was often remarked that a solo ascent was a diminished experience because it had not been possible to share it with others. In June 1827 an English cleric, the Reverend C.B. Woolley, a graduate of Oriel College Oxford, grumpily described himself as 'alone'. Almost a year later, the younger son of the 7th Baron Clifford, who was a cadet at the Piedmont military academy in Turin, recorded his disappointment at the absence of friends: 'The Honourable R.H. Clifford ascended alas alone not having the pleasure of society to sweeten the toils of ascent.' His remarks were echoed by a Polish visitor from Krakow, Leon Like, who found the trip happy and inspiring, but wanted to share his feelings with those he cared for. Next time, he remarked, he would not come alone, but with friends and family.[70]

The idea, as one French woman put it, was to 'travel together'.[71] This explains why so many of the visitors to the volcano travelled in groups – six Italian professors of literature, an entire Caracciolo clan of Neapolitan aristocrats, two generations of the Rothschild bankers, groups of Sardinian and Danish courtiers, and Italian Jewish merchants, nine in number. The professions also travelled together: doctors, engineers, architects (five, from Paris, Warsaw, Coblenz, Lyon and St Gallen, ascended together on a hot August day in 1828); three months earlier a party of Belgian and Swiss artists had made it to the top.[72] And groups of soldiers and sailors, from the same regiments and crews, were regularly to be seen on the slopes of the volcano.

But the commonest groups climbing the mountain were couples and families. Among the many married couples were several men who had made previous ascents and who now brought their wives. Some searched the Visitors' Book for their signatures to confirm their earlier ascent. The Francophone Monsieur Henry brought his rather reluctant wife to see the volcano on 19 September 1827. As she commented,

'I'm not curious, but I have seen the mountain with pleasure ... one must see such a beautiful thing ... but you are not able to go down again except with some sombre thoughts. It's beautiful to see it once.'[73] But he was especially anxious to show 'his dear friend and wife' the entry in the Visitors' Book recording his earlier climb and was, as we have seen, much vexed to find that the page on which he had written had been removed. Unmarried couples also climbed Vesuvius together. George W. Lee 'and his dear friend, the beautiful Milanese' accompanied his friend R.W. Oakley and his 'Carolina', annotating the Visitors' Book with what appears as a four-pointed heart.[74]

Many parties were made up of a loosely knit group of family and friends. In the summer of 1827, Lady Temple led four members of her family to the crater as part of a large party of ten English men and women, including four army officers. Shortly thereafter Justin Audra, a lieutenant of the Vaud Conseil d'État from Lausanne, followed the same path with four members of his family and two other young Swiss women. Two famous stepbrothers, major figures in Parisian science William Frederic Edwards and Henri Milne Edwards, the former the founder of French ethnography, the latter a pioneer in physiological zoology, took time off from their studies in Naples to visit Vesuvius with their wives and a group of friends.[75] Such excursions were not scientific in nature; the presence of family and friends makes clear that they were convivial.

The largest groups of families were local, most notably the members of the Neapolitan aristocracy who held family feasts at the hermitage usually in the months of September and October, and the families of the British merchants, factors and bankers who lived in Naples. The former, members of the Caracciolo, Petti, Petroni and Mastelloni families, were, like other Neapolitans of much humbler status, usually to be found celebrating Mass and enjoying feast days on the volcano. If we plot the months when different groups climbed Vesuvius, we find that the Italians were an anomaly. Nearly all other nationalities ascended in the spring, but the Italians travelled in the autumn (Chart 3).

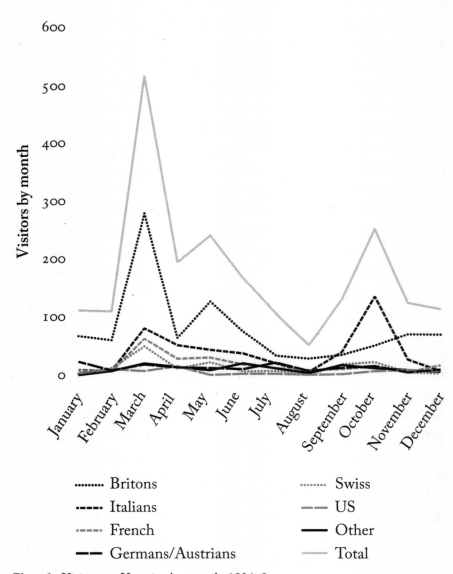

Chart 3. Visitors to Vesuvius by month, 1826–8.
Note: the high March figures are explained by the eruption of March 1828.
Source: MS Ital 139, Houghton Library, Harvard University.

The distinction is explained by the very different relation most Italians, especially Neapolitans, had to the volcano. Like others, they shared an enthusiasm for 'sublime tourism', but for them Vesuvius was part of a culture of feasts, festivals and saints that took place in September and October, taking advantage of the clement, seasonable weather. They journeyed not to peer into the crater, but to celebrate the saints who preserved them, to keep the threats of nature in check, and to share with their families and friends the pleasures of feasting and the enjoyment of benign autumn temperatures. Thus on 26 September Guiseppe Magalotti and friends went to the hermitage to celebrate 'our principal protector the glorious San Gennaro',[76] whose feast day had been held the week before in the cathedral of Naples. Two days later a priest, children and friends from Casoria, a town 10 kilometres north-east of Naples, arrived at the hermitage to enjoy Mass and a celebratory feast, to be followed the next day by members of one of Naples' most illustrious houses, the Cavaliere Antonio Caracciolo di Brienza, his wife and friends. Neapolitans of all classes celebrated their patron on the volcano whose powers he supposedly tamed.[77]

Another rather different group of Neapolitan families often climbed the slopes of Vesuvius together. The English commercial community of Naples was a close-knit society, occasionally riven by rivalries, but united by a common concern to protect their special status in the kingdom, by their Protestant religion and by intermarriage.[78] In 1827, the Neapolitan government taxed twenty-four British enterprises. These included substantial banking and brokerage businesses like Vallin, Routh and Valentine, or Cottrell, Iggulden and Company, which dealt with the shipping needs of British subjects, arranged foreign remittances and promoted local investment, like the steamship company between the mainland and Sicily. But there were also smaller enterprises, like Joseph Kernot's pharmacy in the Strada San Carlo in the centre of Naples. Kernot and his next-door neighbour, Robert Pike, used an ascent of Vesuvius to advertise their wares. Pike described himself in the Visitors' Book as 'from London, patent self-adjusting truss manufacturer and merchant', reminding visitors that his trusses were 'Capital things to wear ascending the mountain or descending either.'[79] Mid-size businesses were like that of Louis Graindorge, a Swiss married to an Englishwoman, who owned the Albergo del Sole in the Largo Castello and a 'British Warehouse' next door which sold English foods, stationery, medicines, beer, riding tackle and sundry other goods in the English taste.[80] By the mid-nineteenth century there were more than 200 British family members resident in the city. This community was quite distinct from the wealthy British aristocrats, like Lady Blessington, who lived for a time in the city, and whose social connections were with travellers of their own class, and with (usually liberal) members of the Neapolitan aristocracy. As Lady Morgan the Irish feminist and novelist commented, the merchant community and the British *bon ton* simply didn't mix.

The effervescent adventurer Colonel Francis Maceroni, trader, balloonist, inventor, soldier and bon vivant, paints a vivid picture of the British commercial community in Naples in his *Memoirs*. Born in Manchester in 1788 to an Italian merchant family, he moved back and forth between England and Italy in the early nineteenth century. He acted as a cicerone in Rome and also served as an officer and aide-de-camp to Murat in the French general's army, but he cut his teeth as a young businessman in Naples. Maceroni was delighted with the British community there, describing them as 'worthy, well-informed, and agreeable men and women, that ever had the happiness of consorting together'. He was astonished by their sociability, comparing them to a club, but with women members. 'Every day of the week, a considerable party met to dine at one or other of their houses'; 'picnics' and outings to such places as Vesuvius 'were continually being arranged', while in the evenings houses 'were open to whist and supper'. The inveterately sociable Maceroni started an archery club – with the English merchants competing with an association of Swiss residents of Naples – as well as organising games of cricket.[81]

Families like the Valentines and Graindorges made regular trips with their friends up Vesuvius. Edward Valentine, the head of the family and president of the 'Tribuno di Commercio', took a party up in the summer of 1827, was twice present with business partners and family friends during the March 1828 eruption, and led a large group of twelve, including five members of his family and two Graindorges, to the summit in October of the same year.[82] The names of members of the British community are scattered all over the Visitors' Book of 1826–8. The English merchants were fond of crude humour – the banker Iggulden and his wife were described as 'spooneys' (simple or ignorant people), while he was also nicknamed 'Wriggle-bum alias Bear in breeches'.[83] And they liked pitting themselves against one another and betting on the result. In January 1828 the Manchester coal importer and madder factory owner James Close returned from the summit to the hermitage, together with a group of six friends, to celebrate winning a wager that he couldn't reach the top of Vesuvius from the house of the head guide in Resina in less than an hour and a half; he made it in 'forty-seven minutes & a half'.[84]

Grand Tourists

But what of the presence of the leisured classes? British historians' accounts of eighteenth-century travel in Italy have centred on the Grand Tourist – a wealthy young man (anywhere between sixteen and twenty-three years of age), often educated at Eton, Westminster or Harrow, and with some experience of residence in an Oxbridge college, especially Christ Church, undertaking an important rite of passage, travelling for instruction and pleasure between adolescence and manhood, often accompanied by an older tutor. The aim was to acquire a sort of cosmopolitan patriotism, grounded in the arti-facts and values of antiquity, that prepared young men for the duties of marriage and public office. But Grand Tourists have also often been defined in a much less precise way, as prosperous travellers

taking journeys of pleasure and instruction along routes used by
Grand Tourists or designated by Grand Tour travel literature. Grand
Tourism, in the strict sense, has always been associated with the
literature on taste and erudition – in art, antiquities and classical
civilisation – whose focus was first Roman, and which then gravitated to Greece and the Middle East. More generally, travellers who
followed Grand Tour routes journeyed for many different reasons
and often with a much more eclectic range of interests. But what
they seem to have shared with 'grand' Grand Tourists was the undertaking of a *voluntary* journey that mixed pleasure and instruction.[85]

Before the middle of the eighteenth-century Vesuvius was of little
importance to Grand Tourists. Visitors to Naples were more interested in the sites to the west of the city such as Virgil's (supposed)
tomb and the Grotto of the Cumaean Sibyl, sites that had direct
associations with classical antiquity. Vesuvius was only important as
the killer of the elder Pliny, the great naturalist who was asphyxiated
trying to help friends and to observe the eruption in 79 CE. With few
exceptions Grand Tour travel writings and memoirs offered only a
perfunctory account of the volcano, said little of their emotional
response to it, and when they did so, viewed it with displeasure. Only
in the later part of the century, as the discoveries of Herculaneum
and Pompeii were progressively uncovered, and as mineralogy and
geology became fashionable pursuits, did the volcano move up the
Grand Tour calendar, become a particular object of interest, and
excite aesthetic approval.

Historians (and, to a lesser extent, literary critics) have tended to see
the Grand Tour as an eighteenth-century phenomenon, severely
curtailed by the Revolutionary and Napoleonic Wars, and largely killed
off in the nineteenth century by a bourgeois tourism of sentiment associated not just with men but women and children. After 1815 when the
European mainland opened up again to prosperous travellers – British
military and naval men had, of course, been active all over Europe and
its seas during the wars – there was a strong sense that the Continent,

and especially Italy, was being overrun by British visitors. After the end of the Napoleonic Wars, as the *Westminster Review* put it, 'the inundation of Britons, like a second irruption of the Goths, poured down upon Italy'.[86] Though, as James Buzard has persuasively argued, such claims became a genre of literary exaggeration (as well as an early case of tourist anti-tourism), it was certainly true that the patrician traveller of the eighteenth century, though as mobile as ever, now had to put up with the presence of a wider range of travellers than ever before. Comments such as Byron's famous complaint about Rome being filled with 'staring boobies, who go about gaping and wishing to be at once cheap and magnificent', or his dismissal of 'a family of children and old women' in the Alps as 'too old and others too young to be the least aware of what they saw' are not only indicative of the sexism and snobbery of aristocratic travellers and commentators, but also remind us that such (supposedly socially superior) critics did not stop travelling.[87] Stories of the Grand Tour may have been replaced by stories of more demotic travel – just as Thomas Cook's tours were later to raise a chorus of condemnation – but Grand Tourists kept on touring.[88]

The nostalgic sense that the Grand Tour had seen better (more exclusive) times, like much such sentiment, makes for poor history, tending to overlook the ways in which tours and tourists changed through the eighteenth century. At the time that many historians see as the peak of Grand Tourism – the period around the American War of Independence (1776–83) – it was already the case that the young aristocrats and their tutors were giving way to family parties (both aristocratic and bourgeois), that tours were getting shorter, and that the preponderance of collectors and connoisseurs of art and antiquity was no longer made up of young men, but of mature scholars and aesthetes.[89] Both guidebooks and personal travel narratives about Italy were also changing, reflecting a more diverse range of interests and a very different sense of history. The prime focus of the tour guide and personal narrative, its constant, remained objects of art and antiquity, but now often included commentary on contemporary society, recent history and 'deep time'. The young William Crackenthorpe, writing to his mother and sister of his tour in Italy in 1815, though admiring the antiquities, could not resist peppering his letters with comments about the current state of Italy and Europe.[90] This shift in focus was not simply a function of feminisation and a move down-market to a more demotic readership (though there were elements of this); it had to do with a changing sensibility among all travellers including those who, two generations earlier, would have qualified as exemplary Grand Tourists.

Though doubtless a few have passed undetected, there are relatively few signatories to the Visitors' Book of 1826–8 who could pass muster as old-fashioned Grand Tourists. We can, of course, place the recalcitrant Crown Prince of Denmark in this category – sent by his father with minders to prepare himself (however inadequately) for adult life. The American Henry Wadsworth Longfellow, who reached Vesuvius on 17 April 1828, might also qualify – a young twenty-one-year-old, undertaking a tour of Europe that lasted three years in preparation for assuming a professorship at Bowdoin College. There were also a number of young Englishmen who fitted the profile: men like Rawdon Lubbock Brown (b. 1806), a former pupil of Charterhouse, who was travelling in Italy in the summer of 1828, ascending Vesuvius on two occasions, in May and August. The trip to Italy was life-changing for Brown who moved to Venice in 1833, remaining there for the rest of his life. He later acted as a cicerone for the likes of John Ruskin and beavered away in the Venetian archives, from which he eventually published a vast Calendar of Venetian State Papers dealing with England. He was one example of a rare but far from endangered species, the Grand Tourist gone native. However, Brown, like the young Honourable Charles Stuart (b. 1810), and Sir Robert Gore-Booth (b. 1805) and the bevy of Old Etonians whose fortunes we will shortly follow, was not accompanied by a tutor, but travelled *en famille*. His companions on his ascent of Vesuvius were first his father, and then later his elder sister, Emma.[91]

In March 1828, immediately before and during the eruption that occurred in that month, several young men, all from Eton College, and most studying at Christ Church College, Oxford – and therefore fitting the classic Grand Tourist profile – climbed the volcano together. In much the same manner as their eighteenth-century predecessors, their paths had already crossed as they travelled through France and Italy. When Arthur Henry Hallam had arrived in Florence in October 1827, he'd been delighted to find two school chums, Charles Coxe and Lord Alexander, the future Lord Caledon, staying in the same hotel, and to meet up with three other old Etonians, Edmund Antrobus, Henry Trench and John Balfour of Balbirnie, who were lodged elsewhere in the city. In Rome, where he spent five months, young Hallam was joined by Henry Browne Beresford, a contemporary at Eton who was in the Bengal Civil Service, and by another school friend, James Milnes Gaskell, who was to become one of his closest companions. Gaskell, in turn, met up with Sackville Casement, another Eton and Christ Church man, who was travelling with Lord Caledon, and introduced Hallam to two more Etonians en route for Naples, Thomas and Robertson Gladstone, the brothers of one of Hallam's best Etonian friends, William Ewart Gladstone, the future British prime minister.[92] Like foxhounds, Old Etonians travelled in packs.

But if this group of young men in some respects resembled their predecessors of the previous century, in others they were very different. Gaskell travelled in the traditional manner, with a tutor, Richard Rothman, but he was in a family party, not travelling on his own but with his parents. The same was true of Lord Alexander. Arthur Hallam too had his parents with him, a paternal aunt (to whom he was very close), and his eleven-year-old sister, Ellen. When the Hallams and the Gaskells went up Vesuvius together, probably at the instigation of James Milnes Gaskell, who had already completed two ascents of the volcano, their party included Gaskell's mother (though not his retiring father), and Arthur's father.[93]

Henry Hallam, Arthur's father, certainly envisaged the journey to Italy of 1827–8 as an occasion to educate his eldest son in the classics. He had taken him on two previous European tours – in 1818 and 1822 – but this was the first to Italy, planned as a year-long educational excursion. Henry, educated at Eton and Christ Church, was well known as a historian, and as an intellectual associated with the Whig *Edinburgh Review* and with the Holland House circle, the home of Whiggery in London. Described as a man of 'system' and by some as a bit of a bore, he was a member of both the Royal Society and the Society of Antiquaries, of which he was vice president.[94] His views on the purposes of travel were very much those of the eighteenth-century Grand Tourist – to get beyond the present into an instructive antique past, made visible by its remnants and given meaning by classical texts. As he wrote to a friend in February 1828 from Rome: 'To enjoy the utmost of Rome, one should exclude the modern – but above all, one shd. exclude English society – he who comes hither with a true Roman feeling shd. keep his countrymen at a distance, even the number (this year a very small one) of those who can distinguish between the eternal city & Brighton'.[95] Hallam was an intrusive parent with strong views about his son's career and future, but in Rome, especially once Arthur was with his school chums, he was forced to concede of his son that his 'mind had been so occupied by other pursuits, that he had thought little of antiquity even in Rome itself'. What mattered to young Arthur were not the remnants of antiquity: 'Who,' he asked, 'can sympathise with two feet of broken wall, or the separated base of an unknown column? The Forum is choked up nearly with mud, disfigured with hovels, and deprived of all effect by piles of dirty linen, hung out to dry!!'[96] What mattered was the Protestant cemetery at Testaccio, where both Keats and Shelley were buried, and about which Arthur composed two sonnets, prefacing them with a quote from Walter Savage Landor, the English poet who lived in Florence: 'If anything could engage me to visit Rome, to endure the sight of her scarred and awful ruins, telling their grave stories in the midst of eunuchs and fiddlers ... it would be that I might spend an hour of solitude, where the pyramid of Cestius points to the bones of Keats and Shelley.'[97] Wordsworth, Coleridge and Shelley (though, interestingly, not Byron) were to become Arthur's lodestars, with their intense commitment to poetry, their belief in the superior powers of the poet, and their interest in what his father, Henry Hallam, disparaging called 'misty metaphysics'. What mattered was that exploration of feeling and emotion that came with a strange land and new acquaintance. What this meant for Arthur and his school friend James Milnes Gaskell was the new feeling of romantic love. But while the eighteenth-century Grand Tourist was likely to embark on a series of grand passions with Italian women, married or no, and, like Augustus Hervey in the mid-eighteenth century, cut a swathe across Italy with numerous lovers in Florence, Genoa and Naples, Arthur and James both fell for the same (more or less respectable) English woman, torturing one another, in the best Romantic fashion, with the exquisite pains of unrequited love. This triangular affection – more strongly felt by James than Arthur (the former left money to the girl friend, Anna Wintour, in his will) – the verses it inspired and the intense late-night conversations it engendered lay, as both young men acknowledged, at the heart of their Italian experience.[98]

Over the following years, the Hallams, father and son, waged a battle which was not resolved at Arthur's premature death in Vienna in 1833. Henry sent Arthur to Cambridge – which at first he hated – to study mathematics (one of the few fields in which his son did not display brilliance); he then enrolled him in the Inner Temple, preparing him for a career in law. He obstructed the publication of his son's Italian Romantic verses and obscured the evidence of his passion. The son resisted. At Cambridge, as a member of the Apostles (a rarified debating club) and a friend of Alfred Tennyson, as well as the suitor of the poet's sister, Emily, Arthur neglected mathematics for 'metaphysics and poetry', which he believed to be 'not only the surest pillars, but even the constituting elements of the Christian

Scheme.' He wickedly parodied his father's sober comments and exhortations: 'That's just the way with Coleridge & the rest of them: they spin a spider's-web of language to catch foolish flies, who think that this mysticism is originality of thought! Read Paley ... Read Locke, read Bacon; but these never *will* be read, when Coleridge, and Shelley are: such authors as favourites, must deprave the mind.' When confronted by his father, Arthur stood firm: 'I am sorry you think my fondness for modern poetry so excessive ... I shall hardly be persuaded to think that I have done wrong in feeding myself with Wordsworth or Shelley'.[99]

Arthur was an exceptional young man, capable of inspiring the strongest emotions – as well as one of the most popular poems of the nineteenth century, Tennyson's *In Memoriam*. But he also personified the nineteenth-century 'Grand Tourist', travelling in the bosom of his family, attracted not to youthful libertinism but to a domesticated, Christian and rather English notion of romantic love, drawn to Italy for what it gave him in the present rather than for what it taught him from the past. His early death in the bloom of youth, of course, also made him an iconic Romantic figure, sharing in this respect, but in almost no other, the fate of Lord Byron.

Military men

Vesuvius's slopes were constantly populated by army and naval officers. Some, and they were almost always from the highest ranks, were, as we have seen, retirees rather than men in active service: famous generals like the indomitable Marshal Soult, the Duke of Dalmatia, still active in French politics, or the Prussian patriot Ludwig Graf Yorck von Wartenburg, now retired to his estates in Silesia; or the British admirals, like William Taylor whose first voyage had been with Captain Cook to Tahiti, and Sir Richard Hussey Bickerton, who had retired to the spa of Bath in the West Country. But these visitors were far outnumbered by much younger active soldiers and sailors.[100]

There was a strong, albeit periodic, British naval presence on Vesuvius. The port of Naples was less commercially significant than Livorno to the north and less strategically important than Malta as a Royal Navy base, but British naval vessels often stopped there, usually en route to the Eastern Mediterranean.[101] Climbing the volcano was a welcome diversion from the confines on board ship. On 12 and 13 May 1827, a sizable party of officers, including one of the ship's surgeons, reached the summit. They were serving aboard HMS *Asia*, a newly commissioned eighty-four-gun ship of the line, and the flag-ship of Admiral Sir Edward Codrington, commander of the Royal Navy's Mediterranean fleet. They were on their way to Greece, where, just a few months later together with their French and Russian allies, they would rout the Turkish fleet at the Battle of Navarino, the last major battle under sail of the British navy. They were accompanied by members of the crew of the naval cutter HMS *Racer*, which also took part in the battle.

In January 1828 men serving on HMS *Mastiff*, a brig on survey duty in the Mediterranean, took time off to visit Vesuvius; a few months later, it was the turn of officers and enlisted men from among the 121 crew members of HMS *Pelican*, an eighteen-gun cruiser, to climb the mountain. In the following year an expedition of seven crew members from the brig *Matilda*, the brig *Hawk* and the brig *Dryad* ended in a quarrel in which three sailors were abandoned on the volcano by their 'ungentlemanly' colleagues.[102]

The presence of soldiers on Vesuvius was more enduring. The constitutional revolt of 1820, which had briefly imposed a constitu-tion on King Ferdinand of the Two Sicilies, was suppressed by an Austrian army which then remained in the kingdom as an occupying force until 1827. They were often on the slopes of Vesuvius and never more so than during the eruption of 1822, which the authorities feared would be interpreted as a sign of hostility to the Austrian occupation. In January of 1827 three different parties of officers in the Imperial Army climbed Vesuvius; the last of these included two

French aristocrats, a Polish count, four Germans and an Italian.[103] But by the spring of 1827, after a flurry of final visits to the hermitage, most of the Austrian troops had left Naples, to be replaced on the volcano by parties of officers from the newly hired regiments of Swiss mercenaries.

By far the most prominent military group on the volcano, where their presence continued until 1848, were the Swiss, most of whom were officers serving in one of the Swiss regiments of the Neapolitan army, four infantry, one artillery and one 'hunters' regiment, bodies recruited en masse from the cantons around Lucerne, Fribourg, Valais and Berne. There had been Swiss regiments in Naples in the eighteenth century, hired by Carlo Borbone in 1734, both as part of his personal guard and to supplement the regular army. By the outbreak of the French Revolution there were about 6,000 Swiss men and officers in the kingdom, but these regiments were disbanded in 1789 and the troops dispersed. Not until Francis I signed a series of contracts with Swiss cantons after his succession in 1825 did the Swiss return. By the end of the decade, the royal army included more than 250 officers and about 6,000 men, gradually bringing the numbers of troops back to their pre-Revolutionary levels. But the purpose of these Swiss soldiers was rather different from that of their precursors.[104] The Neapolitan monarch turned to Swiss mercenaries for political, not military, reasons. The constitutional revolt of 1820 had been led by junior officers – usually the younger sons of the Neapolitan aristocracy – and the royal military academy had become a hotbed of reform. After the uprising's failure, the army was purged, but the revolution of 1820 made clear that the king needed a military force to police his subjects.

The Austrian army that had freed King Ferdinand from his constitutional restraints in 1820 remained as an army of occupation, but they were deeply unpopular and, more importantly from the King's perspective, imposed a considerable financial burden on the Crown. The Swiss were cheaper and, more to the point, owed their allegiance directly to the king rather than to a foreign power. When they arrived in Naples, every soldier was required to take an oath of allegiance to the monarch, to swear to obey his officers and never desert the standard of his regiment. But, in a clause that made clear the king's fear of the *carbonari* who had formed radical and reformist groups, recruits also had to swear that they would never join any secret society. Internal security, not foreign invasion, was the government's first concern. The disposition of the troops made this clear. A full complement of two regiments was always present in the city; the largest force, based at Castel Nuovo, immediately next to the Royal Palace, also housed an artillery battery of six cannon and two howitzers, ready for immediate action to quell any unrest on the streets.[105]

Swiss soldiers were essentially the king's private guard. A patrol accompanied him on every occasion when he travelled about the city or further abroad; but they were also required to accompany all major religious ceremonies, clearing the streets for clerical processions, and to guard the entrances of theatres and other places of public resort. Once a year, on 8 September, during the Fête du Roi or Festa di Piedigrotta, the Swiss troops marched through the city and converged on the main street, the Via Toledo, arriving at the Piazza del Palazzo Reale to cries of '*Vive il Re! Tutto in festa, tutto in gioia*' ('Long live the king! All in celebration, all in joy'). This annual symbolic appropriation of the city's space took place along the routes where the Swiss were to fight and, after bloody street battles, eventually defeat the revolutionaries of 1848.[106]

The rank and file of the Swiss regiments were actively discouraged from mingling with the Neapolitan populace. Zones that they frequented outside the barracks were off limits to civilians; if a soldier suffered from venereal disease – a sure sign of intimacy with the locals – he was severely punished. By far the most popular patrol was that accompanying quartermasters when they were buying provisions: the soldiers were tipped by merchants eager to keep the troops' business, and the trade provided an opportunity to mix with Neapolitans of both sexes. In general, contact was kept to a minimum.

Given the constraints on the Swiss soldiers, it may seem odd that so many managed to find their way onto the slopes of Vesuvius, but those who did are indicative of the fundamental divide that existed between the rank-and-file Swiss soldier and the officers who commanded him. Almost every Swiss soldier who climbed Vesuvius was an officer. In only one case, when a group of sergeant majors climbed the volcano together in March 1828, can we identify any regular Swiss soldier who made the journey to the top. Clearly, officers enjoyed a freedom not available to the ordinary soldier.

Nearly all the Swiss army signatories of the Visitors' Book were lieutenants, young men in their twenties, overwhelmingly from the 2nd (Vonderveid) regiment from the Catholic canton of Fribourg. Only during the eruption of March 1828 were they joined by officers from other regiments, and by a large party of sergeant majors, the most junior ranks to climb the volcano. They were a pugnacious bunch, giving themselves false titles as princes and counts in the hermit's book, appointing one of their number 'Director of Explosions', writing mocking comments and jokes, composing songs and poems, and attacking the British visitors as mean and parsimonious. They notoriously refused to use the services of the Neapolitan guides – a great source of resentment – and directly challenged their authority. In the summer of 1827 two of them urged all visitors to ignore the expensive 'impostures' of the guides, claiming that the ascent could be made unaided. As Swiss they were fully confident of their climbing skills. They organised timed races to the top of Vesuvius – the Konig brothers boasted of taking forty-five minutes up the cone of the mountain and only eight on their return – and gathered in groups at night to drink and sing among the lava flows and embers. Most of these energetic young men climbed Vesuvius on many occasions. When Lieutenant Frederick Wyder of Lausanne reached the summit of Vesuvius with a party of fellow officers on 14 September 1828, it was his tenth time at the top of the volcano.[107]

The Swiss officers became a standing feature of the volcano, regularly mentioned in accounts of its ascent. They flirted with and mocked other visitors. When Emilia Moldinhaver wrote in the Visitors' Book that, though she was from Augsburg she was 'more Italian than German at heart', they scribbled 'Bravo, Bravo, Bravo' and 'What a loss for Germany!'[108] During the eruption of March 1828 they formed 'a society of Swiss officers', as they described themselves, 'to admire the effects of the infernal fireplace (in the vulgar sense)'. They also mocked the Neapolitans as fearful of what they described as imaginary dangers. The mountain made them exuberant, though it did not prevent them from being nostalgic about the peaks of their homeland. One of their verses, in a neat inversion, described Vesuvius as 'cold' when compared with the warmth generated by Mount Rigi, the iconic peak in central Switzerland.[109]

Many of the officers who served in Naples could recall ancestors who fought as mercenaries as far back as the fourteenth century. Most came from the patrician class in conservative Catholic cantons. They had a proud tradition of military prowess, and they were handsomely paid for their services. Typical of this Swiss officer class was Nicholas Joseph de Bumann, who boastfully described himself as 'a bourgeois patrician of the town and republic of Fribourg in Switzerland, currently sub-lieutenant of the second Swiss regiment of Vonderweid in the service of the King of the Two Sicilies', theatrically ending his entry in the book with a bold utterance of fidelity: 'My heart to my lover, my arms to my Prince . . . long live the King!'[110] Bumann was part of the patrician elite that dominated political office in his native canton of Fribourg, and which organised the recruitment of foreign regiments. He also came from a family with a tradition of foreign military service. No fewer than six members of his family served the King of Naples. He himself was an experienced soldier, having fought in Swiss regiments in Spain, Portugal, Russia and France. He was eventually to achieve the rank of brigadier and the governorship of Capua, remaining in the service of the king until 1860. After the fall of the Bourbon dynasty he chose to remain in Naples where he died in 1871.[111] Like many who found themselves on the slopes of Vesuvius, he had come to Naples not to see the volcano, but in pursuit of a career that involved a journey that was neither completely coerced nor unconditionally chosen.

Doctors, surgeons and men of science

Apart from the military men, doctors and surgeons were one of the largest professional groups on Vesuvius. The Visitors' Book records some forty-seven entries of members of the medical profession, thirteen from Britain, ten from Italy and five from the United States of America. Others came from Paris, Nice and Dreux in France; St Petersburg and Copenhagen to the north; and from Stuttgart, Dresden, Göttingen, Königsberg, Zurich and Aschaffenburg in the German-speaking lands. Some were present because of their employment. Dr de Molmer was the personal physician of the Crown Prince of Denmark and Dr Moore a member of the Duke of Buckingham's entourage, while David J. Hall, a surgeon on HMS *Asia*, accompanied his shipmates up Vesuvius in May 1827. Other distinguished medical men who reached the hermitage included Luigi Scatena, who was a professor of surgery in Rome, George Lilburn, an Edinburgh physician and expert in midwifery, Dr George Wilkes, an ear and eye surgeon from New York City, and Harry Deas, professor of surgery at the recently founded Medical College in Charleston, South Carolina, who was later to be president of the institution. On 21 September 1828, M.H. Stapleton, a surgeon and professor of anatomy at Trinity College Dublin, 'ascended the mountain with his bulldog Touser who had a very narrow escape of falling into the crater'.[112]

At least two doctors, George Burrows, who was to become president of the British Medical Association, and James Hope from

Lancashire, were studying in Italy, during something akin to a medical Grand Tour, when they visited Vesuvius. Both men worked with doctors in Paris before moving to Italy. Burrows, whose most famous publications were to be studies of disorders of the brain, went to Pavia to work with Antonio Scarpa, a professor of clinical surgery with a special interest in the nervous system, and with Bartolomeo Panizza, Scarpa's pupil and professor of anatomy; Burrows aimed to enhance his knowledge of neuro-anatomy and neuro-physiology by working with these experts. He also studied cholera on his return to London, using what he had learned in Italy during the outbreak of the disease there in 1832.[113] James Hope, a skilled amateur artist educated at the University of Edinburgh and St Bartholomew's Hospital in London, divided his time in Italy 'among the medical schools and hospitals, the galleries of the arts, and the public buildings'.[114] An ardent advocate of auscultation and of the use of the recently invented stethoscope (whose value he had discovered while working at the hospital La Charité in Paris), he was to write the influential *Treatise on the Diseases of the Heart*, first published in 1832, complete with illustrations by his own hand. These medical men, it should be stressed, were not engaged in a journey of retrospection, but came to Italy to study the innovative work of some of its finest physicians.

Yet in many ways the most remarkable medical visitors to Vesuvius were men whose major intellectual achievements were not in medicine but in related life sciences. As previously mentioned, two notable brothers, William Frederic and Henri Milne Edwards, accompanied by their wives, visited the volcano on 17 December 1827 in a party of nine. William and Henri, born nearly a quarter of a century apart, were the sons of a British Jamaican planter, though by different mothers. William was born in the Caribbean, Henri in Bruges where the family moved at the turn of the century. Both brothers became physicians, studying in Paris, one qualifying in 1808, the other in 1823.

William, who had also been educated (along with William Hazlitt) at the Dissenting academy in Hackney, published his first major work, *De l'influence des agents physique sur la vie*, in 1824 (later translated, in consultation with the author, by the British physician Thomas Hodgkin, as *On the Influence of Physical Agents on Life*). There, in a radical move that equated human and animal development, William argued that 'Man is affected by diverse agents in the measure that is appropriate to his species but in the same manner as other mammals', a view that he supported with a large body of data reporting his experiments.

Yet William Edwards was most interested in working out the complex circumstances that went into producing human diversity both culturally and physically. Unusually, he was a member of both the Académie de Médecine and the Académie des Sciences Morales et Politiques, and the recipient of prizes from both the Académie des Sciences and the Académie des Inscriptions et Belles Lettres. Before and during his trip to Italy, Edwards became interested in both the history of languages and the problem of human types or races. (During his time in Naples he made drawings of the physiognomy of the city's *lazzaroni* – the urban poor.) His views began to shift. A year after his ascent of Vesuvius he published a study of racial characteristics and types entitled *Des caractères physiologiques des races humaines considérés dans leurs rapports avec l'histoire* which, though it expressed a complex notion of racial characteristics and was chiefly concerned with the Gauls and the Franks, became famous for its assertion that human types were permanent, and not subject to environmental factors. In doing so, William laid down one of the major planks in the platform of what was to become the 'science' of race in the nineteenth century. In 1839, along with his brother Henri, the historian Jules Michelet, and scholars in geography, physiology, medicine, natural history, linguistics, archaeology and belles-lettres, William founded (and was the first president of) the Société Ethnologique de Paris. He became known as the father of French ethnography.[115]

While during the 1820s William was concerned with human typologies and their relation to biological or environmental factors, his brother was carving out a career as a protégé of the zoologist Georges Cuvier, performing not dissimilar analyses to his brother, but on marine animals rather than humans. Appointed professor of hygiene and natural history at the École Centrale des Arts et Manufactures, he was to become professor of entomology at the Muséum National d'Histoire Naturelle, and what one admirer described as 'the head of the French School in natural history'. This was largely because of his development of 'physiological zoology' in which creatures were studied in nature rather than in the specimen bottle or as brute matter.[116] Henri was in Naples to study polyps, and was helped by Oronzio Gabriele Costa, a zoologist originally from Lecce, who had a large natural history museum in Naples where he worked on sea snails and studied insect life in the fumaroles on Vesuvius. (Costa played an important part in the research of Charles Lyell, identifying the marine fossils the geologist had found in the highlands of the island of Ischia as the same species to be found in the nineteenth-century Mediterranean Sea, helping to bolster Lyell's argument for terrestrial uplift as a result of volcanic activity.)[117] Costa went on to publish a massive series of volumes on the fauna of the entire Kingdom of Naples. Together with Henri Milnes Edwards he shared an interest in 'physiological zoology' and the two were to travel together in 1844 when Edwards returned to Naples as part of a mission from the French Ministry of Education to compare the fauna of the southern Italian coast with those of France.[118]

Two other scientists who visited the hermitage were important naturalists, both of whom had medical degrees but rarely practised medicine. William Arnold Bromfield (1801–51) qualified at the University of Glasgow in 1823 but had private means and was much given to botanising. His visit to Vesuvius on 16 January 1828, when he wrote in the Visitors' Book 'God save the King',[119] was part of a four-year tour of Germany, France and Italy to collect botanical specimens. Though Bromfield remained in Britain during the 1830s, working on an extensive catalogue of Hampshire plants, he visited the Caribbean and North America on field trips in the 1840s, and in the following decade journeyed in the Near East through Egypt, the Holy Land, Lebanon and Syria, where he died of typhus in Damascus in 1851. His collections were sent to the Botanical Gardens at Kew.[120]

Bromfield left only a sparse published record; his great work on Hampshire flora appeared posthumously in the 1850s, but the British naturalist who followed him up Vesuvius eight days later, William Elford Leach (1791–1836), was a prolific scholar.[121] He came from a prosperous Devonshire family, and studied medicine at Edinburgh and St Andrews, but after completing his studies he took up a post as an assistant at the British Museum in 1813. Specialising in entomology and malacology, he (somewhat ruthlessly) reorganised the museum's collections and within four years was elected to the Royal Society, which was to publish thirty-two of his papers on natural history. Leach was a prodigious worker but suffered from mental illness. In 1822 he left the museum, which bought his collections and gave him an annuity, and moved to Genoa in Italy with his sister Jane. From there he continued to send specimens, notably insects, back to the museum in London. He travelled extensively in Italy and spent time in Rome, where he became a friend of Joseph Severn, the British artist who nursed John Keats in his final illness. Severn was enormously taken with Leach and his sister, writing 'they were the antipodes to each other & attached by great affection'. William, he found, 'seemed to exist in his own particular quality of mind, only to the exclusion of some other quality that as a human creature he ought to have possessed . . . He was like a child in all he did.' Severn was astonished by Leach's 'extacey [sic] of delight' in finding an 'almost invisible insect . . . not bigger than the head of a pin', amazed by his ardour for science.[122] Leach may have been attracted to Vesuvius, which he visited with his sister and brother on 25 January 1828, because of the recent publication of *Fauna Vesuviana* (1827) by Oronzio Costa, who had worked with Edwards, and who was strongly influenced by Leach's work. Leach remained an active collector, while his sister worked tirelessly to treat cholera victims in the Ligurian port, which was one of the first sites of the cholera epidemic that raged through Italy during the 1830s. Leach himself contracted the disease and died outside Genoa in 1836.

Important figures in the biological sciences like Leach and the Edwards brothers – all protégés or friends of the great French anatomist, Georges Cuvier – travelled considerable distances to climb Vesuvius, but local physicians also ascended the volcano. Salvatore De Renzi, who climbed Vesuvius with two friends in October 1828, arrived at the hermitage in the late afternoon before ascending the summit at three o'clock the next morning. As he indicated in the rather mordant poem he transcribed into the Visitors' Book, he had devoted his life to medicine, but his career as a medical practitioner up to that point had not been a happy one, thanks to his politics.[123] Educated at the University of Naples, he had worked as a medical practitioner during the constitutional revolution of 1820, manning an ambulance for General Guglielmo Pepe, the leader of the revolt. Once the old Bourbon regime was restored, he was repeatedly punished for his liberal politics. Twice he was dismissed from appointments which he had won on merit; he was finally given a job teaching the blind. But Dr De Renzi would not be gainsaid – he was a man of prodigious industry, who became obsessed with the effects of the environment on patterns of disease. His pioneering three-volume *Osservazioni sulla topografia-medica del Regno di Napoli*, published between 1828 and 1830, was an extraordinary survey of the kingdom, a vast data bank of information on climate, temperature, humidity, winds, soil types, modes of cultivation, water supplies, diet, buildings, industry and commerce, intended to explore the causes of such habitual illnesses as malaria and also of epidemic diseases such as cholera.[124]

In the *Osservazioni* De Renzi included a calendar of environmental conditions during the year 1828. He noticed that March, the month of the Vesuvian eruption, saw an increase in the number of respiratory complaints, cases of angina and chest pain.[125] His trip on 17 October to Vesuvius, the place he called in the Visitors' Book 'the wonder and terror of the Campania',[126] was a fact-finding expedition, one that he followed up five days later with a further visit to the volcano in the company of Guiseppe Sanchez, head of the Royal Library and author of *Prospetto di geografia fisica e di storia ragionata del Regno di Napoli*. Together they repeated the experiments performed during the earlier visit, and collected large numbers of insects, including many beetles, that they found living in the crevices in the lava. De Renzi wanted to check the height of the volcano (it had changed radically after the eruption of 1822), to test its air, and to compare temperatures on Vesuvius with those in Naples. He took instruments with him on both occasions, barometers and thermometers and a hygrometer, using the data he recorded when writing his description of Vesuvius in the *Osservazioni*. He noted that although the conditions differed during his two visits – the first at night, the second in the daytime – the differences between the temperatures on the volcano and in Naples remained remarkably constant.[127] Though De Renzi commemorated his trips with a poem, they were intended to contribute to a medical and scientific research project, whose broader remit was the health and hygiene of the people of the Kingdom of Naples.

De Renzi's efforts were finally rewarded in the 1830s, when under the new Bourbon monarch, Ferdinand II, he received a number of hospital appointments, was made a knight of the order of Ferdinand I and was nominated inspector of health by royal decree. He organised inoculation campaigns in Naples and the Papal States, founded an important medical journal, and began to study the diseases of cholera, typhus and malaria which he defined as '*malattie populari*' (maladies of the common people). At the same time he began work on a major study of the history of medicine in Italy, focusing on the School of Salerno. De Renzi's political travails were not over, however, as he again suffered in the aftermath of the failed revolutions of 1848, but he lived to see the Unification of Italy which he saw as essential to the progress of medicine, science and public health. His view of Vesuvius – as of the whole Italian peninsula – was that of a scientist determined to contribute to the progressive understanding of the effect of the environment on human well-being.

In addition to the medical doctors, several professors of science and mathematics also climbed the mountain. Robert Saunders, who was professor of mathematics at the College of William and Mary and was to become the school's president, reached the hermitage with two friends from Boston and Philadelphia on 7 February 1827. D'Enrico Giamboni, a professor of mathematics in Perugia, accompanied five other Italians, four from Milan and one from Ferrara, at the height of the 1828 eruption during the night of 21 March.[128] Giamboni was the author of *Elementi di matematica*, a successful mathematics textbook in two volumes printed in Rome, and of two volumes on geometry and algebra published in Naples in 1826 that had recently been adopted by the local Jesuit college of Santa Maria da Caravaggio.[129] Before his appointment at Perugia he had taught at the Collegio Barnabita in Macerata in the Molise and travelled extensively, studying mathematics in the United States.[130]

But perhaps the most famous scientific visitor to Vesuvius to sign the Visitors' Book was Charles Babbage, the independently wealthy mathematician and founding member of the British Association for the Advancement of Science, most famous for his development of the Difference Engine and the Analytical Engine, calculating machines that today are seen as forerunners of the computer. Babbage was eccentric, obsessive, ill-advisedly blunt in his opinions, and given to holding grudges; on the other hand he was loyal to his friends, uxorious, incredibly hardworking, a passionate aficionado of science as an agent of human betterment, and a brilliant mathematician. He arrived in Naples in June 1828 with Edmund Head, a recent graduate of Oriel College, Oxford, who was a passionate student of art and of classical and modern languages, and whom he met while travelling through Germany. (Head, after a brief academic career, was to become Governor General of Canada; in his retirement he published a translation of the Icelandic saga, *Viga Glum's Saga*.)[131]

Like many visitors to Naples, Babbage was there in the first instance because of his health. In 1827 he suffered what he later described as a 'severe affliction from the loss of a large portion of my family'.[132] In a few devastating months, he lost his father, his young wife and two of his children. His friends, members of the government that was financing his Difference Engine project, and medical advisers all urged him to travel on the Continent to help recover from the shock. But he was reluctant to leave his uncompleted machine. Edward Drummond, the secretary to the Chancellor of the Exchequer, Lord Goderich, who was funding Babbage's work, wrote to the scientist, 'I am to express his Lordship's regret that you should have felt any scruples about leaving England, under the circumstances that make it so desirable that you should do so: . . . [don't] for a moment hesitate to give yourself that relaxation which he sincerely hopes may be of service to you.'[133] Babbage's mother, deeply apprehensive about his mental state and fearing that he might take his own life, recruited his best friend, the astronomer John Herschel, to counsel him and persuade him of the need for rest and a change of scene. Even after his return from Italy she feared for his mental health, trying to conceal everything in his house that might lead him to remember his late wife.[134]

Babbage agreed to travel but he ignored the medical advice to rest; instead his chosen cure was 'intense occupation'.[135] His year-long journey through France, Italy and back through Germany was marked by visits to industrial premises, workshops, mines and factories (he was to use these in his work on political economy, *Economy of Manufactures and Machinery*, published in 1832), to scientific academies, and to individual savants and scientists. Travelling through Italy, he talked to professors in Pisa, advised the Grand Duke of Tuscany in Florence, and when he reached Naples he climbed Vesuvius, served on a Neapolitan scientific commission to examine the medical properties of the waters of Ischia, and carried out research on the ruins of the Temple of Serapis in Pozzuoli, 'the most remarkable building upon the face of the earth',[136] to help determine the seismic shifts in the region. He turned his visit to the region into a major geological research project, whose implications, as we shall see, were far-reaching.[137] His achievement was remarkable in view of his deep depression. As he wrote to Herschel: 'I cannot seriously work for more than two hours together, it is the most insufferable exertion and generally when I attempt it leaves me almost knocked up in body ... I am so void of energy that in six months I have not learned a word of German or Italian.'[138]

Babbage's trip to Vesuvius took place on 2 June 1828 during a pause in his researches into the Temple of Serapis. He had employed Salvatore Madonna to watch the volcano and advise him on the best day for an ascent. He and Edmund Head spent the afternoon exploring the slopes of the volcano, 'took a few hours repose in a [the hermit's] hut', and then climbed to the summit. Babbage was determined to descend into the crater to examine the 'miniature volcano' to be seen on its floor. He and Head had brought ropes with them and, though Madonna refused to accompany them, they were lowered into the crater by guides under the head guide's supervision. Babbage was carrying several instruments, including 'one of Troughton's heavy Barometers, strapped to my back looking like a cupid's quiver, though probably rather heavier ... an excellent box sextant ... two or three thermometers, a measuring tape', a flask and a few biscuits. Using the sextant, measuring tape and his walking stick, Babbage calculated the depth of his descent from the edge of the crater and found it to be 174 metres (570 feet). After making a series of observations about the different heights of the volcano's rim, Babbage turned his attentions to a small volcanic cone that was erupting at regular intervals. Timing these, Babbage determined that he had between ten and fifteen minutes in which he could approach the vent without danger and observe 'the slow formation and absorption of . . . vesicles of lava'.[139] He was especially interested in how depth and temperature were connected. Babbage's observations on the depth of the crater and its distance from the highest and lowest points of the rim were subsequently reprinted in the successive editions of Murray's *Handbook for Travellers in Southern Italy*.[140]

Babbage's research, based on meticulous and careful measurement, was intended not just to understand the workings of the volcano, or to answer the long-standing conundrum of what the pillars of the Temple of Serapis revealed about the movement of the earth, but to develop a mathematical model of the relationship between changes in the earth's temperature and its expansion and contraction. Just as Alexander von Humboldt had traced isotherms as a way of modelling the effect of climate on nature, so Babbage tracked and mapped subterranean isotherms as a way of modelling the effect of heat on the earth's surface, using his famous calculating machine to adduce the relations between subterranean heat and rock expansion or contraction.[141] In Babbage's later account it was in examining the volcanic region around the Temple, and in reflecting on his experiences examining viscous lava and firmer, colder ground on Vesuvius, that he came to consider 'other natural causes, constantly exerting their influence, which, concurring with the known properties of matter, must necessarily produce those alterations of sea and land, those elevations of continents and mountains, and those vast cycles of which geology gives such incontrovertible proofs.'[142] He used his local observations to model a more general theory. Though Vesuvius and the Temple of Serapis seemed far from the Difference Engine – both geographically and as objects of different scientific disciplines – they were in fact closely aligned to Babbage's interest in adducing general mathematical laws to unlock the secrets of nature. After his return to Britain, Babbage repeatedly used the story of his ascent into Vesuvius's crater to initiate an account of his views about heat and its effect on the earth's geology.

Babbage's journey to Naples was not only a fact-finding tour, but also convinced him of the need for new forums for the discussion and dissemination of scientific ideas. When he was asked by the

Grand Duke of Tuscany about how to improve science in his domain, Babbage responded by remarking that he had been asked the same question in three major Italian cities, and that his answer was 'better inter-communication amongst its men of science', and that 'the idea of a periodical meeting of men engaged in scientific pursuits naturally arose out of these remarks.'[143] (He then, quite typically, wrote a memorandum on the subject for the Grand Duke.) His words were heeded. Pisa, within the Grand Duchy, was the site of the first Italian scientific congress in 1839 and further conferences followed in Rome and Milan; six years later the venue was the newly opened Vesuvian Observatory, close by the hermitage, not far from where Babbage had napped in 1828 before his ascent of the volcano.

But it was not just the Italian conundrum but the German solution to the spread of scientific knowledge that convinced him of the need for a coordinating society for science, what would become the British Association for the Advancement of Science established in 1831. Arriving in Berlin in September 1828 he was just in time to attend the meeting of scientists convened in the city, a six-day conference chaired by Alexander von Humboldt and attended by 464 scientists whose work combined 'all the branches of physical knowledge, and the historical, geometrical, and experimental philosophy'. As Humboldt pointed out, the object of the conference was to supplement 'the mutual interchange of treatises, or in innumerable memoirs, destined to be printed in some general collection' by bringing 'those personally together who were engaged in the same field of science' into a 'friendly connexion'.[144] This was the model that Babbage took back to London.

One of Babbage's strongest supporters in his efforts to found a British scientific association was also a signatory of the Vesuvian Visitors' Book. James Forbes had always shown a proclivity for science; from a very early age he had kept meteorological and astronomical journals, and no event in his youth delighted him more than his father's gift of a theodolite made by Troughton. As a callow seventeen-year-old and even before his trip to Italy he had submitted two papers to David Brewster, the editor of the *Edinburgh Journal of Science*, one on the heavens, the other on heat and cold.

Forbes was tall, preternaturally thin and dour. One of his biographers describes him as 'aloof, meticulous, cautious, exceedingly well organised, the model of an inductive scientist. He did not make friends readily, and perhaps seemed better fitted for criticism than to construct.'[145] Aristocratic by birth, Tory in his politics and Episcopalian in faith, Forbes was not a sympathetic character, and his career was marked by quarrels, not just with scientific opponents but with former friends like his patron Sir David Brewster, and his collaborator Louis Agassiz. But he was also a skilled and exceptionally well-organised politician, able to mediate between conflicting parties, though his adroitness sometimes verged on the manipulative and certainly served to advance his career.

Naples presented Forbes with an opportunity to make his mark: to write the fullest and most precise scientific description of the region available in English. Forbes was not just ambitious but exceptionally meticulous. As he explained some years later in describing his methods as a note-taker:

> The practice which I have long adopted with advantage is this: to carry a memorandum-book with Harwood's prepared paper and metallic pencil, in which notes, and observations, and slight sketches of every description, are made on the spot, and in the exact order in which they occur. These notes are almost ineffaceable, and are preserved for reference. They are then extended, as far as possible, every evening, with pen and ink, in a suitable book, in the form of a journal – from which, finally, they may be extracted and modified for any ultimate purpose.[146]

Forbes liked this method because it forced him to revise his observations shortly after they were made, and because the act of copying and revising meant that the loss of a pocket-book did not mean the loss of his materials.[147] (Forbes was a scrupulous record keeper: for most of his life he kept copies of the letters he wrote to scientific correspondents.)

Between July 1827 and January 1829 Forbes published eight papers in the *Edinburgh Journal* based on his observations in Italy, including two on Vesuvius.[148] He was not modest. In his accounts of Vesuvius and of Pompeii and Herculaneum he complained about the inadequacy of his predecessors, comparing his own efforts to those of Alexander von Humboldt. Much of his work on the rocks and minerals of Vesuvius derived from Italian scholarship, which he downplayed or criticised while emphasising how his observations were based on 'specimens in my possession'. (His final trip up the volcano with his brother on 2 April 1827 was made to collect 'the best Vesuvian minerals' before their return to Britain.) But his articles gave his readers an accomplished and accessible overview of Vesuvius and the Bay of Naples, using the familiar format that combined a vivid account of an ascent of the volcano with a history of its eruptions. His detailed analysis of the metals and minerals of the volcano was especially effective when combined with his description of the crater:

At our feet and close to us on every side were deep beds of yellow sulphur varying in colour from the deepest red orange, from ferruginous mixture to the palest . . . colours where alum predominated; besides these were white depositions of great size which are decomposed lava in a state of great softness, contrasted with these productions of Beauty, we find the sternest formations of black and purple porphory [sic] which occasionally assume the scarlet hue from the extreme action of heat; add to this the somber grey lava & that of a green colour glittering through with micaceous particles, with the deep brown brescia on Volcanic ashes, and you will have a combination which for grandeur and singularity must be almost unparalleled.[149]

Once back in Edinburgh, Forbes, whose original contributions to the *Edinburgh Journal* had been anonymous and conveyed through a third party, revealed his authorship to David Brewster. Edinburgh's most famous scientist soon became Forbes's mentor, trying to get him elected to the Edinburgh Royal Society, even though he was still a minor, as well as offering him advice on his career and what to study. In 1831 Forbes travelled to London, Cambridge and Oxford. Carrying an armful of letters of introduction from Brewster, he met geologists and mineralogists such as William Whewell and William Buckland, and the astronomer John Herschel. This network of scholars, together with Charles Babbage, was to found the British Association for the Advancement of Science that first met in York in September 1831. From the outset Forbes, urged on by Brewster, was an important figure in the Association. He acted as a liaison between Edinburgh and Cambridge scientists before the first meeting, promoted the Association in an account of its York meeting in the *Edinburgh Journal of Science*, and lobbied hard (and successfully) to secure Edinburgh as the venue in 1834.

In 1833 Forbes was elected professor of natural philosophy at the University of Edinburgh, defeating his mentor, David Brewster. Forbes had mounted a well-organised campaign, orchestrated by his brothers during his absence on a Continental tour. Though the election was probably decided because the Tory Edinburgh city council that made up the electors preferred a Tory Forbes to a Whig Brewster, the contacts and introductions that Brewster had given his protégé enabled him to assemble an impressive dossier of recommendations to endorse their decision. Naturally enough Brewster was incandescent, describing the appointment to Charles Babbage as 'the most scandalous job that the history of science records'.[150]

James Forbes's visits to Vesuvius launched his career as a distinguished physicist and geologist. His articles were widely admired, brought him an important patron in David Brewster, and were subsequently cited by Charles Lyell in his *Principles of Geology*. Once established as a professor and despite what many regarded as his betrayal of Brewster, Forbes embarked on a distinguished career as a scientist in the laboratory, but above all in the field. He made important contributions to the study of radiant heat and light, engaged in a long and acrimonious debate about the nature and movement of glaciers, and eventually became Principal of St Andrews University. His debt to the volcano was immense.

Painters and artists

If natural philosophers viewed Vesuvius as a scientific object, it was also of great aesthetic interest to the many artists who climbed its slopes and portrayed it both in eruption and repose. The artists who signed the Visitors' Book were of many different nationalities – American, Russian, Italian, English, Welsh, German, Belgian and Swiss – some of whom were long-term residents of Naples and very much a part of the local artists' community; others visited Naples regularly from Rome; and some were passing through Naples on an educational tour of Italy. The visitors came from far afield. Robert Weir (1803–89), the Hudson School artist, came from New York, and Colvin Smith (1795–1875), the fashionable portraitist, from Edinburgh. Two other artists, Johann Moritz Rugendas (1802–58), originally from Augsburg, and William Havell (1782–1857), originally from Reading, arrived respectively from Brazil and India, but both travelled to Naples after spending time in Rome, the international centre of art in Italy.[151] The signatories of the book therefore reflected the make-up of the Neapolitan art community – foreign and local artists working in the city, visitors of many nationalities who travelled from Rome, and birds of passage on the artistic equivalent of the Grand Tour.

Weir was in Italy for only a couple of years, a brief stint for an artist's visit. His experience differed from most of the 'foreign' artists in Italy, many of whom spent years studying and painting and tended to remain there for long periods of time – years rather than months, and sometimes for a lifetime. Karl Briullov (1799–1852), who climbed Vesuvius at least twice in the 1820s, and was to paint the massive *Last Day of Pompeii*, spent twelve years on his first visit to Italy, and returned for the last three years of his life. Leopold Robert (1794–1835), the Swiss artist who exhibited in Paris, spent seventeen years in Rome, Naples and Venice before his suicide in Venice in 1835. The Welshman Penry Williams (1802–85), on Vesuvius with the watercolourist William Havell (1782–1857) in the summer of 1828, had arrived in Rome in 1826 and never returned to his native land, except for short visits. August Grahl (1791–1868), a German portraitist who ascended Vesuvius with his friend, Wilhelm Hensel (1794–1861), the future husband of Fanny Mendelssohn, lived in Rome for nine years between 1821 and 1830.[152] This was part of a long-standing pattern. The average length of stay in Italy of British artists between 1760 and 1800 was the same nine years.

There was a very particular ecology to the lives of artists in the Eternal City and, as we shall see, Naples and Vesuvius played a significant part in its development. What drew artists based in Rome to Naples? It was not the baroque art of the city, sometimes copied by local painters, but the city, its people and surroundings, especially Vesuvius. The way to Naples offered an escape from the artistic strictures of Rome, an occasion to paint freely in the open air and to use watercolour and gouache to capture the Neapolitan atmosphere. Figures like the Russian Karl Briullov, the Swiss Leopold Robert, the Englishman Charles Eastlake (1793–1865), the Welshman Penry Williams, the German Franz Ludwig Catel (1778–1856) and the Frenchman Achille-Etna Michallon (1796–1822), the winner of the first Prix de Rome for landscape painting, were all drawn to the Neapolitan picturesque.

The meeting point for artists of all nationalities in Rome was the Caffè Greco on the Via Condotti, 'filled with men of all nations, saluting each other through the fumes of tobacco, coffee and punch',[153] although the French, English and Germans (who were often joined by the Scandinavians) had separate tables. The different foreign communities of artists were known for their boisterous sociability, but there were many restrictions, obligations and limitations on artists' lives. Escape from the Holy City to the surrounding country-side and to Naples and Vesuvius provided the occasion for reinvention and emancipation. Many of the artists working in Italy, especially those from abroad, were young men – usually in their twenties and early thirties – who had been sent there to improve their art through the study of classical antiquity and the Renaissance masters in order that they might contribute to and advance their national school. William Bewick (1795–1866), on Vesuvius in August 1828, had been sent by the president of the British Royal Academy to copy part of Michelangelo's ceiling of the Sistine Chapel;[154] Wilhelm Hensel, with funding from the Prussian administration, was required to make copies of Roman masterpieces, notably Raphael's *Transfiguration*, for the use of students in the Berlin Academy of Arts.[155]

Artists' residences in Rome were funded by academies, rulers and aristocratic patrons. Briullov received four years of support to study in Italy from a group of St Petersburg patrons, the Society for the Encouragement of Artists. Joseph Severn, the young friend who had nursed Keats on his Roman deathbed, had a bursary from London's Royal Academy. The French did things on a grander scale. The Académie Royale de Peinture et de Sculpture in Paris funded six painters, four sculptors and two architects every year, including the prestigious winners of the Prix de Rome, to study at the Villa Medici. In 1813 Joachim-Napoleon Murat, the King of Naples, set up a similar scheme, retained by the Bourbon monarchs, with nine stipends for Neapolitan artists (including three for Sicilians) being awarded to young men lodged with a professor at the Palazzo Farnese.

Not all artists were the beneficiaries of institutional or royal patronage. Penry Williams, from Merthyr Tydfil, was funded by a local ironmaster, Sir Joseph Bailey. Leopold Robert, from Neuchatel, though trained in Paris under Jacques-Louis David, ceased to be a

French citizen in 1816, when the Swiss town came under Prussian rule, and had to turn to patrons from his hometown, but also took out a large three-year loan to fund his studies.[156] And many artists, although they were not directly dependent for support on institutions and patrons in their native metropoles, felt it necessary to keep up a regular correspondence with artists and connoisseurs in cities such as London, Paris, Munich and St Petersburg. Though often funded through stipends or patrons, many artists often felt themselves to be on shaky financial ground. Hensel and Robert, for instance, were plagued by financial insecurities. At the same time, artists in Italy were still attached umbilically to their national schools. Neapolitan painters in Rome looked to Naples, just as British artists looked to London. This is what William Hazlitt, in his excoriating essay 'English Students in Rome', written after his visit with his second wife to the Eternal City in 1825, called 'the great chain of professional intrigue and cabal from one side of the continent to the other'.[157] When the Salon opened in Paris, the French artists in Italy upped sticks and moved en masse back to the capital.[158] British artists clubbed together to freight their submissions to the Royal Academy summer show. Neapolitan artists working in Rome had to exhibit in Naples. The visits to Rome and Naples of art dealers, collectors and rich connoisseurs from the metropoles only served to consolidate the national connections back home.

As Richard Wrigley has shown in his study of nineteenth-century Rome, the experience for artists in the city was at first exhilarating, inducing a sort of fever and frenzy, but could eventually prove oppressive. The young men were exposed, as never before, to extraordinary antique remains and to modern masterpieces. Their early letters, especially when written to their patrons, express their giddy astonishment and awe. This was as it should be: in the academic tradition the experience of the antique and the Renaissance masters was supposed to be revelatory, an incentive to emulation, a lesson in art in the grand manner, and a none too subtle call to produce history painting.

Copying was crucial, an opportunity for the artist to extend his repertoire of subjects and techniques, to improve through osmosis.[159] The single requirement of Neapolitan artists in their first year of study in Rome was to submit a copy of a masterpiece. But copying was tedious, time-consuming and bound to produce what the American literary critic Harold Bloom famously called 'the anxiety of influence': how could one pursue one's own art in the face of past superiority? Henri Fuseli gave this sense of oppressiveness its most famous visual embodiment. In his *The Artist in Despair before the Remains of Antiquity*, a small modern figure, head in hands, is dwarfed by an antique foot and hand of Ozymandian proportions. Fuseli's work dates from the 1770s but was every bit as relevant in the early nineteenth century.

The pressures to produce original compositions, especially those that followed the classical, academic tradition, were considerable and were reinforced by the institutions and patrons who had sent the young men to Italy. Sir Thomas Lawrence, who became president of the Royal Academy in 1819, was never a history painter, nor indeed did he produce 'classical' landscapes. He saw himself as a benevolent adviser and patron, but his correspondence with a group of British artists who were in Italy in the 1820s – Eastlake, Thomas Uwins, Severn and Williams – reads like a succession of school reports commenting on the industry, appropriate conduct and aptitude of his protégés, praising Severn, for example, as 'obviously improving'.[160] Penry Williams was always nervous about Lawrence's approval: 'I look forward', he wrote, 'to the advantage of your observations on my picture with great desire – and am very anxious to know if you will approve of this kind of subject.'[161]

Copies were seen as a means of artistic improvement, but they were also a source of income, one of the many ways in which artists in Italy scraped together a living. The British artist Thomas Uwins, who lived in Naples between 1825 and 1832, 'painted a very careful copy of a beautiful little picture by Correggio' in the Neapolitan royal collection, hoping to 'sell the copy for something handsome if I get it safe to London'.[162] He was also involved in most of the other means of supplementing an artist's income: he produced a steady stream of portraits of Neapolitan notables and visitors, he gave drawing lessons (Lady Blessington was one of his pupils), he acted as a cicerone, taking visitors round the sites, and he painted small views and water-colours to be sold to clients.[163]

Such activities helped pay the bills, but they distracted artists from what they wanted to do, namely pursue their own work. Yet it was difficult to refuse commissions from one's social superiors. Uwins was bullied by the Baroness Rothschild into painting a page for her in the fashionable accessory of the period, the album.[164] And Robert, who was desperate to pursue his own art, had to delay his work in order to cater to the demands of his patron for a couple of pictures he wanted to give as gifts.

Penry Williams's anxieties about the subject matter of his art point to an interest beyond the works of antiquity and the paintings of the Renaissance, a desire to depict contemporary Italy, its light, its landscape and its people. As Joseph Severn complained, 'My passion was Italian Pastoral nature, but I felt bound to study academically.'[165] Less valued in the academies than the history painting that artists were studying and copying, genre painting, and above all landscapes, were what attracted many artists, and though they could pursue both in Rome, they became particularly associated with the hill towns above Tivoli, notably Subiaco and the even more remote Olevano Romano, and with the landscape, further away but in some respects more accessible, around the Bay of Naples.

Painting 'nature', what the Italian painter and politician Massimo d'Azeglio called 'realism', bore a complex relationship to artists' other practices. The object was to immerse oneself in 'nature' and to find ways of capturing this: to draw and paint out in the open air, leaving behind the studio, and to use different techniques – oil sketches on paper, watercolour or gouache – to catch the immediacy of nature's effects. The resulting works were usually small and not intended for gallery display; rather they were stuck up on the artist's studio walls, perhaps to aid the completion of a more finished picture, or to be sold to some visiting client or patron. The relation between this outdoor work and painting in the studio varied greatly. Some artists used their materials to produce new studio compositions; others reworked or 'finished' their open-air sketches, and some treated them as completed works. The precise relation between observed nature and nature in an idealised form differed from artist to artist; on occasion sketches were used to execute landscape history paintings. But the attractions of such art lay in its engagement with Italy not just as a repository of antiquity and Renaissance art, but as a unique landscape inhabited by a picturesque populace. And though the vision of the artist was not the same as the gaze of the scientist, it shared many features, not least in its determination to capture with some precision the effects of changing nature. As the historical landscape artist and theorist Pierre-Henri de Valenciennes made clear in his widely read treatise on perspective, nature was in a constant state of flux, largely because of the daily and seasonal fluctuations in the light and weather. If nature was to be captured accurately, it had to be captured quickly. Valenciennes recommended a maximum of two hours painting during the day, and a mere half an hour for sunrise and sunset, using watercolour or making an oil sketch.[166] Though less admirable than a historical landscape – such as his own depiction of Vesuvius's eruption and the death of Pliny – the 'landscape portrait', as Valenciennes called it, was a faithful representation of nature that captured *local* variation, the distinctiveness of different topography, trees, building materials, clothing and the manners of society. It inhabited the here and now.

The attractions of this sort of art to the (mostly very young) painters in Rome and Naples were social as well as aesthetic. The hill towns around Rome with their craggy cliffs, gorges and woodlands, and the Bay of Naples with its astonishing variety of natural scenery, were places in which artists could engage with as well as depict a variety of local people. When William Havell visited Uwins in Naples in 1828, together they rented a cottage, 'an old deserted house', at the foot of Vesuvius. 'We live,' wrote Uwins, 'most romantically.' They carried pistols at night, though 'for myself I have little fear ... our neighbours are wild mountaineers; but from the wildest of them, I have never received either rudeness or incivility; on the contrary they show on all occasions the greatest readiness to serve us.' 'From the roof of our house,' he added, 'we have every object we can wish for study. The beautiful bay with its lovely islands lies at our feet, and the whole mountain vomits fire and smoke over our heads. If we walk out, we are in a moment amongst the most voluptuous vineyards, witnessing the labours of the peasant, and listening to his songs of gladness.'[167]

Artists in small groups, one artist pairing up with another, left the fetid Eternal City to paint *en plein air*, mounting expeditions to Naples at all times of the year, even in the hottest months. In April 1820 Achille-Etna Michallon, the French artist and teacher of Corot, travelled from Rome to Naples with the Swedish artist Gustaf Söderberg (1790–1875) who, at Michallon's instruction, was fully prepared for outdoor painting. He carried 'a paintbox strapped to his back, a portfolio and folding stool under his arm, and a penknife and eraser attached with twine to a button on his waistcoat'.[168] The two men ascended Vesuvius – there is a fine and typically unusual oil sketch by Michallon in which the dark edges of the crater frame a view of Naples – and befriended Johan Christian Dahl (1788–1857), who was employed by the passionate amateur geologist Christian, Crown Prince of Denmark. In the six months he spent in Naples, Dahl painted Vesuvius repeatedly, producing more than twenty paintings of the volcano. Some were large oil canvasses for his patron and such figures as Jakob Salomon Bartholdy (1779–1825), the Prussian consul-general in Rome, who was a great patron of the arts and a supporter of the Nazarene artists living there. But such paintings were increasingly unfashionable, too redolent of pyrotechnic political revolution to appeal to patrician patrons in the early nine-teenth century. Much more common were smaller works, such as the *View of Vesuvius Erupting*. These were painted for the Crown Prince to give away as gifts to such friends as Teodoro Monticelli, the leading expert on Vesuvius in Naples. Others were painted on paper or card, some as small as a modern postcard, gifts that Dahl gave away to friends and members of the Crown Prince's entourage.[169]

Dahl also befriended Franz Ludwig Catel, an artist from Berlin who arrived in Italy in the summer of 1811 and spent the rest of his life there. Catel's father was a toymaker – Catel himself began as a wood carver – who made a working model of Vesuvius, complete with smoke and fire, that he displayed in his local Christmas market. In the spring of 1812 Catel made his first trip to Vesuvius, travelling with the French archaeologist Aubin-Louis Millan on a journey that would take them through Calabria and into Sicily. He carefully dated his first surviving depiction of the volcano, a small oil sketch of the smoking crater, as April 1812, adding that the picture was 'after Nature'. He was to return repeatedly to Naples and Vesuvius in the following decades.[170]

Catel's images of Naples and Vesuvius followed a familiar pattern, one modelled in part on the works of local artists. He painted many genre scenes, most notably that of the *pifferari* (street pipers), as well as peasants dancing and drinking, fishermen and groups of families – all with Vesuvius in the background (Plate 7). As part of a picturesque prospect of the Bay of Naples, the volcano itself was usually shown in repose, wisps of smoke emanating from its summit.

But when the volcano was in eruption, artists produced entirely different images, often venturing into the crater to portray its sublime, violent pyrotechnics. None of these images were added to the Visitors' Book. They are to be found in the surviving sketchpads, albums and works of artists who were doubtless mindful of the value of their work and did not care to leave it at the hermitage. A few artists, like Thomas Uwins, found the experience of an eruption overwhelming:

'I attempted to draw it, but the attempt only proved that some things in nature are beyond the reach of art, and I put aside my book and pencil for fear I should weaken instead of strengthening the impression the scene had made on my imagination.'[171] But others were bolder. August Kopisch from Breslau climbed Vesuvius on several occasions during his three-year residence in Naples between 1826 and 1829. In March 1827 he penned a song celebrating his ascent to the summit, writing it in the Visitors' Book at the hermitage:

Vesuvius' path is steep at the beginning,
Leaves nothing but toil in sight,
But on top blew in Foehn for salvation,
And provided you views to delight.[172]

Almost exactly a year later he ventured to the lip of the crater during the eruption of March 1828 and produced one of the most remarkable images of the volcano, using a gouache of his own invention. The painting was tiny – only 20 × 30 cm (approximately 8 × 12 inches) – a working study or experiment rather than intended for public view, one whose globules of flying molten rock vividly convey the fiery proximity of the eruption (Plate 8).[173]

Kopisch, a thirty-year-old poet and painter, had trained in Vienna and Dresden before travelling to Italy to recuperate after a skating accident that had damaged his hand, preventing him from painting. He recovered in Naples, not only beginning to paint again, but plunging himself into the cultural life of the city. Inveterately affable and gregarious, he befriended and worked with the composer Gaetano Donizetti, director of the opera at the San Carlo theatre, and with a famous actor and Pulcinella, Filippo Cammarano, whose plays he translated and who returned the favour by including Kopisch as a character in one of his productions. Like many of the artists and writers who visited Naples he was fascinated by its vernacular traditions, customs, costumes and songs, learning the Neapolitan dialect and assembling an important collection of popular Neapolitan verse and music, *Agrumi* (1837). Both from inclination and necessity (it helped pay his bills), Kopisch became a cicerone, a cultural broker or intermediary between German visitors and the sights and sounds of the city and its surroundings. The Prussian ambassador to Naples, Alfons von Voss, with whom he was friendly, steered clients his way, most notably Crown Prince Frederick William of Prussia on his Italian visit of 1828. Kopisch accompanied German artists who visited from Rome, and became a friend and ally (and object of desire) of the gay poet August von Platen, the two enjoying sea bathing together. He was the companion of Wilhelm Waiblinger, the novelist and poet who, supported by the publisher and literary patron Johann Friedrich Cotta, worked as an Italian corre-spondent writing about the sights of Italy – including an ascent of Vesuvius – in a variety of German journals. But Kopisch was perhaps most famous for his 'discovery' in the company of a landscape painter from Heidelberg, Ernst Fries, of the Grotta Azzurra on Capri, a cavernous, watery and brilliantly coloured cave whose beauty, and association with the emperor Tiberius, inspired Romantic writers and poets. (In fact he was guided there by Giuseppe Pagano, whose family owned a hotel on the island thus profiting from German visitors, drawn by the fame of the Grotto, for generations to come.)[174]

Kopisch's role as a cultural intermediary did not end when he returned to Germany in 1831. In the 1830s he published his collec-tion of Italian traditional songs, a German-language version of Dante's *Divine Comedy*, and an account of the Grotta Azzurra. At the same time he was instrumental in opening in Breslau, and then Berlin, a Pleorama of a simulated trip round the Bay of Naples, in which an audience sat in a boat while moving panoramas were scrolled on either side of the vessel to create the illusion of move-ment.[175] Kopisch took Vesuvius back with him to Germany.

On the very day in March 1828 when Kopisch was painting his remarkable gouache of Vesuvius's eruption, three artist friends, one

Belgian, two Swiss, climbed the volcano. Like Kopisch they had plunged themselves into the cultural life of Naples, but whereas the polymathic German had turned to opera, literature and theatre, they became important figures in the local art scene. The Belgian, Frans Vervloet (1795–1872), had won a scholarship to Italy in 1822, spending his first two years in Rome. But in 1824 he moved to Naples, remaining there for thirty years; he was a close friend and collaborator of Giacinto Gigante, the leading Neapolitan artist of the School of Posillipo that specialised in Romantic landscapes of the Bay of Naples. In *Remarks on Modern Painting at Naples*, written in 1855, Charles Napier described Vervloet as a 'naturalized' Neapolitan.[176]

Vervloet's Swiss companions on the journey up the mountain, Rudolf Müller (1802–85) and Friedrich Horner (1800–64), also had close connections to local artists and publishing ventures. Childhood friends in their native Basel, they had moved to Italy in 1822, arriving in Naples in 1824. Müller was an accomplished watercolourist, Horner a painter and (more importantly) a lithographer. They frequently worked together and for lithographic publishers in Naples, notably the company of Cuciniello and Bianchi, contributing to their three-volume *Viaggio pittorico nel Regno delle Due Sicilie* published between 1829 and 1832. Containing 178 views of the kingdom in high-quality lithographs, many taken from the original works of Gigante, and with a text by Raffaele Liberatore suffused with sentiment, it helped shape the image of the kingdom as a Romantic site in the early nineteenth century.

Peppered with anecdotes, filled with the young and old, families and friends, Grand Tourists and military men, doctors and scientists, artists and painters, and many more besides, the Visitors' Book reveals a panoply of visitors in all their variety and richness. When compared with single-author accounts of Vesuvius, it portrays a richer landscape, densely populated with figures whose interactions are as much with one another as with the volcano. Vesuvius itself is less often described than experienced. More important were the emotions felt by visitors, whose response to the volcano was somatic as well as cerebral: they could taste, smell and feel it; it could envelop them, asphyxiate them, warm, burn, bruise or break them, induce a state of intoxication or terror. The intensity of the experience and the proximity of the volcano crowded out more measured responses (of the sort found in travel writings fashioned in the comfort of home) and seems to have enhanced the collective feelings of fellow travellers, for whom this was a shared adventure.

The Visitors' Book complicates the sort of single narrative associated with much of the travel literature of the period. But it also points to two important conclusions. First, it underscores the importance of families – of ties of kinship – that lay at the heart of a sense that friendship, amity and familiarity were shared, tried and tested on the volcano. As we shall see in Chapter 4, though theories of the Romantic sublime (and what our travellers were experiencing was 'sublime tourism') emphasised its character as an *individual* experience, the sublime experience of Vesuvius, notwithstanding Romantic clichés about the virtues of solitude, was valued and understood as something held in common. Secondly, though many visitors to the volcano came from far away, and some of these travellers were engaged in the sort of recreational travel we designate 'tourism', a good many of them were in Naples for other reasons. The Swiss were there to uphold absolutism; merchants and shopkeepers (chiefly French and British) were involved in trade; artists were there to study their vocation; the British long-term residents were there to study Neapolitan literature and culture; diplomats from many nations were engaged in political intrigue; sailors were en route to the East Mediterranean or the Atlantic. There were also significant retirement communities – of British soldiers and sailors who had come to appreciate the Mediterranean during their service; of French soldiers and functionaries who had served under the Muratist regime; of Austrians who had once been in the army of occupation. For many of these visitors to the volcano, their experience was not part of a 'holiday' but an opportunity created by other circumstances, including those over which they had little control.

We are used in the literature about tourism to thinking about the tourist and tourist activity as somehow separate from the everyday, a chance to step out of our quotidian roles, to adopt a different sort of persona. The Romantic era was the first in which travel was valued not just as a source of learning and culture, but as a means of transformative self-discovery. But the relationship between something described as 'tourism' and travel is both complex and ever changing. Patterns of work and travel make possible or enforce many different scenarios of leisure time. The peculiar/particular pattern of visitors to Vesuvius has everything to do with the Revolutionary and Napoleonic Wars and their aftermath, and the way in which they dispersed, divided and diasporised people throughout Europe and the Mediterranean littoral. It was shaped by political forces and lines of commerce, by asymmetries of power and wealth, and by important political differences that were local as well as international.

Being a tourist or visitor requires, as we shall see, the performance of certain rituals, but not the abandonment of other beliefs and identities. Which is why it is important to follow the *filo rosso*, the continuous thread we can detect in the Visitors' Book, both backwards and into the future. So far we have been disaggregating tourists, uncovering their age, gender, occupation, and source of identity or origin. We have also seen what sort of site Vesuvius was, and what it offered. But we also need to treat the volcano as a constituent part of a number of circuits of knowledge and power. In order to do this, we turn first to a key relationship on Vesuvius, that between visitors and guides, and then to the shared values and conflicting imperatives of the travellers up the mountain.

2

GUIDES

On the 28th May we set out for the purpose of seeing Vesuvius –
a sight never omitted by a Visitor to Naples ... We were soon
introduced to our Guide who had borne that Office during the
last 30 years tho' he was still to all appearance a young man. In the
course of his services he had become acquainted with some characters of great interest. He amused me in our ride towards the
Hermitage where we were to repose for a few hours with stories
of Ld. Nelson and Lady Hamilton whom he declared was by far
the most beautiful woman he had ever seen, Madame de Staël,
Murat, Queen Caroline & Bergami ... Here we obtained some
very excellent Lacryma Christi ... and after stretching ourselves a
while on the couch we were summon'd at 2 o'clock by our active
guide to pursue our journey, having advanced as far on donkeys as
they were able to carry us, we were compelled to trust to our own
feet for ascending the higher parts of the mountain ... At length
we stood on the edge of the crater. It was not yet light & the stars
which shone so brightly over us when we left the Hermitage
were obscured by the clouds ... In half an hour the sun rose ...
Our guide now prepared our breakfast roasting some eggs in
the lava ... after breakfast we declared ourselves in readiness to

descend the Crater. Salvatore assured us we should be the 4th party who ever undertook this enterprising journey. Salvatore led the way. I was generally [the] third. The point from which we commenced was so extremely steep that our Guide's assurance of the inevitable destruction attending a false step was not at all necessary. Looking into the Guelph [sic] before us, I could have imagined it of immeasurable depth, for it was still filled with clouds & smoke . . . in this way we descended, Salvatore constantly admonishing us of the dangers and difficulty of the undertaking if he thought us unnecessarily daring, I for one could have assured him he was in error. At length he stopped & informed us with an air of exultation that we were now only 500 ft from the bottom (having descended 1,500), & that no one had ever gone further who had returned. Here we rested, & in some trepidation I resumed my pocketbook to notice the peculiarities around us. In the meantime Salvatore broke with a hammer some curious specimens of lava which lay before us . . . I recalled instantly a note I remembered seeing in the *Pleasures of Memory* where it is mentioned that the echoes of the voice are dreaded in some passes of the Alps for fear of bringing down an avalanche, & I seriously wished my friend to cease his clattering among the lava, but he laughed at my learned apprehensions, & handed me, *un pezzo sceltissimo*, of green lava to admire . . . In fact we now wished to proceed to the bottom but our Guide told us he would not agree, as he was answerable to the Government for all the visitors under his directions.

Sir William Hutt of Gateshead, *Journal of Travels through Italy, Istria, Germany and Belgium*, 28 May 1824[1]

One of the largest groups on Vesuvius consisted of the many guides,[2] nearly all local people from the towns of Resina and Torre del Greco and their surroundings, who shepherded visitors up and down the mountain. Their historical footprint remains small:

they are rarely discussed in the travel literature of the period, their presence often edited out of the journals or correspondence on which these books were based. And, as we have already seen, they were also largely excluded from the Visitors' Book. Most, though not all, guides were illiterate, and those who were not have left almost no historical record. Such men are therefore hard to trace, although their services were virtually indispensable for those bent on ascending the volcano.

An examination of the guides – their relations with travellers, the way in which they worked and organised, the tasks they performed, and their connection to scientific communities both in Naples and beyond – enables us to reconstruct the culture and social dynamics of those on the volcano. But it does much more, for through the experience of the guides we are able to chart how changes in the larger environment – shifting ideas about science, the role of the Neapolitan state, and the organisation of tourist leisure time – transformed the experiences of visitors. For much of the Romantic period, the relationship between travellers, the guides and the volcano was personal, almost intimate. There were gross asymmetries in power and authority – between wealthy travellers and poor guides, savants and their unlearned helpers. But, while they had control of the journey to the summit of Vesuvius, the guides were far from powerless. During the course of the nineteenth century the building of new roads and railways, the establishment of a scientific centre – the Observatory, only a stone's throw from the hermitage – and the development of new technologies came to challenge the guide's expertise. These events marginalised the role of guides as gatekeepers to the mountain, and they also largely eliminated the visitor's romantic adventure, their heroic personal struggle with the volcano.

During the late eighteenth and early nineteenth centuries, the guides (almost all men) worked in a double capacity – as aides to savants seeking to unlock the scientific secrets of the volcano and, more commonly, as the creators of a tourist infrastructure which helped visitors enjoy the sublime experience of a volcano that was in an almost constant state of low eruption.[3] These two functions were not in conflict but rather ran side by side, just as natural philosophical investigation and the aesthetics of sublime travel reinforced one another. Vesuvius was served by guides whose labour, knowledge and expertise made the volcano accessible to a substantial clientele that by the early nineteenth century numbered in the thousands.

First and foremost, guides used their accumulated experience and knowledge of Vesuvius to ensure that visitors were safe, protected from the hazards of the volcano, and able to work or enjoy themselves on its slopes. This partly entailed acting as porters, carriers and aides to travellers, performing menial tasks, but the most experienced guides were also employed by savants to help them carry out experiments and measurements. The guides accumulated experience of the volcano enabled them to predict with reasonable reliability (based on seismic activity, the appearance of the volcano and the water levels in towns surrounding its summit) the immanence of an eruption. And when they were on the volcano they also knew about the behaviour and pattern of eruptive explosions and the vagaries of wind and weather. Long exposure to the volcano (and many guides worked for years) meant that many of them knew the dates of the different features, such as lava flows and fumaroles. Their continued and continuous presence on the volcano meant that they knew the local history of what was a constantly changing landscape, so that many were seen as reliable informants about the history and changing topography of the volcano. It was, after all, 'il nostro Vesuvio', a place in which they had a proprietary interest; in some instances they had actually witnessed the formation of some of the features they described. They also knew where different sorts of rock, lava and crystals were to be found, and could lead visitors, collectors and savants to find the best specimens. They were the inheritors of a long tradition of local examination of Vesuvius and its workings.[4]

Visibility

Recent scholarship in the history of science and post-colonial investigations of travellers and exploration have highlighted the importance of technicians, assistants, guides and servants as participants in
making knowledge, and as the necessary facilitators of experiment,
observation and the recording of data.[5] The role of such assistants,
usually termed 'guides', was especially important, even if they were
not directly involved in 'scientific' investigation, in places which were
otherwise largely inaccessible to outsiders, or whose inhospitable
climes posed acute dangers. Nevertheless such figures were often
rendered or remained invisible in accounts of enterprises to which
they were vital.

There is no better example of this process of erasure than the
German philosopher Immanuel Kant's claim in his *Physical Geography*
(1802) that Horace Bénédict de Saussure, the patrician Swiss savant,
was 'the first mortal to climb to the summit of Mont Blanc'.[6]
The peasant and guide Jacques Balmat and his charge Dr Michel
Gabriel Paccard, who accomplished the first ascent on 8 August
1786, were wiped out with a stroke of Kant's pen. The reader would
not know that two successful ascents of Mont Blanc (both in parties
that included Jacques Balmat, the second of which was exclusively
composed of local guides) had occurred before Saussure finally
reached the top of the mountain in August 1787. But Saussure, a
man of scientific and social standing, spent four and a half hours on
the summit of Mont Blanc carrying out experiments and observations using a battery of instruments. This is what made him Kant's
'first mortal' as well as the most important model for the heroic
scientist before the pre-eminence of Alexander von Humboldt.

In the wake of Kant's 'first mortals' others followed: travellers,
some bent on pursuing scientific investigation, others seeking pleasure
and self-knowledge, all interested in what the much-travelled Sir
Basil Hall called fashionable 'objects of scientific as well as popular

curiosity'.[7] An influx of such visitors was an economic opportunity for locals, especially in places where the indigenous population included many who were poor. The Alps were one such locality, Vesuvius was another. Both were sites of aesthetic pleasure – whether of beauty, the picturesque or the sublime – as well as places of deep scientific interest, at a time when the history of the earth attracted unprecedented attention; the combination of the two engendered a local economy built around the provision of services and expertise. The timing of these developments was very similar in both places. Though there had long been philosophical interest in both sites, it was only from the last quarter of the eighteenth century that they attracted visitors in significant numbers. In Chamonix, at the foot of Mont Blanc, there were no hotels in 1760; but there were three well-appointed inns by the 1780s. Visitor figures to the town rose from a meagre 30 in 1772 to 2,000 in 1785, and by the 1830s numbered more than 4,000 a year. Jacques Balmat, though ignored by Kant, was financially rewarded by the Sardinian authorities who ruled the region because, in the words of the Sardinian envoy in Geneva: 'This [ascent] is regarded in the area as an epochal event which will attract even more foreigners and the curious to the Glacieres.'[8] A similar story, including the support of the local authorities, can be told for Naples. As a Franciscan friar pointed out to Hester Piozzi, the former Mrs Thrale, when she visited Naples in 1785, 'That's our mountain, which throws up money for us, by calling foreigners to see the extraordinary effects of so surprising a phenomenon.'[9] Pietro d'Onofri, in a widely circulated 'Elegy to Carlo Sebastiano di Borbone', the enlightened ruler first of Naples and then of Spain, described Vesuvius as one of the great assets of the Neapolitan kingdom. Vesuvius, he wrote in 1789, was useful 'to *Philosophers* who write about it; to *Printers* who publish their works; to *Booksellers* who sell them; to *Painters* who paint it and to *Engravers* who etch it in copper'.[10]

Pietro d'Onofri not only praised the business of representing Vesuvius but pointed out the volcano's tangible regenerative benefits to the local soil, agriculture and air, as well as its usefulness as a local building material. Even popular piety, he maintained, was strengthened by the fear provoked by Vesuvius's eruptions. What he did not mention, however, was the growing number of ordinary inhabitants of Resina, modern-day Ercolano,[11] a small town at the foot of the volcano, who took advantage of its ongoing, low-level eruptions to supplement their meagre incomes by acting as Vesuvian guides.

The first such guide to be identified by name was Bartolomeo Pumo (though Salvatore Madonna claimed that Pumo was a member of the Madonna family). Also renowned as the 'Cyclops of Vesuvius', presumably because he was both tall and had only one eye, Bartolomeo Pumo was the constant companion and guide to Sir William Hamilton during the British ambassador's sixty-eight ascents of Vesuvius between 1767 and 1794. There can be no question that he was seen as a mere servant: he was caned by an irate Joseph II for some minor annoyance, goaded by the antiquary Johann Joachim Winckelmann, and disparaged as a superstitious nobody by Padre Antonio Piaggio, the cleric whom Hamilton employed to keep a daily record of the volcano's activities.[12]

But not everyone took this view. A Knight of Malta, Louis Jérôme de Goujon de Thuisy, who climbed Vesuvius on numerous occasions in the 1790s, praised Bartolomeo Pumo (he was usually referred to by his first name) as the 'cicerone par excellence',[13] while a Frenchman he guided called him 'the chief officer of the department of Vesuvius'.[14] Hamilton acknowledged learning from Bartolomeo how to cross lava flows, and Pietro Fabris, the artist who worked for Hamilton, appears to have portrayed the guide instructing his patron by pointing out different types of lava flow.[15] When Horace Bénédict de Saussure, the 'first mortal' on Mount Blanc, visited Hamilton and Vesuvius in 1773, he was offered advice by Bartolomeo. Even the criticisms of Padre Piaggio (who was deeply jealous of Bartolomeo's closeness to Hamilton) reveal how the guide had his own ideas about a system 'concerning . . . subterranean channels and the surges of lava that ... came from the summit of the mountain', ideas that he expressed in a disagreement with a local noble. As Piaggio's diary of the volcano – kept for more than fifteen years – reveals, he and Bartolomeo repeatedly traded sleights, rebuffs and insults. Piaggio was able to observe the volcano from his house in Resina, but he was an old man (he began his observations aged sixty-six and died fifteen years later, aged eighty-one) who found it difficult to move about the volcano. But the guide repeatedly ignored his requests for information – he was far more interested in visitors who would pay for his services – and doggedly disagreed with the cleric. When the Abbate Domenico Tata, another clerical observer of the mountain, published a scholarly pamphlet supporting Bartolomeo's views, Piaggio was beside himself with fear and anger: fear that he would lose the confidence of Hamilton and his stipend of £20 a year, and anger that someone should take seriously a 'rustic guide' with native superstitions 'who claims that a new saint, for the sake of four candles that he lights for him, has taken him under his protection'. Bartolomeo, he made clear, had no 'scientific' authority.[16] The guide was stepping on the local savant's territory. Conversely, Bartolomeo was furious when Piaggio went behind his back and used others on the mountain to get information, screaming at him that he had 'offended in matters of his jurisdiction' – and that, with years of experience, no one knew the mountain better than he.[17] In the long term Bartolomeo was the victor. Piaggio had a patron, but the guide had a clientele, one that his successors were able to exploit successfully.

Very little is heard of Bartolomeo after Hamilton's departure from Naples at the end of the century. By 1809 when the German philologist Karl Morgenstern climbed Vesuvius, he was accompanied by a 'little boy' and his brother, the new head guide, Salvatore Madonna. Salvatore was at pains to establish his pedigree; he told Morgenstern that his father, Raimondo Madonna, had replaced Bartolomeo, and in turn was replaced by his son. Salvatore showed Morgenstern a certificate of recommendation signed by Hamilton.[18] For the next thirty years he was to be a commanding presence on the volcano at a time when the number of visitors was growing rapidly, especially after 1815 when the number of British visitors to Naples grew apace.

Bartolomeo may have served as a model for the well-informed guide, but Salvatore was to use his knowledge and authority to create a family business, one that brought many other guides within its orbit, and which shaped the entire experience of visitors to the volcano. Whether Madonna was quite as important as he claimed is unclear, but it is certain that he offered visitors a story that went back to the days before the French Revolution, and that he also understood their need for services that went beyond the basic task of guidance. By the 1820s he appears repeatedly in accounts of the ascent of Vesuvius as the self-proclaimed chief guide, '*il capo cicerone Salvatore Madonna*'.[19] Salvatore was by then in his fifties and had been guiding visitors up the mountain since his teenage years. In 1822, during the terrible eruption of that year, he told Anna Jameson, the governess (and future feminist and art historian) who was chaperoning her pupil on a tour of Europe, that he had been principal guide for thirty-three years.[20] By the third decade of the nineteenth century he was running an extremely sophisticated operation that catered for visitors' every need, from the time they arrived in Resina at the Piazza Fontana to hire guides and asses, until they returned from the volcano.[21] As we shall see, one of the main attractions of Salvatore as a guide for the richer visitors to the volcano was his ability to create order out of the chaos that surrounded the journey from Naples to the summit, via Resina and the hermitage on the flanks of the mountain.

By the 1820s, the journey had acquired a fixed and well-known itinerary, described in many guidebooks and travel memoirs, its first defining moment the scene at Resina when travellers from Naples were engulfed by a tribe of men, women and children with asses, all offering help to get up the volcano. The early guidebooks were brutal in their advice on how to treat the troublesome guides. The Abbé

Jérôme Richard, whose *Description historique et critique de l'Italie* was published in 1766, warned his readers that 'If you show the least awe of their number, of their shouting and brutality, they will fleece you mercilessly ... because they are wicked and self-interested.' The appropriate response was 'not to let them approach you ... you should not fear to beat them away with blows from a stick; nothing but the same manner makes them listen or obey.' Like other commentators he advised against paying the guides before their return from the volcano; otherwise, he asserted, you should expect them to abscond with the money. In his eyes, 'the avidity of these men, their stupid brutishness, their miserable comportment, their confused cries, give a very clear idea of the most gross and most barbaric savages of America.'[22]

Such aggression persisted into the nineteenth century. The travel writer, art critic and amateur painter Louis Simond, a Frenchman who had lived for many years in New York, was shocked by his reception in Resina in April 1828. Surrounded by 'jackasses and their drivers', he was rescued by 'a sentinel' who 'without ceremony belaboured men and asses with his firelock, while our valet-de-place likewise laid about him with his stick'.[23] When in 1834 the fifty-year-old Adélaïde, Countess Chastellux, was engulfed by guides and their animals in Salvatore Madonna's courtyard, he dispersed them by 'hitting them randomly with a long rod'.[24]

At this point in the journey the traditional social hierarchy remained intact – in the streets and courtyards of Resina the guides were viewed as *lazzaroni* to be commanded and chastised; their only recourse was to a type of mob action, a form of plebeian theatre that was at once collective and individual, alarming and picaresque. But the balance of power shifted on the volcano, where many visitors were made aware of their helplessness and dependence on the guides. Visitors expressed ambivalent views towards their guides, whom they often disparaged as ignorant, idle and cowardly, but also praised as kind, solicitous, well informed and shrewd in their guidance. Their attitudes were very like those of the Himalayan climbers towards their Sherpa guides in the twentieth century described by the anthropologist Sherry Ortner.[25]

Salvatore Madonna

Mariana Starke, whose numerous guidebooks to Italy and Europe dominated the Anglophone market between 1800 and the appearance of the famous Murray and Baedeker guides from the 1830s, and who made several ascents of Vesuvius, was the first to suggest to visitors that they could avoid the clamour and assuage their fear of being cheated by asking the head guide 'to pay the guides himself; in order to prevent importunities for more than the proper price'. Up until this point travellers had been urged to give their guides chits or promissory notes that would be paid when they safely returned from the volcano. Dealing with Salvatore Madonna, who sub-contracted the tasks of guidance and porterage at known prices, was far safer than haggling with individuals. The status and importance accorded Salvatore – Starke called him 'Salvatore, the principal, and by far the best-informed cicerone of the Mountain' – enabled him to dominate the visitors' trade.[26] By the 1820s, he had a well-developed family business. His son, also named Salvatore – which explains why some travellers were puzzled at the youth of a guide whom they supposed to have been working on the mountain for thirty years – joined him in shepherding visitors up the slopes of the volcano. Another son, Antonio, is recorded in the Visitors' Book as selling bottles of Lacryma Christi, which he claimed were worth 6 carlini (the equivalent of 2 English shillings), for the knock-down price of 2 carlini.[27] Salvatore's daughter, described by the English evangelical traveller Harriet Morton as having 'a lovely soft, Italian countenance, and is bedecked with ear-rings and necklaces, and such like finery, and possesses a polished gracefulness exceedingly insinuating',[28] was in charge of the sale of Vesuvian rocks and crystals in the family home, 'a fine and large collection of minerals always for sale'.[29] 'The floor, and boxes, and stands,' commented Morton, 'are covered with volcanic products.' As several guidebooks pointed out, the Madonnas offered a shipping service, used by Harriet Morton, which packed and sent 'mineralogical objects' to foreign countries. The distinguished scientist Charles Babbage trusted the Madonnas, using this amenity on his visit to Naples and Vesuvius in 1828, when he 'purchased a good many minerals [from Salvatore], as to the possibility of getting a peep down the volcano's throat'.[30] And Salvatore, to judge from one invoice, also arranged shoe repairs after the ascent, when travellers found that even the stout boots that guidebooks recommended were often badly damaged, torn by the lava and blistered by the heat.[31]

Salvatore was running a vertically integrated family business. Though not the sole guide, he controlled access to the wealthiest visitors to the volcano, offering more and more services to his richest clients. William Bewick, though a humble painter, tagged along with a wealthy party that included Roman, Neapolitan and English aristocrats and courtiers, orchestrated by Salvatore in June 1828. Much to the frustration of Bewick, who was chafing to get up the mountain, the evening began with a trip to a seaside trattoria in Torre del Greco, where the party were served 'a meal of macaroni, fish and champagne' before they embarked on mules towards the hermitage. On the mountain itself Salvatore, who had a reputation for a certain theatricality, stood out, waving his staff and shouting instructions to the other guides, while dressed entirely in impractical white.[32]

Salvatore coordinated the work of other guides, arranging, for example, for baskets of fruit for visitors to be left at different points on the ascent. In 1830, when Charles Greville huffed and puffed his way up the volcano, he was passed by a guide 'with a basket on his head full of wine, bread, and oranges, and while we were slipping, and clambering, and toiling with immense difficulty he bounded up, with his basket on his head, as straight as an arrow all the time, and bothering us to drink when we had not breath to answer'. On the summit

Greville took 'three or four oranges, some bread, and a bottle of wine', paying the guide 3 carlini.[33] This sort of service was already in place during the years of Murat's rule. Amélie Odier, a young Swiss visitor to the volcano, commented in 1812 on the presence at the crater of 'a young boy ... holding a pyramid of oranges on his head and a bottle of wine in his hand.'[34] But Madonna seems to have turned such offerings into a regular system of provision.

Salvatore Madonna, like some of the other guides, kept a book of recommendations to show to his potential customers, but by the 1820s it had become a way to entertain his clients and enrich their experiences on the mountain. It gave him the opportunity to tell (and often embellish) stories about his former clients. The Oxford antiquarian W.T.P. Shortt was greatly impressed by Salvatore on his ascent in 1821, recording that,

> The guide, appeared to be a very intelligent, well-informed character, conversed very freely on the subject of persons of distinction, whom he had conducted to the summit of the mount – particularly Sir Humphry Davy, and many other learned professors; and that he was often commissioned to send specimens of minerals and blocks of lava to them, also to the British Museum.[35]

Madonna's connection with 'learned professors' and their willingness to accept his expertise was largely effected through his friendship and collaboration with Teodoro Monticelli, the secretary of the Academy of Sciences in Naples. As the chief link between the larger scientific community interested in Vesuvius and the men of science in Naples, Monticelli was a vital conduit, steering many learned visitors towards the guide when they visited the volcano. Madonna played an important role in gathering specimens for Monticelli and providing other savants with items for their collections.[36] When the French geologist Ménard de la Groye gave lectures on geology at the Collège de France in Paris, he asked Salvatore to supply him with better examples of the minerals that he had already sent to him.[37] Many teachers and collectors wanted specimens of a certain quality and size and specified what they needed. Madonna could provide them.

As Monticelli grew older (he was born in 1759) and his visits to the volcano became less frequent, he came to rely on Madonna as his eyes and ears, reporting on the state of the mountain. He regularly employed a couple of Madonna's guides to keep him informed and to collect specimens. Monticelli and Madonna developed a mutual trust founded on their shared determination to promote Vesuvius. Monticelli repeatedly mentioned Madonna in his scientific accounts of eruptions (though not in his technical work) and used the term 'perito' or 'expert' to describe him.[38] For Madonna the volcano was his livelihood; for Monticelli Vesuvius was a way of promoting Naples as a centre of scientific knowledge and research. Madonna became the key intermediary between the local savants and the humble guides who laboured on the mountain.[39]

But Madonna knew his authority was fragile, as his frequent assertions of his prowess attest. In his conversation with the young Englishwoman Harriet Morton and her two female companions in 1828, Salvatore stressed his mineralogical knowledge and his work with 'Playfair, Sir Humphry Davy, Buckland, and many eminent geologists'.[40] Ten years earlier, leading Basil Hall and three naval friends to the edge of the crater, when the views had been obstructed by mist and they had been showered with molten rocks, Madonna had regaled Hall with the story of how in the previous year and on a much finer day, he had sat with Basil's father's friend, John Playfair, the mathematician and Edinburgh professor of natural sciences, and the populariser of James Hutton's Plutonist theories of the earth, 'on this very spot, for six hours without intermission'. He added, 'I really believe much as I love Vesuvius and its concerns, the learned Scotch professor loved it as well.' 'Perhaps,' he concluded, 'Mr. Playfair, after a few weeks study, may have understood what was going on here even better than I did, though I had passed my whole life on the mountain.'[41] In a typically adroit move Madonna ostensibly denies his parity with Playfair while strongly implying his superiority. He puts his finger on the sort of knowledge that visitors lacked and that he and other guides enjoyed: a rich recent history of the volcano – its eruptions, its physical and topographical transformations – that only came with continuous daily observation.

This was the sort of information that the youthful Scottish geological enthusiast James Forbes used in one of the articles he published about Vesuvius, the buried cities and the Bay of Naples in the *Edinburgh Journal of Science* in 1828. His acknowledgement of Madonna – 'I shall here write some of the particulars I heard from him' – was generous, as was his praise of him as 'one of the best fitted men for the expedition it is possible to imagine, both from his agility, and his immense stock of information'.[42] Madonna explained to him the changing history (and contours) of the volcano after the major eruption of 1822, and Forbes recycled much of what he gleaned from the guide as well as recommending him in his article on Vesuvius published in David Brewster's *Edinburgh Encyclopedia*.[43] Forbes's account was less a detailed geological analysis than a work in history and topography, eagerly welcomed at a time when information about the effects of the 1822 eruption was still obscure, and as we have seen, it helped launch the highly successful scientific career of one of the founding members of the British Association for the Advancement of Science.

Madonna also helped Forbes gather specimens from the mountain for his personal collection. He performed similar services for many savants while they were together on the volcano. Amateur geologists such as the Crown Prince of Denmark (who spent several months working on the volcano) and the Duke of Buckingham, who spent much of 1828 visiting volcanic sites all over the Mediterranean, relied on his expertise.[44] When, in the same year, Charles Babbage carried out a series of experiments in the volcano's crater, Madonna helped him collect sublimated minerals around the vents of the volcano.[45]

Madonna's storytelling was an important part of his appeal as a guide; his tales connected his clients to nobles, aristocrats and royalty who had visited the volcano, and to the famous savants whose familiarity gave him a certain scientific authority. He cultivated his reputation in imaginative ways. It was common for visitors to impress coins in the lava and cut out their impressions or retrieve the money covered in lava as a souvenir. Madonna had a brand that could be pressed into the lava stamping his name and date, making a memento that visitors carried back home, directly linking him to the visit to Vesuvius (Plate 9). His name became a byword for quality and safety. When the Hungarian poet and Romantic exile Polixena Wesselenyi, enveloped in a cloud of sulphurous fumes, panicked and cried out, 'I'm done for!', her guide offered her reassurance: 'Be brave Madame, you are accompanied by the son of Salvatore.'[46]

Salvatore Madonna achieved an unprecedented visibility as a guide – recommended by name in European guidebooks, appearing not just in travel narratives but in fiction and short stories and the international press.[47] During the eruption of 1834, Salvatore's predictions about its outcome were widely reported in the French and English journals:

> According to the computation of Salvatore, the 'capo cicerone', the stream of lava must have been a mile and a half broad, whilst its extent from the crater was 9 miles [14.5 kilometres] with a depth of 30 feet [9 metres], so that instead of commencing with the base of the houses, it approached and flowed at once over their roofs; entering the doors and windows till the whole were buried, the roofs first falling in with a loud crash.

The lava, Salvatore was reported to have said, 'continued flowing more or less for six days, destroyed about 300 acres of valuable land, and injured or destroyed nearly 800 houses'.[48]

It was during this eruption that Salvatore guided three trips up the volcano with Basil Hall, who had climbed the volcano with him some sixteen years earlier. Now a retired naval captain, Basil was the son of the famous Scottish chemist and geologist Sir James Hall, who had himself been up Vesuvius in 1785. Basil was an experienced traveller – in the China Seas, and off the coasts of South America – a very successful travel writer, a Fellow of London's Royal Society, the Royal Astronomical Society, the Royal Geographical Society and the Geological Society. He had been instrumental in getting the navy to help the most famous novelist in Europe, Sir Walter Scott, to visit Naples in 1831–2 in an (eventually ineffectual) attempt to mend his health.[49] The relationship between the guide and his client is a sign of the stature that Salvatore had achieved. Hall called him 'the prince of guides ... who had kept company with the choicest spirits of Europe'.[50] Hall was eager to witness 'the various effects of the eruption then going on', and his second journey, made alone with Salvatore apart from a boy carrying a *camera lucida*, some refreshments and a tea-kettle, was to that end.

Once up the mountain, Hall was very uneasy: 'To see all these things to any good purpose, it was necessary to go pretty close – much closer than I at all liked, or than I should have ventured under any other guidance than that of old Salvatore.'[51] Marching round the perimeter of the crater, the guide regaled Hall with tales of accidents and mishaps during other eruptions (though, as Hall noted, 'he always made it appear that the only danger arose from neglecting his advice'), while around them, 'The ground was almost constantly in a state of tremor, deep-seated roarings were heard from time to time, enormous jets of red-hot stones projected far into the air every four or five minutes, vast masses of dense smoke issued from the crater, and ... the mountain in its terrific throes gave birth to a river of lava.'[52] As Hall confessed, 'I never felt less in love with scientific research in my life, or more disposed to obey, with the utmost docility,

133

the orders of any leader.'[53] In fact, the group very nearly suffered a serious mishap when 'a huge mass of ancient lava broke away from the cliff above us, and fell thundering into the midst of the party.' The two men leapt clear of the fall, but the young boy, who dived into a crevice in the rock, had to be dug out of the debris.[54] Published accounts like these further enhanced Madonna's reputation.

What rewards did the guides earn for their onerous and dangerous labours? By the early nineteenth century, when official fees were included in such travel guides as *The New Guide to Naples*, the Parisian publications of Galignani and the books of Mariana Starke, a cicerone would expect to receive 12 to 15 carlini, and a donkey and a guide 8 carlini in the daytime but 12 carlini at night (the more usual time to make the journey). Twelve carlini were equivalent to four shillings and six pence. This meant that a guide with a donkey making one trip up Vesuvius, and assuming he was working alone, could earn more than four times the wage of an agricultural day labourer.[55]

Being carried up on what was known as a *'portantina'* was much more expensive: Starke quotes prices ranging from 4 to 6 ducats (40 to 60 carlini) for a crew of six men, a maximum price equivalent to £1. 2s. 6d.[56] Hall, who printed his receipt for his one-man excursion with Salvatore in 1834, paid 7 ducats and 10 carlini (80 carlini all told) for the day, of which 3 ducats (30 carlini) went directly towards the cicerone's service.[57] But as Hall's receipt shows, all the monies spent on the trip went directly to Salvatore. How much he passed on to the boy who accompanied them, to the coachmen and to the boot mender, we do not know. The cicerone, or official guide, held the whip hand because he provided different services and acted as a team leader. When a convoy moved up the volcano he had already determined the size and the remuneration of the crew, in accordance with the bargain he had struck with the visitors. The official rates in the guidebooks do not include the sums paid to the young men, 'robust men accustomed to this exercise',[58] as many as three to a traveller, who pulled, pushed or carried visitors up the final steep slope of hot cinders to the crater. And apart from those the cicerone engaged, there were often hangers-on, like the five men who despite being told they would not be paid, followed Simond 'as guides or guides helpers', and who on their return 'contrived to make us pay more than the customary price'.

Someone like Salvatore Madonna was prosperous by Neapolitan standards. If, as we might plausibly suppose, he and his family earned 3 ducats a day for 200 days in the year, his income of 600 ducats put him in the top few per cent of earners, though, of course, very far from the very wealthiest landowners in the kingdom (96 per cent of the kingdom's population earned less than 200 ducats a year). According to the *catasto* (tax assessment survey) of 1809 undertaken by Murat's regime, Salvatore owned two substantial properties, probably three storeys in height, as well as a stables.[59] The situation of the peasants with their mules, the boys carrying fruit, and the strong men paid to hoist the visitors to the crater was not of the same order. The guide business on Vesuvius had originated when field hands and small proprietors, watching visitors climb the volcano, had offered their services along the route; it was less a systematic trade than a casual by-employment used to supplement income from vine-dressing and spinning flax in their small holdings at the foot of the mountain. Thus Charles de Brosses in his *Lettres d'Italie* described how in 1739 he and his companions had been joined during his ascent of the volcano by local peasants working in the vineyards, who were nevertheless prepared with the 'usual equipment' to take them up through the cinders. He called them '*soi-disant ciceroni*', dressed like Capuchins.[60]

As the number of visitors grew, so did the value of such work. At a time when prices were rising and wages were relatively static, helping travellers was a welcome bonus for the poor. In the 1790s the wife of Bartolomeo Pumo had candles lit to San Ciro, one of the patron saints of Portici (at the foot of the volcano), and kept a lamp lit to Saint Anthony to help bring on eruptions and keep her husband in work.[61] As the Duke of Buckingham noticed, the eruption of 1828 was greeted with delight because it promised much more business, after a period in which Vesuvius had been relatively quiescent since the major eruption of 1822.[62] (These were the years when Thomas Jefferson Hogg, the friend of Shelley, remarked that, 'Vesuvius, I was told, had retired from business.'[63]) In 1831 while working in Naples, the composer Felix Mendelssohn never even contemplated climbing Vesuvius because, as he complained, 'Unfortunately that traitor Vesuvius does not smoke at all, and looks precisely like any other fine mountain.'[64] So when the volcano was active, the guides and porters worked as much as they could. A young Belgian naval officer, who found the climb overwhelming, was shocked to be told by his guide (who may have been exaggerating) that he often made the climb three times a day.[65] Anna Jameson, descending the volcano during the 1822 eruption, was told by her guide, whom she asked to sing for her as he strode along with his hand upon her bridle, that he had climbed the volcano six times that day.[66]

Guide work: guides and their clients

What did the guides do, what services did they render the visitor? At their most basic they were porters, carrying torches if travelling at night, together with food and drink, ropes and straps, for the climb up the cone and into the crater, as well as instruments such as barometers, thermometers and *camera lucida*, like the one used by Basil Hall. But their most important function was to assist human freight: to carry or push and pull travellers to the summit. Famously this was achieved by attaching a belt, harness or girdle around the waist of one guide, who pulled the visitor along in his footsteps, often aided by one or two other guides pushing and holding the traveller so that he or she did not slide back in the cinders. Even a fit young person could benefit from the guide's assistance.

Facilitating the final ascent up the cone of cinders was one stage in the travellers' itinerary that the guides – and especially the head guide, Madonna – tried to make as comfortable and attractive as possible. The guides chose the routes to be followed, offering food and drink at different stations on the way. Many carried eggs to roast in the lava or kettles to heat food. They helped their charges encrust coins with lava as souvenirs, pointed out the finest views, and led them to the most spectacular crystals and lavas.

But above all the guides were employed to secure the safety of visitors, who, with few exceptions, had little idea of the dangers posed by the ever-changing volcano. They were the travellers' risk-managers, selling their skills and knowledge of the mountain to their clients. This made many travellers uneasy. Most were not in the position of Sir William Hamilton, whose trust in Bartolomeo Pumo had grown steadily over the course of many ascents; others were putting themselves in the hands of a stranger. They had to accept that the guides were able to read the weather, and to predict not only if it favoured good views of the summit and crater, but if it would not expose them – in the form of an adverse wind – to clouds of asphyxiating fumes. Most importantly they had to trust that guides were alert to the likely shifts and changes in the volcano during an eruption – the frequency of its explosions (judged not by a stopwatch but through experience), and the likelihood of a collapse of the crater's wall or of the surrounding cliffs of lava. No savant, no matter how knowledgeable of volcanoes in general, had such a knowledge of Vesuvius's particular dangers. It was for this reason that prudent travellers, like James Edward Smith, the president of the British Linnaean Society, 'confided in the prudence and example of our guides, to judge how far we might go, and no further'.[67]

Nevertheless the ascent of Vesuvius was a fraught and complex matter, in which visitors' desire to take advantage of what the guides offered tussled with their hankering to retain personal autonomy and control over their climb. Many were invested in the idea of emulating the part of the heroic explorer. Trust and confidence in a cicerone often wavered, a situation further complicated by the fear that the visitor would be taken advantage of, bilked or mistreated.

So, though many travellers were quite willing to give themselves up and be dragged up the volcano, others were not. This may partly have been because more guides and porters involved greater expense or, at the very least, help from a guide who was already hired implied a larger gratuity at the end of the journey. But more than money was at stake. If on the one hand being hauled up a volcano seemed to abase the guide – Amélie Odier compared his task to that of a horse pulling a cart of wood[68] – it also emphasised the abject dependence of the visitors on those who were dragging them to the crater.

During her ascent of Vesuvius in 1834, the young Swiss woman (and future novelist) Catherine-Valérie Boissier repeatedly resisted the attempts of her guide to make her take hold of the straps that he just as repeatedly offered her. Her *amour-propre* – her self-esteem or pride – meant she was determined to reach the top without assistance. As she struggled and groaned the guide began to mock her gently. She fell, her cheeks burned, she felt as if her arteries were bursting; she fell a second time. She was suffocating with the sulphurous smoke; the wind blew a rain of cinders into her eyes, blinding her. So she gave in, gratefully accepting the guide's assistance, and eventually reached the crater. But her ordeal was not over. On the descent 'my clothes clung to the rocks, and held me in one direction, while the guide dragged me in the other; my shoes were in tatters, my feet were torn; the torrent of suffering which suddenly surged in me made me motionless.' By this point the guide was treating her with compassion, urging her to have no fear, speaking of her as '*poverina*' (poor girl), while she asked for protection, and he invoked the Virgin. When she reached the end of her journey, she declared, 'How blessed I am, on leaving this work . . . with what joy I threw myself on my knees, stammering words of gratitude.'[69] Her account not only captures the fright of a young woman in the midst of an eruption, but also the rather complex ties that harnessed the guide and the visitor.

If relations between guides and their female employees were charged, they were far more so with male clients, who were inclined to think that the dangers of the ascent of Vesuvius were exaggerated by guides seeking custom, and who regarded being dragged up the mountain as an affront to their strength and virility. Paul Crombet was a young Belgian naval officer who, with a group of six naval friends, set out to climb Vesuvius on 27 October 1817. He had ascended the volcano and reached the hardest part of the climb walking side by side with his guide; but as the mountain steepened, his companion pulled out a harness and offered to drag him the rest of the way. Crombet was disconcerted and insulted: 'at my age, to be led to the edge, that seemed to me a little shameful'; he refused the guide's help and insisted on following him. But slipping back, falling over, ending up on his knees, he had to concede that 'fatigue mastered my pride', and he 'reclaimed the help of my guide which I had earlier rejected so haughtily'. Even with his guide's aid he had to pause and take breath. He described himself as 'dying of thirst, frozen by the fresh air, covered in a cold sweat, suffering from a racing heart'; he castigated his own feebleness but, in an effort to keep his masculine pride, also insisted that he and his companions never thought about turning back. Almost prostrate with fatigue, he supported himself on his staff or stretched out on the lava whose rough edges scraped and scratched him. 'No regrets! No fear! No indecision', he kept saying to himself, until he finally reached the top.[70] Looking back on his journey he felt that the fee of one pilastra (12 carlini) that he had paid for a guide and an ass was barely enough, and that it would have been just to double or triple the price.[71]

Elsewhere in his *Souvenirs d'Italie*, Crombet disparaged guides in general as ill-informed and unaware of their own ignorance. But both he and Catherine-Valérie Boissier, though they wished to appear as independent and autonomous travellers in control of their actions, were forced, either by fear or exhaustion or a combination of the two, to recognise their dependence on their guides. Both of their accounts, of course, describe a journey during an eruption, at a time when guides were not only busier but had far more authority because of the dangers to which visitors were exposed. When Crombet and his companions, having recuperated at the crater, wanted to travel further round its perimeter and get closer to the lava flow, their guides warned against such action, explaining how dangerous it would be especially, as they deemed likely, if the wind shifted. Crombet was sufficiently chastened by his ascent to comply willingly with their admonition and to turn back down the mountain. One senses in his account that he had surrendered to his guide: given up his control to the man with local experience and knowledge.

Relations between guides and travellers were coloured by many visitors' inability to see them except through the stereotypical lens applied to Naples' *lazzaroni* – people who were deemed idle, shiftless, superstitious, ignorant and importunate. One traveller writing in the 1830s complacently reported, 'I asked one of the guides whether Signor Diavolo was not down there. The man looked grim and frightened, and said, "*sicuro*", in all faith.'[72] Even Anna Jameson, who had an acute sense of Salvatore's 'intelligent conversation, his assiduity, and solicitude for my comfort', looked on the other guides as showmen delighting in tricks and superficial effects: 'Our guides seemed as proud of the performances of the mountain, and as anxious to show it off to best advantage, as the keeper of a menagerie is of the tricks of his dancing bear, or the proprietor of "Solomon in all his glory" of his raree-show.'[73]

There was a tendency among visitors to question or downplay knowledge shown by the guides. John Owen, an English clergyman and theologian who climbed Vesuvius in the 1790s, had to concede when examining the layers of lava at the foot of the volcano, 'of these the age and circumstances are well known by the cicerones, who explained the phenomena attending them, and assigned to each their regular dates'. But he immediately undercut his acknowledgement, by emphasising that 'Our cicerone was not however a philosopher, he never intermeddled with *causes*; contenting himself with *effects*, he rehearsed his catalogue of signs and wonders; and had only answers to those questions which were connected with what immediately preceded in the dialogue.'[74] No wonder Salvatore was so concerned to explain his connection to the likes of Sir Humphry Davy, to show that he was truly an interpreter of Vesuvius. This may also be why, if Harriet Morton was correct, he addressed his clients not in Neapolitan or Italian, but in French.[75]

There were many visitors who looked on the guides with deep suspicion. When the painter Thomas Uwins, during his fourth ascent of Vesuvius in 1826, took the Scottish artist David Wilkie and his brother-in-law up the mountain, his companions treated their guides poorly and quarrelled with them about the fees they would pay. Uwins heard the guides say that 'We are all heathens, we have no church, no pope, no saints, no Virgin Mary, no holy year, no hope of salvation, and no God.'[76] He was terrified that they would rob and murder them. Similarly, Jane Waldie, another Scottish artist and author of *Sketches Descriptive of Italy in 1816–17*, became petrified when she was left alone with her guide on her return to Portici from the slopes of the volcano: 'It was currently reported, and as moreover, I believe, a fact, that a Russian traveller had been made away with on Vesuvius a few months before by his guide.' She was quick to tell 'my Lazzaroni' that she was carrying no money. But her fears proved groundless; she arrived back 'safe and sound', after 'amicably settling up with him'.[77] The famous Frenchman Louis Coutrel, who took his own life in 1821 by plunging himself into one of the volcano's largest fissures, took care, before he did away with himself, to write in the Visitors' Book that his guide bore no responsibility for his actions, and was certainly not responsible for his death.[78] All of these incidents show the power of the guides over their charges, the consciousness among visitors of their dependence and their deep-seated fears of falling prey to their social inferiors. On the slopes of the volcano, with its unfamiliar, ever-changing landscape of smoke, explosions and lava, travellers were acutely conscious that the guides had the potential not only to save them from hurt but to do them harm.

The group most likely to clash with the guides were young men, often in the army or navy, who were confident that they could manage the climb without local assistance. Two members of the Royal Guard, Antonio Duisomet and Luigi Marsili, complained in the Visitors' Book that so-called ciceroni claimed that an ascent of Vesuvius without a guide was impossible, something they described as both 'false' and an imposition on gullible tourists.[79] The tensions between the guides and certain visitors spilled over during the eruption in March 1828, when numerous Swiss soldiers, mercenaries of the Neapolitan monarch, appeared in large numbers on the mountain. These officers and sergeant majors were hardened military men, who believed that they knew far more about mountains than the Neapolitans, and that guides were unnecessary.[80]

The stereotypes about the guides meant that on more than one occasion they were ignored as cowardly, lazy or up to no good. The Scottish banker Sir James Forbes would not listen to the warnings of his guides when they refused to cross a lava field, 'as we imagined ... that this proceeded merely from their laziness'. Leaving the guides behind, he and his friends plunged on, eager to reach a distant glowing rent in the volcano. Forbes's nightmare began almost immediately and was to continue for several hours. Soon he and his friends were scrambling in the dark on their hands and knees through pieces of lava, 'with the edges and corners as sharp as penknives'. 'All of us,' Forbes admitted, 'experienced many a sore bruise as we got along, sometimes slipping down among the broken fragments, and some-times the ground giving way, and hurling back with us, as we attempted to ascend the heaps which lay in our way.' Once they perceived 'the hopelessness of attaining our main object of reaching the Lava', they 'desisted from so foolish an attempt & agreed to return to the Hermitage'. But the experience took its toll. 'Having been scrambling on the Mountain for 3 or 4 hours, we were all completely tired and excessively hungry.' Forbes helped himself to a large quantity of rum punch to relieve his aches and pains.

> But whether from the fatigue or from being much heated in the course of our Scramble, or more probably from having dipt too deep into the Bowl, it flew up to my head to such a degree, that before we were rose from the table, I was as drunk as an Owl, & absolutely incapable of descending the Mountain from the Hermitage to Portici on foot ... After stumbling and falling at our first outsetting, I was forced to give up attempting to walk alone; and found myself obliged to take the aid of a couple of our Guides, who supported me down the Hill, each under the Arm.

Cut and bruised, his leg swelled up in the following days, and he was forced to call a physician and remain in his lodgings.[81]

This was the sort of story about injuries to travellers that more sceptical visitors, like the Bohemian count Charles-Joseph de Clary-Aldringen, dismissed as exaggerations or outright lies.[82] But the hermit's book makes clear that the risks were real. Falls, minor scrapes and burns were common. Lord Alexander, ascending the volcano in 1828, recorded 'four tumbles going up the mountain'.[83] But these, together with the destruction of shoes, which were often ripped to shreds in the ascent, and the damage to clothing, were comparatively minor matters. More serious were falls into the crater. The English Neapolitan saddler Mr Fish had to be hauled out when he fell into the crater in April 1827.[84] Three months later, George Clarke, a British architect and engineer, travelled up Vesuvius with four Germans, two of whom were architects from Karlsruhe and Hanover: 'Two of whom descended into the crater at the hazard of their lives, one of those who did not descend fell from the highest part above one hundred feet [30 metres] and was much bruised but fortunately for himself escaped well this slight disaster.'[85] A month later James Stewart fell and was badly burned, and shortly thereafter a doctor from Nice almost suffocated when in the crater.[86] In January of the following year a Frenchman from Anvers was 'badly injured', and called on his countrymen to 'remember me my friends' as if he felt his life was in peril, and in the summer and autumn of 1828 there were two deaths, one of a Frenchman, the other of an Italian.[87]

The deaths in 1828 provoked a series of speculations in the hermit's book about the safety of Vesuvius, and visitors became sufficiently alarmed to prompt Salvatore, rather unusually, to respond to their anxieties. With his livelihood at stake, it is not surprising that he replied offering reassurance. Like crossing the Alps, he explained, the ascent of Vesuvius could seem terrifying, but in reality it was safe.[88] As the guides knew, the appeal of the volcano depended to a remarkable degree on maintaining a proper balance between safety and danger: if the journey were too easy, much of its point would be lost; if too hazardous, it would discourage the visitors who were so vital to the local economy. What the guides were selling was a sublime experience, one that was frightening and yet not life-threatening.

One particular point of friction between the guides and their more adventurous clients was the descent into the crater. Guides were paid a fee to take visitors to the top of the volcano, but not to take them down into the crater itself. This was by far the most hazardous place on the volcano, as well as one of the most scientifically interesting, which is why it seems to have attracted the attention of young men (and women). A guide to Naples, published in English and Italian after the major eruption of 1822, when the topography of the volcano changed radically, warned, 'We cannot advise people to undertake the ambitious and very dangerous enterprise of descending into it [the crater]. Why should they? Would it be in order to acquire the right of vainly boasting of a rash action?'[89] Which was precisely the point.

But from the guides' perspective the descent was an opportunity to make extra fees. They usually explained their reluctance to climb down into the crater as a matter of ensuring the safety of their clients and themselves, but many travellers suspected that it was a stratagem either to raise their fees or to avoid the hard work of the descent. Chateaubriand's experience was typical. Having reached the lip of the crater, 'I proposed to my guide that we should descend into the crater. He made several objections; but this was only to obtain a little more money; and we agreed upon a sum, which he received on the spot.'[90] Salvatore told Basil Hall the tale of a young soldier who would not heed his warnings about climbing into the crater: 'Pooh! Pooh! danger . . . what care I for danger - am I not a soldier?' he said, and asked the guide if he was frightened. Such accusations of cowardice were common in such circumstances; they were also the visitors' best bargaining chip. Salvatore eventually agreed to the descent but warned his client that if there were an eruption he should stand still, look upwards and thereby see and evade the falling rock.[91] As they were climbing back out of the crater 'a furious eruption took place, and myriads of stones were shot a thousand feet into the air'. In a panic the soldier forgot the instructions and fled but 'had not run far before he was struck down by three stones, one of which broke his leg, the others stunned him', so that Salvatore had to 'carry him on my shoulders out of the cone'.[92]

A great deal of the guides' expertise had to do with cumulative knowledge about the behaviour of the volcano and could only be exercised *in situ*. It was an informed response, sometimes pre-emptive, sometimes in reaction to immediate circumstances. Guides could teach travellers a few precautionary moves, but by and large their knowledge could not be conveyed directly to their charges who, as we have seen, sometimes resisted their advice, even in circumstances when to do so was very dangerous. If this were true of Salvatore Madonna, it was even more likely in dealings with humbler guides.

This sort of tacit and local knowledge had more than one purpose. First and foremost it was a means to secure people's safety, a matter of urgency and immediacy; invaluable in the moment, it had no larger end and was never intended to be part of any system. But it was also the grounds on which visitors were given a history of the volcano, the veracity of which was always attributed to the guides' continuous familiarity with its activities and changing landscape. This, of course, was Madonna's response to the suggestion that John Playfair's knowledge of Vesuvius was greater than his. And his presence at the side of the British savant was proof that the sort of knowledge that Playfair was seeking was well-nigh impossible without the expertise of Madonna. Bold young men and Swiss army officers may have dispensed with guides, but savants did not.

At the same time, figures like the Reverend John Owen, though they conceded the acuity of the accounts of guides, dismissed their observations as concerned with 'effects', 'signs and wonders' and not, like those of true savants, with 'causes'. As earth sciences shifted away from the mineralogists' concern with the physical and chemical properties of particular rocks and crystals, which could be ascertained in the laboratory, geologists became more interested in the interrelation and positioning of different fossils, rocks and their stratigraphy in the field. The time-honoured practice of crystal collection became less and less important to the savant, though it remained central to the 'curious' visitors with their enthusiasm for 'souvenirs' and brilliant minerals. Crystals of leucite, augite, reddish haematite, garnets, yellowish sulphites, and brilliant lapis lazuli and tourmaline made appealing souvenirs for visitors and eye-catching specimens for the collector's cabinet, but lacked scientific authority unless their place on the mountain was clearly identified. During his visit to Naples in the spring of 1812, the Scottish-American geologist (and maker of the first geological map of the United States) William Maclure was exasperated that local savants did not 'take the trouble or examine the terrain themselves', but bought their minerals from 'stone collectors which [sic] are called *Ciceroni* . . . who are ignorant of everything but brilliant crystals'.[93] Twelve years later, when one of the pioneering figures of mineralogy, Jean-André-Henri Lucas, wanted to put his Vesuvian crystals into the royal collections in Paris, he was opposed by Joseph Barclay Pentland, one of Georges Cuvier's research assistants, on the grounds that the materials had been bought from Salvatore Madonna without any knowledge of their date or place of origin. Too many of Lucas's donations, Pentland complained, 'were taken at random and without having made observations about the position of their location'.[94] This may have been Lucas's failure, but it could not be redressed by turning to the authority of the guide. He might lead the savant to the stones, as Madonna led the young James Forbes – few doubted the capacity of the guides to find different sorts of crystals – but even Madonna lacked the authority to assert their location. For location was not just a topographical referent but one that placed the object within a geological scheme. That required the imprimatur of the man of science.

Guides: their changing role and powers

But what eroded the guides' power in the long term was not just the hostility of those who thought their expertise overrated or redundant, but larger changes in the Kingdom of Naples, which made the volcano far more accessible than ever before. For many years Teodoro Monticelli, the secretary of the Academy of Sciences, had been urging the Neapolitan monarchs to establish a scientific observatory on the slopes of Vesuvius. In 1839, shortly before his death, he got his way. Between 1841 and 1844, a carriage road was built up the mountain, and the Observatory erected on the same extrusion of rock that was home to the hermitage. The new road meant that it was now possible to travel by carriage from the centre of Naples up to the hermitage, bypassing the guides in Resina, a circumstance, remarked the Anglo-Irish writer Selina Bunbury, 'which causes much indignation, and

meets with much opposition from the numerous guides and conductors whose business it has been to supply mules, or ponies or asses'
for the climb.[95] As the *Morning Chronicle* reported, 'No foreigner
comes to Naples without making an ascent of Vesuvius. Thanks to
the fine road the Government has made, the ascent is easily made in
three hours.'[96]

A few years earlier the first railway in Italy had opened with a
stretch of line from the city of Naples to the royal palace of Portici.
Though its prime function – apart from its demonstration of the
modernity of Naples – was to make the royal palace and the surrounding
luxury villas more accessible to their rich owners, it carried a large trade.
The project of a French engineer and using train engines manufac-
tured in Britain, the railway carried more than 130,000 passengers
between its opening in early October of 1839 and the end of the year;
by the 1840s it was transporting over a million a year.[97] From an early
date the railway was seen as part of a tourist economy, catering for
'innumerable foreigners always visiting for the delight of the place, for
its smiling and salubrious climate, [and] for its remarkable wonders of
nature and art'.[98] On the occasion of the 1850 eruption a special train
brought 400 passengers to the foot of the volcano.[99] During the 1858
eruption, which temporarily blocked the road to the Observatory, there
were six trains a day leaving Naples for the slopes of Vesuvius.[100] The
volcano was getting closer to Naples.

In certain respects, the system of guides remained largely un-
altered. Operations were still coordinated by a head guide, though by
the 1850s the Madonna family had been superseded by their relatives,
the Cozzolinos, first Vincenzo, then Pasquale and then Giovanni,
whose services were recommended in John Murray's *Guide*, much as
Starke had recommended Salvatore Madonna, as a means to avoid
the 'rapacious guides' of Resina.[101] The correspondent of the London
Times Henry G. Wreford, who also reported for the *Athenaeum*, the
Daily News and the *London Illustrated News*, and who lived most of
his life in southern Italy,[102] was a friend of Vincenzo Cozzolino and

relied on him for his frequent reports to *The Times* on the state of the volcano. Wreford recommended Cozzolino to his readers, publishing his address (71 Strada Reggia, near the Palace, Portici) because, as he explained, 'all the guides at that place have discovered that they are more or less nearly connected with this hereditary chief, and assume his name.'[103] And when Cozzolino's smallholding and vineyard were destroyed in the 1859 eruption, Wreford launched an appeal for the guide, calling on his former clients to acknowledge his value and past services by helping cover his losses.

There is every reason to believe that Vincenzo Cozzolino was as able a vulcanologist as Salvatore Madonna. Wreford in the *Athenaeum* commented on the guide's identification of 'arsenic and sulphur and iodate of lead, and a variety of other articles with hard names, all of which Cozzolino has at his fingers' ends, or perhaps more correctly, at the tip of his tongue'.[104] At the fifth national meeting of Italian scientists at Lucca in 1843, in a report on recommendations for the future improvement of scientific nomenclature, it was 'suggested that naming practices [of scientific discoveries] should recognize the contribution of persons of ignoble and illiterate condition if they make a contribution to science'. 'Doing so,' the report goes on to say, 'would be compensating for the ingratitude with which the proletarians are repeatedly treated.' 'What geological scientist,' it concludes, 'could deny, by way of example, that he had much profit from humble Vincenzo Cozzolino in exploring Vesuvius?'[105] By the time of Italian unification, Cozzolino was producing daily written reports during eruptions, as well as talking at length to newspaper correspondents, providing up-to-date information on the state of the volcano. He also published a 'Catalogue of Vesuvian Minerals' in three sheets.[106] He had become part of the apparatus of commentary and publicity about the volcano and was even referred to by Wreford as 'a scientific man'.[107]

The tradition of the knowledgeable head guide lived on in the work of Vincenzo's successor. In the spring of 1868 a Cozzolino (either

Pasquale or Giovanni) accompanied two geologists and friends, John Arthur Phillips, a graduate of the École des Mines in Paris, and John Edward Lee, famous for his work on Roman antiquities, up the volcano in order to test Charles Lyell's theory of the formation of volcanoes. Cozzolino, whom Phillips described as 'the excellent descendant and representative of a still more famous guide',[108] provided them with information about the fossil remains on Mount Somma, which they believed refuted Charles Lyell's view that volcanoes were not formed by upheaval of the earth's crust, but by the gradual accumulation of volcanic ejecta.[109]

But the Cozzolino family's relationship to the savants of Naples was quite unlike Madonna's cosy collaboration with Teodoro Monticelli. The royal foundation of the Vesuvius Observatory in 1841, and the inauguration of the building at the Seventh Congress of Italian Scientists in 1845, began a new era of intensive monitoring of the volcano, carried out not by pooling the observations of the guides, but through the development and use of electromagnetic seismographs, invented by the Observatory's director Luigi Palmieri in 1856. These instruments enabled the Observatory and its staff to engage in uninterrupted surveillance of the volcano. When Palmieri used the term 'guida/e' in his annual reports on the activities of the mountain, he never referred to people but only to scientific instruments.

The chief source of scientific information about Vesuvius became the Observatory and its director, Palmieri, dubbed by *The Times* as 'the great Vesuvian authority' and 'the oracle of the Observatory'.[110] The guides were soon at loggerheads with Palmieri. In December 1858 they were incensed that Palmieri, who had left the Observatory and believed a major eruption imminent, had written to the government 'saying that people in the neighbourhood should be cautioned that it is unsafe for them to remain, and begging that a commission might be sent out to examine into the state of the mountain'. His actions threatened their livelihood. 'Who,' they complained, 'should know best the state of the mountain? Palmieri, or we who walk all over daily?'[111] A distinction developed between the local ocular observations of Cozzolino and his colleagues and the 'scientific' data generated by the Observatory. Newspaper reporting on Vesuvius's activities spoke of Palmieri's comments 'which will have much interest for the scientific as well as general reader', while Cozzolino's views were described as 'not certainly scientific, but so far as they go, are very correct'. Even a close friend like Wreford was in two minds about the value of Cozzolino's views: 'His opinion is – and though not a scientific man it is worth something, born and bred as he has been around lava and ashes – that the eruption has not yet reached its climax.' But whereas a generation before, Madonna had confidently asserted his views about the course and intensity of volcanoes, Cozzolino now begrudgingly deferred to the seismometers mounted by Palmieri in the Observatory. These electromagnetic seismographs recorded the intensity, direction and duration of movements within the mountain which were otherwise imperceptible to the human observer. In Palmieri's view their greatest use was in enabling predictions of earthquakes and eruptions. They terrified Cozzolino who, Wreford reported, 'never goes up to the grand cone, he says, without fear, "for the whole mountain rises beneath my feet and from side to side"'.[112] Human experience and intuition were pushed aside by impersonal instrumentation. The bond of trust between the guides and the local savants was broken.

Yet the guides were busier than ever. Improved communications meant that gawping visitors thronged to the slopes of the volcano in unprecedented numbers. There was, wrote one report, 'a continued line of carriages from Naples to the summit of the mountain' during the eruption of 1855; the whole length of the usually quiet road to the Observatory 'was like a fair, and such was the throng of carriages which were moving on in three lines, that it was with difficulty we ever arrived at our destination'.[113] In 1858, the *Englishwoman's Review and Home Paper* (which showed a particular interest in Vesuvian eruptions) spoke of 'hundreds of vehicles round the hermitage', reporting that 'On each night several thousands of persons of all ranks, from the peer to the peasant, urged by curiosity, repair to the scene of this extraordinary spectacle'.[114] Wreford wrote in *The Times* that the scene was like Derby Day: 'Every kind of vehicle is in use, and everyone in Resina is transformed into a cicerone.'[115]

The response of the authorities was to seek to regulate the guides, to control their numbers and activities. An ordinance of 1846 fixed the number of official guides at sixteen, requiring that they should be competent and of good character. They had to carry permits from the police and were required to know at least one foreign language. Prices were fixed, but at levels that were, if anything, lower than those charged under the earlier more permissive regime.[116] It seems that the sort of oversight earlier exercised by Salvatore Madonna and his family was now being eroded by a system of formal government regulation. Madonna had frequently told his clients that he was answerable to the government for the safety of visitors, an explanation or excuse that he often used when declining to undertake what he claimed were risky actions on the mountain. He also used the royal guards, referred to as gendarmes, who were stationed on the mountain to protect visitors from local bandits, to stop travellers who were inclined to disobey his warnings. But the government presence in the era before the Observatory was not obtrusive, apart from the occasional intervention prompted by the monarch's concern that his hunting grounds on the edge of the volcano remain undisturbed.

Better communications meant that visitors to Vesuvius could take a number of routes to the volcano, thus ending the monopoly that Salvatore Madonna and his successors had over access to the mountain. Many visitors still travelled via Resina, in part because the journey was more of an adventure than taking a carriage or train, but the bargaining power of the traditional guides was much diminished. Published guidebooks suggested that it was wise to avoid the importunate guides of Resina, though gripes by travellers about unofficial guides, and Wreford's complaint that 'the tariff of the guide should not only be regulated but enforced',[117] show that the informal system of negotiation was still operating.

But what finally deprived the guides of their importance and income was the funicular railway, that of a celebrated Neapolitan song, first opened in 1880. Earlier road and rail developments had eliminated the need for guides for much of the journey to Vesuvius. The growth of press coverage and the information provided by the government and the Observatory had reduced the value of the information from guides on the ground – their input now presented to the public in a daily sheet issued by the main guide – but the one part of the trip to the volcano that the guides continued to control was the final, painful and precipitous ascent of the cone to the summit. From the first, when a Hungarian banker and a group of engineers proposed a railway, there was fierce local opposition, one that succeeded in extracting a tax on every passenger and an annual fee or concession to the community. The funicular cut the final part of the journey from an hour and a half of sweated labour to a twelve-minute ride seated in a car that carried up to three hundred passengers a day. But its overheads were high and profits low, and the company that ran the railway foundered until it was rescued in 1887 by John Mason Cook, the son of Thomas Cook, the travel agent. Cook, who refused to make the concession payments to the guides, was soon engaged in a major struggle. The guides burned down the station, cut the track and heaved one of the cars into the crater. When he repaired the line, they cut it again. Cook then closed the railway for six months, until the guides came to an agreement in which they received a portion of each rail ticket in return for their services from the upper station of the funicular to the top of the mountain – a distance of only a few hundred yards. In effect the guides became employees or clients of the travel agent, though they continued to supplement their incomes through a lively trade in minerals and lavas.[118]

In the course of a century, the journey to the crater of Vesuvius was transformed from an arduous and dangerous one, redolent of the heroic travels of the famous Enlightenment explorers, to a pleasant jaunt in which steam replaced manpower. Thanks to Cook, the volcano boasted a railway, a restaurant, a hotel and a toll road with levies for all travellers who were not Cook customers. The tentacular control the firm exercised over Europe's transport and tourist industries extended right up to the cone of the volcano. The task of the guides, which had begun as a by-employment, a way to supplement meagre incomes, had quickly become part of a local business, dominated by a few enterprising families from Resina, only to be progressively undermined by the state, which sought to regulate it, and by larger economic forces aided by new technologies that wrested control from the inhabitants of the town.

One effect of these larger changes was to alter fundamentally the relations between guides and visitors. While accounts from the first half of the century often comment on the guides and their relations with the travellers, after Italian unification there is very little said about individual transactions between the guides and their employers. Even Vincenzo Cozzolino seems a paper-thin character when compared with the flamboyant portrait we have of Salvatore Madonna. But then the local guides had become progressively less important, less necessary to travellers. For the likes of Anna Jameson and Paul Crombet, the ascent of Vesuvius during an eruption was an impossibility without a skilled guide, and their feelings of dependence towards them were inevitably emotionally complex. For explorers like Basil Hall, the company of a guide was bound up with the adventure and romance of hazardous exploration. And for a neophyte like James Forbes, collaboration with a guide – learning from his local knowledge – launched a career as a scientist.

The shift in relations between travellers and guides was symptomatic of the altered nature of the climb up the volcano: it ceased to be a Romantic story of personal struggle and physical engagement – the sort of tale that Catherine Wilmot told her incredulous friends when she returned to Naples with her bleeding feet and smouldering,

torn boots. The visitor was distanced, both from the physical environment and from the local people who eased their journey. The
trip had become a matter of 'convenience', of 'speed and comfort',
smoothed by the emollient technologies of the modern road and
railway.

For a period in the early nineteenth century, the mutually beneficial relationship between Salvatore Madonna, the chief guide, and
Teodoro Monticelli, the secretary of the Neapolitan Academy of
Sciences, aligned the interests of the Vesuvian guides and of savants
both local and foreign. The recent history of the volcano and its
mineral products were part of a shared endeavour that promoted
Vesuvius far beyond the Bay of Naples. But shifting priorities, new
institutions and controls, together with new forms of instrumentation, pushed the guides to the scientific margins. H.J. Johnston-
Lavis, the British physician who became the first professor of
vulcanology at the University of Naples in 1893, wrote numerous
reports about the volcano for *Nature* during his thirty years in Naples.
But he only once mentioned guides, when he disparagingly described
them, in true Victorian fashion, as cowardly 'porters'.[119] When he
wanted information beyond that conveyed by his friends, he turned
to the director and engineer of the Vesuvian railway. Over time, the
guides were marginalised and reverted, in the eyes of visitors, into
the stereotypical creatures they had often been accused of being, but
which their skills and labour had resisted. In December 1886, at a
time when the funicular was temporarily not operating, a visitor
arriving at the foot of the volcano's cone was forced to seek help for
his party. 'I was able,' he reported, 'to engage the services of a workman
or idler to lead the most able bodied of the party up the ash cone
to the summit.'[120] Workman, idler: the description could hardly be
lazier, more slipshod and contemptuous. The tradition of undercut-
ting, overlooking or ignoring necessary help clearly lived and lives
on, yet can prevent us from recognising that guides were vital to the
cult of Vesuvius as it flourished in the early nineteenth century.

Part II
Sociability and Taste

3
ON THE MOUNTAIN, ON THE ROAD
Sociability and Travel

I have one want which I have never yet been able to satisfy . . . I have no friend . . . when I am glowing with the enthusiasm of success, there will be none to participate my joy; if I am assailed by disappointment, no-one will endeavour to sustain me in dejection . . . I desire the company of a man who could sympathise with me; whose eyes could reply to mine . . . I bitterly feel the want of a friend. I have no one near me, gentle yet courageous, possessed of a cultivated as well as a capacious mind, whose tastes are like my own, to approve or amend my plans.

> Robert Walton to his sister, in Mary Shelley's
> *Frankenstein: or, The Modern Prometheus*, 1818

Mary Shelley's Arctic explorer, a man driven by a thirst for knowledge, is a suitable companion for her tortured savant, Victor Frankenstein. The two men embody an almost fanatical determination to bring nature to heel, a shared desire to control its powers and subjugate its forces.[1] But Walton also expresses a common anxiety experienced by the Romantic traveller. His frustration at not being able to share his feelings and insights with like-minded friends and companions – the loneliness and isolation he experiences

159

even in the presence of his shipmates – was the frequent experience of travellers in all sorts of unfamiliar surroundings, whether in the ice-cold Arctic or on the scorching flanks of a volcano. Travel enhanced the desire for companionship and familiarity.

In the following pages we will trace both the emotional intensities experienced on the slopes of the volcano and the sorts of attachment that travellers developed on the road. Friendships and antipathies engendered in the often hazardous environment of the slopes of the volcano were not so very different from other forms of Romantic emotion; rather they often marked an intensification of existing feelings of camaraderie and antipathy. But that was the point. Visiting the volcano, exposing oneself to its powers and confronting its dangers, enabled travellers to enjoy, suffer and share with others a heightened intensity of feeling. This experience of the sublime was not just a deeply felt individual emotion; it was frequently experienced as fellow feeling.

The volcano was a crucible in which friendships and antipathies were fashioned with a fiery intensity that could render them sometimes stronger, sometimes more brittle and febrile. The presence of travellers from many different cities and nations, of different occupations, sexes and ages, the babble of different tongues, the presence of many Neapolitans, and the unpredictable, exhilarating and potentially hazardous circumstances in which visitors found themselves were a potent and potentially explosive mix. If on the one hand, the volcano was a place in which friendships were made, consolidated and powerfully reinforced, it also created and intensified hostility to the foreign, unfamiliar and different, and reinforced old clichés and national stereotypes that, though crude, were often deeply felt.

To judge by the entries in the Visitors' Book, both expressions of camaraderie and many of the tensions among visitors to the volcano were fiercer, more ardent, during and in the aftermath of the eruption of March 1828. Many more people were on the mountain, and their behaviour seems to have mirrored the effusiveness and intensity of its volcanic action. Natural pyrotechnics ignited social combustion. The British started quarrelling with the Swiss, the Anglophones with the Francophones, the Swiss with the Neapolitans and especially with the guides, whom they accused, like all Neapolitans, of cowardice, recalling the abject defeat of the Neapolitan army when faced by its foes in 1821. Exuberant expressions of amity and friendship were accompanied by vicious anti-Semitic comments and malicious remarks about individual characters known within the Neapolitan community. Whether this occurred during other eruptions – no evidence survives with the detail to be found in the Visitors' Book – we do not know; but it is reasonable to assume that the same crowded conditions and enhanced hazards were present, and that similar enthusiasms and tensions were therefore in play.

Travel, friendship and identity

Even when travels were less fraught than among the lava flows and periodic explosions of the volcano, they brought home to almost every traveller the importance of existing attachments and friendships, just as they almost inevitably meant that he or she had to learn to deal with people whose nationality, religious faith, language, class and gender were different from their own.

The scholarship on travel and its literatures is remarkably one-sided. Most of it concerns travel and 'the other', the experience and its telling of meeting / confronting / conquering / subjugating / characterising alien people(s). It is understandably concerned with the (often deeply asymmetrical) power relations between travellers and indigenous peoples, 'foreigners' of every class, like the Neapolitan *lazzaroni*, and with the sorts of stereotyping that came easily in an age of nationalism. As we shall see, the Visitors' Book provides much grist to this mill. But less attention has been paid to the processes by which forms of friendship and camaraderie were shaped in travelling – and what they meant – in what were inevitably unfamiliar and changing circumstances. All travellers come with baggage that includes friends, family, prejudices of every sort. Some of it travels with them – a familiar companion, a sense that one's own ways are not just different but superior, or conversely that foreign ways are better – even when some of it remains at home. The ways in which the burden of our attachments is borne is both complex and changing. The most usual way to think of this – in terms of 'identity' – errs on the side of reductionism (What is my identity and how many identities do I have? Which has priority in what situation?) and is a blunt tool, albeit ready to hand, when considering the dynamics of attachments and enmities. In what follows I attempt to explore the different forms of sociability in which friendship and enmity were expressed; my concerns are performative, about what people did rather than who they were, while recognising that how people act is often strongly informed by how they think themselves to be.

Travel inevitably meant absence, either the absence of or from family, friends or fellow countrymen. Issues of nationality and friendship, different but related forms of affinity and attachment, were bound up in complex ways. The young Frenchman Pétrus Borel, whose Italian travel narrative of 1825 took the form of letters to friends back home, reflected on his circumstances as he left France for the very first time:

> It was the first time I set out to leave the soil of my country, from this France where I have never met anyone but friends and brothers. It would be very difficult for a sensitive heart to defend itself, in such a moment, from a painful impression that it is so sweet for us to live in the midst of our friends, dear to us [that] it is so heartbreaking to leave them! Yes, I believe, the pleasure of loving and to be loved this pure, delicious, sublime feeling is perhaps the first and most pressing of our needs.[2]

Leaving France meant being stripped of the warm blanket of reciprocal affections. Borel would have concurred with the views of another visitor to Vesuvius, the Genevan James Augustin Galiffe, who testily complained that 'Abstract *love of country*, divested of all idea of filial piety, fraternal affection, conjugal love, and friendship, is to my conception utterly unintelligible.'[3] Family, friendship, country: they all folded into one another. When the English evangelical Harriet Morton bade farewell to the Bay of Naples, the sadness of her departure was relieved by the thought that she was returning 'homewards' to 'the land of [Protestant] religion, friends, and liberty'.[4] Faith, friendship, politics and Englishness were inextricably combined.

The combination was just as potent on the occasions when travellers sought escape from their obligations. Henry Edward Fox, a member of the Holland House circle and the Fox family who was eventually to inherit the title of the 4th Lord Holland, and who lived in Naples for several years in the 1820s, struggled constantly to escape his obligations to family, country and politics. As he explained vociferously to his family and even more to his English friends living abroad:

> I foresee that I shall not be able to settle as I wish in England – therefore I shall make an existence to [sic] myself elsewhere – I have no local attachments no John Bull feelings – I hate the climate – dislike the manners and feel an almost shameful indifference as to the politics of the country . . . I only feel about myself that I wish I could stop these months from galloping so unfairly past – I dread England & home & duties & lectures.

Fox was, by turns, defiant and guilty: 'It is very melancholy and very wrong,' he wrote to Lady Fazakerley, 'to have no local attachments and inborn patriotism & I do not return as I ought after every foreign trip with the true right blind bolsterheaded [sic] prejudiced John Bull conviction of the superiority of our own,' but 'if I can contrive to dawdle & keep aloof I will.'[5]

More usually, the absence of friends and family sharpened an appreciation of such relationships even when the object of travel was to escape from them. Thus the Duke of Buckingham, the intrepid explorer of Vesuvius, Etna and the volcanic islands of the Mediterranean, was a fugitive not just from his creditors, but from his wife, Lady Anne, who was tired of his profligate ways. Yet he missed her terribly, writing her frequent, self-serving and maudlin letters. She was a constant presence on his journeys; the yacht in which he travelled also bore her name.[6]

Yet even more emotionally pressing for the traveller was the sense that what one needed in unfamiliar and distant places was a friend. How else to make the alien hospitable? This was more than making provision, finding board and lodging, a place to rest one's head. The inn and tavern keeper, the hotelier or, as in the case of the hermitage on Vesuvius, members of the religious orders could take care of that. What the traveller hoped for was the friendship of a stranger.

At first sight such a desire might seem to embody a contradiction in terms. How could such a bond be created? How could one enter into circles of friendship as a stranger? In its purest and most idealised form friendship had long been valued among like-minded and similar persons as 'unreserved', 'true', 'eternal', 'pure and disinterested', 'steadfast', 'constant' and 'unswerving'. It was not a state of transience; there was nothing casual about such acquaintance. Its apogee was reached in a spiritual or religious bond marked by an intense intimacy, in which friends were loved for their own sake, or friendship was understood as somehow either completing the self or involving self-abnegation. Hence the association of friendship with family. It occupied a private sphere of virtue.

This was not universal benevolence, whether Christian or republican (*l'ami du peuple*); it was associated with particular people. Nor was it the instrumentalised friendship of patron and client. Such a view rather disapproved of friendship based on self-advancement, pleasure or profit. Rather this sort of deep friendship was founded on a shared concern for certain ideals and values. The family was supposed to epitomise these sentiments. Beyond the domestic sphere, they were typically found among small coteries that thrived on a shared life of religious, intellectual or artistic endeavour that might well involve frequent and close contact and even cohabitation, the creation of an associative domesticity. In this period it was linked to groups like the Nazarenes, the German artist collective in Rome committed to reviving a spiritual art, Romantic poets like Samuel Taylor Coleridge and William Wordsworth, or the literary and scientific circles around the Schlegel brothers, Friedrich Schiller and Novalis in Jena. Such circles were not impenetrable, though they were very conscious of their special nature and exclusivity.

But this was hardly the only version of Romantic friendship, though it was often held up as an exemplary model to follow. It would be an error to underestimate the capaciousness of Romantic ideas of friendship in an era when the use of the term in English, French (*amitié*) and Italian (*amicizia*) increased markedly,[7] especially in imaginative literature. 'Friendship' was more often approvingly invoked than clearly defined, but that was because it stood at the heart of a congeries of sentiments and manifested itself in a range of actions. The landscape of friendship was never restricted to the topography of male friendship, whose formation went back to Cicero and Aristotle. Female friendship, along with complex family relationships that involved 'friends' as well as relatives, could be every bit as intense, heartfelt and enduring as their male equivalents. Harriet Morton made the long journey from England to Naples with Catharine Buckle 'to seek the health of a dear accompanying friend in a foreign clime – the friend of my youth, the solace of my declining years'.[8] Many male friendships were based on mutual pleasure and affection and were as much about shared experience as shared values.

Travel encouraged travellers to question and rethink their notions of friendship. Romain Colomb, a cousin of Stendhal, arrived at the hermitage on Vesuvius in 1828, where he joined up with three travellers on the slopes of the volcano: 'I made my ascent to Vesuvius with a Dane, a Genoese, and a Hamburgian,' he wrote, pondering a certain irony: 'We are the best friends in the world, and we barely know our names.' The arduous climb to the crater temporarily brought together the men from four different countries.

Colomb's experience led him to reflect on the nature of travel in Italy:

> Nothing is easier in Italy than to find companions to see the curiosities together; These associations are naturally formed in public carriages and at the table d'hôtes [communal dining tables in hotels and inns]; Each foreigner proposing the same purpose, there is agreement and economy for all to combine . . . It may be a pleasant thing for two or three travellers to join together; Sometimes they are more gay; We better notice the objects, and we are more delighted to see them.[9]

It was easier for single men to travel in this manner and strike up casual acquaintances. Women, with a few intrepid and much-remarked-upon exceptions, did not enjoy such freedoms. When they met with fellow travellers it was rarely as an individual but rather as part of a group, often composed of families. But the dynamics of sociability on the volcano were often complex, involving family friendship, male camaraderie, flirtation and romance.

The volcano, friendship, danger and romance

On 22 February 1829, a young man from Liège named Malmadye returned to the hermitage and thumbed through the Visitors' Book to find the names of his thirteen Francophone friends with whom he had climbed the mountain almost a year earlier on 31 March. He was at pains to record his return, and therefore register how important this act of solidarity was to him. The configuration of the original set of entries is striking (Plate 10). All the names are written within an ink-drawn frame, which clearly marks them off from the other recent signatories – four Italians from Milan, two Russian diplomats, and a large party from the English merchant community in Naples. The French signatures are not arranged as a list (the favourite format of the English), nor in the serried ranks that were so often used. Rather they float in space, a bit like stars in the firmament, all in some sense equal, not part of a hierarchy but all connected to one another. Against one name, written in tiny letters, is the following remark: 'My friend, I burn to see you again and to press you to my heart.'[10] The entry attests to the powerful feelings that can be found in a great many of the comments in the Visitors' Book: deep sentiments of friendship, affection and love, affirmed and enhanced by the shared experience of climbing fiery Vesuvius.

These signs of solidarity were not just a matter of profession or nation, though they were common among soldiers and sailors, men whose hazardous lives made trust so important to their safety. They were also, as many remarks make clear, closely bound up with the idea of friendship, especially among the young male visitors to Vesuvius. The Swiss soldier Grutther wrote of his journey with 'his dearest friend, Joseph Villarosa'. In February 1828, Luigi Boncaglia of Imola described the struggle of climbing the volcano through the February snow and high winds with 'my best friend', Giacomo Morelli of Verona. A professor from Milan, Matteo Cantoni, and his friend, Paolo Bonfamiglio, a merchant who had moved to Tuscany, 'intimate friends', shared a meal at the hermitage. Five Italians, a self-described 'company of friends', recorded that on the volcano 'they have had fun' though they had not reached the summit. Similarly, Salvatore Puci, a captain in the Royal Guards, went with 'good company', the Italian term, *buona compagnia*, communicating a stronger sense of amity than the English, to enjoy what he called 'the jovial situation of this site'. Giuseppe Konig, a Swiss soldier whose brother was also serving in Naples, and who was often on the mountain, emphasised on more than one occasion that he was 'exceedingly diverted', and climbed 'not just for the imposing spectacle that Vesuvius offers', but for the company of 'true friends'. His friend Raffaele Garzia confessed that his apprehension of the mountain was dispelled by the 'perfect company' of the two brothers. Three Italian aristocrats described themselves as '*tutti e tre*' (all three – all together); another Italian, Michele Frediani, though disappointed in the view because of fog, was gratified to be 'joining his lovable companions'; yet another spoke of being 'in the very best company', while a party of French and Italian climbers in January 1828 wrote of 'the great satisfaction of the good company'. Friendship was expressed as a group identity or as the deep attachment of two individuals.[11]

Such feelings were not confined to long-distance travellers and military men; they could be found among local men of science. Leopoldo Pilla, a Neapolitan who made more than fifty ascents of Vesuvius in the 1830s, usually in the company of local savants, visiting scientists or dignitaries, and who became a professor of geology at the University of Pisa, was, as we shall see, an assiduous researcher on the volcano.[12] But he also formed powerful and intense personal friendships on his geological excursions. In his travels with the Russian diplomat and amateur geologist Count Trichatcheff, Pilla spoke of how their 'wishes and desires have been in complete agreement', and their hearts formed 'a rare bond of sympathy', sharing the misfortunes and 'delights of the journey'. Travelling on several geological expeditions to Vesuvius, to Pozzuoli and to the volcanic islands of Ischia and Lipari, Pilla formed a series of enduring friendships, none more powerful than that with Alessandro Nunziate, the nineteen-year-old son of an important Neapolitan general. Alessandro, Pilla recorded in his journal, was his 'most loved, most delightful, sweetest friend'. The two of them were 'like two most affectionate lovers [sharing] a deeply moved heart'.[13]

Such amity grew out of shared interests and mutual respect (Pilla admired Nunziate's 'rare gifts of heart and mind') but was also the consequence of shared danger. Looking back on a descent into the crater of Vesuvius in 1840, Pilla fretted at the perils to which he and Count Trichatcheff had exposed themselves. But he also described the day as one of the happiest that he had ever spent on the volcano. Shared risk enhanced fellowship.[14]

There was a long history of this male sociability on the mountain, and this sense that the experience of Vesuvius, and especially of an eruption, was an event that should be shared with one's closest friends. When the English painter Joseph Wright of Derby finally made it up Vesuvius, his biggest regret was the absence of his friend, the clockmaker and geologist John Whitehurst. 'I wished for his company when on Mount Vesuvius, his thoughts would have centr'd in the bowels of the mountain, mine skimmed over the surface only; there was a very considerable eruption at the time, of which I am going to make a picture. 'Tis the most wonderful sight in nature.' Similarly, Sir William Hamilton wrote to the president of the Royal Society, Sir Joseph Banks, that his greatest disappointment was not to be able to share with him the experience of the 1778 eruption: 'I long'd for you, [Daniel] Solander and Charles Greville, for tho I have some company with me on these expeditions sometimes yet they have in general so much fear & so little curiosity that I had rather be alone.'[15] The wrong company, those who lacked intrepidity and scientific inquisitiveness, meant that the sublime experience could not be properly shared. Many years later the poet Samuel Rogers complained about his companion: 'I have been up Vesuvius, going alone if I may say so, when Dent went with me, an unwise thing – but he would have broke his heart if he had not.'[16] Perhaps the most important homosocial moment of the northern Enlightenment in Italy occurred during the eruption of October 1767, when the English envoy to Naples Sir William Hamilton, the great antiquary Johann Joachim Winckelmann, the scholar and libertine pornographer Baron d'Hancarville, and Baron Riedesel, Prussian ambassador to Vienna and author of an important travel guide to Sicily, collectively, and at considerable risk, descended into the volcano's crater.

The heat was so fierce they were forced to strip naked, while they dined on a picnic of pigeons they roasted in the lava streams.[17] John Moore, in his best-selling *View of Society and Manners in Italy*, remarked on the persistence of this male bravura: 'I have heard of young English gentlemen betting who should venture farthest, or remain longest, near the mouth of the Volcano.' It was still around in the 1820s, with young men competing to see how long they could remain in the crater during an eruption.[18]

Such male bravura was a hallmark of many of the Swiss, German and Austrian officers on the slopes of the volcano. But many of the German-language entries in the Visitors' Book also reveal a shared sadness beneath their youthful boisterousness. They are suffused with nostalgia for their homeland, adapting Swiss and German ballads and drinking songs to comment on the volcano and the shared pains of displacement. Here expressions of friendship were less about fulfil-ment than about compensation for an absence, especially the absence of home. As one Swiss, Arthur Hofrath, wrote in the book:

> How different it was, when from Rigi's crest
> Switzerland opened up to my view
> There flowed a volcano through my heart:
> Now speaks to me Vesuvius, whom I climbed
> His song of freedom ringing in my heart
> My mind is tired, my heart is cold![19]

To the Swiss, Vesuvius, despite its volcanic heat, seemed chilly when compared with the warm sensations provoked by Mount Rigi, the 'Queen of Mountains', surrounded by Lakes Lucerne, Zug and Schwyz, and lying in the very heart of Switzerland. Friendship was marked by shared memories of a distant home.

But the nostalgia of the Swiss mercenaries on Vesuvius should not be equated with inertia; on the contrary, their camaraderie was loud and exuberant, made up of raucous groups and clubs of drinkers, whose bellicose good humour could turn nasty, and whose relations with the Neapolitans were always fragile. Friendship for these young men far from home was expressed in drinking contests and races up and down to the summit, with times carefully recorded in the Visitors' Book.[20] The Swiss seem to have been drawn back time and again to the mountain. Perhaps because of their exclusion from Neapolitan society, they made repeated visits to the volcano more often than any other group. Here they could enjoy their exclusive camaraderie. Not surprisingly, their relationship with the guides was uneasy – the young men climbed without assistance and in small groups, almost claiming the mountain for themselves.

How much of this was an attempt to emulate or simulate the Alpine world from which they came is unclear, though occasionally a more sombre tone of melancholy can be detected beneath the soldiers' rambunctiousness. One of a party of Swiss, a Francophone who signed himself Joachim, wrote 'This world is a prison on which everyone wishes to write their name,' adding 'to forget, is to enjoy the present and the future.'[21] He found it hard to divest himself of his memories. One is reminded that nostalgia was a term first applied to the feeling of Swiss mercenaries for their country when far from home. As the Duke of Buckingham remarked, 'Swiss troops, the only soldiers they can depend upon, though well paid, don't like the service, desert, or commit suicide, impelled by the melancholy *mal de pays*, of which one has heard so much as attaching itself to the Swiss troops in France.'[22] The experience of Swiss friendship on Vesuvius was bittersweet.

If the sense of male friendship and solidarity flourished in the face of shared danger, this was also one of the circumstances that enhanced romantic love between men and women. The model here was Corinne and her English admirer, Oswald, Lord Nelvil, in Madame de Staël's bestselling novel *Corinne, ou l'Italie*: 'Oswald and Corinne promised themselves the pleasure of ascending Vesuvius and felt an added delight in thinking of the danger they thus should brave together.'[23]

As we have seen, the hermit's book was full of couples – most married, some lovers – who climbed Vesuvius together.

It was not just danger that fuelled romantic passion. It was the power and force of the volcano itself, the way it ignited the energy, so much admired by de Staël, that fuelled desire and romance. The phlegmatic visitors turned fiery: they shouted, as one Savoyard did on the mountain, 'Love conquers all'; the young men flirted and courted female visitors, and wrote compliments in the Visitors' Book. A young Francophone couple who spent their honeymoon in the hermitage compared their lovemaking to the activity of the volcano, claiming to have enjoyed 'various eruptions'. August Pouget from Toulouse carried on a flirtation in the Visitors' Book with the Comtesse de St Julien until he was rebuffed.[24] The volcano was a stimulus to desire. As the much-travelled poet and playwright W.H. Armstrong wrote in his collection of meretricious erotic verse, *The Lays of Love*, after his ascent of the volcano in January 1828:

In fair Italia's mellow clime –
the clime of soft desire,
Like to its own impassion'd mount
I've burn'd with hidden fires,
And as adown its vine-clad side
The boiling torrents roll –
So, fed with secret flames, has burst
The Lava of my soul.[25]

Again, this sense of the volcano as fuelling the erotic had a long pedigree. Sir William Hamilton described how in December 1770 during what he called 'quite a lady's eruption' he fell for a young woman half his age: 'Nothing can express the glorious scene of Saturday – There were numberless Cascades of fire, the Scoria of the Lava formed arch'd bridges from Space to Space and the Lava ran rapidly under these arches whilst we stood upon them with great security.' As he recalled, 'Mrs. Hampden's beautifull face lighted up by the reflection of the fiery Streams was not a circumstance to be forgot – I was half in love with her before we went to Vesuvius but her courage & the passion she has taken for my favourite object here, has quite undone me.'[26]

Goethe had a similar experience, though at a distance, during his last evening in Naples in June 1787, spent with the erudite and beautiful Duchess of Giovene in a top-floor apartment of the royal palace. Interrupting an intense conversation, the young Italian aristocrat flung open a window shutter, to reveal a view of Vesuvius that took Goethe's breath away:

The mountain roared, and at each eruption the enormous pillar of smoke above it was rent asunder as if by lightning, and in the glare, the separate clouds of vapour stood out in sculptured relief. From the summit to the sea ran a streak of molten lava and glowing vapour, but everywhere else sea, earth, rock and vegetation lay peaceful in the enchanting stillness of a fine evening, while the full moon rose from behind the mountain ridge. It was an overwhelming sight . . . For a time we watched in silence, and when we resumed our conversation, it took a more intimate turn . . . Sitting in the foreground of this incredible picture with the moonlight falling on her face, she looked more beautiful than ever, and her loveliness was enhanced for me by the charming German idiom she spoke.

Forced to leave before the doors of the palace were locked for the night, Goethe concluded, 'And so to beauty, both near and distant, I bade a reluctant farewell, but blessing the Fates who, at its close, had so wonderfully rewarded me for a day unwillingly spent in being polite.'[27]

By fuelling the amorous affections of men and women, young and old, the volcano also reminded visitors of absent lovers. In the summer of 1828 the utopian Christian communist, sign-painter and art dealer Adolphe François Ignace Gouhenant from the Haute-Saône, who was to flee to America in the 1840s, poured out his heart in the Visitors' Book. He wanted Vesuvius to kindle the ardour of his distant lover, calling on the volcano 'to carry to the Heart of my Rosine a spark of its fiery and continual brazier'. An Italian from Pisa, who had lived for ten years in America, England and France, expressed his anguish in the summer of 1827: 'He travels to forget his dear girl but oh . . . it is impossible. She is the hope of my life, she is my dear love my *only* soul. Oh dear and sweet woman may thy name written in this book cause a tear of some gentle heart'd female visiting this spot. She is Luisa Lame, surnamed the fair nymph.' Morandini's mordant *cri de coeur*, written in English, French and Italian, was a little more exaggerated than most – it prompted an English riposte, 'Luisa Lame made a lucky escape from this ass', but echoed the sense of absence or loss felt by many on the volcano.[28]

So much of the appeal of Vesuvius lay in the collective embrace of an experience that, because of the volcano's power, immensity and danger, not merely affirmed but enhanced the higher feelings of friendship and love, though it is notable that such expressions in the Visitors' Book come almost entirely from the male pen.

The hermitage: feasting and carousing, family and friends

Apart from the ascent of the volcano, eating and drinking were the commonest forms of shared activity among the visitors to Vesuvius. The hermit's book is full of comments, many complimentary, some dismissive, of the food and drink served up to travellers. And even those, like many British visitors, who looked askance at Neapolitan food brought their own provisions to enjoy on the slopes of the volcano. Sharing food and drink brought groups together, whether they were consuming a simple plate of Neapolitan bread and cheese or gorging themselves on a feast. Few such events matched the celebration organised by the thirty-year-old German painter, playwright and poet August Kopisch, on 13 November 1828. Twelve German guests had been invited to join the Prussian Crown Prince, the future Frederick William IV, who was visiting Naples, to celebrate the birthday of the Prince's wife, Elisabeth Ludovika (Elise) of Bavaria, who had remained in Berlin. Kopisch celebrated the occasion in a watercolour portraying the table set under an awning, on a lawn just outside the hermitage (Plate 11). Kopisch painted the table before the guests were seated; the only figure to be seen is the hermit, seated under a tree to the right, dressed like a monk or priest. A festooned portrait of the Princess is set at the centre of the table and garlands hang from the adjacent trees. It depicts a shrine to the young Elise, an expression of love and affection for the Princess, capturing a calm moment before the arrival of the chief guests, who were the families of the most important Prussian officials in Naples, the ambassador Alfons von Voss, and the legation secretary Heinrich Alexander von Arnim.[29]

Kopisch had become a good friend of von Arnim and his wife, giving them pictures he had painted; in return, the legate encouraged visiting Germans to employ the artist's services as a cicerone or guide. During the royal visit, Kopisch had acted as a master of ceremonies, arranging theatrical events in Naples, a tour of Herculaneum and Pompeii, and the trip up Vesuvius. As we have seen, the artist from Breslau knew the volcano and the hermitage well. We do not know whether the hermitage feast was his idea or von Arnim's, but it was an unqualified success for both.

Unusually for a dynastic marriage, Prince Frederick William and his wife Elise were deeply in love – he liked to describe her brilliant blue eyes 'as clear as the Neapolitan sky' – and were to remain so until his death in 1861. So, though the birthday feast was a celebration, it was tinged with sadness at her absence. Two days after the event the Prince wrote a letter to her with a vivid description of the feast – the spectacular view, the numerous toasts in Hungarian wine and champagne to his lovely wife, and the climax of the meal, when Kopisch read some (supposedly improvised) verses he had composed about the Crown Princess.[30] After surveying the Prince's trip around the Bay of Naples, Kopisch's final verses mocked the foreigners struggling up the mountain, poked fun at the hermit, but ended with a rousing evocation of the Prince's passion for his wife and his eagerness to return home.[31] At first the diners laughed, but by the end of Kopisch's rendition the Prince and his guests were reduced to sentimental tears. This was the culmination of a visit during which the Crown Prince, von Arnim and Kopisch had become good friends, and which would stand the diplomat and painter in good stead when they both returned to Prussia. Von Arnim's diplomatic career was promoted by the privileged access he had to the Prince, and Kopisch was rewarded with a pension and made a royal art adviser.

Kopisch's feast was an exceptional event, very different from the far more numerous and more modest collations that were chiefly patronised by Italians and Neapolitans. As we have seen, the striking difference between Italians, especially Neapolitans, and other visitors was the former's dense presence on the volcano in the months of September, October and November, whereas most visitors climbed the volcano in the spring. But that was because the Neapolitans were usually on Vesuvius to celebrate saints like San Gennaro, or the Vergine della Neve (who, it was believed, respectively saved Naples and Torre Annunziata from the volcano), by feasting together on the mountain. They often climbed to the summit and peered, like so many visitors, into the crater, but eating, drinking and relaxing in and around the hermitage, or celebrating Mass in its tiny chapel, was their main purpose. Thus on 16 September 1828, 'three Peppinos [three men named Giuseppe] came into this hermitage to have the pleasure of smoking a cigar.'

Such entries in the Visitors' Book reveal how well these visitors knew one another. They were not initiating friendship but celebrating it. They consist, as often as not, of gently satirical, finely drawn portrayals of the members of a party, depicting their foibles, fears and oddities; they are suffused with an intimate affection. Such was the case with Dr Pasquale Campagnoli, who stopped at the hermitage on 29 October 1827 as part of a party of fourteen Neapolitans, husbands and wives, sons and daughters and nephews, and all members of the professional classes or minor nobility (often one and the same thing). The languorous Campagnoli declined to join this bevy of families in their final ascent to the crater, as he thought the pleasure of remaining at the hermitage much greater than the inconvenience of the climb. A man who evidently prided himself on being witty, he took time to pen a series of portraits of his travelling companions, both adults and children. He described Carlo Laruccia, who was accompanied by his father, Luigi, as a 'whimsical guy' (*un ragazzo stravagante*) and a little devil, making a nuisance of himself with the donkey he had chosen for the journey. Dr Antonio Assante, according to Campagnoli, was simply naïve, while his friend Carlo Filo, dark and very tall 'like St Christopher', was a man who hated those who '*far[nno] salamelecchi*', who bow and scrape, fawning with false praise to win favour. (Such behaviour, of course, was the exact opposite of true friendship.) Dr Vito Alberatango was simply helpful to everybody. Campagnoli joked about Federico Langetta, an architect who had come to see '*il salto di Plinio*', hoping that his friend, who had not returned from the summit with the rest of the party, was not about to imitate the great naturalist who died in the Vesuvian eruption of 79 CE.

Once his friends had returned from the summit and re-joined Campagnoli, they all tucked into a meal prepared by the hermit. In Campagnoli's account, Count Villani stuffed himself with salami, bread and fruit, prompting one of his companions to compare him to a goat. Villani's nephew was equally enamoured of the food, praising the hermit's *frittata*.[32] The travellers referred to one another humorously as '*Frati*', as if they were friars or monks all together. The tone is one of playful, affectionate mockery that is found in a number of these entries, often accompanied by ironic but knowing references to poets such as Tasso, and to classical literature and mythology. Some end, like Campagnoli's, with greetings or salutations to future readers of the Visitors' Book. There's a sense in all these entries that friendship is not just being enacted in the journey up the mountain (which often went no further than the hermit's cellar and kitchen) but in the playful banter of the written entry, which is as much a sign of friendship as the events it describes. This sort of domesticated friendship, though it was largely masculine (Campagnoli did not write about the women in the party) was every bit as powerful as the friendship expressed in the competitive rivalries of young men lingering in the crater.

Friendship on the road: camaraderie, gifts, hospitality, bridging difference

Romantic friendship may have been fetishised or idealised as transcendent, but it was also understood as transactional. 'Friendship', wrote one British traveller, is 'formed or cemented by common pursuits, common interest, and common toils, by mutual assistance, and mutual forbearance, and mutual concession.'[33] Or, as another Scottish traveller put it, 'Friendship cannot long exist without a reciprocity of benefits and a union of sentiments.' Friendship was as much a performance as a feeling; it depended on action, demonstrations of selflessness, acts of kindness, offering hospitality, going out of one's way to help someone in misfortune, doing more than was expected or required of someone.

A notable example was the friendship cultivated between Adolphe Monod and Thomas Erskine, who ascended Vesuvius together on a particularly fine day, 14 June 1827. Monod and Erskine were evangelical Protestants, one French, the other Scottish, who during their time in Naples became lifelong friends. The journey up the mountain was part of Erskine's attempt to nurse Monod back into good health, to rescue him from the throes of a deep psychological and spiritual crisis. His kindness and solicitude cemented the friendship that only ended with Monod's death in 1856. Monod came from a prominent family of Protestant pastors – his father and all his brothers were in the ministry. Erskine, his companion, was his senior by nearly fifteen years, an independently wealthy Scottish landowner who had devoted his life to Christian theology and, when he met Monod, was already the well-known author of such tracts as *Remarks on the Internal Evidence of Revealed Religion*. He travelled extensively and had close connections with evangelicals in Paris, Germany and Switzerland. His trips followed the paths of the eighteenth-century Grand Tour, but his concerns were primarily with the spiritual health of the individuals and communities of evangelicals that he visited. The painter Thomas Uwins, a fellow Protestant evangelical who lived in Naples and came to know Erskine there, said of him, 'Of all the men I ever met with, he is the most thoroughly imbued with the Christian spirit. He says a Christian's life should be a daily and hourly manifestation of God, and I am sure he is himself an example of it.'[34]

The young Monod came from an exceptionally ambitious and high-flying Protestant family. His father and brother were distinguished pastors and powerful figures in the French Protestant community in Paris, both known to Erskine. Adolphe found it hard to fulfil expectations. He often lapsed into a deep melancholia – what we would today describe as depression – which took the form of feeling unworthy of his Christian faith and of agonising doubts about his religious belief. His family sent him on a trip to Italy in the autumn of 1825 to relieve his angst and restore his health – the journey, by his own admission, made him much better – but when he arrived at his final stopping place, Naples, in 1826, he was offered the job of serving as the first pastor of the German-French Evangelical Community in Naples, a newly founded religious community led by Swiss Protestants.[35]

Almost from the outset Monod was in a funk: on the one hand he interpreted this offer as a sign from God, a calling, a Christian obligation; on the other, he quickly discovered he hated the job. He found his flock – mostly men of business and commerce – far too practical and lacking in 'spiritual' feeling. He did not respond well to the obstacles thrown in his way by the Catholic authorities, and he hated Naples, complaining about the enervating heat and condemning the city as a place without culture, commerce or faith, solely devoted to music and games.[36] By the time Erskine arrived in Naples in late May of the following year, Monod was bereft; he had suffered an almost total breakdown. Erskine gently nursed him back to health. He took Monod on long walks and, as the Frenchman later recorded, 'ended my melancholy by the counter-example of his perfect peace and his loving charity'. In a letter he wrote on his deathbed, Monod thanked Erskine, commenting that he would never forget his friend's support or the remarks he made as they stood looking at the sun setting over the Bay of Naples: 'Truly the light is sweet, and a pleasant thing it is for the eyes to behold the sun.'[37] A few days after Erskine had bid farewell to Monod to return to Rome, the French pastor wrote to his brother telling him that he was finally on the mend; less than two months later he was in Lyon, beginning a distinguished career as preacher, author and evangelical that culminated in his appointment as pastor of the Reformed Church in Paris. Erskine and Monod remained constant friends, 'brothers in Christ', bound together by their evangelical faith, but also by their experiences together in Naples. The trip up Vesuvius, the long walks the two men took and their many hours of conversation were part of Erskine's successful efforts to end Monod's spiritual and earthly torments. Friendship was its enduring consequence.

Erskine and Monod were brought together by their evangelical faith. This was very much a meeting of the like-minded, although Erskine was exceptionally generous in his devotion to the younger Frenchman. Their closeness was rather different from the sorts of friendship, altogether more ephemeral, that emerged as a result of being on the road. Travel made special demands on friendship; it had a distinctive repertory of actions that connected the journeying traveller with those he met and left along their way. Gift-giving among friends could occur in many circumstances (Erskine gave Monod his writings to reassure him in his Christian faith), but in the context of travel the gift often served as a material reminder of the donor when friends were forced to be apart. Gifts were often associated with departure and separation; they were a material trace of friendship. Thus when the famous naturalist Horace Bénédict de Saussure left Pavia in northern Italy in 1772 to head south to Rome and Naples to visit Sir William Hamilton and to climb Vesuvius, he was delighted to receive from his hosts 'tokens of friendship, laden with books and a thousand little presents which they bestowed on me'.[38] Half a century later, the youthful architect and actor Charles James Mathews proved a droll and amiable companion for Lord and Lady Blessington, travelling with them through France and Italy, climbing Vesuvius on several occasions, and amusing the Blessington entourage with his brilliant mimicry of the Vesuvian guides. When he left the Villa Belvedere in Naples to return home he was given two souvenirs – examples of the many gifts and trinkets fashioned from the detritus of the volcano – to pass on to his mother. Lady Blessington explained, 'They have no other recommendation than that of being the products of this country, and a very trifling memorial of an affection, which, though less flammable than the lava that forms them, retains its warmth much longer; as for you it never can end.'[39]

Once on the road the traveller's greatest need was hospitality. As one American visitor to Naples, Charles Griscom, a professor of chemistry, put it, 'true friendship . . . bids welcome to the coming and speed to the parting guest.'[40] Teodoro Monticelli, the secretary of the Academy of Sciences in Naples, described by Lady Blessington as 'sage and gentle', was famously accommodating to the many scientific visitors to the city and Vesuvius, and made many lifelong friends of his guests. The Danish professor of Syriac at Copenhagen University, Jacob Adler, who helped orchestrate the Crown Prince of Denmark's visit in Naples in 1820, began in formal diplomatic manner by addressing Monticelli as 'Monsieur', but within weeks the Neapolitan had become 'my very dear friend' (*mon très cher ami*). For part of his stay, Adler lived in Monticelli's house, where he said he found 'true friendship without flattery'. Writing after his departure for Rome, he praised Monticelli's hospitality, concluding that, 'Your friendship [is] the most precious thing I will conserve from my visit.'[41] A gift for hospitality was a gift for friendship. Such hospitality, what another traveller called 'gratuitous kindness', made guests and hosts *friends*.

One of the most important parting gifts that a host could give a traveller was a letter of introduction to someone further along the road. Monticelli wrote dozens of such letters introducing his visitors to men of science in southern Italy and Sicily. As we will see in Chapter 11, European natural philosophers visiting the geological riches of Italy were extraordinarily dependent on a network of Italian geologists and mineralogists whose introductions enabled them to enter local scientific communities and get help and information to further their researches. Writing a letter of introduction showed that the author accepted its bearer as a friend; the recipient of the letter was, in effect, invited – though, of course, not required – to initiate a friendship with its bearer. It was a major means by which strangers could become friends.

Travelling did not just lead to befriending hosts, but also to making friends with fellow travellers on the way. This need appeared less pressing if travellers were accompanied by companions who shared their journey, culture and values. It was a persistent complaint in both the eighteenth and nineteenth centuries that the English travelled in groups and showed little interest in others. When Arthur Hallam, the old Etonian, wrote to Milnes Gaskell, his travelling companion with whom he had ascended Vesuvius, reflecting on his experience, he said that his 'dearest link to Italy is the English friendships he formed there'.[42] No wonder that when the Frenchman Romain Colomb talked about the ease with which travelling companions could become friends, he did not include the English. 'Generally the English live alone or between themselves,' he wrote. 'We do not seek them; a certain oddity of character means that the relations with them are difficult or of short duration.'[43] Such views were not confined to the French. Henry Matthews, the British author of *The Diary of an Invalid*, was amazed to find a cricket match ('Eton against the World: and the world was beaten in a single innings') being played in the centre of Naples in 1818, leading him to reflect that 'It is this exclusively national spirit and undisguised contempt for all other people, that the English are so accustomed to express in their manner and content, which have made us so generally unpopular on the Continent.' He concluded, 'Our hauteur is the subject of universal complaint – and the complaint seems but well founded.'[44]

Many, perhaps most, of these friendships on the journey were made with fellow countrymen. Henry Wadsworth Longfellow, on his tour to Naples, met George Washington Greene from Rhode Island on the ship between Marseilles and Livorno; they travelled together and shared lodgings in Rome, and remained lifelong friends. The Danish dancer August Bournonville met the Danish poet Hans Peter Holst on an excursion to the island of Ischia in the Bay of Naples; after they had separately returned to Denmark they collaborated with one another in the theatre and cemented their friendship. Lamartine, lonely in Rome, was delighted to share the costs of travel to Naples with a merchant from Lyon, 'soft, polite and well mannered', whom he met at the table d'hôte of his hotel. In September 1831 the composer Hector Berlioz, who loathed his time in the Eternal City, was snoozing under a laurel tree in the gardens of the Villa de' Medici, when two French friends, also residents of the French Academy in Rome, the architect Constant Dufeu and the sculptor Antoine-Laurent Dantan, woke him and persuaded him to take a month-long trip to Naples with two other friends, a Prussian and a Russian. Naples dispelled his torpor. He was enchanted by its 'noise, brilliance, movement, abundance, action, theatres'. Four days after his arrival he and his companions ascended Vesuvius, Berlioz refusing a donkey and making the walk from Resina to keep company with his new Russian friend.[45]

As Berlioz's experience makes clear, sometimes these friendships were made with travellers of other nationalities. Just as Colomb and the French composer ascended Vesuvius with foreign friends, so in April 1827 a party of four travellers – Baron Edward Rastawiecki, a Polish art historian; a Major Higgins; Carl Striber, a Dane from Calcutta; and the Viennese Heinrich Zimmermann – gathered together and 'toasted in the Hermitage their beloved ones in Italy and Germany with good Lacryma Christi', thus each sharing in their friends' absence. Returning from Naples to Florence, the English physician James Johnson dined en route at a locanda in Acquapendente: 'The company at supper consisted of an Italian, a German, a Frenchman and a Briton. The Italian spoke English, the Frenchman spoke Italian, the Englishman spoke French – and the German spoke a little of all languages. Never was there seen a more happy QUARTETTO.'[46]

Travellers, whether they liked it or not, were forced into the company of others. Unless they were able to travel in the grand style, with their own transport and private rooms for dining, they had to share coaches, cabins, communal dining rooms (the tables d'hôte) and places of public resort like the Piazza della Fontana in Resina, or the rooms of the hermitage. Such circumstances were not conducive to privacy. When the Anglican cleric Walter Shirley crossed the Alps in a diligence (a four-horse stagecoach) on his way to Naples, his companions jammed into the interior were two American students of medicine, a male Milanese opera singer, a Florentine, a Corsican, a Frenchman and a Scottish merchant from Trieste. As Shirley complained, the Milanese and the Florentine 'committed the heinous sin of chattering to each other nearly all the night, while we transalpine people were desirous of sleeping'.[47] But Shirley befriended the merchant, trying to help him secure Bibles in Italian for his employees. These innumerable small meetings, transactions and confrontations were shaped by and helped configure attitudes towards strangers and friends.

National character: sympathy and difference

Such experiences were the occasion for travellers to test the clichés about different national characters with which eighteenth- and nineteenth-century travel narratives abounded. The notion of national character was deeply ingrained, not just as patriotic prejudice (though there was certainly plenty of that), but as a way of analysing different societies. As the philosopher David Hume put it in his essay on national character, 'Each nation has a peculiar set of manners, and . . . some particular qualities are more frequently to be met with among one people than among their neighbours.'[48] Thus when *Cornhill Magazine* published an essay on friendship in the nineteenth century, it began with the assumption that it was nationally inflected. 'Though the causes that go to establish friendship, and endow it with perman-ence and vitality, are everywhere the same, yet the mode in which it is manifested, and the fashions which govern the display of it, are in a large measure regulated by other things'. The British version of friendship might be deeply felt, but it was restrained. 'In this country,' it argued, 'no one looks for the volubility, the effervescence, the ardent chivalry and enthusiastic devotion to an idea, which are natural to the French and Irish – and the passionate effusion, the audacious absence of self-constraint, the sentimentalism, sometimes maudlin, sometimes heroic, which characterize the German.' These, it concluded, 'are according to our insular notion, not only strange, but ludicrous'.[49]

So how could travellers make friends out of strangers, most of whom were seen as having very different habits and manners? These differences were not unbridgeable, though they were difficult to surmount. As we have seen, acts of kindness and hospitality created lasting bonds between people of very different nationalities. Shared interests and knowledge crossed national boundaries. The Neapolitan geologist Leopoldo Pilla became the close friend of the Russian diplomat Count Trichatcheff, at first because of their shared scientific interests, but also because of what he described as a bond of 'sympathy'. To be mindful of difference was not to see it as an impenetrable obstacle to amity. Many travellers of different nationalities and faiths discussed the issue. This was particularly true of Protestants and members of the Roman Catholic Church. After Shirley had made his crossing of the Alps, he visited a Dominican monastery not far from Alessandria on the north Italian plain. He went to see its frescoes, but he was taken round by a young monk who was about his age, in his early thirties. As they walked round the buildings, they chatted about their respective faiths, agreeing to differ, while sharing their commitment to the Christian faith. The monk gave Shirley coffee in the sacristy. 'After which he asked me for my name and address and gave me his, declaring that we should be friends for life, and that he would correspond with me in Latin.'[50] A bridge was built. Three years later, Shirley, though an evangelical, angered his friends by supporting the civil rights of Catholics in England through the Catholic Emancipation bill.

Shirley's accommodating spirit was very much in line with the conduct recommended by Dr John Moore, the Scottish author of two extremely successful travel books of the late eighteenth century, *A View of Society and Manners in France, Germany and Switzerland* (1779) and *A View of Society and Manners in Italy* (1781). Moore's volumes, which were frequently reprinted in England, Scotland, Ireland and North America, as well as being translated into French, German and Italian, were not just a witty and well-recounted travelogue. Moore argued for a certain sort of traveller, someone who relied on conversations with local people and not just on visual impressions (he recommended the table d'hôte), who looked beyond

superficial observations, and who regarded 'the foreign' sympathetic-
ally. As Moore wrote, 'By being received with hospitality, conversing
familiarly, and living in the reciprocal exchange of good offices with
those whom he considered as enemies, or in some unfavourable point
of view, the sphere of his benevolence and good will to his brethren
of mankind will enlarge.'[51] Moore was well aware of the debate about
the limits and extent of sympathy among Scottish philosophers. He
shared Adam Smith's views in *The Theory of Moral Sentiments* about
the difficulty of establishing sympathy with strangers or with those
who seem different or distant, a much harder task than expressing
fellow feeling for family and close friends. But he advocated stratagems to bring strangers closer together. Moore, it is important to
emphasise, did not deny difference; he urged a different, sympathetic
response on the part of the traveller. 'Travellers are too apt,' he
complained, 'to form hasty, and for the most part, unfavourable opinions of national characters. Finding the customs and sentiments of
the inhabitants of the foreign countries through which they pass,
very different from their own, they are ready to consider them as
erroneous, and conclude, that those who act and think in a manner
so opposite to themselves, must either be knaves, fools, or both.'[52]
Different was not necessarily worse.[53]

Some travellers took Moore's admonitions to heart. The New
York cleric William Berrian, in his *Travels in France and Italy in
1817 and 1818*, declined to pass judgment on the character of Italians,
writing, 'We must have been long among a people, admitted cordially
into their society, acquainted and intimate with their language and
prepared by habits of accurate observation, before we can give a just
view of their character. Few strangers can pronounce decisively upon
it without presumption.' This did not prevent him, however, from
condemning his Neapolitan guides as 'gross, immoral and degraded'.[54]

Berrian's casual dismissal was more common than his more
thoughtful reflection on how to judge national character. In general
Moore's advice fell on deaf ears, as travellers continued passing

(usually adverse) judgments on their Italian hosts and their fellow travellers of other nationalities in equal measure. In short, not everyone was happy at having to live with the foreign. The sentiment of one of four Belgian visitors to Vesuvius inscribed in the hermit's book, 'The more I live abroad, the more I love my country', was far from uncommon.[55] There were deep antipathies among travellers, not least because so many had been caught up in the political and national conflicts that had torn Europe apart for more than a quarter of a century, and which still lingered, in the struggles between autocratic and legitimist regimes and liberals and reformers. One favourite topic of conversation after 1815 was the relative prowess of soldiers and sailors of the different nationalities: was one Frenchman worth two Prussians? When the antiquary William Gell was in Colmar, the 'French landlord . . . gave me his estimate of the comparative military prowess of the different peoples of Europe. He reckoned one Frenchman equal to four Germans – one Frenchman equal to two Russians – one Englishman equal to six Frenchmen on the sea – the French and English upon land *un peu près le même chose.*'[56] The form that these hostilities assumed, though they were sharpened by recent conflicts, was usually fashioned by long-standing notions of national character, views about the peculiar manners of particular peoples or nations.

Travel writing was often shaped by what one critic has called 'the commentary of opposition' in which the foreign and familiar, seen as very different from one another, are viewed as rival ways of being and living. Rarely are they treated, as Moore might have wished, as matters of indifference rather than occasions for moral judgment, almost invariably in favour of the familiar. The table d'hôte, seen by Moore as the occasion to learn and appreciate foreign manners, had a very different effect on William Webb, an Anglo-Irishman travelling to Italy in 1822–3. Dining in Lyon with twenty others – 'I was the only Englishman' – he was disgusted by the exaggerated manners of 'nasty foreigners'. 'The Continentalists,' as he called them, designate us English as devotees to the comfortable. Now this touches on morals and also on manners, and on these most variously. Foreigners are far more ceremonious than we, because they have not the tact from which love of comfort emanates ... all their manners, in proportion as they declare themselves, are in the same bad taste. With all this overacting, which does not at all touch on the real decencies of life, is associated a clownishness and a coarseness in all the details of in-door demeanour, which disgusts plain John Bull with his dinner, when in a company that comports itself in such a pot-boy style.[57]

This sort of disparagement of the foreign was not confined to the English. One German woman traveller confided, 'The French nation despises all other nations whatsoever – with the exception of the English, whom – as it is not in their power to despise them – they hate.'[58] The French traveller Colomb, who, as we have seen, was much struck by English singularity, also criticised their dealings with money: 'They spend much', he wrote, 'but without nobility. The continual precautions which they think they ought to take for small things are painful and pitiful; they find the means of being prodigious and of appearing miserly.'[59] This affluent miserliness was brilliantly satirised by Alexandre Dumas in his account of the dealings between the English and the *lazzaroni* in his Neapolitan travel book, *Le Corricolo*. Dumas's Britons believe that money opens every door, but they are terrified of being duped. The American chemist Charles Griscom was repeatedly struck by Anglo-French hostility, by the singularity of French manners – their politeness, gallantry and licentiousness, and their preference for Americans over the English.[60]

If many were critical of their fellow travellers, they were equally derogatory about Italians and Neapolitans. William Webb, in characterising the Italians, also made the French seem worse: 'Indolence is the paramount vice, and the parent of all other vice in Italy. Yet it is the listlessness of genius, and contrasts favourably with the hung-on-wires volatility of Frenchmen, an animal quickness which has to do with cleverness, but not with lofty talent.'[61] Writing of the Neapolitans, the Marquis de Sade, no less, remarked that 'It is sad indeed to see the most beautiful country in the universe inhabited by the most degraded species.'[62] In this, and little else, he shared the views of the Scottish painter Jane Waldie, who believed that 'Uniting the cunning and craft of their Greek origin with the ingrafted vices of their Roman conquerors, sunk in indolence, effeminacy, and meanness, the general Neapolitan character exhibits as disgusting a moral picture as is displayed in the frequency of bodily deformity.'[63]

The travel literature of this period is littered with stereotypical examples of English aloofness, charming French duplicity, German torpor, Italian indolence and the like, together with broad brush characterisations of different national types, some of which are highly inconsistent. At the same time, these very works often contain anecdotes and stories whose narratives defy national stereotypes and characterisation through moments of personal kindness and acquaintance. Similarly, the Visitors' Book on Vesuvius contains many accounts of shared experience and friendship, but also clear evidence of national conflict.

Much of the latter occurred during the period around the eruption in the spring of 1828, when the energy and violence of the mountain and the crowds of visitors seem to have intensified feelings. As the most numerous groups on the volcano and the most visible of travellers, the 'English', a term that was usually used to include the Welsh, Scots and Irish, excited much criticism. To their detractors, the English were cold, silent, arrogant and tight-fisted. An entry in the Visitors' Book exclaimed:

I am angry to tell you that . . . to complain about the parsimony of the English. I, who know you, am not surprised, knowing that most of those who travel do it out of economy. Pay to the monk like the others, to support, by the sacrifice of a few carlini, the honour of old England.

A friend of John Bull yours forever.[64]

This produced the immediate chauvinist riposte: 'Please learn to write English to prove that you know the Nation' (*l'on vous prie d'apprendre à écrire l'anglais pour prouver que vous connaissez la Nation*), while the following day a small party of English merchants and shopkeepers, 'Natives of Albion' resident in Naples, including regular visitors to the volcano, wrote in an entry headed 'April Fools' Day' that they 'felt astonished that there should be such illiterate ... *Rascals* among the foreign servants. The orthography of it proves it to have been written by One, The Charge, even was it true, would have been much better written this night.'

The assertiveness of the English provoked criticism and mockery. A French entry derided the way 'the English milords' signed their names in the Visitors' Book.[65] They had a habit of listing their names below one another on the left side of the page (usually entered by one member of the party), taking a great deal of space, but omitting any commentary, salutation or statement of feeling about the ascent. The visual effect is orderly and authoritative. No comment seems necessary; it is enough that Englishmen have been there. Not surprisingly, when they did offer remarks, their uncharacteristic expressiveness was mocked.

It is difficult to gauge how deeply felt these squabbles were. Just as travellers of different nationalities bantered and played with stereotypes in their conversation on the road, so the Visitors' Book set up a good-humoured Anglophone–Francophone rivalry, conducted by those who were not altogether familiar with either language. At one point a visitor wrote in very large letters, 'Long live France, beautiful women and good wine' (*Vive La France, Les jolies femmes et le bon vin*), only to be followed by 'Long live the English woman' (*Vive La Anglaise*) in another hand. After a further and unflattering comment about the English, a final remark adds: '*Tout le monde sait que . . . tirate avanti*' (Everyone knows that . . . plough on).[66]

But these often light-hearted remarks were also accompanied by real antipathies. A sarcastic English remark about two American visitors to the volcano, Robert M. Oakley from Poughkeepsie in New York State, and James Ferguson from Catahoula in Louisiana – 'who understands enough of Geography to tell where those two places are?' brought a swift response. Signed 'Yankee Doodle', it reminded readers of how the Americans, led by General Andrew Jackson, had defeated a superior English force at the Battle of New Orleans in 1815: 'I guess as how Johnny Bull ye don't know our Geography, but I'll tell ye Catahoula is a considerable sort of a place, about 350 mile above New Orleans where old Hickory & the Kentucky Boys licked Packenham and the Veterans of the Peninsula.'[67]

The hostility between the Neapolitan guides and the Swiss officers on the volcano was also deeply felt. The Visitors' Book reveals an ongoing quarrel in which the Swiss complained about the exorbitant fees and charges of the guides and the hermits, the way they exaggerated the difficulty of the ascent of the volcano and, as they believed, tricked their clients into hiring unnecessary guides. The guides countered by accusing the Swiss of 'avarice'. In response the Swiss condemned the Neapolitans as lazy, devious and, as they claimed during the eruption of 1828, cowardly. The last charge was especially galling in the light of the 'rout of Rieti' in 1821, when the Neapolitan army had turned tail and run from the Austrian forces sent to restore the absolutist monarchy, which was the Swiss mercenaries' employer. Whereas for most visitors, as we have seen, the guides and helpers who led and dragged them up the volcano were a necessary (and sometimes welcome) aid to their ascent of Vesuvius, for the Swiss the Neapolitans were a distraction whose presence made it hard to equate their gatherings with similar events in their homeland.

Much uglier was the vein of anti-Semitism in the Visitors' Book. When Charles (Carl) Rothschild, the head of the Naples branch of the family bank founded in 1821, and his wife Charlotte, their youngest son and four other friends ascended the volcano on 21 March 1828 to view the recent eruption, someone wrote in English 'Jew Thief' against Charles's name and added 'Damn'd Jews' to the entire entry. A day later, the visitor H. Goldschmitt was stigmatised (again in English) as 'an infernal Jew', though another visitor responded 'No Christian could pen this'. The Rothschild bank was unpopular in liberal circles in Naples, as it had handled the financing of the Austrian army of occupation after 1821, and the presence of Jews in the city, a community that was centred on the banking house, was seen as a recent development. But these anti-Semitic entries, written in English, probably emanated from the British commercial community in Naples and not from Neapolitans. They express both racial bigotry and a sense that the Rothschilds were a powerful intrusion upon English economic power in the city. They also tapped into a long-standing hostility to finance and banking among the British commercial classes.[68]

In short, friendship and the deeply felt attachments to nation (and religion) were all powerfully expressed through encounters on the slopes of the volcano. If anything, Vesuvius seems to have intensified the expression of feelings. As we have seen, visitors expected to experience a heightening of sentiment on the volcano. That was one of the main reasons for going there. The *mise en scène*, the tensions generated in a perilous environment, encouraged the flamboyant expression of a range of emotions – fear and dread, elation and exhilaration. When trying to capture these feelings, to give them expression, visitors repeatedly turned to the language of the sublime, a well-established script that expressed and kept their emotions in check. This was the common currency of most Vesuvian travellers – and it is to the sublime that we now turn.

4
VESUVIUS AND THE SUBLIME
Sublime Tourism, Aesthetic Effects and Science

The topography of the sublime

Visitors to Vesuvius – Neapolitans and foreigners of every language and nation, learned savants and tourists – all agreed, almost without exception, in seeing the volcano and the sensations that it provoked as 'sublime'. In this they followed a broader trend. In the Romantic era the aesthetic language of 'the beautiful', 'the picturesque' and especially 'the sublime' came to saturate travel literature and to haunt the sensibility of lovers of nature. But their usage in much travel literature was slipshod and haphazard. Broadly speaking, a landscape was sublime if it provoked feelings of fear, terror, awe and admiration because of its wildness, vastness, limitlessness, scope and power. Harmony, smoothness and order – often imposed by man – prompted the attractions of the beautiful. And the picturesque, with its roughness, asymmetry and variety, occupied a position either between the two or as a combination of them both.

My definitions here are deliberately simplistic and vague (though we will be refining our notion of the sublime) because Romantic journals, notebooks and letters describe a wide variety of relations between the feelings of the sublime, and those prompted by other aesthetic categories such as the beautiful and the picturesque. Quite often the sublime is treated as a sort of beauty; on some occasions, the different effects are elided, as when sublimity is treated as 'lovely' or 'enchanting'. When the Cambridge professor of mineralogy Edward Daniel Clarke took time off from Vesuvius to visit the Amalfi coast, he described it as 'sublime', but also as 'picturesque' and 'romantic'.[1] The line between the picturesque and the sublime was often vague or non-existent. Travellers were only sometimes savants and philosophers, and even if they were, their object was less to define their terms than to convey an (often imprecise) impression.

Nevertheless their accounts contain echoes of numerous authors on the sublime, not just Kant and Burke, but the source of much writing on the sublime, the Roman-era Greek author Longinus, as well as such eighteenth-century commentators as Joseph Addison, James Thomson, Lord Kames, Archibald Alison and Hugh Blair. Few, however, acknowledged their sources, and many would have derived their knowledge of such terms from the periodical press and magazines. Only rarely was someone as explicit as the English traveller Margaret Grenville, who said of a Vesuvian eruption that she witnessed in 1761–2, that it 'perfectly answered Mr. Burke's idea of the sublime'.[2]

Concepts like the sublime gave travellers a descriptive language that enabled them to see environments and landscapes as embodying certain sorts of feeling, or as triggering particular emotions. The sublime encompassed events as well as places. According to the Scottish critic Hugh Blair, it included 'the grandeur of earthquakes and burning mountains; ... great conflagrations ... stormy oceans and overflowing waters ... tempest of winds of thunder and lightning [and] all uncommon violence of the elements'.[3] All were sublime because they were examples of unfettered natural power, a force that provoked fear and awe. This was what Kant called the dynamic sublime, which overwhelmed the observer with its sheer presence, as opposed to what he dubbed the mathematical sublime, which stupefied the viewer by its plenitude, its overwhelming extent, scale and number.

Paradoxically, a common feature of descriptions of the sublime was their invocation of the cliché that the sublime is unrepresentable, an assertion usually made just before the author embarks on a long description. The Reverend William Coxe, author of the highly successful *Travels in Switzerland*, was particularly egregious in this regard. Time and again he tells his reader, 'I have not yet met with such astonishing scenes of wildness, horror, and majesty, as occurred in this day's journey', only to add that, 'Description generally fails in representing the most ordinary exhibitions of nature; how inadequate then must it be to the singular combination of sublime objects, which I shall now attempt to delineate?'[4] Similarly, Patrick Brydone in his extremely successful *A Tour through Sicily and Malta*, first published in 1774, ruefully confesses of Mount Etna that 'here description must ever fall short, for no imagination has dared to form any ideas of so glorious and so magnificent a scene', before going on to regale the reader with an astonishingly vivid (and frequently reprinted) rendering of the sublimity of the Sicilian volcano that extends over more than a dozen pages.[5] One cannot help thinking that such professions are a none too covert way of promoting the literary skills of the author.

Though writers on the Alps and on the volcanoes of southern Europe used the language of the sublime, there were important (and obvious) differences between descriptions of fiery volcanoes like Vesuvius and Etna and glacier-covered mountains like Mount Blanc. The volcano, at least when erupting, was characterised by loud and unexpected noises (usually compared to cannon fire), and by movement – of lava and ash – and agitation. It was an image of instability. The goal of a volcanic ascent, as Cian Duffy has emphasised in his study of the natural sublime, was to observe the crater, a bubbling, burning, viscous mass of indeterminate depth, a sort of fluid barrier between the atmosphere and the underworld.[6] In contrast, Mount

Blanc and indeed all high snow-covered mountains were characterised by what the Swiss savant Horace Bénédict de Saussure called 'an abode of cold and silence'.[7] Though avalanches and glaciers (repeatedly compared to lava flows) were signs of movement and mobility Alpine mountains were, on the whole, associated with a massive, adamantine illegibility. Perhaps this is what Voltaire was thinking about when he wrote to Sir William Hamilton in Naples, memorably contrasting the 'eternal calm' of his beloved Alps with volcanoes 'full of caprice ... too lively, that often become angry without reason'.[8] Vulcanism was less about grandeur, monumentality or stability, which entailed a certain static quality, than about violence and (e)motion: sublime action rather than sublime being. As David McCallam in his study of volcanoes in eighteenth-century Europe puts it, 'The volcano constitutes the mountain as event.'[9] And if one of the themes of the alpine sublime was imperviousness, the activity of the volcano – the outpouring of its innards, the extrusion of its viscera – entailed a certain active liminality, a crossing of boundaries in which the interior secrets of nature were (threateningly) exposed.[10] It is not surprising that, although both the Alps and volcanoes were co-opted by the French revolutionaries, the volcano – a sudden violent force of destruction that nevertheless had regenerative power – was much the most common metaphor and analogy with political change, and that fear of volcanic eruption also became a metaphor for fear of revolution.

All of which is to say that the sublime feelings associated with volcanoes were chiefly those of fear and danger, whereas those of high mountains were awe and exaltation, what the Swiss naturalist Jean de Luc described as 'a kind of sensation of immensity it is impossible to explain'. Whether in the form of a Rousseauian reverie on a pristine natural order or as a piece of natural theology, accounts of the Alps expressed the transformative spiritual effects of mountain air. As the Genevan Marc-Théodore Bourrit put it in his *New Description of the Alps*:

Only one idea remains, but it is strong, it is the Sovereign of nature, who seizes all the faculties of your soul, His idea is sublime; nothing distracts; only He reigns here: that one feels is so strong, so transcendent, that one feels oneself changed. Neither the temples where one gives adoration, nor the view of its altars, produces nearly as profound a feeling of his presence.[11]

No wonder the radical English poet Percy Bysshe Shelley was provoked to describe himself in the visitors' book at Chamonix as 'Democrat, Philanthropist, and Atheist', and to write a poem, 'Mont Blanc', as a materialist challenge to this sort of natural theology.[12]

A further difference in accounts of the alpine and volcanic sublime is that alpine sublimity was figured as solitary, whereas volcanic sublimity was, as we have already seen, figured as social. Saussure's comment during the first evening of his unsuccessful attempt of 1785 to climb Mont Blanc is often cited: 'The repose and profound silence which reigned in this vast expanse, enlarged still further by the imagination, inspired me with a sort of terror; it appeared to me that I alone had survived in the universe; and that I saw its corpse stretched out at my feet.'[13] The reader would hardly know that the Genevan stood only a few metres from a cabin that contained eighteen sleeping (and probably snoring) men. In contrast, the Vesuvian sublime was rarely represented as that of the isolated individual confronting nature, but as an experience that was best shared.

Though the natural sublime assumed different forms, for many commentators the volcanic sublime was its most intense and complete manifestation. The Scottish artist Jane Waldie was certain that 'No earthly scene of sublimity and horror is comparable to that exhibited at the mouth of a raging volcano.'[14] Humphry Davy concurred. In his extremely popular lectures on geology delivered at London's Royal Institution between 1805 and 1811 the youthful Davy, who had yet to witness a volcanic eruption, spoke eloquently of volcanic power:

The general aspect of a volcanic district, even in its most quiet state, must be highly impressive, but when the subterranean fires are displayed in their full energy, when they burst forth from the interior of the earth desolating and destroying, then the effect must be beyond comparison the most awful and the most sublime of the phenomena belonging to our globe.[15]

Volcanic eruptions, after all, ticked nearly all the boxes of sublimity – irresistible force, infinity, magnificence and vastness, astonishment, uncertainty, surprise and wonder, loud noises, darkness and obscurity. They provoked a whole range of powerful feelings – horror, as Waldie remarks, but also dread, terror and apprehension; in fact any species of fearfulness, a sense of shock and awe in the face of overwhelming power. In letters to his future wife, Jean-Marie Roland de la Platière wrote of 'the appalling horror' of the scene during an eruption on Vesuvius in the 1770s and about the 'horrible racket' produced by 'a hell unapproachable from all sides'.[16] The German playwright August von Kotzebue, who witnessed an eruption in November 1804, described it as 'awful and horrid', and as one of 'the sublimest spectacles of nature'. A Frenchman who entered the crater in the 1820s called it 'the Heart of Our Fate' and described Vesuvius as 'the eternal Arbiter' making 'of the sky a hell, and of hell a sky'. Five visitors from Campobasso in the Molise recorded that they 'remained stupefied by the repeated shocks, and by the balls of smoke, and flames that this visible inferno erupted'. The painter Vigée-Lebrun described a scene *'effrayante et sublime'* (frightening and sublime). In similar fashion Sir William Hamilton, writing to his nephew, Charles Greville, described the major eruption of 1779 as 'most sublime but terrible'. More than a generation later, when Davy finally witnessed a Vesuvian eruption, he predictably echoed these and his earlier sentiments, by describing an eruption as 'most sublime'.[17]

As we have seen, this sublime experience was rendered all the more poignant by observing the contrast with the rich and fertile land that surrounded it. Its depiction was well scripted and much commented upon. The Irish clergyman Martin Sherlock in his *Letters of a Traveller* (1781) described the view from the top of Vesuvius as 'the most perfect union of the sublime and beautiful in nature'.[18] Mrs Hester Piozzi wrote in the winter of 1785 of Vesuvius: 'One need not stir out for wonders, while this amazing mountain continues to exhibit such various scenes of sublimity and beauty.'[19] This was the place that Goethe described as 'this peak of Hell which towers up in the middle of paradise'.[20] So the journey up the mountain and into the volcano – what one French visitor described as crossing 'the great divide' (*le grand partage*) – played out what had long been a trope of the Bay of Naples as a place of contrasts, exceptionally graced by nature – not least in the rich soils produced by the volcano – but also blighted by natural disaster, misrule and human failure.

This combination of beauty and sublimity was seen by visitors as pleasurable and – a term taken from Edmund Burke's account of the sublime – as 'delightful'.[21] The volcano, one Swiss army officer wrote, 'leads finally to joy, and finally to delight'.[22] One British visitor, the Hon. R.H. Clifford, remarked that 'The idea of horribly beautiful is explained when you reach the verge of the crater of M. Vesuvius.' In October 1828, John Gartley recorded that 'This grand and formidable mountain afforded me the sublimest pleasure I have yet felt – how beautiful and awful are the workings of the volcano.' Italian and Francophone visitors were even more forthcoming. They praised the 'most elegant spectacle' of the eruption, wrote about the 'pleasure of terror and wonder' they experienced before 'the terrible Majesty of Nature' of the '*orrendo vulcano*' which threatened to 'submerge' the world. One Italian visitor claimed that 'It is impossible to explain how much this beautiful terror pleased me', while others 'admired the immense force of nature and its admirable effects'.[23] One French visitor was reduced to a series of expostulations that mirrored the explosions of the volcano: 'How beautiful! How majestic! How terrible!'[24]

Such remarks about the pleasure and delight provoked by the volcano make clear the important distinction between naked fear and the aesthetic emotions of the sublime. Sublime pleasure was the feeling produced in the aftermath of a moment of shock, awe, fear or terror. It was a second order response, prompted when the viewer recognised that they were not in direct danger. As Edmund Burke explained in his much-read *A Philosophical Enquiry into the Origin of our Ideas of the Sublime and Beautiful*, 'When danger or pain press too nearly, they are incapable of giving any delight, and are simply terrible; but at certain distances, and with certain modifications, they may be, and they are, delightful.'[25] The distinction is one between the terror felt by the inhabitants of Herculaneum in 79 CE before they were consumed in a pyroclastic flow, and the sublime feelings of Romantic visitors provoked by contemplating a slow-moving flow of burning lava. In antiquity the volcano was a killer; by the early nineteenth century it had become an object of sublime tourism.

Like many such responses, the experience of the sublime was highly scripted. We can see this most clearly when the right frame of mind or the appropriate series of emotions that were supposed to ensure a sublime response were prevented, inhibited or interrupted. Lady Morgan's ascent of Vesuvius during her Italian tour of 1819–20 was ruined by a chance encounter. On reaching the summit 'which a few days before had been liquid fire, and from which smoke and a sulphureous vapour were emitted at frequent air-holes', her party 'came unexpectedly upon a group of English dandies, of both sexes, of our acquaintance – the ladies with their light garments something the worse for the adventure, and all laughing, flirting, and chattering over a chasm, which exhibited the lava boiling and bubbling up within a few feet below where they stood.' Morgan could barely conceal her irritation:

This was very pleasant, but it was very provoking! To have travelled so far! – to have endured all the exhaustion of inordinate fatigue, and other annoyances equally out of the sphere of daily habits of ease, in the vain hope of snatching at a new and a strong sensation (the great spell of existence) – of meeting Nature, all solitary and sublime, in the awful process of one of her profoundest mysteries!

All of this was eclipsed by 'a réchauffé of the St Carlos party of the preceding evening, and the sight of faces seen for nothing in the Paris circles during the preceding winter'. It was, she ruefully concluded, 'a terrible sacrifice of the sublime to the agreeable!' 'It was in vain', she complained, that 'the mind returned to its sublime and terrific object ... There was no awe mingled with its contemplation! It was vain to gaze on the thin and trembling crust which vaulted the crater, and separated the spectator from an abyss of flame! There was no recoil of the imagination.' Instead 'inquiries, compliments, and recognitions, mingled with the deep subterranean murmurs of the volcano; parties were made, for distant days, on the brink of the engine of instant destruction; and the surprise most audibly evinced, was that of a rencontre so strange!' It was not the presence of others that inhibited Lady Morgan's experience of the volcanic sublime which, as we have seen, was 'social', but the completely inappropriate response of the 'English dandies', who undercut serious emotional engagement with their frivolity.[26]

Whose sublime?

The pleasures of the sublime were not, according to an increasing number of commentators, a mere function of a sense of physical security, but were rather an elevation of feeling, a sense of expansive mental powers, less a quality that inhered in objects like the volcano than an affective experience that was a quality of mind. As the German philosopher Immanuel Kant put it in his *Critique of Judgment*: sublime objects 'raise the energies of the soul above their accustomed height, and discover in us a faculty of resistance of a quite different kind, which gives us courage to measure ourselves against the apparent almightiness of nature'.[27] Or as Prince Maximilian put it, rather more simply, as he reflected on his ascent of the volcano, 'The sublime must stand high; this is a desire of the human mind; it elevates in order to be elevated.'[28] If in the eighteenth century the sublime was, more often than not, seen to reside in the volcano, by the nineteenth sublimity had gravitated to the observer.[29] Typically, the Welsh clergyman Thomas Watkins, climbing Vesuvius at night in January 1788, declared, 'never did I behold anything so dreadfully sublime'; for him, sublimity was attached to the mountain. But thirty years later, Anna Jameson's account of her experience emphasised a subjective sublimity: 'I can hardly write, my mind is so overflowing with astonishment, admiration, and sublime pleasure.'[30]

The debate among philosophers about the precise nature and timing of this subjective sublimity (what John Keats, apropos of William Wordsworth, referred to as 'the egotistical sublime') was fiercely complex: was it simultaneous with the feeling of fear, or did it follow later? What did it mean to say that a feeling of safety and security was a necessary condition of sublimity? In the confrontation with nature did reason or imagination elevate man to a pre-eminence over nature? But what came to matter was less the processes of the subjective sublime than the question of who could enjoy it, and what that enjoyment entailed. Many natural philosophers, following a series of remarks by Kant, came to conclude that the capacity to experience an aesthetic response to nature was not given to all, and that it was a consequence of an educated, moral culture. As Kant put it, without such a sensibility, 'what we call sublime, merely strikes the untutored mind as terrifying'. He pointed to the contrast between the responses of the learned savant and the rude peasant to Mount Blanc. Horace Bénédict de Saussure, he noted, used his 'soul-stirring sensations' for 'the instruction of men', reacting quite differently from a Savoyard peasant, who 'in the indications of the dominion of nature in destruction, and in the great scale of its might . . . will only see the misery, danger, and distress which surround the man who is exposed to it'.[31] More generally Kant concluded that ignorance and the inability to understand how man can confront and transcend the powers of nature was a sign of superstition; conversely, the aesthetic of the sublime raised man 'above the fear of such operations of nature, which he no longer regards as outbursts of His wrath'. In this way he achieved 'emancipation from superstition [which] is called enlightenment'.

Such critics distinguished two classes of people in relation to the volcano, those who were distinguished by either their embrace of or distance from an educated moral culture. How one responded to the volcano – with sublimity or superstition – placed the observer in a particular category. Many savants and enlightened thinkers were determined to dispel the idea that volcanic activity was evidence of an active, vengeful and rebarbative deity, whether pagan or (more usually) Christian, intervening in and deploying nature to a moral purpose. In his *Theory of the Earth* (1788), the Scottish savant James Hutton took explicit aim at the view that volcanic eruptions, like other disasters, were portents of divine wrath: 'Volcanoes are not made on purpose to frighten superstitious people into fits of piety and devotion, nor to overwhelm devoted cities with destruction.'[32] Rather their effect, he argued, though ostensibly terrifying and sometimes highly destructive in the short term, should be seen as an example of a benign natural order, their eruptions an instance of a self-regulating nature. As that ur-text of the Enlightenment, Diderot's *Encyclopédie*, put it: 'Volcanoes must be looked at like the air vents of the earth, or like the chimneys by which it gets rid of the burning matters which devour its bosom . . . Volcanoes are therefore a blessing of nature.'[33] The object of the natural philosopher was to chart, understand, perhaps explain and, if possible, exploit these natural processes (for example by identifying the properties in volcanic soil that made it so fertile). This was an aim of most of the many scientists who made their way to and up Vesuvius, among them Alexander von Humboldt, Joseph Louis Gay-Lussac,

Leopold von Buch, Humphry Davy, Déodat de Dolomieu, Charles Babbage and Charles Lyell.

What was needed, therefore, was an understanding of the systematic workings of nature, one that placed volcanoes in their proper (scientific) context. This was the message that Davy offered his London lecture audience as the climax of his geological survey. 'Volcanoes when superficially examined appear rather as accidents than as orderly events in our system,' he explained, 'But when they are accurately considered, it will be found that their effects are not unimportant in the economy of things and that they bear a distinct subservience to the general harmonious series of natural operations.' It followed that 'the earthquake and the subterraneous fire have their uses in our system. They at first terrify and destroy, but a few years only pass away and their desolating effects disappear; the scene blooms with the fairest vegetation and becomes the abode of life'. Hence Davy concluded in his remarks at the end of his tenth lecture on geology:

> Even the most terrible of the ministrations of nature in their ultimate operation are pregnant with blessings and with benefits. Beauty and harmony are made to result from apparent confusion, and all the laws of the material world are ultimately made subservient to the preservation of life and the promotion of happiness.[34]

Understanding what Davy called the 'system' dispelled ignorance and fear. As Adam Smith put it in his *Essays on Philosophical Subjects*, feelings of wonder and fear were the direct products of our inability to understand the interconnected causes of a phenomenon, a particular problem in the case of the inscrutable forces of nature. Philosophy 'by representing the invisible chains which bind together all these disjointed objects ... soothe[s] the imagination, and ... render[s] the theatre of nature a more coherent, and therefore a more magnificent spectacle than otherwise it would have appeared to be.'[35]

Such emancipation from superstition was achieved through an understanding of the processes by which the spectacle of nature was produced. As Davy explained in his first geological lecture, 'The beauty, the majesty and the sublimity of the great forms of nature have their effect in the imagination rather increased than diminished by being connected with the view of philosophy.' As he went on to explain:

> The imagery of a mountain country, which is the very theatre of all science, is in almost all cases highly impressive and delightful, but a new and higher species of enjoyment arises in the mind when the arrangements in it, their harmony and subserviency to the purposes of life are considered. To the geological enquirer every mountain chain offers striking monuments of the great alterations that the globe has undergone. The most sublime speculations are awakened, the present is disregarded, past ages crowd upon the fancy, and the mind is lost in admiration of the designs of that great power who has established order in which at first view appears as confusion.[36]

As Davy's final remarks make clear, this view was not incompatible with Christian or deist views of the world, but it supposed an autonomous and self-regulating nature.

Enlightenment and superstition

The contrast between the enlightened and superstitious versions of the volcano is very clearly depicted in the work of the most important artist portraying Vesuvius in the later eighteenth century, the Frenchman Pierre-Jacques Volaire.[37] Volaire, born in Toulon, lived for eighteen years in Naples, married and died there in 1799. During his time in the city he produced a steady stream of pictures of the volcano in eruption, depicting the eruptions of 1767, 1771, 1774, 1779 and 1794. His sublime large-scale oil paintings – with vivid reds, yellows and golds pouring from the mouth of the volcano, their huge moonlit skies and gesticulating figures – were and probably still are the best-known images of Vesuvius from the eighteenth century. Almost all of Volaire's works were night scenes – Vesuvian tourism was nocturnal – and many, like the works of Joseph Wright of Derby, who was in Naples in the spring of 1774, and in a manner first developed by the Neapolitan artist Carlo Bonavia, contrasted the fiery reds and golds of the erupting volcano with the silvery light of the moon. Volaire's illustrious patrons included diplomats like Sir William Hamilton, Cardinal de Bernis (the French ambassador in Rome), the Austrian ambassador, and François Cacault, a consular official in Naples who also traded in pictures for Parisian clients. He sold pictures to two famous English collectors, Charles Townley and Henry Blundell, on their 1777 visit to Naples, to Mrs Piozzi when she was there in the 1780s, to French aristocrats like the enormously rich tax farmer Bergeret de Grancourt, and to the Vicomte de Saint-Pardoux, on his Grand Tour of 1777. His royal patrons included the Duke of Savoy and Ferdinand IV of Spain.[38] Most of Volaire's works claimed to depict a specific moment or event, and sometimes claimed to have been produced on the spot and with a high degree of exactitude. The Neapolitan diplomat and savant Michele Torcia dedicated an account of the 1779 eruption to the Russian Count Domaschneff, the Tsar's Chamberlain, in which he commented on the risks the painter ran during the eruption of that year in pursuit of 'fidèles images' of the volcano. (Only a very few of Volaire's paintings were fantasy pictures, such as those that combined the effects of the eruptions of 1771 and 1779.) They were repeatedly praised for their accuracy.

Volaire's pictures, for all their startling effects and apparent verisimilitude, told tales that chimed with the attitudes and beliefs of the philosophical travellers and enlightened figures who were his chief patrons and customers.[39] Most, though not all, of Volaire's paintings adopt one of two points of view: either close to the volcano on the so-called Atrio del Cavallo, between the crater of Vesuvius and Mount Somma; or at a distance, looking south-east towards Vesuvius from the Ponte della Maddalena and the city of Naples. In the former case, as in the painting inscribed *Vue de l'Éruption du mont Vésuve du 14 mai 1771* (Plate 13), we see the insouciant artist depicted on the left of the picture, sitting on a rock, his sketchpad in hand. (Note, by the way, the precision of the title.)

Below and to the right two standing figures, one accompanied by a dog, and a seated gentleman gesture towards the eruption. Their comportment could have come out of a genteel dancing master's manual; the poses are casual but authoritative, in a manner that indicates that they are engaged in observing a natural phenomenon that might inspire sublime feelings, but that does not entail fear (Plate 14). Here the gentleman savant (and potential patron) is portrayed as he would wish to have been seen. It is therefore not surprising that the image was widely disseminated in the form of an engraving after the painting was published in one of the most influential works on Italy, Saint-Non's *Voyage Pittoresque*.

The view from the Ponte della Maddalena at the southern edge of Naples was, however, very different (Plate 15). As can be seen in a painting of 1777, now in the North Carolina Museum of Art,[40] a pell-mell crowd of terrified Neapolitans, some in carts filled with their possessions, most on foot, are fleeing across the bridge from the eruption. Everywhere there are signs of popular belief that the safety of the people lay in their supplication to San Gennaro, the most important patron saint of Naples, who supposedly had the power to hold back (as he had famously done in 1631) the power of Vesuvius. His statue, erected on the bridge in the 1760s, stands at its apex, his hand raised towards the volcano. A fleeing man turns back on the bridge to raise an image – presumably of the saint – to ward off the eruption. And at the end of the bridge a group prostrate themselves before another image of the saint nailed to a parapet, pleading for his intercession. The figures are almost grotesque:

bodies, especially of the women, are contorted, their faces grimace with fear, or they roll their eyes towards the heavens. The painting depicts a persistent cliché about the Neapolitan populace – that they were superstitious and fearful rather than modern and enlightened. Volaire's paintings thus establish the difference and distance between the philosophical traveller or *érudit*, who was his patron, and the Neapolitans he depicted.

Volaire's work was the most conspicuous instance of this topos, but not the only one. It can be found, for example, in the work of a German artist resident in Naples, Jacob Philipp Hackert. His dramatic painting of the 1794 eruption features both a penitent religious procession and a swooning dishevelled woman. Similarly, one of the plates by Pietro Fabris, who illustrated Sir William Hamilton's lavish and sumptuous publication on his volcanic work, *Campi Phlegraei* (1776), shows a group of Neapolitan *lazzaroni*, gesturing towards the volcano and holding up a devotional image to ward off the wrath of Vesuvius. It is noticeable how often Hamilton included details about popular and superstitious responses in his reports to learned societies like the Royal Society about the different eruptions. Their agitated presence, hardly justified in understanding the nature of Vesuvian eruptions, seems to have served as a foil for the cool deliberations of the knowing savant. Indeed, in response to his reports, the London Royal Society praised Sir William Hamilton for his 'philosophical fortitude in the midst of the Horrors of Vesuvius' and expressed their admiration for his 'resolution' and 'constancy' in observing a phenomenon that he had 'so minutely as well as philosophically accounted for and described'.[41]

Plate 38 by Fabris in the *Campi Phlegraei* perfectly captures Hamilton's self-presentation as the enlightened savant (Plate 16). The image depicts an incident on 11 May 1771 – three days before Volaire's trip up the volcano – when Hamilton took the Neapolitan King Ferdinand and Queen Maria Carolina to see what he described as a 'curious phenomenon'. The lava, Hamilton wrote, ran into the valley, between Somma and Vesuvius, disgorged itself into a hollow way, formed a beautifull cascade of fire of more than 50 feet [15 metres] perpendicular fall, and escaping pure and in its fluid state from under the Scoriae, fell into the hollow way, and produced the finest effect, that can be imagined. The original Drawing for this Plate was taken that night on the spot.

We see Hamilton, like Volaire's savants, gesturing towards the cascading lava, explaining to the royal couple what they could see. Courtiers and servants look on, a sedan chair and two horses await the monarchs, and Fabris, again like Volaire, can be seen sketching the scene in the left foreground. This is not just an image of a 'curious phenomenon', but a representation of a certain sort of witnessing. It portrays not only the volcano, but the experience of being there, and it scripts the encounter between the eruption and the visitor as one of enlightened sociability and sensibility. The image was intended to instruct its audience in the appropriate sublime response to the powers of nature, one that showed an unflinching determination to reveal the secrets of nature. And it places Hamilton in the very best possible light: as a sagacious savant explaining the workings of nature to people of power and consequence.

We know that Hamilton had a special regard for this image, as he used it in order to have a working model of Vesuvius made, a light and sound box fronted by a transparency of Fabris's plate.[42] Hamilton showed this 'mechanical device' to visitors to Naples when the volcano was not erupting, and he sent two versions to England, one, predictably, to the Royal Society in London, the other, less probably, to David Garrick, the actor and manager of the Drury Lane Theatre, a gift that, as we shall see, may have had a major impact on the development of technologies of the moving image.

The contrast between the cool savant and the frightened *lazzaroni*, between enlightenment and superstition, made no attempt to understand the position of many native Neapolitans towards the volcano, except as a failure of understanding. The enlightened savant and artist regarded the volcano as a tableau, a scientific object and an instance of the (benign) workings of nature. This was not the vision of many Neapolitans, whose relation to the volcano was far more intimate and less distant. As a guide explained to a French traveller in the mid-nineteenth century, short-term visitors saw only the volcano's powers of destruction. Yet 80,000 people, he claimed, lived from and on Vesuvius in the surrounding towns, exploiting its fertility.[43] At the most basic level, the volcano was part of a cyclical nature that the native inhabited. Hester Piozzi recalled a conversation she had with a woman on the slopes of the volcano; she feared that the volcano would overwhelm the house and smallholding of the woman, who replied without concern:

> Let it go. We don't mind now if it goes tomorrow; for as we can make it answer, by raising our vines, oranges &c against it for three years, our fortune is made before the fourth arrives; and then if the red river comes, we can always run away, *scappar via*, ourselves and hang the property. We only desire three years of use of the mountain as a hot wall or forcing house, and then we are above the world, thanks to God and St Januarius.[44]

This response was largely unintelligible to Piozzi, who reflected that 'an odd jumble of past and present days, past and present ideas of dignity, events, and even manner of proportioning out their time, still confuse their heads'. She could not imagine a view without a linear, progressive conception of time.

For most enlightened commentators, the invocation of San Gennaro, and the importance attached to the thrice-yearly liquefaction of his blood in Naples cathedral, was the touchstone of Neapolitan superstition. Yet this completely failed to see how the city and the saint had over many years cemented a pact in which Naples uniquely celebrated San Gennaro, lavishly creating shrines, displaying images and relics, and building the saint into the ceremonial fabric of the city. He was Naples' local saint. In return he was expected to protect the city, to warn it of disaster and shield it when threatened. The bond was deeply charged with emotion, a fervent attachment both to the saint and to the city. This explains why, when the liquefaction was delayed or did not occur, the women in attendance abused and vilified the saint, much to the shock of most outside observers. It was not just fear of the misfortunes that would follow from the failure of the miracle. The saint was failing to keep his side of the bargain with his faithful Neapolitan followers. Though the focus of this reciprocity were the festivals of liquefaction, the process was ongoing. San Gennaro, Naples and the volcano were all bound together, creating a distinctive local symbiosis whose fortunes might fluctuate but which would never change. The combination of fear – understandable in those who lived in the shadow of the volcano – and resignation was beyond the ken of those steeped in Enlightenment science.

Sublime sensation, cool observation and the figure of the scientist

Not that the savant viewed the volcano without feeling. How, we might ask, were sublime descriptions of volcanoes as sites of emotional intensity connected with a more deliberate and colder language associated with the meticulous tasks of scientific observation? Observation was central to scientific practice in the Enlightenment and entailed an active engagement of the senses and intellect.[45] As the Genevan pastor and botanist Jean Senebier commented in *L'art d'observer* (1775), 'Attention alone renders the observer master of the subjects he studies, in uniting all the forces of his soul, in making him carefully discard all that could distract him, and in regarding the object as the only one that exists for it at that moment.' Goethe endorsed this view that scientific investigation demanded painstaking attention: 'As soon as an observer gifted with acute senses happens to pay attention to objects, he becomes both inclined to make observations, and excellent at them.' The aim, however, was not to observe individual curiosities – the modern savant was very concerned to distinguish himself from the casual collector and admirer of nature – but to use particulars to reconstruct a picture of nature and, above all, to understand its general laws by identifying 'uniform particulars' to create what Davy had called 'system'. When the Swiss savant and Alpine explorer Horace Bénédict de Saussure ran into Sir William Hamilton's nephew, Charles Greville, a lifelong collector of gems and crystals, in 1775, he dismissed him because 'he was not a serious student and did not attempt to generalize'.[46]

A grid of local facts needed to be fashioned into a systematic view of nature. The capacity to scale up was vital. This entailed precision, repetition and comparison in order to construct a general object – not Vesuvius or Etna or Stromboli, but volcanoes. So scientific knowledge depended, in the first instance, on a mass of detailed observations such as those of Vesuvius undertaken between 1779 and 1794 by Padre Antonio Piaggio at the behest of Sir William Hamilton. Such knowledge was not intended to prove but to discover – to produce rather than test general hypotheses about nature through patient discernment.

Curiosity, wonder, aesthetic appreciation – these were the feelings that were known to draw the traveller or tourist to the spectacles on the slopes of Vesuvius, but how were they to be persuaded to see nature as the savant intended, not just as an emotional stimulus, but as part of the order of things? One way to achieve this was for savants to portray the sublime and aesthetics more generally as the precursor and stimulus to a more sober analysis. As John Playfair, the Scottish mathematician and natural philosopher who spent several hours on the slopes of Vesuvius with Salvatore Madonna, explained in his *Illustrations of the Huttonian Theory of the Earth* (1802), 'as soon as he [the savant] has recovered from the general impression made by the novelty and magnificence of the spectacle before him, he begins to discover the footsteps of time.'[47] The excitement stimulates rather than inhibits inquiry.

Secondly, skilled observation became increasingly associated with the idea of genius, with virtuosity and ingenuity, both in fashioning more precise instruments and in deftly recording nature. Tabular results may have been prosaic and routine, but their recovery and constitution, especially when it put the observer at risk or in danger, was not. In the Romantic era a self-consciously heroic view of the natural philosopher as travelling investigator was fully elaborated, first in such figures as Saussure and the French geologist Déodat de Dolomieu, and most famously embodied in the person of the Prussian aristocrat and hero of the young Charles Darwin, Alexander von Humboldt. Humboldt's remarkable journey through the Americas between 1799 and 1804, and the even more remarkable abundance of his publications with their account of indigenous peoples, luxuriant tropical flora and exotic fauna (electric eels, capybaras, monkeys and the like), and spectacular natural features (precipitous slopes, wide prairies and high volcanoes) caught the European imagination. The trials and privations inflicted on Humboldt and his travelling companion, Aimé Bonpland, in the cause of science, most famously in their ascent of the volcano Chimborazo, then thought to be the highest mountain in the world, was the stuff of legend. Overcome with altitude sickness, they may not have reached the summit, but they exemplified the spirit of scientific inquiry. As a student, Darwin copied out and read aloud passages from Humboldt, and kept seven volumes of his *Personal Narrative of Travels to the Equinoctial Regions of the New Continent during the Years 1799–1804* in his cabin during the voyage of the *Beagle*.

Savants sought to resolve the problematic relation between powerful aesthetic feelings and defined meticulous observation, not by fighting the sensations associated with the sublime, but by making such feelings the handmaiden of science, while crafting themselves as heroic, sublime figures enduring danger and discomfort in the pursuit of philosophical truths. Their sublimity derived from their actions in nature, including the prosaic activities of measurement and precise description that seemed so removed from an aesthetic that spoke of boundless horizons, obscurity and darkness. The natural sublime became something not just apparent to the naked eye, but an aestheticised, invisible universal system, revealed through the savant's painstaking and painfully accumulated data. Its appeal lay in its penetration into the hidden and largely unknown depths beneath the surface of the earth.

Such views were consonant with the enthusiasm for scientific inquiry and the admiration its practitioners enjoyed. Humphry Davy, whose discoveries and lectures at the Royal Institution made him into the most visible spokesman for the sciences in the Anglophone world, and who was to spend months experimenting on the slopes of Vesuvius, promoted an exuberantly optimistic view of the powers and progress of science that was also mirrored in the literature of exploration and conquest. 'Science,' the youthful Davy rhapsodised, 'bestowed upon [humanity] powers which may be called almost creative; which have enabled him to change and modify the beings surrounding him, and by his experiments to interrogate nature with power, not simply as a scholar, passive and seeking only to understand her operations, but rather as a master, active with his own instruments'. Such circumstances, he concluded, would make any inquiring mind 'ambitious of becoming acquainted with the most profound secrets of nature; of ascertaining her hidden operations; and of exhibiting to man that system of knowledge which relates so intimately to their own physical and moral constitution.'[48]

More powerfully than any other natural philosopher, Davy, the friend of poets and artists, made the case for scientific inquiry as an imaginative and aesthetic practice: 'Imagination, as well as reason, is necessary,' he wrote, 'to perfection in the philosophic [i.e. scientific] mind. A rapidity of combination, a power of perceiving analogies, and of comparing them with facts, is the creative source of discovery.' This made the savant a man of feeling, the scientist an artist: 'Discrimination and delicacy of sensation, so important to physical research, are other words for taste; and love of nature is the same passion as the love of the magnificent, the sublime and the beautiful.'[49]

As Davy's private notebooks reveal, his private views about the powers of science were less assured than his public utterances, which were very much about promoting natural philosophy and savants like himself. Reflecting on the paucity of current scientific knowledge – its inability to grasp the vast scope and complexity of the universe and of the earth itself 'an endless field of investigation' – he pondered the globe's unknown interior, the ignorance about the causes of volcanoes: 'We have learnt some truths with respect to the surface but there is an immensity beneath us. Geology in every sense of the word is a superficial science.'[50] But this niggling sense that scientific knowledge had only scraped the surface of the natural world only served to encourage investigators, explorers and scientists to even greater exertions.

While much travel literature used the conventional imagery of male sexuality to laud such single-minded efforts to conquer, pene-trate and reveal the secrets of nature, not everyone was convinced that the sublimely motivated researches of the savant were an unqualified benefit to mankind. In her best-selling novel of 1818, *Frankenstein: or, The Modern Prometheus*, Mary Shelley, the daughter of the brilliant feminist theorist Mary Wollstonecraft and the anarchist philosopher William Godwin, famously created not only a living creature – a monster – fabricated by man, but the figure of the inexorably driven scientist determined to triumph over nature whatever the costs. In subsequent versions of Shelley's story, notably the theatrical adapta-tions staged shortly after the novel's publication, her subtle and complex portrait of the savant Victor Frankenstein, and the agonies he undergoes, is flattened into a popular figure (still with us) of the mad scientist. But she makes clear in her cautionary tale that Victor's scientific hubris, his sense that nature is a malleable and manipulable object that can be bent by human reason, unleashes forces in society that Frankenstein, as a scientist, cannot control or repair. The sublime comes with a health warning.

5
VESUVIUS
Travellers and Tourists in a Shifting Ecology

The slopes of Vesuvius were a distinctive ecology, a landscape of splendour and desolation, at once hazardous and beautiful, and constantly shifting, full of what Giuseppe Maria Mecatti, the author of *Racconto storico-filosofico del Vesuvio*, called 'most notable mutations'. Every major eruption changed the configuration and appearance of the landscape. After the eruption of 1767 the cone emerged higher than it had been when the eruption began. The eruption of 1794 made it hazardous for several years to descend into the crater and its lava flows buried a large part of the town of Torre del Greco before they reached the sea; the eruption of 1822, like that of 1631, blew the top off the cone, lowering it by about ninety-three metres, and destroying 165,000 square metres of woodland and over 100,000 square metres of vineyards. In 1872 the towns of San Sebastiano and Massa di Somma, north-west of Vesuvius, were badly damaged, and about a dozen people, including a party of medical students, were killed when a huge fissure opened up on the flank of the volcano. But, in between these spectacular explosions, Strombolian eruptions, repeated moderate effusive-explosive events producing new cones of ash and cinders, lava flows and lava fountains, constantly changed the landscape. Regeneration also transformed the topography.[1] As

Vivant Denon remarked in 1778, 'The most recent lavas show only ferruginous and bituminous cinders that are the colour of clinker. After a century, this calcination becomes less sharp and is first covered with moss or litchen ... and soon broom and lavender begin to grown on it. Then each type of vegetation comes in turn, and so on, until the next lavas arrive.'[2] Denon's observations were astute but his timeline was overextended. Lichen (*stereocaulon vesuvianum*) covers lava within seven to ten years; flowers emerge four years later, and then the shrubs of yellow broom, celebrated in Leopardi's famous poem about Mount Vesuvius.

This shifting landscape was reconfigured not just by the volcano itself, but also by human endeavour. In the nineteenth century the construction of a paved road up to the hermitage, the opening of the Observatory immediately adjacent to it in 1844, the building of railways, both to Portici and then the funicular up the volcano itself – all of these developments, fuelled by the Neapolitan state, scientific inquiry and the growth of tourism, altered the environment in ways that affected social relations on the mountain.

Vesuvius hosted a distinctive ethnography, one that mixed local *lazzaroni* and peasants with an occupationally diverse population of visitors not just from Naples itself but from all over Europe and the Americas. It was built around the dangers and attractions of the volcano, an economy of visitors and guides, and was largely shaped by a script in which travellers enjoyed a sublime experience of the volcano through the good offices of locals. The journey to the crater provoked a range of intense emotions and feelings: the excitement, awe, terror, fright, fear, exultation, thrill and elation associated with the sublime; but also love, lust and pleasure, as well as melancholy, nostalgia, wistfulness, longing, yearning and homesickness. It amplified friendships and camaraderie, strengthening loyalties and allegiances, just as it revealed enmities and antipathies. And it afforded the opportunity for visitors to display their courage, fortitude, fearlessness and intrepidity, one that they did not always take.

The relations between visitors and guides shifted between the late eighteenth and late nineteenth centuries. As numbers grew in the first half of the nineteenth century, so enterprising locals from a small group of families came to dominate the services offered to visitors. The use of their skills as guides and specimen collectors by men of science in Naples linked them to a larger world of mineralogical and geological research. The volcano was accessible to a growing public, but visitors, with some exceptions, had to rely on the skills and help of guides to enjoy it safely. Relations were fraught but often personal. Visitors shared their experiences not only with one another but also with their guides, who were their employees but also their instructors.

Gradually, however, the human skills and labour of the guides were replaced by new technologies and modern 'improvements'. The guides adapted as best they could, but the connection between them and the local scientific community and with the curious traveller was transformed.

The ecology and ethnography of the mountain changed because they were not autonomous but connected to circuits of power and knowledge that spread much further afield. As the politics of the Kingdom of Naples and of the Two Sicilies changed, so did the composition of military and naval visitors to the volcano. During the Napoleonic occupations and under Murat there were precious few Britons on Vesuvius and a great many French; after 1815 the English visitors came back with a vengeance. The Austrians abounded after 1821 but were replaced by the Swiss in 1827. As American commercial and strategic interests in the Mediterranean grew, so too did the presence of American civilians.

The Neapolitan regime's attitudes towards science were ambivalent. The Bourbon monarchy looked askance at public education – schooling was poor, literacy low, and Protestant visitors were repeatedly shocked by the almost total absence of that most rudimentary form of reading, the vernacular Bible. Yet at the same time, the Bourbons were eager to appear modern and scientific. They built the first Italian railway, were promoters of steam packets between the mainland and Sicily, and built panopticon prisons, like that of Santo Stefano, of which Jeremy Bentham would have been proud. The volcano's Observatory was also the first of its kind, heralding a new era in volcanic science; it placed scientists constantly on the volcano, and its second director, Luigi Palmieri (Macedonio Melloni, the first, was fired because of his reformist politics), introduced a regime of instrumental regulation – using technologies brought from Paris. The guides were marginalised in this research; crystal collecting continued, but there was much less amateur involvement in the collection of information about the volcano.

The final change in the habitat of Vesuvius came in the form of a new kind of tourism. It was still possible to enjoy the Romantic sublime experience of the ascent of the volcano. One night in May 1877, the Tuscan writer Renato Fucini made a dramatic guided ascent up and into the crater whose description in his *Napoli a occhio nudo* could have been written by any Romantic visitor of the first half of the nineteenth century. But when he arrived back the following morning at the hermitage, Fucini was confronted by a landau drawn by four horses, containing a party wearing glazed kid gloves and sunglasses, and carrying sun umbrellas.[3] These impeccably dressed travellers looked on Fucini and his dishevelled, dirty friends with condescending commiseration. For his part Fucini felt he had the last laugh – how could anyone ascend Vesuvius like this? – but the landau and its passengers were the upmarket harbingers of a new, more comfortable experience of the volcano, one that became available to the ordinary traveller as well as a wealthy visitor and stripped it of much of its romance.

Already in the 1850s, as a result of the new road, there were unprecedented crowds watching the volcano erupt. The growth of organised tourism, most famously under the watchful eye of Thomas Cook, brought not just more visitors (Cook's first tour to Naples was in 1866), but a greater degree of outside regulation. At the base station of the funicular Thomas Cook and Sons built a structure housing the steam engine that powered the railway, a stables and a restaurant, where guests were asked to sign a 'register of travellers' that sadly does not survive. As one visitor wrote,

> We enter the adjoining restaurant, where we do justice to an excellent lunch which is provided for us. Our wants are attended to by an English-speaking waiter, whilst a post office, in the building, supplies the intrepid adventurer with post-cards, bearing a printed heading of Mount Vesuvius, in fancy letters, on which he may advise his friends in other parts of the globe of his safe arrival on the volcano. What more can one desire?[4]

In 1903 the opening of a new electric railway at Pugliano made it possible to travel all the way from Naples to the foot of the funicular by train. All that remained for the local guides was the 150 metres between the top of the funicular and the crater of the volcano. This was not just a loss for the guides. As one visitor admitted, 'The romance of an ascent in earlier years has vanished.' The *Saturday Review* complained that 'Vesuvius has been turned into a kind of hotel bar for Naples', presided over by the firm of Thomas Cook, 'Lord of Vesuvius'.[5]

Studies of tourism are often framed as a modernising and democratising historical narrative, in which tourism begins as an aristocratic activity (the Grand Tour of the eighteenth century), reaches a bourgeois audience in the age of Romanticism, and becomes a form of mass consumption with the advent of railways, public holidays, and leisure entrepreneurs like Thomas Cook in Britain and Carl Stangen in Germany. If we look solely at numbers, then this is a plausible story. Foreign visitors to Naples numbered in the hundreds in the eighteenth century, in the low thousands in the 1820s (6,000 or so) and had reached 60,000 by the last decades of the nineteenth century. But more, of course, does not mean the same. The relationship between the traveller and the local environment is very different whether they are an eighteenth-century French official (Francois Cacault, the patron of Volaire), a nineteenth-century Swiss mercenary, like Lieutenant Nicholas Joseph de Bumann, or a female member, possibly a schoolteacher, of one of Thomas Cook's organised excursions to the slopes of the volcano. We tend to think of the schoolteacher, a leisure traveller whose sole purpose is recreational, and who has purchased a bundle of amenities and a period of time 'away', as the 'real' tourist of these three visitors. But the tourist as holidaymaker was only one iteration of the travelling visitor, whose numbers, as we have seen, could include many who may have taken a few hours away from work to ascend the volcano, but who were by no means on vacation.

Today the United Nations World Tourism Organization (UNWTO) collects figures on travel and tourists.[6] These make clear that, in the halcyon days before Covid-19, travel and tourism accounted for a huge part of the world's economy: 11.7 per cent of world GDP; 8 per cent of world exports, and 8 per cent of employment in 2000. But the UNWTO statistics reveal a problem that lies at the heart of many tourist studies, namely the difficulty of distinguishing something called 'tourism' from travel more generally conceived. Currently the UNWTO statistics for inbound international tourism use four categories: 'leisure, recreation and holidays'; 'visiting family and relatives, health, religion, other'; 'business and professions'; and 'not specified'. Though the leisure category is still by far the largest, the trend over the last ten years has been for it to shrink as a percentage of all tourism, and for the rather miscellaneous 'visiting family' category to grow at its expense. Studies also indicate that these UNWTO categories are exceptionally porous, and that increasingly travel involves a combination of more than one and often several of these factors. It is becoming clear that tourism and travel are not confined solely to commoditised leisure.

We face then, something of a paradox. On the one hand, it does not seem difficult to identify *homo touristicus*, a species that comes in many stripes but is easily spotted by its characteristic plumage, its habitat, collective behaviours and appurtenances (once a copy of Byron's poems, a sketchpad and a Baedeker guide, or more recently a camera, a mobile phone and a selfie stick). Nor is it difficult to identify clearly defined commodities sold as souvenirs and memorabilia (lava models, for instance) or services sold to visitors (guides, board and lodging). The travel agents of the nineteenth century like Thomas Cook brought these all together in the form of 'tourist experiences' or 'holidays' with their fixed itineraries scheduled through vouchers, pre-paid tickets and hotel bookings. But if we want to get beyond this sort of superficial observation of tourists and their activities (every bit as shallow as the views often attributed to tourists themselves), it is important to disaggregate them, not just in the sense of distinguishing different types of tourist activity or national origin (a common practice), but in terms of what they bring to their travels. Being a tourist requires the performance of certain rituals, not the abandonment of other beliefs and identities.

Both tourism and travel come to have different valences in societies where mobility of all sorts has become a commonplace of everyday life. In the social science literature, enhanced mobility and travel have been added to the ever-expanding list of the features of modernity, leading anthropologists and sociologists to rethink the questions of travel and tourism. Some have argued that if travel has become as much the norm as the exception, we should view 'home' as a nodal point rather than a fixed entity. Why should we assume that cultures are somehow fixed and local, rather than mobile and protean, moving in both time and space? As the cultural anthropologist James Clifford puts it, 'Virtually everywhere one looks, the processes of human movement and encounter are long-established and complex. Cultural centers, discrete regions and territories, do not exist prior to contacts, but are sustained through them, appropriating and disciplining the restless movements of people and things.'[7] Though individual curiosity and the enjoyment of leisure time contribute to these developments, movement and cultural contact are fuelled by three much larger processes: the growth of international trade, finance and knowledge exchange; the development of empires; and the waging of war. The less historically minded social sciences tend to assume this is a very recent development. But such forces were central to the Romantic era, an epoch dominated by international warfare, imperial struggles, and an unprecedented movement of men and resources.

John Urry, one of the most distinguished sociologists of tourism, has recently emphasised how the growth in mobility and travel in general, as well as the establishment of networks using new media, have begun to change the nature of tourism, so that recreational and social travel has become increasingly less distinct from other sorts of mobility. In a world where families are dispersed, where people travel for work over long distances, and where migration, exile and emigration are a frequent experience, tourism has increasingly become implicated in extended kinship chains and networks of sociability, especially the sustaining or reinforcement of friendship. Different patterns of work and travel make possible many different scenarios of leisure time. Urry refers to this as the 'de-exoticising' of tourism, which he claims has become less associated with 'time away' and 'time out' than with the sustaining of ongoing relationships at a distance, through periodic 'face-to-face' encounters. Tourism has lost its autonomy.[8]

Part III

Travel Writing, Politics and Revolution

6
VESUVIUS AND NAPLES IN TIME, SPACE AND HISTORY

Mediations: Vesuvius and Naples in travel literature and images

Though we may define 'Vesuvius' and 'Naples' in terms of their topography and geography – our sense of them as places – their identity has always been shaped by forces that extend beyond their immediate boundaries. This was recognised during the Romantic era when the temporal and spatial coordinates of Naples and Vesuvius were understood to be vast and virtually unfathomable, to stretch beneath and far beyond what could be observed by the naked eye. The geologist, the mineralogist, the antiquary, the archaeologist and the serious travel writer excavated and uncovered multiple layers of a disturbingly deep history, while the sciences that they embodied connected the processes that shaped the region to larger forces found throughout the globe. Their writings and many graphic images in a variety of media illuminated and projected differing views of the city and the volcano, furnishing information and fashioning visions that were enjoyed vicariously by an enormous number of readers and viewers.

The creators of these works were drawn to a distinctive location that was often described in meticulous detail. They were also go-betweens, intermediaries who connected Naples to a larger world.

229

Many were Neapolitan, many were not, but their collaboration – even when reluctant – was vital to the shaping of 'Romantic Vesuvius'. Though the heart of this study is the volcano itself – the volcanic and human activity at its crater, on the flanks of the mountain and in the surrounding towns, including the buried cities – we also need to examine the processes by which 'Romantic Vesuvius' was constantly breaching its boundaries, flowing out into a much larger world, escorted on its way by politicians, merchants, savants of every stripe, impresarios, artists and literary figures. This process was not unidirectional; knowledge and taste moved both ways. 'Romantic Vesuvius' was a place located within elaborate networks, some local, others extending from the Baltic to the Americas. Changes in the material environment, in technologies of representation and in systems of power and knowledge moved the idea of the volcano in new directions, making Naples and the volcano into different kinds of place.

One of the greatest forces that moved Vesuvius beyond the Bay of Naples was the publication of an astonishing volume of travel literature in multiple languages, and the widespread dissemination of graphic representations of the volcano – not just paintings and prints, but through the newer technologies of the diorama and panorama. Though very little of this material attended to current politics – indeed, it often avoided the subject altogether – and it seems to have been chiefly concerned with taste and aesthetics and with individual emotional responses to the environment, these travel narratives and images were nevertheless informed by values and assumptions that characterised and passed judgment on Naples, its people and their volcano. Even while writers and artists were descanting on the astonishing beauty of the Bay of Naples, shaping an itinerary that guided readers and viewers to its choicest spots, they were fashioning a view of the city and its surroundings as a backward and primitive place (part of its picturesque attraction) best understood as being not only close to nature but even a part of it. Travel writers wanted to refashion Naples, one of the largest cities in Europe, as an environment in which the differences between nature and culture were almost indistinguishable.

Travel literature was far and away the most popular form of non-fiction in the Romantic era. As C.G. Worde, the aptly named assistant librarian to the British Museum, put it in 1795, 'One of the most distinguishing features in the literary history of our age and century, is the passion of the public for voyages and travels. Of the books that have lately been published, there are none, novels alone excepted, that, in point of number, bear any proportion to them.'[1] The Romantic era saw the publication and consolidation of a canon of works by distinguished travellers to Italy and the South – many of them literary figures who wrote about the region. One of the most enduring and influential, though chiefly for a prosperous and erudite readership, was the work of the Frenchman Jean-Claude Richard de Saint-Non, who with the help of several distinguished writers and artists put together *Voyage pittoresque, ou Description des royaumes de Naples et de Sicile*, first published in 1781–6 but still in print in the 1830s. These beautifully produced folio volumes (not easily packed into a traveller's luggage) were a shared point of reference for many aristocratic travellers; they also appeared in many German editions. Two other French authors were the lodestars of many eighteenth-century travellers, the astronomer Jérôme Lalande whose *Voyage d'un françois en Italie* appeared in 1769, and the magistrate and man of letters Charles Dupaty, whose *Lettres sur Italie*, filled with feeling and sensibility, appeared in the first of many editions in Rome in 1788.[2] As one French traveller remarked, the most finely wrought account of Italy was the work of Dupaty, but Lalande's work was the most comprehensive.[3] In the nineteenth century, readers were apt to supplement these works with Stendhal's *Rome, Naples et Florence* (1817), Chateaubriand's much-excerpted *Voyage en Italie* (1827), and the travels of the great German writer and scientist Johann Wolfgang von Goethe, whose famous *Italienische Reise* (Italian Journey), though it refers to a trip to Italy of 1786–8, was published in 1816–17.

The English canon contains more travellers than literary lions. Two works that focused on southern Italy helped shape views of the region. Patrick Brydone's enormously successful *A Tour Through Sicily and Malta*, which first appeared in 1773, went through numerous English editions into the nineteenth century, and became a European bestseller with translations into Dutch, French and German. Henry Swinburne's *Travels in the Two Sicilies*, published seven years later, was repeatedly reprinted in the 1780s, and was quickly translated into German and French. In the nineteenth century three important English guides to Italy, Henry Coxe's *A Picture of Italy* (1815), the Catholic John Chetwode Eustace's *A Tour Through Italy* (1813), later retitled *A Classical Tour*, and Joseph Forsyth's extremely lively *Remarks on Antiquities, Arts and Letters during an Excursion to Italy in the Years 1802–03* (1813), were all often cited or plagiarised by travellers. Many of these works were plundered by later guidebooks, such as those published in Paris by the foreign-language publishing house of Galignani, whose *Traveller's Guide Through Italy* proudly boasted of its incorporation of earlier accounts.

Travel writing in the Romantic era was an extraordinarily protean genre, and in the early nineteenth century there were several books that combined travel narrative and information within a work of fiction. Long stretches of sentimental storytelling were punctuated by travel descriptions that could have been (and probably were) lifted from guidebooks. None was more popular than Madame de Staël's novel, *Corinne, ou l'Italie* (1807), with its doomed relationship between a British aristocrat and Corinne, an Italian (who turns out to be half British). De Staël not only described Italian antiquities, sites and landscapes (including Vesuvius, where a pivotal scene in the novel occurs); she coached her readers in the appropriate emotional responses to her Italian surroundings. Published in Paris, and then in

London, Berlin, New York and Boston within a year of its first appearance, it was constantly invoked by travellers as an invaluable guide to the peninsula, and especially to Naples. As Anna Jameson put it in her *Diary of an Ennuyée* (1826) – another work that combines travelogue and fiction – it was 'a fashionable *vade mecum* for sentimental travelers in Italy'.[4]

Paradoxically, by the early nineteenth century accounts in guidebooks and travel literature of Naples and its surroundings, including Vesuvius, had become standardised, even as they became more diverse. On the one hand a core of information and interpretation, chiefly derived from writings on antiquities and the Grand Tour, was repeatedly rehearsed in travel narratives. On the other, it was now surrounded by new and more variegated materials: subjective responses, personal experiences, and commentary about the current state of politics and the contemporary world. In his diary that covers his visit to Naples in 1814–15, the Whig Member of Parliament and coalmine owner William Ord tried to keep the two separate, recording his traditional tourist observations on the right page, reserving the left for comments and thoughts on current affairs and contemporary politics. He found the distinction couldn't hold. By the time Napoleon escaped from Elba, Ord was mixing the entries indiscriminately.[5]

A routine itinerary, of the sort recorded on the right-hand page of Ord's diary, had emerged in the wake of the travel narratives and guidebooks intended to shepherd the visitor to the sites of Naples and its environs. First and foremost was the '*coup d'oeil* of matchless beauty',[6] the extended panorama of the Bay. Within this prospect and the bounds of the city itself, travellers were directed to the Via Toledo, the city's bustling main thoroughfare, to the Royal Museum with its rich display of antiquities, and to the spectacle both on and off the stage of the theatre of San Carlo. To the south and east, the visitors' itinerary took in Vesuvius, Herculaneum, the Palace at Portici, Pompeii and the more distant temples of Paestum. To the north and west, there were an especially large number of natural and historic sites: the Grotto of Posillipo, Virgil's Tomb, the bubbling volcanic Solfatara, the Grotta del Cane with its mephitic gases and, further afield, Pozzuoli and its antiquities, most notably the Temple of Serapis, the Cave of the Sybils, Baiae and Monte Nuovo, the small volcano that had emerged in 1538.

Northern travellers to Naples looked not just on Vesuvius and sites of great beauty but also on the city itself as natural elements in a landscape of compelling richness and abundance. 'Naples,' wrote one early nineteenth-century visitor, 'owes its fame, the character of its inhabitants, and perhaps its very existence, to the superlative loveliness of its situation. In no spot on earth are the skies brighter or the waters more pellucid and serene.'[7] Such hyperbole was commonplace; the excesses of nature prompting excessive prose. Forsyth in his 1813 guide was unrestrained in his praise and extolled Naples and its environs for their charms:

> What variety of attractions! – A climate where heaven's breath smells sweet and wooingly – the most beautiful interchange of sea and land – wines, fruits, provisions, in their highest excellence – a vigorous and luxuriant nature, unparalleled in its productions and processes – all the wonders of volcanic power spent or in action – antiquities different from all antiquities on earth – a coast which was once the fairyland of poets, and the favourite retreat of great men. Even the tyrants of the creation loved this alluring region, spared it, adorned it, lived in it, died in it.[8]

The emphasis was on nature rather than on man, or on the powers of nature over man. For some commentators, like Jean Henry Westphal, the author of a French *Guide* to accompany a map of the environs of Naples (1828), nature was the region's sole attraction. Like so many travel writers he acknowledged Naples as a place of variety and abundance with its 'immense number of objects, sites and enchanting points of view, which it is hardly possible to meet in any other country in the world', but, he added, 'the true enjoyment that Naples confers' is the admiration of 'beautiful nature', that one 'is able to obtain in the midst of inexhaustible riches' because 'nature has done everything'. The rest is paltry: 'the works of men, both ancient and modern, are, with a few exceptions, hardly worthy of great attention.'[9]

Though Westphal overstates his case, he is typical in how he treats so much of Naples, even its culture, as if it were a part of 'nature'. The presumed visitor is, in Forsyth's words, 'a mere student of nature . . . an artist, a man of pleasure', or anyone 'that can be happy among people who seldom affect virtue'. Naples is represented as a site of aesthetic and social pleasure, a place to explore one's feelings; it is not sober, pious, serious or scholarly, but exciting, giddy and stimulating, full of 'gaiety, bustle and confusion'. Seen from afar it is an astonishing spectacle, 'a whole vast city, involved in one mighty globe of the richest light, and surrounded by hills and waters, all partaking in various degrees of its brilliancy'.[10] Plunged into its midst, the visitor was swept along 'the bustling streets of Naples, where carts, calishes and carriages of all descriptions roll impetuously & incessantly onward amid shoals of foot passengers equally heedless and bustling'.[11] 'Parading the streets,' commented one traveller, 'seems to be the principal occupation of every individual.' Even the busy streets are seen as sites of performance and theatricality rather than industry.

The notion that the Bay of Naples was a place of *otium* not *negotium* (pleasure rather than business) went back to antiquity and was reinforced by the experiences of travellers usually coming from the north and from the ancient city of Rome, the traveller's chief point of comparison. To the English painter Elizabeth Frances Batty, the Eternal City was 'the abode of dullness and monastic monotony'.[12] One young traveller, William Crackenthorpe, wrote to his mother, 'In the one the streets are totally depopulated, in the other they are more crowded than in the Strand in London; desolation and wretchedness are the striking features of Rome, bustle and noise those of Naples.'[13] Those who preferred Rome favoured 'the *severe majesty* that seems to preside as the genius of the place, [that] proscribes frivolity, and inspires loftiness of thought and gravity of deportment.' Naples, a 'total contrast' with Rome, was a place of energy and motion.[14]

In the Romantic era, the Bay of Naples became more and more popular as a destination largely because it fitted so well with the purported objects of Romantic travel. All those qualities that the literary scholar Chloe Chard in her recent collection of travel writing, *Tristes Plaisirs*, identifies as the chief attractions that drew the traveller to Italy – its topographical excess, its abundance of culture and nature, its ability to provoke both pleasure and a sense of danger, its capacity to hold men and women in thrall – were more powerfully present in the Bay of Naples than anywhere else on the peninsula. There was nowhere better to explore what Chard has called 'the adventure of the self'.[15]

This shift towards the subjective was part of two larger trends in the Romantic era. The cult of sensibility emphasised (and praised) the capacity of individuals to exercise sympathy and explore their own feelings through contact with the unfamiliar and strange, whether it be foreign lands, unfamiliar landscapes, the remnants of lost civilisations or charming natives. Ironically it had flourished in the wake of a brilliant parody of such feelings in Laurence Sterne's *Sentimental Journey* of 1768. Sterne proved so influential that Swinburne felt impelled to insist that his account of southern Italy was not a fanciful fiction: 'I am writing the account of a real Tour', he grumpily complained, 'and not an imitation of Sterne's Sentimental Journey.'[16] Swinburne's annoyance was mirrored in the views of many reviewers, who complained that the object of observation in travel narratives was more usually found in the exploration of authors' psyches than in the topography through which they travelled.

Few travel narratives ever attained Sterne's inventive playfulness, but his work encouraged the publication of numerous travel accounts, many of which struggled, often unsuccessfully, to justify their origin-ality, while they followed on what was known as 'the beaten track' of visitors to Italy. As early as the 1760s, the historian and novelist Charles Pinot Duclos ruefully conceded on his Italian journey that 'These places have been described in such a large number of books that I will say nothing about them, except that I walk through them with great pleasure.'[17] The problem of belatedness – that one had arrived at a scene viewed and described many times before – encouraged authors to explore their inner reflections in the pursuit of singularity. When upbraided for producing yet another travel narrative, Shelley's friend Thomas Jefferson Hogg reverted to special pleading: 'The journal of a traveller is his life during the period of his travel; it is consequently amusing, not only on account of the countries of which he treats, but as a piece of autobiography.'[18] Claims that the author's feelings lay at the heart of the travel account were not only an excuse to explain away the pursuit of a familiar path; they also informed the experience of travel – what places mattered and why.

This was because the development of a picturesque aesthetic provided a visual syntax of emotion, which meant that the natural environment – whether violent eruptions, waterfalls and torrents, dark woods, rolling hills, or rich, populated pastureland – were seen as objects of both art and feeling. 'The general Effect of a survey of nature is delight,' wrote Charles Davy, 'whilst every species of Landscape, like every different species of Melody excites its own peculiar genuine emotions, nor are they limited to the imagination only, they make their passage through it to the heart.' Alexander Cozens, a British landscape artist and drawing master, the teacher of, among others, the wealthy Romantic aesthete and novelist William Beckford, was even more specific. He identified sixteen sorts of land-scape and the accompanying emotions they provoked. The tops of high mountains, for example, elicited 'surprize, terror, superstition, silence, melancholy, power, strength', all qualities associated with the sublime. A hollow or chasm, like a cave or crater, prompted 'greatness, awe, surprise, danger, Banditti ... and superstitious fear'. In contrast, varied landscapes with no dominant feature were associated with 'chearfulness, amusement, equality of fortune' and 'friendship' while open lands with cities and cultivation prompted 'public happiness. Liberty curiosity grandeur. Admiration'.[19]

Cozens's schema is only a more complex and subtle version of the language of 'the beautiful', 'the picturesque' and 'the sublime' that saturated travel literature. As we have seen, such terminology and the definition of their accompanying feelings exercised the great philosophers, including Immanuel Kant and Edmund Burke, but their usage in much travel literature was careless and promiscuous, mixing equivalent sorts of emotion. But their general importance lay in giving travellers and travel writers a descriptive language which led them to see environments and landscapes as embodying certain sorts of feeling, or as triggering particular emotions.

A repertory of sites in Europe (and beyond) were identified in travel literature, guides, memoirs, fictions and a variety of graphic media as exemplary locations offering the most complete experiences of 'nature'. These places shared the possibility of a heightened aesthetic experience because they seemed to combine the full range of aesthetic forms, and by playing off the sublime and the beautiful, offered a more intense experience of both. Such special regions included, but were never confined to, much of Switzerland, and especially the Alps, the valley of the Rhine, the Jura and Pyrenees mountains, Vesuvius and the Bay of Naples, and Sicily and Mount Etna. Each country had its own natural hotspots; in Britain, for example, they included the Wye Valley, the Peak District, the Lake District and the Highlands of Scotland. These sites offered aesthetic plenitude. James Johnson, physician and author of *A Change of Air* (1831), writing about the Bay of Naples, regaled his readers with a cluster of impressions: 'gaze on the sublimest scenes of varied beauty, fertility and grandeur, that ever burst on the human eye; or shudder at the desolating ravages of active or exhausted volcanoes . . . we are over-whelmed, distracted by the tumultuous tide of impressions, half of which we can neither receive, dispose of, nor retain!'[20] In similar fashion the enormously successful guidebook to Switzerland, Johann Gottfried Ebel's *Manuel du voyageur en Suisse*, which first appeared in 1793 and went through more than twenty-three editions in French,[21] began by praising Switzerland as the country that had it all (apart, Ebel had to admit, from volcanoes and oceans): 'All that is great, extraordinary, astonishing, sublime; anything that can inspire fear or terror; all bold, sad, or melancholy that nature likes to spread in its compositions, all that it offers in its immensity of scenes romantic, pleasant, sweet and pastoral, seems to be gathered in this country to make it the garden of Europe.'[22] As Charlotte Smith, the radical author and English translator of Alexander von Humboldt, put it in a letter to a friend, 'I do not mind dying, but I want to see the Alps and Vesuvius first.'[23] In both cases the traveller was offered an abun-dance of nature and a surfeit of feeling. Catering to a Romantic demand for intense experience, the travel literature guided readers to sites that prompted the deepest emotions.

But this emphasis on personal feeling should not lead us to over-look the politics that underpinned such aesthetic views. As Cozens's schema makes clear, a highly cultivated and a well-populated land-scape was beautiful, a sign of liberty and modernity that prompted feelings of admiration, very different from the sublime feelings provoked by wild nature. The rough-hewn picturesque, found in ramshackle ruins, uncultivated grounds and the ragged appearance of the poor, may have had a pleasing aesthetic effect but did not excite moral approval. As Anna Jameson put it in her *Diary of an Ennuyée*, 'Civilization, cleanliness and comfort are excellent things, but they are sworn enemies of the picturesque . . . but in Italy the picturesque is everywhere.'[24] And, she might have added, especially in southern Italy and Naples.

Nature and culture: the backward south

We have already seen that Naples and Vesuvius were regarded as places of great natural beauty, as sites rich with history, culture and nature. This enthusiasm, however, was not accompanied by an admiration for the contemporary Neapolitan kingdom and its inhabitants. On the contrary, discussion of them, both then and now, have been dominated by what has been called 'an imaginative geography' or 'a moralised geography' that emphasises the backwardness of the south – its poverty and lack of economic development, its superstition and its archaic institutions – characterising it as a place teetering on the edge of civilisation. As the poet and operatic librettist Auguste Creuzé de Lesser famously put it in 1806, 'Europe ends at Naples and ends there quite badly.'[25] In eighteenth- and nineteenth-century travel literature, studies of national character and works on geography, political philosophy and political economy, this sense of Italy's backwardness, of incompleteness or even of stasis became an *idée fixe*. The borders of this moralised geography were unclear. Sometimes they encompassed the Italian peninsula and the territories south of the Alps as a whole, sometimes the Kingdom of Naples. But as with many such distinctions, what mattered was the nature of the dichotomy rather than its precise boundaries.

Notions of southern inferiority came to have a long and varied history, whether in the politics of the period immediately after Italian unification, in the corpus of writings known as *meridionalismo* or in the racialised analyses of southern criminality. More recently, social scientific writing has stigmatised the absence of civic consciousness in the south, while in the political sphere, the region has been subject to the banalities and stereotypes of the early Lega Nord (Northern League, now simply 'The League') political party. As the historian John Davis elegantly puts it, southern Italy has become 'a prisoner of its own notoriety'.[26]

1. One of many popular representations of the *calesso* to Resina, the invariably crowded carriage that was the easiest way to reach the foot of Mount Vesuvius.

2. A young traveller's drawing of the hermitage, from the sketchbook of her Italian tour, *c.* 1820.

3. Guides pull and push visitors to the edge of the crater of Vesuvius.

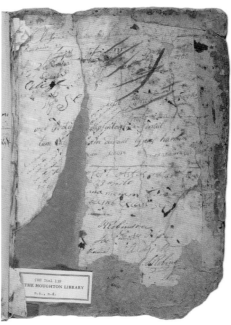

4. Front and rear inside cover of a visitors' book, a well-worn and much-used album whose entries were often inserted at random.

5. Visitors address the hermit: 'Good Friar you ask me to write in your book …' Note the comment on the entry in another hand: 'I wish that the Poet had told us the name of the stupid Mule, which could be so tame as to allow so much writing to be made "on his backside".'

6. The popular festivities and colourful costumes celebrating a miracle of the Virgin at the Easter festival at Sant'Anastasia, on the north slopes of Vesuvius, was a frequent subject of such artists as Gaetano Gigante, Leopold Robert, Pietro Fabris and Anton Sminck Van Pitloo. Penry Williams, the artist of this work, was on Vesuvius in the summer of 1828.

7. The German artist Franz Catel was a frequent visitor to Naples, painting Vesuvius in both eruption and repose. He took a particular interest in Neapolitan dress and customs.

8. August Kopisch lived in Naples for three years and was a frequent visitor to Vesuvius. This remarkable small gouache was painted observing the eruption of March 1828.

9. Lava medals were made from metal moulds inserted into the lava. They were commemorative items and souvenirs; more than seventy survive in the collections of the Vesuvius Observatory. This medal celebrated Vesuvius's chief guide, Salvatore Madonna.

10. A constellation of friends' signatures from 31 March 1828. They are annotated by Malmedye of Liège who returned to the volcano on 22 February 1829 and fondly recalled his friends.

11. The feast for Crown Prince Frederick William of Prussia to celebrate his absent wife's birthday. The view is from outside the hermitage looking northward towards the Bay of Naples. August Kopisch's watercolour depicts the table arranged with garlands and a picture of the Princess shortly before the guests arrive. The only figure is the hermit seated on the right.

12. A nineteenth-century gouache of the Bay of Naples and Vesuvius, typical of the many images sold to visitors and collectors.

13. One of many versions of Vesuvian eruptions painted by the French artist resident in Naples, Pierre-Jacques Volaire.

14. The insouciance of the savant and the gentleman observer in the face of volcanic power. Volaire portrays the onlookers as fearless.

15. The flight of the *lazzaroni*. In direct contrast with his portrayal of fearless gentlemen, Volaire depicts terrified and superstitious Neapolitan *lazzaroni* fleeing the eruption.

16. Sir William Hamilton explains the volcano to King Ferdinand and Queen Maria Carolina, the monarchs of Naples, 11 May 1771. The creator of this image, Pietro Fabris, can be seen sketching, seated on a rock on the lower left.

17. Vesuvius singled out. Despite its small size, Vesuvius is distinguished by its red colouring and as the only erupting volcano in the centre of a cross-section of much larger mountains and volcanoes.

18. A lava medal supporting the revolution of 1820, made by the Catalan geologist Carlos de Gimbernat. These medals ruined Gimbernat's career and drove him out of Naples.

19. Portrait of Déodat de Dolomieu, the French aristocratic geologist widely regarded as the leading expert on volcanoes in the late eighteenth century.

20. Bust of Teodoro Monticelli, secretary of the Academy of Sciences in Naples, the most important promoter of Vesuvius as a site of scientific investigation in the early nineteenth century.

21. The Temple of Isis in Pompeii as a ruin, and as imagined before the 79 CE eruption. Such before-and-after images were common in the representations of the Romantic era.

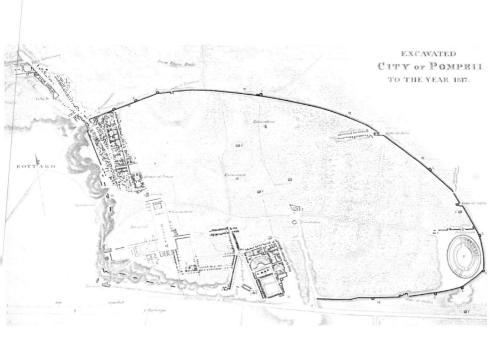

22. Sir William Gell's 1819 map of Pompeii. Note the large area of the city that remained unexcavated.

23. The aristocratic French Grand Tourist Pierre Bergeret de Grancourt and his protégé, the painter Jean-Honoré Fragonard, together with their wives contemplate a skeleton at Pompeii.

24. This painting is based on an elaborate report of the discovery of the skeletons of a woman and three children in 1812 by the French antiquary Aubin-Louis Millin. It is a characteristic mix of accuracy and licence. The jewellery precisely follows the excavation report, but it places the family in a chariot rather than an alcove, and adds a mirror, chest and lyre, signs of wealth but also symbols of human vanity.

25. Karl Briullov's huge painting, executed between 1827 and 1833, was exhibited in Rome, Milan, Paris and St Petersburg, and may have inspired Bulwer-Lytton's *Last Days of Pompeii*.

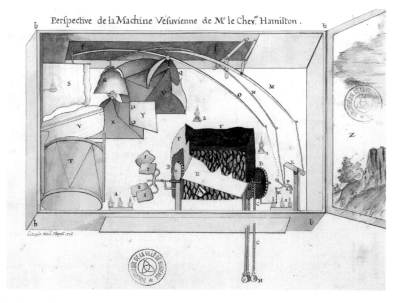

26. Sir William Hamilton's attempt to replicate the sound and motion of Vesuvius. It was fronted by a transparent version of Pietro Fabris's Plate 38 in Hamilton's sumptuous and lavishly illustrated publication *Campi Phlegraei* (see Plate 16). Built in the 1770s, it used candlelight and a clockwork-powered drum to simulate the movement and sound of a Vesuvian eruption.

27. Philippe de Loutherbourg's Eidophusikon, a machine that uses the same techniques of clockwork and changing light as those employed by Hamilton to create the illusion of a Vesuvian eruption.

28. Alessandro Sanquirico's stage design for the final scene in Pacini's opera *L'ultimo giorno di Pompeii*, 'The Eruption of Vesuvius'. A staging of the opera was seen by Karl Briullov and may have helped inspire his painting (see Plate 25).

The pre-unification characterisation of a backward south had both a historical and geographical dimension. On the one hand it was often presented as a fall from grace, as decline or decay from a magnificent classical civilisation, prosperous, martial and often free, that had been Etruscan, Greek or Roman. But it was also seen as a failure to embrace the future, to modernise. As Goethe put it, 'Italy ... has lagged very badly behind other countries with respect to mechanics and technology, which are after all the basis for a more modern and comfortable way of life.'[27] Nature and geography were implicated in this criticism. Commentators as far back as antiquity had emphasised that the climate and soil of the Campagna made the region into a paradise, a site of natural plenitude and abundance whose fertility readily yielded the fruits of the earth. Yet poverty abounded. Enlightenment philosophers, most notably the Baron de Montesquieu in his *The Spirit of the Laws*, attributed this situation to the climate. Cold northern climes made men more vigorous, the harshness of their environment encouraged industry – in some ways made it necessary for survival – while warm climates encouraged laziness or enabled indolence.[28] This cold/hot north/south dichotomy extended to politics: vigorous northerners were more freedom-loving, while easy-going southerners acquiesced in their servitude. Montesquieu's analysis was frequently applied both to Italy as a whole, and to the south of the peninsula in particular. Though often criticised – most notably by David Hume and other members of the Scottish Enlightenment who explained north–south differences as the result of different sorts of political arrangements – and sometimes qualified, Montesquieu's views were deeply embedded in much of the writing on Italy and Naples in the eighteenth and early nineteenth centuries. They reinforced a sense of superiority of the (usually northern) traveller, and the feeling that Neapolitans were an undeveloped people, close to nature, more emotional, less rational, more primitive, embodying an uncultivated human nature.

The natural metaphors used to describe the crowds in the city reinforced this view: they moved in 'shoals', like fish in the Bay. The

Scottish painter Jane Waldie compared her entry into the city of Naples, with its 'brilliancy and noise . . . [that] dazzled and confounded our senses', to the move from 'silent enjoyment of the mildest beauties of nature' into 'the midst of a living volcano – a burning mountain – emitting eruptions, and flames, and smoke and smells, and noises, on all sides and without end'.[29] For some, like the historian Thomas Babington Macaulay, Naples was a modern city: 'It is the only place in Italy that has seemed to me to have the same sort of vitality which you find in all the great English ports and cities. Rome, Pisa, and Genoa are mere corpses, dead and gone . . . Naples is full of life and bustle.' But it was this view that Forsyth's guide sought to rebut, contrasting the London crowd, 'uniform and intelligible: it is a double line in quick motion – it is the crowd of business' with 'the crowd of Naples' that consisted 'in a general tide rolling up and down, and in the middle of this tide a hundred eddies of men. Here [in London] you are swept on by the current, there you are wheeled round by the vortex.'[30] The crowd, he insists, is turbulent but not progressive, a part of nature not culture. The volatility of the landscape, and of Vesuvius in particular, was seen as shaping a distinctive Neapolitan temperament: boisterous, voluble, theatrical, unpredictable, easily angered and quickly appeased, one that eschewed the calculating rationality of the northern European. Climate, economy and character were all connected.

In her vivid and exuberant account of Naples in her three-volume study of Italy, Lady Morgan, playwright, essayist, Irish radical, feminist and proponent of Italian unification, described the essence of the city thus:

> Its great, its distinguishing feature is the singular and sublime character stamped on its region by Nature! In this point of view Naples stands alone; taking her perilous position on the brink of destruction, reposing her luxurious villas on the edge of a crater, and raising her proud towers on the shifting surface of an

eternally active volcano. Such fatal but inevitable engines rarely allure the proximity of man: they are found lording the desolation where human interests end, amidst the ice deserts of Kamtschatka, the altitudes of the Andes, the outskirts of the world; but the gay, brilliant, fantastic city, which pours its restless, busy, bustling population at the foot of Vesuvius, with an electric fluid for its atmosphere, and rivers of flame, and showers of ashes, for its ordinary phenomena – such a city is well worth visiting, though it had not one attraction besides that of its awful and uncertain site.[31]

In Morgan's telling it is almost impossible to draw a boundary between the city and the volcano, to judge whether its 'bustling population' is some kind of natural or social force; what we are led to understand, however, is that the city and the volcano are dazzling, hazardous and in constant motion. She captures the positive, if somewhat contradictory, attractions of the region to the outsider.

This enthusiasm was entirely compatible with the view that southern Italy was backward; indeed it was exactly this that made it attractive to the northern traveller eager to escape the strict constraints of measured deliberation and to explore new feelings and experiences. The barely clad but voluble *lazzaroni*, the pageantry not just of the popular rituals and ceremonies but of everyday life, the noise of the city – commented on by almost every visitor – the ubiquitous filth, poverty and exuberance: all seemed quaint and picturesque to the orderly northerner. Little wonder that, as Nelson Moe remarks in his study of 'the southern question', the northern commentator's vision 'alternates between denunciation of backwardness and exultations of picturesqueness'.[32] They were two sides of the same coin.

Neapolitan and visiting painters did much to create the image of the Neapolitan picturesque, especially in small-scale works in watercolour, tempura and gouache, media that conveyed the vividness of the Neapolitan scene. Though tempura and gouache had a long history, they became the media of choice for Romantic Naples.

TRAVEL WRITING, POLITICS AND REVOLUTION

Used on paper or cardboard, drying with great rapidity, and enabling an image with high gloss and transparency, they could produce the brilliant colours and evoke the extraordinary light that flooded the Bay of Naples. Among their early practitioners were Pietro Fabris (1740–92), born in England of Italian ancestry and often employed by Sir William Hamilton, and Jacob Philipp Hackert (1733–1807), a German trained in Berlin and Paris who became a court painter to the Habsburg Neapolitan Queen Carolina in 1786. The development of Naples' distinctive style of landscape art was always an international affair. In 1819, two schools of drawing were founded there, one by the German Jakob Wilhelm Huber (1787–1871), the other by the Dutchman Antonie Sminck Pitloo (1790–1837); both had a decisive influence on their students, many of whom were drawn from the local military school of topography.

Fabris, Hackert and two Neapolitan painters, Alessandro D'Anna and Saverio Della Gatta, were all to produce striking paintings of Vesuvian eruptions in 1779 and 1794 as well as a great many landscapes of the Bay, usually populated with carefully rendered human figures.[33] Their landscapes and genre painting shaped the production of painting in Naples for more than a generation. Their work was patronised by the Bourbon court and served a wealthy clientele, both Neapolitan and foreign, but was the peak of a much larger mountain of work that catered to the growing number of foreign visitors to Naples in the nineteenth century.

Quick to execute, relatively inexpensive, portable, whether in the luggage of the returning visitor or of the itinerant artist, these brightly coloured works were distributed in large numbers. They portrayed the Bay, local customs, festivals and costumes, as well as Vesuvian eruptions. They varied enormously in quality, from the more impressionistic and much-admired works of Giacinto Gigante and his close friend Achille Vianelli of the so-called Posillipo School, through the recognisable *vedute* of Luigi Gentile and the vivid Vesuvian eruptions of Camillo De Vito, to a vast tranche of anonymous pictures, some brilliantly rendered but many more appearing like shop work that came off a production line, produced in a standard format, usually measuring 35 × 50 cm (14 × 19 in).[34] The images were also to be found on fans, ceramics and other tourist memorabilia. Francis Napier, the British diplomat, captured this market and its consumers in his snobbish but revealing *Notes on Modern Painting at Naples*:

> For the wanderers of every country, whose fortune is too slender for the acquisition of superior works, or whose intelligence is incapable of appreciating their value, there is a copious manufactory of views repeated cheaply from good originals, and preserving with tolerable fidelity the tints and outlines of a scene, which the rudest pencil may scarcely obliterate or disguise. These productions, which give bread to many necessitous painters, and pleasure to many uncritical travellers, may be viewed with charity, even by the cultivated eye, as the ministers of fading memory.[35]

According to statistics compiled for the Seventh Congress of Italian Scientists held in Naples in 1845, there were by then 148 painters, 72 draftsmen (*disegnatori*), 155 engravers and 48 lithographers in the city.[36] These artists, though of very different abilities and skills, shaped the international image of Naples in the period. They depicted pellucid skies, shoeless *lazzaroni* and costumed street vendors and rural labourers, a rich popular religious culture, sweeping vistas and a violently erupting volcano; in doing so, they attracted foreign artists drawn to Naples less by its famous baroque art than by the opportunity to paint its people, sights and scenery *en plein air*. It is hard to find a foreign artist in Italy in the early nineteenth century who did not spend some time in the region of Vesuvius. If they were not sketching views of the volcano from the city, or depicting its street life, they climbed the volcano, painting it in oil, watercolour or gouache, or foraged on its slopes and visited nearby villages, sketching the local landscape, peasantry, bandits and colourful religious festivals.

Though many of these artists looked on the *lazzaroni* of the city and the labourers in the countryside with a sympathetic eye, celebrating the diversity of people's appearance and costume and the richness of their local traditions, they nevertheless reinforced the stereotype of the Kingdom of Naples as backward and its people as unsophisticated and unmodern.

This northern vision of the south and its inhabitants was part of a much larger trend to be found in the travel writings of the period, many of which were constructed around an idea of historical development and enlightened progress, in which a core group of (northern) European countries represented the most advanced, free and commercial societies and the ideal to which other more distant and recently explored societies should aspire. The scope of this vision was not European but global: as the politician and philosopher Edmund Burke put it in a letter to the Scottish historian William Robertson, 'now the Great Map of Mankind is unrolled at once: and there is no state or Gradation of barbarism, and no mode of refinement which we have not at the same instant under our view.'[37] Geography revealed a chequered history of development. It was possible to ask 'what time is this place?' and to conclude that Naples had not yet arrived in the modern present.

This all-encompassing vision, of which Italy was only a part, was embodied in the early nineteenth century in the massive collections of travel literature published in English, French and German. John Pinkerton's vast *A General Collection of the Best and Most Interesting Voyages and Travels in All Parts of the World: Many of which are now first translated into English* appeared in seventeen volumes between 1808 and 1814. Its geographical scope was remarkable, ranging from the Arctic to Australasia, including one volume on Italy, and ending with an annotated bibliography of travel writings that runs to a staggering 255 pages. Similar projects were launched in France, notably Gilles Boucher de la Richarderie, *Bibliothèque universelle des voyages, ou notice complète et raisonnée de tous les voyages anciens et modernes dans les différentes parties du monde* published in six volumes in 1808 and, in a rather different register, in Germany with Eberhard August Wilhelm von Zimmermann's *Taschenbuch der Reisen* which appeared annually between 1802 and 1813.

Collected histories such as Pinkerton's imposed a universal grid of time and space upon both nature and culture, an imperialising discourse that quite explicitly saw travel writing and the travelling that made it possible as a form of global conquest. This travel literature constructed what the anthropologist Johannes Fabian describes as 'a system of coordinates (emanating of course from a real centre – the Western metropolis) in which given societies of all times and places may be plotted in terms of relative distance from the present'.[38] The attitude is captured in the work of the French jurist and philosopher Joseph Marie Degérando, *Considération sur les méthodes à suivre dans les observations des Peuples Sauvages* (1800): 'The philosophical traveller, sailing to the ends of the earth, is in fact travelling in time; he is exploring the past; every step he makes is the passage of an age.'[39] Like the voyager moving towards the end of the world, the traveller moving southwards through the Italian peninsula moved backwards in time.

The view that the most useful way to think about Naples was in terms of its backwardness invited rebuttal, for instance from the Neapolitan aristocratic revolutionary Giuseppe Ricciardi. He spent years in exile in Paris and London, was not impressed by the deep inequalities in England and France, and maintained that the Neapolitan sciences, arts and letters were every bit as advanced as in northern and eastern Europe.[40] His periodical *Il progresso delle scienze, delle lettere e delle arti* (1832–47), published in Naples, went out of its way to print extended summaries of the intellectual achievements of the kingdom.[41] And Ricciardi made a fair case. Too often northern European accounts of Naples ignored the exceptionally rich culture of Enlightenment Naples. The city hosted the first university chair of political economy in Europe, included a reading public consisting of lawyers, administrators, university teachers and reform-minded nobles, and published Enlightenment classics locally translated into Italian from French and English. From the mid-eighteenth century, Antonio Genovesi, who held the chair in political economy, and the many pupils and followers he encouraged, fostered the investigation of the role and nature of commercial society, the importance of general education, and the development of public opinion. The aim was to get university teachers and lawyers to engage in a debate that would have practical consequences for the kingdom. Ricciardi's publications in the early nineteenth century were part of a tradition that extended back to the mid-eighteenth century of creating a history and genealogy of Neapolitan reformist inquiry.[42]

As many commentators have pointed out, some Neapolitan intellectuals, though they were impatient at the crude and misinformed views of many foreign commentators on Naples, were complicit in the contrast between north and south. In making the case for improvement, these reformers looked to other societies and economies, but they were aware that the problem of underdevelopment was by no means uniquely Neapolitan. At the same time, they pointed to specific legal, political and economic practices – the endurance of southern feudalism before its abolition by the French, the rigidity of certain institutions, the absence of proper elementary education – as the greatest obstacles to progress. In their analyses they were closer to David Hume than the Baron de Montesquieu, more sociological than geographical.

The perspective of external critics, it needs to be stressed, was often the expression of a set of feelings – anger, irritation, alarm and incomprehension – seeking to control or subordinate what they thought of as an unruly place and disorderly populace, and to bend them to their will. During the periods of French occupation (1799 and 1806–15) their officials railed against the intractability of the populace; throughout the Romantic era British diplomats complained about the resistance to British commercial privilege and dominance. The Austrian chancellor and orchestrator of counter-revolutionary Europe, Prince Metternich, famously characterised Neapolitans as 'a semi-barbarous people of absolute ignorance and boundless cruelty, hot-blooded as the Africans, a people who can neither read nor write, whose last word is the dagger'.[43] Yet this was in 1820, at precisely the moment when an almost bloodless revolt established a regime that had a written constitution and that, for all its problems, was only ended by Austrian bayonets. At the very same time, the British envoy in Naples, William A'Court, wrote a dispatch to Lord Castlereagh in London conceding that the Neapolitans had much to be discontented about, but described them as incapable of governing themselves. How to save 'this beautiful country from itself?', he asked rhetorically. Then he provided his answer: 'The volcano [the Constitutional regime] which threatens everyone's safety, must be extinguished at any cost.'[44]

What is striking, whether reading the frustrated and angry responses of diplomats and politicians or the blander comments of foreign travellers, is the sense of the inscrutability and inaccessibility of Naples and its peoples, the difficulty of pinning down a natural and social environment that was constantly in motion. This is the obverse of the need to stamp them with a fixed set of characteristics; it revealed a weakness and failing on the part of the powerful outside observer. As Henry Swinburne (1743–1803) explained in his *Travels in the Two Sicilies*:

When allowances are made for difference of seasons, diversity of studies, occasional information, and many other accidental helps, we shall find an ample field still remain [sic] for our curiosity to range in: to say nothing of the revolutions, moral, physical, and political, effectuated by the hand of Time, which, however slowly and imperceptibly it may perform its operations, acts with irresistible force upon the state both of nature and of man.[45]

These general reflections, Swinburne thought, were especially applicable 'in the southern parts of Italy, where the elements ferment with more than ordinary violence, where changes in government have succeeded each other with uncommon rapidity, the variations are more precipitate, the effects more striking'. This meant that 'the face of things has been so much altered, that the descriptions given by the ancient classics can seldom interfere with those of a modern writer.' Even before the tumultuous changes of regime that racked Naples and Europe with the outbreak of the French Revolution, Naples was already understood as exceptionally volatile and inscrutable. Forty years later, Lady Morgan put it more pithily: 'The ruins of time and man are mingled with the fragments of an overwrought creation.' Nature was 'changing, combining, exhausting, renewing, and recreating, but never destroying'.[46] (Morgan was a liberal and an optimist.) For the outside observer, the region embodied a fecund unpredictability that was unquestionably volcanic. It was extremely difficult for them to find the sort of linear, progressive history that they wished to stamp on Naples, its people and the volcano.

The attitudes of Neapolitans themselves towards '*il nostro Vesuvio*', the source of this unpredictability, were complex. It was the symbol of the city and kingdom – almost all of the kingdom's rulers were painted with the smouldering volcano in the background; it was built into the civic and religious life of most Neapolitans through the story of the city's leading patron saint, San Gennaro, whose blood, preserved in a vial in the cathedral, flowed, like the volcano's lava, three times a year. The volcano was a source of both fear and pleasure, the destroyer of homes and crops, a replenisher of the earth, a symbol of the country, an ally that brought curious wealthy foreigners to Naples. It was literally embedded in the city, its rocks and stones providing the pavements and streets on which its people travelled daily, its buildings, as we have seen, constructed of volcanic rock. Even its darkest moments, its savage eruptions in anger, had their bright side; all but the worst eruptions attracted visitors and onlookers.

Though always a clear and present danger, a persistent reminder of the arbitrary and unpredictable nature of human existence, it was also a source of local pride – an integral part of the unique vista that Stendhal and others declared the most beautiful in the world.

It is notable that outside observers were often confused about Neapolitan attitudes towards the volcano. The frequent assertions that Neapolitans were deeply indifferent to Vesuvius and its activities were accompanied by comments on how knowledgeable even humble local people were about the volcano; remarks about the fearfulness and superstition surrounding the mountain appear alongside comments on the affection in which the volcano was held. Attempts to somehow wrestle Neapolitan attitudes towards Vesuvius onto a Procrustean bed were doomed to failure.

Unpredictable violence: nature and politics in Naples and Europe

Naples and Sicily had their fair share of disasters in the eighteenth and nineteenth centuries. Of the 130,000 deaths in Europe from earthquakes between 1693 and 1786, nearly all occurred in Sicily and on the southern Italian mainland. Though the memory of the Lisbon earthquake of 1755 has eclipsed those in Sicily and Calabria, casualty levels in Sicily in 1693 and again in 1783, extending also into Calabria, were every bit as high as in Portugal. Lisbon, however, was one of Europe's largest cities, at the crossroads of the New World and Europe. The publicity that surrounded the Lisbon earthquake was unprecedented, a European catastrophe as media event that cultivated new forms of scientific inquiry and a more sympathetic and emotive account of natural disaster.[47] But the extent and nature of the suffering in Italy was just as great.

Other disasters were equally devastating. The famine and plague of 1763–4 killed between 30,000 and 50,000 people in Naples and perhaps 200,000 throughout the kingdom. These catastrophes dwarfed the paltry number of victims of volcanic action. The greatest number of deaths resulting from a Vesuvian eruption in the period was an estimated eighteen victims during the spectacular eruption of 1794. Before then, there had been no significant death toll from either Etna or Vesuvius since the Vesuvian eruption of 1631, the largest since 79 CE, which took approximately 4,000 lives. In more recent times the eruption of 1906 killed 216 victims.[48]

Vesuvius, then, was not a major modern killer. This is not to trivialise the power of volcanic eruptions. Within the Romantic era, two eruptions – Laki in Iceland (1784) and Tambora in modern Indonesia (1815) – had devastating effects and caused a massive loss of life. The nine-month-long Laki eruption is thought to have been responsible for about 10,000 deaths through disease and famine in Iceland. Tambora's eruption, the most powerful in recorded human history, is thought to have killed about 10,000 to 12,000 victims in its immediate aftermath, but because of its impact on global weather patterns – the 'year without a summer' – may have caused a further 50,000 deaths, or even more, as a result of disease and harvest failure.[49] And on the Bay of Naples itself, we should not trivialise the repeated, corrosive effect of the regular eruptions on the life of those who lived in the shadow of the volcano and whose homes, small-holdings and vineyards were frequently damaged or destroyed. Many outside observers were struck by the determination with which farmers and the residents of nearby towns like Torre Del Greco patiently and, in a way that recognised the cycles of destruction and abundance, painstakingly rebuilt their dwellings and replanted the land. We have already seen Hester Piozzi's incredulous response to her conversation with a woman on the slopes of Vesuvius. She found it hard to understand how someone could have been so accepting of their fate.[50] To an outside observer, thinking in terms of risk and progress and fetishising the ownership of land rather than its use, this seemed foolish, but to the Neapolitans it was part of the rhythms of life.

These losses, no matter how frequent or powerfully felt, were not sufficient for Vesuvius to be recognised as a catastrophic force. As we shall see, archaeology did that: as the buried cities slowly revealed their secrets, and especially after the 1760s, when more and more bodies were found, it became much easier to imagine a Vesuvian disaster of epic proportions. The literary, historical and visual imagination, fuelled by the sympathetic sensibility first awakened by the Lisbon earthquake, fed this imagining, so that by the mid-nineteenth century it would be seriously suggested that the eruption of 79 CE had in fact killed 250,000 people. Antique Vesuvius came to define the volcano's modern identity.

In the Age of Revolutions, human disasters were every bit as devastating, violent and shocking as their natural counterparts. In trying to make sense of the radical political changes in the late eighteenth and early nineteenth centuries, contemporaries had frequent recourse to analogies or metaphors that drew on the forces of nature. Because of their unprecedented and therefore inexplicable nature, human calamities were described and explained as if they were natural disasters – floods, inundations, plagues, earthquakes and volcanic eruptions – events that transcended human agency. Vincenzo Cuoco began his influential account of the abortive revolution in Naples in 1799 by asserting, 'The great political revolutions occupy the same place in the history of man as extraordinary phenomena do in the history of nature.'[51] The volcano, naturally all-powerful, capricious, unpredictable and potentially devastating, was a compelling (and obvious) analogy to the violent social and political forces that swept across Europe and beyond. When an urbane essayist, moralist and member of the Académie Française, Pierre-Marc-Gaston the Duc de Lévis, ascended Vesuvius in September 1827 the experience immediately reminded him of the analogy between revolutionary and volcanic force.[52] An aristocratic liberal supporter of the French Revolution in its early days, he soon became disillusioned and in August 1792 fled into exile in England. In 1795 he took part in the abortive Quibéron expedition and royalist invasion of France, in which he was seriously wounded, though he escaped the fate of many of his aristocratic colleagues, who were summarily executed after they surrendered.[53] His mother and two sisters were also victims of the Revolution, ending up on the guillotine. As he watched the burning volcano, he recalled the terrible destruction he had witnessed and reflected on the human willingness to countenance such enormities.

The experiences and trauma that the Duc de Lévis had suffered – revolution, exile, civil war with its atrocities, the loss of close family and many friends – were far from exclusively French misfortunes. The revolution in France had ramifications throughout Europe. It inaugurated a long period of political perturbation in Naples marked by regime change, internal strife and foreign invasion. The immediate aftermath of the French Revolution, especially the execution of Louis XVI and his wife, Marie Antoinette, the sister of Queen Carolina, led the Neapolitan monarchs to turn their backs on any species of reform while it simultaneously encouraged reformers and radicals in the kingdom, who plotted in the 1790s to overthrow the absolutist regime. There were over 400 arrests of Jacobin conspirators in 1794. In 1799 the French invaded and set up a republic, chiefly supported by a liberal elite. Even before they had arrived in Naples, the flight of the monarchs, courtesy of the British navy and Admiral Nelson, to Palermo had unleashed chaos, killing and disorder. Those thought to be sympathetic to the French and to reform were singled out and sometimes killed. The Duca della Torre, an enlightened liberal, chemist and expert on Vesuvius, was murdered with his brother, and his house, Vesuvian and art collections, and laboratory destroyed.

The republic barely lasted six months, torn apart by civil strife, with atrocities perpetrated on all sides and not least by the French army, whose policy of 'military execution' systematically killed the inhabitants of loyalist towns and villages. The regime was incapable of survival without French military support. The republic fell to the counter-revolutionary forces of the Santa Fede (holy faith) in the summer of that year, triggering a series of reprisals, some in the form of judicial punishment and execution (3,818 tried, 216 executed, 492 exiled; the rest were given lesser sentences), others through summary justice at the hands of the loyalists. Aristocrats, lawyers and university professors were prominent victims. The pivot back to reactionary absolutism did not last long. By 1806 the French were back, establishing administrative autarchy and abolishing feudalism under the rule of Joseph Bonaparte and Joachim Murat. The Bourbons returned in 1815, but were forced to accept a constitutional monarchy in 1820–1 until rescued by an invading Austrian army. Minor plots and conspiracies continued until the unsuccessful risings of 1848. The prisons and dungeons on the volcanic islands of the Mediterranean were filled with political prisoners. Though there were some short periods of stability, the tension between the radical *carbonari* – the secret societies of the period, whether revolutionary or constitutionalist – and those who were terrified that any change signalled immanent revolution, was constant.

War was often civil war, a fight among and between civilian populations, waged not on big battlefields but within the interstices of daily life. Western France (the Vendée), Saint-Domingue in the Caribbean, Spain, the city of Naples in 1799, and Calabria within the Kingdom of Naples all saw brutal conflicts, cycles of atrocity and reprisal, in which armed civilians fought one another and regular troops in a guerilla war (a new term for a new type of warfare) which often involved the rape, torture, mutilation and summary execution of prisoners and civilians, the wholesale massacre of local communities, the burning and pillaging of towns and villages. No conflict was more brutal than the republican suppression of the royalist revolt in the conservative Vendée in the west of France. Between 220,000 and 250,000 civilians were slaughtered in the years 1793–4. And no conflict is better known than the Spanish guerilla war of 1808–14, thanks to the bleak and despairing intaglio prints of the 'disasters of war' by Goya. But the war between the French and the bands of guerillas and bandits in Calabria between 1805 and 1811, though it never reached the scale of the Vendée (some 5,500 bandits were killed, executed or imprisoned), was aptly compared to the events in Spain that prompted Goya's masterpieces. French prisoners were roasted alive and then fed to other French captives; in retaliation whole towns were razed to the ground; massacres of civilians occurred in half a dozen towns; prisoners were routinely executed.[54] As Ridolfo Ianelli, a Neapolitan who supported the French and fought against the partisans, put it: 'This is a new type of war against all decency that makes good men tremble.'[55]

Many of these conflicts occurred because of foreign invasion or regime change. Who ruled and according to what rules changed often. There were continuities of both personnel and practice, but also veering changes, confusion and unclear expectations. The future all too often seemed indeterminate or frighteningly uncertain. The republics and monarchies established by the French revolutionaries and by Napoleon were extraordinarily divisive – welcomed by some, especially liberal elites, loathed by others, notably the hierarchy of the Catholic Church and the peasantry – and the expectations and revulsion they provoked remained a bone of contention long after Napoleon was finally dispatched to St Helena. The French occupation of the Italian peninsula provoked popular risings not just in the Abruzzi, Molise and Calabria, within the Kingdom of Naples, but throughout the peninsula – in the north in Piedmont, Lombardy and the Veneto, and in central Italy in Tuscany, Umbria, Le Marche and Lazio. It ignited or reignited long-standing conflicts – between rulers and peasants, reformers and reactionaries, philosophers and the clerical hierarchy, and between local jurisdictions and central power, whether foreign or not. It often gave them a new, burning intensity.

Even with the triumph of the counter-revolution in 1815, these conflicts remained unresolved; the restoration of the *ancien régime* was never absolute, even when there were ultra-reactionaries who hoped for a complete reversion. The experiences of Naples – occupation by the French, the attempt to impose Napoleonic administrative and legal uniformity, the raising of liberal, constitutionalist hopes among minor aristocrats and members of the professions, including the army and some of the clergy while at the same time reinforcing a sense of nationalism – were repeated across Europe.

The revolutionary volcano

The intensity of the violence, its capriciousness and ferocity made it easy to compare with the punishing forces of nature. Volcanic eruptions were particularly favoured because of their spectacular nature, and because – like earthquakes – they revealed powerful but hidden forces which disrupted what might appear as tranquillity. Thus when Napoleon overthrew the Directory and seized power in France on 18th Brumaire (9 November) in 1799, he told the Council of Five Hundred, 'Representatives, you are not surrounded by ordinary circumstances. You are sitting on a volcano.' Bonaparte's remarks drew on what had become a familiar metaphor during the Revolution, that of the volcano as a revolutionary force for change.[56]

On 18 October 1793, two days after the guillotining of Marie Antoinette, the Théâtre de la République in Paris staged a new play entitled *The Last Judgment of Kings* by the republican atheist Sylvain Maréchal.[57] The play is set on a volcanic island – a smouldering summit can be seen at the back of the stage – inhabited by a single French political exile, a victim of royal persecution, who has been stranded for twenty years. He has taught its 'savage' inhabitants not to fear the volcano or to countenance monarchs or priests. A rock bears the inscription, 'It is better to have for a neighbour | A volcano than a King | Liberty . . . Equality'. A party of sans-culottes, republicans from the different nations of Europe, brings monarchs from the Holy Roman Empire, Spain, Poland, Prussia, England, Naples,

Russia and Sardinia, along with the Pope, onto the island stage. The parade of shackled rulers was almost invariably the most popular part of the play. The sans-culottes enumerate their monarchs' crimes and failings and ask 'nature', that is the volcano, to complete the removal of hereditary monarchy and the priesthood: 'Hurry to finish the work of the sans-culottes; breathe fire on this scum of society, and make kings return forever to the void from which they will never have to leave.' Incapable of productive labour or of feeding themselves, the rulers soon begin to quarrel; the Pope and Catherine the Great exchange blows, the monarchs scramble and fight over a last crust of black bread. (As Maréchal explained in his commentary, this was payback: the stage had often mocked the conduct of the plebs; now the plebs could watch and mock the conduct of kings.) But these regal altercations are abruptly ended by a volcanic eruption, a massive onstage explosion, that consumes them all. As the stage directions stipulate: 'The volcano begins its eruption; it throws rocks onto the stage, hot coals . . . There is an explosion. The fire besieges the rulers on all sides; they fall, swallowed in the entrails of the half-opened earth. The volcano had done its job.'[58]

The Last Judgment of Kings was no one-off wonder. It had the regime's backing; the Committee of Public Safety granted it funds to buy saltpetre and gunpowder for the volcanic explosions, 10,000 copies of the play were printed, and an edition of 6,000 copies was distributed among the troops in the revolutionary army. The play was also performed in many provincial cities (how many is not quite clear), with performances in Lille, Metz, Le Mans and Grenoble. It was only the most conspicuous instance of the frequently reiterated view, especially common in the years of the Terror, that revolution was a natural phenomenon, albeit facilitated by human intervention, and that volcanic eruptions were the perfect model of natural, revolutionary processes. The play, as the literary critic David McCallam makes clear, portrayed the volcano as a revolutionary force, even beyond its power as metaphor.[59] By destroying monarchy and the papacy it created a new revolutionary order. The volcano had, as Maréchal's title with its clever, tongue-in-cheek allusion to Christian theology makes clear, administered the last rites and final judgment on the *ancien régime*.

But the volcano was more than just a killer of kings. What made volcanic action an especially potent metaphor was the widespread recognition that volcanic eruption was not just destructive, but regenerative. In the hands of revolutionaries like Joseph Fouché and the Abbé Grégoire, the rather bland remark of the English historian Thomas Babington Macaulay, that 'the richest vineyards and the sweetest flowers always grow on the soil which has been fertilised by the fiery deluge of a volcano',[60] became a rallying cry for the purgative destruction that they believed necessary to make a better world. As Grégoire declaimed during the crisis of 1792, 'The nations are throwing themselves in the path of liberty. The volcano is about to break forth, which will transform the globe.'[61] Two years later, another popular play staged in Paris, *Barra, ou La mère républicaine*, made the message clear:

> The revolutions of governments, like great crises in nature, topple everything, in order to regenerate everything. Sorrow, no doubt, for those who are struck by the explosions of one or the other volcano! But, while children and fools hit the wall that they blindly collide with, wise men submit with grace to the imperious law of necessity. Happy! For from the midst of chaos we are plunged into, one can see ... the emergence of order and perfection.[62]

The analogy persisted into the nineteenth century. So when the Catalan geologist Carlos de Gimbernat wanted to celebrate the uprisings and revolutions of 1820 in Spain and Naples, he made stamps to plunge into the soft lava of Vesuvius to make medals to distribute to friends (Plate 18).[63] In the following year, Shelley repeatedly compared volcanic eruptions to revolutionary uprisings.[64]

The poet and supporter of Greek independence Kondratii Ryleev, executed (holding a book of Byron's poems) in July 1826 for his part in the Russian Decembrist plot to force the Tsar to adopt a constitution, was described by a friend as one whose eloquence meant that 'his words flowed like a stream of lava'. He wrote in 1824, 'The peoples [of] . . . Western and Southern Europe have made attempts to throw off the yoke of despotism. The kings united and by force tried to suppress aspirations to liberty. They triumphed, and now a deathly silence hangs over Europe, but it is like the temporary silence of Vesuvius.'[65] Radical political change would inevitably re-emerge like the subterranean forces that poured forth in a Vesuvian eruption.

In short, the connection between volcanoes, Vesuvius and revolution became a commonplace, even amongst those who feared the return of revolutionary vigour. This was especially true after the Restorations of 1815. The European rebellions and revolutions of 1820, 1830 and 1848, indeed any threat of democracy or popular revolt, were all compared to volcanic eruptions. Tocqueville's famous and prescient remark made in January 1848, 'I believe that at the present moment we are slumbering on a volcano', had by then become a cliché. The smouldering and sometimes quiet volcano seemed very much like the hidden, simmering political energies in favour of radicalism and reform that always threatened to rupture the fragile surface of the early nineteenth-century conservative political consensus. Thus the historian Jules Michelet in his *History of the French Revolution* looked back to 1789: 'What were then the subterranean revolutions of the earth, and what incalculable forces fought each other inside it, which made this mass raise the mountains, pierce the rocks, split the marble strata, and shoot forth to the surface.'[66] Michelet went further. In his book *The Mountain*, written in the 1860s, he argued that conflicting versions of the earth's development were shaped by the political experience of savants, drawing a direct analogy between political experience and different theories of the earth:

These revolutions [in understanding] of the globe have been in perfect accordance with the political events which simultaneously transpired. They were singularly modelled on the character of the two generations who succeeded each other in this same half century. Men who had been present at the terrible eruption of the revolutionary volcano, at the catastrophes of the great wars, at the national outbursts of 1813, at the immense earthquake in which the Napoleonic empire was swallowed up – could discover nothing else but violent cataclysm in the primeval history of the globe. They examined with the eyes, the same eyes which had witnessed these political events.

But these largely European geologists and mineralogists were challenged, in Michelet's view, by British savants: 'Immovable England, which had not experienced our great social convulsions, judged the globe from a different point of view. What had she seen in her own bosom? A progressive constitution, built up gradually without violent change, a well-balanced government undergoing little modification.' Hence their commitment to 'peaceful transformations', their suppression of 'the revolutionary in Nature, and their decree that the Earth shall perform all her operations without violent excesses; that insensibly, through a vast period of years, she shall modify and transform herself.'[67] Michelet's account is, as we shall see, overdrawn and confused, mixing generations and places. But it epitomises the power of the association between political change and the forces of nature.

The analogy between the volcano and revolution, with its implication that the latter was part of a process of purgative regeneration and was therefore ultimately a public good – an interpretation that derived from an Enlightenment idea of erupting volcanoes as benign agents restoring the balance of nature – did not go uncontested. Volcanoes in general, and Vesuvius in particular, were inexorably drawn into political debate. In the early nineteenth century an enlightened and revolutionary vulcanism came to be opposed by a more conservative version that, harking back to Christian ideas of divine punishment of the wicked and the redemption of true believers, saw volcanic action as the reconstitution of a proper natural and political order – a return, not a going forward or rupture. And while the revolutionary volcano was very much a creature of the present – it was erupting or threatening to erupt *now* – the conservative volcano was a creature of the past, whose narrative power was drawn from the eruptive events of 79 CE and their incorporation into a series of fables shaped around the fate of the buried cities and their inhabitants. The volcano was an apt image of the power, caprice, uncertainty and displacement that contemporaries saw as part of the spirit of their age, and Vesuvius, imagined Vesuvius, antique Vesuvius rather than the lavas and rocks on the Campanian shore, became a site of political contestation.

Part IV

Vesuvius and the Earth Sciences

7

VESUVIUS AND VOLCANOES

Vesuvius has produced a kind of scientific fermentation of writings on Vesuvius, and its horrible lava, which will produce philosophical-intellectual eruptions of books, discourses, letters, reports.

Francesco Antonio Astore, 1794[1]

*L**e Corricolo*, written by the French dramatist, journalist and novelist Alexandre Dumas about his visit to Naples in 1835, remains one of the wittiest travel books about the region. In a pause from its breathless dialogue, Dumas turned his attentions to Vesuvius towering over the Bay of Naples. He portrayed the smoking mountain as a brilliant actor whose calculated performance gives it bigger billing than its more physically impressive rivals Etna and Stromboli. 'In nature as in art, in the creations of God as in the work of man, in the volcano as in drama,' Dumas writes, 'alongside real merit there is reputation.' Taking advantage of its 'admirable position and magnificent *mise en scène*', Vesuvius, he records, burst into prominence in 79 CE and followed this up with more than fifty eruptions, making so much noise and smoke that it 'eclipsed' its rivals. Dumas describes the volcano's dramatic first entry – the debut of its 'carrière volcanique' – as 'a master stroke':

> To wrap the countryside and the sea in a dark cloud; to spread terror and night over a vast expanse; to send ashes to Africa, Syria, Egypt; to eliminate two cities such as Pompeii and Herculaneum; to asphyxiate from a distance a philosopher such as [the elder] Pliny and to force his nephew to immortalize the disaster in an admirable letter – you have to admit that's not too bad a beginning for a volcano.

But that was just for starters:

> From that time Vesuvius never neglected anything to justify the fame it had acquired in such a terrible and so unexpected way. Sometimes bright as a mortar flare and vomiting torrents of lava from nine mouths of fire, sometimes pumping up seawater and throwing out bubbling sprays to the point of drowning three thousand people, sometimes crowning a plume of flames that rose in 1779, according to some calculations, to eighteen thousand feet [5,500 metres] in height, its eruptions, which one can follow exactly in a collection of coloured prints, all have different characters and always offer the most grandiose and picturesque views.

Vesuvius, Dumas concluded, 'is not just famous, it's popular'.[2]

Dumas anthropomorphises Vesuvius as an actor, a performer in pursuit of fame, ever ready to play an outlandish trick. The volcano, he implies, adopts diverse characters, offering different performances to hold the attention of its audience, even when they themselves are its victims. Dumas is, of course, mocking the idea that nature exists to do man's bidding, but he also captures how the fame of Vesuvius lies as much in its human as in its natural history. As far as he is concerned the natural feature, the fiery mountain to the south of

Naples, is of no consequence until it bursts onto the human stage in 79 CE. Thereafter, nature performs for man. Though a repeated performance, it is far from stale, enlivening and enriching its history, one that pulls us back inexorably to its Roman point of origin.

By the time that Dumas was writing, nearly all of the world's volcanoes had been identified by European scientists. Claude Nicolas Ordinaire's *Histoire naturelle des volcans*, published in Paris in 1802 and immediately also published in an English translation in London, contained a global map of vulcanism that showed volcanoes in Kamchatka, Japan, Java, Sumatra, Ecuador, Peru and Mexico, as well as those in the Canary Islands and the isle of Bourbon (Réunion) off Madagascar.[3] Beautiful, often hand-coloured atlases and maps, with titles like *Atlas universel*, *A Comprehensive Atlas* or *Comparative View of the Principal Mountains of the World*, published by Marmocchi in Florence, Adam and Charles Black in Edinburgh, James Reynolds in London, Henri Duval in Paris, by the Coltons in New York and by Thomas Bradford in Boston, and all modelled on Alexander von Humboldt's famous cross-sectional maps of the Andes, invited adults and schoolchildren to think globally about volcanoes. Arranging them by continent and relative height, they invariably included a profile of Vesuvius, though at little more than 1,280 metres [4,200 feet] the volcano was dwarfed not only by Etna (over 3,050 metres – 10,000 feet), but by the vast peaks of the South American Andes and of the Siberian Kamchatka peninsula, whose biggest volcano was more than three times as high as its Neapolitan rival. But, paradoxically, early nineteenth-century knowledge about the great volcanoes in Iceland, South America, Asia and the Pacific 'ring of fire' only seems to have enhanced the importance of Naples' neighbour. John Emslie's highly stylised image of mountains and volcanoes that appeared in the popular school book *Atlas of Physical Geography* (1851) depicts Vesuvius as dominated by larger peaks, but it is not overshadowed. On the contrary, Emslie places the volcano at the centre of the image, colouring its slopes and ejecta a brilliant red and gold that pushes other much larger mountains and volcanoes, painted muddy brown and marked only by wisps of white smoke, into the background (Plate 17). For many European readers and viewers, Vesuvius epitom- ised 'the volcano', at a time when, as we shall see, more than two generations of scientific research had elevated volcanic action from a marginal process in the history of the earth to a far more important agent that urgently needed investigation and understanding.

Vesuvius had many advantages over its bigger and more spectacu- lar rivals. It was repeatedly active; it was easy to access; and, though a natural wonder, it had a human history. Today, Vesuvius produces some local weather and a will-o'-the-wisp trail of sulphurous smoke. It has largely been inert since the major eruption of 1944 that coin- cided with the Allied arrival in the Bay of Naples, and which destroyed the famous funicular railway to its summit as well as more than seventy American aircraft based near Pompeii. Since then we have had more than seventy-five years of inactivity. The situation could hardly have been more different in the Romantic era. There were major eruptions in 1760, 1766–7, 1779, 1794, 1822 and 1834, spectacular events (called 'Plinian' after the famous victim of the 79 CE eruption) that produced the vast ash clouds that so attracted artists, lava flows that destroyed property (though they moved too slowly to kill people), and pyroclastic flows and torrential floods that were far more dangerous to human life. But equally important were the ongoing low-level eruptions (usually referred to as Strombolian) that, with occasional breaks after the powerful eruptions of 1766–7 and 1822, meant that the volcano's activity was a constant reminder of its potentially lethal powers. As we can see from Chart 4, from the mid-eighteenth to the mid-nineteenth century, Vesuvius was almost constantly in a state of low-level eruption.

So, as Dumas reminds us, Vesuvius was repeatedly drawing atten- tion to itself, even when its activity was not devastating. It was far more spectacular than it appears today, yet usually not life-threatening. This made it a perfect object for sublime tourism, a place to admire

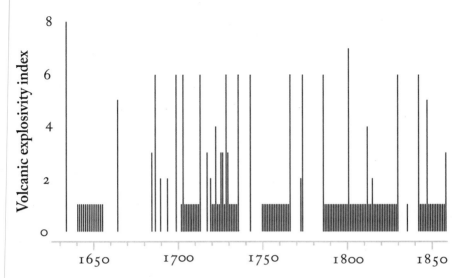

Chart 4. Vesuvian eruptions, 1631–1850.
Note: adapted from Alwyn Scarth, Vesuvius: A Biography, *Princeton NJ, 2009, pp. 231, 258.*

nature and its power, experience the smallness of man, but also to test oneself in the face of nature (knowing that, in all probability, one was not in mortal danger). The experience in 1820 of Lady Morgan was typical. 'The mountain,' she wrote, 'though it never raged with that fury which adds alarm to admiration, was sufficiently active to excite an incessant interest.'[4] Its dynamism made it all the more attractive: the volcano was a shapeshifter, its constant motion a source of new views and sights, new crystals and lavas.

And Vesuvius was privileged by its location. The volcano was close (15 kilometres as the crow flies) to one of Europe's largest and liveliest urban populations: Naples had over half a million inhabitants by the end of the eighteenth century. The political, legal and administrative centre of the Kingdom of Sicily, it was for much of the period the final destination of travellers taking an Italian tour. After his accession in 1732, Charles III of Bourbon had embarked on a series of extravagant improvements to the city, typical of an enlightened despot: the remodelling of the old palace; the building of new palaces in Naples, at Capodimonte, where the famous Farnese collections were displayed, Caserta (Reggia) and Portici; the erection of a huge hospital for the poor (Albergo dei Poveri); the building of new roads; and the opening of the San Carlo theatre, one of the finest opera houses in Europe. University reform and the founding of academies followed. The excavations at Herculaneum and Pompeii, which were to change fundamentally contemporary views of Vesuvius, were also a royal project designed to promote Naples and its rulers.

Vesuvius was also a key element in the prospect of the Bay of Naples, which had become, in the words of Stendhal in *The Charterhouse of Parma* (1839), 'the world's most renowned beauty spot'. A young American spoke for many other visitors when he wrote in 1794:

What a scene for contemplation ... it is impossible any other spot can combine such an extensive variety of prospects (on all sides one sees the beauties & wonders of nature or the monuments of art). The vast range of Apennines dazzling the eye with their snow-clad summits – Here Vesuvius rearing its smoking head above the clouds – there Craters of extinguished Volcanoes formerly scattering destruction around now filled with groves of trees, with palaces and cottages – on one hand the Mediterranean bound by the almost imperceptible line of the horizon, on the other the beautiful fields of Campania, with a horizon almost as extensive as the sea, presenting an immense and unbroken plain, diversified with innumerable towns, Palaces, Country Seats & Villages.[5]

The richness, plenitude and variety of the prospect made it a major Romantic attraction.

Beauty, but also convenience. According to Alexander von Humboldt, the great German scientist who visited Vesuvius on two occasions – once in 1805 in the company of the Parisian chemist

Joseph Louis Gay-Lussac and the Prussian geologist Leopold von Buch, and again in 1822 – no volcano was easier to climb, more accessible or, because of its persistent eruptions, offered more new material to study.[6] Vesuvius was, as the English chemist Humphry Davy put it, the 'grand laboratory of nature', but it was, in its own way, also small and suburban. The other major European volcano active in the period, Etna, on the island of Sicily, was much less reachable, and at more than twice the height of Vesuvius, was a far more difficult climb. (Vesuvian visitors outnumbered those to Etna by a factor of more than ten to one).[7] Further afield, the volcano was dwarfed by such Andean peaks as Chimborazo, which Humboldt had attempted to climb in 1802, only to turn back suffering from altitude sickness at over 5,800 metres (19,000 feet), and by Tambora, the Indonesian volcano that in 1815 produced the most devastating eruption in human history and the infamous 'year without a summer'.

But these volcanoes were far away, more rebarbative and more hazardous, likely to be the destination of the dedicated natural philosopher rather than the casual visitor. The journey to Vesuvius from Naples was only a matter of a few hours, though the last part of the trip up the cone and to the crater was extremely arduous and time consuming. By the early nineteenth century there was a well-developed infrastructure of scientific facilities, institutions and collections, as well as an organised system of guides that catered both to the tourist of the sublime and the serious savant. For much of the period, the experience of ascending Vesuvius remained an exhilarating adventure, a fragile equilibrium between danger and convenience, orchestrated by local Neapolitan guides. By the late nineteenth century, the journey had lost some of its Romantic aura, but no active volcano in Europe was easier to reach, or more accessible.

Though Vesuvius had long been an object of interest to natural philosophers, especially after the devastating eruption of 1631, the growth of the earth sciences, including the new discipline of geology, saw a radical uptick in scientific writings on Vesuvius and its volcanic hinterland from the mid-eighteenth century. Scholarly articles, learned accounts in the journals that came out of the academies, institutes and societies in Paris, London, Berlin, Göttingen, Geneva and Naples itself, examined the chemistry and physics of the volcano's rocks, soils and gases, the structure of its crystals and minerals, reported in detail on the dynamics of eruptions and lava flows, and speculated on the role of volcanoes like Vesuvius in the history of the earth. These were international conversations, conducted in several languages (though most often in French) among savants from all over Europe and the New World. When the Polish aristocrat and man of science Count Stanislao Dunin Borkowsky wrote a paper in 1816 on sodalite, the beautiful, rich-blue mineral found on Vesuvius, it appeared in two Paris journals, *Annales des mines* and *Journal de physique, de chimie, d'histoire naturelle et des arts*, in London's *Annals of Philosophy* and in *Annalen der Physik* published in Halle.

A nineteenth-century bibliography devoted to such studies of Vesuvius identified more than 550 books and articles, many supported with engravings and diagrams, published between 1760 and 1840. These were the products of scholarly networks, built through the epistolary exchange of information, the gift, sale or exchange of specimens of rock, crystal and lava that emanated from the volcano, and they were held together by travel and field work. Scholars had long relied on networks of correspondents to acquire and spread knowledge, but by the early nineteenth century such clusters had acquired an unprecedented density and profusion. They relied on the unceasing expeditions of restless natural philosophers like the dashing Frenchman Déodat de Dolomieu, famed for having visited more volcanic sites than any other of his contemporaries, but also on more sedentary stay-at-homes, like Teodoro Monticelli, the secretary of the Royal Academy and the Academy of Sciences in Naples, who operated a global clearing house of Vesuvian specimens and information. Between 1807 and 1845 Monticelli wrote and received thousands of letters with correspondents in Europe and North and South America.

The scholarly and technical literature about Vesuvius, though it was increasingly addressed to savants, both academic and amateur, found its way into journals and periodicals for a large lay audience. The famous accounts of Sir William Hamilton, the British plenipotentiary to Naples, of the Vesuvian eruptions of the 1760s, 1779 and 1794 were originally published in the *Transactions of the Royal Society*, but they were quickly reprinted in newspapers and periodicals.[8] Visitors to Naples, even those with little or no knowledge of volcanoes, had ready access to accounts like those of Hamilton long before their arrival.

Every major eruption (and many minor ones) spawned accounts written by Neapolitans or by visiting travellers and scientists. Their daily progress was carefully monitored, each new explosion and lava flow recorded in precise detail. Local scrutiny reached an international readership through these reports that were printed or excerpted in the pages of the European newspaper and periodical press. The eruption of 1779, for instance, was covered not just by the British press but the *Gazette d'Amsterdam*, *Courrier d'Avignon*, *Gazette de Leyde*, *Gazette de Cologne* and, above all, the *Gazette d'Utrecht*.[9] By the early nineteenth century, newspaper correspondents from northern Europe were regularly filing stories of Vesuvius's activities. In the 1820s, the German Romantic poet Wilhelm Waiblinger had his Italian travels financed by the publisher and literary patron Johann Friedrich Cotta. He worked as an Italian correspondent writing about the sites of Italy – including Vesuvius – in a variety of German journals, notably Stuttgart's (and Cotta's) *Morgenblatt*. Henry G. Wreford, an Englishman who lived on Capri, sold Vesuvian copy to *The Times* of London and a raft of other British journals. By the mid-nineteenth century, papers like *The Lady's Newspaper* and the *Englishwoman's Review and Home Paper*, whose chief clientele was female, were publishing detailed descriptions of Vesuvian eruptions. Reports of the violence of the volcano were readily available to be read in the safe surroundings of the parlours, libraries, clubs and cafés of the European and American bourgeoisie.

8
GEOLOGIES
Vulcanism, Local and Global

From the mid-eighteenth century, the knowledge accumulated by earth sciences was growing at an unprecedented rate. The questions of how the global landscape had developed, the processes in its development, and the age of the earth were all given a vigorous and contentious airing. By the early nineteenth century a new science had emerged, geology, devoted to the causes and history of telluric change. How did the local history of Vesuvius come to connect to these larger global developments?' To understand how this occurred at the end of the eighteenth century, we need to examine the growth of the earth sciences in Europe and the New World and their shifting concerns, but also chart the ways in which local volcano-watchers came to frame their observations within debates that extended beyond Naples and into the scientific societies and academies of cities like Paris, London and Berlin. This was a two-way street: if locals learned to see the volcano in new and broader ways, the preoccupations and ideas of naturalists and savants in institutes, academies and universities outside Italy led to an increased focus on its volcanic regions. This was far, of course, from being the whole story of Romantic geological history – one that is still dominated by the discovery and use of fossil remains and the slow march

274

towards Darwinian evolution – but it was one important episode in a burgeoning inquiry into the history of the earth. And it meant that by the early nineteenth century, attempts to connect the local world of Vesuvian vulcanism with the new sciences could be fully realised.

Vesuvius had long been an object of fascinated observation that dated back into classical antiquity. But the devastating eruption of 1631, after a prolonged period of quiescence, provoked an unprecedented outpouring of commentary on the volcano. Much of this was religious in nature, an attempt to interpret theologically the volcano's sudden and brutal intervention into the everyday lives of the people of the Bay of Naples. But from the seventeenth century on, there were also a growing number of attempts to understand the natural causes of volcanic eruptions. As we shall see, local observers accumulated a good deal of information about the day-to-day workings of the volcano and speculated as to their causes.[1]

The state and history of the earth sciences

William Whewell (1794–1866), the son of a master carpenter and later Master of Trinity College Cambridge, was regarded by his contemporaries as an intellectual prodigy and polymath. A great coiner of terms, he was the first to make current the word 'scientist' as a general description of those who studied the natural world. The author of writings in the sciences, political economy, philosophy, education, the history of science as well as translations of Greek and German poetry, he was also a geologist. His first book was an *Essay on Mineralogical Classification and Nomenclature*; appointed professor of mineralogy at Cambridge in 1828, he became a member, and then later president, of London's Geological Society. In 1832 he wrote a special report on mineralogy for the recently founded British Association for the Advancement of Science.[2] Whewell was therefore an apt reviewer of the first volume of Charles Lyell's *Principles of Geology*, perhaps *the* canonical, albeit controversial, work on the earth sciences in the nineteenth century when it appeared in 1830.

Whewell used the occasion to look back with some satisfaction on the history of geology since the late eighteenth century. He praised the 'hammer bearing philosophers' whose inquiries ranged 'from the plains of the Mississippi to the coasts of New Holland', painting a vivid picture of geologists striding the continents. 'Their disciples have been taught, their converts and teachers formed, with the hammer in their hands, with the knapsacks on their backs ... in long and laborious journeys amid privation and difficulty; with a perpetual personal exercise, both of the most minute discrimination of differences, and of the widest sweep of combination.' As a result, Whewell concluded, 'a mass of knowledge has been collected, most remarkable both in its quantity and in its kind.'[3] Note that Whewell had little to say about the state of *theorising* about the planet. In this he was at one with many of his contemporaries, following what Lyell called 'that fashion ... of discountenancing almost all geological speculation'.[4] Whewell's geology was first and foremost a field science. That given, he reached a bullish conclusion: 'Geology has flourished,' he declaimed, 'and is flourishing'.[5]

Geology was a comparatively new discipline. The term 'geology', though originally used by Ulisse Aldrovandi, the naturalist and physician from Bologna, as early as 1603, only came into general usage in the early nineteenth century, growing out of the older sciences of mineralogy, geognosy (knowledge of the earth's interior, closely associated with the mining of metals and coal) and physical geography (the observation of large-scale features of the earth's surface). As one early nineteenth-century geologist explained, there were two main branches of the earth sciences: 'Geognosy embraces the subordinate sciences of Mineralogy, Chemistry, and the study of the relative position of Rocks ... Geology has for its business a knowledge of the processes which are in continual or occasional operation within the limits of our planet.'[6] As the French geologist Déodat de Dolomieu put it to his students at the École des Mines, 'I can say that one can be a mineralogist without being a geologist, but I would add that one cannot become a geologist without being a mineralogist.'[7] The earth sciences were concerned not only with the history of what happened when, but with identifying the scientific processes that produced changes in the nature of the earth.

Whewell's enthusiastic characterisation of the state of geology captures the sense throughout Europe that the earth sciences, and geology in particular, had made enormous strides since the late eighteenth century. Whewell was mindful, as he explained to his readers, that these advances had been achieved through the combined endeavours of 'the four principal scientific nations of Europe'. In Germany, he pointed to the contribution of the Mining Academy established in the Saxon town of Freiberg, and to the work of one of its brilliant professors, Abraham Gottlob Werner (1749–1817), a mineralogist who not only developed a theory of rock classification (a 'succession of formations'), but trained a future generation of scholars and engineers that included, among many others, the Edinburgh professor Robert Jameson, and two famous and independently wealthy Prussians, Alexander von Humboldt (1769–1859) and Leopold von Buch (1774–1853), who devoted their lives to scientific study.[8] In France he picked out the work of the gifted anatomist and palaeontologist Georges Cuvier (1769–1832), and his colleague, the mineralogist and mining engineer Alexandre Brongniart (1770–1847), who together produced one of the first and finest in-depth accounts of a geological region, the Paris Basin. In Italy he pointed to the many local scholars who had helped Lyell to identify the most recent deposits of rocks, minerals and fossils that were a vital link between the topographical present and the recent geological past.[9] Whewell did not mention Giambattista Brocchi (1772–1826), the curator of the Natural History Museum in Milan and the author of *Conchiologia fossile subapennina* (1814), by name, but his writings, a rigorous combination of extensive field work in the Italian Apennines and careful examination of fossil shells and contemporary molluscs, had a great influence on Lyell's thinking.[10]

Whewell's review was excessively complimentary to the English – it saw German and French geologists as dependent on British innovations, especially William Smith's geological mapping – but it gave readers a crisp sketch of the international landscape of geology, especially those branches principally concerned with stratigraphy – the analysis of the layers of rock – and with the contribution of research into fossils as means of distinguishing them.

But this was only a part of the growing area of earth sciences. An even fuller picture appeared across the Channel in the 1834 Annual Bulletin of the Société Géologique de France, written by Ami Boué, one of the recently founded society's secretaries. Boué, who came from a wealthy French Protestant family, had an exceptionally cosmopolitan upbringing. Born in Hamburg, schooled in Geneva, taking a medical degree in Edinburgh, studying sciences at the Universities of Paris and Berlin, and with a special interest in the Balkans and eastern Europe, he was perfectly positioned to survey the current state of earth sciences. His report, running to more than 500 pages, surveyed general natural history, chemistry, mineralogy and physical geography and palaeontology as well as geology, and reported on findings not just in Europe and the New World, but Africa, Asia and Antarctica.[11] More modestly, in the same year Leopoldo Pilla, the Neapolitan geologist we have already encountered on the slopes of Vesuvius, completed a two-part, wide-ranging overview of more than a hundred pages on the state of Italian mineralogy and geology. Published in a new periodical entitled *Il progresso delle scienze, delle lettere e delle arti*, edited by his young radical friend Giuseppe Ricciardi, Pilla's review deliberately set out to publicise and explain a large body of scientific work that had appeared in the scholarly journals of academies, universities and institutes, making it available to a more general reader. Like Whewell, he also had a patriotic agenda, claiming Giovanni Arduino from the Veneto as the father of modern stratigraphy, Lazzaro Spallanzani, the author of *Travels in the Two Sicilies* (1798) as the founder of modern vulcanology, and Scipione Breislak, the author of the first geology textbook in Italian, as the first effective critic of Werner's theories of rock formation.[12]

My general point here is that the period was one of exceptional intellectual activity: great (and sometimes sensational) discoveries were made – fossil skeletons of extraordinary creatures, remarkable natural features – and geologists accumulated an enormous amount of information about different parts of the earth. Nevertheless, as Whewell's relative silence on general formulations about the history of the earth implies, there was still a strong sense that much remained to be discovered, explained and understood. As Lyell ruefully remarked about this state of 'imperfect insight', 'much still remains to be done, and the curiosity of many generations of men must multiply almost indefinitely their observations and experiments, ere the geologist can be enabled to restore to our imagination, the picture successively presented at remote periods, by the earth's surface and its inhabitants.'[13] Empirically strong, analytically precarious and conceptually wobbly, when geology scaled up from the local to the global, it entered, as Lyell himself was at great pains to point out, a realm of unsubstantiated a priori assertion and assumption.[14]

Nevertheless the geological sciences were extraordinarily popular in the age of Romanticism. Theories of the earth were the work of philosophers, but field work and collecting were accessible to all. For every learned mineral, fossil rock and lava collector there were many more enthusiastic amateurs, notably physicians and apothecaries, genteel men and women, clergymen and government functionaries. To a certain extent drawing such a distinction is false. Though the learned collectors included professors in universities, mining and scientific academies, many 'enthusiastic amateurs' were as erudite as their professional counterparts. European aristocrats – among them the Duke of Buckingham in England, Goethe's employer and friend Karl August the Grand Duke of Saxe-Weimar, the Danish prime minister Joachim Moltke, the French aristocrat and exile Jacques-Louis Comte de Bournon, and the Russian exile Count Gregorii Razumovsky, whose collections were purchased by Yale University in 1825 – not only accumulated enormous collections but made their own contributions to the earth sciences. These grandees were only the most visible manifestation of a much broader phenomenon of natural history collecting.[15]

In 1780 Baron Sigmund Zois, a leading figure of the Slovene Enlightenment, wrote to the French naturalist Picot de Lapeyrouse in Toulouse complaining that the passion among the Austro-Hungarian aristocracy for minerals had created a scarcity that was inhibiting less privileged collectors.[16] Dealers in mineral and fossil specimens were to be found not just in the major cities of Europe such as London, Paris, Stockholm, Dresden, Turin and Naples, and in university cities like Heidelberg, but also in smaller cities and towns like Berne in Switzerland, Verona in the Veneto and Derby in the English Midlands, where the doctor, poet, inventor and philosopher Erasmus Darwin, the grandfather of Charles, purchased many of the specimens in his collection.

Natural history societies proliferated through Europe – they were especially numerous in the German-speaking lands – developing their own collections and publishing papers in mineralogy, geology and botany. Many of the scientific academies contained sections devoted to the earth sciences. Enthusiasm for these pursuits was fed by the travel and discovery narratives of intrepid men of science that filled bookshops and library shelves from the Baltic to the Mediterranean. Horace Bénédict de Saussure on the Alps, Alexander von Humboldt's vivid account of his painful and painstaking exploration of the volcanoes of the New World, and Lazzaro Spallanzani's tales of his geological travels in volcanic Italy were European bestsellers, translated into several different languages. Such epic accomplishments inspired the much less heroic peregrinations of the weekend rock and fossil hunter. Booksellers published mineralogical and geological works for the general public, for schools and for the young. (After 1777, the study of natural history, including mineralogy, was required in all Hungarian schools.) Brongniart's *Traité élémentaire de minéralogie* (1807), as its title page explained, was aimed at teaching in '*les lycées nationaux*'; the interlocutors in Delvalle Lawry's *Conversations in Mineralogy* (1822) were young women.[17] A similar book, *Conversations on Geology* (1828), featured discussions between an all-knowing mother and her two children, Edward and Christina.[18] Works like Robert Bakewell's *An Introduction to Geology*, first published in 1813 and still in print in revised form at the end of the 1830s, were based on courses of public lectures; similarly William Thomas Brande published his Royal Institution Lectures as *Outlines of Geology* in two different editions in 1817 and 1829.[19] Geological lectures delivered at the intellectually exalted Collège de France in Paris were published to ensure that their audience extended beyond their immediate auditors.

The podium presented special opportunities in an age that was well known for the theatricality of science.[20] Humphry Davy's geological lectures at the Royal Institution from 1805 (the first in Britain) ended with a spectacular eruption designed to show the chemical reactions that lay behind volcanic explosions, but which was interpreted by his audience as a re-enactment of the Vesuvian eruption of 79 CE.[21] In Oxford, William Buckland lectured to both students and women surrounded by maps, charts and large fossil specimens or took his auditors out into the fields around the university.[22] In Naples Giuseppe Vairo, professor of chemistry at the Royal University, taught geo-chemistry to his students in the open air 'smoking laboratory' of the Solfatara, the sulphurous volcanic beds in Pozzuoli.[23] In Cambridge, Edward Clarke, the professor of mineralogy who had acted as a cicerone on Vesuvius in the 1790s, used a model of the volcano to demonstrate its workings, and simulated its pyrotechnics by using a blow-pipe of his own invention.[24] The line between academic instruction and spectacular entertainment – were the dioramas of Vesuvius in public pleasure gardens instructive, entertaining, or both? – was not easy to draw.

Contours of geological activity varied from country to country. In Britain they were shaped by a large body of amateur enthusiasts and collectors, men and women from all walks of life within the genteel classes and sometimes beyond. In France they were more confined to a professional elite of academics and government functionaries. As Lyell put it in his notes for his geological lectures at King's College London, 'In France though the numbers [of savants] are few they are systematically organised . . . Compare [the] French to a small standing army – English to desultory multitudinous host of irregulars'.[25] In fact, throughout Europe there were independently wealthy students of geology with no formal professional or academic position. But in France, Germany and Italy, rulers interested in exploiting mineral resources and university professors in the sciences played a more important role than in Britain.

What were the issues that fascinated and divided these geological enthusiasts? The cliché that nineteenth-century geology was a struggle between science and religion, chiefly about the length of the earth's history – was it the biblical span of a mere 4,000 years, much longer, or even infinite? – has largely been discredited.[26] Certainly in Britain and the United States there were so-called 'physico-theologians' who read the biblical chronology literally, and the Catholic Church in Italy took the side of the Neptunists – those who saw water as the key geological agent – against the Plutonists who favoured fire, because their views were more compatible with the biblical Flood.[27] But most men of science, including most Christians, recognised that the history of the earth was much, much longer. The key issue was whether, in the memorable words of the famous Scottish savant James Hutton, the earth revealed 'no vestige of a beginning, no prospect of an end', that it was a self-equilibrating mechanism, what he called 'a beautiful machine', or whether it was an object with a history which stretched back into deep time but had an (as yet unde-tected) moment of origin.[28] Most geologists took the latter view.

But, regardless of these positions, geologists were chiefly pre-occupied by the processes by which the earth and its inhabitants changed. Were these cyclical – repeated cycles of destruction, consoli-dation and elevation – or progressive, as in the view that life on earth was gaining in complexity, or that the earth was undergoing a constant process of cooling? Were they catastrophic, the result, for example, of global inundation, as the anatomist Georges Cuvier concluded on the basis of surviving fossil evidence? Or were they gradual, the consequence of repeated, continuous processes over extended periods of time, as Charles Lyell maintained? And what were the key forces behind such changes? Were they aqueous or igneous: what were the roles of water and fire? And what exactly were the processes – phys-ical and/or chemical – that caused them? Such was the great debate at the end of the eighteenth century.

There was general agreement that the starting point in answering such questions was observation in the present. As Alexander von Humboldt put it, 'geological reasoning can be supported only on the analogy of facts that are recent, and consequently well authenti-cated.'[29] But were they sufficient to explain the earth's history? Some, like Cuvier, whose reading of the fossil record pointed to at least one major rupture in the history of the earth, argued that currently observable geological action was not adequate to explain the cata-clysms of the past; others, most notably and vehemently Lyell, saw change as incremental, and the workings of the present as adequate to explain earlier change. These positions, identified by the historian Jules Michelet as Continental and English, should be seen as oper-ating on a spectrum with many savants occupying a place in between.

In these disputes, 'actual causes' – erosion, sedimentation, volcanic and seismic activity: changes in physical geography occurring in the time of human history and contained within the human record – were clearly crucial. The object of their examination was to develop a timescale that could then be projected back to a pre-human world. Accounts of 'actual causes' were sometimes based on texts, written records of events in the earth's history, as in the German bureaucrat and historian Karl von Hoff's monumental five-volume *History of the Natural Changes at the Earth's Surface that are Attested by Tradition* (1822–41). But they were also recorded through direct observation, as in the work of Mario Gemmellaro, one of the brothers who devoted their lives to studying Mount Etna, whose mapping of the volcano and its many cones made clear that volcanic eruptions could be traced back into a pre-human past.[30] This vast accumulated volume of research, observation and erudition recovered an earth that was and had been dynamic and changing. The uplift of the earth's crust, the changes of sea level, the folding of mountains, the reconfiguration of the landscape through gradual erosion or violent eruption, became the matter of scientific observation and dispute.

Fire and water

Where then did volcanoes and Vesuvius fit into this story? To understand this we need to see how the relative importance of volcanoes in the study of the earth shifted in the late eighteenth and early nineteenth centuries. Werner's extremely influential classification of rocks treated volcanic materials as unimportant and superficial. Water, not fire, was considered as the crucial agent in rock formation, whether in the form of a biblical flood, a receding ocean or marine inundation of the land. Volcanoes were not considered important in the formation of mountains; on the contrary, mountains made volcanoes. But from the 1750s, the field work of a number of French naturalists in the regions of the Auvergne, Vivarais and Velay in the Massif Central revealed the presence of numerous extinct volcanoes; soon others were discovered in northern Italy, Germany and Portugal. Volcanic action was baked into the history of the earth. Nicolas Desmarest, a French government official who had travelled in the Auvergne, argued that columnar basalt, found both in the Auvergne and in spectacular form in the Giant's Causeway on the north coast of Ireland, was composed of volcanic rocks, because such prismatic forms could be found emanating from the extinct cones of the volcanoes in the Auvergne. The potential implications of such views, which came to be shared by other savants in France, Italy and Germany, were far-reaching: they implied a much greater role for heat in the development of the earth, and that volcanoes were not superficial, recent phenomena but had a much longer history. Desmarest's views were reinforced by his observation of both extinct and active volcanoes in Italy (the only live volcano he ever saw was Vesuvius), but they remained controversial, triggering an intense debate about the nature and role of basalt. When, in 1788, the members of the recently founded Naturforschenden Privatgesellschaft (Natural History Society) in Berne set the essay prize question, 'What is basalt? Is it volcanic, or is it not?', they knew they were posing one of the most controversial questions of the day.[31]

The responses to this question were complex, but generally fell into one of three positions. The first argued that basalt was not volcanic but rather an aqueous precipitate formed as the global ocean receded. This was the so-called 'Neptunist' view taken by Werner and many of his followers. The second maintained that basalt was an igneous rock but was produced by the solidification of subterraneous, not volcanic, lava. The third position argued that basalt was indeed an igneous rock produced by volcanoes. (Both of these last two views, despite their difference, were characterised as 'Plutonist'.) Charles Daubeny, the author of *A Description of Active and Extinct Volcanos* (1826), represented these different positions by placing them on what he called 'The Geological Thermometer', an image scaled from 1 to 100 that showed 'the opinions attributed to various geologists with respect to the origin of rocks'. At the highest temperature were the Plutonists, then shading towards the middle were the Vulcanists, while at the bottom were the Neptunists. Count Buffon and Hutton were at the top, while Werner and his followers were at the bottom. Significantly, many geologists occupied complex intermediate positions.[32] The situation was further complicated by the fact that some, in fact most, geologists came to concede that basalt was volcanic but continued to take the view that the most powerful force in shaping the earth was aqueous. Thus Déodat de Dolomieu in his lectures on geology at the École des Mines in 1796 made a distinction between 'earths formed by precipitation and those that owe their origin to fire'.[33]

We do not need to adjudicate among these views to recognise that they made living volcanoes vital sources of evidence about the processes that created rocks and potentially might explain the history of the earth. Rudolf Erich Raspe (1737–94) is best remembered as the author of the remarkable *Baron von Münchausen's Narratives of His Marvellous Travels and Campaigns in Russia*. His reputation as a literary hack and con man has obscured his scientific pedigree. He was elected to London's Royal Society and praised by Goethe for his important study of hitherto unknown volcanic basalts in Germany. Immersed in the controversy over basalt, he looked for help to Sir William Hamilton in Naples, seeking information about Vesuvian lava. 'Do any of the cooled lava flows of the Vesuvius display toward their end something similar to prismatic basalt?', he asked. Hamilton's response was ambiguous: 'concerning the basalt, I have, since investigating lavas, always considered it as a type of lava', he wrote. 'However', he concluded, 'I have never found any kind which is columnal or polygonal like basalt, among the numerous types of lavas of the Vesuvius, Sicily, and the island of Ischia.' Raspe never visited Vesuvius (though the fictional Münchausen, like the classical philosopher Empedocles, did throw himself into the crater of Etna), but a tour of Vesuvius and the Italian and Mediterranean volcanic regions became essential for those who wished to engage in the debate about the nature and history of the earth.[34] Vulcanists like Scipione Breislak were convinced (not always correctly) that experiencing the powerful forces of Vesuvius and Etna would persuade savants of the central importance of volcanoes. Important Italian natural philosophers were indeed converted: after he had visited southern Italy in 1811, Giambattista Brocchi accepted that basalt was of volcanic origin, and explained the presence of marine fossils as the result of submarine volcanic activity. Spallanzani and Arduino had earlier taken similar views, though this did not mean that they were full-blown Plutonists.[35] But the important point is that the extraordinary levels of volcanic activity, not just of Vesuvius itself but of the Bay of Naples, including the Campi Flegrei, provided the geological visitor with a remarkably rich catalogue of 'actual causes' to work on, and the presence of numerous sites of antiquity enabled them to connect the historical and the geological record. This was true not just of Pompeii and Herculaneum but also at Pozzuoli, where three pillars of the so-called Temple of Serapis were pitted by borings of sea molluscs, indicating that the building (in fact a market) had at some point fallen below sea level and later re-emerged above the water. Lyell chose an engraving of the site as the frontispiece to his *Principles of Geology*. There seemed to be no better temporal marker of gradual shifts in the earth's crust.[36]

The case of Naples

We get a strong sense of the importance of Vesuvius and the Bay of Naples for the geologist from the ecstatic (if sometimes pompous) account of George Julius Poulett Scrope (1797–1876) of the joys of working in southern Italy. Scrope, the son of a Russia merchant, spent the winter of 1817–18 in Naples with his parents and became fascinated by the volcano and its surroundings. He returned in 1819–20, and after a period of researching extinct volcanoes in France came back to witness the most violent Vesuvian eruption of the nineteenth century in 1822. A member of London's Geological (1824) and Royal (1826) Societies, in 1825 he published *Considerations on Volcanoes*, which set out a general model for volcanic processes and their role in explaining the development of the earth. Some years later he wrote, 'The volcanic action going on in the vicinity of Naples, where all its phenomena can be conveniently and agreeably watched, affords a valuable field of observation to the student of natural dynamics.' Not just Vesuvius but Stromboli and Etna, he observes, are 'in almost continual and very energetic activity,' while everywhere 'the traces of former action at various periods lie scattered around in profusion, and are mingled in the most interesting manner with the vestiges of man's occupation of the same fertile and delicious sites.' The mingling of 'the relics of human art' and nature is especially revealing. 'We gather as much knowledge of the past history of Vesuvius from the disinterment of Pompeii and Herculaneum, as we do of the history and manners of their former inhabitants. The beautiful Temple of Serapis at Pozzuoli is quite as interesting to the geologist as to the antiquary.' Citing his own experiences, Scrope said, 'The combination of both studies . . . affords a gratification of the most intense character, quite peculiar to this favoured and favourite district.' He pictured himself enjoying 'the luxury of geologising in the extinct craters of the Elysian Fields, with a Virgil in one hand and a hammer in the other', and as standing on the promontory of Misenum, where the younger Pliny observed the eruption of 79 CE, 'surrounded by the written monuments of classical antiquity, and viewing, through the transparent medium of that delicious atmosphere, Vesuvius and the Solfatara yet smoking, with a hundred circling hills that mark out so many extinct volcanoes, whose craters and sides are studded with relics of Roman villas and Grecian cities'.[37]

As European savants like Scrope turned their attention to the Italian volcanoes (Lyell was especially enamoured of Etna), they intersected with older local traditions of volcano-watching. In Naples, especially after the devastating eruption of 1631, local savants had understandably devoted a great deal of attention to the workings of Vesuvius, seeking to understand both the sources of its heat and what triggered the ignition of an eruption. The answers to these questions were rarely what we today would think of as dispassionate, empirically grounded accounts, though they were often based on carefully compiled observations. They were bound up with Christian theological concerns, with humanist histories and with the moral and political state of the city and its inhabitants. Famously the eruption of 1631 was seen as the occasion when San Gennaro interceded to rescue Neapolitans from the volcano, an intervention that the Counter-Reformation authorities used not only to consolidate the local reputation and power of the saint, but to urge that 'from the sight of these fires, everyone might learn to root out vice and sin, to live well, and heed conscience'. As the author Gioseffe Mormile pointedly put it, 'Is man's intellect so stubborn that he cannot grasp that the fires of Hell will be minister and castigator of his crimes?'[38] Yet even when commentators accepted the miraculous intervention of San Gennaro, this did not preclude them from viewing the eruption as a natural phenomenon rather than a portent or prodigy, or from inquiring after its natural causes.

Thereafter, a succession of Neapolitan observers wrote histories of the volcano based on the testimony of classical texts and modern witnesses, tabulating its eruptions. They debated the relative importance of sulphur, nitre, bitumen and charcoal in igniting the volcano, and the depth of the sources of heat. They also provided foreign savants with detailed accounts of successive eruptions. After the 1737 eruption, for example, a member of the Academy of Sciences, the physician and medical professor Francesco Serao, produced an official account in both Latin and Italian with accompanying images, which was then published in French in Paris and in English in London. In fact, the *Istoria dell'incendio del Vesuvio accaduto nel mese di maggio dell'anno 1737* was, as a note added to the French edition makes clear, a collaborative work of members of the academy, seen as an exemplary case of trustworthy knowledge produced through intellectual collaboration. It was still in print in 1778.[39]

There was a striking continuity in many of these accounts which emphasised local, ongoing scrupulous observation, the sort of knowledge that could only be acquired through a local informant on the spot. Thus Gaspare Paragallo, in his *Istoria naturale del Monte Vesuvio* (1705), castigated his predecessors for failing to observe that eruptions involved more than sulphur and bitumen; Giuseppe Valletta, in writing to the Royal Society in London in 1712, stressed the importance of witnessing ongoing Vesuvian eruptions, while Giuseppe Mecatti, the author of a series of 'Observations' and 'Historical-Philosophical Accounts' covering eruptions in the 1750s and early 1760s, preened himself on having kept a very detailed diary of 'what the lava did'. The priest, royal librarian and curator Abbé Giovanni Maria della Torre, the most important local observer of Vesuvius in the mid-eighteenth century, laid great emphasis not only on the frequency of his visits to the volcano, but on his elaborate system of note-taking. In his *Storia e fenomeni del Vesuvio* (1755), he explained that each observation he made was 'without having first seen my preceding observations'. After each trip he set aside his notes 'with no further glance'. Only when he began to write up his findings did he search for patterns and correlations, drawing his conclusions 'without the preconceptions of any particular system'.[40] In 1794 Domenico Tata boasted that he had been studying Vesuvius continuously for nearly forty years. So when Sir William Hamilton hired Father Antonio Piaggio to keep a daily record of Vesuvius's activities (a diary now deposited in the archives of the Royal Society in London), he was following a local tradition as well as an international trend, one that privileged the ongoing observations of an informed observer in situ. And, like a good local, Hamilton, after explaining that his ascent of Vesuvius in May 1779 was his fifty-eighth and that he had 'been four times as often on parts of the mountain without climbing to its summit', complained about naturalists who, after giving Vesuvius the '*coup d'oeil*', thought themselves qualified to pronounce on every aspect of the volcano.[41]

The tradition lived on. When Leopoldo Pilla and a colleague launched their magazine *Lo spettatore del Vesuvio e de' Campi Flegrei* in 1832, they took aim at foreign visitors who after a brief visit to the volcano drew what they condemned as the 'overly precipitous conclusions' and 'exaggerations' of ill-informed observers. Only a few scholars passed muster as 'outsiders' whose assiduous observations qualified them as acceptable witnesses to Vesuvius's activities.[42] These included Sir William Hamilton, William (Guglielmo) Thomson, a British doctor and mineralogist who (having fled Oxford because of a homosexual scandal) lived in Naples and Palermo between 1792 and his death in 1806, and his friend Scipione Breislak, the radical Roman geologist who lived in Nola and Naples in the 1780s and published on the geology of the Campania. Claims to be well-informed were proprietorial. Local savants usually referred to accounts of '*il nostro Vesuvio*'. The volcano may have been 'a laboratory of nature' as both Hamilton and Humphry Davy put it, but it was also the prized possession of local naturalists. As we will see, there was always a tension among Neapolitans who wanted their volcano to feature in the international annals of science and who drew foreigners towards Vesuvius, but who were also sceptical of the capacity of those without an intimate knowledge of the volcano to understand its workings properly.

The English-language scholarship on Vesuvius in the second half of the eighteenth century is dominated by the contribution of Sir William Hamilton.[43] In many respects, as I have already indicated, Hamilton went native in Naples: his reports on individual eruptions, which he usually submitted to the Royal Society in London, but which were more widely circulated in magazines such as *The Annual Register*, followed the model of such accounts by other and earlier Neapolitan observers. He drew on the ideas and researches of local experts like Serao, Ignazio Sorrentino – a secular clergyman from Torre del Greco who published a compendium of eruptions between 1682 and 1734, whom Hamilton described as 'a very accurate observer of the phenomena of the volcano' – and Abbé Giovanni Maria della Torre 'who has wrote so much and so well upon the subject of Mount Vesuvius' and was 'a great observer of the mountain'. He also cited the work of Gaetano De Bottis, the professor of natural history at the University of Naples, 'a very accurate observer of the phenomena attending Mount Vesuvius', whose account of the 1761 eruption was 'well worthy the attention of the curious', and whose projected 1779 account, Hamilton predicted, 'will undoubtedly be executed with the same accuracy, truth, and precision, as have render'd that Author's former publications upon the Subject of Mount Vesuvius so universally and deservedly esteem'd'.[44] On occasion he simply took, unacknowledged, the findings of local experts, such as those of Giuseppe Vairo, a professor of chemistry, on the extraction of alum from lavas.[45]

The tone of Hamilton's comments could sometimes be condescending, and it is clear that he was conferring his imprimatur on local experts to a foreign audience. He was self-consciously aware of his role as an international intermediary.[46] At the same time he claimed the authority of the long-term resident who could observe the volcano almost continuously, contrasting his observations with the aperçu of the casual visitor: 'While the Volcano is in an active state, the crater changes in form perpetually, so that Travellers accounts of this part of the Volcano can seldom agree.'[47] Yet he also distanced himself from his local informants, most of whom were clerics, antiquaries and functionaries whose horizons were bounded by the Kingdom of Naples.

Much of what Hamilton reported on Vesuvius, the Bay of Naples and the volcanoes of southern Italy was not new. The claim that volcanoes demonstrated a history of the earth beyond the biblical span had already been expressed by, among others, Hamilton's guide on Etna, Giuseppe Recupero. Hamilton shared with De Bottis the view that the sources of heat dwelt deep in the earth and not near its surface. His descriptions of particular eruptions were matched by those of his colleagues. But Hamilton's work repeatedly pushed a particular message: that the entire Neapolitan region demonstrated that volcanoes were major and continual forces in the creation of the earth's landscape. As he explained in his 'Remarks upon the Nature of the Soil of Naples, and its Neighbourhood', sent to the secretary of the Royal Society in October 1770, 'when I first came to Naples, my whole attention, with respect to Natural History, was confined to Mount Vesuvius, and the wonderful phaenomena attending a burning mountain.' Gradually, however, his perspective widened: 'in proportion as I began to perceive the evident marks of the same operation having been carried on in the different parts [of Campania] ... and likewise in Sicily in a greater degree, I looked upon Mount Vesuvius only as a spot on which Nature was at present active.' What he was observing was a more general process, 'in which one of her [Nature's] great operations (an operation, I believe, much less out of her common course than is generally imagined) was effected'.[48] As he put it more pithily: 'Mountains are produced by volcanos, and not volcanos by mountains.'[49]

Hamilton enjoyed a number of advantages as a naturalist observer. He was a well-connected aristocrat, diplomat and courtier, versed in the arts and etiquette of epistolary self-presentation, embedded in the circuits of European knowledge and taste. The observations of the classically educated Hamilton – whose letters to the Royal Society are littered with antique references and allusions – carried authority, both in Britain and in the larger European scientific community. And he was able to present them in a striking format. The first two folio volumes, entitled *Campi Phlegraei*, published in 1776, and the *Supplement* that appeared three years later were not the first works on Vesuvius to be published with illustrations and maps, but nothing so lavish had ever appeared before. The original *Campi Phlegraei* contained fifty-four engraved plates hand-coloured in gouache by local artists and based on drawings made by the artist Pietro Fabris, whose work was personally supervised by Hamilton. The costs were exceptional: Hamilton claimed to his nephew, Charles Greville, that the volumes put him £1,300 out of pocket. Special sets were presented to the Royal Society, to King George III and to Sir Joseph Banks, a good friend who was to become president of the Royal Society in 1778.[50] Claims about the Europe-wide impact of these luxurious volumes should be treated sceptically. They could originally only be obtained from Pietro Fabris in Naples, at the price of 60 ducats. By the time they reached the London bookshops they cost 12 guineas and in Paris they cost 16 livres, beyond the budget of all but the wealthiest naturalists and far more likely to be bought by wealthy bibliophiles. The appearance in 1781 in Paris of *Oeuvres complètes de M. le Chevalier Hamilton*, officially commended by the Academy of Sciences, was justified on the grounds that the *Campi Phlegraei* volumes were so scarce and expensive that they were not easily accessible to savants and natural philosophers. The French edition was shortly translated into German and Dutch.[51]

But the Paris edition points to an important shift in the under-standing of Hamilton, which is also discernible in the *Supplement* to the *Campi Phlegraei* published in 1779. In 1776, when returning to England from Naples, Hamilton spent some time in Paris. There he met with, among others, Europe's most famous naturalist, the Comte de Buffon, who gave him comparative information on volcanic materials on the Isle de Bourbon in the Indian Ocean (modern-day Réunion).[52] He may also have met the editor of his French edition, Jean-Louis Giraud Soulavie. Soulavie, a priest and savant from the Vivarais in what is now the department of the Ardèche, was the author of a multi-tome *Natural History of Southern France*, whose fourth volume, *The Physical Chronology of the Eruptions of the Extinct Volcanoes of Southern France*, appeared in the same year as his edition of Hamilton's works. In the Hamilton edition Soulavie included not only the *Campi Phlegraei* but a letter to the Royal Society that Hamilton had written after his Paris trip entitled *An Account of Certain Traces of Volcanos on the Banks of the Rhine*, in which he iden-tified volcanic materials, basalts and lavas near Bonn and Koblenz that were also to be found on Vesuvius. This was the first (and only) publication of Hamilton on a volcanic region outside Italy; it marked a point at which his researches extended beyond the Bay of Naples, and fed into much larger debates on the effects of volcanic action. This was precisely the aim of Soulavie who added nearly 200 pages of notes to his edition of Hamilton's text. As he explained, 'In the History of Nature, as in all kinds of knowledge, we only acquire new views by the comparison of several objects.'[53] Soulavie argued that when Hamilton's work on Italy and Germany was placed alongside the research of Desmarest, Faujas de Saint-Fond and himself on the Auvergne, Vivarais and Velay, it demonstrated that volcanic products displayed a remarkable similarity that was the result of the uniform nature of volcanic activity. This could only be adduced by comparing observations made on the spot by a number of reliable informants.

As Martin Rudwick has shown, Soulavie was an exceptionally enterprising and energetic provincial savant, a self-promoting mapmaker and model builder as well as author determined to make it in the Parisian salons.[54] His work was full of speculations that amounted to a precocious geo-history, though one that failed to command widespread recognition or acceptance. His concern with comparison was to discover parallels with his own very local research, to enable him to generalise on the basis of many particulars about the epochs of the earth. His edition of Hamilton therefore conferred considerable benefits on the editor as well as the author. But for our purposes, Soulavie's importance lies in how his interpretation of Hamilton's work pushed it beyond the boundaries of the Bay of Naples. Hamilton knew the benefits of this. Soulavie claimed that the Englishman had written to him, giving his formal approval of the edition. Hamilton was also a subscriber to Soulavie's monumental *Histoire naturelle de la France Méridionale*. And Hamilton, as his footnotes to the *Supplement* of the *Campi Phlegraei* make clear, had also been reading Barthélémy Faujas de Saint-Fond's beautifully illustrated recent work, *Recherches sur les volcans éteints du Vivarais et du Velay* (1778), which made explicit the links between prismatic basalts and extinct volcanoes.[55] Indeed Hamilton, according to Faujas, wrote to him in January 1779 with information about prismatic basalt ejected from Vesuvius. Hamilton's story is therefore one of a growing commitment to placing the Vesuvian story in an expanding context – first beyond the volcano itself and into the volcanic phenomena of southern Italy and Sicily, and then in one that was at least European and perhaps global. As we shall see, many Neapolitan commentators on Vesuvius followed this same trajectory.

In Naples itself Hamilton often acted as a cicerone, taking visitors up the volcano. But relatively few of them were men of science. Saussure visited him in 1773, and Hamilton was much concerned to emphasise that the Swiss expert 'agreed perfectly with me in my opinion, as to the Volcanick origin of this part of this country'.[56] As a neophyte naturalist, he needed and cherished such an endorsement. He also took Déodat de Dolomieu and the Scottish chemist Sir James Hall to the summit in 1784. But most of the visitors he accompanied on the slopes of the volcano were dignitaries like Catherine the Great's son, the Grand Duke Paul of Russia, and his much-loved wife, both of whom huffed and puffed their way up Vesuvius. Or they were amateur enthusiasts like his old schoolfriend, August Hervey, the Bishop of Derry, who was injured in the eruption of 1766. The savants among the Grand Tourists that he escorted were sometimes interested, like his nephew, Charles Greville, in mineralogy, and were always up for the drama of an eruption, but they most probably shared the sentiments of Horace Walpole who, as an ardent bibliophile, purchased a copy of *Campi Phlegraei* but told Hamilton that he wished he had not changed his 'taste in painting and Antiquity for Phenomena'. Walpole conceded that when it came to nature, his first response was to 'admire and revere, but am not more struck, probably less, with the dissection than with the superficies'.[57]

Hamilton was far from being the only savant guide on Vesuvius. The Abbé della Torre (not to be confused with the Duca della Torre, an important aristocratic observer of the volcano) was known to Parisian savants as a reliable and informative guide.[58] In the later years of the century Hamilton, no longer a young man, had to cope with an English rival, Edward Daniel Clarke, the future professor of mineralogy at Cambridge, who acted as a guide to British visitors during his two and a half years, residence in Naples. But he, like Hamilton, was accompanying the curious Grand Tourist rather than the discerning savant.

Hamilton's final contribution to the literature on Vesuvius was his letter to the Royal Society about the 1794 eruption, the most dramatic, devastating and long-lasting of the eighteenth century, but it is important to see it in the context of a growing Neapolitan literature and scientific culture concerned with the volcano. No eruption, apart from that of 1631, produced so much comment and commentary.[59] In part this was because of the extent of the eruption and the range of its disruption. Not only was a large part of the shoreline town of Torre del Greco smothered in a huge lava flow, but the eruption that began on 15 June continued until almost the end of the month, producing what was later estimated to be 40 million cubic metres of ejecta, in the form of ash, cinders and lapilli (rock fragments). Much of Naples and many of the towns on the northern side of the volcano were covered in ash; the sky was darkened and the light obscured for more than a week. And in July the atmospheric effects of the volcano prompted a series of damaging mudflows not just towards the coast, but also on the northern slopes of the volcano into towns such as Ottaviano and Somma, killing livestock and destroying trees and crops. Human casualties were surprisingly low, but the effects on the livelihoods of Neapolitans were long-lasting. Crops did not recover for two years, though the Duca della Torre was astonished when he visited Torre del Greco a year after the eruption to discover how much local rebuilding had already taken place.[60]

The 1794 eruption not only raised questions about what had triggered the event, but also issues of public health. Were the deposits of ash poisonous? What was the state of the air? What was the effect on the health of the population, on the well-being of livestock and the growth of crops? It raised questions both chemical and medical. The eruption's different forms, a succession of explosions, its many deposits, its electrical storms and its mudslides, together with its longevity raised many scientific questions of which the most intriguing and puzzling was the role of electricity. The large number of accounts of the eruption and the precision with which they were made – recording detailed times for different events, checking temperatures and barometric pressures, measuring the size and depth of lava flows – together with the chemical and physical analysis of the volcano's materials made the eruption one of the most carefully scrutinised in Vesuvius's history.

By the 1790s accounts of Vesuvian eruptions by local eyewitnesses had become a familiar genre. The famous Neapolitan political economist Ferdinando Galiani, under the pseudonym Onofrio Galeota, wrote a parody of the genre after the eruption of 1779, entitled *The most frightening description of the frightening fright that frightens us all with the eruption of Vesuvius.*[61] Galiani's satire attacks popular incredulity, but also points to the limitations of science. Another pamphlet with the same title and nom de plume (though not written by Galiani) appeared in 1794. Accounts of the eruption in that year were published under the name of one of the hermits, Salvatore Caneva, and of the gardener, Simone Giros, at the recently completed royal Villa Favorita in Resina.[62] Some of the publications fêted San Gennaro, maintaining that he had once again intervened to save the city, and others attacked the scientific and philosophical analysis of the eruption. After a long and sympathetic account of the many religious processions prompted by the eruption, 'Un Legista Napolitano' (Neapolitan Lawyer) mocked the language of physics and modern philosophy in a published letter to his brother in the provinces, condemning the 'sophisticated reasoning' and 'deadly maxims' of the 'capricious philosophy' of the eighteenth century. Urging him to pray to an all-knowing God, he concludes his message: 'Stay healthy, and pity only our fears, which the most refined philosophy will never be able to remove from us.'[63] As we have already seen, there was a long-standing difference between the enlightened savant and the traditionally pious Christian in their views of the volcano and its workings, but the French Revolution gave these interpretations an unprecedented political edge.

'Philosophical' accounts of the 1794 eruption were therefore under some pressure, though they made up most writing on the volcano. Who produced this important body of work? Many were medical men, like Pasquale Manni (1745–1841), the doctor and botanist who also published works on typhus, smallpox inoculation, meteorites and the silk industry, or Biagio Sotis (b. 1779) from Fondi, who studied philosophy and medicine in Naples, but also published Greek and Latin poetry, botany, history, archaeology, numismatics, inoculation and health statistics.[64] Michele Arcangelo D'Onofrio was a professor of medicine and military doctor, who wrote not just several accounts of the 1794 eruption, but also on the telegraph, plague and earthquakes.[65] These polymathic physicians were matched by polymaths from other disciplines, including Francesco Antonio Astore, a gifted linguist who composed poems in Latin, French and English as well as Italian and who wrote a series of extraordinarily erudite dialogues on the 1794 eruption between himself and a figure reputed to be the Duca della Torre.[66] Though a conservative critic of the radical Enlightenment, Astore came to support the republic of 1799, writing a Republican Catechism dedicated to its leader, Francesco Mario Pagano, and serving in the regime's Supreme Court. When the Bourbons returned, he paid for his enthusiasm with his life.[67] A few commentators on the eruption were lawyers, like Ciro Saverio Minervini, a longtime critic of clerical power, who also published on mineralogy, agriculture, geography, numismatics and philology.[68] Others were of a more scientific bent. The mason and radical Antonio Barba, a professor of physics at the university, also studied motion, electricity and the brain;[69] Ferdinando Viscardi described himself as an experimental physicist.[70] Domenico Tata, a professor of physics and mathematics from the Molise, had already studied several Vesuvian eruptions, as well as the activity of other volcanoes like Etna.[71] Luca Cagnazzi de Samuele held chairs of mathematics and physics, as well as of statistics and political economy. Apart from volcanoes his publications included studies of pedagogy and poverty, money and meteorology, and demography. He was the author of a textbook on political economy, and the inventor of the tonograph, an instrument to measure and preserve the intonation and inflection of the human voice.[72]

In short, most of the 'philosophical' commentators on Vesuvius in the 1790s were polymathic intellectuals who made up part of the enlightened elite of late eighteenth-century Naples. Astore was the pupil of the first professor of political economy in Naples, Genovesi. He also studied with Abbé della Torre, who was the teacher of the physicist Barba. Pasquale Manni was the pupil of Domenico Cirillo, the brilliant botanist and physician, who was to pay with his life for his support of the 1799 Neapolitan republic; the Duca della Torre moved in the circle around Gaetano Filangieri, the author of the famous Enlightenment text *The Science of Legislation*. These were often second-generation Neapolitan philosophers, many of whom were involved in supporting the republic of 1799, and who, if they survived the bloodbath of the counter-revolution, would go on to serve the French during the ten years of their occupation. They made up an identifiable community, many publishing their work on Vesuvius and a diverse range of issues connected with economy and reform in the *Giornale letterario di Napoli*, a monthly periodical whose liberal sympathies were well known. Some, like the Duca della Torre and Astore, were killed during the events surrounding the 1799 republic; others went into exile, like Scipione Breislak and Cagnazzi de Samuele.

Probably the two most cited accounts of the 1794 eruption were those of the Duca della Torre and the geologist Scipione Breislak. Breislak collaborated with Antonio Winspeare, the aristocratic military engineer who had been in charge of the rescue operations after the devastating Messina earthquake of 1783.

The Duca della Torre, one of the founding sponsors of the Enlightenment journal *La scelta miscellanea*, published in Naples in the 1780s, had made Vesuvius a particular obsession. In 1795–6, in the wake of his two published accounts of the recent eruption, he published his *Gabinetto vesuviano* which included more than twenty different images of eruptions (including four for 1794), a chronological narrative of eruptions since 79 CE, and an account of his own investigations of the most recent eruption. He described in considerable detail the seismograph he built and used to record seismic activity, and explained how he had combined its findings with the use of an electrometer to suggest when eruptions might occur. The *Gabinetto* also included an inventory of his Vesuvian mineral collection, classified and arranged with the help of William Thomson, the British mineralogist living in Naples, together with an extensive bibliography of the books and tracts on Vesuvius that the Duke had collected and housed in a special library.[73]

The Duca della Torre clearly had one of the most important collections of Vesuviana in Naples. But none of it was to survive. On 19 January 1799, after the Bourbon royal family had fled from Naples to Sicily and days before the French invading army arrived, della Torre and his brother were abducted by a mob of anti-Jacobins led by the Duke's hairdresser, who believed him to have been in treasonous communication with the French. The palace of the Duke was completely destroyed – the family collection of paintings, many of them masterpieces, went up in flames, along with all his scientific equipment, described by his son as 'a mechanical laboratory capable of carrying out any research work; a workshop filled with beautiful instruments for the art of watchmaking in which my father was perfect; the most complete physics cabinet, a choice collection of works on Vesuvius, and a chemical laboratory equipped with many machines.'[74] Later that night the Duke and his brother were tied to cannon and shot; their bodies were then covered with pitch and set on fire. (Was this, one wonders, a cruel allusion to della Torre's Vesuvian obsessions?)

In their account of the 1794 eruption, Breislak and Winspeare, both of whom survived the turmoil of the 1790s, emphasised their continuous observation of the volcano, maintaining that one or both were present over a period of twenty days. Their professed aim was not merely a detailed description of the eruption, but to throw 'light on [the] theory of volcanic eruptions'. Theirs was a 'memoria', a record of what they recalled and remembered, rather than a 'narrative', a history. Unlike many of their predecessors, whose accounts of earlier eruptions assumed the form of a chronology, Breislak and Winspeare linked contemporary observations to particular historical examples; their account was analytical rather than diachronic, dealing with such topics as lavas, gases, minerals and topographical measurements.[75]

Most of the scientific accounts of the eruption of 1794 were concerned with its immediate effects, and these were not only scientific but social. Their authors, regardless of their level of scientific expertise – and this varied widely – were understandably concerned, as enlightened reformers who believed in the power of government-led social engineering, with maintaining the well-being of Neapolitans – hence the many discussions about the effects of the ash and cinders that clouded the atmosphere and covered the houses, farms and fields in Naples and its surroundings. But the debate about the 1794 eruption also revealed an awareness of the larger scientific debates going on throughout Europe about the role of heat and volcanoes in shaping the shifting contours of the earth.

One sign of a growing openness between the scientific communities of Naples and the rest of Europe was the royal decision in 1789 to send a group of six talented young mineralogists on an ambitious tour, starting in the Habsburg Empire, to study mining techniques and the metal industries in Europe. The aim was to enable them to acquire the expertise necessary to help mining initiatives in the Kingdom of

Naples. This was very much a project in applied science, with the men supervised by Giuseppe Parisi, an energetic reformist general in the corps of military engineers, to whom they had to report on a monthly basis.[76] But these men, though they were brought home to develop mines and military facilities in Calabria, had much larger interests. Most had studied medicine at the university in Naples; several of them were also chemists. Matteo Tondi and Andrea Savaresi gave private lessons in chemistry and both were supporters of the new chemistry associated with Lavoisier. Tondi's *Istituzioni di chimica* was the first Neapolitan publication of the French chemist's system.

The group of Neapolitan students began their studies at the mining school at Schemnitz (in present-day Slovakia), and though their itinerary through Europe was curtailed by the events of the French Revolution and by the bitter personal antipathies that developed among them, they remained abroad until 1796, collecting specimens, keeping journals, and buying instruments and books. When Matteo Tondi returned to Naples from Trieste, his baggage included thirty-five cases of minerals and forty-eight manuscript volumes of his findings and notes.[77] And when another of the travellers, Giuseppe Melograni, published his geological textbook in 1809, based on a course given to a group of Neapolitan architecture students, he frequently cited the notebooks of his European trip, especially those that recorded his findings in Germany and Britain.[78]

After the return of the six young men, the Bourbon government set up a royal mineralogical museum in 1802 based largely on materials collected by Tondi (though at this point he was a political exile in Paris) and his friend and fellow traveller Carmine Antonio Lippi. The catalogue was produced by Melograni, using the classificatory systems of Werner and the Parisian mineralogist René-Just Haüy. Over the next generation the directors of the museum, who also held the chair of mineralogy in the university, included Vincenzo Ramondini (another of the travellers) and, after his return to Naples in 1812, Matteo Tondi.

Of course these colleagues all missed the eruption of 1794, and their professional formation in Germany, dominated by the teachings of Abraham Gottlob Werner, led them to take Neptunist positions that criticised vulcanism and emphasised the importance of aqueous forces in the process of mountain formation.[79] Notoriously, Carmine Antonio Lippi published a series of papers in the second decade of the new century in which he argued that the destruction of Herculaneum and Pompeii was not the result of a Vesuvian eruption, but of a series of floods that buried the cities with detritus. This was not just a specific claim but one that, in a deliberately provocative fashion, pushed the Neptunist agenda. Lippi claimed to 'have demonstrated that all the mountains in strata, and composed of volcanic materials, & non-volcanic ... find their origin in water ... Similarly all the mountains of volcanic tufo [are] the product of humidity ... Here, then, is what I call Neptunian volcanic mountains, of which, that is, the material is volcanic, but the genesis is due to floods.'[80] Though his views were much criticised in Naples, notably by members of the Academy of Sciences in Naples, his old friend Tondi came vigorously to his defence.[81]

But this debate was symptomatic of a change. Discussions in the pages of a new journal, the *Giornale letterario di Napoli*, and subsequent polemics that went on into the new century, were mindful of, and sometimes made direct allusions to, larger debates in Europe about the place of vulcanism in the earth's history.[82] Thereafter, local investigation of Vesuvius and international science were unbreakably connected. But the link was not sustained, as one might have expected, by the professor of mineralogy and head of the mineralogical museum. Tondi had a great deal of international experience – in exile after 1799 he had worked for several years in Paris at the Muséum National d'Histoire Naturelle and acted as the assistant to two of France's most distinguished scientists, the geologist Déodat Gratet de Dolomieu and the mineralogist René-Just Haüy – but he showed little interest in volcanoes and seems never to have spent time working on Vesuvius.[83]

The very large collection of Vesuvian rocks and minerals that can be seen in the Naples mineralogical museum today was largely the addition of later collections, those of Teodoro Monticelli and Tondi's pupil Arcangelo Scacchi. Indeed, it was Monticelli, the permanent secretary of the Neapolitan Royal Academy of Sciences established by Joseph Bonaparte in 1807, who became the key go-between, connecting the international scientific community to local naturalists and to the volcano itself.

Putting Vesuvius in context was a process that involved not just local scholars, but experts who tried to tie together the rapidly accumulating body of information about volcanoes across Europe and beyond. It depended, as the following chapters will reveal, not just on sedentary figures like Monticelli, but also on travelling scholars like Déodat de Dolomieu whose ambitions were comparative, committed to developing a general account of vulcanism rather than the history of a single place.

Part V

Geological Lives: The Politics of Vulcanism

9
DÉODAT DE DOLOMIEU AND TEODORO MONTICELLI

I n the last section we saw how the earth sciences became both central to scientific investigation and fashionable, and what effect this
had on the study of Vesuvius, connecting larger trends in scientific
knowledge with the assiduous field work of Neapolitan and Italian
investigators of the volcano. Though this was an essential part of the
culture of vulcanism and Vesuvius, there is a danger that it will make
the story appear to be merely an account of scientific problem-
solving rather than a matter of understanding how scientific knowledge is made in a complex and messy world. To understand this we
need to move from a study of abstractions to a study of people, from
ideas to life histories, and from concepts to practices.

The next two chapters use the lives of two naturalists and earth
scientists, the French noble Déodat de Dolomieu (1750–1801) and the
Neapolitan functionary Teodoro Monticelli (1759–1845), to examine
two scientific careers, and the different ways in which the volcano was
treated as a scientific object. This was not just a matter of scientific
observations and inferences, but about how the two men framed and
understood their inquiry. For Dolomieu, concerned to develop theories
about the nature of volcanic action and its effects on the formation of
rocks and crystals, Vesuvius was an important case study, a particular

instance of a general phenomenon. For Monticelli, Vesuvius was a scientific site or object whose value lay as much in its use as a promoter of Neapolitan scientific culture as in its geological importance. Each studied, presented and used the volcano in different ways.

The Frenchman, deeply committed to field work and to the distinctiveness of individual geological sites, saw himself as someone whose observation of an exceptional number of active and extinct volcanoes placed him in a unique position. Though today we remember Dolomieu as the naturalist whose name was given to an alpine carbonite rock and the range of mountains, the Dolomites, where it is found in such abundance, in his lifetime he was known as the geologist who had visited and studied more volcanoes than any other naturalist. His travels and his collections of lavas, minerals and rocks were legendary. When he died prematurely in November 1801, his final travelling companion, the Danish geologist T.C. Bruun-Neergaard, exclaimed, 'Dolomieu is no more! What a blow for natural history, for mineralogical philosophy, for geognosy, and above all for the science of volcanoes!'[1]

If Dolomieu was closely associated with the science of volcanoes, or more precisely with the processes of vulcanism, Monticelli was intimately connected to Naples and Vesuvius. His long tenure as the secretary to the Royal Academy of Sciences, his assiduous encouragement of research into Vesuvius, his coordination of a vast international network of volcanic scientists, and his determination to develop a broad-ranging local scientific culture built around the volcano made him into a local, internationally recognised expert. He became, as one young admirer put it, a 'cult' among mineralogists, praised by Alexander von Humboldt as 'the learned and zealous observer of the Volcano',[2] while Humphry Davy compared Monticelli's achievements as a vulcanist to those of the famous Swiss scientist Horace Bénédict de Saussure, as a scholar of the Alps.[3]

Both Dolomieu and Monticelli were ardent vulcanologists. In order to pursue their passions – writing to a fellow savant in Sicily,

Dolomieu described natural history as their 'shared mistress'[4] – they had to face a whole series of obstacles. Both had to navigate the radical and abrupt changes in regime that fundamentally altered political and scientific institutions and the contexts in which they could pursue their studies. Their achievements and misfortunes make clear that the study of volcanoes – indeed, almost any form of scientific investigation – was inevitably shaped by the political and social volatility of the age. As we shall see, Monticelli, for reasons of temperament as well as circumstance, was rather more successful at negotiating these obstacles. But on the cusp of the nineteenth century both men were political prisoners of the Bourbon regime, Dolomieu in a tiny windowless cell in Messina in Sicily, and Monticelli in the Castello Santa Caterina, a Saracen fort on the island of Favignana, 17 kilometres off the western coast of Sicily. Dolomieu's premature death, shortly past his fiftieth year, was directly attributable to his imprisonment by the Bourbons for twenty-one months between June 1799 and March 1801.

The two men's work involved contrasting styles of scientific inquiry. Dolomieu was a restless spirit, a figure in almost perpetual motion, travelling constantly between Paris, his family seat near Grenoble, Italy and its islands, the Pyrenees, the Alps, and Malta (to his day job as one of the Knights of St John). His correspondence is full of itineraries, either projected or completed. Monticelli, apart from a brief sojourn in Rome, never seems to have left the Kingdom of Naples, and rarely left its capital city. He preferred to sit at the centre of an extraordinarily extensive network of naturalists and savants that was sustained by a common interest in geology, volcanoes and Vesuvius.

To a certain extent these differences were also matters of personal temperament. Dolomieu was a flamboyant character, given in his letters to a certain theatricality and self-importance. Thus, when speculating on what to do with his mineral and rock collections, he devised a proposal to donate them to the Congress of the United States, but only on the condition that a century later (and only if France was free from despotism) the Congress would send a comparable collection of scientific specimens back to France. He had a razor-sharp intellect, wrote beautifully, never suffered fools gladly, and, though praised for his charm, was impatient, argumentative and assertive. (He had killed a man in a duel before he was twenty.) Everywhere he went he seems to have attracted admirers and detractors in equal measure.

Dolomieu had a reputation as a libertine with lovers, both married and single, in many different cities, including Paris, Rome and Florence. He cut a striking figure, slender, muscular, nearly 1.95 metres (6 foot 4 inches) tall with blue eyes, an aquiline nose and blond hair (until it turned white during the French Revolution). In one posthumous tribute his final travelling companion, Bruun-Neergaard, described him as a man who 'loved society very much, and was very agreeable to the fair sex, who usually formed a circle around him'.[5] Some authorities think that he was the model for the Vicomte de Valmont in the novel *Liaisons dangereuses* by his friend, Pierre Choderlos de Laclos. Certainly, another of his companions, the notoriously dissolute Alexandre Comte de Tilly, saw him as a man of sexual intrigue, comparing him to Lovelace, the libertine villain of Samuel Richardson's novel, *Clarissa*.[6] His preferred milieu was the mixed-sex salon rather than the (male) academy: in Paris at the salon of the Duchesse d'Enville, in Rome (where he was frequently in the 1780s) at the salons of the Spanish ambassador, of Maria Pizzelli, the Countess Piccolomini – who was his lover – and of Angelika Kauffmann, who painted his portrait. Here his companions were antiquaries, artists, men of letters, aristocratic French travellers, women of intellect and beauty, and diplomats.[7] Almost all were agreed on Dolomieu's *mondanité*. He was sociable, attractive, quick-witted and charming, his knowledge capacious but lightly worn; his writing was both elegant and incisive. Though from a pious, cash-strapped, provincial noble family, he moved with confidence in aristocratic circles.

Monticelli, on the other hand, was famous for his probity, tranquil demeanour, charm and general affability, his extraordinary facility in making deep and lasting friendships with men and women, and people of all nationalities. His affections, though strongly felt, were more muted. He seems to have led a chaste life, reserving his personal affections for his brother's son, whose career as a diplomat he assiduously promoted. He moved in aristocratic circles and was a longstanding member of the most cosmopolitan salon in Naples, that of his patron Francesco Ricciardi. But he was a man of modesty, not brilliance, who took less pride in his own achievements than in those of others.

The two men also had very different relations to Vesuvius. Dolomieu's were vexed and complex. On his first visit to the volcano in the 1770s he was accompanied by Sir William Hamilton, whom Dolomieu saw as a rival and populariser, ill-versed in both chemistry and physics. He returned in the autumn of 1784, making four ascents of the volcano in ten days, sometimes in the company of the Scottish chemist Sir James Hall, helping him to collect specimens that Hall would later use in experiments on his return to Edinburgh. But Dolomieu was disappointed in his findings. The major eruption of 1779 had buried in lava parts of the mountain he particularly wished to investigate, and he failed to find the minerals he wanted that had been described by the Parisian mineralogist Roman de Lisle. In Naples, visiting mineral vendors (a group he despised and distrusted), he also could not find what he wanted. Two years later, Dolomieu was further frustrated in his desire to examine the volcano. He had been banned from the Kingdom of Naples for allegedly having spread rumours on his earlier visit of a secret deal between the Neapolitans and Russians, with the complicity of the Knights of St John. Naples, he was supposed to have said, would give up its claims to Malta in favour of the Russians. Fearing arrest if he landed, Dolomieu could only watch from a ship in Naples harbour as the volcano erupted. Thereafter, his close friend, collaborator and correspondent Giuseppe Gioeni became the vehicle for Dolomieu's knowledge and observations about Vesuvius.

Dolomieu had first met Gioeni, a protégé of Giuseppe Recupero and his successor as professor of natural history at the University of Catania, when he visited Etna in 1781. Gioeni spent much of the 1780s in Naples, where he had been invited by Sir William Hamilton, and had become tutor to the monarch's son. In these years Gioeni worked on a comprehensive study of the minerals of Vesuvius which eventually appeared in 1790 as *Saggio di litologia vesuviana* and was translated into German three years later. Dolomieu has been described as the 'authoritative supervisor' of Gioeni's work, which began with a comparative overview of the literature on volcanoes (very much Dolomieu's perspective) and was organised on a table devised by the Frenchman 'for the methodical distribution of volcanic materials'. Before its appearance, Dolomieu had peppered Gioeni with advice, warnings and information about how to structure his study and how to distinguish different volcanic products. Thanks to the Frenchman's tutelage the work was a great success and secured Gioeni corresponding memberships of academies in Göttingen, Berlin, Milan, Padua and London.[8]

The problem with Vesuvius, from Dolomieu's point of view, was a problem of accessibility. Much of his reputation came from his exploration of previously understudied volcanic sites and his analyses, supported by his collections, of rare individual configurations of minerals and lavas. He may have had problems reaching the volcano due to the political ban on him, but Vesuvius was just too popular and too crowded. The presence of Hamilton, whom Dolomieu dismissed as a 'half-connoisseur', did not help. But what especially irked him were the rock and lava vendors. As he told Gioeni, 'Above all, beware of anything sold by merchants: they bring stones from foreign countries, which they then sell as lava from Vesuvius; generally only rely on what you have collected yourself.'[9] For Dolomieu, Vesuvius was a vexed case, but a vital piece in the complex jigsaw of volcanic matter and the processes of its creation that he worked so hard to assemble. As we shall see, it did not sit easily with his conception of himself as a heroic scientific explorer and pioneer.

No such problem confronted Monticelli. After his return to Naples from imprisonment and exile in 1806 he worked quickly under the French to become the go-to person for those savants, both local and international, who were interested in studying the volcano. He made himself into a facilitator rather than a gatekeeper, never passing judgment on a naturalist's experience or credibility, but rather enabling them, as best he could, to study the volcano and its activities. He used his country house in Boscotrecase on the southern slopes of the volcano to entertain visitors and to carry out research. Though the number of his ascents of Vesuvius diminished by the third decade of the century – his last recorded visit was with the Prince of Denmark in 1828 – he had long-established relations with the guides at Resina and especially with Salvatore Madonna, arranging for savants to work with him, and encouraging them to rely, in a way of which Dolomieu would not have approved, on his skills in finding crystals and lavas. Though, as we shall see, he contributed a great deal to research on the volcano; in the eyes of many he became a guardian of the mountain. It was his job to shepherd visiting royalty and high aristocracy up the volcano. After the shocking suicide of the French army officer Louis Coutrel, who threw himself into one of the burning crevices on the slopes of the volcano on 11 January 1821, it was Monticelli who penned and published a formal account of the incident, reassuring future visitors of their safety, and exonerating the guides of any blame.[10] Though a savant and a leading member of the Academy, Monticelli was very much a part of the Vesuvian economy that Dolomieu viewed with such suspicion. But that was because he saw himself not just as a naturalist, but as pursuing a particular vision of the Kingdom of Naples.

10
DÉODAT DE DOLOMIEU
The Hazards of Vulcanism

J'écrirai au Baron Zois . . . s'il aime les productions volcaniques, je suis son homme.

(I will write to Baron Zois . . . if he loves volcanic products, I'm his man.)

Dolomieu to Philippe Picot de Lapeyrouse, June 1783[1]

Le premier Vulcaniste du monde.

(The number one vulcanologist in the world.)

Spallanzani on Dolomieu, as reported in
Senebier to Pictet, 7 March 1797[2]

Déodat de Dolomieu's distinguished career reveals the virtual impossibility of isolating the work of the natural philosopher from the complex politics of the times. Dolomieu's life as a scientist was marked by a number of transitions – from the *ancien régime* to the Revolution, from the aristocratic amateur savant to membership of what Charles Lyell later called 'the small standing army' of public scientific officials, and from the disciplines of physical geography and mineralogy to geology. Aptly, he gave the very first course on geology at the École des Mines in 1795. But as Dolomieu was to discover

316

through his membership of the scientific expedition that accompanied Napoleon's invasion of Egypt in 1798, such transitions were far from smooth. The story of his fate during and after his attempt to return to France from the Middle East is a grim warning of what could be at stake in scientific inquiry, and of the difficulties confronted by savants trying to negotiate a volatile political landscape.

On 17 March 1799 the *Belle Maltaise*, an old corvette with 120 people on board, limped into the harbour at Taranto in Puglia. For more than a week passengers and crew had worked to keep the leaking ship afloat, caulking its seams, tossing overboard its ten cannons and much of a cargo that included 4,000 pounds of coffee and 11 Arabian stallions. The vessel had set sail for France ten days earlier from the Egyptian port of Alexandria, its complement including some forty sick and wounded French soldiers, and two French generals, Jean-Baptiste Manscourt du Rozoy and Thomas-Alexandre Dumas, the Haitian-born commander of Napoleon's cavalry, who had commissioned the vessel to take them back to France. Also on board were Déodat de Dolomieu and his star student Louis Cordier, both of whom had been members of the scientific expedition that had accompanied the French army of invasion of Egypt. Dumas and Dolomieu had each, in their different ways, fallen out with Napoleon. Bonaparte, justifiably, suspected Dumas's commitment to the Egyptian expedition, while Dolomieu had grown disillusioned with the project: 'My association with a military enterprise, which put me (even in an indirect fashion) under the orders of a general, was tiresome to my imagination, even if the general was Bonaparte.'[3] Neither man was well, their health compromised by the climate and threatened by the plague that ravaged the French army.

The French passengers, all hoping to return to their homeland, were out of luck. Many on board thought they were landing in the recently established Neapolitan republic, a client state of the expanding French empire, but the flags that fluttered over Taranto's harbour fortress told a different story. Puglia was back in the hands of the Santa Fede, the ardent and sometimes fanatical supporters of the Bourbon dynasty and the Catholic Church. Seeking help from a friendly power to help them on their journey, instead the Frenchmen found themselves prisoners of war, incarcerated in Taranto's mediaeval fortress.

Soon they were transferred to an old seminary between the town and the sea. Only the generals remained in the citadel. Dolomieu spent his time reading Pliny's *Natural History*, while his protégé, Cordier, gave lessons in mineralogy to his fellow prisoners. After nine weeks of confinement they were all shipped off to Messina, the Sicilian city across the straits from mainland Italy. Only Manscourt and Dumas remained in Puglia, imprisoned in adjoining dank cells of the fifteenth-century fortress, whose humid atmosphere and clammy air irreparably damaged the health of the French-Haitian commander, who was also convinced that the prison doctor was poisoning him.[4] Such circumstances explain two of the lifelong obsessions of Dumas's son, the novelist Alexandre Dumas: the horrors of incarceration and the political fate of the Kingdom of Naples and Italy. As Alexandre would later write, 'The day ... when Ferdinand the first imprisoned my father, he made me a citizen of Naples.'[5]

This was not Dolomieu's first trip to Messina. In February 1784 he had visited the city to examine the effects of the disastrous earthquakes and tsunamis of the previous year that had destroyed much of the town, damaged the Duomo, wrecked the harbour, flattened surrounding villages, and killed between 35,000 and 50,000 people. On that occasion he came of his own free will as a scientific investigator eager to explain why some towns and villages had been so badly damaged while others escaped relatively unscathed. The trip was one of Dolomieu's series of expeditions – to Sicily, the Aeolian Islands, the Pyrenees and northern Italy – as an amateur naturalist obsessed with volcanoes, mountains and the history of the earth. Fifteen years later his circumstances were very different. When all the Frenchmen were repatriated, returning home via Livorno after a month in Messina, Dolomieu was not among them. Instead he was separated from his companions, including Cordier, and incarcerated in a local prison for political prisoners, locked up in solitary confinement in a 3- by 4-metre cell (10 by 12 feet), illuminated only by a dim shaft of light that emanated from a small opening above its door.

The local Knights of Malta, members of the ancient Order of St John, had secured Dolomieu's incarceration, though he was nominally held by King Ferdinand of Naples. They were furious at what they saw as Dolomieu's betrayal of the Order, in which he had been enrolled as a young man. On the voyage from France to Egypt, Napoleon had captured the island of Malta and, knowing of Dolomieu's connections to the Knights, had ordered him to handle the treaty of surrender, an accord that Napoleon failed to honour. This was only the latest if most egregious example of what many within the Order regarded as Dolomieu's cavalier attitude towards the customs and values of the Maltese knights. Dolomieu's past had caught up with him.

The Knight of Malta and the *ancien régime*

Dolomieu had been christened Dieudonné Sylvain Guy Tancrède de Gratet de Dolomieu on 24 June 1750. The names, indicating his vows to serve God and linking him to the famous eleventh-century Crusader, together with the presence of his godfather and uncle Guy, a cavalry officer and Knight of Malta, make clear the career that his family had chosen for him. Dolomieu was a younger son of a pious, provincial noble family. His parents, like many other French nobles, paid a fee (in their case 6,200 livres) when he was two years old for his rite of passage into the Order of St John, a Catholic lay religious order, which he then joined as a teenager.[6] He had no choice in the matter; he was to follow in a family tradition of service in the Order. The family's aim was less for the young man to lead a life of 'Poverty, chastity and obedience', vows more honoured in the breach than in their observance, or to defend the Christian faith, than to give Dolomieu the chance to earn a decent gentlemanly living. The Knights still performed military and charitable duties, but the Order had largely become a form of charitable support for the titled classes. About half its wealth lay in French properties and more than half the Knights were French.

Dolomieu's relations with the Knights of Malta were always complex and difficult. In 1768, aged eighteen, he quarrelled with a fellow noviciate and, in the ensuing duel at Gaeta, north of Naples, killed his opponent. He was condemned to life imprisonment in Malta, but his sentence was commuted as a result of the intervention of the representatives of the Pope and Louis XV. He went home to France, did not return to the island until 1776, and was only made a Knight of the Order in 1778. Thereafter, his rise through the ranks was both swift and precarious. In 1780 he became the 'commandeur' in charge of the 'commanderie Saint Anne Saint Priest', a cluster of Templar properties in the Haute-Vienne in west-central France. These, doubtless to the satisfaction of his parents, gave him a tidy income: the rents were 12,000 livres a year in 1787, of which only 4,500 livres were remitted to the Knights in Malta.[7] But Dolomieu was soon complaining that his 'bigger fortune [was] acquired at the price of my liberty and independence', though this did not prevent him from using these funds to finance his many geological expeditions, leading his uncle to fret at his frequent absences from Malta. In 1783 he became Lieutenant of the Grand Marshal and Governor of Valletta but complained that the job produced only 'boredom' and 'torment'.[8] The politics of the Order were a toxic brew of intergenerational conflict, factionalism (chiefly based on the nationalities of the Knights), and deep personal antipathies that often became long-lasting grudges.[9] Dolomieu was far from immune, and was soon known as a troublemaker: he quarrelled with the Grand Master, whom he accused of 'a propensity to despotism',[10] and engaged for several years in a protracted and bitter struggle with his lifelong enemy Bailli Charles Abel de Loras, the Grand Master's faithful servant and the dupe of Cagliostro. Dolomieu portrayed himself as a reformer, and as a victim 'the object of envy and the most infamous persecution'.[11] He promoted the building of the library in Valletta, opened a school to teach bread-making, built a scientific observatory and imported 20,000 francs' worth of telescopes and scientific equipment.[12] But, as he repeatedly complained, few of his fellow Knights were interested in science, and most were fearful of reform, which they saw as a threat to their privileges. He became embroiled in labyrinthine quarrels and protracted litigation with his rivals, repeatedly visiting the Papal Court in Rome – he made eight trips between 1784 and 1791 – to defend himself from accusations made by a growing number of enemies from among the Knights. His presence in Paris during the early days of the Revolution fuelled rumours that he was a Jacobin, that he planned to lead a local rising against the Knights, and that he wished to destroy the Order. None of this was true: he had an uncle and a younger brother in the Order and wanted to keep the income he had from the French estates he administered. But his conversations on the island with his fellow Knights in which he spoke of 'ignorance and the chains of despotism' and expressed puzzlement at their inability to entertain the notion that there should be equality before the law cannot have helped.[13] Given this history, and his implacable enemies within the Order, it was not surprising that Dolomieu was incarcerated in appalling conditions.

But how had the restless young man turned to the sciences of the earth and to vulcanology?[14] How did a soldier become a savant? After his return to France in the early 1770s, Dolomieu had been recruited into a regiment of *carabiniers* stationed at Metz. Here he took his first lessons in chemistry, physics, mineralogy and metallurgy, paying 2 louis a session to the local apothecary, Jean-Baptiste Thyrion, most of whose students were army officers from the artillery and engineering regiments stationed in the town.[15] (Thyrion's daughter soon became Dolomieu's lover and was a lifelong friend.) Thyrion was especially interested in the chemistry of minerals.

Among those Dolomieu met in Thyrion's shop and laboratory and on collecting trips in the surrounding countryside were the great amateur mineralogist and collector the Comte de Bournon, and the Duke de La Rochefoucauld.[16] The Duke, an enlightened aristocrat, was a member of the Academy of Sciences, a friend of the greatest naturalist of the age, Georges-Louis Leclerc, Comte de Buffon, and was passionately interested in chemistry and mineralogy. He published scientific papers, had his own laboratory in Paris, and sponsored the translation of scientific works from German.[17] He soon became Dolomieu's patron and close friend and was a key figure in his development as a natural philosopher. It is clear from Dolomieu's correspondence that he went to great lengths to cultivate and retain La Rochefoucauld's patronage, even though at times he claimed to find it irksome. He was eventually to ingratiate himself with the family and to become a member of the household.

La Rochefoucauld and his mother the Duchess d'Enville were at the centre of a distinguished circle of philosophers, savants and writers that moved between the salon the Duchess ran from the family hôtel on the rue de Seine in Paris, and the chateau at Roche-Guyon, some 75 kilometres from the capital. This country seat boasted an observatory, small theatre and magnificent 12,000-volume library. Though the circle was known for its scientific interests – the Duchess took lessons in geometry and had her own mineral collection – it was also the meeting place of such important thinkers and politicians as Turgot (who when dismissed from government in 1776 went straight to the chateau at Roche-Guyon), Condorcet and the Abbé Mably. A centre of support for the American Revolution – the Duke de La Rochefoucauld was a good friend of Tom Paine and Benjamin Franklin, and translated the American constitution into French at the latter's request – the circle was a fount of the reformist politics that Dolomieu was later to embrace with enthusiasm.[18] But equally important were the scientific connections that Dolomieu made through La Rochefoucauld and Buffon, who actively

322

worked together to promote their clients into the Academy of Sciences.[19] The circle included Nicolas Desmarest, who had accompanied the young Duke up Vesuvius in 1765, and who was the acknowledged expert on the extinct volcanoes of the Auvergne, and Barthélemy Faujas de Saint-Fond, a protégé of Buffon's, who was the first to arouse Dolomieu's interest in vulcanism and who became his lifelong friend. (After Dolomieu's death Faujas erected a monument made of prismatic lavas in his garden with the inscription *'Dolomieu, mon élève, mon maître, mon ami'* – 'Dolomieu, my pupil, my master, my friend'.)

Whether or not Dolomieu saw his pursuit of mineralogy as the path to his social advancement, he quickly acquired a lifelong passion, embarking on his new scientific interests with characteristic energy and dedication. Eager to impress the Duke de La Rochefoucauld with his growing skills as a mineralogist and chemist, he sent him elaborate reports of his findings on his travels and specimens for the Duke's collections, constantly thanking him for his support and dropping heavy hints about his desire to be elected to the Academy of Sciences. Through the good offices of the Duke, he also corresponded with Louis-Jean-Marie Daubenton, the collaborator of Buffon, an official at the Jardin des Plantes and an enthusiastic mineralogist, who would eventually sponsor Dolomieu as a corresponding member of the Academy of Sciences. Before returning to Malta in 1776, Dolomieu orchestrated a flurry of solicitation to his mineralogical friends, clearly anxious not to lose the patronage of La Rochefoucauld and his colleagues once he was back on the island.

Throughout the 1770s and 1780s Dolomieu shuttled between Malta, France and the volcanic regions of the Mediterranean. His vulcanological travels were prodigious. He made his first scientific Italian trip in 1776, taking in Vesuvius and the Apennines. Two years later he travelled to Portugal as the secretary of Camille de Rohan, the ambassador for the Knights of Malta in Lisbon. His reports on the presence of basalt there finally earned him a corresponding membership of the French Academy of Sciences. In 1781 he was in Sicily and the Aeolian Islands examining active volcanoes. The following year he travelled with his friend, Picot de Lapeyrouse, through the Pyrenees. In 1784 his studies took him to northern Italy, Elba, Rome and the Papal States, Tuscany and the Kingdom of Naples. Pondering a new expedition in 1785, he began to think that Italy was 'a country that I knew already too well'[20] and that he needed somewhere new; he contemplated a trip to the Americas or to the East Indies. In the end he lowered his horizons, opting to spend several months studying Mount Etna and travelling through Calabria. Despite being banned from the Kingdom of Naples, he was back in Italy in 1787, boasting that only a balloonist could travel further in less time. He claimed to have gone for nine days without sleeping, and to have spent sixty-four hours in the saddle in the mountains round Genoa.[21] He led, he confessed, 'a truly wandering life', and had travelled over all of Italy. 'If God gives me the patience and time to write up my observations, I would be able to lead the travelling naturalist to all the nooks of this beautiful country.'[22] Only the outbreak of the Revolution inhibited his wanderings which became chiefly confined to the regions of France, the Vosges, Piedmont, the much-studied Auvergne and the Alps, where he spent much time with Swiss collaborators and friends. When he was recruited for Napoleon's Egyptian expedition, he had already been planning journeys to Corinth and Constantinople.

Detailed findings from Dolomieu's travels were laid before his fellow savants in a series of publications. Two of his early works were printed as appendices in the books of his friend Faujas de Saint-Fond: his account of Portuguese basalts appeared in Faujas's *Recherches sur les volcans éteints du Vivarais et du Velay*, and a catalogue of '*produits volcaniques*' of Mount Etna that Dolomieu had sent to Faujas and to the Duke de La Rochefoucauld in 1782 was included in the former's *Minéralogie des volcans*, a book that, as we shall see, played a special role in Dolomieu's life. Among a steady stream of publications in the 1780s and early 1790s were articles in the journal *Observations sur la physique, l'histoire naturelle et les arts* (later the *Journal de physique*), edited by his close friend Lamétherie, and studies of the Mediterranean volcanic islands and of the devastating earthquake in Calabria of 1783.[23]

These publications and the travels that made them possible established Dolomieu's reputation as a naturalist who had seen more volcanic features than any other living person. While in the 1770s Dolomieu betrayed some anxiety about his erudition, which he was often overeager to display to others, by the 1780s he had developed a sense that he now belonged to an august body of savants whose erudition and skills were much greater than most mineralogists and small collectors. He complained bitterly about having to collect materials for less erudite but wealthier amateurs, like his patron the Duke de La Rochefoucauld.

Central to this self-perception were his collections of lavas, rocks and minerals, which served as an aide-memoire of his travels and attachments. 'To each of my stones,' he wrote to his fellow naturalist Lapeyrouse, 'is attached the remembrance of one of the circumstances of my life; they recall my quests, the friends they have secured me, the pleasures they have given me.'[24] They were also a research tool which he used to make meticulous comparisons and distinctions between volcanic substances from different locations. When he wanted to convince the naturalist he most admired, Horace Bénédict de Saussure, about the specificity of certain igneous rocks, he assured him that if he could see the specimens in his collection, he would be convinced of their identity. Time and again he warned his fellow naturalists against buying specimens, especially those offered by dealers; only rock and minerals found *in situ* by the naturalists themselves could count as reliable evidence. Correct labelling was essential. Dolomieu built his reputation not just on the range of his observations, but on their precision.

Originally most of Dolomieu's collections were kept at his house in Malta. He spoke of them as the chief impediment to leaving the island, as powerful a constraint on his departure as the presence there of his ageing and ailing uncle. By 1789 he had twenty-two huge cartons of specimens scattered through Europe. A year later he moved the bulk of his collections from Malta to Marseilles, storing them with the port's Swedish consul, but he still had materials in Grenoble, Lyon, Geneva and Venice. He was distraught when he heard that six cases from Venice had probably been lost at sea. After the Revolution, when he was teaching at the government's École des Mines in Paris, he tried to persuade the government to pay for the consolidation of his collections on the grounds that they were essential to instruct his students. Before he left for Egypt he boasted that he had more than 500 separate drawers of geological specimens, overwhelmingly volcanic materials.

During these years, his circle of friends and correspondents, ranging from northern Europe to Sicily, grew apace, and he became part of a network of geological and vulcanological savants exchanging information and, above all, samples of rocks and lava. Dolomieu was always slightly wary of such exchanges, especially as they usually involved duplicates in collections, which were bartered off while the collector kept the best samples for themselves. He gave his correspondents the sense that it was almost a privilege to be able to engage in such exchanges with him. But this network sustained Dolomieu as a man of science. He rarely omitted an opportunity in his letters, which he pointedly signed in this period 'Naturalist and Frenchman', to distance himself from Malta and its feudal order, and to place himself in the international community of scientific savants.[25]

The Revolution

By the spring of 1791 Dolomieu had abandoned Malta and the Knights, spending the next seven years in France, immersed in Revolutionary politics, and then working as an instructor and inspector for what became the École des Mines. He was an early and enthusiastic supporter of the Revolution (his friend Faujas de Saint-Fond even thought him briefly a Jacobin), though, like several liberal aristocrats, he came to favour a constitutional monarchy rather than an anti-monarchical republic.

But the escalating violence and radicalism of the Revolution turned Dolomieu's world upside down. In September 1792, his friend, patron and fellow mineralogist, the Duke de La Rochefoucauld, was stoned and stabbed to death in Dolomieu's presence at Gisors, some 32 kilometres (20 miles) from the Duke's ancestral home at the Château de la Roche-Guyon. In the same month the Order of the Knights of Malta was officially suppressed and its properties confiscated. Dolomieu lost his most important patron and his income. His family was imprisoned in Grenoble; his mother never recovered from the experience and died shortly after her release. Friends were executed, imprisoned or went into exile. Dolomieu's hair turned white.

Over the previous twenty years Dolomieu had skilfully crafted a space for himself to pursue his fascination with volcanoes and the history of the earth, using the financial resources of the Knights of Malta, and the aristocratic patronage networks that lay at the heart of *ancien régime* science. He had established himself as a leading amateur savant by stint of his virtuosity and industry. Now his world was in tatters. Like many a noble (and many a savant) he thought it wise to keep out of the limelight.

For much of the next two years after La Rochefoucauld's assassination, he remained at Roche-Guyon with the mother and the widow of the Duke. Afraid to travel, he was also fearful of Paris. After spending six days back in the capital, he wrote to a friend, 'I swear that that visit made such an impression of terror, of fear, that I am still not free of it ... anxiety and mistrust are imprinted there on all faces, we are afraid to speak to each other, we do not dare to risk an opinion, egoism exercises an absolute empire over everyone; there are no longer any ties or friendship.'[26] In his provincial retreat Dolomieu concentrated on writing. But whereas in 1792 he had still signed his publications as 'Commandeur Déodat de Dolomieu', by 1794 he had become 'le citoyen Dolomieu', who complained that he had no means of support and was beginning to experience a growing survivor's guilt.[27]

But after the Terror his reputation as a geologist rescued him. In 1794 he agreed to write the section on mineralogy for Panckoucke's *Encyclopédie méthodique*, accepting the famous publisher's terms, because, as he said, 'all that remains of my ancient fortune does not suffice to pay for a bad dinner.'[28] (He nevertheless did not complete the project.) He began working for the Conseil des Mines, inspecting their sites, though he was soon complaining that 'If I did not serve my tastes at the same time as I carried out the duties of my job, I would have quit a long time ago.'

Dolomieu was being pushed, a little unwillingly, into the market-place and public employment. In 1795 he was appointed to the Conseil des Mines and elected to the mineralogical and natural history section of the newly founded Institut National, which was intended to replace the pre-Revolutionary academies. Like other naturalists, he survived because he could plausibly claim to have skills useful to the Revolutionary regime. For the next three years he divided his time between field trips inspecting French mines (he used his official duties as an opportunity to visit new areas of volcanic and mineralogical interest) and lecturing on geology to students in the École des Mines. As he ruefully remarked, 'The sciences which, at another time, were for me a relaxation have become the trade [*métier*] which gives me something to live on; and yet I'm doing it with pleasure.'[29]

But public employment limited the freedom of action that Dolomieu could enjoy. As one of France's most eminent earth scientists and the author of a study of the formation of the Nile Delta published in 1793, he was understandably recruited to Napoleon's Egyptian expedition, an extraordinary exercise in scientific imperialism. One hundred and fifty-one savants and their assistants in such fields as mineralogy, zoology, botany, mathematics, physics, astronomy and medicine were all recruited to examine and dissect the Arab state. But things did not go well for Dolomieu. He did little mineralogical work; a number of his friends were killed, and he fell out with Napoleon. He was eager to return to France. His capture and removal to Messina only made matters worse.

In Messina Dolomieu was stripped of nearly all his possessions and papers. His remaining belongings were confined to four shirts, three precious books and a broken comb. He was deliberately deprived of pen and paper. His cell included a wooden bed frame and mattress, a chair, a table, a plate, a single, flickering lamp, and two receptacles, one for water, the other to relieve himself. His mattress and sheets were constantly damp, his rations were meagre, and he had no exercise. As he himself put it, he paced up and down the cell like a wild beast in a cage. He often contemplated suicide, complaining that his circumstances were worse than those of a prisoner on a chain gang, who at least had company, or a man standing on the gallows, who at least knew when his misery would end.[30]

But Dolomieu's angry and anguished response to his circum-stances stimulated his resourcefulness. He set out to refurbish his cell, to fill it with the capacious world of natural history, to recreate the ideas, practices and friendships that had drawn him to geological science in the first place. And he did so through writing. He fash-ioned a pen from a piece of whittled wood and made ink from lamp-smoke mixed with water, neatly filling in the margins and white spaces between the lines of the three printed books he had managed to keep. Writing became his greatest distraction, though he was plagued by the fear that his script, crowding the ever-smaller margins of his books, would eventually leave him with no more space.

Most of Dolomieu's journal was written in and over the 511 pages of a book entitled *La minéralogie des volcans: ou Description de toutes les substances produites ou rejetées par les feux souterrains*, written by

Faujas de Saint-Fond and published in 1784. Faujas, as Dolomieu noted in one his vignettes, 'was he who introduced me to the study of volcanoes'.[31] He was a long-standing friend and collaborator. The book that served as Dolomieu's journal was not only a handy work of reference – it was a systematic study that opened with thirteen chapters on the different sorts of basalt – but the token of a friendship that had begun some twenty years earlier, when Faujas had included a letter from Dolomieu about volcanic basalts in Portugal in his *Recherches sur les volcans éteints du Vivarais et du Velay* (1778). This book, a work by an avowed Plutonist, was part of the efforts in the late 1770s, to which Desmarest, Soulavie and Sir William Hamilton contributed, to extend the findings about the extinct volcanoes of central France and to assert the general importance of volcanic action in the ongoing development of the earth. Dolomieu continued to support this enterprise. The final section of Faujas's *Minéralogie des volcans* was an extended catalogue of volcanic materials from Etna, collected by Dolomieu in 1781 and sent to Faujas and the Duke de La Rochefoucauld. His book not only enabled Dolomieu to record his thoughts and feelings but embodied the sort of scientific relationships that Dolomieu thought so important.

And what did Dolomieu write in the lines between Faujas's printed text? Like many a prisoner before him, he kept a journal to mark the passage of time, focusing on his relationship with his jailor (portrayed as an arbitrary and despotic figure) and on his frustrations and disorientation at being deprived of news and information. But Dolomieu's quotidian observations were eclipsed by his impassioned account of the contrast between his present circumstances and the taste and habits, '*mes goûts et mes habitudes*', of his earlier life. His story is by turns melodramatic, sentimental and self-aggrandising, yet also heartfelt and revealing. Darkness and light, constraint and freedom, closure and openness, confinement and movement, scarcity and abundance: Dolomieu builds his account around a series of powerful, emotionally freighted contrasts. The claustrophobia of his cell is heightened by his painstaking description of its frugal, mundane details – the measurements of his cell, the inventory of his possessions, the fetid air, the sole source of light – the sort of meticulous account one would expect from a skilled scientific observer, a careful inventory of incarceration. In contrast his (idealised) account of his earlier life is bursting with ideas, feelings and a sense of vast but traversable spaces, the heavens studded with a panoply of stars or the panoramic view from the top of mountains. Its cumulative effect is a powerful indictment of the injustices its author was suffering, the cruelty of his confinement, the enormity and unjustness of his punishment. Yet, as he wrote repeatedly and doggedly at the end of his entries, '*Et, cependant, je vis encore*' – 'and yet I still live'.

As historian of science Alix Cooper has shown, Dolomieu's *cri du coeur* was not just an agonised plea for freedom, but the assertion of a particular scientific identity, one built around the direct engagement of the geologist with nature, in which travel – voyaging – was central to the identity of the savant and his enterprise.[32] Movement is freedom and progress, an understanding reinforced by the metaphors and images that Dolomieu uses about 'the precipitous march' and 'rapid development' of the sciences and their 'general impulse' to expand and grow. Earth sciences might need laboratories, libraries and museums but at heart geology was a field science; only out in the mountains could real insight be found. Dolomieu conjures up a romantic picture of his impulse to follow and search out an irresistible nature:

> The passion that entices me to the contemplation of Nature was so strong that each year, when the spring restored life to the vegetable kingdom and gave new impulse to all organised beings, all the beauties of art lost their attractions for me. The confines of Paris seemed narrow, its atmosphere dense and heavy. My imagination had need of more space, my feelings desired other objects, and my taste other pleasures.[33]

These feelings impelled him to flee the city and seek a wilder nature:

> Each year I dashed towards some chains of mountains, and would
> go on their summits to seek those profound emotions that always
> procure the view of very grand objects/ends, and [I would] give
> myself over to a meditation on the formation of the globe, on the
> revolutions that it has experienced, on the causes which have
> changed and modified their forms, and which have produced the
> state that we now see. My thoughts became grander and my
> conceptions more extended, as I raised myself higher: my horizon
> had fewer boundaries.[34]

For Dolomieu the satisfaction of his curiosity was both an emotional
and aesthetic necessity; it was a 'desire', a taste ('*goût*') that defined
his sense of self. Deprived of it he lost both his identity and purpose.

Many natural philosophers of the period described their scientific
inquiries as motivated by different sorts of feeling, but this did
not preclude them from setting rigorous standards for what constituted proper conduct and rigorous observation. In his prison journal
Dolomieu figured scientific inquiry as a journey that expressed both
bodily and intellectual freedom. But, as he had made clear four years
earlier in his lectures to his students at the École des Mines, the geologist required particular moral qualities and skills, ones that would be
tested in the arduous circumstances of the field. What mattered was
character and expertise. The geologist required patience, persever-
ance, courage, a passion for truth and an active curiosity. Geological
inquiry could reach its destination by following a path that required
'this active curiosity, this ardour for discoveries, this strong enthusiasm which only considers the goal to which one wants to reach,
without ever being put off by intermediate obstacles'. Dolomieu's
geologist is a heroic traveller able to resist 'extreme fatigue', to 'with-
stand all temperatures', accustoming himself, he says, 'as I have done,
to sleeping as well on sand and stone, as in the most sumptuous bed'.

'He will frequently,' adds Dolomieu, 'endure hunger, thirst, and we must tell him that straw, for going to bed, will most often be a luxury item difficult for him to obtain.'[35]

Such determination was necessary but not sufficient to make a successful explorer. Scientific observation needed system and sustained attention. So Dolomieu accompanied his animated descriptions of the arduousness of field work with more sober advice to his students about journal- and record-keeping, about how to collect and conserve specimens. His final word to his students comes from the man he idolised and took as a role model, Horace Bénédict de Saussure: 'Saussure ends his diary by saying that the study of geology is not made for the lazy, nor for the sensual.'[36]

Dolomieu's account of himself in his prison notes was of a piece with his earlier thoughts on how to understand and value geological work. It made him into an exemplary geological fieldworker and asserted his (entirely justified) claim to have contributed to modern scientific knowledge. Even as he explains how he has been denied his part as the travelling savant, he reasserts himself as a contributor to the advance of modern scientific knowledge: 'I followed with extreme pleasure the rush of science . . . every day brought a discovery; every day announced to me where a conquest [was] made over ignorance . . . I joined my efforts to this general impulse, and I was happy to be counted among those who gave this great development to the human spirit.'[37]

Here, there is a shift of register away from the intrepid individual explorer and towards an emphasis on participation in a shared enterprise, one made more apparent by Dolomieu's decision to record the names of his 'principal friends' inserted between the lines of Faujas's text. In all he named sixty-three from Paris, four from Geneva, six from England, seven from Italy, and individuals from Denmark and Hamburg in Germany. As Cooper points out, it was a veritable scientific network across Europe. In addition to the list, Dolomieu wrote short character sketches of many of them, vignettes that described their qualities, and what they had done with or for him. Thus he basked in the friendship and praise of Horace Bénédict de Saussure, 'to my honour, I can say he has befriended me', and singled out the polymathic doctor and naturalist Jean-Claude Lamétherie, the editor of the *Journal de physique* that published many of Dolomieu's papers, as 'the first and the most important of my friends'. Much of this commentary was addressed directly to his friends, as if they were present with him in his cell. As he wrote of Lamétherie, 'my heart guesses everything that happens in yours with regard to me and everything you do for me.'[38] He frequently speaks of what will happen when he and his friends meet again. Although his friends are inaccessible and far away, the way in which Dolomieu interacts with them makes them feel present, a gathering of the like-minded to cheer him in his dark and dank cell.

Dolomieu's friends came from different periods of his life as well as different places: from his small hometown, Dolomieu north of Grenoble, from Malta, the Paris salons, the scientific circles of Geneva, and the expedition to Egypt. Among the women – a minority on the list – some were former lovers, others the partners of men he admired. Dolomieu never married and his envious descriptions of several couples read like the sentimental comments of a lonely libertine. From his comments, two patterns among Dolomieu's friends stand out. The first is how many came either from the La Rochefoucauld circle or from the institutions in which Dolomieu worked – the Agence and the École des Mines and the Institut de France. Several of them, like the physicist and inventor Alexis-Marie de Rochon, the inventor of the prismatic micrometer, and Faujas de Saint-Fond, belonged to both. But secondly, and perhaps more importantly, he often depicts his friends as having the personal qualities and ethics that made them both outstanding companions and men of science. Gillet de Laumont, one of the founding figures of the Agence des Mines, is described as someone with an 'ardent head, warm and open heart, loving with transport the sciences, with passion the enterprise that he established, and without reserve to those to whom he became attached'.[39]

Dolomieu praises his protégé, travelling companion and pupil, Louis Cordier, who was to succeed Faujas as the professor of geology at the Muséum National d'Histoire Naturelle, for his 'measured, always attentive, always obliging' manner towards him, while he addresses Alexandre-Charles Besson, another member of the École des Mines, as 'my old friend' whose heart he appreciates as much as his cabinet. Besson had one of the great Parisian mineral collections, and had also lent Dolomieu money when he was hard up. 'You miss dinner in order to buy some rocks; but you ignore the rocks to be able to help your friends.'[40] His colleagues at the École, like the mineralogists Alexandre Brongniart and Abbé René Just Haüy, are repeatedly described as methodical, patient, perspicacious, judicious and fair. Dolomieu expresses a special affection for his friends in Geneva, whom he first met through the good offices of the Duke de La Rochefoucauld, and whom he visited on many occasions in the 1790s as he spent more and more time studying the Alps. He praises Marc-Auguste Pictet, the physician and naturalist who wielded enormous influence as the editor of *Bibliothèque Britannique*, a journal that circulated throughout Europe, as the man who 'brought into public affairs the great gift of conciliation' and into private life 'the charms of friendship', crediting him with all the 'virtues of a good citizen and a good father' as well as 'all the strength of soul of a true *philosophe*'.[41] The deep friendships that we saw among many visitors to the slopes of Vesuvius also sustained Dolomieu in captivity and helped him endure his solitary confinement.

Dolomieu's collective sketch of the world of scientific savants is, of course, Panglossian, and never alludes (except perhaps for one tart remark about Faujas's skills at sucking up to whomever had power)[42] to the intellectual conflicts, personal antipathies and factional infighting that were characteristic of a scientific elite that was desperately trying to preserve itself, both collectively and individually, at a time of repeated and wrenching political change.

But to be fair, the international scientific community showed remarkable unity and determination in seeking to secure Dolomieu's release. As soon as Cordier returned to France, he began a campaign on Dolomieu's behalf, presenting his patron's plight to a meeting of members of the Institute in October 1799, and getting them to petition the Directory to secure his release. Working with Dolomieu's brother-in-law, the Marquis Étienne de Grès, a politician and avid mineralogist, and with Dolomieu's lover from Metz, Jennie Tyrion, the group contacted Sir Joseph Banks, the president of the Royal Society, and Dolomieu's Danish friend, the geologist Frederic Münter. At the same time Pictet, the Swiss editor of the *Bibliothéque Britannique*, also called on Banks to help secure Dolomieu's release.[43] The Institut d'Égypte in Cairo, where Dolomieu had worked, urged the French government to act, and one of its members, Jean-Lambert Tallien, urged the Governor General of Malta to intervene on Dolomieu's behalf. As he wrote, 'Nations ... can wage war against each other, but men who devote themselves to science must never cease to be friends: in the midst of the tumult of passions, the clash of various interests, a true philanthropic man remains consoled to see less public calamities through the union, esteem and continued relations of philosophers of all countries.'[44] Such sentiments were echoed by Sir Joseph Banks. Though he felt that the Royal Society could not act in an official capacity 'to break the Chains of the Meritorious Dolomieu',[45] he went to considerable lengths to secure his release, writing both to Sir William Hamilton and his wife Emma, urging them to help. He told Sir William, 'You have no idea how much sensation his confinement has made in the Literary world here, and how anxious men of Science feel in all parts of Europe for his Liberation. In my little way of correspondence I have already had more than 30 signatures of men of Letters anxiously enquiring whether it is possible anything can be done to save him.' It was Dolomieu's determination to overcome every obstacle in the pursuit of science that justified support for his release: 'That Dolomieu has long ago devoted himself to Science is well known. In the pursuit of it he has brav'd the danger of Calabrian Banditti, & encounter'd a thousand other difficulties which very few men would have voluntarily subjected themselves to.'[46] As Banks pointed out to Emma Hamilton, his release would 'be for the honour of the Court of Naples, for the advancement of Science, for the benefit of humanity'.[47]

The effort to get Dolomieu released was concerted, a clear sign both of his international importance and the solidarity that could sometimes be shown among the community of savants. It also, and implausibly, portrayed 'curiosity' – scientific inquiry – as somehow transcending the partialities of nation and regime. But its effects were nugatory. Though both the Hamiltons lobbied the Neapolitan monarchs, and Cornelia Knight, one of Dolomieu's old lovers from Rome who was now in the entourage of Queen Maria Carolina, also spoke on his behalf, all they were able to achieve was an amelioration of his conditions of confinement. Knight was able to send him food and clothing; he was moved to a better cell with more light; and he was allowed writing materials and to send and receive correspondence. Only a series of victories on the battlefield for Napoleon and the ensuing armistice finally obtained Dolomieu's release on 15 March 1801.[48]

On his release Dolomieu tried to return to his old ways. He taught a course based on the book he had written during his confinement, *La philosophie minéralogique*, at the Muséum National d'Histoire Naturelle, and in August embarked with the Danish geologist Bruun-Neergaard on an expedition to the Alps. 'I need rest,' he said, 'and will look for it in the mountains.'[49] Returning to the house of his sister and brother-in-law in Burgundy, he put the finishing touches to his *La philosophie minéralogique* and began planning a trip to Saxony to visit the famous mineralogist Gottlob Werner in Freiberg and present him with a special collection of minerals, and to visit geological sites in Denmark, Sweden and Norway. But he was worn out, plagued by bouts of fever and weakened by the effects of his imprisonment. He died on 28 November 1801, a mere eight months after his release.

It would be easy to dismiss Dolomieu as a vainglorious character, unwilling to accept the sorts of dependence necessary to all but the very rich. There was often an air of theatricality about his conduct and the insistent way in which he repeatedly identified his uniqueness. For him *curiosité* became a way of being, a mode of self-presentation, almost a transcendent value that defined his relations with others. It rested on certain principles – particularly the centrality of personal but systematic observation – but was always more than a technique. As one of his admirers put it, 'He could make almost a dozen leagues in a day ... almost always on foot. Intrepid and indefatigable, he left [behind] the most robust men and the most accustomed to the mountains, the guides of Chamonix. The rain, winds, snows, nothing stops him. His efforts and his courage were extreme.'[50] The pursuit of scientific truth was perhaps his highest emotion, a love affair, though one in which he was the dominant partner. His correspondence strongly suggests that his was a quest of 'discovery', 'conquest', 'impulse', seeking what he called the 'shared mistress' of natural history; and he was eager to show others how accomplished he was in achieving his goal.

But this came at a price. Dolomieu, as his frequent complaints attest, was always jealous of his 'liberty and independence', his freedom of action. He came to resent the obligations he had to La Rochefoucauld, even though he loved him as a friend; he was eager to point out that taking employment was never his choice, and that he only endured it because it enabled him to continue his geological pursuits. When he dedicated his 1784 work on the Calabrian earthquakes, he ostentatiously remarked that he could have dedicated it to one of the grand men of France, 'to display his sumptuous titles, his imaginary virtues', but that he preferred to name an old friend, a commander in the Knights of Malta.[51] He failed to fulfil his only commercial publishing commission. He chafed under the administrative and organisational constraints of a large-scale project like the scientific expedition to Egypt. As he ruefully admitted, it was his desire to escape these – to enjoy his freedom – that explained his early flight from Egypt and his consequent capture and imprisonment.

In short, Dolomieu valued his freedom to follow his pursuits more than anything else and failed to accommodate himself either to the subordinate position of a patron's client in the *ancien régime*, or to feel comfortable as a functionary or government employee. He was never an institutionalised man, and it was only in his confinement that he came to see that the chains of friendship he had forged were not fetters but as much a part of the scientific enterprise as his personal heroic achievements.

I have the sense that what made Dolomieu such a famous savant were not just his palpable skills as a scientific investigator of volcanoes, but his total and unbounded commitment to *curiosité* as a practice of rigorous observation. For him *curiosité* was a transcendent value that should override other concerns because of its capacity to recover demonstrable truth. This was something that savants wanted to believe but knew to be untrue. They were aware that its practice was bound up with other, sometimes conflicting, values and was fashioned or circumscribed by the contexts in which it occurred. Vesuvius and other volcanoes were never purely 'scientific objects' subject to the disinterested scientific gaze. And the savant was never, as Dolomieu somehow hoped, free to pursue their intellectual pursuits unconstrained by political and social circumstance. And Dolomieu's misfortunes – *'la bizarrerie de ma destinée'* – precisely proved the point. Yet paradoxically this made it easy to put Dolomieu on a pedestal, to celebrate and idealise him as a heroic martyr to science, the greatest vulcanologist of his age.

11
TEODORO MONTICELLI
International Vulcanism and Neapolitan Politics

A s we have seen, many Neapolitans regarded Mount Vesuvius with proprietorial affection, usually describing it as '*il nostro Vesuvio*'. The volcano belonged not only to the city, the country and the monarch, but held a special place in their hearts. When Montesquieu spoke of '50,000 men in Naples who ... fall into the most terrible depression at the slightest puff of smoke from Vesuvius', he could not have been wider of the mark.[1] Vesuvius was Neapolitan and Neapolitans were Vesuvian. Vesuvius was one of Naples' greatest assets.

No one knew this better or took more advantage of this knowledge than Teodoro Monticelli, the secretary of the Academy of Sciences in Naples, a figure who presided over the volcano for more than thirty years, publishing papers and books on individual eruptions, co-authoring a vast tome on its minerals and metals, assembling and distributing collections of Vesuvian rocks that were dispersed throughout Europe and the New World, and acting as a learned guide and facilitator for visiting dignitaries, diplomats, ardent amateur geologists and mineralogists, and friends and savants of every stripe. Monticelli was a passionate promoter of '*il nostro Vesuvio*' who fought tirelessly to ensure that the volcano featured prominently in international geological debates. This, as we shall see, was a form of volcanic patriotism, one designed not just to promote knowledge about Vesuvius but to further a particular vision of Naples as a centre of culture and science. Monticelli used the volcano and its products in many different ways – as an enticement, a vehicle for propaganda, a token in an international economy of scientific prestige – and most ingeniously as a shield, protecting himself and other Neapolitan intellectuals in a politically volatile environment that was often hostile to the sorts of scientific inquiry he and his friends promoted.[2]

The source of Monticelli's power and influence was not so much his intellectual prowess as his remarkable ability as a facilitator, intermediary and fixer. After his youthful republican aspirations – which led to his imprisonment between 1795 and 1801 – he returned to Naples in 1806 after a spell of study in Rome. He survived a succession of regime changes, including the Bourbon restoration of 1815, the constitutional revolution of 1820–1, and the further restoration that followed. He accumulated honours and influence throughout his career as a watchful servant of Bourbon absolutism (as well as being ennobled in Denmark and Brazil), while becoming a lifeline for his exiled and disgraced friends, whether in the kingdom or abroad. He was a survivor, but one who consistently pursued a reformist vision of Naples and an agenda for its modernity.

Monticelli's early work had been on husbandry – he had written a catechism for smallholding farmers, a treatise on beekeeping while in prison on Favignana, and an environmental study, *Sull'economia delle acque da ristabilirsi nel regno di Napoli* (*On the restoration/recuperation of the economy of water in the Kingdom of Naples*), which some modern scholars see as an early work of Italian environmentalism.[3] Monticelli never lost interest in these questions, but from 1808 onwards he published a succession of geological works, of which the two most important were an extraordinarily detailed study of observations and experiments made on Vesuvius between 1821 and 1823,[4] which ran to 163 pages, and the *Prodromo della mineralogia vesuviana*, a comprehensive analysis of its rocks and minerals.[5] Both of these were written in collaboration with Nicola Covelli, a brilliant young chemist who had studied for three years in Paris with Abbé René Haüy, the father of modern mineralogy, and with the chemist Alexandre Brongniart, a collaborator of Georges Cuvier. Covelli was also the pupil of Matteo Tondi, whom he had first met in Paris. In these publications Monticelli and Covelli measured the fallout of pyroclastic deposits (a topic that Monticelli had already discussed in his account of the 1813 eruption), developed a historical classification of volcanic types according to their different mineral content and age, and disagreed with the likes of Alexander von Humboldt and von Buch over whether volcanoes were the product of processes of elevation rather than eruption.[6]

Monticelli's achievements as a scientist are difficult to assess. On a visit to Naples in 1812, the distinguished geologist Giambattista Brocchi, an admirer and friend of Monticelli, commented that although his passion and zeal as a collector was admirable, Monticelli depended on the expertise of others: 'He complies with the findings that are given to him by the erudite, and by his friends who are learned in science.' The Genevan naturalist Stefano Moricand and the Roman naturalist and lithographer Giovanni Dell'Armi both advised Monticelli to be more precise and 'scientific' in his descriptions. Monticelli's two most important publications, the detailed account of the 1822 eruption and the *Prodromo*, were written in collaboration with Nicola Covelli, described by a fellow geologist as '*la main droite*' of Monticelli, and seen as a far better-educated scientist.[7] The *Prodromo della mineralogia vesuviana* with its obvious debt to Haüy and its detailed diagrams of crystals seems more likely to have been led by the chemist Covelli than Monticelli, but we have no real evidence of how the cooperation worked. Sadly Covelli's premature death in 1829 ended their collaboration. Thereafter Monticelli produced no major work, though he continued to publish short papers – letters and memoranda – right up until his death.[8]

Though Monticelli became an assiduous vulcanologist, his horizon was bounded by the Kingdom of Naples, and was largely confined to Vesuvius and the Campi Flegrei. He seems never to have travelled outside the Italian peninsula. Unlike most of the important geologists of his generation, he never crossed the Mediterranean into Greece, the Holy Land and Egypt, nor did he make it northwards over the Alps to France and Germany. Monticelli's friends, like the Irish geologist and factotum of Georges Cuvier, Joseph Pentland, and the Roman lithographer and naturalist Giovanni Dall'Armi, repeatedly encouraged him to expand his studies beyond Vesuvius and its immediate vicinity and urged on him the importance of providing samples for chemical analysis in Paris and Sweden.[9] Moricand in Geneva frequently pressed a dilatory Monticelli to send him materials for publication in the Genevan journal *Bibliothèque universelle*, as he knew that it circulated throughout northern Europe.[10] But Monticelli's chief concerns were local and his observations were not theoretical but resolutely empirical. As he and Covelli wrote about the eruption of 1822:

We consulted the ancient and modern writers about our volcanoes and the papers of foreign people on the same topics, as well as the most famous authors of Geology and Mineralogy; however having found that geologists are divided into two tendencies, one of which ascribed most external and internal terrestrial phenomena only to waters, and the other one only to fire, we simply tried to study their doctrines, without embracing any one of them; we only intended to give exact reports of things observed by us.[11]

To a certain extent this was a characteristic gesture of many geologists of the 1820s who wished to privilege empirical observation over speculative theory. But at heart Monticelli was a Plutonist, as he revealed in his uncharacteristically dyspeptic response to Carmine

Antonio Lippi's claims about the aqueous inundation of Herculaneum and Pompeii. Probably Monticelli took a publicly neutral position because his prime concern was less to adjudicate between Neptunists and Plutonists than to ensure that, whatever the larger geological narrative, Vesuvius and the Neapolitan kingdoms would feature within it. For, passionate as Monticelli was about mineralogy, geology and vulcanism, his first commitment was to realising a particular vision of Naples.

When savants like Humphry Davy and Alexander von Humboldt arrived in Naples, they headed not to Professor Tondi or to the royal mineralogical collections but to the door of the man the German scientist dubbed 'the learned and zealous observer of the Volcano'.[12] For Carlos de Gimbernat, the Catalan geologist who worked on the slopes of Vesuvius for nearly two years between 1818 and 1820, Monticelli was 'the most zealous savant in advancing knowledge relative to Vesuvius'.[13] In Paris, the mineralogist Alexandre Brongniart spoke of Monticelli and the pleasure of working with 'an observer as skilful and as active as you'.[14] For Davy, who worked closely with him, Monticelli's achievements as a vulcanologist were comparable to those of the Swiss scientist, Horace Bénédict de Saussure, as a scholar of the Alps.[15] Crucially Monticelli, with his institutional backing and personal enthusiasm, was treated as a trusted and reliable informant, as well as a facilitator. Whatever the level of his scientific expertise, he became accepted as the gatekeeper to the volcano.

In short, Monticelli was what we would today describe as an inveterate networker. As the secretary of both the Bourbon Royal Society and of one of three academies that made up that body, the Academy of Sciences, he was the public face of both institutions, the chief correspondent with other academies, libraries and museums in Italy and beyond. He stood at the intersection of a large body of local knowledge and the greater scientific community and used the promotion of such connections to further a much larger political project, one that looked towards the establishment of constitutional regimes

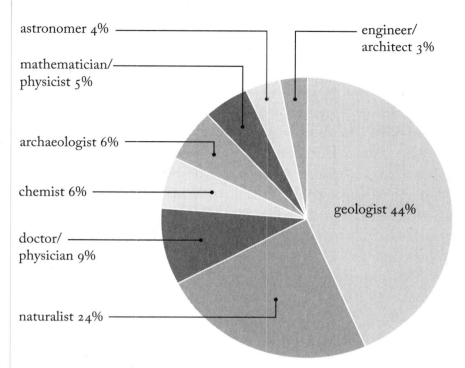

astronomer 4%

engineer/
architect 3%

mathematician/
physicist 5%

archaeologist 6%

chemist 6%

geologist 44%

doctor/
physician 9%

naturalist 24%

Chart 5. The distribution of Teodoro Monticelli's scientific correspondence by field.
Source: Teodoro Monticelli Mss, Biblioteca Nazionale, Naples.

with an educated and enfranchised public, and even towards an entire peninsula united in a single nation.

Monticelli belonged to three different but overlapping networks. One connected Italian savants of mineralogy and geology in Sicily, Naples, Rome, the Tuscan cities, and the towns of northern Italy and the Veneto: Milan, Turin, Bologna, Pavia, Padua. Like-minded, similarly positioned natural philosophers and university professors, connected through correspondence, the exchange of specimens and shared international visitors, they not only shared an interest in earth sciences, but became good friends. The help and hospitality they extended to the travellers who journeyed down and up the Italian peninsula was one way in which they connected to a second network that made up a larger scientific community, an international network of scholars from the New World – the United States and later Brazil – as well as from all over Europe: Britain, France, Belgium, Sweden, Norway, Denmark, Russia, Poland, the German-speaking lands and Greece.

This network consisted of a series of clusters, of which there were at least four. The most important and powerful was that centred on Paris and included brilliant scientists like the zoologist and palaeontologist Georges Cuvier; his collaborator, the mineralogist Alexandre Brongniart; the geologist Pierre Louis Antoine Cordier who had been Dolomieu's favourite pupil; the chemist Joseph Louis Gay-Lussac; his friend Alexander von Humboldt; and Brochant de Villiers, another of Dolomieu's students and a professor of mineralogy. This constellation of illustrious talent frequented the Muséum National d'Histoire Naturelle, its adjunct the Jardin des Plantes, and the École des Mines. The second cluster was British, centred on London, the Geological Society, the Royal Society and the Royal Institution, with offshoots to the universities. Though it included such famous figures as the chemist Humphry Davy, mathematicians like John Herschel, Charles Babbage and William Playfair, and geologists such as Charles Lyell, William Buckland and Charles Daubeny, it also embraced a number of amateurs and women. The third cluster was more diffuse, spread through the Scandinavian countries, Russia and the German-speaking lands of north Europe, and included the Danish court, Swedish, Saxon and Silesian mining engineers, the University of Uppsala, the famous chemist John Jacob Berzelius and his pupils in Stockholm, as well as amateur collectors, mineral dealers and university professors in Jena, Heidelberg and Göttingen. A fourth and final group was to be found in the New World, based in the colleges of New England, sustained by such American Grand Tourists as Senator Stephen Van Rensselaer of New York, who visited Monticelli in Naples in 1819, as well as by chemists and physicians associated with the National Institute for the Promotion of Science in Washington, which was to become the Smithsonian Institute.

These two networks of men of science, one Italian, the other international, were connected through Monticelli to a third of a rather different character, which consisted of a generation of Italian administrators and functionaries who had supported royal initiatives under the *ancien régime* to dispel an almost ubiquitous feudalism, and to erode the special privileges of the nobility and the Catholic Church. Generally predisposed to French revolutionary ideals and to the views of the French ideologues and Napoleonic functionaries, if they survived Admiral Nelson's and the Bourbons' pogrom of the Neapolitan intelligencia in 1799–1800, they went on to promote reform during the regimes of Joseph Bonaparte and Joachim Murat (1806–15). After the Bourbon Restoration many remained in office and continued to share a desire for comprehensive reform in which they hoped that the sciences – not just 'natural', but medical, social and political – would achieve a universal salubriousness.

Monticelli used the prestige he acquired as a vital intermediary in the first two networks not only for self-advancement (and protection) but to promote the aims of the third network for scientific reform. Vesuvius was vital to this, making Monticelli indispensable to a monarch who, though a political and religious reactionary, wished to be seen as a technological and scientific modern. It was Monticelli's task to use the magnet of Vesuvius to introduce foreign dignitaries and savants to the scientific culture of Naples.

The volcano and the Bay of Naples gave Monticelli certain advantages within the world of mineralogy and geology. No site was so spectacular – so sublime – and yet so accessible to the European savant and the tourist. In Sicily, the Gemmellaro family presided over Etna, a far more impressive mountain, but it was both less accessible and much harder to climb. And, as we have seen, Vesuvius was its own greatest publicist, its activities the object of public and scientific fascination. Naturalists wanted detailed accurate descriptions of the volcano's many eruptions, reliable information about its lavas and crystals, and specimens and collections of Vesuvian materials for study, display in their museums and cabinets, and as objects of chemical analysis. Scientists from throughout Italy and in much of Europe and North America constantly solicited specimens from the volcano, and pressed Monticelli to send them accounts of Vesuvius and its eruptions. They believed that such articles would increase the visibility of their journals. Monticelli was only too happy to provide.

And, of course, savants wanted access to Vesuvius itself. The logistics were never as complex as a visit to Etna, but Monticelli was able to ensure a scientist's smooth passage, often offering them accommodation, providing them with guides and information, as well as granting them access to his collections. Monticelli's advantages were complemented by his extraordinary gift for friendship. His correspondence is littered with effulgent expressions of gratitude and thanks for his help and hospitality. In the spring of 1820, for example, Humphry Davy wrote from Rome to Monticelli, to thank him for his hospitality during a recent sojourn in Naples, concluding his letter by remarking that 'the things that you have done for me, and the things we did together I will never forget.'[16] One might cynically dismiss such gratefulness as an understandable response from those who needed Monticelli's help and connections to pursue their studies, but there was much more happening here. Monticelli was capable of great shrewdness in his dealings with foreign naturalists, but his conduct was often not instrumental. Meeting a curious young Danish naval lieutenant in Naples in July 1818, he assembled for him a small collection of lava, together with Greek and Roman coins for his brother. Visitors to Naples repeatedly felt overcome by his kindness and his candour. A radical educational reformer, scientist and journal publisher from Palermo, Ferdinando Malvica, a youthful protégé of Monticelli's, described himself as 'overwhelmed by his affectionate and generous favours', addressing him as *padrone ed amico veneratissimo* (master and most highly respected friend). Another acquaintance, the poet Vincenzo Monti, described him to a friend as 'highly cultivated' with an 'aura of goodness and courtesy'.[17]

Monticelli's gift of friendship was never circumscribed by convention. He had a lifelong interest in the education of women; asked by an American geologist what he would like in return for his gift of Vesuvian materials, he requested publications on female education.[18] He also cultivated friendships with women who were geological enthusiasts. He provided Delvalle Lowry, the English author of a popular introduction to mineralogy, *Conversations on Mineralogy* (1822), with volcanic specimens, and for a decade carried on a correspondence with Lowry's friend, Anna Wilbraham, an ardent vulcanologist who was in Naples in the spring of 1826, 1827 and 1828, climbing Vesuvius on many occasions; she even provided Monticelli with a drawing of the new cone of the volcano created during the minor eruption of 14 March 1827. Her cousin, Emma Bethell, had carried out chemical experiments in England on Vesuvian rocks provided by Monticelli and sent him her results together with a set of English rocks, and a copy of Conybeare and Phillips's *Treatise on English Geology*.[19] Later she received more volcanic specimens from Monticelli, brought back to England by Anna Wilbraham.

Wilbraham took it upon herself to keep Monticelli abreast of English developments. She sent him a detailed account of William Wollaston's goniometer, an instrument to measure accurately the angle between crystal surfaces, introduced him to the work of Lyell, and sent him the first two volumes of *Principles of Geology*. She also kept him informed of deliberations at the meetings of the British Association for the Advancement of Science.[20] She translated some of his work into English and had it published in the *Cambridge University Gazette* and then in the *Literary Gazette* in London.[21] Their friendship was personal as well as geological. Wilbraham confided in Monticelli, explaining to him how fortunate she had been to find a husband (an older man and member of the Grosvenor family) who, though ignorant of science, had supported her studies, while Emma Bethell had been unable to find a suitable partner. This sort of easy intimacy with women was a marked feature of Monticelli's correspondence. Lady Blessington, who saw him often during her residence in Naples, described him as 'sage and gentle'. The Queen of Denmark, with whom he exchanged gifts of paintings, addressed him as '*Amatassimo* [sic] *Signore*' (Beloved Sir).

Monticelli needed all his diplomatic skills when required, as he often was, to conduct important foreign visitors on a tour of Vesuvius and of its collections. When royalty or the grand aristocracy were present, the Neapolitan court ensured that Monticelli was in attendance. One elegy written shortly after his death in 1845 claimed (not altogether accurately) that Monticelli had entertained the Grand Duke of Tuscany, the Dukes of Saxe-Weimar and Saxe-Coburg, the King of Greece, the Grand Duchess Elena of Russia, Prince Albert and the Duke of Hesse-Cassel, as well as his good friend Christian Frederick of Denmark. With the exception of Monticelli's scientific work with Christian Frederick, 'a philosopher prince', these meetings, whether over his Vesuvian collections or on the mountain itself, were ceremonial rather than scholarly, occasions on which Monticelli, often surrounded by foreign courtiers and diplomats, acted as a major-domo whose task was to show off the natural and cultural treasures of the kingdom. Typically, this did not prevent him forming close friendships with the scholars in these princely entourages. We have already seen how Jacob Adler, who was Christian Frederick's secretary and professor of Syriac at Copenhagen University, became a lifelong friend. Similarly, Johann Nepomuk von Ringseis, a professor of medicine who accompanied Crown Prince Ludwig of Bavaria as his personal physician on three trips to Italy, and first met Monticelli in 1825, wrote regularly to his '*Signore estimatissimo*' (most esteemed Sir) conveying greetings from his wife, swapping specimens and even trying to persuade Ludwig that he should buy Monticelli's entire mineral collection.[22]

What really mattered to Monticelli was not the formal hosting of grandees and their entourages, but entertaining and aiding the steady stream of natural philosophers of every stripe that passed through Naples. As his friend, the great Italian naturalist Giambattista

Brocchi, commented in a letter, 'your house is a true school for all the learned foreigners [who pass through Naples]'.[23] He took enormous pleasure in his hospitality. When his collected works were published in 1841, Monticelli inserted a brief account of 'Excursions made on Vesuvius in the company of illustrious subjects and celebrated learned foreigners' made between 1817 and 1820.[24] He boasted of how he had introduced the Crown Prince of Denmark to Humphry Davy, and how they worked together studying lavas at the same time as the French mineralogist Alexandre Brongniart and his son were examining the volcano. Davy and Giambattista Brocchi were also studying the properties of volcanic waters, provided by the Catalan geologist working for the King of Bavaria, Carlos de Gimbernat, who was on Vesuvius to investigate their potential medicinal value. This was Monticelli's *beau idéal*: a Dane, an Englishman, two Frenchmen, a Catalan and an Italian from the Veneto all working away simultaneously on the slopes of Vesuvius or using his microscopes at his country house at Boscotrecase on the southern slopes of the volcano.

The life

Teodoro Monticelli was born in 1759, the younger son of minor nobility from Brindisi, who, like many a younger son who did not go into the military, entered the church. In Brindisi, Lecce, Naples and Rome he was educated in philosophy and mathematics, and was taught by the followers of Antonio Genovesi, who held the first chair in political economy in Europe, established in Naples in 1754. Like many students of the major figures of the Italian Enlightenment, Monticelli was an early supporter of the French Revolution. He became a radical Jacobin and freemason in the 1790s, a member and teacher in the Società Patriottica Napoletana, linked to the private academy of the defrocked priest Carlo Lauberg, who taught applied mathematics and chemistry for revolutionary ends 'to promote public education and extirpate ancient prejudices'. He was also a regular visitor at the salon of Elenora de Fonseca Pimentel, the charismatic poet, editor of the revolutionary *Il monitore napoletano*, and later martyr for the Republican Revolution of 1799. Arrested in 1794, he was released two months later but then re-arrested in January 1796, when he was offered the bishopric of Salerno if he would betray his fellow radicals. Refusing to do so, and narrowly avoiding a death sentence, he spent the next six years first in the Castel Sant'Elmo high above the city (and in a windowless cell), and then as a prisoner on the remote island of Favignana off the north-west coast of Sicily, where he had been sentenced to ten years of confine-ment. Like many of his radical friends, Monticelli suffered the experience of prolonged incarceration either on the mainland or on the many volcanic islands that served as a gulag for opponents of the Bourbon governments.[25]

Thanks to what his admirers described as his 'serene affability', Monticelli seems to have enjoyed a degree of freedom on Favignana courtesy of his good relations with the commander of the Castello Santa Caterina, an isolated, bleak fortress that housed political prisoners, built on a rocky outcrop 300 metres above the island's coastal plain. He used his time to write a treatise on the agricultural advantages of beekeeping. His incarceration probably saved his life: he was not able to be a part of the brief government of the Neapolitan republic set up by the French in 1799, and radically purged by the Bourbons and Horatio Nelson. Freed in 1801 as part of the amnesty negotiated at the Treaty of Florence, he returned to study and work in Rome (where he first studied geology and developed a lifelong friendship with his teacher, Carlo Giuseppe Gismondi), and then returned to Naples as professor of ethics in 1806. With the (second) French occupation of Naples, Monticelli's fortunes flourished, and in 1807 he was made head of the Collegio del Salvatore and a member of the Ministry of Education. In the following year he became permanent secretary of the Academy of Sciences, was given the title of Cavaliere, and was appointed to the

Internal Commission of General Statistics for the kingdom, responsible for agriculture.[26]

These were also the years in which Monticelli formed some of his
lasting friendships with leading reformers. He was especially close
to Francesco Ricciardi, the Count Camaldoli (1758–1842), a liberal
lawyer who had defended many of the republicans in the political trials
of 1800, and who became Minister of Justice under Murat. Ricciardi
was largely responsible for the adoption of a (somewhat Neapolitan)
version of the French legal system – the 'Code Napoleon' – in Naples,
using his powers to increase the authority and autonomy of the magis-
tracy. Described by one of the French officials sent to modernise
Naples as 'the only truly enlightened person I have had the pleasure to
meet in Naples', he was also president of the Academy of Sciences.[27]
When Ricciardi retired from politics in 1821, Monticelli became a
regular member of the circle that often gathered at the Villa Ricciardi,
a neo-classical palace with beautiful botanical gardens set on the hills
above Naples in the village of Vomero.[28] The villa (described by Lady
Blessington as 'the delightful residence of our excellent friends, the
Ricciardis, where we met many clever people of both sexes') was a
gathering place for reformers, intellectuals and foreign visitors – poets
and botanists, lawyers and novelists, antiquaries and politicians, liberal
clerics and geologists – brought together not just by Ricciardi himself
but by his entire family. The true *salonnière* was his wife Luisa Granito
who, like her husband, had pleaded for the lives of republicans in 1799.
She was a poet, linguist and intellectual with a strong attachment, like
Monticelli, to women's education. She orchestrated readings and theat-
ricals, and taught her children herself, nursing them in a more revolutionary politics than that of her husband. Her second son, Giuseppe,
became a follower of Mazzini and Babeuf, committed to a strongly
anti-clerical democratic and republican politics. He spent much of
his life before Italian unification in exile, though this did not prevent
him from editing *Il progresso delle scienze, delle lettere e delle arti*, the
wide-ranging progressive Neapolitan periodical, whose contributors

included Leopoldo Pilla. His father Francesco Ricciardi was not merely the titular head of the scientific academy. The count's addresses to the scientific academy display an extraordinary variety of interests, ranging from the potentially beneficial qualities of Vesuvian gases and soils to zoophytes (coral ornaments were an important Neapolitan craft), from astronomical observations to French philosophy, and from population statistics to phrenology.[29] The Ricciardis also entertained many of Monticelli's scientific friends.

The French regimes of the so-called '*decennio*', the ten years of French rule in Naples between 1805 and 1815, had been especially hospitable to political and educational reform. These included the revival of the Royal Academies, including that of science, the reform of the university and establishment of new chairs and disciplines, the foundation of the Accademia Pontaniana, a body of the great and the good, and the promotion of the Istituto d'Incoraggiamento, which had as its explicit purpose the application of the sciences of mathematics, physics, chemistry and economics to government administration and to the economy, especially agriculture. All of these developments helped shape an agenda that appealed to reforming Neapolitans, even when they were unhappy about French interference, and about the terrible economic burden placed on the kingdom by its obligations to pay for French armies. These institutions also helped shape an elite in the French manner, a body of administrators, technocrats and scientists, of which Monticelli was a minor but ubiquitous member. In particular, there was a large overlap between the membership of the Academy of Sciences, the Accademia Pontaniana and the Istituto d'Incoraggiamento. Monticelli and Ricciardi were members of all three.

Under the French, Neapolitan savants like Monticelli had assumed positions of power, quite often taken administrative office and promoted legal and educational reform (though with limited success). After 1815 the intervention of the Austrians prevented the Bourbons from completely purging the Muratist administration to which Monticelli belonged and he, along with most of his friends, remained in office. But the failure of the abortive constitutional regime of 1820–1, supported by many of the Muratists, meant that many of his long-standing friends were dismissed or forced into exile. Monticelli survived, most probably because he had made himself indispensable as the link between Vesuvius and foreign visitors and dignitaries. The youthful ardent Jacobin had mellowed into a pragmatist, willing to accept the restored dynasty because his positions gave him influence and power that could be used in the pursuit of reform. For the last thirty years of his life he was secretary of both the Bourbon Royal Society and the Academy of Sciences, in continuous correspondence with savants from Europe and the New World. In 1845, on the last day of the Seventh Congress of Italian Scientists held at the newly opened Observatory on the slopes of Vesuvius (a project he had ardently promoted but whose inauguration he had been too ill to attend), Monticelli died in his eighty-sixth year. His funeral in Naples was attended by many of the Congress's participants. Posthumous panegyrics are rarely reliable, but they seem to have agreed on his 'serene affability', and his 'aura of modesty'.[30]

Monticelli and Vesuvius

Monticelli was determined to insert Vesuvius (both materially and intellectually) into the international geological narrative, because he saw international interest in the volcano as a means to promote Naples as part of a modern, scientific world. He wanted this perception to be both local and international. This involved several interconnected stratagems: acting as a fixer between the volcano, the local scientific community and foreign visitors to Naples; bringing Vesuvius to the attention of a local and international public through the display of collections, accounts of Vesuvius's activity, and the international circulation of specimens; and finally, protecting and ensuring the status of Vesuvius as a scientific object in the face of criticism and hostility from the local church and other conservative forces.

Almost every important geologist and major public figure who came to Naples between 1808 and 1840 met Monticelli, who frequently accompanied them on an ascent of Vesuvius. His surviving correspondence is littered with letters of introduction from geologists like Alexander von Humboldt and Humphry Davy recommending savants from Britain, Germany, France, Scandinavia and the New World. In his dealings with this international clientele, Monticelli was a master of the small significant gesture: at Christmas 1814 he entertained Sir William Gell, who became the greatest English-language expert on Pompeii, at his country house at Boscotrecase on the southern slopes of Vesuvius, and took the Englishman on his very first visit to the ruins;[31] he helped Davy on his first visit to Vesuvius in 1814–15, sent him compounds to Rome for his experiments en route to Naples in 1819, and managed all his affairs during the eruption of 1819–20.[32] When an ill-equipped Humboldt arrived in Naples in 1822, from a diplomatic mission in Verona, Monticelli lent him instruments and log tables to pursue his work.[33] When Charles Lyell arrived in 1828, two years before the publication of his ground-breaking *Principles of Geology*, he was unable to observe all of Vesuvius because of its eruptive state, so Monticelli provided him with drawings of the parts of the volcano he could not see.[34] He made travel arrangements for the Oxford geologist William Buckland and his wife in 1826, and made a lifelong friend of the Danish archaeologist Charles Jurgensen-Thomsen, by providing him with accommodation during his visit to Naples in the 1820s.[35]

This was typical. Monticelli helped not just geologists, but scientists of every stripe, agronomists, botanists, physicists and chemists, doctors and philosophers, cartographers and geographers, mathematicians and statisticians, and the many amateurs and polymaths who were typical of the scientific culture of the period. When the Duke of Buckingham, an ardent amateur geologist, arrived in Naples in the spring of 1828, Monticelli offered the services of his secretary as a guide to the volcanic islands that the Duke was eager to visit in his custom-built (and unpaid for) yacht. Buckingham was delighted with Emmanuele Donati's services – Donati found and identified specimens, supervised an archaeological dig, and worked tirelessly on the Duke's behalf on Capri and Corsica. When the two men parted in Genoa, Buckingham gave Donati 10 pounds for travel expenses and a gold snuff box, and arranged to pay him 50 pounds. 'He is sorry to go,' the Duke wrote, 'and I am equally sorry to lose him, as he has been a very active, quiet, unassuming companion, and has been of great use to me.'[36]

Monticelli also drew visitors into the scholarly life of Naples. He persuaded Charles Babbage, in Italy to recuperate from the loss of his father, wife and son, to sit on a commission – to which the Catalan geologist Carlos de Gimbernat also contributed – into the curative powers of the waters of Ischia.[37] He had the chemist and botanist Charles Daubeny, author of *A Description of Active and Extinct Volcanoes* (1826), speak about his research to the Royal Academy of Sciences. He even persuaded a rather nervous Christian, Crown Prince of Denmark, an amateur obsessed with geology, to present his findings about Vesuvius to a special session of the Academy. Brokering such events gave the Academy greater kudos in the eyes of the court, even as it enhanced its reputation among the foreign visitors and dignitaries who were drawn into its affairs.

A central feature of Monticelli's hospitality was a visit to his collection of Vesuvian lavas and minerals. On 25 January 1820, for example, Crown Prince Christian visited Monticelli's collection with Humphry Davy, describing it as 'unique' for '*objets volcaniques*'; he was also struck by its collection of fossils from northern Europe which he thought much richer than was usually found in Italy. Originally housed in Monticelli's home, the Museum moved to the Palazzo Penne in the centre of Naples in 1825, and at his death contained 6,600 specimens from Vesuvius and a further 1,400 minerals from other volcanoes in the Azores, Sardinia and Iceland. This was an entirely separate collection from the royal cabinet of minerals, which had its own curator.

Like many others, Christian was fascinated by the collection, which included many volcanic substances that he could not recognise or name. As was often the case, this visit prompted a request that Monticelli put together a collection of 'the most interesting specimens' for the visitor.[38] As the Duke of Buckingham, another passionate aristocratic collector, commented, 'the collection of Vesuvian minerals is immense and beautiful, and supplies all of Europe'.[39]

So one way to ensure Vesuvius's place in the grand narrative of geology was through a process of dispersal: to distribute samples of the volcano to schools, cabinets, academies, universities and laboratories. Monticelli was big in the rock business. Visitors to his collection were given samples, but Monticelli, either for a fee or as part of a system of gift exchange, also distributed larger collections of minerals all over the world. Quite often he was solicited for samples, often in return for election to an academy or in response to a gift of samples from other geological sites. Thus Charles Frederic Bachmann, the director of the Jena Mineralogy Society, accompanied news that they had awarded Monticelli with a diploma with a request for specimens of Vesuvian rocks.[40] Monticelli received minerals from northern Europe, including Copenhagen, Stockholm, Norway, southern England, the lower Rhine, Bohemia and Geneva; from the Mediterranean: Marseilles, Trieste, Udine, Catania and Malta; and from the New World: Mexico and Baltimore. He supplied minerals not just to London, Paris and Copenhagen, but to Jena, Dresden, Marseilles, Turin, Philadelphia, Middlebury Vermont, Washington and Rio de Janeiro, as well as to many Italian museums and collections.

The circulation of these material objects worked through a network of exchange and information (letters, offprints and books) that included more than 150 correspondents in Germany (Berlin, Jena, Göttingen, Freiberg, Dresden, Heidelberg and Bonn), London (the British Museum, the Royal Society and the Geological Society), Paris (the Académie des Sciences, the Jardin des Plantes, the École des Mines, the Muséum National d'Histoire Naturelle and the Institut Historique),

Scandinavia (Copenhagen, Helsingfors, Uppsala, Stockholm), Russia (St Petersburg), as well as in the New World in Vermont, New York, Washington (the National Institute for the Promotion of Science), Buenos Aires, Rio de Janeiro and Mexico City.

Some of these transactions were at the behest of rulers, diplomats and government officials, others were often facilitated by diplomatic staff who arranged to shepherd valuable specimens through ports and customs. Some were simple commercial transactions with mineral and rock dealers in London, Freiberg, Göttingen, Heidelberg and Vienna. But most of Monticelli's transactions were either with academies and museums, or, on a much smaller scale, with private individuals, often in response to gifts – as small as a single rock – or to direct requests for a few specimens. Many grew out of contacts first made in Naples.

The entire range of such exchanges, small and large, personal and official, can be followed in the ongoing development of the relationship between Humphry Davy and Monticelli. In February 1816, Davy sent some Cornish minerals to his Italian friend because, as he wrote to his mother, when he had been in Naples, Monticelli had been 'excessively civil' and 'gave me a very fine collection of minerals from Vesuvius'.[41] Three years later, when Davy returned to Naples, Monticelli gave him 'a list of substances wanting for his collection', and Davy wrote to his young assistant Michael Faraday in London asking him to arrange a reciprocal gift, which he would pay for.[42] Monticelli had already put together another 'magnificent collection' for Davy, which the Cornishman asked him 'to send to the Royal Institution', suggesting that if they had any duplicates that were on Monticelli's wish list they should give them in exchange.[43] When the collection arrived in London it was catalogued by Michael Faraday. In the autumn of 1820, and newly appointed as the president of the Royal Society in London, Davy received from Naples two cases of minerals, samples of sea salt, and several bottles of wine. Davy, on his part, told Monticelli that he was waiting for a means of safe passage before sending him several precious stones from Ceylon, which were later brought to Naples by William Hamilton, the British envoy.[44]

The scale of these exchanges changed radically in June 1821 when Davy first proposed that the British Museum should buy Monticelli's entire Vesuvian collection.[45] As he made clear from the outset, they were only interested in his volcanic specimens, not in his collection as a whole. By the following spring Davy had Treasury approval to pay £500 for the collection – he had consulted Henry Fitton secretary of the Geological Society and Lord Compton on the fairness of the price – and designated Compton, who was then resident in Rome, to ensure that the right rocks reached London.[46] (In the summer of 1819 Compton, then in England, had received a shipment of minerals from Monticelli, and had reciprocated with a gift of British specimens.)[47] After some negotiation – Monticelli persuaded the British government to pay for the packing and shipping – the deal went through, and the collection arrived in London some time in 1823.

It is not clear how much of Monticelli's collection was acquired by the British Museum, but the sale must have left a gaping hole. Why did he sell such a large part of it and why, indeed, did Davy broker the transaction? Monticelli's collection was his private property, not the possession of one of the academies or of the Crown. He had been complaining bitterly a few years earlier about how costly his Vesuvian ventures had become. Writing to Paolo D'Ambrosio, an old friend who was the Neapolitan envoy in Copenhagen, he complained that he had 'lavas, tuffs, pumices, volcanic glasses, scoriae and sublimations' that would have filled a dozen cabinets but 'I have no room to house them and no money to make them [the cabinets], each costs at least 16 ducats. I have become poor from frequent expenses . . . It is cheering for me, the admiration shown by the crowd of foreigners who come to visit it. But . . . [I] keep on living philosophically and with every kind of hardship'.[48] However justified – and there was certainly an element of special pleading in Monticelli's comments – we don't know if Davy was conscious of Monticelli's financial plight or was interested in helping him, or perhaps even taking advantage of his circumstances. In their correspondence the two men only spoke of the contribution to science the purchase would make. But Davy was very direct with his Italian friend: he made clear that if he wanted more than £500, the deal would fall through. In their correspondence there was a significant shift – Davy began writing in Italian, shifted to French (in which he was more comfortable) and ended up describing the final deal in English, which he certainly knew that Monticelli did not understand.[49] Whatever the case, there seem to have been significant benefits for Monticelli. The detailed list of materials, probably drawn up by and certainly in the hand of his colleague Nicola Covelli, served as the basis for the *Prodromo della mineralogia vesuviana* that they jointly authored and published in 1825, while Monticelli himself was now well enough off to buy the substantial Palazzo Penne in the centre of Naples and to use it to exhibit his remaining collections which, it is claimed, eventually numbered some 16,800 minerals, fossils and rocks.

Davy and Monticelli continued to correspond after the sale of 1823 – exchanging gifts of food, writings and a few specimens – but they never met again.[50] Davy was preoccupied with Royal Society business and was then hampered by ill health. He wrote frequently to Monticelli in 1827–8 when he was recuperating in Rome, promising that they would renew their researches on Vesuvius together. But this, as Davy knew, was wishful thinking; he was too ill for such strenuous activity. The last surviving letter he wrote to the Neapolitan was in February 1828 from Terracina, halfway between Rome and Naples.[51] He never made it further south, and died the following May.

Networks

The transactions between Monticelli and Davy reveal the complex interplay of self-advancement and camaraderie, vanity and idealism, cooperation, collective endeavour and ambition that informed dealings among the savants fascinated by the minerals, rocks and fossils that promised to reveal the secrets of the earth. While royalty, grand aristocracy and public figures of renown seem almost to have demanded Monticelli's help (and specimens) as of right – in much the manner that Alexander von Humboldt did in 1822 – and though there was certainly a thriving market for geological specimens of all sorts, most of the savants he dealt with engaged in a polite game of give and take that was a way of nurturing relationships that were (at least ostensibly) of mutual benefit.[52]

Monticelli was an exceptionally amenable and hospitable colleague, who went out of his way to help the many foreign visitors who came through Italy in pursuit of learning, aiding, as we have seen, not just geologists and mineralogists, but those interested in archaeology and antiquity, agriculture and economics, literature and art. In this respect he resembled many friends within Italy who acted as hosts to an itinerant army of international savants, and with whom he was in frequent correspondence.

Like Monticelli these men combined a university professorship with the custody and nurturing of local natural history collections that were displayed to foreign visitors. Stefano Borson became professor at the Sardinian mining school at Moutier after teaching mineralogy at the University of Turin. His massive catalogue of the Turin collections, almost entirely his own work, included 9,866 specimens: 6,027 minerals, 1,486 rocks, 748 marbles and pietre dure, and 1,605 fossils. Fillipo Nesti taught in Florence and curated the zoological and mineralogical collections in the Museo di Fisica e Storia Naturale in Florence, which he proudly showed Georges Cuvier when the latter visited in 1809. Similarly, Paolo Salvi was professor of geology in Pisa, Luigi Canali professor of physics and chemistry in Perugia, and Carlo Giuseppe Gismondi professor of mineralogy in Rome. All three presided over important local collections; Gismondi oversaw two, one at the university, the other at the Collegio Nazzarino.

Like Monticelli, none of these figures confined their intellectual interests to geology or mineralogy. Ranieri Gerbi, another professor from Pisa, studied astronomy, physics, insect life and hydraulic systems, and published poetry. He was president of the First Congress of Italian Scientists held in Pisa in 1839. Carlo Gemmellaro, who guided visitors up Etna, was a literary figure and an expert on coins and archaeology. His Sicilian colleague Francesco Ferrara was a professor of physics who wrote extensively on history, archaeology and natural history.

During the first three decades of the nineteenth century, these scholars and polymaths developed into a network. Gismondi was Monticelli's teacher in Rome and inspired his interest in minerals and geology; he also moved to Naples for a year in 1816 to help reorganise Monticelli's collections. Canali in Perugia first contacted Monticelli in 1817, after he had read about him in a periodical article; similarly Marco Antonio Fabroni, a scholar in Arezzo, wrote to Monticelli in 1823 requesting Vesuvian minerals after reading a paper in a French journal by the famous chemist Joseph Louis Gay-Lussac that praised the Neapolitan's work. The savants set up mineral exchanges with Monticelli, sending him samples of rocks that he had requested from all over Italy in return for Vesuvian minerals, crystals and lavas. The exchange with Nesti in Florence began in 1811, with Ranzani in Bologna in 1820, with Fabroni in Arezzo and with Nicolò Da Rio in Padua in 1824, with Gemmellaro in Catania in 1825, and with Vitaliano Borromeo Arese in Milan in 1830.

The links in the network were consolidated not just by an exchange of local specimens, but by the mutual distribution of books, pamphlets and periodicals and the proceedings of the various local academies. There was an economy of prestige in which savants in the different cities arranged for the election of their counterparts to be corresponding members of their institutions, which also entitled them to copies of the academies' proceedings. Their motto might have been the words with which Mario Gemmellaro, writing from Sicily, ended a letter to Monticelli: *'comandateme, amatemi, e credetemi'*, 'command me, love me, and believe me'.[53]

In certain respects these geologists and mineralogists were resolutely local. The ambit of their research and publications was largely confined to their immediate surroundings (the major exceptions were Scipione Breislak and Giambattista Brocchi). Gismondi was a figure of enormous stature but only ever published a single article, on the subject of minerals in the vicinity of Rome; Borson travelled extensively in France but limited his publications to studies of Piedmont. Even a well-travelled savant like Carlo Gemmellaro, who served as a surgeon in the British army and navy and who attended Humphry Davy's lectures on geology at the Royal Institution in London, focused his attentions on Sicily and Catania. As Pietro Corsi has pointed out, the object of such studies was to feed local information – observations and collections – into some of the larger scientific issues, while retaining a strong sense of place.

But this did not preclude the belief that what the savants were producing was 'Italian' science. The naturalist-antiquary Giuseppe Giovene from Molfetta near Bari wrote to Monticelli that he would always act for 'the honour of science, of the nation, and of the patria'.[54] When Luigi Canali wrote to Monticelli from Perugia asking for Vesuvian materials, he justified his request by arguing that he needed *'le cose italiane'* (Italian things) to teach his students 'Italian' science. After reading in a foreign journal about a new discovery made by Monticelli's collaborator Nicola Covelli, Niccolò Da Rio complained, 'What a disappointing thing that one must discover from a French journal what is happening in Italy.'[55] Pietro Carpi and a famous professor of medicine from Pavia, Antonio Scarpa, praised Covelli and Monticelli's *Prodromo della mineralogia vesuviana* as a triumph for *Italian* science.[56] Giacinto Cavena, a member of the Academy of Sciences in Turin, wanted to procure 'a free and easy scientific and literary communication among the diverse parts of our Italy'.[57] This was the only means by which the larger picture of Italian geology could be constructed.

This sense of 'Italy' was both political and experiential. The generation of savants born between the 1750s and 1770s were well travelled within the Italian peninsula and had lived under a variety of regimes, many of which aspired, under French rule, to a sort of Italian nationhood. Take the geologist of that generation with the highest international profile, Scipione Breislak. Breislak began his studies in Rome, moved to Nola and Naples where, as an expert in mining and nitre, he was attached to the royal military academy, carrying out extensive research throughout the Kingdom of Naples. Though a royal employee, his politics were republican and in 1798 he moved back to his native city to serve as the Roman Republic's Minister of Finance. With the collapse of the Republic in 1799 he was forced into political exile, fleeing to Paris, where he worked with such savants as Georges Cuvier and Alexandre Brongniart. In 1802 he returned to Milan where he was appointed by the government of the Italian Republic as the inspector of the manufacture of powders and saltpetre, a position that enabled him to continue his geological researches. He published works on the lithology and geology of the Campania, Rome and the province of Milan, and his work was translated into French and German.[58] His *Introduzione alla geologia* (1811) is regarded as the first Italian geological textbook. He persistently urged Monticelli to publish his work in journals that were available outside Italy in order to promote Italian geological science.[59]

Brokers and go-betweens

Scipione Breislak had exceptionally good connections outside Italy, especially in Paris. But the most important figures in making international connections for the Italian savants were two outsiders with loose ties to the network,[60] namely the young Irishman Joseph Barclay Pentland (1797–1873), who for many years was Cuvier's intermediary in his dealings with both Britain and Italy, and the Genevan watch manufacturer, amateur botanist and geologist Moïse-Étienne Stefano

Moricand (1779–1854). Their range of contacts among the savants was greater than that of the Italians, and they were far more assiduous in getting the group to work together.

Pentland, though he held no official position and had no salary, worked for Cuvier in the Jardin des Plantes, collaborating closely with Buckland in Oxford,[61] with London's Royal Society, and with many savants on the Italian peninsula. He shared fifty-four contacts with Monticelli, twenty-two of whom were British and seventeen from Paris and its environs. He was an exceptionally energetic and ebullient character (for a while he served as secretary to the British consul in Bolivia), who bombarded the much more phlegmatic Monticelli with schemes and ideas. After a first Italian trip in early 1822 (before the major eruption of Vesuvius in October–November of that year) Pentland set up an exchange between Cuvier and Monticelli, giving the latter detailed instructions about what Paris needed. He encouraged links with Nesti in Florence and an exchange between Monticelli and Vitaliano Borromeo Arese, a Milanese savant who had acquired Breislak's geological collection. Urging a connection with the Milanese, he urged Monticelli on: 'I think that located at the two extremities of Italy you can be useful the one to the other, and as the advancement of science is your common goal I don't doubt you would concur – as I said before Borromeo has very little of things from Vesuvius and I think that you are [would be] very much richer in the mineralogy of Piedmont, Lombardy and Switzerland.' Pentland also got Monticelli to coordinate a southern Italian search for specimens of sea turtles and medusa that Cuvier wanted for his research (Gemmellaro was able to provide the turtles), as well as to organise a hunt for porpoise fossils. In return he bombarded Monticelli with gifts – French fossils and minerals, copies of works by Alexander von Humboldt and Cuvier, proceedings of the French academies, and a series of models of fossils, approved by Cuvier, which were intended to help Italian researchers identify the materials that they found. He even arranged with a French and a London dealer in scientific instruments for Monticelli to purchase equipment he needed in exchange for supplying them with Vesuvian lavas and crystals. His customary tactic was to flatter Monticelli – 'You have here in me a friend, a man who is beholden to you for your goodness towards him' – and immediately follow such plaudits with multiple new requests. At the same time he urged Monticelli to broaden the scope of his work, to extend it beyond Vesuvius to cover the whole of the Neapolitan kingdom and to focus on geology rather than mineralogy.[62]

The Swiss Moïse-Étienne Stefano Moricand, born in Geneva, had spent the years of his youth in Italy in the watch and clock trade.[63] As a young man he had become fascinated with gems and crystals, and when he returned to Geneva he began to study them, and to support the natural history museum that was established there in 1818. He continued to make frequent trips to Italy (he visited Monticelli in 1815 and 1819), and was a good friend of Breislak, Gismondi and Brocchi, writing gossipy letters about their research and travels. Between 1816 and 1819 he published three short papers on lavas and crystals in the *Bibliothèque universelle*, the widely read Genevan periodical edited by Marc-Auguste Pictet, all of which were heavily indebted to Monticelli. When Monticelli's co-author, Covelli, visited Moricand's collection in Geneva in 1825, he described it as second only to Monticelli's in the number and quality of Vesuvian minerals.[64]

Though concerned to establish his scholarly credentials (about which he was always anxious), and though an enthusiastic mineralogist and botanist, Moricand was also an important dealer who sold minerals and offered his services to savants. He had contacts in Germany, Russia and the New World as well as France. In 1817 he introduced Ernst Odeleben, the German dealer who sold minerals to Goethe, to Monticelli, who also bought specimens from him. He plied Monticelli with information about the prices of crystals in different parts of Europe, sent him boxes of minerals from northern Italy and journals and books from Geneva. In return he solicited specimens for the Geneva museum and strontium sulfate crystals, which he especially valued as their beauty and rarity made them powerful bargaining chips in trading for other minerals.[65]

Pentland linked the Italian geologists to Paris, reinforcing a connection that in some cases went back to the era when the universities of northern and central Italy were under French control. (Several of the savants knew Cuvier from the time he spent in Italy as inspector general of the Imperial University in 1809–10 and 1813. After Ranzani met Cuvier in Bologna in 1810, he spent fourteen months at the Frenchman's invitation working in Paris.) Moricand, as Breislak knew, was a vital link to the major mineral dealers in northern Europe, while he and his colleagues in Geneva – often referred to as 'the Athens' of Europe – helped propagate Italian science north of the Alps. The first contacts of these outsiders, and many other foreign savants with Italian geologists, were as travellers, visitors and collectors; their contributions to sciences within Italy were vital as they helped bind the Italians even more closely together and cemented their connections with the scientific community throughout Europe. As Dorinda Outram reminds us, 'In natural history, perhaps more than in any other scientific discipline, the exchange of tangible objects or information about them, in the shape of specimens, casts, drawings and verbal descriptions, was of crucial importance in research.'[66]

Pentland and Moricand connected many Italian geologists and mineralogists to one another and to scholars and institutions throughout Europe. But Monticelli also had a go-between who connected him to northern Europe. Paolo D'Ambrosio was a personal friend of Monticelli, an embittered Neapolitan diplomat who compensated for exile in Scandinavia (as he saw it) by a hyperactive determination to cultivate scientific interests between the North and the South.[67] He set up exchanges of northern minerals – chiefly from Iceland, Greenland and Sweden – in return for collections of Neapolitan volcanic rocks. He urged Monticelli to send gifts to the officials who established the mineralogical museum in Copenhagen. These included the prime minister Joachim Godske Moltke, the museum director and famous con man Bedemar Vargas, and the mining engineer Eric Thomas Svedenstierna, who had been an industrial spy for the Swedish government in Britain. D'Ambrosio was proactive: on a number of occasions he entrapped Monticelli, making promises to Scandinavian savants on his behalf (and without his knowledge) to further connections to Danish and Swedish industry. He also linked Monticelli to the Heidelberg professor of mineralogy Karl Casar von Leonhard, whose scholarly interests did not preclude him from becoming one of the biggest mineral dealers in northern Europe. And he set up what was described as '*une belle relation minéralogique*' between Monticelli and Wolfgang von Herder, the Saxon government official and ironworks proprietor.

D'Ambrosio was greatly impressed by Scandinavian and German 'cameralism' – by the conscious attempt to manage and develop resources for the benefit of the state – and by the scientific culture that sustained it. He urged this as a model that could be emulated in Italy and Naples and saw the exchange of information as vital to its nurturing. Writing to Monticelli, he contrasted the rich periodical culture of Denmark and the German-speaking lands with the paucity of journals in Italy. He urged Monticelli to start a multilingual scientific journal, modelled on the Swiss *Bibliothèque universelle des sciences, belles-lettres et arts*, remarking that 'If the richness of a nation is always in proportion to the number of contracts, then the culture is in proportion to the number of journals.'[68]

Monticelli knew that to join or create an international network required a certain finesse. In 1812, when he was relatively unknown among mineralogists and geologists, he introduced himself to Parisian savants by sending Brochant de Villiers, a professor at the École des Mines, a small sample of Vesuvian minerals. These were an unsolicited gift, accompanied by a request for advice about how to acquire non-Vesuvian materials in the French capital. Monticelli was seeking to set up a correspondence, open up a channel of communication, one that he made clear would enable the Parisians to obtain Vesuvian rocks and crystals. Similarly, as we have seen, Monticelli's London connection began with a number of personal gifts to Humphry Davy, and with the obligation Davy incurred by depending on Monticelli for hospitality during his first trip to Naples. Thereafter a succession of British geologists turned to Monticelli for hospitality and help in acquiring geological specimens.

Monticelli was also approached by people or institutions with whom he was totally unacquainted. Thus John White Webster, the Harvard professor of geology and chemistry better known as the murderer of his creditor George Parkman[69] than for his scientific prowess, approached Monticelli in 1821 seeking Italian minerals for his lectures and collections, and promising (and sending) two boxes of specimens to Naples in return. Institutions behaved in a similar manner. We have already seen how Charles Frederic Bachmann, the director of the Jena Mineralogy Society, combined news that the society had awarded Monticelli a diploma with a request for specimens of Vesuvian rocks. In all these cases of first contact, the correspondent spoke of a commitment to the furtherance of knowledge as their aim. One spoke, for instance, of asking for Monticelli's help 'for the love of lithology'. Invariably they offered something in return for their request, though almost never money. What was involved was a gift exchange, a '*baratto*', an exchange in kind, framed as a way of spreading scientific information.

The ways in which institutions, especially academies, established links with one another were formal and ritualised. Writing in response to a letter from Monticelli in May 1835, the secretary of the Lisbon scientific academy, Costa de Macedo, agreed to his request for a mutual correspondence. He and Monticelli promised to implement a regular exchange of publications, especially of each institution's proceedings. Then de Macedo raised the question of exchanging geological specimens, especially duplicates. The relationship was sealed by the mutual election of the secretaries as corresponding members of the other academy.[70] Exactly the same pattern occurred with the Academy of Sciences in Turin, the Accademia Gioenia in Catania in Sicily, and the Istituto Brasileiro in Rio de Janeiro.[71]

Such exchanges were also transactions in an economy of prestige. Corresponding memberships of academies were status symbols, almost invariably included on the title pages of publications. The French geologist Ménard de la Groye, who had helped Monticelli develop Parisian connections, was much put out by the Neapolitan's failure to secure him a membership of the Naples academy. De la Groye prodded and hectored him, reminding Monticelli of how many other academies had elected him, and offering to send him minerals if he secured his election. When finally appointed, he complained about the slow delivery of his diploma, but magnanimously remarked that it would encourage his efforts for science and especially for 'Italian naturalists in general'.[72]

Academy secretaries were the go-betweens, often acting as intermediaries between other local savants and those working through the other academy. The links in the network were consolidated not just by an exchange of local specimens, but by the mutual distribution of books, pamphlets and periodicals and the proceedings of the various local academies, and by the exchange of information about travellers, other possible contacts, mineral dealers and their prices, and new discoveries. In Mario Gemmellaro's case, for example, he asked Monticelli for instruments, comparative temperature data, information on a new book on Sicily published in Paris, and the whereabouts of Brocchi; in return he sent Monticelli a collection of Etna materials, reports on the volcano's activity, and information about the price of agate.[73]

Academy officials often exploited these institutional connections for their personal benefit. In 1843 (and in his eighty-fourth year!) the ever-industrious Monticelli wrote to Francis Markoe, one of the founders and the corresponding secretary of the National Institute for the Promotion of Science in Washington, requesting a correspondence between the Institute and the Neapolitan academy. Monticelli was already a corresponding member of the Institute, thanks to the support of Frederick Hall, the first professor of mathematics and natural philosophy at Middlebury College in Vermont, who had been in Naples in 1836. Markoe, who knew of Monticelli's reputation – he had bought a large collection of Italian minerals from Henry Stephen Fox, the British ambassador in Washington who had earlier seen diplomatic service in Naples – followed up an official reply with a note in which he pointed out that 'in addition to any official intercourse wh. may become necessary between us on behalf of the Academy and the Institute . . . I shall be most pleased to interchange letters with you . . . letters marked "private".' Markoe's intentions were clear. He pointed out that he had a 'valuable geological cabinet' of some 8,000–9,000 rocks and fossils, adding, 'I have also a splendid Cabinet of minerals, about 7,000 specimens, & for 6 or 8 years I have been diligently engaged in enlarging & improving it by rare, beautiful, and valuable specimens.' But he didn't like the poor quality of his Vesuvian collection; he only wanted 'first rate' specimens and hoped that Monticelli 'through your superior knowledge & facilities', could find him between fifty and a hundred suitable minerals.[74] Markoe was prepared to purchase or exchange specimens. He sent Monticelli a series of gifts: a copy of Captain Wilkes's account of *The Narrative of the United States Exploring Expedition 1838–42* and two mineralogical works by professors at Harvard and Yale. Eventually the deal fell through – Markoe was able to secure another collection and by the time Monticelli received the American's last letter he was on his deathbed – but the correspondence meant that four Neapolitan scientists – including the botanist and dear friend of Monticelli, Michele Tenore – were made corresponding members of the Institute while Markoe was elected to the Naples academy. The line between personal and institutional interests was often hard to draw.

Frictions

In Chapter VII of the first book of *On War*, his masterpiece published in 1832, the Prussian general Carl von Clausewitz introduced the idea of friction, 'the influence of an infinity of petty circumstances' that deflect or distort the aims of a military commander. These nagging difficulties, he emphasised, were never concentrated at a single point, but were scattered throughout any system. The same applies to networks: though they are rightly praised as vehicles driving towards accomplishment, this should not lead us to overlook the obstacles they face(d), and the difficulties that were thrown in their way. In the case of Monticelli and his colleagues, maintaining connections furthering the cause of mineralogy and geology was not an easy task. Within Italy, though it had been somewhat easier under the French occupation, after 1815 it was difficult to generate and spread scientific knowledge through the Italian peninsula and beyond. As the Swiss collector and dealer Moricand complained, 'how disagreeable it is for those who are interested in the circulation of scientific news, to see that circulation hampered in Italy by the lack of accord among the posts of the different states; it is stupid that the costs of sending journals to Italy exceeds the value of their subscription ... a book that crosses all of France by post for 10 centimes ... costs eight times more to travel a shorter distance in Italy.'[75] In an autocratic and divided world, censorship, suspicious customs officials, high duties, multiple (and expensive) postal systems, spies and poor communications meant that letters, books, specimens and journals were constantly destroyed, damaged, impounded, suppressed or simply lost. In 1823 the head of the Academy of Sciences in Turin asked Monticelli to secure an exemption on the duties on the importation of foreign books, so he would not have to pay the tax on academic and scientific books they wished to send to him.[76] Long-distance communication was little better. An exchange that Monticelli's friend Dall'Armi arranged with Dr Schonberg in St Petersburg was particularly unfortunate: the

Russian minerals sank to the bottom of the Baltic, and the Italian specimens were confiscated by Russian customs as their documentation did not contain an evaluation.[77]

Many letters took months and even years to reach their destination – '*a passo di tartaruga*', 'at the pace of a tortoise', as one correspondent put it.[78] The Swedish mining engineer and mineral dealer Eric Svedenstierna[79] stopped writing to Monticelli about the Swedish chemist Berzelius's chemical experiments on rocks from Naples, because he had had no communication for more than a year. The American senator and geological enthusiast Stephen Van Rensselaer refrained from sending books to Naples, as he believed they would be confiscated by customs.[80] Nicolò da Rio in Padua complained that it took longer to send things to Naples than to France: 'in general, communications with '*Italia Meridionale*' [southern Italy] are more difficult than with Paris.'[81] Camillo Ranzani from Bologna was embarrassed when materials designed to begin relations with Monticelli got lost.[82] Stefano Moricand attempted to send minerals from Verona to Naples. Like many others he didn't trust shipping overland, which was also more expensive, and spent time, as he explained to Monticelli, looking for a ship from Venice to Messina or Barletta. Moricand began the process in September 1815, but the materials had still not arrived in Naples in May 1816. Such delays were normal. It took three years for minerals from the London dealer John Henry Heuland to arrive in Naples. A shipment of two boxes of minerals and two books from another London dealer and Geological Society Member, John Mawe, was delayed for two years, because they had no letter of advice. Vesuvian minerals destined for Heidelberg were routed through Livorno and Rotterdam. The professor there, Leonhard, a major dealer as well as scholar, was shocked to find when he opened the cases that the minerals were intended for the Crown Prince of Denmark and should have been sent to Copenhagen. It became clear that the case intended for Leonhard was lost; as he bitterly complained, 'everything I've tried to do is in vain.'[83]

The chief topic of much network correspondence concerned the logistics. Which port and which agent should you use to ensure successful transmission? Should materials be sent by land or sea? How should specimens be packaged so they did not end up, as Lavinio Spada de Medici of Rome complained, crushed and looking like chickpeas? A number of Monticelli's correspondents gave him detailed instructions about how to wrap and transport precious specimens. Moricand, for example, explained that specimens should first be wrapped in fine and soft paper, then silk paper; then placed on a bed of oakum which should also surround them. They should then be wrapped in strong paper 'enveloping everything' and placed inside a case.[84]

The negotiations between the secretaries of the scientific academies and between individual savants were rather like the elaborate courting rituals of exotic birds. They were precisely defined and carefully choreographed, the rules apparent to all, but they were also the source of much anxiety. The formalities were so often thwarted by unforeseen circumstance – the loss of a letter, the failure to receive a box of specimens – that provoked fear that the relation would break down, that a slight might have been incurred, a conciliatory or communicative gesture misunderstood or overlooked. When William Phillips, Quaker, printer and founding member of the Geological Society died in 1828, leaving his widow with a recently arrived and unacknowledged box of specimens from Monticelli, his friends were called in to tell her of the protocols she should follow. 'My opinion', wrote the Reverend Francis Lunn, member of the Royal Society and chaplain to the Duke of Buckingham, 'is that the case you have received was intended as a present, and that a letter to acknowledge its receipt will be sufficiently satisfactory under existing circumstances' (Lunn's euphemism for Phillips's death). But, he added, 'if you wish to do more it will not be difficult for you, without injury to the collection to select a few English minerals of which there must be duplicates, and which are more valuable to Monticelli, than those which we call foreign'.[85]

Correspondents frequently asked if they had provided the materials that were wanted or complained that they had not been told what to provide. They fussed over who should pay the costs of postage, transport and duties. One letter writer even asked 'please write in small characters on fine paper' in order to reduce the costs of postage.[86] Everyone knew how difficult communication might be, how many obstacles remained in the way of achieving the sort of mutual beneficial admiration that was the goal of the academies. The economy of prestige, both personal and institutional, the sense that a satisfying exchange was or could be successfully accomplished to the satisfaction of all parties, was always at risk, which is why the correspondence between savants so often oscillated between the sycophantic and the nagging – between hyperbolic praise for the other party and a persistent complaint that they were not quite delivering what they promised. It was not so much that transactions were slow, but that they were uncertain, and that undermined trust.

In such a situation the traveller who could carry books, letters and boxes of specimens was vital to the health and strength of intellectual inquiry. Operating with a system of exchange in which the traveller was given letters of recommendation but was expected in return to perform favours that linked the author and the recipient, Italian savants passed travellers on to one another as they made their way down and back up the peninsula. Nesti in Florence, for example, wrote letters of introduction to Monticelli for several international colleagues: Ashurst Majendie, an English member of the geological society; Mr Saybrot, a naturalist from Philadelphia; Mr Fowler, an American educated at the École des Mines in Paris who eventually donated his mineral collection to Princeton University; Herr Dietz of Vienna; and Hermann Abish, a geological professor from Estonia.[87] Monticelli, in turn, was a vital source of letters for savants like Giambattista Brocchi, Humphry Davy, Charles Daubeny, William Buckland, John Frederick William Herschel and Otto Baust, a mining engineer from Freiberg, who wanted to visit and meet geologists and naturalists in Messina, Palermo and Catania.[88]

Many of these travellers, armed with letters of recommendation, were asked to convey parcels and packages. During his tour in Europe in 1819–20 the New York mineralogist and politician Stephen Van Rensselaer (1764–1838) brought Monticelli two books on crystals from Paris that he had been given by their author, Brochant de Villiers, the geologist at the École des Mines who had been Monticelli's first Parisian contact.[89] A year later the Swedish mining engineer Eric Thomas Svedenstierna, who had a sideline in selling minerals, had a young army officer posted to Naples bring Monticelli twenty specimens of Swedish and Russian rocks from Stockholm.[90] When Moricand first approached Monticelli he sent a small deposit of rare lava via Joseph Liboschitz, the Lithuanian doctor, composer and naturalist who was Tsar Alexander I's personal physician.[91] Liboschitz had journeyed from St Petersburg via Geneva to Naples. Camillo Ranzani in Bologna persuaded the pharmacist and botanist Antonio Orsini from Ascoli to carry a volume of scientific pamphlets and two volumes of his small elementary work on zoology to Naples.[92]

Just as erudite travellers brought him books, rocks and crystals, so Monticelli used his visitors to convey books and pamphlets. The English astronomer John Frederick William Herschel took copies of Monticelli's *Prodromo della mineralogia vesuviana* to his friends in Catania.[93] Scipione Breislak received materials in Milan through a Milanese aristocrat, Count Porro, who had been visiting Naples, and via the Crown Prince of Denmark, who was eager to meet him after his visit to Vesuvius in 1820.[94] There were, of course, other means by which scientific knowledge circulated, but most, as the savants often found to their cost, were deeply uncertain. Friends, beholden and sympathetic, made the best couriers; only a diplomat, who enjoyed immunity from inspection and search, was better.

Though there was a strong ethos of collaboration between the travellers and the Italian savants, we should not idealise these relationships. As he travelled through Italy in 1828–9, the Duke of Buckingham was often critical of the collections he visited and the savants he talked to. After dining with Professor Borelli, a mineralogist at the University of Turin who worked closely with Borson, Buckingham expostulated, 'It is extraordinary how ignorant these philosophers are of everything out of the immediate range of their pursuits. Many of the most interesting localities Borelli did not even know by name.' Similarly he was dissatisfied with the mineral collection 'arranged after the system of Brongniart, by Mr Borson', complaining that 'Its collection of volcanic materials is paltry, and not separated from the rest.'[95] (After Buckingham's departure Borson promptly wrote to Monticelli, asking him for specimens from Vesuvius.)[96] At Naples Buckingham's complaints also focused on the local nature of the collections. After praising Monticelli's Vesuvian collection, he grumbled that 'His general collection is meager and bad.'[97] Local strength was parsed by Buckingham as a general weakness.

Conversely, the Italian savants, though they desperately wanted foreign visitors to draw on their local expertise, often felt a certain superiority towards them, because their guests were bound to be less knowledgeable of local conditions. In Catania Gemmellaro used his local knowledge to jealously guard his intellectual independence. In the 1820s a number of Neapolitan intellectuals mounted a campaign to dispel what they saw as the often superficial and frequently misinformed foreign misapprehensions about both the volcano and the kingdom that surrounded it. Someone like Leopoldo Pilla, a protégé of Monticelli's (though they were to fall out later), who became professor of geology at Pisa, and who died on the battlefield fighting for the Revolution in 1848, started a series of publications, *Lo spettatore del Vesuvio*, designed to reveal the scientific value of Vesuvius to foreigners, whose visits, he argued, were too brief, too superficial and too dependent on other accounts to be properly informed. He was particularly disparaging of the very successful guide written by Canadian geologist and alpinist John Auldjo, *Sketches of Vesuvius*, published in Naples and London in both English and French. In 1827 Gabriele Quattromani produced the *Itinerario delle due Sicilie* (also published in a French edition), as a 'Mappa Statistica' of the two kingdoms with the overt object of rebutting most foreign accounts which he dismissed as '*romanzi*' (novels). Much of the data in the *Itinerario* came from reports of commissions on the Neapolitan infra-structure to which Monticelli had contributed. Breislak, in urging Monticelli to publish his results and ensure that they were circulated widely, warned him that otherwise 'foreigners who rush to Vesuvius in a crowd', and who didn't know much about the volcano, would 'take advantage of your observations and pass them off as their own property'.[98] He offered to circulate Monticelli's work through journals published north of the Alps. This concern with the outsider's point of view was persistent: the argument for the publication of Monticelli's various papers into three volumes of collected works in 1841 was that it would increase their visibility among foreigners.

The politics of Neapolitan earth sciences

Such visibility was all the more important after 1815 because of the delicate position that science and new knowledge occupied in the world of Restoration absolutism. Under the French, Neapolitan savants like Monticelli had assumed positions of power, quite often taken administrative office, and promoted legal and educational reform. But this positive, reformist environment and its proponents, though it survived the Restoration, came under suspicion from the Crown and the Church. Neapolitan monarchs, like their counterparts elsewhere in Europe, were eager to win the international prestige that came with the support and development of science and technological innovation. Certainly, the Bourbons were not hostile to new technologies. Naples, after all, had the first steamship service and the first railway in Italy. (It also had some state-of-the-art panopticon prisons.) But the rulers wanted, like the panopticon, to exercise surveillance and control; they were terrified of unleashing the forces of reform and of liberalism, especially those that might produce political change. This was one reason (though clearly not the only one) why Monticelli and his colleagues were so eager for international recognition and involvement; it bolstered the argument that 'science' helped promote Naples and the prestige of its rulers. As we have seen, the list of visitors to Vesuvius touted by Monticelli included savants of the calibre of Humboldt, Buch, Davy and Lyell, but he also often enumerated the large number of kings and queens, princes and princesses who made the pilgrimage up the mountain. From all points of view the Crown Prince of Denmark was the ideal visitor – unalloyed royalty but also a passionate enthusiast for the new science of geology.

Looking outward was a way of looking in. This is very clear in Monticelli and Covelli's *Prodromo della mineralogia vesuviana* published in 1825. Its dedication to the king, written in the deferential, not to say fawning, language of such prefaces, praises the monarch's achievements as a patron of the arts and science. Surveying all the scholarly and scientific institutions in Naples – its academies, cabinets of minerals, physics, chemistry, zoology and pathology – it attributes their success to royal munificence. At the same time, it underscores their importance to German, French and English visitors, and uses them to advocate the teaching of the useful sciences, promoted through observation and experiment.

There was, of course, a deep ambiguity in claiming that scientific investigation, including that of Naples' greatest foreign attraction, Vesuvius, enhanced the prestige and caché of the nation, an equivocation neatly concealed in the term 'nation'. Did such a term refer – as any autocratic ruler, however enlightened, would assume – to the dominion of the Prince, or, as many savants throughout the peninsula believed, to the body of people? It was possible, indeed, in the context of Restoration Naples, desirable, to fudge the issue of who was the beneficiary of science.

Monticelli was in a good place to do so, both through the academies and as a member of government bodies investigating education, steam navigation, bridges and roads, waterways, forestry and hunting. What emerges in his writings is a larger vision of science and learning that harks back to his Jacobin and French roots. What one sees is not a kingdom but an environment, both natural and human, of great potential and abundance (a trope about Naples that goes back to Pliny), whose failures are attributable to a misuse of resources. Wasteland, swamps and marshland, deforestation and erosion: all were obstacles to farming and cultivation, as well as hazards to the health of livestock and human inhabitants. Monticelli was obsessed with what is best called 'good husbandry', promoting schemes to drain marshland, reclaim wastes and to canalise and control water flow, and set up tanks and other means of water conservation. What was important was not maximising profit or making short-term gain so much as securing the long-term well-being of the rural community, making nature yield its bounty. Medical science and the investigation of public hygiene were crucial to this process; environmental degradation went hand in hand with endemic diseases, most notably malaria. Part of the reform process involved opening up access to resources, hence concern with the development of a better infrastructure of roads, waterways and bridges – but it also sought to break up monopolies, always a problem in a society that remained quasi-feudal and corporatist.

The analyses of Monticelli and his colleagues were not couched as criticisms of authority – indeed, in one sense, they emanated from authority itself – nor could they afford to excite the attentions of the censor. And their ability to secure change, much less reform, was seriously limited. When Monticelli republished his *Sull'economia delle acque da ristabilirsi nel regno di Napoli* in 1821 (just as the new constitutional government had created a free press), he complained bitterly that its first edition of 1809, under the Muratist regime, had been largely ignored.[99] As John Davis points out, the parlous state of Neapolitan finances and the intractable problems posed by the intervention of central powers in local power struggles made it exceptionally difficult to implement reform, even when the regime was willing.[100]

For most reformers the greatest political stumbling block came in the realm of human capital rather than natural resources. Figures like Monticelli viewed education as the means by which human resources could best be mobilised. Instruction was to dispel ignorance, create skills, eliminate poverty and enhance wealth. As the report of the commission on reorganising public education penned by Vincenzo Cuoco eloquently put it: 'Only education will enable us to retain our ancient greatness and ancient glory. Nature has bestowed on us all the capital we need. We do not lack for industries, but we do lack the knowledge to develop them; yet this, too, education can provide ... The purpose of educating the masses is to make possible communication between the many and the few.'[101] Hence the reformers' fascination with education methods, especially those of the Swiss educator Johann Heinrich Pestalozzi, with his commitment to accessible and universal education, and with the Bell and Lancaster systems of schooling which, by training pupils to teach their peers, promised to reduce the cost of education and make it more accessible to the poor. Monticelli was particularly interested in Pestalozzi and sent collections of Vesuvian minerals to Pestalozzi schools.

Science was one thing, but education was another, especially after the failed constitutional revolution of 1820. Moderate as were the changes introduced in 1820 – freedom of speech and of the press, and the creation of a freely elected legislature – they produced the fierce backlash that had been avoided in 1815. The biggest changes after 1821 came in the army, but the educated classes were also badly hit. They had, after all, provided many of the seventy-two delegates to the legislature: eight were professors of 'science' and nine were doctors. Public employees and teachers were purged, students at the University of Naples were rusticated. The Catholic Church's powers over education were enhanced; censorship returned; a junto for public education was established. The Minister of Police railed that 'The fanaticism of innovation was spread by books. These were the source of the poison that was present in the guise of reform, regeneration, progress and freedom. It was in this way that the spirit of revolution brought desolation to our people, undid morality and destroyed religion.'[102]

Monticelli was closely allied to and personal friends with many members of the regime of 1820–1, but he survived. The next ten years of his career were unquestionably the most active. He moved to the Palazzo Penne, entertained many foreign visitors, became rector of the university and, after the accession of Francis I in 1825, was extremely active on governmental commissions. He seems to have played a double game. It is the nature of such stratagems that they are hard to prove, but there are telling signs – all Vesuvian – that even as he ingratiated himself with the court, he remained, at the very least, a sympathiser and fellow traveller with the constitutional reformers. These were also the years when he received calls for help and re-habilitation from some of his old radical friends.

Monticelli used the fruits of Vesuvius – some of its most beautiful gems and crystals – as gifts to gain favour at court. Working through Caterina de Simone, the Queen's lady-in-waiting, who was notorious for taking bribes and gifts from clerics and civil servants, he gave the Spanish wife of Francis I, Maria Isabella, several gifts of gems, including a collection of jewel studs; he was even invited to a royal audience to offer his opinion on a gemstone necklace she had acquired. Monticelli was not a rich man, and he would never have been able to afford the sort of gems that he gave the royal consort if he had not obtained them from Vesuvius, but, because of the identification of the kingdom with the volcano, he could present the gift of products of Vesuvius as a patriotic act, one in which the Spanish-born princess could share by the public display of the gems.

Yet even as he was ingratiating himself with a royal consort who was terrified of *carbonari* (radicals and reformers), he was sending his secretary, Emmanuele Donati, with the Duke of Buckingham on a tour of the Mediterranean. Donati, who, as we have seen, was greatly admired as a geologist by the Duke of Buckingham, was also a radical.

He was arrested on his return to Naples, accused of making contact with fellow radicals on his journey, and suspected of involvement in the Cilento insurrection of June 1828, a rising of a number of *carbonari* factions in the mountains south of Salerno. (As a rather shocked Duke of Buckingham was to discover, and as Monticelli knew to his own cost, almost every inhabited volcanic island in the Mediterranean was not just a vulcanologist's paradise, but a secure site where political prisoners were exiled and incarcerated.) How involved Donati was with the plot is unclear, though he did meet with a group of radicals in Malta that the government believed to be behind the rising. At all events, Donati was forced into exile, and ended up living in lodgings in London's Tottenham Court Road. It had been the value of his technical knowledge about volcanoes that had enabled him to embark on a journey that proved his political undoing. In the following years Donati eked out a rather meagre existence in London and Paris, often acting as an intermediary between English and French savants and Monticelli.

As in his secretary's case, for Monticelli Vesuvius, geology and politics were intertwined. One of the Vesuvian objects he included in the collection that he sold via Humphry Davy to the British Museum was a piece of dark grey trachyte lava that has been pressed into a mould to create an impression that reads, 'Alliance of Crown and Liberty Sealed with the Burning Lava of Vesuvius. March 1820 by C. Gimbernat' (Plate 18).[103] This was not just a transformation of nature into culture, but of nature into politics.

Carlos de Gimbernat was a Catalan geologist, a liberal whose father had been fired on political grounds from the medical school he founded in Madrid. He studied science and medicine in Madrid, went to Oxford where he befriended the radical Thomas Beddoes, who was an early patron of Humphry Davy, attended geological lectures in Edinburgh, worked with Dolomieu in Paris and attended Werner's famous mining school at Freiberg. He had been sent on an official mission to Naples by Maximilian Joseph of Bavaria to investigate the potentially medicinal properties of Vesuvian gases. Arriving in the city at the time of the November 1818 eruption, Gimbernat stayed for twenty-nine months and made more than sixteen ascents of the volcano. He worked with Monticelli and Humphry Davy, using an apparatus of his invention to collect solutions that Davy and Brocchi examined at Monticelli's summer house in Boscotrecase. But Gimbernat became embroiled in the constitutional revolt of 1820, sending detailed and enthusiastic reports to his employer, and making a series of medals that he gave to his friends and associates. He claimed to have produced two sorts of medal: one, like that in the Monticelli collection, that celebrates the agreement in March 1820 by the Spanish king Ferdinand VII, to uphold the liberal Spanish constitution of 1812; the other, which he described as a votive rather than commemorative medal, was inscribed 'Es liebe Konig Max. Joseph. Baiern und Witterbach [sic] Jan 1820'. His lava medal sent to London celebrates the reinstatement of the liberal Spanish Constitution of 1812 by Ferdinand VII of Spain in 1820, an event that helped precipitate the constitutional revolution in Naples in July of that year, a revolution that also adopted the Spanish constitution. He may have been hedging his bets by producing another that praised his patron, Maximilian Joseph 'Long live the King', but the stratagem, if such it was, failed.[104]

The gravity of Gimbernat's offence in celebrating Spanish and Neapolitan revolution was made clear by the response in Munich to news of his actions. Once Bavarian officials learned of his lava medals, he was deprived of his stipend and refused access to the king, his son Prince Ludwig and Bavarian court officials in Rome. Gimbernat desperately sought rehabilitation, pointing out that he had made medals praising his royal employer. He sent a collection of Roman minerals to the Academy of Sciences in Munich, and a huge collection of volcanic materials from Vesuvius that he claimed weighed more than 1,000 kilos. But all to no avail. He remained in Italy, eking out an existence writing studies of the medicinal qualities of thermal baths for cities like Montecatini, Lucca and Pisa. Then he moved to the Savoy Alps, but was denounced to the Piedmontese authorities, threatened with arrest and forced to flee to Switzerland. Gimbernat's career was ruined by the lava medal he had created.[105]

This cautionary tale serves to emphasise the risks that Monticelli was taking by including Gimbernat's lava medal in the materials he sold to London. The care with which Monticelli's collection for the British Museum was assembled, along with its detailed inventory, leaves no doubt that the inclusion of this political slogan was deliberate not accidental. After 1821 the possession in the Kingdom of the Two Sicilies of any item that seemed to embody or express sentiments and ideas associated with the *carbonari* was punishable by a mandatory ten years of exile. No one could have undertaken Monticelli's action lightly. But clearly Monticelli wanted to make a point to Humphry Davy and the British Museum. Vesuvius served him as he had served the volcano, and both worked in the service of Naples.

Monticelli died as the Seventh Congress of Italian Scientists got under way in Naples, holding its first session in the hall that contained the Royal Geological Museum that had been established in 1801. He predeceased the violence of 1848, which would probably have made his political trimming impossible, and left to posterity an underappreciated inheritance. His achievements were personal rather than scholarly and are only revealed through his correspondence, which his family gave to the Museo San Martino and was deposited in the National Library of Naples in 1929. His letters attest to an extraordinary conscientiousness about Neapolitan science and Vesuvius. Even after his eightieth year he was approaching scientific institutions in the United States of America and in Brazil, working to set up exchanges and to secure access for Neapolitan savants to resources in the New World.

All of this came at some personal cost. Count Ricciardi promised Monticelli a stipend after his recovery from cholera in the 1830s, noting that Monticelli had received no payments for his many years of service as secretary to the Academy of Sciences. We have seen that in the 1820s he complained to his friend Paolo D'Ambrosio about the extraordinary expenses he incurred entertaining naturalists and assembling collections. His only major asset was his collection, a large part of which went to the British Museum. The profit and advantage that he gained from this sale, notably the new residence at the Palazzo Penne, led him to believe that he could improve his finances by selling large collections of Vesuvian minerals to institutions or princely collectors. He often badgered his friends, asking them for suggestions about potential buyers. At different times he tried to sell to museums in London, Paris, Brussels, Munich and Rio de Janeiro, enlisting his contacts in the different cities. Anna Wilbraham offered him advice from London and Pentland from Paris. He won the support of Markoe in Washington for an American sale and of Ringseis in his efforts to get Ludwig of Bavaria to buy a collection, but they all fell through. Part of Monticelli's problem was that his collections were mineralogical rather than geological and, as almost all his correspondents explained, geology had become the prevailing fashion. As the physician and good friend Dr Thomas Hodgkin wrote to him, 'among amateurs and perhaps among savants geology has become more popular than mineralogy chez nous, who lack volcanoes while we find their products in Europe ... there are secondary formations and tertiaries and alluvial and deluvial deposits that are attracting the most attention, because of interesting organic remains of animals and vegetables.'[106] Anna Wilbraham gave him the same message. His collection remained in his hands at his death, bequeathed to his nephew, the Neapolitan consul in Malta. It remained his greatest asset and was eventually sold for 3,500 ducats via the good offices of Scacchi to the Royal Mineralogical Museum where most of its specimens remain today.

Part VI

Vesuvius and the Buried Cities

12
THE SPECTACLE OF CATASTROPHE

Stand at the bottom of the great marketplace of Pompeii, and look up the silent streets, through the ruined temples of Jupiter and Isis, over the broken houses with their inmost sanctuaries open to the day, away to Mount Vesuvius, bright and snowy in the peaceful distance; and lose all count of time, and heed of other things, in the strange and melancholy sensation of seeing the Destroyed and the Destroyer making this quiet picture in the sun. Then, ramble on, and see, at every turn, the little familiar tokens of human habitation and every-day pursuits; the chafing of the bucket-rope in the stone rim of the exhausted well; the track of carriage-wheels in the pavement of the street; the marks of drinking-vessels on the stone counter of the wine-shop; the amphoræ in private cellars, stored away so many hundred years ago, and undisturbed to this hour – all rendering the solitude and deadly lonesomeness of the place, ten thousand times more solemn, than if the volcano, in its fury, had swept the city from the earth, and sunk it in the bottom of the sea ... The least among these objects, lends its aid to swell the interest of Vesuvius, and invest it with a perfect fascination. The looking, from either ruined city, into the neighbouring grounds overgrown with beautiful vines and luxuriant trees; and remembering that house upon house, temple on temple, building after building, and street after street, are still lying underneath the roots of all the quiet cultivation, waiting to be turned up to the light of day; is something so wonderful, so full of mystery, so captivating to the imagination, that one would think it would be paramount, and yield to nothing else. To nothing but Vesuvius; but the mountain is the genius of the scene. From every indication of the ruin it has worked, we look, again, with an absorbing interest to where its smoke is rising up into the sky. It is beyond us, as we thread the ruined streets: above us, as we stand upon the ruined walls, we follow it through every vista of broken columns, as we wander through the empty court-yards of the houses; and through the garlandings and interlacings of every wanton vine. Turning away to Pæstum yonder, to see the awful structures built, the least aged of them, hundreds of years before the birth of Christ, and standing yet, erect in lonely majesty, upon the wild, malaria-blighted plain – we watch Vesuvius as it disappears from the prospect, and watch for it again, on our return, with the same thrill of interest: as the doom and destiny of all this beautiful country, biding its terrible time.

Charles Dickens, 'A Rapid Diorama', from
Pictures from Italy, 1845

B y the early nineteenth century volcanic eruption had become a powerful political metaphor used, as we have seen, to justify the sweeping political and social transformations of revolution, and as a threatening image to alert conservatives to the subterranean but potentially devastating effects of popular discontent. Not surprisingly, given the frequency with which Vesuvius and Etna exploded in the era of Romanticism, the focus was on contemporary eruptions. But from the mid-eighteenth century the debate about the fraught relations between Vesuvian nature and Neapolitan culture, between eruptions and the social order, took a historical turn, back to the eruption of 79 CE.

If you had asked a savant or a chronicler before the Romantic era about Vesuvius as a force of death and destruction, they would almost certainly have pointed to the eruption of 1631 as the most devastating of modern history. That year loomed large and dwarfed its antique predecessor not just because it was of more recent memory, but because knowledge about the earlier eruption was sketchy. The surviving record of the eruption in 79 CE was meagre – some comments from Strabo, Martial and Virgil, and an account written a hundred years after the event in Dio Cassius's *Roman History*. Most famously, the nephew of the famous naturalist the elder Pliny sent two revealing letters to the historian Tacitus in response to a request for an account of his uncle's death. (Pliny died of asphyxia on the beach at Stabia, south of Pompeii, during an attempt to rescue friends from the eruption.) The younger Pliny's first letter focused on the demise of the elder Pliny and portrays him in a heroic light, making him a model for a type that we have come across repeatedly, the intrepid and fearless savant. Sailing back across the Bay of Naples towards the eruption, bent on rescuing friends, Pliny 'hurried towards the place from which everyone was fleeing and steered a straight course right into the danger, so fearlessly that he dictated notes on all the changes that he observed as the disaster unfolded'. The younger Pliny adds some details – famously about the volcanic cloud resembling an umbrella pine, the accompanying earthquakes and the hail of pumice – but is surprisingly vague about what he acknowledges to have been a 'catastrophe that destroyed the most beautiful regions of the earth, a fate shared by whole cities and their populations'. Doubtless this was why Tacitus, ever the vigilant historian, asked for further information, prompting a second letter that described the chaotic scene – 'women shrieking, children crying and men shouting ... calling for their parents, some for their children, some for their wives ... bewailing their own fate, or those of their relatives' – as well as adding details of the eruption and its accompanying tsunami.[1] Clearly a horrific disaster had occurred, but the search for more written evidence of what happened was largely unsuccessful, and before the early eighteenth century, the archaeological record was nugatory.

How excavations changed the stories of Vesuvius

The slow but gradually accelerating excavations of Herculaneum and Pompeii during the eighteenth century revealed the full extent of the volcano's power, uncovering the effects of what came to be seen as the most devastating eruption in recorded history. Begun at Herculaneum in 1738, in Pompeii in 1748 (the site was not identified as Pompeii until 1756) and supervised by a Spanish and a Swiss mining engineer, they revealed an astonishing trove of buildings, art and artifacts, statues, frescoes and papyri.[2] The museum, established in 1758 at the Portici palace at the foot of the volcano and later moved into Naples, though it contained major works of antique art, was also filled with ordinary objects of use, revealing a more accessible classical antiquity, one that exposed the everyday life of the ancients, exciting human sympathy as much as recondite scholarship. From the 1760s, as more bodies were discovered, the extent of the eruption of 79 CE became apparent. The volcano was written into the history of human catastrophe. The findings also linked natural history and the study of antiquity in a particular blend that flourished in the collections and museums of the city. There was no better place to examine the complex interplay between the forces of nature and the workings of human society.[3]

The discovery of the buried ancient cities of Herculaneum, Pompeii and Stabia was tremendously exciting to historians and antiquaries, though in the first instance knowledge about the buried cities was largely confined to those with an expertise in antique culture and history. Its first impact was on European taste, enhancing, even if it did not originate, a neo-classicist aesthetic in art, architecture, dress and personal adornment that swept the Continent. But, as the extent of destruction and loss of human life was gradually revealed – a process that took decades rather than years – the relation between the volcano and the ruins, between the killer and its victims, became a matter of enormous interest (one might fairly call it a Romantic obsession), playing out the contemporary confrontation between great, all-powerful forces, whether natural or man-made, and the fate of ordinary people. The violence and unprecedented revolutionary struggles of the era had, as we have seen, been brutally disorienting. Private lives were sucked up into the larger processes of history; to an unprecedented degree ordinary people were made aware of giddying change and their place within it. The events of 79 CE and their aftermath were a place where it was possible to explore ideas and feelings about history, time, rupture, death, loss and nostalgia: sentiments, hopes and anxieties in and about the present that were projected back into the past. And, as we shall see, though accounts of the classical eruption and its effects became part of a conservative story that was more nostalgic than ideological, they also became overtly committed to Christian values and the rejection of a cluster of attitudes – polytheism, atheism, paganism, sexual licence – that were associated with antiquity and modern revolution. If the contemporary eruption had been largely co-opted as an agent of progressive change, the destruction of the buried cities became a conservative leitmotif.

But we are getting ahead of ourselves. Our story must be told in a drama with three acts. The first has to do with objects, the second with bodies and the third with the combination of the two into sententious narratives and stories. This required a redefinition of antiquity that embraced everyday life and the ordinary object as much as the heroic monument, one that encompassed an entire environment, and not just a few artifacts. It also depended on the discovery of human relics, skeletal remains and impressions in the tufa that framed the burial of the cities as not just a natural disaster but a human tragedy. Then, by juxtaposing human and object remains of the 'city of the dead' (a phrase attributed to Sir Walter Scott, though it preceded him),[4] writers, poets and antiquaries fashioned stories about the final hours of the city that fed back into versions of Roman life and culture, but also offered lessons on the present condition.

Objects

When knowledge of the rich extent of the archaeological findings at Herculaneum first reached the international community of anti-quaries and savants in the early eighteenth century, the focus was on the miraculous conservation of a huge number of classical artifacts.[5] The treasure trove was unprecedented in its richness and variety; the eruption of 79 CE had yet to be seen as a human tragedy. A letter published in the *Transactions* of London's Royal Society in 1751–2 describes at great length the underground theatre of Herculaneum, the surrounding sites, statues, busts, artifacts, inscriptions, frescoes, metal wares and marbles, before concluding that the body count from the eruption was negligible: 'That it was not a sudden over-whelming, and that the inhabitants had time to escape with their lives, tho' not with their goods, is proved by not finding dead bodies, where they have thitherto dug.' The author goes on to concede that 'some human bones were found, tho' few,' imagining them to be the remains of 'some miserable bedridden wretch or other, who could not escape, or of a person dying suddenly thro' fright; which I think is not difficult to imagine, when one considers what a scene of horror they must have had before their eyes.'[6] This is an early example of sympathy for the victims of the volcano, but in a small circle. In contrast, a century later William Hazlitt, the son of the famous Romantic critic, put the death toll at an astonishing 250,000 in his *Classical Gazetteer*, a well-received primer for students, praised for its accuracy.[7] Neither of these imaginings is remotely right, but they capture how much the story of Vesuvius and the buried cities had changed between the mid-eighteenth and mid-nineteenth centuries.[8]

Before the French Revolution, the visitors to Herculaneum and Pompeii were chiefly fascinated by the surviving artifacts, excavated from the sites, many of which had been removed from their place of discovery and placed in a series of rooms in the nearby palace at Portici. The extraction of antiquities from Herculaneum was hampered by the heavy load of carbonised debris (more than 20 metres in depth) under which the city was buried, as well as by the presence of the modern town of Resina (today Ercolano) built on the site of the buried city; later excavations at Pompeii were much simpler, as the town had been buried by ash. By 1755 the Neapolitans had inventoried 738 frescoes and 1,647 objects.[9] Three years later a display in a suite of rooms in the Portici palace opened as the Herculanense Museum. Some of the newly excavated objects were monumental works of classical sculpture like the famous equestrian statues of the official and benefactor Marcus Nonius Balbus, but most were of a much humbler nature.

The excavation of Roman remains and the discovery of the artifacts and ruins of antique life was hardly peculiar to the sites of the buried cities. In the city of Rome and its surroundings it was a veritable industry. But there was a strong sense that Herculaneum and especially Pompeii were somehow different, strange and unfamiliar. Part of this singularity lay in the sense that what they revealed was a complete picture of Roman life, one that included not only public buildings such as amphitheatres, temples and baths, but also private, domestic and intimate spaces. As Madame de Staël put it in *Corinne*, a novel that often doubled as a guidebook, 'in Rome, one finds hardly anything but the debris of public monuments, and these only recount the political history of bygone centuries; but at Pompeii it's the private life of the ancients that you see before you just as it was'.[10] These objects of everyday life conveyed an entirely different sense of classical culture – and one seemingly much closer to the present – than that conveyed by the great works of classical civilisation, whether textual or in the form of antiquities. As the future revolutionary

Jean-Marie Roland de la Platière (1732–93) explained, the most striking findings were not the statues in bronze and marble, of a type that any antiquary would have known well, but the remarkable range of everyday things exhibited. Captivated and engrossed, he sent his fiancée, the future Madame Roland, an extraordinary inventory of what he saw, a list whose copiousness captured his excitement:

> tools and utensils of arts and crafts, those of the toilet, the household; the kitchen ... measurements of weights, scales, musical instruments, writing tablets, desks, scent bottles, rouge, mirrors, scrapers, hair needles, similar to those that common women still use throughout Italy, rings, bracelets, boxwood and horn combs; many small pieces of ivory, braid, nets etc.; all things sought in the work; many of whom we believe to be the inventors, and which we only imitate from afar; such still axes, scissors, forces, levers, flutes, taps, spoons, ink horns, writing nibs ...; hinges, spars, bits, boiling pots, saucepans, strainers etc; the cups with their saucers, like our coffee cups; an infinite number of other vases, various kinds of surgical instruments; and how many other tools and utensils of every kind of metal, the use of which we do not even know.[11]

The remains of antiquity were no longer confined to classical texts by heroic authors or individual works of great art; they encompassed the entire panoply of its material culture. Classical erudition was no longer the sole vehicle to understanding antiquity; it had become an aid to the imaginative reconstruction of the past. Objects – ordinary objects – were more eloquent than texts, and the story that they told was not aesthetic but what we today would call 'ethnographic'. As Stendhal put it, before the object 'one has the sense of being transported into antiquity, and so long as one has the habit of trusting only one's eyes, instantly knows it better than any scholar'.[12] When Winckelmann wrote in 1762 about the household

398

objects found at Herculaneum, he praised them for their beauty and taste, treating them as aesthetic objects. A half century later the French poet and dramatist Auguste Creuzé de Lesser preferred the Pompeian 'instruments of all the mechanical arts . . . observers cannot get enough of them' – to classical statues.[13]

Writing at the end of the eighteenth century, a young, unidentified American, someone well versed in classical literature and history, captured perfectly the shift in sensibility. The problem, he recognised, was that 'In the heroic character of illustrious people one hardly can realize any of their scenes of domestic life. There is a natural curiosity in wishing to see everything that has been rendered famous by its connection with them but we can't easily imagine or it does not readily occur that those people have wants & feelings like ourselves.' But the objects of the buried cities enable us to do so.

> Here in beholding such objects evidently the relics of some great calamity one feels for the sufferings of humanity and the ravages and desolation caused by a destructive conflagration are at once brought to the mind. We may be astonished in viewing the prostrate Columns of Superstitious Grandeur or the fallen monuments of Ancient Magnificence but here the heart is softened and acknowledges its connection with the great family of mankind.

Perhaps, he concluded, 'it is the most interesting collection of Antiquities in the world, & enables one to form a juster idea of the arts and sciences, domestic and ornamental of the ancients, & of their customs & manners than the most laboured descriptions – indeed, it should be seen, not described.'[14] The display of these artifacts created a bond of sympathy between the eighteenth-century observer and the first-century Roman, eliciting an emotional response. At the same time the objects made it possible to envisage a new sort of antiquity, one that was accessible to almost any viewer. The much-travelled Frances Trollope spoke for many in her *A Visit to Italy* (1842) when she remarked, 'I shall never feel sent back to ages past by the columns and pediments of ancient Rome as I did by the shop-counters, the oil jars and ovens of Pompeii.'[15]

It is notable that before the nineteenth century the emphasis of commentators is less on Pompeii (and Herculaneum) as environments – places of living – than on the objects that identified classical civilisation as every bit as prosaic and ordinary as modern everyday life. This is partly explained by the wholesale removal of the best images and artifacts from the sites where they were discovered. They were displayed first in the Portici palace, close to the foot of the volcano, and then, after 1816, in the Palazzo degli Studi that housed the Real Museo Borbonico in Naples itself. The sites from which they came were valuable to Neapolitan rulers as sources of cultural booty, much less as historic environments.[16]

The disparate nature of findings excavated from the buried cities complemented the emphasis of many antiquarians and students of classical culture in the early eighteenth century, who saw objects as more reliable sources of historical evidence than texts, and who looked to the material and visual record of the past as the means to build a picture of a culture. In this sense they did not represent a departure from current antiquarian interests so much as reinforce a trend.[17] Of course, the response was not unambiguous. For some, the paintings discovered in Herculaneum and Pompeii were disappointingly crude and primitive; the architecture of the cities did not conform to what were taken as classical principles; and the phallic drawings and objects pointed to a licentiousness that troubled many.

Figures as diverse as the English antiquary Horace Walpole, the German student of Greek art Abbé Winckelmann, the French aristocratic connoisseur the Comte de Caylus, and the Italian art historian Scipione Maffei were all critical of the conduct and handling of the findings at Herculaneum and Pompeii by the Neapolitan monarchy. Their objections were twofold. Their first complaint was about the secrecy surrounding the excavations – the lack of access and information about the archaeological sites. Carlo Borbone and his successors pursued (an often unsuccessful) balancing act between control and transparency. They wanted exclusive ownership of the cities' antique treasures and the exclusive power to interpret them. This absolutist antiquarianism envisaged the sites and their treasures as the means to enhance the prestige of the monarchy as the proprietor of one of the greatest collections of antiquities in Europe. Naples' rulers also needed to display and grant access to them if they were to contribute to the monarch's prestige, but they did so begrudgingly. It infuriated amateurs and antiquaries, many of whom travelled especially to Naples to see the discoveries, that note-taking and sketching in the Portici palace museum were prohibited. It also angered them that the King tried, albeit unsuccessfully, to monopolise the publication of the archaeological findings in a series of extremely expensive volumes that took years to reach the press.[18]

But even worse was the practice of removing antiquities and frescoes from their original location to place them in the museum. Antiquaries, especially those from northern Europe, had come to see that the value of objects rested not just in the things themselves but in knowing their location, their relation to both other objects and to spaces and places in which they were found. In this respect the antiquary and the geologist were following parallel paths. (Often, as in the famous case of Sir William Hamilton, the antiquary and the geologist were one and the same person.) Just as the study of the earth's history depended upon being able to place rocks and minerals in situ, and in relation to one another, so too the value of objects as evidence for the history of human culture required that they be contextualised and given a clear location. But this was not, in the first instance, the concern of the Bourbons; instead the most obviously attractive works were often ripped from the walls, and treated as a sort of royal booty.[19]

But, as Goran Blix puts it in his study of the cultural politics of Pompeian archaeology, this was about to change: 'Between 1750 and

1830, Pompeii is transformed from a grave to be robbed into the image of a lost civilization; in the process, a sweeping change has occurred – in the nature of the objects exhumed, in the value attached to the artifacts, and in the gaze of the beholder.'[20] It took time for this to happen, not least because the work of excavation was unsystematic, haphazard, often crude rather than conservationist, and often interrupted because of political conflict or the financial difficulties of the Crown. Important buildings were unearthed in the 1760s and 1770s – the Porta Ercolano, theatre, Temples of Isis and Escapulus, the House of the Gladiators, House of the Surgeon and the House of Diomedes – but it was only in the early nineteenth century that a proper sense of a complete civic environment was revealed. During the French occupation, Caroline Bonaparte, the wife of the King of Naples, Marshal Murat, took a special interest in Pompeii and made clear that she wanted to delimit the perimeter of the city, establish its exact dimensions, name individual dwellings and streets, and establish inventories of dwellings' contents.[21] As Sir William Gell's map of 1817 makes clear,[22] such a task remained far from complete (Plate 22), but it turned Pompeii itself into an object of inquiry and interest, and not just a container or hunting ground for antiquities.

The role of architects and archaeologists was vital to this process. In 1809 Queen Caroline employed the French architect François Mazois to conduct and publish an accurate survey of the city, which eventually appeared as *Les ruines de Pompei*, published between 1824 and 1838. Mazois's magnum opus was only one of a growing number of illustrated books, prints and engravings that made it altogether much easier to understand Pompeii as a developed urban environment. Jacob Philipp Hackert, the German artist who enjoyed the patronage of the Neapolitan court, and who had painted several pictures of Vesuvian eruptions, produced a series of views of Pompeii between 1792 and 1794 that were widely circulated after his brother had engraved them. Francesco Piranesi published his engravings after his father's drawings in *Antiquities de Pompeia* in 1804. In the second decade of the new century, Carl Theodor Muller produced a series of lithographs based on works by the Swiss artist W.J. Hubner, which were published collectively as *Collezione di vedute pittoresche del' antica città di Pompei*. These views became the model for many subsequent prints of Pompeii in the nineteenth century.[23]

By the 1830s Mazois's volumes competed with other architectural works, including *Pompeiana; the Topography, Edifices and Ornaments of Pompeii*, published between 1817 and 1832 by the English antiquary Sir William Gell, *Delineations of the Celebrated City of Pompeii* (1818), by the engineer James Pattison Cockburn and the engraver William Bernard Cooke, and *Suite des vues pittoresque des ruines de Pompeii* of the architect Henry Wilkins, published in Rome in 1819. After the restoration of the monarchy, French architectural students who won the Grand Prix de Rome were required to complete a 'restauro', a plausible drawing of how a classical building might once have looked. Pompeii was a favourite subject. In 1824, for example, Felix Emmanuel Callet produced drawings of the forum of Pompeii both in its (imagined) former and present state.[24]

The effect of these architectural and archaeological investigations, many using such technologies as the *camera lucida*, was twofold. Their publication enabled both visitors and those at a distance who had never seen Pompeii to imagine the city as a whole, an ensemble of streets and buildings that had once been a living urban environment. As the Russian poet Konstantin Nikolaevic Batyushkov remarked after his visit to Naples in 1819 (he made four trips to Pompeii and two to Vesuvius), Pompeii was the 'cemetery of an entire city'[25] and not just a set of ruins. This vision was very much enhanced by the practice, in the manner of Callet, of accompanying detailed drawings of buildings and streets with imagined versions of them prior to the eruption of 79 CE, scenes that included the presence of Romans going about their daily business. As Blix puts it: 'The major publications of engravings from Pompeii testify to the instant and un-canny character of archaeological resurrection: Saint-Non, Francois Mazois, William Gell and [much later] Carl Weichardt, all drew sumptuous recreations right beside their drawings of the actual ruins.'[26]

The sense that Pompeii was the cultural artifact, rather than the objects within it, underpinned both the increasingly frequent complaints about the removal of findings from the site, and the competing suggestion that the city should become a museum in its own right. Pompeii became a sort of microcosm of the ancient world. As the architect and director at Pompeii, Carlo Bonucci, put it rather soberly in his guidebook of the 1820s, Pompeii was valued 'as a model of the product of the manners, religion, and government of the ancients'.[27] Bulwer-Lytton's description in his best-selling novel *The Last Days of Pompeii* (1834) was more sensational, and captures what was to become a cliché:

> Pompeii was the miniature of the civilization of that age. Within the narrow compass of its walls was contained, as it were, a specimen of every gift which luxury offered to power. In its minute but glittering shops, its tiny palaces, its baths, its forum, its theatre, its circus – in the energy yet corruption, in the refinement yet the vice, of its people, you beheld a model of the whole empire. It was a toy, a plaything, a showbox, in which the gods seemed pleased to keep the representation of the great monarchy of earth, and which they afterwards hid from time, to give to the wonder of posterity.[28]

The view that the integrity of the buried cities should be maintained dated back to the critics of the early excavations (and removals) from Herculaneum. These antiquaries wanted the site and its findings to be conserved together as a means of understanding antiquity. As early as 1739 Charles de Brosses, savant and president of the Parlement de Bourgogne, had written to a friend that 'by excavating and leaving everything in place, the city would become an unequalled museum', a thought that at that point was nothing more than a fantasy.

But, from the 1760s, when the scope of Pompeii became increasingly apparent, there were more frequent calls for conservation by antiquaries like Sir William Hamilton. In the 1770s, the Scottish physician Dr John Moore suggested that Pompeian houses should be fully reconstructed and have their roofs restored. Such longings – for such they were – were even more frequent in the nineteenth century. Chateaubriand had complained in 1826 about the removal of ordinary things from Pompeii, saying that if they remained *in situ* they would comprise a museum of 'the private life of the Roman people'.[29] He envisaged rebuilt and restored houses, filled with impedimenta of everyday life. 'One would learn more', he asserted, 'about the domestic history of the Roman people, the state of Roman civilization in a few restored promenades of Pompeii, than by reading all the works of antiquity.'[30] Few however went as far as J.M. La Riche, author of *Vues des monuments antiques de Naples* (1827), who suggested that local people should dress in antique costume in return for being housed in restored Pompeian buildings, or as Louise Colet, the writer and lover of Flaubert, who suggested that the entire city should be covered with a huge glass dome, somewhat in the manner of the Crystal Palace. Nevertheless at least one English genteel tourist was reported as having spent several days, dressed in Roman costume, staying in one of Pompeii's less dilapidated buildings, and Alexandre Dumas claimed to have spent eight days living in the House of the Fauna when writing his play *Caligula* in 1835.[31]

Bodies

But if what we have been describing is a living antiquity – a world of utensils and furnishings, mundane activities such as cooking, drinking, eating and selling, of work and leisure – into which viewers and visitors could project themselves through a process of recognition of what was familiar (in more senses than one), Pompeii was also, superabundantly, a place of death. By the early nineteenth century, the number of bodies/skeletons of Vesuvius's victims that had been recovered in Herculaneum was relatively small (the large number of bodies on the beach at Herculaneum were only discovered in the 1970s). The body count in Pompeii was much higher. In the 1760s and 1770s, new excavations there led to the discovery of bodies on a variety of sites – in the gladiators' barracks, the Temple of Isis, the Villa of Diomedes – that attracted international attention. As Andrew Wallace-Hadrill has explained, this was also the moment at which, for a variety of reasons, there was a decisive shift in the pattern of interest, away from the buried city of Herculaneum, which had revealed such spectacular hidden treasures, and towards Pompeii, whose more easily uncovered remains exposed the life and death of antiquity. As he memorably puts it: 'The memory of Herculaneum was buried, with its backfilled tunnels; now Pompeii was the place to let the imagination run riot. Instead of dark tunnels and charred timbers, the visitor could meet ancient life' – and, we might add, death.[32]

The discovery in 1766 of what proved to be the gladiators' quarters, with a cache of arms, thirty-four bodies, including several women with jewellery, and four men with their legs manacled to the floor, sparked a fascination with their fate. The Emperor Joseph II's stage-managed visit to Pompeii in April 1769, which involved the (re)exhumation of a female skeleton in an underground room in the quarters, subsequently named after the Emperor, was symptomatic of a new interest in human remains, whether skeletons, such as those found in the gladiators' barracks, or human impressions in the volcanic ash.[33] Examining the female skeleton, Joseph II purportedly 'for a long time . . . stood reflectively before these tokens of an intense human drama'.[34] The wealthy French tax farmer Bergeret de Grancourt, visiting the same spot several years later, wrote, 'In the room downstairs where they must have done the washing, we could see all the implements, the stove, the washtub etc, . . . and a heap of volcanic ash upon which rested the skeleton of a woman, as if, having tried to escape from the choking ashes coming in from all sides, she had finally fallen backwards and died'[35] (plate 23.)

These remains were, I believe, the first to be the subject of a sententious narrative, appropriately written by Sir William Hamilton. In his account of these discoveries, sent in a letter to the Society of Antiquaries in London, and published as *Account of the Discoveries at Pompeii* in 1777, Hamilton writes of the washerwoman (he has ascribed this identity to her solely on the basis of her presence in the room) as waiting 'for death with calm resignation, and true Roman fortitude, as the attitude of the skeleton really seems to indicate'. (How, one might ask, does a skeleton indicate 'resignation'?) He goes on to add, 'It was at my instigation that the bones were left untouched on the spot where they were found.'[36] Hamilton's concern to have the scene remain intact is as much about preserving the story he has constructed as it is about the conservation of the room.

Between 1771 and 1774 at the suburban villa usually referred to as the Villa of Diomedes, a further large group of skeletons was found – more than twenty women and children in the cellar, as well as a male figure under the portico surrounding the garden, who, as he was clutching a lot of coins and holding a key, was quickly identified as Diomedes himself. Francesco La Vega, the director of the excavations, cut and removed from the cellar several of the impressions of human forms in the lava that were transferred to the museum at Portici. The bones remained, many of them stolen by later visitors.[37] But one set of impressions, though they no longer survive, had a lasting effect on the narrativisation of Pompeii. Charles-Mercier Dupaty, a French lawyer and civil servant, described the fragments as follows: 'one [impression] represents half of her bosom; it is of perfect beauty; another, a shoulder; another a portion of her shape, and all concur in revealing to us that this woman was young, and that she was tall and well made, and even that she escaped in her shift; for some pieces of linen are attached to the ashes.'[38] Admired by many male visitors including Chateaubriand (1804), this fragment inspired

Gautier to write his novella of necrophilic fetishism, *Arria Marcella* (1852), in which a young man falls in love with the impression of the hip and bosom of a Pompeian victim from the Villa of Diomedes.[39]

It was not until the 1860s that the practice of making plaster of Paris casts of the victims became common, and thereby revealed their death agonies in all their vivid enormity, but from the beginning the remains made more and more visitors conscious of the terrible details of human suffering. In a report to the Royal Society in 1795, William Hamilton wrote of one skeleton: 'Having engaged the men that were digging to take off the piece of hardened tufo, that covered the head, with great care, and, as in a mould just taken off in plaster of Paris, we found the impression of the eyes, that were shut, of the nose, mouth and of every feature perfectly distinct'.[40] These fragile impressions, though they often crumbled to dust, had a more powerful effect than the skeletons themselves and prefigured the famous plaster of Paris casts made by Giuseppe Fiorelli, the Director of Excavations, after the Risorgimento.

The skeletons, the impressions in the ash which revealed the death agonies of the volcano's victims – all apparently so striking, so intimate and shockingly revealing of the feelings of those who died centuries earlier – profoundly affected how visitors saw the volcano and their presence under its shadow, exciting a deep sense of sympathy and compassion for these ancient victims. As Harriet Dennison wrote in her journal in 1816: 'What an awful scene it must have been! The very thought of what the people must have suffered makes one shudder.'[41] She was echoing the sentiments of many others. Dr John Moore remarked, 'It is impossible to view these skeletons, and reflect on this dreadful catastrophe, without horror and compassion', a sympathy that was reinforced by evidence that the volcano's victims were not just the heroes of classical antiquity, like Pliny the Elder, but ordinary citizens going about their everyday activities – working, baking bread, attending the theatre – before they were immolated in the sudden eruption.[42]

This sense of identification reinforced an awareness that, though the volcano might now be an obligingly incandescent object of sublime taste, it would one day again exercise its unstoppable capacity for destruction: what happened in 79 CE would certainly happen again. The excavation of the past revealed an impending future, binding together the visitor and the volcano's victims. Jane Graham daughter of a West Indian planter, the wife of the future Lord Wedderburn, wrote that 'From the top [of Vesuvius] there is the most heavenly prospect of the Campagna Felice, but one is struck with horror to see what beautys what fertile plains Vesuvius has yet to destroy when one sees in the heart of these rich Meddows streams of antient Lava – upon the whole it is more dreadful than pleasing to see'. Mrs Piozzi made the connection explicit: 'How dreadful are the thoughts which such a sight suggests! How very horrible the certainty, that such a scene might be all acted over again tomorrow; and that, who today are spectators, may become spectacles for travelers of a succeeding century, who mistaking our bones for those of the Neapolitans, may carry some of them to their native country back again perhaps.'[43] There was a growing sense even among the most transitory of visitors that in contemplating both the volcano and its classical victims, they were contemplating the inescapable fact of their own mortality. The antiquary Sir Richard Colt Hoare ran the gamut of emotions:

> then weep over the unhappy fate of the antient Cities of Stabia and Pompeii, & look with horror on the fiery Mountain above them which destroyed them . . . and reflect with surprise on the boldness of the present age in erecting their numerous palaces on the very spot of the destroyed city, & grieve lest the same cause should again bury under the Earth the valuable Museum so lately restored to life from the ashes of the . . . cities.[44]

Vesuvius, as Lady Blessington remarked, was 'like a sleeping giant in grim repose, whose awakening, all dread'.[45]

Dialogue with the dead: Vesuvius and the buried cities, depiction and narration

Before the French Revolution, most of the bodies found at Pompeii were viewed with a mixture of sympathy and horror. The story in which they were placed was one of victimhood and loss. But in the early nineteenth century, commentators began to embellish on the findings of artifacts and human remains, constructing narratives about the circumstances of the eruption in 79 CE and sententious stories about the lives of the victims. They were helped in doing so by the way in which the relationship between Vesuvius and the buried cities was understood. The vestiges and ruins of the buried cities were different not purely in their content – the access they gave to the everyday lives of the ancients – but also in their relation to time and history. The ruins of ancient Rome not only connoted a moment of imperial grandeur, but betrayed their weathering and erosion, both natural and human, over the centuries. They were, in Constanze Baum's happy phrase, *ruins of duration*, embodying a narrative history, changes through time that could be characterised as stories of loss, decay and corruption or even decline and fall. Their presence in the Eternal City, where many of the edifices of Christianity were built with the stones of a recycled antiquity, was both a vestige of an earlier civilisation and a reminder of the city's transformation into the capital of Catholic Christianity. They survived in the present as part of a punctuated historical continuum. The buried cities, however, were, to evoke Baum again, *ruins of suddenness*.[46] Though we now know that the destruction wreaked by Vesuvius took place over several days, there was a strong commitment in the Romantic era to the idea that the eruption was a single devastating act of nature that stopped daily life in its tracks.[47] As Madame de Staël puts it in *Corinne*, 'The amphorae are still prepared for the next day's banquet; the flour that was going to be kneaded is still there . . . Nowhere else can be seen so striking a picture of the interruption of life.'[48]

410

The volcano erases the cities; nature buries culture. But Vesuvius both destroys and conserves a single unique moment; it arrests time. Our knowledge that the volcano was the creator of this frozen moment (the cold image does not seem apt, but I can think of none better) inevitably informed how the vestiges and traces of the buried cities were understood. Ruins of suddenness invite reflection on the moment of destruction, not on the history of the ruin. And what the excavations achieve, albeit in a gradual and painstaking manner, is the recovery of that moment in all its vividness, a recuperation that promises to breathe life back into what Mazois characterised as a 'tableau of private life'.[49] The past becomes an all-encompassing 'present moment',[50] visualised by the observer in the here and now, monopolising the field of vision of the contemporary onlooker. As August Goethe, the son of a more illustrious father, remarked, at Pompeii past and present shared a friendly handshake.[51] The proximity of this past and the present – so close they could shake hands – was reinforced by the similarity of many of the everyday objects – cooking utensils, medical instruments – with contemporary tools, and by the sense that the houses of the buried cities had only very recently been vacated. As Chateaubriand remarked, it was 'as if the inhabitants left fifteen minutes ago'.[52]

The gap between the moment when Vesuvius simultaneously 'erased and froze'[53] the city and the occasion of its modern observation was compressed or even obliterated. The work of archaeological recuperation was seen to constitute what Bulwer-Lytton and others called 'a resurrection' or a 'revival', an end to a tragic 'interruption' so that antique life resumed in the present. It is as if, in Sabrina Ferri's words, 'their rediscovery and archaeological exploration redeemed them from the catastrophic fate that had befallen them.'[54] Herculaneum and Pompeii are artifacts of the past, items of history, but they were not treated historically; rather they became contemporary sites and sources for imaginative reanimation. The time both before and after their realisation is relatively unimportant.[55] (It is

411

notable, much to the frustration of archaeologists, how much the language and action of conservation is overshadowed by talk of resurrection.)

The buried cities become a stage or setting into and onto which the reflecting observer can project an imaginative narrative and characters of the past. They are not blank pages or empty canvasses, but much more like crime scenes, littered with evidence, that excite two powerful emotions: the desire to solve the crime, to know what happened – we know the killer (Vesuvius) but not the circumstances of death – and the urge to sympathy, to feel for the victims, and even to bring them back to life. And they create discomfort, occupying that eerie zone between life and death.

The thin line that separated this special moment and the present could be crossed imaginatively. Someone like the aristocratic aesthete William Beckford, standing in the Temple of Isis, could fall 'into one of those reveries' thereby 'transporting myself seventeen hundred years back, [and] fancied I was sailing with Pliny the elder'.[56] (Rich aesthetes kept only the best company.) More commonly, those wandering the ruins were often confronted with the uncanny feeling that they were about to come face to face with Pompeians. Madame de Staël, that great shaper of visitors' imaginations, comments, 'When you stand in the centre of the crossroads . . . it is as if you are waiting for someone, as if the master is about to arrive, and the very semblance of life in this place makes you even more sad at feeling its eternal silence.'[57] Such sentiments were echoed by Louise Demont, a companion of Queen Caroline on her visit to Pompeii in 1814:

While you are wandering through the abandoned rooms, you may, without any great effort of imagination, expect to meet some of the former inhabitants, or perhaps the master of the house himself, and almost feel like intruders, dreading the appearance of anyone in the family. In the streets you are afraid of turning a corner, lest you should jostle a passerby; and on entering a house the smallest sound startles, as if the proprietor were coming out of the back apartments.[58]

Many visitors recounted experiences where they abruptly come upon Neapolitans in the ruins who seemed to them to be or to resemble ancient Pompeians. A young American visiting Pompeii in November 1796, for instance, was startled to find a working cobbler in one of the buildings; only when the workman addressed him in his native Neapolitan did he realise that he was a man of the present.[59]

These assumptions – about the frozen moment and imaginative time travel – are brilliantly mocked in one of the cleverest early nineteenth-century satires on the responses of visitors to Naples and the Campagna Felix by Gottlieb Lewis Engelbach, a minor art critic of German descent who worked in London's Audit Office. His account, published in 1815, masquerading as (and containing many of the elements of) a personal travel narrative, portrays his protagonist as deeply confused about how to understand the history of Pompeii's remains. 'In viewing the remnants of remote ages,' he writes, 'we are generally capable of tracing the period of their duration from exterior marks left upon them by the hand of TIME. But here, I confess, my ideas of time were so strangely assailed and bewildered . . . What, said I, is this string of events this something, which history intercalates between the catastrophe and the discovery?' For Engelbach's protagonist this space is unintelligible as it betrays 'a total absence of external means to assist that faculty of our mind, called memory; a faculty which, under such conditions, would, I suspect, be either intirely [sic] wanting, or turn out quite another sort of thing – What then becomes of your time, of history, our age, our actions?'[60] What he completely misunderstands is that such a history is irrelevant or immaterial; what matters is the ability to make the imaginative move that drags a special moment into the present.

Later, on another visit to Pompeii, Engelbach portrays the line between the archaeological past and the present as exceptionally permeable. A group of visitors, his English narrator, a Russian staff surgeon, a French painter and two merchants, one Turkish, the other German, accidentally tumble down into an unexplored crypt and in an ice-cellar discover a Pompeian, Eupator, lying in a sarcophagus filled with ice from Etna. The figure revives and understandably wishes to know about the state of the volcano and the fate of his family. He inhabits both his own time and the present. But, as the visitors regale him with a potted history of modernity – printing, spectacles, gunpowder, Isaac Newton, credit, watches, the Americas, balloons and the telegraph – encouraging his entry into an improved world – the Pompeian turns his back on a present that can provide him with no solace for his misfortunes. History is as irrelevant to the volcano's victim as it is to the contemporary observer.[61]

But Engelbach who, as Mary Beard points out, played with the idea that Pompeii was not an ancient ruin but a modern forgery,[62] was not able to curb the impulse to narrativise Pompeii, to subject it to imagination treatment 'which penetrates and discovers the finest secrets that meditation and study can reveal to us.' When Bulwer-Lytton wrote in 1834 of his desire to 'people once more those deserted streets, to repair those graceful ruins, to reanimate the bones which were yet spared to his survey, to traverse the gulf of eighteen centuries, and to wake to a second existence the City of the Dead!'[63] he was giving voice to sentiments that had been common since the end of the Napoleonic Wars, when a veritable orgy of storytelling about Pompeii began. As Jon Seydl puts it in his rehearsal of the events of the 1820s that contributed to what he calls 'the Last Days phenomenon', 'This sequence of events should ... be understood ... as a cascading cultural shift in which accounts of Pompeii move from a focus on mass destruction to more particularised stories that culminate in the cataclysm.'[64] It is striking how discoveries made in the 1760s and 1770s only receive the full narrative treatment after 1815. Only in the second decade of the nineteenth century did the presence of a female skeleton in the gladiators' barracks spawn stories of a lover's tryst or a prostitute on call.[65] Similarly, the remains at the Temple of Isis became a story about priests sharing a final meal. Most famously, a small niche on the left exterior side of the Porta Ercolano, first excavated in 1763, had become, according to Mariana Starke in 1802, 'the sentry box of the guard', where, according to Sir William Gell in his *Pompeiana* (1817–19), 'was found a human skeleton, of which the hand still grasped a lance. Conjecture has imagined this the remains of a sentinel, who preferred dying on his post to quitting it for a more ignominious death, which, in conformity with the severe discipline of his country, would have awaited him.' This tale naturally found its way into Bulwer-Lytton's narrative of the eruption: 'his stern features were composed even in their awe, remained erect and motionless at his post', a moment that was later rendered (in slightly more sentimental fashion) by Edward Poynter in his painting *Faithful Unto Death*.[66] The original record of the excavation of the gate makes no mention of any skeleton, and from a very early date the niche was identified as a tomb or altar, but by the early nineteenth century and for the following forty years, the story of the soldier rooted to his post was to remain one of the most frequently told tales of the last days of Pompeii.

As we have noted, in the early nineteenth century it became comparatively unusual to see the sorts of representation of contemporary volcanic eruptions produced by Volaire and his Enlightenment colleagues in major exhibitions and collections. Such depictions lived on as tourist souvenirs and as part of the portfolio of many local Neapolitan artists such as those of the Posillipo School, but, as Nicholas Daly has pointed out, 'many representations . . . focus less on the spectacle of the volcano per se, and more on the collision of the volcano with humanity, and the moment of destruction and preservation.'[67] In fact there is a marked move away from the depiction of contemporary eruptions and towards the portrayal of the historic eruption of 79 CE. This is partly explained, of course, by the progress of the excavations of the buried cities and the richness of their findings, but this of itself cannot explain the shift. When the largest eruption of the nine-teenth century took place in 1822, it was used in London to promote Burford's panorama of Vesuvius and Pompeii, not the contemporary explosion. The same was true of the Vauxhall Gardens transparency of the following year, and of John Martin's huge canvas depicting the Destruction of Herculaneum and Pompeii exhibited in the Egyptian Hall in 1822.

In this explosion of Vesuviana, across a whole variety of media, the volcano became not the prime object of interest but a sort of *deus ex machina* in a moral tale or fable. Bulwer-Lytton's *The Last Days of Pompeii* (1834) remains the best known of a series of literary works that included Thomas Babington Macaulay's prize-winning poem *Pompeii* (1819), Edwin Atherstone's verses, *The Last Days of Herculaneum* (1821), Thomas Gray's novel, *The Vestal, or a Tale of Pompeii* (1830), and the lengthy and lurid *The Last Night of Pompeii* (1832) by the American Sumner Lincoln Fairfield. But the last days and their tales of woe and misfortune were also a favoured topic of academic painting.

In 1812 the skeletons of a woman and three small children were discovered, together with a quantity of jewellery, near the Mammia tomb. Joseph Franque, a French painter living in Naples, recreated the moments before their death in his *Scene during the Eruption of Vesuvius* exhibited at the Paris Salon in March 1828 (Plate 24). The painting was based on an elaborate report of the find by the French antiquary Aubin-Louis Millin, who combined breathless narrativ-ising with a detailed description of the artifacts found at the site:

A mother fled, dragging after her a part of her family: two daugh-ters, and an infant whom she clutched in vain against her breast. There was no longer any hope; still gasping for breath in the midst of swirling clouds of burning cinders, and pressing against the walls of the portico, they fell exhausted by fatigue and suffering. The ash covered them, burying them all in the same tomb; their remains were mingled, and almost indistinguishable from one another. One could almost see this unfortunate family embracing one another in their last breath.

Franque's painting is a characteristic mix of accuracy and licence. The jewellery precisely follows the excavation report, for example, representing a curled serpent's ring on the daughter's right hand, but it places the family in a chariot rather than an alcove, and adds a mirror, chest and lyre, signs of wealth but also symbols of human vanity.[68]

Franque was a professor in the Accademia di Belle Arti in Naples, and it is possible that his painting, which was completed in 1826, was seen by a young Russian artist, Karl Briullov, who was to produce what became the most famous of all the visual representations of Pompeii's final days, *The Last Day of Pompeii*, painted between 1827 and 1833. Briullov had come to Naples with his brother, Alexander, who trained as an architect and had an abiding passion for Pompeii. The two, like many artists before them, had been sent to Italy on scholarships – in this case awarded by the Society for the Encouragement of Artists in St Petersburg – for a four-year visit to the peninsula. Karl, wilful, brilliant and supremely talented, had been the star pupil at the St Petersburg Academy, showered with medals and prizes, but had quarrelled with its director. Together with Alexander, he turned to the recently founded Society, which was not an academy with fixed rules, but a body of the great and good (including patrons and collectors) who wished to encourage the arts in Russia. The brothers had arrived in Rome in May 1823.

At first, Karl followed the usual path of an artist visiting Italy: he copied old masters – though few were so ambitious as to take as their model Raphael's *School of Athens* – he worked on a couple of history paintings, but he also executed several private commissions, chiefly genre paintings and sketches of Neapolitan life that he sent back to clients in Russia. But his ambitions changed in 1827. In that year he resigned his stipend from the Society, which had grumbled about the content of his picture *Italian Midday*, the portrayal of a voluptuous, vivacious and smiling peasant woman admiring a bunch of grapes she appears to have plucked from a vine. 'The aim of any artist,' they wrote to him, 'should be to portray a model with gracious proportions whereas your model could not be considered gracious since she belongs to the lower class.' (They had not complained about his *Italian Morning*, which had portrayed an altogether more patrician and classical – though bare-breasted – woman at her morning toilette.) Karl was able to forego their stipend and dismiss their complaints as a plea for empty uniformity because in 1827 he met the extremely beautiful, very rich Countess Yulia Samoilova, who, whether or not she was his lover, became his admirer, muse and patron, funding and fuelling what became a powerful mutual attachment. She accompanied the two brothers to Naples in 1827, though there is no evidence that she climbed the volcano.[69]

The sources of Karl's fascination with Vesuvius and Pompeii are hard to disentangle. His brother was one obvious influence. Alexander had sketched out a restoration scheme for Pompeian baths as early as 1826 and was to design the small Pompeian dining room in the private quarters of the Winter Palace in St Petersburg. The two brothers had already been in Naples in May 1824 with a party of Russian officials and diplomats, spending a night on the volcano, recorded in a series of watercolours by Alexander.[70] Briullov had also seen in Naples a performance of Giovanni Pacini's opera *L'ultimo giorno di Pompei*, whose spectacular climax included a re-enactment of the eruption of 79 CE with vivid visual effects, and temples and buildings that crashed onto the stage.[71] The performance used the technique that, as we shall see, became common in the nineteenth century, of brilliantly illuminating the stage from the rear to create depth and clarity. Painters of the period, many of whom worked in theatres, adopted this device, especially in large history paintings. But Briullov's inspiration seems to have come primarily from his own experience of the buried city: 'The sight of these ruins involuntarily forced me to be transported to the time when these walls were still inhabited ... You cannot go through these ruins without feeling in yourself some completely new feeling that makes you forget everything, except for the terrible incident with this city.'[72]

Who commissioned Briullov's canvas is unclear, but Count Anatole Demidov, a rich Russian industrialist and art collector who lived for much of the time in Florence, eventually paid Briullov 40,000 francs for the painting. Whatever its origin, Karl's interest in the subject quickly developed into an obsession. He spent six years working on the painting, producing his first sketches in 1827, studying documents and artifacts in museums in Naples before beginning the painting itself in 1830. The huge canvas – approximately 456.5 cm × 651 cm (179.7 in × 256 in) – was first exhibited in Rome, and then in Milan, where it was seen by the British writer Bulwer-Lytton, and Paris, where it won the Salon's First Gold Medal, before reaching its destination, St Petersburg, in August 1834 (Plate 25).[73]

Briullov's *The Last Day of Pompeii* was a triumph: it excited the praise of Italian and Russian critics (the French were lukewarm), gained him election to the academies of Bologna, Milan, Rome and Florence, and earned the praise of the public who crowded to see the canvas when it was publicly displayed.[74] For Nicolai Gogol, Briullov's painting was 'one of the most brilliant phenomena of the nineteenth century'; Sir Walter Scott, 'having contemplated it in silence for more than an hour' declared it an 'epic in colours'. The painting made Briullov's reputation – the Tsar summoned him back to Russia to be professor of painting at St Petersburg – but it also marked his apogee. Profoundly depressed after its completion, he never again created a history painting that either satisfied him or commanded the same sort of public success. He spent years on a large painting of *The Siege of Pskov*, a patriotic history painting, but abandoned work on it in 1843. Back in Russia he became a fashionable portrait painter, a caricaturist, and an habitué of literary, musical and artistic circles, but never really fulfilled his earlier promise as a history painter. He quarrelled with the Tsar and felt uncomfortable as a courtier. He acquired a reputation as a heroic drinker. In 1849 he left Russia for good, spending his last three years chiefly in Italy, producing portraits and the many genre scenes that seem to have been his special passion.

The power and effect of Briullov's painting in part derives from its size, but also, as Gogol observed in an essay devoted to the picture, from its composition and illumination.[75] The early sketches for the composition are far more compressed, the space of the figures far more confined, than in the final version of the painting, the image much darker. Briullov stretched the space occupied by the figures, opened up the sky by pushing back the tumbling buildings, and made the whole into a series of brilliantly illuminated vignettes, each of which, although they contributed to the whole, could be viewed or read as discrete representations with their own story and moral. As Gogol put it, 'He has seized hold of lightning and flooded the picture with it . . . so that everything should be picked out by it, so that not a single object should be hidden from the viewer.' On the right we can see the younger Pliny pleading with his mother to escape the city (Briullov has transposed the scene from Misenum to Pompeii itself); next to them two young men, one a soldier, carrying a man, presumably their father, in a desperate attempt to take him to safety (some have suggested that the figure represents the elder Pliny); in the lower centre lies a dead mother with her child, while close by is an open bundle of her scattered possessions, including a key and a mirror; above her, a pagan priest looks back towards the volcano, his left arm wrapped around his possessions. On the left of the canvas is a Christian priest and close by him, a mother and her two children. On the steps of the tomb to the left (the painting is aptly set in the Via dei Sepolcri), surrounded by panic-stricken figures, we can see the head of Briullov himself, and above him a box containing paints, brushes and a palette. As Ingrid Rowland has reminded us, the painting is full of allusions to figures and poses derived from Raphael,

Poussin and classical sculpture, deliberately placing its creator within a long classical tradition,[76] but it also connects the antique and the present, not only in the figure of Briullov himself, but in several female figures whose faces are those of his beautiful patron, Yulia Samoilova.

Some scholars have placed Briullov's painting in the context of what has been termed 'the school of catastrophe', the efflorescence of writing and painting in the 1820s depicting epic disasters from classical and biblical history. Works by the English artists J.M.W. Turner, John Martin and Francis Danby of the *Plagues of Egypt*, *The Deluge*, the *Destruction of Pompeii and Herculaneum* respectively, and of the apocalypse, portrayed all-powerful natural forces overwhelming a sea of stricken humanity. No doubt Briullov's picture fits into this pattern, but it was also different. As Gogol pointed out, when he contrasted Briullov's painting with John Martin's *Belshazzar's Feast* (1820) and *The Fall of Nineveh* (1829), 'in which great catastrophes are presented in fearsome grandeur', *The Last Day of Pompeii* combined epic scale with an intimacy that could not be felt in the British pictures: 'The overall impression from these [English] pictures is striking and is full of an exceptional unity; but ... they are like distant views; they only convey a general impression. We are aware of the terrible position of the crowd, but we cannot see the person on whose face would be expressed the full horror of the destruction that he himself is witnessing.' Turning back to Briullov, Gogol concluded that, 'The concept that is here presented to us in distant perspective is suddenly placed full-square before our eyes by Briullov ... and we ourselves seem to be caught up in its world.' These sentiments are echoed in the words of another of Briullov's commentators, Bulwer-Lytton, whose novel *The Last Days of Pompeii* may well have been inspired by viewing Briullov's picture in Milan.

This picture is full of genius, imagination and nature. The faces are fine, the conception grand ... the most natural touch is an infant in its mother's arms: her face impressed with a dismay and terror which partake of the sublime; the child wholly unconscious of the dead event – stretching its arms toward a bird of gay plumage that lies upon the ground struggling in death, and all the child's gay delighted wonder is pictured in its face. This exception to the general horror is full of pathos, and is the true contrast of fine thought.[77]

Lytton seems to have misremembered the scene, or to have viewed a version that was later altered – in the extant version of the picture the mother lies dead, the child looks stricken, there is no bird – but the effect is clear; catastrophe is rendered domestic and intimate, and therefore all the more touching.

This is why, in Gogol's crucial phrase, we are not so much outside observers of the scene; rather 'we ourselves seem to be caught up in its world'. Briullov represents a very specific time and place – 24 August 79 CE, the Via dei Sepolcri outside the gates of Pompeii – and, like other painters of the catastrophic school, goes to considerable lengths to secure a degree of historical accuracy – his figures refer to particular skeletons found in the city, the tombs and artifacts match surviving objects – but it is the sense that we share in, or are a part of, this disastrous scene that is vital to its power. This requires not only a sympathetic attachment to the inhabitants of the ancient world, but also a sense that the viewer's future might also involve catastrophic misfortune. At the very simplest level we might think of such identification as an awareness of human frailty and mortality, a reminder – like the mirror, a vanitas symbol that lies at the bottom centre of the painting – of the brief and transitory nature of human life. But, and here Briullov is far from alone, it is the sense of the precipitous, sudden and violent intervention of an unstoppable force, its brutal intrusion into the rhythms and patterns of everyday life, that make this event so terrifying. Briullov renders graphically 'the interruption of life' that other commentators found so shocking. His painting is not just about death, but about a particular sort of death, one that seems to entail the destruction not just of individuals, but the obliteration of the very fabric of life – of kin and family, work and play, and of religious faith. It makes clear that what can be observed in the present are, as we have seen, *ruins of suddenness* rather than *ruins of duration*.[78] The young future Russian socialist Alexander Herzen saw the force of the Vesuvian eruption depicted by Briullov as analogous to the unstoppable absolute power of the Russian Tsar over his people: 'On an enormous canvas the crowds closely packed, terrified people, in disorder, trying vainly to save their lives … they will perish under the force of a wild, senseless, merciless power … against which any resistance is futile. The inspiration for this force Briullov took from St Petersburg.'[79] Such analogies between natural and political force were, as we have seen, common in the early nineteenth century, though they more usually referred to the forces launched by the French Revolution.

Vesuvius was important, not so much as a modern sublime spectacle but as both the destroyer and conservator of a classical world. What are we to make of the extraordinary proliferation of narratives and moral vignettes about the destruction of Pompeii? A great many of the stories – whether Bulwer-Lytton's *Last Days*, Thomas Gray's novel *The Vestal*, or the verses of Sumner Lincoln Fairfield – depict the eruption of 79 CE as providential punishment for the sins of Pompeii: a city of slavery, greed, luxury and debauchery, a pagan, polytheistic culture given to sexual excess. This providentialist narrative is one that links such depictions to catastrophes depicted in the Bible, and rendered so vividly by the likes of John Martin, J.M.W. Turner and Francis Danby: the Fall of Nineveh, Belshazzar's Feast, the Plagues of Egypt and the Destruction of Sodom. Thus Fairfield in his poem *The Last Night of Pompeii* claims that we should feel 'little regret and less astonishment at the terrible overthrow of cities as excessive and not so venial in their crimes as Gomorrah'.[80] Bulwer-Lytton follows suit: as the volcano showers the city, a Christian cries,

'Behold! The Lord descendeth to judgment! He maketh fire come down from heaven in the sight of men! Woe! woe! Ye strong and mighty! . . . Woe to the idolater and the worshipper of the beast! Woe to ye who pour forth the blood of saints, and gloat over the death-pangs of the sons of God!'[81] Pompeii is sin city.

This connection is made even more explicit by the importation – for which, as Mary Beard argues, there is no historical evidence – of Christians into these Pompeian narratives.[82] Repeatedly Christians are portrayed as victims – of pagan priests, or imperial persecution, or abstract injustices, rescued, like other virtuous characters, at the very last minute by the action – the eruption – of the volcano. Glaucus, Lytton's hero, avoids death in the amphitheatre, the innocent virgin avoids rape by the priest of Isis in Fairchild's poem, the virtuous wife in the opera *L'ultimo giorno di Pompei* is spared from being buried alive. The volcano does not just chastise the wicked; it also aids the virtuous and Christian. Even when it causes their death, as in Briullov's painting or Gray's novel, it shows them as having the sorts of virtue that will grant them ultimate salvation. We are presented with antithetical views of life, crudely associated with stock characters: the cruel and sexually predatory pagan priest, memorably Arbaces in Bulwer-Lytton; the miser scrambling for gold on the ground or hugging his riches to his chest, as portrayed by Briullov; the cowardly pagan – all these contrasted with the mother seeking to protect her child, the children seeking to protect elderly parents, or the loving couple holding one another in their arms. Wicked individuals, virtuous families. Destruction is the result of pagan sin; the embrace of family pieties and Christianity offers redemption and a future. A certain Christian view has, then, in the 1820s hijacked the volcano and the city of the dead.

But there was also something else going on in these narratives of Pompeii. For if Vesuvius represents a punitive, destructive force, there is also a way in which the recuperation of the buried cities constitutes a sort of resurrection, a triumph not only over the forces of revolution, but an occasion for the assertion of continuity, of historical survival in the face of terrible forces. The language of resurrection, survival and continuity was used repeatedly, sometimes before the aftermath of the French Revolution, but much more frequently thereafter. Charles Dupaty talks of the 'triumph over time' of a grain of corn at Herculaneum; a generation later, Felicia Hemans, in her verse on the mould of a mother and child, exclaims:

> Oh! I could pass all relics
> Left by the pomps of old,
> To gaze on this rude monument,
> Cast in affections mold.
> Love, human love! What art thou
> Thy print upon the dust
> Outlives the cities of renown
> Wherein the mighty trust![83]

In quite a common image, Thomas Gray in *The Vestal* compares Pompeii to the story of Sleeping Beauty, a beautiful creature in slumber waiting to be awakened not with a prince's kiss, but by the shovel of the archaeologist.[84] Gautier's novella *Arria Marcella* is also about the effect in the present of something from the distant past – 'the curve of a breast has survived through the centuries when so many empires have vanished without leaving a trace'. Human flesh triumphs over the lava and ash that destroyed it. For Bulwer-Lytton what survives is not flesh but the Christian soul. At the end of *The Last Days*, Glaucus, writing of his conversion to Christianity, asserts, 'We know that we are united in the soul, as in the flesh, for ever and ever! Ages may roll on, our very dust be dissolved, the earth shrivelled like a scroll; but round and round the circle of eternity rolls the wheel of life – imperishable – unceasing!' Goran Blix, in his study of the politics of archaeology, perfectly captures the appeal of Pompeii in the early nineteenth century:

This city embodied a contradiction that lay at the heart of archaeology's power of enchantment: it had been abruptly annihilated
and just as suddenly resurrected, and this stark contrast of violence
and redemption provided an irresistible melodramatic script for
the comprehension of history; while conceding that history was a
violent process that littered the past with vibrant cultures, it also
dissociated ruin and amnesia and suggested that lost worlds
might leave imperishable traces. Loss and memory were cemented
into a single felicitous narrative at Pompeii.[85]

The frieze that adorned Berlin's Neues Museum when it opened
in 1855 encapsulates these stories about Pompeii. Executed by the
sculptor Hermann Schievelbein, it portrays the destruction of the
ancient city, drawing directly on Briullov and Bulwer-Lytton rather
than on the historical record. But Pompeii is not just an end, it is also
a point of origin, a beginning, portrayed both by the line of Christians
retreating from the city and the group of Pompeians who, having fled
the town with numerous artifacts, present them to the architect of
the Museum, Friedrich Andreas Stüler, and its first director, Ignaz
von Olfers. The place of the frieze, between ancient and more recent
works of art, establishes it as a link in a historic chain of development
in which the Christian era succeeds that of the ancient world. The
presence of Christians in the destruction of Pompeii, here as elsewhere, was vital to the themes of resurrection and historical continuity, while the gifts to Stüler and Olfers underline the importance of
the museum as a conservator of the past.[86]

It is easy to see why, in a post-revolutionary or even anti-
revolutionary age, artists and writers should want to populate the
time between the moment at which Vesuvius destroyed/conserved
the buried cities and their present. The ruins of Rome, as we have
seen, made it easy to construct a history between their creation and
their contemporary presence. A classic example would be Edward
Gibbon's musings while contemplating ruins in the Eternal City: 'It

was at Rome, on the fifteenth of October 1764, as I sat musing amidst the ruins of the Capitol, while the barefooted friars were singing Vespers in the temple of Jupiter, that the idea of writing the decline and fall of the City first started to my mind.'[87] Roman ruins and singing friars shaped a ready-made history in the way that Pompeii did not. The story of Christian persecution and eventual triumph, what Byron referred to as 'from Jove to Jesus',[88] was written into the city's stones, into a narrative of centuries. It was not, of course, that observers were not able to summon up imaginatively the dying gladiator in the Colosseum, the killing of innocent Christians in the amphitheatre, or even ancient spectres, to leap imaginatively into the past, but they did so within a known historical trajectory. This, as we have seen, the buried cities of the Campagna lacked: they were envisaged as the creation of a single moment, a sudden confrontation between the powers of nature and the works of man, vividly conveyed by the likes of Briullov, one that both broke and arrested the continuum of human history. One way to overcome this rupture was through a process of recuperation and resurrection, through the painstaking work of the archaeologist and antiquary, whose task re-established the connection and memory of a lost and buried culture. But the findings at Herculaneum and Pompeii were also troubling; their artifacts were redolent of a society whose religious and social practices could not stand as a model for modern Christian society. Two stratagems neutralised that threat. The first interpreted the eruption of 79 CE as a divine act of punishment, reviving an old trope about the explanation of volcanic action, one clearly at odds with the Enlightenment view of vulcanism as a benign (at least in the long run) natural process. Such providentialism had to be distinguished from earlier 'superstition' about the workings of the volcano, even though it shared some of its features. The second stratagem involved the importation of history into the tableau of the buried cities, but in the form of imaginative reconstruction. Christians, regardless of the historical evidence, had to be present to set up a pseudo-historical narrative that underpinned a moral fable.

It is instructive to try a thought experiment here, one in which the archaeological remains of Pompeii were not the result of an eruption, a natural disaster, but were merely exceptional survivals of the antique world. (This would preclude the corporeal remains of those killed in the disaster.) The density and character of its artifacts would, as we have already seen, have made the site remarkable, but without knowledge of the 'intervention' of Vesuvius, our sense of the sudden arrest of history, I suspect that we would see the ruins very differently, and be much less disposed to create the sort of moralised fables with which the ruins are populated. Vesuvius and Pompeii are joined at the hip or, to change the metaphor, the killer and their victim both remain at the scene of the crime. There is the then, '79 CE', and the then in the now. Capturing that moment, as we shall see, became something of a preoccupation of the showmen and artists of the nineteenth century, as they converted its sublimity into a commodity.

13
VESUVIUS
The Spectacle of the Sublime in 'the Age of Contrivances'

In *L'ultimo giorno di Pompei* on the edge of each wing was a huge column made of canvas and surmounted by its own capital. Balancing these on the other side of the stage there were six similar columns, the whole forming a larger underground hall, constructed in such a way that in the shaking of the soil that preceded the eruption of the volcano, the great columns broke apart in various ways, the pieces falling on the stage ... In this way the scene disintegrated in the eruption, and it is impossible to express in words how it succeeded in being so true to life.

At the same time as the ceiling fell in ... there fell from the flies at the back of the stage innumerable pieces of rock made out of cardboard coloured with red lead and heightened by red powder mixed with huge quantities of sawdust, so that they appeared to be stones and ashes from Vesuvius. Simultaneously nine curtains of ash-coloured gauze on which were painted billowing clouds of fire and smoke rose one after the other to display the great eruption, which was pictured on a large transparent oil-cloth drop curtain four hundred palmi long, wound round a drum 8 palmi in diameter. This drop curtain was painted with tongues of flame and balls of fire, reflecting red and giving the illusion that you

were looking at real flames rather than a transparent curtain ...
Shortly afterwards, fiery lava was seen to be moving towards the
ruins on the stage with such verisimilitude that the people in the
stalls were terrified.

> Letter to his Excellency, the Marchese Luigi Imperiale,
> Superintendent of Theatres and Spectacles, Naples, June 1846,
> on the performance of Pacini's opera *L'ultimo giorno di
> Pompei* at the San Carlos Theatre[1]

The early nineteenth century was sometimes called by contemporaries 'the age of contrivances', a period marked by exceptional technical ingenuity. The term has a double resonance, pointing positively to imaginative inventiveness but also recognising that contrivances involve an element of trickery and deception. Those who used the term were often thinking of the exhilarating but slightly troubling culture of spectacle in which a range of novel techniques, technologies and machinery were used to create images, three-dimensional objects and environments of unprecedented verisimilitude. These presentations were not just staged in such traditional venues of exhibition and performance as the art gallery, the theatre, the opera and the pleasure garden. They were also held in exhibition halls that hosted a variety of special performances whose common features involved, in the words of the visual critic Tom Gunning, 'direct stimulation and shock of display, the inciting of visual curiosity and pleasure, and the solicitation of attention through surprise and astonishment'.[2] An advertisement for a three-part entertainment held in the Subscription Rooms at the small Devonshire town of Hatherleigh in 1857 that culminated in a simulated Vesuvian eruption makes its aims clear:

> The intention has been to join Scientific amusement with
> intellectual recreation ... an opportunity of seeing some of
> the most AWFUL AND MAGNIFICENT SCENES
> EVER WITNESSED AND SOME OF THE MOST

WONDERFUL AND BEAUTIFUL TABLEAUX ... and such as will call down universal EXPRESSIONS OF ASTONISHMENT AND DELIGHT.[3]

The most famous of these spectacular exhibitions were the 'oramas': the panorama – in both its static 360-degree and mobile linear formats – and the diorama, with its manipulation of light to create a sense of change through time. By the mid-nineteenth century they were to be found in the capitals and major cities of Europe and the New World. Though these 'attractions' emphasised seeing, witnessing and looking as their chief aesthetic experience (sight, after all, was what Wordsworth dubbed 'the most despotic of our senses'), they often involved mixed-media and appealed to a broad range of faculties, notably hearing, using sound and music (as opposed to words). They were frequently staged on a large scale, not least to create an immersive reality and to 'transport' members of the public, so that 'the spectator might be so effectually deceived ... as to be induced to take the produce of art as real nature'.[4] Their target audience was not the gentleman connoisseur and savant and their aim was not the expression of taste; rather they sought a larger and more mixed public that included the less genteel, young people and women, and their object was to stimulate and to instruct.[5]

They were part of what Tony Bennett has called 'the exhibitionary complex'. He argues that

The emergence of the art museum was closely related to that of a wider range of institutions – history and natural science museums, dioramas and panoramas, national and, later, international exhibitions, arcades and department stores – which served as linked sites for the development and circulation of new disciplines (history, biology, art history, anthropology), and their discursive formulations (the past, evolution, aesthetics, man) as well as for the development of new technologies of vision.[6]

431

No matter how large and spectacular, a display was chiefly judged by its ability to appear real; accuracy was at a premium. These attractions portrayed battles and historic events, townscapes and landscapes, combining a commercialised patriotism celebrating national victories and the splendour of large cities with a virtual tourism that singled out nature's greatest wonders. They all referred to a real event or place. The occasional attempt to create a fictional spectacle usually ended in failure. The public demanded simulacra of the real world, the opportunity to enjoy a surrogate experience.

Large, spectacular, immersive, playing on the powerful emotions of shock and surprise, such attractions were often called 'sublime'. And it is therefore no surprise that one of their frequent preoccupations was natural disaster – floods, fires and other catastrophes – and that one of their most common subjects was a volcanic eruption, especially those associated with Vesuvius. Whether in the form of a transparency, a panorama, a diorama, a cosmorama (an image usually viewed through an optical device), an Eidophusikon (a display that combined changing light and physical motion) or a model or painting incorporated into an environment – most usually in the theatre or in a pleasure garden – Vesuvian attractions were staged in London, Liverpool, Dublin, Paris, Toulon, Bremen, Hamburg, Dresden, Leipzig, Berlin, Dessau, Breslau (now Wroclaw), Vienna, New York, Boston, Philadelphia, Milan, Florence and Naples itself. By the 1830s it was commonplace to end performances of Pacini's *L'ultimo giorno di Pompei* and Daniel Auber's opera *La muette de Portici*, both works frequently performed throughout Europe, with a grand finale featuring a Vesuvian eruption. René-Charles Guilbert de Pixérécourt's drama *La Tête de mort; ou, Les Ruines de Pompeïa*, enjoyed 116 consecutive performances in Paris in 1827–8, every one of which ended with an eruption that completely engulfed the stage.[7]

One of the earliest and simplest ways in which an active Vesuvius was represented was through a 'transparency', a large picture executed with a mixture of translucent and regular paints on light-weight cloth – silk, linen, calico or muslin – and often illuminated from the rear. The technique was an old one, used in baroque spectacles, though it reached new levels of sophistication in the early nineteenth century when transparencies were combined with other materials and techniques. An early example was the transparency of the Vesuvian eruption of October 1767 sent by Sir William Hamilton to the Royal Society, together with a written account, maps and diagrams of the event.[8] He described it as 'a view of a current of lava from Mount Vesuvius; it is painted with transparent colours, and, when lighted up with lamps behind it, gives a much better idea of Vesuvius, than is possible by any other sort of painting.'[9] If the Duchess of Anhalt-Dessau (whose husband built his own volcano in his gardens at Worlitz in Germany) is to be believed, this was the transparency displayed in a specially darkened room when she visited the British Museum in October 1775.[10] Writing to thank Hamilton for his gift, the future president of the Royal Society Sir John Pringle commented that 'The representation of that grand and terrible scene, by means of transparent colours, was so lively and striking, that there seemed to be nothing wanting in us distant spectators but the fright that everybody must have been fired with who was so near.'[11] Note that Pringle focuses on the response to the experience of the eruption, the issue of sublimity rather than on the scientific accuracy of its representation. There is no evidence in the surviving descriptions of any mechanism to animate this image, though one assumes that the claim about its superiority to 'any other sort of painting' probably depended on flickering light that conveyed a sense of motion.

Hamilton's transparency of Vesuvius was only one of several displayed in London. The artist Hugh Deane, who had been in Naples in the 1770s, showed eruptions in rooms in Covent Garden and at the Exeter Exchange Exhibition Room in 1780 and 1786, displays made up of 'transparencies, machinery and the sound of rumbling underground convulsions and peaks of thunder'. Deane's exhibit claimed to be 9 metres high and 4 metres wide (12 by 9 feet) but was dwarfed by the transparency displayed in the summer seasons at Vauxhall Pleasure Gardens in the 1820s, which extended upwards to a full 24 metres (80 feet), and included a mechanism that enabled 'nightly eruptions'. Vesuvius was to be found in other pleasure gardens. Liverpool Zoological Gardens displayed Vesuvian eruptions in the 1830s, while through the 1830s and 1840s, Surrey Zoological Gardens, whose artificial lake was converted into a version of the Bay of Naples, staged eruptions that emanated from behind a huge canvas of the volcano painted by the theatrical scene painter and friend of Charles Dickens, George Danson.[12] Every summer evening, a dazzling firework display simulating an eruption announced the immanent closure of the gardens.

These outdoor displays were a response to the extraordinary popularity of two new technologies, the panorama and the diorama. Though there are disputed claims about who invented the panorama, there is no doubt that the first building erected to house one was built by the Irish artist Robert Barker on the edge of London's Leicester Square in 1793. Over the next seventy years more than 120 different panoramas were opened in Europe, the bulk of them in the years between the 1790s and the 1830s. It is estimated that visitors to Paris panoramas between 1800 and 1820 numbered between 30,000 and 50,000 each year. In 1824 one London commentator exclaimed, '*The Ramas!* – One would think the population of the British metropolis had turned Turks, and this was the season of Ramadan; for we have the Diorama, Cosmorama, Panorama, Peristrephic-panorama, and Naturorama, all inviting the public to pay for a peep.'[13]

The panorama, an all-encompassing cylindrical painting in a circular building seen from a central viewing platform, was immediately recognised as producing remarkable effects on the viewer. As Alexander von Humboldt put it, 'The paintings on all sides evoke more than theatrical scenery is capable of because the spectator, captivated and transfixed as in a magic circle and removed from distracting reality, believes himself to be really surrounded by foreign nature.'[14] The distinction between the real and its representation, deliberately concealed in the totalising environment or field of vision, seemed to have collapsed. As Wordsworth put it in the *Prelude*, the panorama conveyed 'absolute presence of reality, / Expressing as in a mirror sea and land, / And what earth is, and what she hath to show' (II, 249–51). The effect was at once startling and disorienting, described by one historian of the panorama as 'see-sickness'.[15]

But the panorama had one major weakness when it came to rendering an event rather than an object, namely its inability to convey change or movement through time. As the aptly named periodical *The Literary Panorama* commented as early as 1810, 'Neither motion nor sound can be comprised in a Panorama; and thus we perceive that even this, the nearest approach to a visible reality, stands in need [of] various allowances, and of the exercise of candour by the spectator.'[16] Novel technologies age fast. The interest in witnessing natural events like an eruption of Vesuvius remained high but was confronted by a diminishing reality effect that could only be sustained by simulating change through time.

No one was more aware of this than Sir William Hamilton, who was acutely sensitive, as we have seen, to the importance of demonstrating his special relationship to the volcano to both an erudite audience and a larger public. In the early 1770s Hamilton came up with his own solution to the problem of representing volcanic motion. The independent scholar Bent Sorensen has unearthed a detailed description in the archive of the Académie des Sciences, Belles-Lettres et Arts de Bordeaux, made by the French naturalist François de Paule Latapie, when he was in Naples in 1776, of what was referred to as Hamilton's 'mechanical contrivance'.[17] The mechanism, roughly 80 × 130 × 50 cm (32 × 51 × 20 in) deep, is fronted by a transparent version of Plate 38 of Pietro Fabris's plates for Hamilton's sumptuous and lavishly illustrated publication *Campi Phlegraei* (1776) (Plate 16). Contained within the box is a clockwork mechanism that rotates an irregularly perforated cylinder containing a lamp, and animates three arched levers, two raising and lowering covers to lamps whose position corresponds to the summit of the volcano and the fracture below it, the last operating a mallet which hit a drum to make the sounds of the eruption (Plate 26).

Hamilton's mechanical contrivance was emphatically not intended to reveal the processes of eruption; it had little or no explanatory value, and was the record of an event or, more accurately, the record of the witnessing of a volcanic spectacle. Its scientific claims were purely observational – that it was a true and accurate rendering of a phenomenon (note the claim that Fabris's drawing was made on the spot), made truer and more accurate by virtue of representing an eruption in motion.

Hamilton could easily have chosen a more distant view of the volcano, using one of the many spectacular images of the eruptions earlier than that of 1771, but instead he chose a view that is close to the eruption, and that shows him as the enlightened savant, explaining to the monarchs what can be observed. The viewer, however, has no access to what Hamilton is telling the royal couple. Rather he or she is invited to share in the sublime experience of those depicted in the image. The purpose of the technology was to evoke that experience as accurately as possible; it simulated witnessing, and it scripted the encounter between the eruption and the visitor as one of enlightened sociability and sensibility. For all its complicated mechanisms, the message of Hamilton's device is very much in line with the paintings of artists like the Chevalier Volaire, intended not just to evoke the power of the volcano, but also the sublime control of the enlightened savant.

Why did Hamilton have the devices made? His aims are not altogether clear. He seems to have shown his contrivance to visitors to Naples in the years between 1771 and 1779 when the volcano was relatively quiescent, and he was always mindful of the impact that his accounts, whether verbal or visual, had back in London among the savants of the Royal Society. He also sent a transparency and accompanying instructions about machinery to David Garrick, the manager of the Drury Lane Theatre, who had spent time in Naples in the winter of 1763–4 during his tour of Italy and who was also, like Hamilton, a member of the Society of Dilettanti, a club of Grand Tourists who promoted the arts and the study of antiquity. Hamilton may have had in mind Garrick's set designer, the Frenchman Philippe de Loutherbourg, who had been transforming the staging and sets of theatrical productions since his arrival in London in 1771. Though it is not possible to establish a direct connection, there is a remarkable resemblance between Hamilton's contrivance and Loutherbourg's so-called Eidophusikon (from the Greek meaning an image of nature).[18] The Eidophusikon, described in advertisements as 'imitations of natural phenomena represented by moving pictures', was larger than Hamilton's device. It consisted of a theatrical box measuring 2 × 1.5 × 2.5 metres (6.5 × 5 × 8 feet), and used back-lit scenery, semi-transparent colours on strips of linen, models, cork and pasteboard, and lamps with rotating colour filters, together with a clockwork 'winding machine' to simulate motion and movement through time.[19] One of five scenes exhibited at its opening in 1781 was, almost inevitably, 'Sunset, a View over Naples'. The later history of this machine is one of its gradual transformation from an 'elite entertainment to commonplace variety show',[20] but its technologies continued on the stage. Clarkson Stanfield, a prolific artist and set designer, used what was called an Eidophusikon, 'shewing the Beauties of Nature, and Wonders of Art', to display an eruption of Vesuvius in his mixed-media staging of *Zoroaster; or, the Spirit of the Star* at Drury Lane Theatre in the spring of 1824.[21]

Hamilton seems to have been astonishingly prescient in sending his device to Garrick, for it was in the world of the theatre that new ways of modelling nature originated. De Loutherbourg was credited (or condemned as) the person who transformed London staging, enveloping actors in a complex machinery of scenery and illusion that achieved unprecedented verisimilitude.[22] As the *Morning Chronicle* put it in February 1776, he was 'the first artist who showed our theatre directors that by a just disposition of light and shade, and critical preservation of perspective, the eye of the spectator might be so effectually deceived in a playhouse as to be induced to take the produce of art for real nature'.[23] He and his successors reconfigured the stage from a space of performance to a space of illusion. They greatly increased the depth of the stage, very often bolstered and darkened the proscenium arch, using it as a framing device, included colossal architectural elements, and employed gas and spotlighting. The effects could be seen, for example, in the staging of Pacini's *L'ultimo giorno di Pompei* in Milan (Plate 28) which characteristically uses a brilliantly illuminated backstage – in this case the light of the eruption – to create a sense of depth, a device that, as we have seen, was also used by Karl Briullov in his massive painting of the same subject.

These innovations in staging and lighting were largely responsible for the transformation of the nineteenth-century theatre with its preference 'for show over sentiment', and for the importance (reflected in salaries and the attention they received on playbills) of the artists, like Clarkson Stanfield and David Roberts, who staffed 'the spectacle departments' of theatres in London and Paris. Other innovations that started in the theatre included the moving panorama – huge scrolled canvasses – that created the illusion of travel or movement and which were first introduced as theatrical backdrops (the first recorded instance is in 1800) before they became freestanding entertainments.[24] They were the precursors of freestanding moving panoramas (peristrephic panoramas, as they were called) like J.R. Smith's 'Moving Panorama Tour of Europe', a journey that began in London and ended peering into the crater of Vesuvius. Similarly the dioramas opened in Paris and London by Louis Daguerre (himself originally a scene painter at the Théâtre de l'Ambigu-Comique and the Paris opera) and by the architect Karl Schinkel and Carl Gropius in Berlin used the partly opaque, partly translucent colours, gum-based paints, colour wheels, silk screens, lighting techniques and pulley systems that were first developed in the theatre. Schinkel's Berlin perspective-optical cycles, which used 'strong lamp illumination both in front of the picture and behind', were described by the artist Ludwig Catel as presenting the viewer 'as if in front of a traditional theatre stage before which the enchanted mirror reveals itself'.[25]

The dioramas invented by Daguerre were seen as the most successful illusions in motion.[26] Huge paintings – as large as 21 × 14 metres (70 × 45 feet) in size – displayed in specially darkened exhibition spaces (there were premises in both London and Paris), they were painted on both sides with opaque and translucent paint so that when they were illuminated from different angles, using a system of shutters and screens, the view underwent a gradual and subtle transformation. Less concerned with accuracy than the circular panorama, their fame lay in their reproduction of the *effects* of nature. The response to these was described by Lady Morgan, the Irish feminist and novelist we have already met in Naples, on a visit to the London diorama in the 1830s:

> Effects so opposite in character, so natural, so picturesque in effect, produce an illusion so perfect that the mind, when left to itself, is never for a moment awakened to the belief that this wondrous exhibition is not the thing it represents, that those salient monuments, those remote perspectives, those lessening isles, those faint gleams, and fainter shadows, are all the effect of light and shade – all produced on a flat surface, and by ordinary colours; and as long as silence continues unbroken, it is impossible to detect the cheat to which the senses so implicitly submit.

Her awareness of the power that the diorama had to convey motion led her to reflect on how the genius of earlier artists like the Neapolitan painter of the sublime Salvator Rosa would have been enhanced if they had possessed the new technology. In Rosa, she wrote, 'the rock had been shattered by the flash [of lightning] before its abrupt sharp fragments were represented . . . trees are blasted, not blasting – lights are dimmed, not dimming – shadows are deep, not deepening. 'The image is static. 'Could Salvator have represented this world of sublime destruction in the act of being destroyed,' she concluded, 'how near to the terrible agency of nature would this great master of terror have approached! But his art reached not the out-pouring of a river of flames of a volcano, or the falling of an avalanche over an Alpine village with all its details of movement, and its horrible but rapid progress of destruction.'[27]

Daguerre never produced a full-scale diorama of either the Bay of Naples or Vesuvius, though his techniques were employed in many polyorama panoptique, smaller viewing boxes whose favourite subject was Vesuvius in eruption. In the absence of a surviving moveable diorama, the organisers of the exhibition on Daguerre and dioramas, held in Paris in 2017, chose to present a modern diorama by the French artist Jean Paul Favand; his chosen subject was an erupting Vesuvius.[28]

One German artist whom we have already met on the slopes of Vesuvius, August Kopisch, used a somewhat different technique to represent the volcano when he returned to his native Breslau in 1831. He helped create a huge pleorama – a simulated trip round the Bay of Naples, in which a paying audience sat in an enclosed boat while moving panoramas were scrolled on either side of the vessel to create the illusion of a voyage across the gulf 'just as it would pass before one's eyes if one went on board ship near Procida on a bright and beautiful day and took a leisurely trip past several miles of the most beautiful scenery in Europe, to the foot of Vesuvius and back.'[29]

The pleorama – which later moved to Berlin – was not the first such representation of the Bay of Naples to be exhibited in Breslau; in 1826 the Silesian painter Johann Augustin Siegert (1786–1869), who had earlier shown a panorama of Mount Etna, exhibited two dioramas, one of which was of the Bay of Naples, illuminated in such a way that the light shifted from dusk to night to daybreak.[30] But the pleorama, a collaboration between Carl Ferdinand Langhans (1781–1869), an architect who planned the exhibit, and Kopisch, who provided sketches that he had made in Naples, was altogether on a greater scale.[31] Kopisch wrote an accompanying eighty-page booklet explaining the trip's itinerary, and painted 'the Apennines, Vesuvius and its eruption of ash, the peninsula of Sorrento and the isles of Capri, Ischia and Procida'. As the magazine *Der Hausfreund* reported, 'One hears the rumblings of the majestic volcano, sees its terrible clouds of smoke and ghastly rain of ash in a myriad of startling colours as night falls; the total effect is startling and wonderful.'[32]

Langhans and Kopisch offered their customers a flamboyant exercise in cultural mediation: a virtual trip in which 'those who have toured the Bay of Naples by ship will be able to refresh their pleasant memories . . . those whose familiarity with the region is derived solely from travellers' accounts and a classical education will find their longing to set eyes on it fulfilled in the most pleasant fashion.'[33] The power of this sort of experience is brought out in the journal of a young Yorkshire gentleman visiting Naples with his brother in 1823: 'We went on the water to see Naples from near the Spot from whence we had seen it represented in the Panorama in London, and were bound to acknowledge the resemblance wonderfully correct.'[34]

Volcanic eruptions were among the greatest spectacles of nature and had the added bonus that they embodied violent motion. Fiery volcanoes – and in this respect they resembled the majestic snow-covered alpine glaciers that were also so often represented – were ideal subjects whose power stemmed from their intense light.

How were these 'attractions' interpreted and how did they affect Romantic notions of nature, volcanoes and the sublime? The subject matter of these entertainments and technologies was never confined to the depiction of the volcano. They were experiments in spectacle and showmanship, triumphs of modern technology which celebrated their ability to stun their audiences and viewers with their verisimilitude, and their power to manipulate time and space. Such spectacles were not just sensational but controversial. Opinions within the art world were divided. Some artists, like Sir Joshua Reynolds and Benjamin West, were fascinated with new possibilities; others were ambiguous – both admiring and critical – chiefly on the grounds that art was a matter of imagination, not of imitation.[35] Critics, especially in France, dismissed what they saw as something mechanical and therefore incompatible with art. Viollet-le-Duc condemned Daguerre's invention because 'the diorama stinks of the machine'.[36] Romantics like Coleridge disparaged what they saw as 'the tyranny of the eye'. Nevertheless devices like the panorama had many supporters, though they tended to emphasise their didactic rather than aesthetic virtues. Humboldt praised them for the opportunities they afforded those who could not travel. John Ruskin, despite his hostility to the mechanical, praised Burford's panorama in Leicester Square, as 'an educational institution of the highest and purest value, and ought to have been supported by the Government as one of the most beneficial school instruments in London. There I had seen, exquisitely painted, the view from the roof of Milan cathedral, when I had no hope of ever seeing the reality, but with a joy and wonder of the deepest.'[37] A report made in 1800 by the French Institut National des Sciences et Arts supported panoramas as objects of instruction and utility.[38] As the Scottish physician and populariser of science Neil Arnott pointed out, such devices 'become the means of conveying most impressive lessons of historical fact and moral principle'.[39]

Much was and has been made of the way such simulacra, in Lady Morgan's words, made it 'impossible to detect the cheat to which the senses so implicitly submit'. Tales of gullible observers believing in the reality of what they saw, or acting as if what they saw was real, were, like tales of the credulity of early cinemagoers, not uncommon.[40] But these stories obscure the way in which these early attempts at virtual reality were praised and promoted by the impresarios who displayed them to the public, implicitly asking them to share in the pleasures of the illusion. There was no attempt to conceal the mechanisms by which the illusions were created; on the contrary, their ingenuity was often explained in the advertising and guides that promoted and accompanied their performance. The creator of the European travelling panorama that ended in the crater of Vesuvius, John Rowson Smith, saw his device as a piece of modern technology that he compared with 'the telegraph, the railway and the Steam-Boat'.[41] Numerous puffs for panoramas dwelt on the ingenuity of their artistic creators.

As *Blackwood's Magazine* remarked about the 1824 panorama of Vesuvius, 'We have seen Vesuvius in full roar and torrent, within a hundred yards of a hackney-coach stand, with all its cattle, human and bestial, unmoved by the phenomenon.' Six years later *The Times* made a similar point about the dioramas in Regent's Park. 'Thanks to the contrivances of modern ingenuity, the "long drawn aisles and fretted vaults" of the Cathedral at Rheims are now fixed snugly in the Regent's-park, and the rocks of Mont St Gothard, torn from their old foundations, are reposing quietly in the same vicinity.'[42] The recognition that vision and viewing was a matter of perception, of point of view, and that this human faculty could be manipulated to produce certain effects, lay at the heart of these attractions.[43] They managed the experience of the (complicit) viewer through their presentation; their focus was not so much on the nature or natural processes they represented – the fiery explosions of the volcano or the serpent-like flow of lava – as on the human ingenuity and technological inventiveness that brought them within the purview of a paying public. The magic of the experience now lay not in the wonder of nature but in the skills of the inventor whose achievement – the manipulation of time and space as well as nature – made the sublime experience into a commodity that was domesticated and controlled.

It was not just that views travelled; so too did viewers, as Charles Dickens explained in a gently mocking piece in *Household Words* about the virtual traveller Mr Booley. 'It is very gratifying to me,' said he, 'to have seen so much at my time of life, and to have acquired a knowledge of the countries I have visited, which I could not have derived from books alone. When I was a boy, such travelling would have been impossible, as the gigantic-moving-panorama or diorama mode of conveyance, which I have principally adopted (all my modes of conveyance have been pictorial), had then not been attempted.' But the situation had changed radically. 'It is a delightful character-istic of these times, that new and cheap means are continually being devised for conveying the results of actual experience to those who are unable to obtain such experiences for themselves: and to bring them within the reach of the people – emphatically of the people; for it is they at large who are addressed in these endeavours, and not exclusive audiences'. 'Some of the best results of actual travel,' he concludes, 'are suggested by such means to those whose lot it is to stay at home. New worlds open out to them, beyond their little worlds, and widen their range of reflection, information, sympathy, and interest. The more man knows of man, the better for the common brotherhood among us all.'[44]

Visual, inexpensive, widely accessible, educational: these were the much-vaunted virtues of virtual travel. They imply a capaciousness that was not, however, borne out by what was often mentioned as a further advantage of such forms of conveyance, namely avoiding 'the nausea of crossing the Channel, the roguery of continental innkeepers, and all the other and indescribable miseries of foreign travel'.[45] These included 'the insolence of public functionaries ... the visitations of armed banditti, charged to the muzzle with sabre, pistol and scapulary ... the rascality of custom-house officers, who plunder, passport in hand, the indescribable *desagremens* of Italian cookery, and the insufferable annoyance of that epitome of abomination, an Italian bed.'[46] What, after all, was the point of suffering such unpleasantness and physical discomfort, if the visual pleasures of travel came so easily to hand?

We are a far cry from the suffocating fumes, intense heat and peri-odic explosions faced by visitors bold enough to climb up the cone of

Vesuvius, reach the summit and peer into its crater. Romantic travellers expected to experience a level of what today is euphemistically called 'discomfort'; by the mid-nineteenth century an armchair traveller could experience a largely disembodied visual experience whose promoters told him was every bit as real as 'the real thing'. The process was one of disengagement with the environment in order to ensure immersion in the image or the commodified experience. In this way it bore affinities with the sort of travel and tourism promoted by Thomas Cook. Cook went to great lengths to seal off his clients from indigenous environments and their difficulties. English-speaking representatives at all the major railway stations, baggage arrangements that cut out local porters, coupons that avoided handling foreign money and knowing rates of exchange, meals prepared by English cooks, were all provided on the grounds of comfort, convenience and 'efficiency'. And, as we have seen, all these sorts of amenities eventually found their way up towards Vesuvius's crater. The same sort of sanitised experience was praised in the *Art Journal* of 1861 which lauded the panorama of the Bay of Naples as 'even more pleasant to look upon in Leicester Square, than is the reality with all its abominations of tyranny, licentiousness, poverty and dirt'.[47]

Whether as a virtual experience, or as part of a package deal for the traveller, Vesuvius, the Bay of Naples and the buried cities had become, by the 1850s and 1860s, a common cultural property of bourgeois Europe – one spectacle among many in the shows staged in European metropolises, one property amongst many in the itineraries of tourism. The development of the steamboat and the steam train – technologies in which the Kingdom of Naples was a pioneer – and the organisational skills of northern European Protestants like Mr Thomas Cook and Herr Carl Stangen, both of whom smoothed the passage of visitors into the Mediterranean, meant that though the volcano and the cities remained objects of geological inquiry and continued to be tied in complex ways to the communities that surrounded them, they had now also become the properties of the travel agent and the foreign tour operator. And, though paintings, prints and sketches had long been ways of conveying an image of the Bay of Naples and the volcano to a viewer, the new contrivances in the metropoles of Europe were different. They invited their clients to share in the power of manipulating the world, of taming nature, and celebrating their control over the envir-onment. They were peddling a comfortable illusion, one that im-agined a nature – 'out there' – separate from man and subject to his control, and deliberately overlooked the fact that, as those who had clambered to the top of the volcano had learned, man was in nature and subject to its forces.

CONCLUSION

In the course of this book we have travelled from the slopes of Vesuvius, gnarled and torn by some of nature's most powerful forces and populated by a diverse throng of guides and visitors, along the networks shaped by travellers of every kind and formed by itinerant and sedentary savants, through the maze of antique ruins both real and vividly imagined, and have ended in the strange spectacular spaces of Europe's metropolises, sites of both entertainment and science, in which objects of representation were meticulously presented in order to excite certain effects in a paying audience. This has been a journey outward from the volcano, but also forward through time. Though it is important to recognise the ways in which Vesuvius was transformed during the course of this journey – how technology, science, commerce and the modern state transformed its relation to the larger world – we also need to understand that focusing on these developments may lead us to overlook or ignore a history that does not fit into a reassuring story of human progress. We can see that much of the writing and representation of Vesuvius constituted and still often constitutes at best an omission and at worst a suppression of its plenitude and richness. The variety of travellers and their complex motivations and powerful emotions are flattened by a 'progressive'

447

history of tourism; the guides and servants are overlooked in 'scientific' accounts; the cult of the sublime excludes children, the humble and the uneducated, and discards alternative accounts of the volcano as 'primitive'; the active relation between human communities and the volcano recedes in the realm of scientific publication and rigorous instrumentation, and the somatic experience of 'being on the volcano' is evacuated by comfortable tourist amenities and the stunning illusions of virtual reality. These are the processes by which the volcano became both a scientific subject and a spectacle, a regulated object of human contrivance rather than of unruly nature.

Romantic and subsequent science made remarkable and undeniable progress but only nibbled at the edges of the problem of man's relation to nature. These achievements have implied a greater human ability to master natural forces than has been the case, encouraging a certain attitude which supposes 'nature' to be the handmaiden of human endeavour. The persistent human desire to believe that 'nature' can be subjugated by man can take many different forms, ranging from the confidence of the enlightened savant like Sir William Hamilton that he (almost invariably he) has the special ability to understand nature as a benign force, to the complacence of Charles Dickens's Mr Booley, who can delight in a virtual experience in nature without any of its bodily encumbrances. Such comforts are illusions based, as many commentators have noted, on the assumption that we, 'humankind', are not in nature and bound by it, but separate from it and therefore able to exercise a degree of control over it. Such views serve to suppress our begrudging recognition that there are forces that, even if we analyse and explain them, cannot be constrained by us. We can deploy certain environments – the museum, the theatre, the panorama – and use certain technologies to fix and tame the volcano, but the slopes of Vesuvius were one of the places where we had and have to confront our powerlessness. It is tempting to speculate that the Romantic obsession with Vesuvius was part of a deep ambivalence about 'nature', one that saw in the volcano a striking instance of nature's powers over man but also strove to use the case of the most famous volcano in Europe to argue for the possibility of a human and spiritual triumph over natural forces.

I have emphasised not just the volcano as destination but the often circuitous, contingent and diverse processes of travel. This is not merely a matter of recounting motion – the movement of travellers, the circulation of ideas and objects – through time and space. What has been more important are the many sorts of connection and affiliation made through the volcano, as a facilitator of friendship and fellow-feeling, a hands-on experience, scientific object, site of pleasure, political metaphor and symbol, and conflicted source of representation. None of these was a discrete area of experience. They were connected – in different configurations that changed through time – by people and objects that created shifting and deeply consequential attachments.

What happened on the volcano – its constant movement that might include dramatic eruptions, the give and take between visitors and guides, the struggles with a rebarbative mountain, the friendships and conflicts among the visitors, the making of images and lava medals, the taking of measurements and soundings, the presence of the government or the intrusion of multinational bodies like Thomas Cook – made Romantic Vesuvius an environment that encompassed both nature and culture. It may have been represented as a world apart – as was so much of wild nature – but it was not. It was a world inhabited and lived in, whose material properties were as much a part of society as the people it affected. Vesuvius fitted into the life experiences of a heterogeneous body of people, some of whom were close to the volcano – earned a livelihood from it, spent their lives studying it, enjoyed or suffered, however briefly, an intense connection with it, or used it to achieve some particular end. Others were connected at a distance, some of whom travelled to the volcano, while some enjoyed it virtually, or in the form of the laboratory specimen or an eye-catching crystal in a collection. The sheer variety and number of such actors and the ways in which they were bound together is remarkable.

We have seen throughout this book that there were complex groups with strong affinities and vested interests in the volcano. It might be better not to describe them as 'communities', with its cuddly sense of unanimity, or as 'networks' which conveys a sense of abstract instrumentalism – though I have used both terms. We are talking about families eking out a living on the margins of society, some much more successfully than others; Neapolitans of every stripe bundling the volcano and the city's religious traditions; university professors and rich amateur enthusiasts of geological and vulcanological sciences, tussling with one another to a common purpose; travellers whose emotional needs, desire for belonging and sense of disorientation were sometimes but not always met by their experiences of travel; and an urban public enjoying simulacra of nature.

Some individuals connected these groups. Before the French Revolution, Sir William Hamilton linked elite savants in Naples, Paris and London, just as Teodoro Monticelli was to do in the early nineteenth century. The artist August Kopisch found in Vesuvius a medium to express his exuberant talents as an artist, a writer and an impresario whose work engaged the German-speaking lands of central Europe. In the early nineteenth century Salvatore Madonna, working with Monticelli, connected his fellow guides – in ways they may have resented – to a clientele that included affluent travellers and determined savants from all over Europe and the New World. But these individuals were only some of the numerous actors whose actions, prompted by motives as diverse as greed, thrill-seeking, curiosity, making a living, friendship, politics and patriotism, promoted a 'matrix of movement'[1] of people, images, ideas and objects that went to make up Romantic Vesuvius.

Over the course of the nineteenth century, the connections between those on the mountain and those beyond its immediate purview broke down. We can see this in personal terms – the end of the special relationship between humble people on the mountain and savants that did not survive beyond the lives of Salvatore Madonna and Teodoro Monticelli. But the process was more fundamental. The rather delicate (and brief) balance between closeness and distance, engagement and detachment, a matter of mutual interest and benefit, was gradually upset by technological and scientific change and the triumph of a vision of the volcano as an external natural object that was viewed or acted upon rather than lived in. This was part of a much larger nineteenth-century view of man's relation to the natural world, one that saw it as a story of progressive conquest, the 'capture' of almost every aspect of nature, even its wildest and most powerful forms. This was not just the achievement of intrepid European explorers. Their footsteps were followed not only by later travellers and tourists, but in the great nineteenth-century compendia of travel literature. Their findings were systematised in the global atlases that measured and compared rivers, mountains and volcanoes. Urban spectacles secured an orderly tableau of nature; volcanic eruptions occurred punctually at regular intervals. Zoological gardens 'tamed' their animal inmates. All of these developments acted as an (illusory) form of reassurance, helping to promote the idea of a universal nature separate from man, and cumulatively subject to his bidding.

What I have learned in researching and writing this book is how important it is not to treat the relations between the volcano and human actors as amenable to a single or simple resolution. I find myself increasingly irritated by authors claiming to have written '*The* true history of x', a wilful refusal to recognise that there are many true stories, told by different narrators, for different purposes at different times. It is precisely because historical actors can tell their own stories that the historian, as a narrator and analyst concerned with verisimilitude, should not shy away from the complexity this necessarily produces. As for the rumbling, convulsive volcano, Vesuvius speaks for itself. We should listen with respect. Even its silence speaks volumes.

ENDNOTES

Introduction

1. Quoted in Peter Fritzche, *Stranded in the Present: Modern Time and the Melancholy of History*, Cambridge MA, 2004, p. 44.
2. James Clifford, *Routes: Travel and Translation in the Late Twentieth Century*, Cambridge MA, 1997, p. 3.
3. Rebecca Ford, 'Images of the Earth, Images of Man: The Mineralogical Plates of the *Encyclopédie*', in *Histoires de la Terre: Earth Sciences and French Culture 1740–1940*, ed. Louise Lyle and David McCallam, Amsterdam, 2008, pp. 57–73.
4. Visitors' Book to Vesuvius, MS Ital 139, Houghton Library, Harvard University (hereafter VB).

Prologue: The Journey to Vesuvius

1. Elena Auricchio and Elena Sarnataro, 'Un'escursione al Vesuvio: momenti e figure di un itinerario', in *Il Vesuvio e le città vesuviane 1730–1860: in ricordo di Georges Vallet*, Naples, [1998], pp. 197–214.
2. [C. Flandin], *Études et Souvenirs de Voyages en Italie et en Suisse par C. Flandin*, Paris, 1838, p. 60.
3. Antoine-Laurent Castellan, *Lettres sur l'Italie, faisant suite aux Lettres sur La Morée, l'Hellespont et Constantinople*, Paris, 1819, p. 284.
4. *Notes on Naples and its Environs: and on the road to it from Rome by a Traveller*, London, 1838, p. 70.
5. Alexandre Dumas, *Le Corricolo*, Paris, 1846, p. 2. For *Le Corricolo* see Dominique Bertrand, 'Ce volcan en éruption de livres: Dumas face au Vésuve', in *Le Vésuve en éruption: Savoirs, représentations, pratiques*, ed. Émilie Beck Saiello and Dominique Bertrand, Clemont-Ferrand, 2013, pp. 179–89.
6. British Library, Add MS 64101, f. 64.
7. Jane Waldie, *Sketches descriptive of Italy in the years 1816 and 1817: with a brief account of travels in various parts of France and Switzerland*, 3 vols, London, 1820,

vol. 3, p. 158; Adélaide-Louise-Zéphirine de Damas, *Voyage en Italie, par la comtesse de Chastellux née de Damas*, Paris, 1834, p. 275.

8. Valérie Boissier de Gasparin, *Voyage d'une ignorante dans le midi de la France et l'Italie*, 2 vols, Paris, 1835, vol. 2, pp. 288–91.

9. *The Letters of Percy Bysshe Shelley*, vol. 2, *Shelley in Italy*, ed. Frederick L. Jones, Oxford, 1964, p. 489.

10. Countess Blessington, *The Idler in Italy*, 2 vols, 2nd edn, London, 1839, vol. 2, p. 195.

11. Marianne Talbot, *Life in the South: The Naples Journal of Marianne Talbot, 1829–32*, ed. Michael Heafford, Cambridge, 2012, p. 14.

12. [August Bournonville], Helene Darling, 'August Bournonville's Letters from France and Italy, 1841, Part Three', *Dance Chronicle* 25, 3 (2002), pp. 355–6; John Auldjo, *Sketches of Vesuvius with a short account of its principal eruptions, from the commencement of the Christian era to the present time*, Naples, 1832, p. 6; Northumberland Archives, ZMI B 52/3/1, Sir Charles Miles Lambert Monck, 'Journal of a tour through France, part of Switzerland, Italy and Sicily, in company with Lord Wallace and my son, but in Sicily alone', vol. 2, 17 December 1830.

13. Quoted in Chantal Grell, *Herculanum et Pompéi dans les récits des voyageurs français du XVIIIe siècle*, Naples, 1982, p. 183.

14. Madame de Staël, *Corinne, ou l'Italie*, Book XIII, ch. 4.

15. Selina Bunbury, *A Visit to the Catacombs, or First Christian Cemeteries of Rome: and a Midnight Visit to Mount Vesuvius*, London, 1849, p. 27.

16. On the early history see Auricchio and Sarnataro, 'Un'escursione al Vesuvio', pp. 202–3.

17. [Bournonville], 'August Bournonville's Letters', p. 355.

18. *Galignani's Traveller's Guide Through Italy*, 7th edn, Paris, 1824, p. 475.

19. VB, 5 March 1828.

20. August von Kotzebue, *Travels through Italy in the Years 1804 and 1805*, 4 vols, London, 1806, vol. 2, pp. 14–15.

21. Harriet Morton, *Protestant Vigils; or, Evening Records of a Journey through Italy in the Years 1826 and 1827*, 2 vols, London, 1829, vol. 2, p. 70.

22. See, for example, Joseph Hulmandell, 'The Hermitage at Mount Vesuvius' (lithograph), in *Twenty-Four Views of Italy drawn from nature, and engraved on stone*, London, 1818; John Auldjo, 'L'eremo del Vesuvio' (lithograph by Wenzel), in *Sketches of Vesuvius*; Antonio Senape, 'Romitaggio del Vesuvio'.

23. 'L'Hermite n'est qu'un aubergiste': [Madame de Staël], *Les Carnets de Voyage de Madame de Staël, contribution à la genèse de ses œuvres*, ed. Simone Balayé, Geneva, 1971, p. 121.

24. James Fenimore Cooper, *Gleanings in Europe: Italy*, Albany NY, 1981, p. 149.

25. 'ein frommer Räuber': August Kopisch, 'Seiner Königlichen Hoheit dem Kronprinzen von Preussen. Auf dem Vesuv am 13. November 1828', in Kopisch, *Gesammelte Werke*, 4 vols, Berlin, 1856, vol. 2, p. 5.

26. For a memorable example of Britons' attachment to their own cuisine and hostility to Italian food, see the verses of the artist Thomas Jones, written in Rome and published in the *Gentleman's Magazine* (February 1797), printed in 'Thomas Jones, Memoirs, 1742–1803', *Walpole Society* 32 (1951), p. 143. This antipathy to Italian cuisine was not confined to the English. Many Germans also disliked the use of olive oil instead of butter, and the ubiquitous presence of garlic, which also offended the English palate. Dieter Richter, *Napoli Cosmopolita: Viaggiatori e comunità straniere nell'Ottocento*, Naples, 2002, pp. 74–6.

27. VB, 29 October 1827; 14, 18 October 1828.
28. William Brockedon, *Travellers Guide to Italy or, Road-book from London to Naples*, Paris, 1835, p. 204.
29. Lady Morgan, *Italy by Lady Morgan*, 3 vols, London, 1831, vol. 3, p. 166.
30. Paolo Gasperi and Silvia Musella, *Un Viaggio al Vesuvio: Il Vesuvio visto attraverso diari, lettere e resoconti di viaggiatori*, Naples, 1991, pp. 108–9.
31. David Sutherland, *A Tour up the Straits, from Gibraltar to Constantinople: with the leading events in the present war between the Austrians, the Russians and the Turks, to the commencement of the year 1789*, London, 1790, pp. 64–5.
32. Earl of Ilchester (ed.), *The Journal of Elizabeth, Lady Holland (1791–1811)*, 2 vols, London, 1908, vol. 1, p. 27.
33. Beinecke Library, Yale University, Osborn D358, 'Travel Journal of Harriet Dennison, 1815–16', not foliated.
34. VB, 15 October 1827, 30 March 1828.
35. *Army and Navy Chronicle* (19 November 1835).
36. Henry Swinburne, *Travels in the Two Sicilies by Henry Swinburne, Esq. in the years 1777, 1778, 1779, and 1780*, 4 vols, 2nd edn, London, 1790, vol. 1, p. 82.
37. 'le vent, la fumée et la raideur du talus, coupent la respiration d'une manière fort incommode': [Romain Colomb], M.R.C., *Journal d'un voyage en Italie et en Suisse pendant l'année 1828*, Paris, 1833, p. 164.
38. J.B. Ferraro, *A New Guide of Naples, its Environs, Procida, Ischia and Capri. Compiled from Vasi's Guide, several more recent publications, and a personal visit of the compiler to the Churches, Monuments Antiquities etc. by J.B. Ferarro, Professor of Languages*, 1st edn, Naples, 1826, p. 422.
39. [Greville, Charles C.F.], *The Greville Memoirs: A Journal of the Reigns of King George IV and William IV by the late Charles C.F. Greville*, ed. Henry Reeve, 3 vols, London, 1874, vol. 1, p. 299.
40. *Morgenblatt* (3 June 1828).
41. [Abraham Reeves Jackson], 'Newspaper Letters of another "Innocent Abroad": Dr. Abraham Reeves Jackson', *Mark Twain Journal* 33 (1995), p. 35.
42. [Buckingham and Chandos, Richard, 1st Duke of], *The Private Diary of Richard, Duke of Buckingham and Chandos, KG*, 3 vols, London, 1862, vol. 1, p. 311.
43. For analogies between volcanic eruptions and industrial processes see David McCallam, *Volcanoes in Eighteenth-century Europe: An Essay in Environmental Humanities*, Oxford, 2019, pp. 116–19. Perhaps even more frequently, volcanic action was compared to the sounds of battle, a familiar experience for many of those who visited Vesuvius.
44. [David Wilkie], *The Life of Sir David Wilkie with his Journals, Tours, and Critical Remarks on Works of Art; and a Selection of his Correspondence*, ed. Allan Cunningham, 3 vols, London, 1843, vol. 2, p. 271.
45. University of St Andrews Archives, Forbes Mss Dep7, Box 14, Journal 2, Forbes Journal, 19 July 1826–24 November 1826, f. 168.
46. Auldjo, *Sketches of Vesuvius*, p. 12.
47. *Notes on Naples and its Environs*, pp. 195–6.
48. [J.M.L. Borel], *Lettres écrites d'Italie à quelques amis; Par J.M.L. Bor**, Paris, 1825, p. 140.
49. Maximilian (Emperor of Mexico), *Recollections of My Life by Maximilian I, Emperor of Mexico*, London, 1868, pp. 32–6.
50. Talbot, *Life in the South*, vol. 1, p. 133.

51. Henry Matthews, *The Diary of an Invalid, being the Journal of a Tour in Pursuit of Health in Portugal, Italy, Switzerland and France in the years 1817, 1818, 1819*, 2nd edn, 1820, p. 220.

52. [Charles Mercier Dupaty], *Travels through Italy, in a Series of Letters written in the year 1785, by President Dupaty. Translated from the French by an Englishman*, London, 1788, pp. 331–2. The original French text is better: 'Lorsque j'eus contemplé cette obscurité et cette splendeur, cette nature affreuse, stérile, abandonée, et cette nature riante, animée, féconde, l'empire de la mort et celui de la vie, je me jetai à travers les nuages, et je continuai à gravir.'

53. British Library, Add MS 64101 f. 66v, Louis Jérôme de Goujon de Thuisy.

54. Nathaniel Parker Willis, *Pencillings by the Way, written during some years of residence and travel in Europe*, Auburn, 1854, p. 43.

55. Brinsley Ford Archive, Paul Mellon Centre, London, transcriptions Wedderburn Papers.

56. Quoted in *Il Vesuvio e le città vesuviane 1730–1860*, pp. 297–8.

57. VB, 14 December 1827.

58. Henry Sass, *A Journey to Rome and Naples, giving an account of the present state of society in Italy, and containing observations on the fine arts*, London, 1818, p. 187.

59. Maximilian, *Recollections*, vol. 1, p. 40.

Chapter 1. Close at Hand: The Visitors' Book and Vesuvius

1. For an earlier discussion of such books see my 'Visitors' Books and Travel Narratives: The Case of Romantic Vesuvius', *Studies in Travel Writing* 25, 3 (2023), pp. 350–75.

2. VB.

3. VB, 28 April 1828.

4. John Scott, *Sketches of France, Switzerland and Italy*, London, 1821, p. 344.

5. [Étienne de Jouy], *L'Hermite de la Chauseé d'Antin, ou Observations sur les mœurs et les usages parisiens au commencement du XIX siècle*, 2 vols, 2nd edn, Paris, 1813, vol. 1, pp. 146–50, 168, 170–1; Kevin James, 'The Album of the Fathers and the Father of all Albums: Inscribing Wonder and Loss in the Grande Chartreuse', in *Continental Tourism, Travel Writing and the Consumption of Culture*, ed. Bryan Colbert and Lucy Morrison, London, 2020, pp. 52–5.

6. Kotzebue, *Travels through Italy*, vol. 2, p. 16.

7. Ernest Wadsworth Longfellow, *Random Memories*, Boston, 1922, p. 170.

8. [Ernest Wadsworth Longfellow], *Letters of Henry Wadsworth Longfellow*, vol. 1, *(1814–1836)*, ed. Andrew Hilen, Cambridge MA, 1966, p. 259.

9. Jouy, *L'Hermite*, vol. 1, p. 168.

10. British Library, Add MS 64101 f. 66; VB, 9 October 1828.

11. Jouy, *L'Hermite*, vol. 1, p. 146.

12. Blessington, *The Idler in Italy*, vol. 2, p. 205.

13. Henry Coxe, *Picture of Italy; being a Guide to the Antiquities and Curiosities of that Classical and Interesting Country; containing sketches of Manners, Society and Customs, and an itinerary of Distances in Posts and English Miles, best Inns &c with a Minute Description of Rome, Florence, Naples, & Venice, and their Environs. In which are prefixed Directions to Travellers, and Dialogues in English, French and Italian*, London, 1815, p. 337.

14. Stendhal, *Oeuvres intimes*, Paris, 1982, vol. 1, p. 796.

15. National Library of Scotland, Ms 1542, Journal of Sir William Forbes 1792–93, f. 71.
16. [Elizabeth Wynne Fremantle], *Travels in the Two Sicilies 1817–1820*, ed. Nigel Foxell, London, 2007, p. 7.
17. Kotzebue, *Travels through Italy*, vol. 2, pp. 14–15.
18. 'Visit to Mount Vesuvius of Professor Morgenstern [1809]', *New Monthly Magazine and Universal Register* (June 1818), p. 389.
19. William Webb, *Minutes of Remarks on subjects picturesque, moral and miscellaneous, made in the course along the Rhine, and during a residence in Swisserland [sic] and Italy, in the years 1822 and 1823*, 2 vols, London, 1827, vol. 2, p. 53.
20. Joel Fineman, 'The History of the Anecdote: Fiction and Fiction 1', in *The New Historicism*, ed. H. Arram Veeser, New York, 1989, pp. 49–76 at p. 61.
21. Catherine Gallagher and Stephen Greenblatt, *Practicing New Historicism*, Chicago, 2000, p. 50.
22. Gallagher and Greenblatt, *Practicing New Historicism*, p. 49.
23. 'Spallanzani's Travels in Italy', in *A General Collection of the best and most interesting voyages and travels*, ed. John Pinkerton, 6 vols, Philadelphia, 1810–12, vol. 5, p. 62. Spallanzani is contrasting Vesuvius with the journey to Etna.
24. For visitors' books and albums see Kevin J. James and Patrick Vincent, 'The Guestbook as Historical Source', *Journal of Tourism History* 8, 2 (2016), pp. 147–66 esp. pp. 153–4.
25. See, for example, Manchester Metropolitan University Archives, Sir Harry Page Collection, album no. 100, f. 56.
26. See, for instance, Manchester Metropolitan University Archives, Page Collection, no. 39 Misses Walker, 1830, ff. 2–2v; no. 158, Anon., n.d.; no. 219, Anon., 1814–40, f. 51; no. 270, S. Ryder, 1826.
27. VB, 19 September 1827.
28. [James D. Forbes], *Life and Letters of James David Forbes*, ed. John Campbell Shairp, Anthony Adams-Reilly and Peter Guthrie Tait, London, 1873, p. 306.
29. VB, 14 May 1828. On the occasion of Dixon's sixth ascent.
30. VB, 2 July 1827. 'Kennst du das Land wo die Citronen blühn? / Und unter dunklem Laub die Gold-orangen glühn?'
31. A distinction vividly elaborated in James Buzard, *The Beaten Track: European Tourism, Literature, and the Ways to 'Culture', 1800–1918*, Oxford, 1993.
32. Carlo Ginzburg and Carlo Poni, 'The Name and the Game: Unequal Exchange and the Historiographic Marketplace', in *Microhistory and the Lost Peoples of Europe*, ed. Edward Muir and Guido Ruggiero, Baltimore, 1991, pp. 5–6.
33. As a point of comparison, John Ingamells's *A Dictionary of British and Irish Travellers in Italy, 1701–1800*, London and New Haven, 1999, which serves as the database for Stanford University's Grand Tour project, contains approximately 6,000 entries over the course of a century.
34. Captain Jousiffe, *A Road-book for Travellers in Italy*, Brussels, Paris and London, 1840, p. 131.
35. VB, 24 April 1827, 1 April 1828, 10 June 1828, 24 October 1828.
36. [Thomas Uwins], *A Memoir of Thomas Uwins, R.A. late Keeper of the Royal Galleries by Mrs Uwins with letters to his brothers during his seven years spent in Italy*, 2 vols, London, 1858, vol. 2, pp. 90–1.
37. [William Bewick], *Life and Letters of William Bewick (artist)*, ed. Thomas Landseer, 2 vols, London, 1871, vol. 2, p. 98.
38. VB, 25 April 1827, 24 September 1827, 1 November 1827, 28 March 1828.

39. VB, 25 June 1827.
40. This entire case can be followed in Geraldine Roberts, *The Angel and the Cad: Love, Loss and Scandal in Regency England*, London, 2015.
41. VB, 22 April 1827 (Rastawiecki), 12 July 1827 (Burrows), 5 August 1827 (Mülner), 12 February 1827 (Childe), 2, 9 December 1827, 28 March 1828 (Frosmont), 29 September 1828 (Läpple), 18 March 1828 (Cesa), 22 March 1828 (Klentz), 1 April 1828 (Krivtsov), 26 August 1828 (Palazzolo), 29 September 1828 (Hagendorn), 22 April 1829 (Calba), 30 August 1827 (Esten).
42. R.F. Trisco, *The Holy See and the Nascent Church in the Middle Western United States, 1826–1850*, Rome, 1962, pp. 234–5; W.B. Posey, *Frontier Mission: A History of Religion West of the Southern Appalachians*, Lexington KY, 1966, p. 260.
43. VB, 14, 25 June 1827, 15 October 1827, 18, 21 March 1828, 22 April 1828.
44. Clifford, *Routes*, p. 3.
45. VB, 8, 22 April 1827.
46. Andrew Oliver, *American Travelers on the Nile: Early US Visitors to Egypt*, Cairo, 2014, pp. 125–30.
47. 'William Arnold Bromfield', *Oxford Dictionary of National Biography*.
48. Silke Friedrich, *Johann Moritz Rugendas: Reisebilder zwichen Empirie und Empfindung*, Frankfurt, 2017.
49. VB, 17 June 1828. See Fritzche, *Stranded in the Present*, for an illuminating analysis of what he calls 'private ordeals and public dramas' in the Romantic era.
50. VB, 13, 14 March, 10 December 1827; 22 March, 25 April 1828.
51. VB, 13 February, 6 March, 15 June, 27 September 1827; 9 March 1828.
52. VB, 14 December 1827, 15 August 1829.
53. VB, 23 March 1828, 6 September 1828.
54. Northumberland Archives, ZMI B.52/3/1, Monck, 'Journal of a tour', vol. 2, 11 February 1830.
55. *Morganblatt* 134 (4 June 1828).
56. VB, 3 June 1828.
57. National Library of Scotland, Hall Mss 6327, f. 8v.
58. VB, 17 December 1827; 26 April 1828.
59. National Library of Scotland, Ms 1541, Journal of Sir William Forbes 1792–93, f. 91.
60. Joseph Forsyth, *Remarks on Antiquities, Arts, and Letters, during an excursion in Italy in the years 1802 and 1803*, London, 1813, p. 335.
61. Forsyth, *Remarks on Antiquities*, p. 420.
62. Élisabeth Vigée-Lebrun, *Souvenirs*, 2 vols, Paris, 1869, vol. 1, pp. 204–8.
63. [Catherine Wilmot], *An Irish Peer on the Continent (1801–1803), Being the Narrative of the Tour of Stephen, 2nd Earl Mount Cashell, Through France, Italy etc. as related by Catherine Wilmot*, ed. Thomas U. Sadleir, London, 1920, pp. 150–2.
64. Harriet Morton, *Protestant Vigils; or, Evening Records of a Journey in Italy, in the Years 1826 and 1827*, 2 vols, London, 1829, vol. 2, pp. 73–5.
65. Scipione Fougasse, *Chez une Femme Illustre suivi de quelques souvenirs de l'Auteur*, Paris, 1866, pp. 188–90; VB, 20 October 1827.
66. Fougasse, *Chez une Femme Illustre*, pp. 184–8.
67. Morgan, *Italy*, vol. 3, p. 168.
68. [W.T.P. Shortt], *A Visit to Milan, Florence and Rome. The Subterranean Cities Herculaneum and Pompeii, and the crater of Vesuvius in 1821. By W.T.P. Shortt, A.B. of Worcester College Oxford*, London, 1823, pp. 57–8.

69. VB, 22 April 1828: 'pour la première fois et la dernière'.
70. VB, 12 June 1827, 20 May 1828, 12 September 1828.
71. VB, 13 March 1828: 'venir ensemble'.
72. VB, 10 May 1827 (professors); 29 September 1828 (Caracciolo); 22 March 1828 (Rothschilds); 17 June 1828 (Sardinian courtiers); 25 April 1828 (Danish courtiers); 23 May 1828 (Jewish merchants); 26 August 1828 (architects); 22 March 1828 (artists).
73. VB, 19 September 1827: 'Je ne suis pas curieuse mais j'ai vue le mont avec plaisir ... il faut le voir quelle belle chose ... mais vous ne pouvez redescendre qu'avec des idées sombres. C'est beau de le voir une fois.'
74. VB, 7 June 1828 (Lee and Oakley): 'sa chère amie la Belle Milanese'.
75. VB, 2 May 1827 (Temple); 19 September 1827 (Audra); 17 December 1827 (Edwards).
76. VB, 26 September 1828: 'il nostro principale Patrono il glorioso S. Gennaro'.
77. VB, 28 September 1828 (Casoria); 29 September 1828 (Caracciolo).
78. Barbara Dawes, *La comunità inglese a Napoli*, Naples, 1988.
79. VB, 7 May 1827.
80. On these and other amenities provided specifically for an English clientele see Mariana Starke, *Information and Directions for Travellers on the Continent*, 5th edn, Paris, 1826, especially pp. 386–7; Jousiffe, *Road-book*, pp. 123–5.
81. [Francis Maceroni], *Memoirs of the Life and Adventures of Colonel Maceroni*, 2 vols, London, 1838, vol. 1, pp. 135–6; vol. 2, pp. 6–8.
82. VB, 18 June 1827; 18 March, 20 March, 27 October 1828.
83. VB, 22 March 1828.
84. VB, 27 January 1828.
85. The literature on the Grand Tour is vast; for an overview see my 'Whose Grand Tour?', in *The English Prize: The Capture of the Westmorland, An Episode of the Grand Tour*, ed. Maria Dolores Sanchez-Jaurequi Alpanes and Scott Wilcox, New Haven, 2012, pp. 45–62.
86. *Westminster Review* (3 April 1825).
87. Buzard, *The Beaten Track*, pp. 12, 83–4, 91–2.
88. The same point is made about French aristocratic travellers in Gilles Bertrand, *Le Grand Tour Revisité. Pour une archéologie du tourisme: Le Voyage des Français en Italie (milieu XVIIIe siècle–début XIXe siècle)*, Rome, 2008, p. 108.
89. These points were made as early as 1985 in John Towner's pioneering attempt to put some numbers to the literary story of the Grand Tour, but have been largely ignored by historians of Grand Tour literature. See John Towner, 'The Grand Tour: A Key Phase in the History of Tourism', *Annals of Tourist Research* 112, 3 (1985), pp. 297–333.
90. Cambridge University Library, Add Ms 8908, Crackenthorpe Papers, ff. 61–8.
91. VB, 25 April 1828 (Denmark); 17 April 1828 (Longfellow); 6 May, 26 August 1828 (Lubbock Brown); 29 December 1826 (Stuart); 12 May 1828 (Gore-Booth).
92. Martin Blocksidge, *A Life Lived Quickly: Tennyson's Friend Arthur Hallam and his Legend*, Brighton, 2011, pp. 62–3, 68–9; [James Milnes Gaskell], *An Eton Boy: Being the Letters of James Milnes Gaskell from Eton and Oxford, 1820–1830*, ed. Charles Milnes Gaskell, London, 1939, p. 136; [Arthur Henry Hallam], *The Letters of Arthur Henry Hallam*, ed. Jack Kolb, Columbus OH, 1981, pp. 181–2, 184–5, 189–91, 195–201, 204–8.
93. VB, 19, 23 March 1828.
94. 'Henry Hallam', *Oxford Dictionary of National Biography*.
95. Blocksidge, *A Life Lived Quickly*, p. 63.

96. Arthur Hallam to William Ewart Gladstone, 15 December 1827, [Hallam], *Letters of Arthur Hallam*, p. 186.
97. Blocksidge, *A Life Lived Quickly*, p. 66.
98. The affair is well covered in Blocksidge, *A Life Lived Quickly*, pp. 66–75; [Gaskell], *Eton Boy*, pp. 136–7.
99. Blocksidge, *A Life Lived Quickly*, p. 92.
100. VB, 5 March 1828 (Soult); 14 March 1827 (Wartenburg); 24 March 1828 (Taylor); 13 March 1827 (Bickerton).
101. For the British naval presence in this period see Robert Holland, *Blue-Water Empire: The British in the Mediterranean since 1800*, London, 2012.
102. VB, 16 January 1828 (*Mastiff*); 27 May 1828 (*Pelican*); 28 January 1829 (*Matilda*).
103. VB, 30 January 1827.
104. For numbers see Albert Maag, *Geschichte der Schweizertruppen in neapolitanischen Diensten 1825–1861*, Zurich, 1909, p. 62.
105. Henri Ganter, *Histoire du service militaire des regiments suisses à la solde de l'Angleterre, de Naples et de Rome*, Geneva, n.d., pp. 27 seq., 106, 110, 129, 137, 150.
106. For policing and the Swiss regiments see P. de Vallière, *Honneur et Fidelité. Histoire des Suisses au Service Étranger*, Lausanne, n.d., pp. 722 seq.
107. VB, 26 March 1828 (explosions); 20 June 1827 (imposture of guides); 29 October 1827, 29 May, 22 October 1828 (Konig brothers); 14 September 1828 (Wyder).
108. VB, 12 July 1827 (Moldinhaver): 'più Italiana che Tedesca di cuore'; 'Che perdita per la Germania'.
109. VB, 26 March 1828 (cheminée): 'pour admirer les effets de la cheminée Infernale (sense vulgaire)'; 26 March 1828 (Rigi verses).
110. VB, 6 July 1827: 'Bourgeois patricien de la ville et République de Fribourg en Suisse, actuellement Sous-lieutenant au 2 régiment Suisse de Vonderweid au service de S.M. le Roi des Deux Siciles'; 'Mon Coeur à ma belle et mon bras à mon Prince . . . Vive le Roi'.
111. See Maag, *Geschichte der Schweizertruppen*, pp. 698–9.
112. VB, 25 April 1828 (Molmer); 22 March 1828 (Moore); 13 May 1827 (Hall); 22 June 1827 (Scatena); 17 July 1828 (Lilburn); 29 April 1827 (Wilkes); 8 March 1827 (Deas); 21 September 1828 (Stapleton).
113. 'George Burrows', *Oxford Dictionary of National Biography*.
114. [James Hope], *Memoir of the late James Hope, M.D. by Mrs Hope*, London, 1843, p. 45.
115. On the complex story of William Edwards's place in the history of ethnography and concepts of race see Claude Blanckaert, 'On the Origins of French Ethnography: William Edwards and the Doctrine of Race', in *Bones, Bodies and Behavior: Essays in Behavioral Anthropology*, ed. George Stocking, Wisconsin, 1990, pp. 18–55; Elizabeth William, *The Physical and the Moral: Anthropology, Physiology, and Philosophical Medicine in France, 1750–1850*, Cambridge, 1994, pp. 224–33; Martin S. Staum, *Labeling People: French Scholars on Society, Race and Empire*, Montreal, 2003, pp. 129–34; Toby Appel, *The Cuvier-Geoffrey Debate: French Biology in the Decades before Darwin*, Oxford, 1987, pp. 215–22.
116. Accounts of Henri's life are all based on [Henri Milnes Edwards], *Notice Historique sur Henri Milnes Edwards, member de l'académie des sciences, par M. Bertelot*, Paris, 1891.
117. Leonard G. Wilson, *Charles Lyell, the Years to 1841: The Revolution in Geology*, New Haven and London, 1972, p. 228.

118. On Edwards and Costa see Rossella De Ceglie, *'L'anello mancante': L'opera di O.G. Costa nella biologica italiana del primo Ottocento*, Bari, 1999, pp. 21–5. More generally on Costa see Salvatore De Renzi, *Della vita e delle opere di O.G. Costa*, Napoli, 1868. For Salvatore De Renzi, who was also on Vesuvius, see below at 123.

119. VB, 16 January 1828.

120. 'Arnold Bromfield', *Oxford Dictionary of National Biography*.

121. For Leach's life see 'William Elford Leach', *Oxford Dictionary of National Biography*.

122. [Joseph Severn], *Joseph Severn: Letters and Memoirs*, ed. Grant F. Scott, Aldershot, 2005, pp. 600–1.

123. For De Renzi's life see Vincenzo Cappelletti-Federico Di Trocchio, 'De Renzi, Salvatore', in *Dizionario Biografico degli Italiani*.

124. Salvatore De Renzi, *Osservazioni sulla topografia-medica del Regno di Napoli: Cenni sulla topografia-medica della città di Napoli, e delle provincie di Napoli, di terra di Lavoro, ed di principato ultra*, 3 vols, Naples, 1828–30.

125. De Renzi, *Osservazioni*, vol. 2, p. 119.

126. VB, 17 October 1828: 'La meraviglia ed il terrore della Campania'.

127. De Renzi, *Osservazioni*, ch. 10: 'Luoghi prossimi alle Capitale che influsiscono sulla sua atmosfera', vol. 2, pp. 24–8.

128. VB, 7 February 1827 (Saunders); 21 March 1828 (Giamboni).

129. Giovanni Ferraro, 'Manuali di geometria elementare nella Napoli preunita', *History of Education and Children's Literature* 3, 2 (2008), pp. 103–39 at p. 132.

130. J.C. Poggendorff, *Poggendorffs biographisch-literarisches Handwörterbuch für Mathematik, Astronomie, Physik mit Geophysik, Chimie, Kristallographie und verwandte Wissensgebiete*, Leipzig, 1863, vol. 1, p. 891.

131. D.G.G. Kerr, *Sir Edmund Head: A Scholarly Governor*, Toronto, 1954, especially pp. 4–5, 237.

132. Charles Babbage, *Passages from the Life of a Philosopher*, ed. Martin Campbell-Kelly, New Brunswick NJ, 1994, p. 228.

133. British Library, Add MS 41536, ff. 92–92v.

134. Royal Society Archives, HS2 John Herschel Correspondence, vol. 2, items 215, 216, 227, 233, 236: Elizabeth Babbage to John Herschel, 8, 15 September 1827; 1 July, 10 September, 19 November 1828.

135. British Library, Add MS 41536, f. 233.

136. Babbage, *Passages*, p. 348.

137. Babbage, *Passages*, pp. 160–5, 348–9.

138. Royal Society Archives, HS2 Herschel Correspondence, vol. 2, Babbage to John Herschel, 9 May 1828 [Naples], 226. It should be added that the young Babbage was plagued by ideas of his own idleness, which he was prone to exaggerate (see for example Royal Society Archives, HS2 Herschel Correspondence, vol. 2, Babbage to Herschel [post 12 January 1814], 21).

139. Babbage, *Passages*, pp. 160–4.

140. For example, John Murray, *Handbook for Travellers in Southern Italy*, 3rd edn, London, 1858, p. 183.

141. This argument is best developed in Brian Dolan, 'Representing Novelty: Charles Babbage, Charles Lyell, and Experiments in Early Victorian Geology', *History of Science* 36 (1998), pp. 299–327.

142. Charles Babbage, *Observations on the Temple of Serapis, at Pozzuoli, near Naples, with an attempt to explain the causes of the frequent elevation and depression of large portions of the earth's surface in remote periods. And to prove that those causes continue*

in action at the present time. With a Supplement. Conjectures on the physical condition of the surface of the moon, London, 1847, pp. 22–3.

143. Babbage, *Passages*, pp. 323–4.
144. Charles Babbage, *Reflections on the Decline of Science in England, and on some of its causes*, London, 1830, pp. 81–5.
145. Frank F. Cunningham, *James Forbes: Pioneer Scottish Glaciologist*, Edinburgh, 1990, p. 2.
146. James D. Forbes, *Travels through the Alps of Savoy and other parts of the Pennine Chain with observations on the phenomena of Glaciers*, Edinburgh, 1845, pp. 5–6.
147. For note-taking as a practice see Marie-Noëlle Bourguet, 'A Portable World: The Notebooks of European Travellers (Eighteenth to Nineteenth Centuries)', *Intellectual History Review* 20, 3 (2010), pp. 377–400.
148. [Forbes], *Life and Letters*, p. 43. The list omits his final contribution on Posillipo.
149. [James D. Forbes], 'Remarks on Mount Vesuvius', *Edinburgh Journal of Science* 7, 1 (1828), p. 13. Based on his journal: University of St Andrews Archives, Forbes Mss Dep7, Box 14, Journal 2, Forbes Journal, 19 July 1826–24 November 1826, ff. 167–9.
150. Quoted in Jack Morrell and Arnold Thackray, *Gentlemen of Science: Early Years of the British Association for the Advancement of Science*, Oxford, 1981, p. 433. The campaign that Forbes organised can be followed in the same volume, pp. 431–3.
151. VB, 3 February 1827 (Weir); 3 April 1827 (Smith); 4, 6 September 1828 (Rugendas).
152. VB, 15 June 1827 (Briullov); 10 August 1828 (Havell, Williams); 14 September 1828 (Grahl, Hensel).
153. Quoted in Derrick Pritchard Webley, *Casting to the Winds: The Life and Work of Penry Williams (1802–1885)*, Aberystwyth, 1995, p. 42.
154. 'William Berwick', *Oxford Dictionary of National Biography*.
155. R. Larry Todd, *Fanny Hensel: The Other Mendelssohn*, Oxford, 2009, pp. 118–19.
156. Pierre Gassier, *Leopold Robert*, Neuchatel, 1983, p. 99; [Leopold Robert], *Leopold Robert – Marcotte d'Argenteuil Correspondance 1824–1835 Publiée par Pierre Gassier avec la collaboration de Maryse Schmidt-Surdez*, Neuchatel, n.d.; Steven Bann, 'Leopold Robert and the Afterlife of Antiquity', in *Regarding Romantic Rome*, ed. Richard Wrigley, Oxford and Berne, n.d., pp. 69–70.
157. William Hazlitt, *Criticisms on Art. 2nd Series, edited by his son*, London, 1844, p. 218.
158. *Marcotte d'Argenteuil Correspondance*, p. 20, Leopold Robert to Marcotte d'Argenteuil, 12 September 1827: 'Beaucoup d'artistes français qui étaient à Rome sont déja partis pour se trouver à l'ouverture du Salon.'
159. Richard Wrigley, *Roman Fever: Influence, Infection, and the Image of Rome, 1700–1870*, New Haven and London, 2013, especially pp. 11, 18, 25–6, 30, 32, 37–9.
160. Royal Academy Archives, Sir Thomas Lawrence Mss 5/293, Lawrence to Eastlake, 29 December 1828.
161. Royal Academy Archives, Lawrence Mss 5/308, Williams to Lawrence, 17 February 1829.
162. [Uwins], *Memoir*, vol. 1, p. 327.
163. [Uwins], *Memoir*, vol. 1, pp. 266, 280–1, 350, 379, 385.
164. [Uwins], *Memoir*, vol. 2, pp. 48–9.
165. [Severn], *Letters and Memoirs*, p. 652.
166. Pierre-Henri de Valenciennes, *Éléments de perspective practiques à l'usage des artistes*, Paris, 1799, pp. 405, 410–12, 417–19; Philip Conisbee, Sarah Faunce,

Jeremy Strick and Peter Galassi, *In the Light of Italy: Corot and Early Open-air Painting*, New Haven and London, 1996, pp. 80–1. Valenciennes also recommended that artists depict volcanoes at night.

167. [Uwins], *Memoir*, vol. 2, pp 132–4.
168. Quoted in Conisbee et al., *In the Light of Italy*, p. 189.
169. [Johan Christian Dahl], *Johan Christian Dahl 1788–1857: Life and Works*, ed. Marie Lodrup Bang, 3 vols, Oslo, [1987], vol. 2, entries 217, 218, 232, 237, 251, 256, 257, 262, 263, 270, 274, 284, 289, 296, 300, 316, 338, 393, 450, 451, 510, 1032, 1284.
170. [Franz Ludwig Catel], *Franz Ludwig Catel: Italienbilder der Romantik*, Hamburg, n.d.
171. [Uwins], *Memoir*, vol. 1, p. 301.
172. VB, 17 March 1827:

Des Vesuvs Bahn ist Anfangs steil,
Läßt nichts als Mühe blikken,
Doch weten oben föhnt ein zum Heil
Und verschaffet Euch Blikke zum Entzükken.

173. *August Kopisch: Maler, Dichter, Entdecker, Erfinder*, Berlin, [2016], p. 81.
174. For Kopisch's Italian career see Dieter Richter, 'Dichter, Künstler: Lebenskünstler – August Kopischs romantische Existenz', in *August Kopisch: Maler*, pp. 31–45.
175. *August Kopisch: Maler*, pp. 186–9.
176. Lord Napier, *Notes on Modern Painting at Naples*, London, 1855, pp. 111–19 for Vervloet's career.

Chapter 2. Guides

1. Tyne and Wear Archives, DX 985/1, Sir William Hutt of Gateshead, 'Journal of travels through Italy, Istria, Germany and Belgium', no foliation [1824].
2. See my earlier discussion in 'Visiting Vesuvius: Guides, Local Knowledge, Sublime Tourism and Science, 1760–1890', *Journal of Modern History* 93 (March 2021), pp. 1–33.
3. For Vesuvius's eruptive activity in the period see the tables in Alwyn Scarth, *Vesuvius: A Biography*, Princeton NJ, 2009, pp. 231, 258.
4. The excavation of this tradition, developed in the aftermath of the 1631 eruption, is a central theme of Sean Cocco, *Watching Vesuvius: A History of Science and Culture in Early Modern Italy*, Chicago, 2013.
5. The literature on this subject is now enormous but see Steven Shapin, 'The Invisible Technician', *American Scientist* 77 (1989), pp. 554–63 for a founding text. For a recent overview of this literature see Iwan Rhys Morus, 'Invisible Technicians, Instrument Makers, Artisans', in *A Companion to the History of Science*, ed. Bernard Lightman, Chichester, 2016, pp. 97–110. Here I am chiefly concerned with workers in the field, rather than in the laboratory.
6. Cited in Peter Hansen, *The Summits of Modern Man: Mountaineering after the Enlightenment*, Cambridge MA, 2013, p. 113.
7. Basil Hall, *Patchwork*, 3 vols, 2nd edn, London, 1841, vol. 1, p. 54.
8. Hansen, *Summits of Modern Man*, p. 96.
9. Hester Lynch Piozzi, *Observations and Reflections Made in the Course of a Journey through France, Italy and Germany*, Dublin, 1789, p. 305.
10. Pietro d'Onofri, *Elogio estemporaneo per la gloriosa memoria di Carlo III. Monarca delle Spagne e delle Indie*, Naples, 1789, p. xcviii.

11. The town's name was changed in the 1960s, doubtless to link it more closely to the tourist attraction of the excavations at Herculaneum.

12. Noah Heringman, *Sciences of Antiquity: Romantic Antiquarianism, Natural History, and Knowledge Work*, Oxford, 2013, pp. 109–13.

13. British Library, Add MS 64101, Louis Jérôme de Goujon de Thuisy narrative, f. 64.

14. Houghton Library, Harvard University, MS Fr 178, 'Lettres sur L'Italie', f. 166.

15. Heringman, *Sciences of Antiquity*, pp. 110, 112.

16. Heringman, *Sciences of Antiquity*, p. 112.

17. 'Offeso in materia di sua giurisdizione'. Relations between Pumo and Piaggio can be followed in [Piaggio], Carlo Knight, 'Un inedito di Padre Piaggio: Il diario Vesuviano 1779–1795', *Rendiconti della Accademia di archeologia, lettere e belle arti* 62 (1989–90), pp. 59–132.

18. 'Visit to Mount Vesuvius of Professor Morgenstern [1809]', *New Monthly Magazine and Universal Register* (June 1818), pp. 387–8.

19. Morton, *Protestant Vigils*, vol. 2, p. 69.

20. Mrs [Anna] Jameson, *The Diary of an Ennuyée*, Boston, 1860, p. 220.

21. Note that throughout I use the term 'visitor' or 'traveller', not 'tourist'. Though there were those whom we might now call 'tourists' – Grand or otherwise – on Vesuvius they were only one of several sorts of visitor, including Neapolitan residents (of many nationalities), and foreigners in Naples in a military, diplomatic, scientific or commercial capacity.

22. Abbé Jérôme Richard, *Description historique et critique de l'Italie, ou Nouveaux mémoires sur l'état actuel de ses gouvernements, des sciences, des arts, du commerce, de la population et de l'histoire naturelle*, 6 vols, Paris, 1766, vol. 4, pp. 424–5.

23. Louis Simond, *A Tour in Italy and Sicily*, London, 1828, pp. 420–1.

24. Damas, *Voyage en Italie*, p. 275.

25. For a similar ambiguity in a very different context see Sherry Ortner, *Life and Death on Mount Everest: Sherpas and Himalayan Mountaineering*, Princeton NJ, 1999.

26. Starke, *Information for Travellers*, p. 257.

27. VB, 25 April 1827.

28. Morton, *Protestant Vigils*, vol. 2, p. 68.

29. Beinecke Library, Yale University, Osborn D469, 'Travel Diary Anon, 1826–27', entry for 25 November 1826.

30. Babbage, *Passages*, p. 160.

31. Hall, *Patchwork*, vol. 3, p. 101.

32. [Bewick], *Life and Letters*, vol. 2, pp. 99–102.

33. Greville, *The Greville Memoirs*, vol. 1, p. 298.

34. Amélie Odier, *Mon Voyage en Italie 1811–1812*, ed. Daniela Vaj, Geneva, 1993, p. 267.

35. Shortt, *A Visit to Milan*, p. 57.

36. Royal Institution, Davy Letters Project (hereafter DLP), Humphry Davy to Teodoro Monticelli, n.d. 1822 (23 April 1822), www.davy-letters.org.uk, accessed 20 June 2018.

37. Biblioteca Nazionale, Naples, Teodoro Monticelli Ms (hereafter Monticelli Ms) M.89, Ménard de la Groye to Teodoro Monticelli, 1 September 1818. For de la Groye see https://explore.psl.eu/fr/le-magazine/focus/menard-de-la-groye-geologue-et-explorateur.

38. [Teodoro Monticelli], *Opere dell'abate Teodoro Monticelli*, 3 vols, Naples, 1841–3, vol. 2, p. 51.

39. For the importance of such intermediaries in science studies see Kapil Raj, 'Go-Betweens, Travelers, and Cultural Translators', in Bernard Lightman (ed.), *A Companion to the History of Science*, Chichester, 2016, pp. 39–57.
40. Morton, *Protestant Vigils*, vol. 2, p. 69.
41. Hall, *Patchwork*, vol. 2, pp. 180–1.
42. University of St Andrews Archives, Forbes Mss Dep7, Box 14, Journal 2, Forbes Journal, 19 July 1826–24 November 1826, f. 170.
43. *The Edinburgh Encyclopedia conducted by David Brewster LLD, FRS with the assistance of gentlemen eminent in science and literature*, 18 vols, Philadelphia, 1832, vol. 18, p. 477. Though Forbes was always generous in his acknowledgement of Madonna (and other guides), his biographer largely suppresses the guide's importance and contribution.
44. [Christian VIII], *Kong Christian VIII.s Dagbøger og Optegnelser. II 1. halvbind 1815–1821*, ed. Albert Fabritius, Finn Friis and Else Kornerup, Copenhagen, 1973, 26–7 May 1820; Buckingham, *Private Diary*, vol. 1, pp. 313–14.
45. *Opere dell'abate Teodoro Monticelli*, vol. 2, p. 120.
46. Quoted in Adriana Pignatelli Mangoni and Vincenzo Cabianca, *Viaggio tra i Vulcani d'Italia e di Francia tra Illuminismo e Romanticismo*, Naples, n.d., p. 134.
47. See, for example, 'Drifting and Dreamings Part II', *Dublin University Magazine* 18, 105 (1841), p. 273.
48. *The Times* (19 January 1835); *Blackburn Standard* (28 January 1835); *Morning Post* (25 September 1834).
49. 'Sir Basil Hall', *Oxford Dictionary of National Biography*.
50. Hall, *Patchwork*, vol. 3, pp. 86, 90.
51. Hall, *Patchwork*, vol. 3, p. 93.
52. Hall, *Patchwork*, vol. 3, pp. 93–4.
53. Hall, *Patchwork*, vol. 3, p. 98.
54. Hall, *Patchwork*, vol. 3, p. 98.
55. In 1824 a ducat was worth 3 shillings 9 pence in pounds sterling; there were 10 carlini to a ducat, and 10 grane to a carlino. Labourers engaged in harvesting and viticulture earned between 20 and 25 grane a day; field hands, if they were involved in any supervision, might make 30 grane; building workers, especially those with more skills, were better paid at 40 grane a day. (R. Romano, *Prezzi, Salari e Servizi a Napoli nel secolo XVIII (1734–1806)*, Milan, 1965, pp. 23, 32, 36.)
56. *Galignani's Traveller's Guide Through Italy*, p. 474; Starke, *Information for Travellers*, p. 257.
57. Hall, *Patchwork*, vol. 3, p. 101.
58. 'Gens robustes et accoutumés à cet exercice'. P.C. Briand, *Les Jeunes Voyageurs en Europe, ou Description Raisonnée des divers pays compris dans cette Partie du Monde*, 5 vols, Paris, 1827, vol. 2, p. 113.
59. Archivio di Stato Napoli, 1809 catasto provvisorio, secondo versamento, fascicolo 933.
60. Charles de Brosses, *Lettres familières écrites d'Italie en 1739 et 1740*, 2 vols, Paris, 1885, vol. 1, p. 352.
61. [Piaggio], Knight, 'Un inedito di padre Piaggio', 120. She was trying to counteract the powers of San Gennaro who protected the Neapolitans from eruptions.
62. Buckingham, *Private Diary*, vol. 1, p. 307.
63. Thomas Jefferson Hogg, *Two Hundred and Nine Days; or, the Journal of a Traveller on the Continent*, 2 vols, London, 1827, vol. 2, p. 55.

64. [Bartholdy, Felix Mendelssohn], *Letters of Felix Mendelssohn Bartholdy from Italy and Switzerland*, trans. Lady Wallace, New York and Boston, 1866, p. 143.
65. [Crombet, Paul], *Les Souvenirs d'Italie de Paul Crombet, officer belge de la marine royale des Pays-Bas (1817–26)*, ed. Vicomte Charles de Terlinden, Brussels, 1941, p. 42.
66. Jameson, *Diary of an Ennuyée*, p. 224.
67. James Edward Smith, *Sketches of a Tour on the Continent*, 3 vols, London, 1807, vol. 2, p. 121.
68. Odier, *Mon Voyage*, p. 266.
69. Boissier de Gasparin, *Voyage d'une ignorante*, pp. 297–305.
70. [Crombet], *Les Souvenirs d'Italie*, pp. 36–7.
71. [Crombet], *Les Souvenirs d'Italie*, pp. 38–9.
72. *Notes on Naples and its Environs*, p. 215.
73. Jameson, *Diary of an Ennuyée*, pp. 222–3.
74. John Owen, *Travels into different parts of Europe in the years 1791 and 1792 with familiar remarks on Places-Men-and Manners*, London, 2 vols, 1796, vol. 2, p. 107.
75. Morton, *Protestant Vigils*, vol. 2, p. 73.
76. [Uwins], *Memoir*, vol. 1, pp. 301–2.
77. Waldie, *Sketches descriptive of Italy*, vol. 3, pp. 168–9.
78. The fullest account of this famous incident is Teodoro Monticelli, *Notizia di una escursione al Vesuvio,e dell'avvenimento che vi ebbe luogo il giorno 16 Gennajo; in cui il francese Coutrel si precipitò in una di quelle nuove bocche*, Naples, 1821. The Visitors' Book entry was reproduced in the *European Magazine*. See 'Letter from Dr. Gimbernat respecting a French traveller who perished in the crater of Vesuvius', *European Magazine* 80 (1821), p. 361.
79. VB, 20 June 1827.
80. Many visitors commented on the unwillingness of the Swiss to use guides. See, inter alia, Odier, *Mon Voyage*, p. 159.
81. National Library of Scotland, Ms 1542, Journal of Sir William Forbes 1792–93, ff. 91–9.
82. Mattieu Magne, '"Mon Dieu que ce Vésuve est beau!" Le récit de l'ascension dans le journal d'un aristocrate de Bohême au cours de son voyage de 1816', *Cahiers de la Méditerranée* 89 (December 2014), p. 291.
83. VB, 10 March 1828.
84. VB, 23 April 1827.
85. VB, 4 July 1827.
86. VB, 30 August, 20 September 1827.
87. 'Fortement blesse . . . souvenir de moi mes amis': VB, 16 January 1828.
88. VB, 29 June 1828.
89. Ferraro, *A New Guide of Naples*, p. 426.
90. Chateaubriand's account was published in English in *New Monthly Magazine* 3 (1815), pp. 315–16.
91. These are precisely the instructions given to Werner Herzog by the Cambridge geologist Clive Oppenheimer, during the filming of Oppenheimer and Herzog's *Into the Inferno* (2016).
92. Hall, *Patchwork*, vol. 3, pp. 95–7.
93. [William Maclure], *The European Journals of William Maclure*, Philadelphia, 1988, pp. 495, 497.
94. Monticelli Ms P.35, Joseph Barclay Pentland to Teodoro Monticelli, 23 February 1824.
95. Bunbury, *A Visit to the Catacombs*, p. 25.

96. *Morning Chronicle* (15 October 1857).
97. P.M. Kalla-Bishop, *Italian Railways*, Newton Abbot, 1971, p. 16; Carlo Ilarione Petitti, *Delle strade ferrate italiane e del migliore ordinamento di esse. Cinque discorsi*, Capolago, 1845, p. 127.
98. Petitti, *Delle strade ferrate*, p. 131.
99. Among other press reports, *Elgin and Morayshire Chronicle* (12 April 1850).
100. *Glasgow Herald* (23 March 1864).
101. John Murray, *A Handbook for Travellers in Southern Italy Being a Guide for the Continental Portion of the Kingdom of the Two* Sicilies, London, 2nd edn, 1855, p. 201, recommending Pasquale. The third edition of 1858 recommends Vincenzo, the eighth edition of 1883 (p. 191) recommends Giovanni, while the ninth edition of 1892 (pp. 96–8) makes no mention of any guide by name and focuses on the services provided by Thomas Cook and Sons.
102. For Wreford see his obituary in *The Times* (29 March 1892).
103. *The Times* (22 November 1867), reprinted in *Leeds Mercury* (3 December 1867).
104. *Athenaeum* (25 June 1859).
105. 'Raccomandazioni per migliorare in futuro la Nomenclatura', *Atti Quinta Unione scientifica italiana 1843*, p. 823.
106. Federigo Furchheim (ed.), *Bibliografia del Vesuvio. Compilata e corredata di note critiche estratte dai più autorevoli scrittori vesuviani*, Cambridge, 2011, p. 42.
107. *The Times* (22 November 1867).
108. John Phillips, *Vesuvius*, Oxford, 1869, p. 127.
109. *The Times* (8 April 1868). Wreford had obviously talked at length to the two Britons. His help is acknowledged in Phillips, *Vesuvius*, p. viii.
110. *The Times* (14 February 1868).
111. *Athenaeum* (1 January 1859).
112. *The Times* (2 January 1868).
113. *Lloyd's Weekly News* (20 May 1855); *Lady's Newspaper* (26 May 1855).
114. *Englishwoman's Review and Home Paper* (12 June 1858).
115. *The Times* (11 June 1858).
116. Auricchio and Sarnataro, 'Un'escursione al Vesuvio', pp. 211–14.
117. *The Times* (19 October 1868).
118. Paul Smith, 'Thomas Cook & Sons Vesuvian railway', *Japan Railway and Transport Review* (March 1998), pp. 10–11.
119. *Nature* (24 January 1889).
120. Letter to *The Times*, published 9 December 1886.

Chapter 3. On the Mountain, On the Road: Sociability and Travel

1. Although Frankenstein retains his determination to pursue his goals to the last, while Walton eventually accedes to his crew and abandons his quest.
2. [Borel], *Lettres écrites*, p. 1.
3. James Augustin Galiffe, *Italy and its Inhabitants: An account of a tour through that country in 1816 and 1817*, 2 vols, London, 1820, vol. 2, p. 292.
4. Morton, *Protestant Vigils*, vol. 2, p. 112.
5. British Library, Add MS 61937 Fazakerley Papers, Fox to Fazakerley, 15 February, 8 October 1825.
6. The printed version of Buckingham's private diary excluded much of this material but the manuscript version in the Huntington Library, Stowe Mss ST88, makes clear his emotionally fraught state.

7. At least according to Google Ngram.
8. Morton, *Protestant Vigils*, vol. 1, p. 1.
9. Colomb, *Journal*, pp. 167–8.
10. 'Mon ami, je brûle de te revoir et de te presser sur mon Coeur': VB, 31 March 1828.
11. VB, 20 May 1828 (Grutther); 13 February 1828 (Boncaglia); 25 September (Cantoni); 19 March 1828 (*compagnia*); 27 May 1828 (Puci); 29 May, 22 October 1828 (Konig); 29 October 1827 (Garzia); 22 October 1827 (*tutti e tre*); 19 March 1828 (Frediani); 30 January 1828 (*bonne compagnie*).
12. For Pilla's life and career see Bruno D'Argenio, 'Leopoldo Pilla (1805–1848): A Young Combatant Who Lived for Geology and Died for his Country', *Geographical Society of America*, Special Paper 411 (2006), pp. 211–23.
13. Leopoldo Pilla, *Notizie storiche della mia vita quotidiana a cominciare dal 1mo gennaio 1830 in poi*, ed. Massimo Discenza, Venafro, 1996, pp. 218, 345.
14. Pilla, *Notizie storiche*, pp. 218, 345.
15. Daniel Solander was a Swedish botanist who accompanied Banks on many of his journeys, and acted as his secretary. Charles Greville was Hamilton's nephew and heir, who introduced him to his mistress Emma Lyon/Hart, later Hamilton's second wife. See [Joseph Banks], *The Scientific Correspondence of Sir Joseph Banks*, ed. Neil Chambers, 6 vols, London, 2007, vol. 1, item 130.
16. Beinecke Library, Yale University, Osborn 12794, Samuel Rogers Correspondence, Samuel Rogers to Sarah Rogers, Naples and Rome, 26–31 March 1822.
17. David Constantine, *Fields of Fire: A Life of Sir William Hamilton*, London, 2001, p. 38.
18. John Moore, *A View of Society and Manners in Italy*, 2 vols, 2nd edn, London, 1779, vol. 2, p. 215.
19. VB, 26 March 1828:

Wie anders war's, als mir von Rigi's Rücken
das Schweizerland sich aufthat meinen Blicken
da hat ein Vulkan mir das Herz durchwallt:
Nun spricht der Vesuv mir, zu dem ich klimm
Mir laut ins Herz mit seiner Freiheitsstimm - -
Mein Geist ist müd', mein Herz ist kalt!

20. The Swiss were not the only ones: VB, 8 March 1827: Mr William Goff 'Went up in 14 minutes 39 sec & ¼ & came down in 1 minute 13 sec & ¾!!!!'; VB, 25 March 1827: Mr Edward Every [Eggington, Co Derby], 20th Regiment, Captain [George] Campbell [92nd regiment], Captain Macpherson, Late of the Royal, Mr J Campbell, Mr C Story 'Ascended from the base of the cone to the crater in 28 minutes, descended in three'.
21. VB, 23 March 1828.
22. Buckingham, *Private Diary*, vol. 1, p. 271.
23. De Staël, *Corinne*, Book XI, chapter 2.
24. VB, 11 March 1828, 'Diverses eruptions'; 29 June 1828, 'Love conquers all'; 9, 13 March 1828 (Pouget).
25. Captain W.H. Armstrong, *Lays of Love*, London, [1832], p. 53.
26. Quoted in Constantine, *Fields of Fire*, p. 60.
27. Johann Wolfgang Goethe, *Italian Journey*, ed. and trans. Elizabeth Meyer & W.H. Auden, London, 1982, pp. 324–5.
28. VB, 24 July 1828 (Gouhenant); 31 August 1827 (Morandini).
29. The watercolour is reproduced in *August Kopisch: Maler*, pp. 112–13.

30. Printed in *August Kopisch: Maler*, pp. 110–11.
31. Kopisch, 'Seiner Königlichen Hoheit dem Kronprinzen von Preussen', vol. 2, pp. 3–7:

Herauf bemüh'n die Last der Erdenleiber,
Wo auch Du kamest fröhlich angeritten
Ich kehr' zurück, wo Deutsche, Franken, Britten

Auf einem Thier, das ungern folgt dem Treiber
Zum allerweltlichsten der Eremiten,
Der allen Reisenden ein frommer Räuber,
Der, niemals einsam, Thränen flaschenweise
Verkauft um stündlich wandelbare Preise.

Hier prangt, inmitten herrlicher Gefilde,
Ein Bild, das Dich erfüllt mit sanftem Triebe:
Du ziehst es vor jedwedem andern Bilde
Dem weit zurück ein jedes Nachbild bliebe!
Du schaust entzückt. Die allgewalt'ge Milde
Mit Nachtigallensehnsucht lockt zu Liebe
Dich sanft zurück bis in die Winterwolke
Zu deiner hohen Frau, zum treuen Volke!

So töne laut beim hohen Freudenmale
Ein Lebehoch dem hohen Gast der Höhe,
Elisabeth! Im Klange der Pokale,
Die glücklich Ihn zurückersehnet sehe!
Die mit der Liebe allerreinsten Schaale
Sein harret am umschneiten Tegern-Seee,
In dem nicht mehr die klaren Silberwellen
Wie hier im Golf um alle Borde schwellen!

32. Che giornata fortunata
Su' quest' Eremo passai
Fu eccellente la frittata
Ch'il Romita ci donò
Sig. Ant. Assanti.

33. John James Blunt, *Vestiges of Ancient Manners and Customs Discoverable in Modern Italy and Sicily*, London, 1823, pp. 292–3.
34. [Uwins], *Memoir*, vol. 2, p. 48. For Thomas Eskine's life see *Oxford Dictionary of National Biography*.
35. James L. Osen, *Prophet and Peacemaker: The life of Adolphe Monod*, Lanham, MD, 1984.
36. His state of mind can be followed in his letters of the period: Adolphe Monod, *Choix de Lettres à sa Famille et des Amis*, 3rd edn, Paris, 1885, pp. 1–16.
37. *Letters of Thomas Erskine of Linlathen from 1840 to 1870*, ed. William Hanna, Edinburgh, 1877, p. 106.
38. Quoted in Douglas W. Freshfield, *The Life of Horace Benédict de Saussure*, London, 1920, p. 128.
39. [Countess Blessington], *The Literary Life and Correspondence of the Countess of Blessington*, ed. R.R. Madden, 3 vols, London, 1855, vol. 2, p. 325.

40. John Griscom, *A Year in Europe Comprising a Journal of Observations . . . in 1818 and 1819*, 2 vols, New York, 1825, vol. 1, p. 203.
41. Monticelli Ms A.40, 52, 56.
42. *The Letters of Henry Arthur Hallam*, ed. Jack Kolb, Columbus OH, 1981, p. 214.
43. Colomb, *Journal*, pp. 167–8.
44. Matthews, *Diary of an Invalid*, pp. 171–2.
45. *Mémoires Inédits de Lamartine, 1790–1815*, Paris, 1870, p. 168; Hector Berlioz, *Voyage Musical en Allemagne et en Italie*, 2 vols, Paris, 1844, vol. 2, pp. 175–80; David Cairns, *Berlioz 1803–1832: The Making of an Artist*, London, 1989, pp. 463–7.
46. James Johnson, *A Change of Air, or the Pursuit of Health; An Autumnal Excursion through France, Switzerland and Italy in the year 1829*, London, 1831, p. 223.
47. Thomas Hill (ed.), *Letters and Memoir of the Late Walter Augustus Shirley, D.D*, London, 1849, pp. 77–8.
48. David Hume, *Essays, Moral, Political and Literary*, ed. Eugene F. Miller, Indianapolis, 1987, p. 197. Hume, as he stressed, allowed a fair amount of flexibility in his analysis.
49. 'The Ethics of Friendship', *Cornhill Magazine* 10 (1864).
50. Hill (ed.), *Letters and Memoir of Shirley*, p. 80.
51. Moore, *View of Society and Manners*, vol. 2, p. 495.
52. Moore, *View of Society and Manners*, vol. 1, p. 459.
53. On Moore see my 'Between Distance and Sympathy: Dr John Moore's Philosophical Travel Writing', *Modern Intellectual History* 11, 3 (2014), pp. 655–75.
54. William Berrian, *Travels in France and Italy in 1817 and 1818*, New York, 1821, pp. 365, 130, 192.
55. VB, 14 May 1828: 'Plus je vis l'étranger, plus j'aimai ma patria'. Cf. a French signatory, 30 September 1828: 'Plus j'ai vu des Pays plus que j'aime ma patrie'.
56. Beinecke Library, Yale University, Osborn D293, Notebook of Sir William Gell, f. 22v.
57. Webb, *Minutes of Remarks*, vol. 1, p. 373.
58. Webb, *Minutes of Remarks*, vol. 1, p. 311.
59. Colomb, *Journal*, p. 168.
60. Griscom, *A Year in Europe*, vol. 1, pp. 248, 286.
61. Webb, *Minutes of Remarks*, vol. 1, p. 85.
62. Marquis de Sade, *Journey to Italy*, ed. and trans. James A. Steintrager, Toronto, 2020, p. 189.
63. Waldie, *Sketches descriptive of Italy*, vol. 3, p. 136.
64. VB, 31 March 1828: 'Gentlemen je suis fâché de vous dire que [next line crossed through] de plaindre de la parcimonie des anglais. Moi, qui vous connois, je m'en suis point etonné sachant que la plupart de ceux qui voyagent la font par économie. Au moine payer comme les autres, pour soutenir, par la sacrifice de quelques carlins, l'honneur de la old ingland.'
65. VB, 5 March 1828.
66. VB, 29 June 1828.
67. VB, 7 June 1828.
68. For the Rothschilds in Naples see Francesco Barbagallo, 'The Rothschilds in Naples', *Journal of Modern Italian Studies* 5 (2000), pp. 294–309, and Marco Rovinello, 'Un grande banchiere in una piccola piazza: Carl Mayer Rothschild e il credito commerciale nel Regno delle Due Sicilie', *Società e Storia* 110 (2005), pp. 705–39.

Chapter 4. Vesuvius and the Sublime: Sublime Tourism, Aesthetic Effects and Science

1. William Otter, *The Life and Remains of Edward Daniel Clarke, Professor of Mineralogy in the University of Cambridge*, 2 vols, London, 1825, vol. 1, pp. 144–6.
2. Quoted in Jeremy Black, *Italy and the Grand Tour*, New Haven and London, 2003, p. 55.
3. Hugh Blair, *Lectures on Rhetoric and Belles Lettres*, 2 vols, London, 1783, vol. 1, pp. 47–8.
4. William Coxe, *Travels in Switzerland. In a Series of Letters to William Melmouth, Esq.*, 3 vols, London, vol. 3, p. 71.
5. Patrick Brydone, *A Tour Through Sicily and Malta. In a Series of letters to William Beckford, Esq. of Somerly in Suffolk*, 2 vols, Dublin 1780, vol. 1, p. 132. His description runs from pp. 132 to 144.
6. Cian Duffy, *The Landscapes of the Sublime, 1700–1830: Classic Ground*, Basingstoke and New York, 2013, p. 69. But see Alessa Johns, 'Representing Vesuvius: Northern European Tourists and the Napoleonic Culture of War', in her *Bluestocking Feminism and British-German Cultural Transfer, 1750–1837*, Ann Arbor, 2014, pp. 88–120, on the refusal of many women to share this sublime moment.
7. Douglas W. Freshman, *Life of Horace Benedict de Saussure*, London, 1920, p. 202.
8. Voltaire, *Oeuvres Complètes*, ed. T. Besterman et al., 147 vols, Geneva, 1968–2022, vol. 124, D.18429.
9. McCallam, *Volcanoes*, p. 233.
10. Noah Heringman, *Romantic Rocks, Aesthetic Geology*, Ithaca NY, 2004, p. 32; McCallam, *Volcanoes*, pp. 113–16 for a fascinating discussion of the transgressive properties of lava.
11. Quoted in Hansen, *The Summits of Modern Man*, p. 79.
12. On Shelley and Mont Blanc see Nigel Leask, 'Mont Blanc's Mysterious Voice: Shelley and Huttonian Earth Science', in *The Third Culture: Literature and Science*, ed. Elinor S. Shaffer, Berlin, 1998, pp. 182–203.
13. Hansen, *The Summits of Modern Man*, p. 80.
14. Waldie, *Sketches descriptive of Italy*, vol. 3, pp. 164–5.
15. The series were delivered in 1805, 1806, 1808, 1809 and 1811: [Humphry Davy], *Humphry Davy on Geology: The 1805 Lectures for the General Audience*, ed. and intro. Robert Siegfried and Robert H. Dott Jr, Madison WI, 1980, p. xiv.
16. His description is reproduced in Grell, *Herculanum et Pompéi*, p. 183.
17. Kotzebue, *Travels through Italy*, vol. 2, p. 11; VB, 28 March, 18 July 1828; Élisabeth Vigée-Lebrun, *Souvenirs 1755–1842*, ed. Geneviève Haroche-Buzinac, Paris, 2008, p. 80; Hamilton to Greville, 10 August 1779, *The Collection of the Autograph Letters and Historical Documents formed by Alfred Morrison*, 2nd series, 1882–93, *The Hamilton and Nelson Papers*, vol. 1, *1756–1797*, [London], 1893, p. 59.
18. [Martin Sherlock], *Letters from an English Traveller Martin Sherlock Esq. translated from the French original printed at Geneva*, London, 1780, p. 35.
19. Piozzi, *Observations and Reflections*, p. 307.
20. Goethe, *Italian Journey*, p. 206.
21. VB, 23 March 1827 (Gillman and Goff families): 'All for the third time having descended into the crater all highly delighted.'
22. VB, 12 July 1827: 'Doch später führt Endlich zur Freud/Und endlich zum Enzücken'.
23. VB, 20 January 1828 (Clifford); 25 October 1828 (Gartley); 22 March 1828 (during an eruption when most of the hyperbolic comments were made).

24. Alfred Driou, *Naples, les magnificences de son golfe et les curiosités de ses rivages*, Limoges, 1862, p. 157.

25. [Edmund Burke], *The Writings and Speeches of Edmund Burke*, vol. 1, *The Early Writings*, ed. T.O. McLoughlin, James T. Boulton and William B. Todd, Oxford, 1997, p. 217.

26. Morgan, *Italy*, vol. 3, pp. 167–8.

27. Immanuel Kant, *Critique of Judgment*, trans. James Creed Meredith, rev. Nicholas Walker, Oxford, 2007, para. 28.

28. Maximilian, *Recollections*, p. 103.

29. McCallam, *Volcanoes*, pp. 120–3.

30. Jameson, *Diary of an Ennuyée*, p. 213.

31. Kant, *Critique of Judgment*, para. 29.

32. James Hutton, 'Theory of the Earth', *Transactions of the Royal Society of Edinburgh* I (1788), p. 275.

33. 'Les volcans doivent être regardés comme les soupiraux de la terre, ou comme les cheminées par lesquelles elles se débarassent des matieres embraseés qui dévorent son sein . . . Les volcans sont donc un bienfait de la nature.'

34. *Humphry Davy on Geology*, pp. 136, 139.

35. Quoted in Andrew Ashfield and Peter de Bolla (eds), *The Sublime: A Reader in British Eighteenth-century Aesthetic Theory*, Cambridge, 1996, p. 240.

36. *Humphry Davy on Geology*, p. 13.

37. Emilie Beck-Saiello, *Le Chevalier Volaire: un peintre français à Naples au XVIIIe siècle*, Naples, 2004.

38. The patrons can be followed in Volaire's catalogue raisonné produced by Emilie Beck-Saiello, *Pierre Jacques Volaire 1729–1799 dit le Chevalier Volaire*, Paris, 2010.

39. See, notably, the outstanding analysis of Susan M. Sivard, 'Upheaval and Transformation: The Volcano in American and European Art, 1765–1865', PhD thesis, Columbia University, 2011, pp. 6–7, 45–69. My account replicates many of her arguments.

40. Another version of the painting, purchased from Cacault in 1810, is in the Musée des Beaux Arts in Nantes.

41. British Museum, Add Ms 40714, f. 47, Matthew Maty to Sir William Hamilton, 5 July 1768. Quoted in Ian Jenkins and Kim Sloan (eds), *Vases and Volcanoes: Sir William Hamilton and his Collections*, London, 1996, p. 68. For an excellent account of the relations between the enlightened savant and the sublime see David McCallam, 'Exploring Volcanoes in the Late French Enlightenment: The Savant and the Sublime', *Journal of Eighteenth-century Studies* 29 (2006), pp. 47–59.

42. Bent Sorensen, 'Sir William Hamilton's Vesuvian Apparatus', *Apollo* 159 (2004), pp. 50–8.

43. Abbé C. Chevalier, *Naples Le Vésuve et Pompéi*, 4th edn, Tours, 1887, p. 117.

44. [Hester Lynch Piozzi], *Glimpses of Italian Society in the 18th Century, from the Journal of Mrs Piozzi*, London, 1892, p. 251.

45. The following discussion draws heavily on Lorraine Daston, 'Observation and Enlightenment', in *Scholars in Action: The Practice of Knowledge and the Figure of the Savant in the 18th Century*, ed. Andre Holenstein, Hubert Steinke and Martin Huber, 2 vols, Amsterdam, 2013, vol. 2, pp. 657–77.

46. Saussure was a harsh critic. Greville's mineral collection, with more than 15,000 items, was sold at his death to the British Museum for over £13,000.

47. [John Playfair], *The Works of John Playfair Esq., with a Memoir of the Author*, 4 vols, Edinburgh, 1822, vol. 1, p. 122.

48. Humphry Davy, *Discourse Introductory to a Course of Chemistry*, London, 1802, p. 16.
49. Humphry Davy, *Collected Works*, ed. John Davy, 9 vols, London, 1839–40, vol. 8, p. 308.
50. Royal Institution, HD12/1123, quoted in Richard Holmes, *The Age of Wonder: How the Romantic Generation Discovered the Beauty and Terror of Science*, London, 2008, pp. 355–6.

Chapter 5. Vesuvius: Travellers and Tourists in a Shifting Ecology

1. These changes are best followed in Antonio Nazzaro, *Il Vesuvio: Storia eruttiva e teorie vulcanologiche*, Naples, 1997.
2. Quoted in Scarth, *Vesuvius*, p. 236.
3. Renato Fucini, *Napoli a Occhio Nudo. Lettere ad un Amico*, Florence, 1878, pp. 121–38.
4. *The Sunday at Home: A Family Magazine for Sabbath Reading* 31 (1897).
5. *The Quiver* (1892), p. 47; *Saturday Review* (21 September 1878).
6. United Nations World Tourism Organization, Statistics of Tourism: https://www.unwto.org/statistics.
7. Clifford, *Routes*, p. 3. Another anthropologist, Tim Ingold, makes a similar point in slightly different language: 'To reach a place, you need cross no boundary, but you must follow some kind of path. Thus there can be no places without paths, along which people arrive and depart; and no paths without places, that constitute their destinations and points of departure.' Tim Ingold, *The Perception of the Environment: Essays on Livelihood, Dwelling and Skill*, London, 2022, p. 253.
8. Chris Rojek and John Urry, *Touring Cultures: Transformations of Travel and Theory*, London, 1997, pp. 1–3; John Urry, *Sociology Beyond Societies: Mobilities in the Twenty-first Century*, London, 2000, p. 50; Urry, 'Social Networks, Travel and Talk', *British Journal of Sociology* 54, 3 (2003), pp. 155–75. See also the comments in Adrian Franklin and Mike Crang, 'The Trouble with Tourism and Travel Theory?', *Tourist Studies* 1, 1 (2001), pp. 5–22.

Chapter 6. Vesuvius and Naples in Time, Space and History

1. Quoted in Shef Rogers, 'Enlarging the Prospects of Happiness: Travel Reading and Writing', in *The Cambridge History of the Book in Britain, vol. 5, 1695–1830*, ed. Michael F. Suarez and Michael L. Turner, Cambridge, 2010, p. 781.
2. Bertrand, *Le Grand Tour Revisité*, especially p. 69.
3. 'Ce qu'il y a de plus élégant sur l'Italie est le voyage du Président Dupaty, et de plus complet, celui de M. Lalande'. [Auguste Creuzé de Lesser], *Voyage en Italie et en Sicile, fait en MDCCCI et MDCCCII, par M. Creuzé de Lesser, Membre du Corps Legislatif*, Paris, 1806, p. xi.
4. Jameson, *Diary of an Ennuyée*, p. 120.
5. Northumberland Archives, 324/12, William Ord Diary 1814–1815.
6. J.G. Lemaistre, *Travels after the Peace of Amiens, through France and Switzerland, Italy and Germany*, 3 vols, London, 1806, vol. 1, p. 404. Using language employed by many others.
7. [Thomas Roscoe], *The Tourist in Italy by Thomas Roscoe illustrated with drawings by J.D. Harding*, 2 vols, London, 1832, vol. 2, p. 175.
8. Forsyth, *Remarks on Antiquities*, p. 283.

9. Jean Henry Westphal, *Guide pour accompagner la carte des environs de Naples*, Rome, 1828, pp. 5–6. 'Cependant, celui qui admire la belle nature, et parcourt de tous côtés et sans plan précis, ces campagnes, trouvera une quantité immense d'Objets, de sites et de points de vue enchanteurs, qu'il est a peine possible de rencontrer dans aucun pays du monde. C'est la vraie jouissance que présente Naples, et qu'on est à même de procurer au milieu [sic] des richesses inépuisables: la nature a tout fait; les ouvrages des hommes, tant anciens que modernes sont, à quelques exceptions près à peine dignes d'une grande attention.'

10. [Roscoe], *The Tourist in Italy*, p. 207.

11. Tyne and Wear Archives, DX 985/1, Sir William Hutt of Gateshead, 'Journal of travels through Italy, Istria, Germany and Belgium', no foliation [1824].

12. Elizabeth Frances Batty, *Italian Scenery from Drawings Made in 1817*, London, 1820, p. 128.

13. Cambridge University Library, Add Ms 8908, Crackenthorpe Papers, f. 66, William Crackenthorpe to his mother, 10 February 1815.

14. *Galignani's Traveller's Guide Through Italy*, p. 514.

15. Chloe Chard, *Tristes Plaisirs: A Critical Reader of the Romantic Grand Tour*, Manchester, 2014, p. 13.

16. Swinburne, *Travels*, vol. 1, p. xvii.

17. Charles Pinot Duclos, *Voyage en Italie, ou Considérations sur l'Italie*, Paris, 1791, p. 120: 'Ces lieux ont été décrits dans un si grand nombre d'ouvrages que je n'en dirai rien, sinon que je les parcours avec beaucoup de plaisir.'

18. Hogg, *Two Hundred and Nine Days*, vol. 1, p. viii.

19. See the more extensive account by Kim Sloan in *Alexander and John Robert Cozens: The Poetry of Landscape*, New Haven and London, 1986, especially. pp. 56–60. Sloan emphasises Alexander Cozens's concern to use this sort of analysis to develop a landscape of 'virtue'.

20. Johnson, *Change of Air*, p. 204.

21. World Cat lists these French editions, published in Zurich, Paris, Geneva, Basel and London. In addition there was an English edition of 1818, and several editions in German after its original publication in 1793.

22. J.G. Ebel, *Manuel du Voyageur en Suisse*, 3rd edn, 3 vols, Zurich, 1817, vol. 1, p. 9.

23. [Charlotte Smith], *The Collected Letters of Charlotte Smith*, ed. Judith Phillips Stanton, Bloomington, 2003, p. 105.

24. Jameson, *Diary of an Ennuyée*, p. 321.

25. [Creuzé de Lesser], *Voyage en Italie et en Sicile*, p. 96: 'L'Europe finit à Naples, et même elle y finit assez mal.'

26. John Davis, 'Casting off the "Southern Problem": or the Peculiarities of the South Reconsidered', in *Italy's 'Southern Question': Orientalism in One Country*, ed. Jane Schneider, Oxford, 1998, p. 205.

27. Quoted in Nelson Moe, *The View from Vesuvius: Italian Culture and the Southern Question*, Berkeley and Los Angeles, 2006, p. 16.

28. This explains the frequent comparison, made for example by Sir William Hamilton, between the Neapolitan poor and the inhabitants of Tahiti. Both were seen as able to feed themselves without engaging in hard labour, a circumstance that clearly unnerved Enlightenment thinkers.

29. Waldie, *Sketches descriptive of Italy*, vol. 3, p. 36.

30. Forsyth, *Remarks on Antiquities*, p. 293.

31. Morgan, *Italy*, vol. 3, p. 153.

32. Moe, *The View from Vesuvius*, p. 17.

33. Melissa Calaresu, 'From the Street to the Stereotype: Urban Space, Travel and the Picturesque in Late Eighteenth-century Naples', *Italian Studies* 62 (2007), pp. 189–203; Calaresu, 'Collecting Neapolitans: The Representation of Street Life in Late Eighteenth-century Naples', in Melissa Calaresu and Helen Hills, *New Approaches to Naples, c.1500–c.1800: The Power of Place*, Farnham, 2013, pp. 175–202.

34. Lucio Fino, *Gouaches napoletane nelle collezioni private*, Grimaldi, Naples, 1998; Giancarlo Alisio, Pier Andrea De Rosa and Paolo Emilio Trastulli, *Napoli Com'Era nelle Gouaches del Sette e Ottocento*, 5th edn, Rome, 2004.

35. Napier, *Notes on Modern Painting*, p. 163.

36. *Napoli e i Luoghi Celebri delle sue Vicinanze*, 2 vols, Naples, 1845, vol. 2, statistical appendix, p. xvii. The book was published by the government and was intended to promote the Kingdom of Naples at the time of the congress.

37. [Edmund Burke], *The Correspondence of Edmund Burke*, 10 vols, Cambridge and Chicago, 1958–78, vol. 3, p. 351.

38. Johannes Fabian, *Time and the Other: How Anthropology Makes its Object*, New York, 1983.

39. J.M. Degérando, *The Observation of Savage People*, trans. F.C.T. Moore, London, 1969, p. 63.

40. See, for example, his strictures on the English in his *The Autobiography of an Italian Rebel*, London, 1860, p. 117. The English translator of this work was reduced to incredulity at Ricciardi's critical remarks.

41. Moe, *The View from Vesuvius*, p. 22; Marta Petrusewicz, 'Before the Southern Question: "Native" Ideas of Backwardness and Remedies in the Kingdom of Two Sicilies, 1815–49', in *Italy's 'Southern Question': Orientalism in One Country*, ed. Jane Schneider, Oxford, 1998, pp. 27–46.

42. For this tradition see Melissa Calaresu, 'Constructing an Intellectual Identity: Autobiography and Biography in Eighteenth-century Naples', *Journal of Modern Italian Studies* 6, 2 (2001), pp. 157–77.

43. [Klemens Wenzel Lothar von Metternich], *Memoirs of Prince Metternich, 1815–1829*, ed. R. Metternich, trans. A. Napier, Bentley and Son, London, 1881, vol. 3, p. 386.

44. Quoted in Rosa Maria Delli Quadri, *Nel Sud Romantico. Diplomatiche e Viaggiatori Inglesi alla Scoperta del Mezzogiorno Borbonico*, Naples, 2012, p. 118.

45. Swinburne, *Travels*, vol. 1, p. xiii.

46. Morgan, *Italy*, vol. 3, pp. 153–4.

47. For which see Mark Molesky, *This Gulf of Fire: The Great Lisbon Earthquake or Apocalypse in the Age of Science and Reason*, New York, 2015; Grégory Quenet, 'When Geology Encounters a Real Catastrophe: From Theoretical Earthquakes to the Lisbon Disaster', in *Histoires de la Terre*, ed. Louise Lyle and David McCallam, Amsterdam, 2008, pp. 37–56; Theodore E.D. Braun and John B. Radner (eds), *The Lisbon Earthquake of 1755: Representations and Reactions*, Oxford, 2005.

48. J.-C. Tanguy, Ch. Ribière, A. Scarth and W.S. Tjetjep, 'Victims from Volcanic Eruptions: A Revised Database', *Bulletin of Vulcanology* 60 (1998), 137–44.

49. Tanguy, Ribière, Scarth and Tjetjep, 'Victims', pp. 138, 140–1. Gillen D'Arcy Wood, *Tambora: The Eruption that Changed the World*, Princeton NJ, 2014, elaborates the global effects of the eruptions.

50. [Piozzi], *Glimpses of Italian Society*, p. 251.

51. Vincenzo Cuoco, *Historical Essay on the Neapolitan Revolution of 1799*, trans. David Gibbons, ed. Bruce Haddock and Filippo Sabetti, Toronto, 2014, p. 15.

52. VB, 12 September 1827.

53. *Biographie universelle, ancienne et moderne, ou, Histoire, par ordre alphabétique, de la vie publique et privée de tous les hommes qui se sont fait remarquer par leurs écrits, leurs actions, leurs talents, leurs vertus ou leurs crimes*, 85 vols, Paris, 1811–62, vols 23–4, pp. 407–11.

54. For an overview see Philip G. Dwyer, '"It Still Makes Me Shudder": Memories of Massacres and Atrocities during the Revolutionary and Napoleonic Wars', *War in History* 16, 4 (2009), pp. 381–405.

55. Quoted in Milton Finley, *The Most Monstrous of Wars: The Napoleonic Guerrilla War in Southern Italy, 1806–1811*, Chapel Hill NC, 1994, p. 118.

56. McCallam, *Volcanoes*, pp. 159–95 for a rich and brilliant discussion of the volcano and revolution between 1789–94. More generally in the visual arts see Sivard, 'Upheaval and Transformation', ch. 4, pp. 204–61.

57. P. Sylvain Maréchal, *Le jugement dernier des rois, prophétie en un acte, en prose*, Paris [1793/94].

58. Maréchal, *Le jugement dernier des rois*, pp. 26–7, 36. On the play see Mary Ashburn Miller, *A Natural History of Revolution: Violence and Nature in the French Revolutionary Imagination, 1789–1794*, Ithaca NY, 2011; McCallam, *Volcanoes*, pp. 167–73; Sanja Perovic, *The Calendar in Revolutionary France: Perceptions of Time in Literature, Culture, Politics*, Cambridge, 2012.

59. McCallam, *Volcanoes*, p. 169: 'The volcano goes from being a privileged metaphor of revolution to being its principal agent.'

60. [Thomas Babington Macaulay], *The Miscellaneous Writings of Lord Macaulay*, 2 vols, London, 1860, vol. 1, p. 57.

61. Quoted in William Edward Hartpole Lecky, *A History of England in the Eighteenth Century*, 8 vols, Longmans, London, 1878–90, vol. 6, p. 99.

62. Quoted in Miller, *A Natural History of Revolution*, p. 70.

63. The actions of Gimbernat and the misfortunes that ensued can be followed in [Carlos Gimbernat], Lluis Solé Sabarís, 'Diario inedito del geologo Catalan Carlos de Gimbernat (1768–1834)', *Llull* 5, 8–9 (1982), pp. 111–31.

64. G.M. Matthews, 'A Volcano's Voice in Shelley', *English Literary History* 24, 3 (1957), p. 224.

65. Richard Stites, *The Four Horsemen: Riding to Liberty in Post-Napoleonic Europe*, Oxford, 2014, p. 274.

66. Quoted in Goran Blix, *From Paris to Pompeii: French Romanticism and the Cultural Politics of Archaeology*, Philadelphia, 2009, p. 226.

67. Jules Michelet, *The Mountain, from the French of Michelet, by the Translator of 'The Bird'* [W.H.D. Davenport-Adams], London, 1872, pp. 115–18.

Chapter 7. Vesuvius and Volcanoes

1. 'Il Vesuvio ha prodotto un specie di fermentazione scientifica di scritti sul Vesuvio, e la sua lava orribile, che produrrà eruzioni filosofico-intellettuali di libri, discoursi, lettere, relazioni …': [Francesco A. Astore], *Dialoghi sul Vesuvio in occasione dell'eruzione della sera de' 15 Giugno 1794*, Naples, 1794, p. 4.

2. Dumas, *Le Corricolo*, ch. XXIV.

3. Claude Nicolas Ordinaire, *Histoire Naturelle des Volcans*, Paris, 1802.

4. Morgan, *Italy*, vol. 3, p. 166.

5. Massachusetts Historical Society, Ms SBd-40 Anon Travel Diary, Naples 1796–7.

6. Marie-Noëlle Bourguet, *Le Monde dans un carnet. Alexander von Humboldt en Italie (1805)*, Paris, 2017, p. 129.

7. I reach this conclusion by comparing figures in the Vesuvian Visitors' Book to the figures supplied by Mario Gemmellaro to the Royal Geological Society: Royal Geological Society, LDGSL/36 Italian tracts on Sicily and Etna.

8. For magazine coverage of the 1767 eruption see: *Universal Magazine, London Magazine, Scots Magazine, Gentleman's Magazine, Critical Review, Monthly Review, Monthly Miscellany*. For 1779: *Westminster Magazine, Scots Magazine, London Magazine, Edinburgh Magazine*. For 1794: *Walker's Hibernian Magazine, Scots Magazine, Universal Magazine, Weekly Entertainer*.

9. Anne-Marie Mercier-Faivre, 'Éruptions dans la presse: l'image du Vésuve dans la presse européene francophone du XVIIIe siècle', in *Le Vésuve en eruption: Savoir, representations, practiques*, ed. Émilie Beck Saiello and Dominique Bertrand, Clemont-Ferrand, 2013, pp. 83–98.

Chapter 8. Geologies: Vulcanism, Local and Global

1. Cocco, *Watching Vesuvius*.

2. 'William Whewell', *Oxford Dictionary of National Biography*.

3. [William Whewell], '[Review of] *Principles of Geology* . . . by Charles Lyell', *British Critic* 9 (1830), p. 180.

4. [Charles Lyell], '[Review of] *Memoir of the geology of central France* . . . by G.P. Scrope', *Quarterly Review* 36 (1827), p. 441.

5. [Whewell], '[Review of] *Principles of Geology*', p. 182.

6. George Poulett Scrope, *Considerations on Volcanos, the probable causes of their phenomena, the laws which determine their march, the disposition of their products, and the connection with the present and past history of the globe*, London, 1825, pp. iii–iv.

7. Déodat de Dolomieu, 'Discours sur l'étude de la Géologie', *Journal de Chimie, d'Histoire Naturelle et des Arts* (1794), p. 259.

8. Whewell had himself studied in Freiberg in 1825.

9. [Whewell], '[Review of] *Principles of Geology*', pp. 187–91.

10. Gian Battista Vai, 'Light and Shadow: The Status of Italian Geology around 1807', in *The Making of the Geological Society of London*, ed. C.L.E. Lewis and S.J. Knell, London, 2009, pp. 179, 192–7; P.J. MacCartney, 'Charles Lyell and G.B. Brocchi: A Study in Comparative Historiography', *British Journal for the History of Science* 9 (1976), pp. 177–89; Martin J.S. Rudwick, *Bursting the Limits of Time: The Reconstruction of Geohistory in the Age of Revolution*, Chicago, 2005, pp. 522–9.

11. Ami Boué, *Bulletin de la Société Géologique de la France: Résumé des Progrès des Sciences Géologiques*, Paris, 1834.

12. Leopoldo Pilla, 'Cenno Storico sui progressi della Orittognosia e della Geognosia in Italia', *Il Progresso delle Scienze, delle Lettere e delle Arti* 2 (1832), pp. 37–81, 3 (1832), pp. 165–234, 5 (1833), pp. 5–41. Vai, 'Light and Shadow', has a recent scholarly evaluation. He points out that more than 200 scientific papers by Italian 'geoscientists' were published between 1777 and 1837, of which half were on volcanoes and earthquakes (p. 182).

13. [Lyell], '[Review of] *Memoir of the geology of central France*', pp. 473–4.

14. Adelene Buckland, *Novel Science: Fiction and the Invention of Nineteenth-century Geology*, Chicago, 2013, especially pp. 110–13.

15. For a good general sense of this phenomenon see Wendell E. Wilson, 'The History of Mineral Collecting 1530–1799: With Notes on Twelve Hundred Early Mineral Collectors', *The Mineralogical Record* 25, 6 (1994).

16. [Déodat Dolomieu], Alfred Lacroix, *Déodat Dolomieu (1750–1801). Sa Correspondance, sa vie aventureuse, sa captivité, ses œuvres*, 2 vols, Paris, 1921, vol. 1, p. 108.
17. Alexandre Brongniart, *Elémentaire de Minéralogie, avec des applications aux arts; ouvrage destiné à l'enseignement dans les lycées nationaux*, Paris, 1807; Delvalle Lawry, *Conversations in Mineralogy*, London, 1822.
18. Much of this literature is discussed in the excellent study by Ralph O'Connor, *The Earth on Show: Fossils and the Poetics of Popular Science, 1802–1856*, Chicago, 2007, especially pp. 128–33, 145–6.
19. For Bakewell see O'Connor, *The Earth on Show*, pp. 119–21, 128–32. Brande published his lectures as *Outlines of Geology, being the substance of a course of lectures delivered in the Theatre of the Royal Institution in the year 1816*.
20. For which see the classic article by Simon Schaffer, 'Natural Philosophy and Public Spectacle in the Eighteenth Century', *History of Science* 21, 1 (1983), pp. 1–43.
21. [Davy], *Humphry Davy on Geology*, pp. xxxix–xl.
22. O'Connor, *The Earth on Show*, p. 116.
23. Corinna Guerra, 'If You Don't Have a Good Laboratory, Find a Good Volcano: Mount Vesuvius as a Natural Chemical Laboratory in Eighteenth-century Italy', *Ambix* 62, 3 (2015), p. 250.
24. Brian Dolan, 'Governing Matters: The Values of English Education in the Earth Sciences, 1790–1830', PhD thesis, Cambridge University, 1995, pp. 52–3, 64, 98.
25. Martin Rudwick, 'Charles Lyell F.R.S. (1797–1875) and his London Lectures on Geology 1832–33', *Notes and Records of the Royal Society of London* 20 (1975), p. 249.
26. Most notably in the two monumental works of Martin J.S. Rudwick, *Bursting the Limits of Time* and *Worlds before Adam: The Reconstruction of Geohistory in the Age of Reform*, Chicago, 2008.
27. Andrea Candela, 'On the Earth's Revolutions: Floods and Extinct Volcanoes in Northern Italy at the End of the Eighteenth Century', in *Geology and Religion: A History of Harmony and Hostility*, ed. M. Kölbl-Ebert, London, 2009, p. 90.
28. James Hutton, *Theory of the Earth, with Proofs and Illustrations. In Four Parts*, London and Edinburgh, 1795, pp. 15, 200, 272.
29. Quoted in Rachel Laudan, *From Mineralogy to Geology: The Foundations of a Science, 1650–1830*, Chicago, 1987, p. 188.
30. For von Hoff and Gemmellaro see Rudwick, *Worlds before Adam*, pp. 91–9.
31. Cited in Martin J.S. Rudwick, *Bursting the Limits of Time*, pp. 94–5, 203–26, who provides a full history of these developments. See also Davis A. Young, *Mind over Magma: The Story of Igneous Petrology*, Princeton NJ, 2003, pp. 16–49; Laudan, *From Mineralogy to Geology*, pp. 181–5; Haraldur Sigurdsson, *Melting the Earth: The History of Ideas of Volcanic Eruptions*, Oxford, 1999, pp. 133–6; McCallam, *Volcanoes*, pp. 70–7.
32. Charles Daubeny, *A Description of Active and Extinct Volcanos; with remarks on their origin, their chemical phaenomena, and the character of their products*, London, 1826, p. 452.
33. 'Terrains formés par la voie humide et les terrains qui doivent leur origine au feu', quoted in Thérèse Charles-Vallin, *Les aventures du chevalier géologique Déodat de Dolomieu*, Grenoble, 2003, p. 176. For an overview of the terms used here see Rhoda Rappaport, 'Dangerous Words: Diluvialism, Neptunism, Catastrophism', in *The Advancements of Learning: Essays in Honour of Paolo Rossi*, ed. John Heilbron, Florence, 2007, pp. 101–31. And for their application to debates about volcanoes see McCallam, *Volcanoes*, pp. 80–5.

34. On Raspe and Hamilton see Sigurdsson, *Melting the Earth*, pp. 141–3.
35. Ezio Vaccari, 'Wernerian Geonosy and Italian Vulcanists', in *Abraham Gottlob Werner and the Foundation of the Geological Sciences: Selected Papers of the International Werner Symposium*, ed. Helmuth Albrecht, Freiberg, 2002, pp. 25–6.
36. See the outstanding Luca Ciancio, *Le Colonne del Tempo: il 'Tempio di Sarapide' a Pozzuoli nella storia della geologia, dell'archeologia e dell'arte (1750–1900)*, Florence, 2009.
37. George Poulett Scrope, 'Review of *Principles of Geology* . . . by Charles Lyell, 3rd edition. In 4 vols, 1835', *Quarterly Review* 53 (1835), p. 421.
38. Cocco, *Watching Vesuvius*, p. 114.
39. Cocco, *Watching Vesuvius*, p. 114.
40. Cocco, *Watching Vesuvius*, p. 114.
41. [Sir William Hamilton], *Supplement to the Campi Phlegraei, being an account of the great eruption of Mount Vesuvius in the month of August 1779*, Naples, 1779, p. 2, fn. a. By 1794 Hamilton had reached his sixty-eighth ascent.
42. F. Cassola and E.L. Pilla, *Lo Spettatore del Vesuvio e de' Campi Flegrei* 1 (July–December 1832), pp. 4–5, 34.
43. Jenkins and Sloan (eds), *Vases and Volcanoes*; Constantine, *Fields of Fire*; Mark Sleep, 'Sir William Hamilton (1730–1803): His Works and Influence on Geology', *Annals of Science* 25, 4 (1969), pp. 67–96; Heringman, *Sciences of Antiquity*, chapter 2.
44. [Sir William Hamilton], *Campi Phlegraei. Observations on the Volcanos of the Two Sicilies as they have been communicated to the Royal Society of London by Sir William Hamilton*, 2 vols, Naples, 1776, vol. 1, pp. 23, 27, 60, 63; vol. 2, reference to Plate XIII; [Hamilton], *Supplement to the Campi Phlegraei*, p. 1.
45. Guerra, 'If You Don't Have a Good Laboratory', p. 257.
46. David Nolta, 'The Body of the Collector and the Collected Body in William Hamilton's Naples', *Eighteenth-Century Studies* 31, 1 (1997), p. 110.
47. [Hamilton], *Campi Phlegraei*, vol. 2, reference to Plate IX.
48. [Hamilton], *Campi Phlegraei*, vol. 1, pp. 86–7.
49. [Hamilton], *Campi Phlegraei*, vol. 1, p. 36.
50. On Hamilton's strategies see Karen Wood, 'Making and Circulating Knowledge through Sir William Hamilton's *Campi Phlegraei*', *British Journal for the History of Science* 39, 1 (2006), pp. 67–96; Heringman, *Sciences of Antiquity*, pp. 77–122.
51. [Sir William Hamilton], *Oeuvres Complètes de M. le Chevalier Hamilton . . . Commentée par M. L'Abbé Giraud-Soulavie*, Paris, 1781, p. x.
52. [Hamilton], *Supplement to the Campi Phlegraei*, p. 8.
53. 'Dans l'histoire de la Nature, comme dans toutes les espèces de connaissances, on n'acquiert de nouvelles vues que par la comparaison de plusieurs objets': [Hamilton], *Oeuvres Complètes*, p. 278.
54. Rudwick, *Bursting the Limits of Time*, pp. 215–22.
55. [Hamilton], *Supplement to Campi Phlegraei*, pp. 5, 22.
56. [Hamilton], *Campi Phlegraei*, vol. 1, p. 4.
57. Horace Walpole to Sir William Hamilton, 18 February 1776, in *The Hamilton and Nelson Papers*, vol. 1, p. 47.
58. As Soulavie makes clear in [Hamilton], *Oeuvres Complètes*, p. 309.
59. For the eruption and its coverage see Filippo Russo and Francesco Formicola, *L'Eruzione del Vesuvio del 1794. Inquadramento geo-vulcanologico*. Vesuvioweb, at http://www.vesuvioweb.com/it/wp-content/uploads/Filippo-RUsso-e-Francesco-Formicola-Laruzione-del-Vesuvio-del-1794-vesuvioweb-2012.pdf; Nazzaro, *Il*

Vesuvio, pp. 167–8, 294–301; Scarth, *Vesuvius*, pp. 212–23; Furchheim (ed.), *Bibliografia del Vesuvio*, pp. 248–9.

60. Russo and Formicola, *L'Eruzione del Vesuvio del 1794*, p. 43: Torre writes, 'Fui sorpreso dal vedere molti nuovi edifici innalzati sulla lava ancora calda, dei quali alcuni erano di già abitati' ('I was surprised to see many new buildings erected on the still hot lava, some of which were already inhabited').

61. *Spaventosissima descrizione dello spaventoso spavento che ci spavento tutti coll'eruzione del Vesuvio*: see Anna Maria Salvadè, 'Fra satira e scienza: Ferdinando Galiani vulcanologo', in *Geografie e Storie Letterarie*, ed. Stefania Baragetti, Rosa Necchi and Anna Maria Salvadè, Milan, 2019, pp. 141–6.

62. Salvatore Caneva, *Lettera dell'eremita del S. Salvatore sito alle falde del Vesuvio per dare ad un amico suo un succinto ragguaglio dell'accaduta Eruzione la sera de' 15 Giugno*, Naples, 1794; Simone Giros, *Veridica Relazione di Simone Giros giardiniere della Real Villa Favorita, circa l'ultima eruzione del Vesuvio accaduta al 15 Giugno per tutto Luglio dell'anno 1794*, Naples, 1794. Caneva's letter was also included in a selection of materials about the eruption published in Leipzig: Furchheim (ed.), *Bibliografia del Vesuvio*, p. 128.

63. *Seconda Lettera di un Legista Napolitano ad un suo fratello in provincia*, Naples, 1794, pp. 15–16.

64. Biagio Sotis, *Dissertazione fisico-chimica dell'ultima eruzione vesuviana*, Naples, 1804; P. Pasquale Manni, *Saggio fisico-chimico della cagione de' baleni e delle pioggie che osservansi nelle grandi eruzioni vulcaniche. In occasione dell'eruzione del Vesuvio a Giugno 1794*, Naples, 1794. For Sotis see *Poliorama Pittoresco. Opera Periodica. Anno Ottavo – Semestre Primo*, Naples, 1844, pp. 255–6. For Manni see http://scienza-salento.unile.it/biografie/pasquale_manni.htm.

65. Michele Arcangelo D'Onofrio, *Dettaglio istorico della peste di Noja in provincia di Bari*, Naples, 1817; Michele Arcangelo D'Onofrio, *Lettera del professore di medicina Michele Arcangelo in cui si da la descrizione del telegrafo* [Naples], 1794; Michele Arcangelo D'Onofrio, *Lettera ad un amico in provincia sul tremuoto accaduto a 26 Luglio*, Naples, 1805. D'Onofrio wrote *Relazione ragionata della eruzione del nostro Vesuvio*, Naples, 1794, and *Nuove Riflessioni sul Vesuvio con un breve dettaglio de' Paraterremoti*, Naples, 1794.

66. [Astore], *Dialoghi sul Vesuvio*.

67. Nino Cortese, 'Francesco Antonio Astore', in *Dizionario Biografico degli Italiani*.

68. Ciro Saverio Minervini, 'Due Lettere al M. Rosini, 17 e 21 Giugno, 1794', *Giornale Letterario di Napoli* XI (1794), pp. 86–97. Graziano Palamara, 'Ciro Saverio Minervini', in *Dizionario Biografico degli Italiani*.

69. Ruggiero di Castiglione, *La Massoneria nelle due Sicilie e i 'fratelli' meridionali del '700*, 6 vols, 2nd edn, vol. 1, Rome, 2008, pp. 209–10.

70. Ferdinando Viscardi, *Breve riposta alla lettera del Signor Abate Tata de' 21 Agosto 1794. Di Ferdinando Viscardi, regio operatore di fisica sperimentale*, Naples, 1794.

71. Pasquale Palmieri, 'Domenico Tata', in *Dizionario Biografico degli Italiani*.

72. C. Paola Scavizzi, 'Luca Cagnazzi de Samuele', in *Dizionario Biografico degli Italiani*; Biagio Salvemini, *Economia politica e arretratezza meridionale nell'età del Risorgimento. Luca de Samuele Cagnazzi e la diffusione dello Smithianesimo nel regno di Napoli*, Lecce, 1981.

73. Toni Iermano, 'Ascanio Filomarino', in *Dizionario Biografico degli Italiani*.

74. 'L'Uccisione di Ascanio e Clemente Filomarino', *Archivio storico per le province napoletane* XXV, 1 (1900), pp. 74–5.

75. Scipione Breislak and Antonio Winspeare, *Memoria sull'Eruzione del Vesuvio accaduta la sera de' 15 Giugno 1794*, Naples, 1794.
76. Anna Maria Rao, 'Esercito e Società a Napoli nelle riforme del secondo Settecento', *Studi Storici* 28 (1978), pp. 623–77, especially pp. 657–62.
77. Pietro Corsi, 'Matteo Tondi', in *Dizionario Biografico degli Italiani*.
78. [Giuseppe Melograni], *Manuale Geologico di Giuseppe Melograni*, Naples, 1806, p. 13.
79. Vaccari, 'Wernerian Geonosy and Italian Vulcanists', pp. 24–5, 30.
80. 'Ecco, quindi, quel che io chiamo montagne volcaniche nettuniane, delle quali, cioè il materiale è volcanico, ma la genesi e dovuta alle inondazioni': Carmine Antonio Lippi, *Fu il fuoco o l'acqua che sotterrò Pompei ed Ercolano?*, Naples, 1816, p. 236.
81. Fabio D'Angelo, *Dal Regno di Napoli alla Francia. Viaggi ed esilio tra Sette e Ottocento*, Naples, 2018, pp. 215–18.
82. The *Giornale* published papers on volcanoes and the chemical content of rocks (XVII, pp. 58–80; XLI, pp. 59–67), and in its review of Giovanni Andres's fifth volume of *Dell'origine, de' progressi e dello stato attuale d'ogni letteratura* on natural history dealt extensively with the basalt debate and geological formation (LIV, pp. 64–8).
83. Fabio D'Angelo, 'Les Institutions scientifiques à l'heure française', in *Le royaume de Naples a l'heure française. Revisiter l'histoire du decennio francese (1806–1815)*, ed. Pierre-Marie Delpu, Igor Moullier and Mélanie Traversier, Villeneuve-d'Ascq, 2018, p. 245; Fabio D'Angelo, 'Les hommes de science napolitains en exil en France, des passeurs scientifiques et politiques (1799–1820)', *Revue d'Histoire du XIXème siècle* (2016), pp. 39–57.

Chapter 9. Déodat de Dolomieu and Teodoro Monticelli

1. T.C. Bruun-Neergaard, *Journal du dernier Voyage du Cen. Dolomieu dans les Alpes*, Paris, 1802, p. 1.
2. In 1829 Engelsbach-Larivière, a young naturalist from Luxembourg, having spoken of Monticelli as the subject of a 'cult' among mineralogists, described Humboldt as 'at the centre of your admirers', adding that Humboldt was not one to give praise readily. Monticelli Ms E.0003, Engelsbach to Monticelli, 10 August 1829.
3. Buckingham, *Private Diary*, vol. 1, p. 314; DLP, Davy to Monticelli, Rome, 8 April 1820.
4. [Dolomieu], Lacroix, *Dolomieu*, vol. 2, p. 116.
5. Bruun-Neergaard, *Journal du dernier Voyage*, pp. 151–2: 'Aime beaucoup la société, et était très-agréable avec le beau sexe, qui faisait ordinairement un cercle autour de lui.'
6. Charles-Vallin, *Les aventures*, pp. 45–7.
7. For Dolomieu in Rome see Gilles Montègre, *La Rome des Français au temps des Lumières*, Rome, 2011, pp. 122–6, 404–7, 524–8, 531–4.
8. For Gioeni see Giuseppina Buccieri, 'Giuseppe Gioeni', in *Dizionario Biografico degli Italiani*.
9. Lacroix, *Dolomieu*, vol. 2, pp. 223–3.
10. Monticelli, *Notizia di una escursione al Vesuvio*.

Chapter 10. Déodat de Dolomieu and the Hazards of Vulcanism

1. [Dolomieu], Lacroix, *Dolomieu*, vol. 1, p. 108.
2. Marc-Auguste Pictet, *Correspondance: sciences et techniques*, ed. Jean Cassaigneau, Jean-Michel Pictet and Jean-Claude Pont, 4 vols, Geneva, 1996–2004, vol. 1, p. 726.

3. 'Mon association à une entreprise militaire, qui me mettait (quoique d'une manière indirecte) sous les ordres d'un général, fatiguait mon imagination, et cependant, ce général était Bonaparte': [Dolomieu], Lacroix, *Dolomieu*, vol. 1, p. 23.
4. The entire episode is well told in Tom Reiss, *The Black Count: Glory, Revolution, Betrayal, and the Real Count of Monte Cristo*, New York, 2012, pp. 266–80, 290–303.
5. Quoted in C. Samaran, 'Alexandre Dumas Napolitain', *Europe* 48, 490 (1970), p. 126.
6. Charles-Vallin, *Les aventures*, pp. 14–15.
7. Charles-Vallin, *Les aventures*, p. 127.
8. Lacroix, *Dolomieu*, vol. 1, pp. 107, 172.
9. A useful account of the Order and of Dolomieu's role within it can be found in Roderick Cavaliero, *The Last of the Crusaders: The Knights of St John and Malta in the Eighteenth Century*, Valletta, 2001, especially pp. 168–70, 175–80, 188–90, 196–8.
10. Lacroix, *Dolomieu*, vol. 1, p. 113.
11. Lacroix, *Dolomieu*, vol. 1, p. 169.
12. Charles-Vallin, *Les aventures*, pp. 100, 110.
13. Lacroix, *Dolomieu*, vol. 1, p. 248.
14. On Dolomieu's scientific career see Kenneth L. Taylor, 'Dolomieu', in *The Complete Dictionary of Scientific Biography*, vol. 4, Princeton NJ, 1971, pp. 149–53.
15. For Thyrion see John Perkins, 'Creating Chemistry in Provincial France before the Revolution: The Examples of Nancy and Metz. Part 2. Metz', *Ambix* 51, 1 (2004), pp. 48 seq.
16. Perkins, 'Creating Chemistry', pp. 56–9.
17. For the Duke's scientific interests see, E. Jovy, 'La Correspondance du Duc de Rochefoucauld-d'Enville et de George Louis Le Sage Conservée à la Bibliothèque de Genève', *Bulletin du Bibliophile* (1917), pp. 461–90; (1918), pp. 35–55, 135–51.
18. R. Galliani, 'Le duc de la Rochefoucauld et Thomas Paine', *Annales Historiques de la Révolution Française* 52 (1980), pp. 425–36.
19. For the salon see Antoine Lilti, *Le Monde des salons: sociabilité et mondanité à Paris au 18e siècle*, Paris, 2005, pp. 42–3, 176, 262.
20. Lacroix, *Dolomieu*, vol. 1, p. 150.
21. Lacroix, *Dolomieu*, vol. 1, p. 178.
22. Lacroix, *Dolomieu*, vol. 1, p. 192.
23. See *Dictionnaire des journaux 1600–1789*, http://dictionnaire-journaux.gazettes18e.fr/journal/1089-observations-sur-lhistoire- naturelle-sur-la-physique-et-sur-la-peinture.
24. Lacroix, *Dolomieu*, vol. 1, p. 114 : 'À chacune de mes pierres est attaché le souvenir d'une des circonstances de ma vie; elles me rappellent mes courses, les amis qu'elles m'ont procurés, les jouissances qu'elles m'ont données.'
25. Lacroix, *Dolomieu*, vol. 1, p. 101; Alix Cooper, 'From the Alps to Egypt (and Back Again): Dolomieu, Scientific Voyaging, and the Construction of the Field in Eighteenth-Century Natural History', in *Making Space for Science: Territorial Themes in the Shaping of Knowledge*, ed. Crosbie Smith and John Agar, Basingstoke, 1998, pp. 47–8.
26. 'L'inquiétude, la méfiance y sont empreintes sur toutes les figures, on redoute de se parler, on n'ose hasarder une opinion, l'égoïsme exerce un empire absolu sur tout le monde; il n'y a plus ni liaison ni amitié; tout est faction, tout est parti; il faut adopter une livrée et se livrer ensuite à toute exagération du chef qui l'a adoptée' : Lacroix, *Dolomieu*, vol. 2, p. 56.

27. In 1797 he wrote, 'Il n'y a que la culture des sciences qui ne donne point de chagrins; mais souvent on n'a pas la tête assez libre, assez délivrée d'inquiétudes pour s'y livrer tout entier. Que ne puis-je me borner à ne penser qu'à mes pierres!' ('There is only the culture of the sciences which does not give rise to sorrows; but often one does not have a sufficiently free head, sufficiently liberated from anxieties to give oneself over to it entirely. Why can't I confine myself to thinking only of my stones!'): Lacroix, *Dolomieu*, vol. 2, p. 163.

28. Lacroix, *Dolomieu*, vol. 2, p. 64.

29. 'Les sciences qui, autrefois, étaient pour moi un délassement sont devenues le métier qui me donne de quoi vivre; et cependant je le fais avec plaisir': Lacroix, *Dolomieu*, vol. 2, p. 138.

30. See 'Contraste de ma situation actuelle avec mes goûts et mes habitudes', 'Journal de Captivité', in Lacroix, *Dolomieu*, vol. 1, pp. 3–44.

31. Lacroix, *Dolomieu*, vol. 1, p. 49.

32. Cooper, 'From the Alps to Egypt', pp. 39–63.

33. Lacroix, *Dolomieu*, vol. 1, p. 4: 'Chaque année, lorsque le printemps venait rendre la vie au règne végétal et donner une nouvelle action à tous les êtres organisés, toutes les beautés de l'art perdaient leurs attraits pour moi. L'enceinte de Paris me paraissait étroite, son atmosphère épaisse et pesante.'

34. 'Chaque année je m'élançais vers quelques chaînes de montagnes, et j'allais sur les sommets chercher ces émotions profondes que procure toujours la vue des très grands objets, et me livrer à la méditation sur la formation du globe, sur les révolutions qu'il a éprouvées, sur les causes qui ont changé et modifié ses formes, et qui ont produit l'état où nous le voyons. Mes pensées devenaient plus vastes et mes conceptions plus étendues, à mesure que je m'élevais plus haut: mon horizon avait moins de bornes.'

35. 'Discours sur l'étude de la Géologie, prononcé par Déodat Dolomieu, Membre de l'Institut National, à l'ouverture de son cours sur les gisements des Minéraux, commencé en Ventôse de l'an 5', *Journal de Physique, de Chimie* 2–45 (1794), pp. 256–72.

36. 'Discours sur l'étude', *Journal de Physique*, p. 262.

37. Lacroix, *Dolomieu*, vol. 1, p. 6: 'Je suivais avec un plaisir extrême la marche précipitée des sciences ... chaque jour amenait une découverte; chaque jour m'annonçait ou une conquête faite sur l'ignorance ... Je joignais mes efforts à cette impulsion générale, et je me trouvais heureux d'être compté parmi ceux qui donnaient ce grand essor à l'esprit humain.'

38. Lacroix, *Dolomieu*, vol. 1, p. 47: 'Mon coeur devine tout ce qui se passe dans le vôtre à mon égard et tout ce que vous faîtes pour moi.'

39. Lacroix, *Dolomieu*, vol. 1, p. 49: 'Tête ardente, coeur chaud et ouvert, aimant avec transport les sciences, avec passion l'établissement qu'il dirige, et sans réserve ceux à qui il s'est attaché.'

40. Lacroix, *Dolomieu*, vol. 1, p. 50: 'Vous vous passez de dîner pour pouvoir acheter des pierres; mais vous vous passez des pierres pour pouvoir obliger vos amis.'

41. Lacroix, *Dolomieu*, vol. 1, p. 60: 'Porter dans les affaires publiques le don et la conciliation, et dans la société les charmes de amabilité; posséder toutes les vertus d'un bon citoyen et d'un bon père de famille, et toute la force d'âme d'un vrai philosophe.'

42. Lacroix, *Dolomieu*, vol. 1, pp. 48–9.

43. Pictet to Banks, 24 September 1799, Pictet, *Correspondance*, vol. 1, p. 21; [Banks], *Scientific Correspondence*, vol. 4, item 1517.

44. 'Nations . . . peuvent se faire la guerre, mais les hommes qui s'adonnent aux sciences ne doivent jamais cesser d'être amis: au milieu du tumulte des passions, du choc des intérêts divers, il reste à l'homme véritablement philanthropique une consolation de voir diminuer les calamités publiques par l'union, l'estime et les relations continues des philosophes de tous les pays.'

45. Sir Joseph Banks to Marguerite Ursule Fortunée Briquet, April 1802, [Banks], *Scientific Correspondence*, vol. 5, item 1642; Banks to Dolomieu, 16 July 1801, [Banks], *Scientific Correspondence*, vol. 5, item 1600.

46. Banks to Sir William Hamilton, 8 November 1799, [Banks], *Scientific Correspondence*, vol. 4, item 1519.

47. Banks to Emma Hamilton, 8 November 1799, [Banks], *Scientific Correspondence*, vol. 4, item 1520.

48. For Dolomieu's thanks to Banks see Dolomieu to Banks, 14 Prairial An IX, [Banks], *Scientific Correspondence*, vol. 5, item 1598.

49. Lacroix, *Dolomieu*, vol. 2, p. 21.

50. 'Il pourrait faire jusqu'à douze lieues par jour . . . presque toujours à pied. Intrépide et infatigable, il laissait les hommes les plus robustes et les plus accoutumés aux montagnes, les guides de Chamonix. La pluie, les vents, les neiges, rien ne l'arrêtait . . . Ses fatigues et son courage furent extrême.' Fortunée B. Briquet, *Ode sur la Mort de Dolomieu, précédée d'une notice sur ce Naturaliste*, Paris, An X, p. 10.

51. 'J'aurois décoré cette épître du nom de quelque grand de la terre, y faire l'étalage de ses titres fastueux, de ses vertus imaginaires; mais j'y préfère le nom de mon ami, d'un ami de vingt ans.' Déodat Dolomieu, *Mémoire sur les Tremblements de Terre de la Calabre pendant l'année 1783*, Rome, 1784, dedication.

Chapter 11. Teodoro Monticelli: International Vulcanism and Neapolitan Politics

1. But then much of what he had to say about Naples bore an indelible ideological imprint which modern critics have exposed but rarely transcended.

2. An earlier sketch of Monticelli can be found in my 'Scientific Networks, Vesuvius and Politics: The Case of Teodoro Monticelli in Naples, 1790–1845', *Incontri* 34, 1 (2019), pp. 54–67.

3. See Giuseppe Foscari, *Teodoro Monticelli e l'Economia delle acque nel Mezzogiorno moderno*, Salerno, 2009; Constanza D'Elia, *Bonifiche e stato nel Mezzogiorno (1815–1860)*, Naples, 1994, pp. 26–32, 55–61.

4. Nicola Covelli and Teodoro Monticelli, *Storia de'Fenomeni del Vesuvio avventi negli anni 1821, 1822 e parte del 1823*, Naples, 1823, reprinted in [Monticelli], *Opere dell'abate Teodoro Monticelli*, vol. 2, pp. 167–330.

5. Teodoro Monticelli and Nicola Covelli, *Prodromo della mineralogia vesuviana*, Naples, 1825.

6. Nazzaro, *Il Vesuvio*, p. 231; Antonio Nazzaro and Angela di Gregorio, 'The Contribution of the Neapolitan Geologist, Teodoro Monticelli (1759–1845) to the Development of Geology', in *Volcanoes and History: Proceedings of the 20th INHIGEO Symposium, 19–25 September 1995*, ed. Nicoletta Morello, Genoa, 1998, pp. 423–5.

7. A. Bylandt Palsterkamp, *Resumé préliminaire d'ouvrage sur le Vésuve*, Naples, 1833, pp. 9–10.

8. Furchheim (ed.), *Bibliografia del Vesuvio*, pp. 117–21.

9. Monticelli Ms D.22, Dall'Armi to Monticelli, 27 December 1825.

10. Monticelli Ms M.251, Moricand to Monticelli, 22 November 1815; M. 258 14 July 1816.
11. Quoted in Nazzaro and di Gregorio, 'The Contribution of the Neapolitan Geologist', pp. 426–7.
12. Monticelli Ms E.0003, Engelbach to Monticelli, 10 August 1829.
13. Monticelli Ms G.050, Gimbernat to Monticelli, 11 December 1818.
14. Monticelli Ms M.288, Muséum National d'Histoire Naturelle to Monticelli, 31 January 1824.
15. Buckingham, *Private Diary*, vol. 1, p. 314; DLP, Humphry Davy to Teodoro Monticelli, Rome, 8 April 1820.
16. DLP, Humphry Davy to Teodoro Monticelli, Rome, 7 March 1820.
17. Monticelli Ms M.06, M.11, Ferdinando Malvica to M, 20 August 1833, 24 April 1834.
18. Monticelli Ms H.007, Frederick Hall to Monticelli, 2 April 1841; H.024 Alexander Hammett to Monticelli, 20 May 1841.
19. Monticelli Ms B.27–30, Emma Bethell to Monticelli, 25 June 1820, 3 August, 15 December 1823, n.d.
20. Monticelli Ms W.13, Anna Wilbraham to Monticelli, 27 July 1832; W.14 27 July 1833.
21. *Literary Gazette*, 19 (1835), p. 602.
22. Monticelli MS. R.238–43, Von Ringseis to Monticelli, 30 March 1830; December 1832; 15, 18 April, 20 June 1833; 10 June 1837.
23. Monticelli Ms B.92, Brocchi to Monticelli, 27 January 1821.
24. *Opere dell'abate Teodoro Monticelli*, vol. 2, pp. 72–80.
25. Castiglione, *La Massoneria nelle due Sicilie*, pp. 42–6.
26. On Monticelli's life see Francesco Paolo De Ceglia in *Dizionario Biografico degli Italiani*; Nazzaro and di Gregorio, 'The Contribution of the Neapolitan Geologist', pp. 415–39; Foscari, *Teodoro Monticelli e l'Economia delle acque*, pp. 59–88.
27. On Ricciardi see John A. Davis, *Naples and Napoleon: Southern Italy and the European Revolutions 1780–1860*, Oxford, 2006, pp. 144 n. 6, 170, 184, 233, 240–3, 284, 299–300, 305–8, 313–14.
28. The site on which the villa, completed in 1817, was built was a gift of sequestered church lands from Murat to his minister.
29. See for example [Ricciardi, Francesco, Count Camaldoli], 'Discorso letto dal Presidente Conte Ricciardi nella tornata dell'Accademia alle Scienze del 14 Febbraio 1832', *Scritti e Documenti Varii di Francesco Ricciardi Conte di Camaldoli*, Naples, 1873, pp. 425–35.
30. Amilcare Mazzarella, 'Della Vita e delle Opere di Teodoro Monticelli', *Giornale Euganeo di Scienze, Lettere ed Arti* 2, 3 (1846), p. 495.
31. Beinecke Library, Yale University, Osborn D293, William Gell, 'Journal 9 August 1814–31 May 1815', f. 83.
32. DLP, Davy to Monticelli, n.d.; 19 November, 15 December 1818; 21 March, 4 April, 17, 24 October 1819.
33. Monticelli Ms H.62, Humboldt to Monticelli, 1822.
34. Charles Lyell, *Principles of Geology; or the modern changes of the earth and its inhabitants*, 9th edn, New York, 1853, p. 379.
35. Monticelli Ms B.108, Buckland to Monticelli, n.d.; DLP, Davy to Monticelli, 20 February 1826; Monticelli Ms T.007, Charles Jurgensen-Thomsen, 13 September 1824.
36. Buckingham, *Private Diary*, vol. 2, pp. 31, 38, 49, 236.

37. Babbage, *Passages*, p. 165.
38. Albert Fabriius, Finn Friis and Else Kornerup (eds), *King Christian VIII's dagøger og Optegnelser. I halvbind 1815–1821*, Copenhagen, 1973, pp. 204–5.
39. Buckingham, *Private Diary*, vol. 2, p. 38.
40. Monticelli Ms B.03, Charles Frederic Bachmann to Monticelli, n.d. 1832.
41. DLP, Humphry Davy to Grace Davy, 14 September 1814.
42. DLP, Humphry Davy to Michael Faraday, 3 April 1819.
43. DLP, Humphry Davy to Michael Faraday, 3 April 1819.
44. DLP, Humphry Davy to Monticelli, 22 October 1820.
45. DLP, Humphry Davy to Monticelli, 20 June 1821.
46. DLP, Humphry Davy to Monticelli, 23 April 1822; Davy to Lord Compton, November 1822.
47. Monticelli Ms C.148, Compton to Monticelli, n.d.; D.200, D.201, D.203 Margaret Douglas Maclean Clephane to Monticelli, 19 June 1818; 17 June 1819; 10 August 1821.
48. Quoted in Nazzaro and di Gregorio, 'The Contribution of the Neapolitan Geologist', p. 422.
49. DLP, Davy to Monticelli, 23 April, 4 November 1822. Most of the letters to Monticelli in his archive written in English are accompanied by translations not in his hand.
50. DLP, Davy to Monticelli, 13 December 1824; 8 October 1825; 12 January, 20 February 1826; 4 March, 4, 25 November, 3, 18 December 1827.
51. DLP, Davy to Monticelli, February 1828.
52. The following discussion has benefited greatly from the network analysis 'Acting at a Distance', in Emma Spary, *Utopia's Garden: French Natural History from the Old Regime to Revolution*, Chicago, 2000, pp. 49–98.
53. Monticelli Ms G.25, Mario Gemmellaro to Monticelli, 4 October 1825.
54. Monticelli Ms G.54, Giuseppe Giovene to Monticelli, 22 October 1825. More generally see Maria Toscano, 'The Figure of the Naturalist-Antiquary in the Kingdom of Naples: Giuseppe Govene (1753–1837) and his Contemporaries', *Journal of the History of Collections* 19, 11 (2007), pp. 225–37, especially p. 231.
55. Monticelli Ms D.07, Nicola Da Rio to Monticelli, 17 May 1820.
56. Monticelli Ms C.49, Pietro Carpi to Monticelli, 1 October 1825.
57. Monticelli Ms A.28, Giacinto Cavana to Monticelli, 16 December 1829.
58. Luigi Gennari, 'Breislak, Scipione', in *Dizionario Biografico degli Italiani*.
59. Monticelli Ms B.67, Scipione Breislak to Monticelli, 29 April 1819.
60. For the importance of such figures in networks see the classic articles Mark S. Granovetter, 'The Strength of Weak Ties', *American Journal of Sociology* 78 (1973), pp. 1360–80; 'The Strength of Weak Ties: A Network Theory Revisited', *Sociological Theory* 1 (1983), pp. 201–33.
61. For which see William Anthony S. Sarjeant and Justin B. Delair, 'An Irish Naturalist in Cuvier's Laboratory: The Letters of Joseph Pentland, 1820–1822', *Bulletin of the British Museum (Natural History)* 6 (1980), pp. 245–319.
62. Monticelli Ms P.26, 27, 30, 32, 34, 35, 37, 38, 40, 42, 48, 49, Pentland to Monticelli, 22 August, 3 October 1822; n.d.; 24 August, 22 November 1823; 23 February, 24 June, 24 July, 22 October 1824; 26 September 1829; 15 October 1841; 22 May 1843.
63. For his life see Abraham S. Breure and Emmanuel Tardy, 'From the Shadows of the Past: Moricand Senior and Junior, Two 19th-century Naturalists from Geneva, their Newly Described Taxa and Molluscan Types', *Revue Suisse de Zoologie* 123 (2006), pp. 113–38.

64. Monticelli Ms C.213, Covelli to Monticelli, 12 July 1825.
65. Monticelli Ms M.249–51, 253, 257–8, 260, 262, 266, 268–9, 274–5, Moïse-Étienne Stefano Moricand to Monticelli, 24 December 1814; 22 September, 22 November 1815; 28 January, 12 May, 14 July 1816; 3 January, 22 June, 27 July 1817; 8 February, 5 June, 17 July 1818; 14 May, 2 June 1820.
66. Dorinda Outram, *Georges Cuvier: Vocation, Science and Authority in Post-Revolutionary France*, Manchester, 1984, p. 84.
67. For D'Ambrosio's life see Pietro C. Ulloa, *Elogio di Paolo D'Ambrosio già Ministro Delle Due Sicilie in Danimarca e Svezia*, Naples, 1835.
68. Monticelli Ms D.39–59 for D'Ambrosio's exchanges with Monticelli.
69. Simon Schama, 'Death of a Harvard Man', in Schama, *Dead Certainties: Unwarranted Speculations*, New York, 1991, pp. 73–318.
70. Monticelli Ms C.187–207, Costa de Macedo to Monticelli, 11, 25 June, 9 July 1836; 6 March, 29 April, 31 August, 6 December 1837; 18 February, 8 May, 27 October 1828; 20 February, 13 September 1839; 16 July 1840; 14 July 1841; 15 July 1842; 18 February 1843.
71. See Monticelli Ms A.008–10, Accademia Gioenia to Monticelli, 19, 20 July 1824; I.004-5, Istituto Brasileiro to Monticelli, 21 September 1843.
72. Monticelli Ms M.88, 90, Ménard de la Groye to Monticelli, 2 June 1816; 6 June 1819.
73. Monticelli Ms G.22, 24, 25, 26, 27, 28, 33, Mario Gemmellaro to Monticelli, 8 March 1824; 30 May, 4 October 1825; 21 June, 8 July 1826; 28 June 1827.
74. Monticelli Ms M.051, M.053–4, Francis Markoe to Monticelli, 4 May 1844; 11 January, 10 September 1845.
75. Monticelli Ms M.268, Moricand to Monticelli, 5 June 1818.
76. Monticelli Ms A.024, Antonmaria Vassalli Eandi to Monticelli, 1 February 1823.
77. Monticelli Ms D.026, Dall'Armi to Monticelli, 16 January 1827.
78. Monticelli Ms D.25, Dall'Armi to Monticelli, 14 July 1826.
79. Monticelli Ms S.163, Svedenstierna to Monticelli, 5 July 1821.
80. Monticelli Ms V.7, Van Rensselaer to Monticelli, 7 July 1824.
81. Monticelli Ms D.10, Da Rio to Monticelli, 4 July 1837.
82. Monticelli Ms R.03, 04, Ranzani to Monticelli, 7 May 1820, 23 July 1823.
83. Monticelli Ms L.39–42, Leonard to Monticelli, 1 July 1831; 9 March 1833; 1 December 1834; 3 July 1835.
84. Monticelli Ms M.267, Moricand to Monticelli, 3 April 1818.
85. Francis Lunn, autograph letter signed to Mrs William Phillips, 25 November 1828, https://jnorman.com/pages/books/32322/francis-lunn-autograph-letter-signed-to-mrs-william-phillips.
86. Monticelli Ms M.265, Moricand to Monticelli, 20 August 1817.
87. Monticelli Ms N.06, 08, 09, 11, 12, Nesti to Monticelli, 25 September 1818; 18 October 1819; 9 September 1827; 30 April, 18 September 1833.
88. Monticelli MS. B.85, Brocchi to Monticelli, 2 May 1819; B.108, William Buckland to Monticelli, n.d.; F.18, 20, Francesco Ferrara to Monticelli, 26 July 1824; 1 June 1826; G.23, Mario Gemmellaro to Monticelli, 20 June 1824.
89. Monticelli Ms V.14, Stephen Van Rensselaer to Monticelli, n.d. 1819.
90. Monticelli Ms S.161, Eric Thomas Svedenstierna to Monticelli, 1 June 1820.
91. Monticelli Ms M.249, Moricand to Monticelli, 24 December 1814.
92. Monticelli Ms R.03, Camillo Ranzani to Monticelli, 7 May 1820.
93. Monticelli Ms M.40, Carmelo Maramigna to Monticelli, 4 July 1824.
94. Monticelli Ms B.63, 71, Scipione Breislak to Monticelli, 26 February 1817; 16 June 1821.

95. Buckingham, *Private Diary*, vol. 2, pp. 264–5.
96. Monticelli Ms B.61, Stefano Borson to Monticelli, n.d.
97. Buckingham, *Private Diary*, vol. 2, p. 38.
98. Monticelli Ms B.067/065, Breislak to Monticelli, 29 May 1819.
99. For the complex context of the issue of water and the environment see the brilliant discussion in Stefania Barca, *Enclosing Water: Nature and Political Economy in a Mediterranean Valley, 1796–1916*, Cambridge, 2010, especially pp. 36, 53–7.
100. Davis, *Naples and Napoleon*, p. 285.
101. Quoted in Davis, *Naples and Napoleon*, p. 185.
102. Quoted in John A. Davis, 'Italy', in *The War for the Public Mind: Political Censorship in Nineteenth-century Europe*, ed. Robert Justin Goldstein, Westport CN, 2000, p. 87.
103. The item is available under 'Gimbernat' on the Natural History Museum website, though the inscription is incorrectly translated as 'Alliance of Thunder and Liberty'.
104. Gimbernat may have learned how to make such medals from the Duca de la Torre, who had made several such medals in the 1790s and whose son was also on Vesuvius during the eruption of 1819–20. Such lava medals were to become common in the nineteenth and twentieth centuries. Salvatore Madonna, the chief guide on Vesuvius, had them made with his name inscribed on them as tourist souvenirs. Two from the 1930s celebrate Mussolini and Hitler – and many, as in these examples, carried a political message. They can be seen in the Royal Mineralogical Museum in Naples, the Volcanic Observatory in Naples, the Museum of Natural Sciences in Barcelona, the National Museum of Romanticism in Madrid and the Royal Ontario Museum. See Maddalena De Lucia and Massimo Russo, 'One Hundred and Twenty Years of Italian and Vesuvian History in the Lava Medals Collection of the Observatorio Vesuvino', *Epitome* 4 (2011), p. 144.
105. The entire saga can be followed in Sabarís, 'Diario inedito del geologo Catalan Carlos de Gimbernat'.
106. Monticelli Ms H.051–2, Thomas Hodgkin to M, 27 October 1829; n.d.

Chapter 12. The Spectacle of Catastrophe

1. The two letters have been frequently reprinted as well as appearing on such websites as http://www.pompeii.org.uk/s.php/tour-the-two-letters-written-by-pliny-the-elder-about-the-eruption-of-vesuvius-in-79-a-d-history-of-pompeii-en-238-s.htm.
2. Christopher Charles Parslow, *Rediscovering Antiquity: Karl Weber and the Excavation of Herculaneum, Pompeii, and Stabiae*, Cambridge, 1998.
3. Alain Schnapp, 'The Antiquarian Culture of Eighteenth-century Naples as a Laboratory for New Ideas', in *Rediscovering the Ancient World on the Bay of Naples, 1710–1860*, ed. Carol Mattusch, Washington DC, 2013, pp. 11–34.
4. The historian Thomas Babington Macaulay used the term in his prize-winning poem 'Pompeii': *Pompeii. A Poem which obtained the Chancellor's Medal at the Cambridge Commencement July 1819 by Thomas Babington Macaulay of Trinity College*, Cambridge, 1819.
5. Knowledge of the findings dates back to the first decade of the century, but a general familiarity among antiquaries with the extent and importance of the discoveries dates from mid-century, which is when Naples became 'the capital of curiosities'.
6. *Transactions of the Royal Society of London* 47 (1751–2), pp. 131–42; quote at p. 141.

7. William Hazlitt, Jnr, *The Classical Gazetteer*, London, 1851, p. 369.
8. By 1832 160 skeletons had been found, leading Sir William Gell to estimate a death toll of *c.* 1,300. By 2002 1,047 bodies were accounted for. Giuseppe Fiorelli, the Neapolitan archaeologist and after 1863 director of the Naples National Archaeological Museum, estimated the number of dead at about 2,000. Estelle Lazer, *Resurrecting Pompeii*, Abingdon, 2009, p. 76. For the most recent estimates see McCallam, *Volcanoes*, pp. 18–19.
9. Grell, *Herculanum et Pompéi*, p. 39.
10. De Staël, *Corinne*, Book XI, ch. 4.
11. Roland de la Platière, *Lettres écrites de Suisse, d'Italie, de Sicile et de Malthe*, 6 vols, Amsterdam, 1780, vol. 4, p. 234.
12. Stendhal, *Rome, Naples et Florence*, Paris, 1987, p. 341.
13. [Creuzé de Lesser], *Voyage en Italie et en Sicile*, pp. 174–5.
14. Massachusetts Historical Society, Ms SBd-40, Anon Travel Diary, Naples 1796–7.
15. Quoted in Catharine Edwards, 'The Roads to Rome', in *Imagining Rome: British Artists and Rome in the Nineteenth Century*, ed. Michael Liversidge and Catharine Edwards, London, [1996], p. 15.
16. As Moormann points out, these practices continued throughout the nineteenth century. Erik Moormann, *Pompeii's Ashes: The Reception of the Cities Buried by Vesuvius in Literature, Music and Drama*, Boston, 2015, pp. 49–50.
17. For an illuminating overview of antiquarianism in the eighteenth century see Giovanna Ceserani, 'Antiquarian Transformations in Eighteenth-century Europe', in *World Antiquarianism: Comparative Perspectives*, ed. Alain Schnapp, Los Angeles, 2013, pp. 317–42.
18. Alden R. Gordon, 'Subverting the Secret of Herculaneum: Archaeological Espionage in the Kingdom of Naples', in *Antiquity Recovered: The Legacy of Pompeii and Herculaneum*, ed. Victoria C. Gardner Coates and Jon L. Seydl, Los Angeles, 2007, pp. 37–57.
19. Recent scholarship has been kinder to the Bourbons, pointing out the place of the excavations in a larger project of cultural Enlightenment in Naples, the novelty of royally sponsored excavations, and the 'modern' layout of the museum display of antique artifacts. See Arturo Fittipaldi, 'Museums and Safeguarding an Artistic Heritage in Naples in the Eighteenth Century: Some Reflections', *Journal of the History of Collections* 19, 11 (2007), pp. 191–202, especially pp. 195–6; Alexander Echlin, 'Dynasty, Archaeology and Conservation: The Bourbon Display of Pompeii and Herculaneum in Eighteenth-century Naples', *Journal of the History of Collections* 26 (2014), pp. 145–59.
20. Blix, *From Paris to Pompeii*, p. 10.
21. Moormann, *Pompeii's Ashes*, p. 48; Lucio Fino, *Ercolano e Pompei tra'700 e'800. Acquerelli disegni stampe e ricordi di viaggio*, Naples, 2005, p. 112.
22. There were earlier plans in 1776 and 1785. See Moormann, *Pompeii's Ashes*, p. 43.
23. Fino, *Ercolano e Pompei*, pp. 130–40.
24. Fino, *Ercolano e Pompei*, p. 172.
25. Cited in Fino, *Ercolano e Pompei*, p. 145.
26. Blix, *From Paris to Pompeii*, p. 87.
27. [Charles Bonucci], *Pompéi décrite par Charles Bonucci; un précis historique des excavations depuis l'année 1748 jusqu'à nos jours. Traduction de la troisième édition italienne par C.S.*, Naples, 1828, 'au lecteur'.
28. Edward Bulwer-Lytton, *The Last Days of Pompeii*, London, 1850, p. 8.

29. Quoted in Luciana Jacobelli, ' "Ricostruire" Pompei', in *Pompei. La Costruzione di un mito. Arte, letteratura, aneddotica di un'icona turistica*, ed. Luciana Jacobelli, Rome, 2008, p. 21.
30. Quoted in Anthony Vidler, 'The Architecture of the Uncanny: The Unhomely Houses of the Romantic Sublime', *Assemblage* 3 (1987), p. 16.
31. Mary Beard, 'Taste and the Antique: Visiting Pompeii in the Nineteenth Century', in *Rediscovering the Ancient World on the Bay of Naples*, ed. Carol Mattusch, pp. 215–16 for these and other examples of re-creation and re-enactment; Blix, *From Paris to Pompeii*, p. 215.
32. Andrew Wallace-Hadrill, 'Ruins and Forgetfulness: The Case of Herculaneum', in *Pompeii in the Public Imagination from its Re-discovery to Today*, ed. Shelley Hales and Joanna Paul, Oxford, 2011, p. 378. He might have been thinking of the comment made by the neo-classical architect and populariser of Pompeian designs, William Adam, about Herculaneum: this town, 'once filled with temples, columns, palaces, and other ornaments of good taste is now exactly like a coalmine worked by galley slaves who fill in the waste rooms they leave behind'.
33. On (re)exhumations or 'staged' exhumations see Luciana Jacobelli, 'Ospiti Illustri e Falsi Scavi a Pompei', in *Pompei. La Costruzione di un mito*, ed. Jacobelli, pp. 43–57; Beard, 'Taste and the Antique', pp. 221–2; Lazer, *Resurrecting Pompeii*, pp. 5–6.
34. See Eugene Dwyer, 'Science or Morbid Curiosity? The Castes of Giuseppe Fiorelli and the Last Days of Romantic Pompeii', in *Antiquity Recovered*, ed. Coates and Seydl, p. 174.
35. Bergeret de Grancourt, Pierre Jacques Onésyme, *Journal inédit d'un voyage en Italie: 1773–1774 / Bergeret et Fragonard (par Bergeret de Grancourt)*, Paris, 1895, p. 315.
36. [Sir William Hamilton], *Account of the Discoveries at Pompeii communicated to the Society of Antiquaries of London by Sir William Hamilton*, London, 1777, pp. 6–7. William Beckford offers a similar sketch of resignation: see William Beckford, *Dreams, Waking Thoughts and Incidents*, ed. Robert J. Gemmett, East Brunswick NJ, 1971, p. 217.
37. Moormann, *Pompeii's Ashes*, pp. 180–1.
38. [Charles Mercier-Dupaty], *Lettres sur l'Italie en 1785*, 2 vols, Paris and Rome, 1788, vol. 2, p. 190.
39. Compare Felicia Hemans's altogether more maternal and less sexualised verse of 1828, 'Impression of a Woman's Form, with an Infant Clasped to the Bosom, Found at the Uncovering of Herculaneum':

Oh! I could pass all relics
Left by the pomps of old,
To gaze on this rude monument,
Cast in affections mold.
Love, human love! What art thou
Thy print upon the dust
Outlives the cities of renown
Wherein the mighty trust!

40. Sir William Hamilton, 'An Account of the Latest Eruption of Mount Vesuvius', *Philosophical Transactions* 85 (1795), pp. 92–3.
41. Beinecke Library, Yale University, Osborn D358, 'Travel Journal of Harriet Dennison, 1815–16', 23 February 1816.
42. John Moore, *A View of Society and Manners in Italy, with Anecdotes Relating to Some Eminent Characters*, 3 vols, Dublin, 1786, vol. 3, p. 12.

43. Piozzi, *Observations and Reflections*, p. 331ro.
44. Cambridge University Library, Ms 3550 Colt Hoare, f. 14.
45. [Blessington], *Literary Life*, vol. 1, p. 102.
46. Constanze Baum, 'Ruined Waking Thoughts: William Beckford as a Visitor to Pompeii', in *Pompeii in the Public Imagination*, ed. Hales and Paul, p. 45. A similar distinction is made in Sabrina Ferri, *Ruins Past: Modernity in Italy, 1744–1836*, Oxford, 2015, p. 44: 'Whereas the ruins produced by time evoke simultaneously the disappearance of the past and its duration into the present; the ruins of catastrophe inhabit a constant present.'
47. Lazer, *Resurrecting Pompeii*, p. 66.
48. De Staël, *Corinne*, Book XI, ch. 4.
49. François Mazois, *Les Ruines de Pompéi*, 4 vols, Paris, 1824–38, vol. 2, p. 4.
50. Charlotte Roberts, 'Living with the Ancient Romans: Past and Present in Eighteenth-century Encounters with Herculaneum and Pompeii', *Huntington Library Quarterly* 78, 1 (2015), pp. 61–85, especially p. 64.
51. Moormann, *Pompeii's Ashes*, p. 153.
52. See Vidler, 'The Architecture of the Uncanny', pp. 16–17.
53. Ferri, *Ruins Past*, p. 11.
54. Ferri, *Ruins Past*, p. 53.
55. For lack of interest in the pre-history of the buried cities see Moormann, *Pompeii's Ashes*, p. 70.
56. Beckford, *Dreams*, p. 218.
57. De Staël, *Corinne*, Book XI, ch. 4.
58. [Louise Demont], *Voyages and Travels of her Majesty, Caroline, Queen of Great Britain, by one of Her Majesty's Suite*, London, 1821, pp. 292–3.
59. Massachusetts Historical Society, Ms SBd-40 Anon Travel Diary, Naples 1796–7.
60. [Gottlieb Lewis Engelbach], *Naples and the Campagna Felice in a Series of Letters Addressed to a Friend in England, in 1802*, London, 1815, p. 109.
61. [Engelbach], *Naples and the Campagna Felice*, pp. 271–381. At the end of the letter the account is revealed as a dream.
62. Beard, 'Taste and the Antique', p. 224.
63. Bulwer-Lytton, *Last Days*, preface to the first edition.
64. Jon L. Seydl, 'Decadence, Apocalypse, Resurrection', in *The Last Days of Pompeii*, ed. Victoria C. Gardner Coates, Kenneth Lapatin and Jon L. Seydl, Malibu, 2012, p. 20.
65. Lazer, *Resurrecting Pompeii*, p. 18.
66. Behlman, 'The Sentinel at Pompeii: An Exemplum for the Nineteenth Century', in Coates and Seydl, *Antiquity Recovered*, pp. 161–2; Lazer, *Resurrecting Pompeii*, p. 14; Moormann, *Pompeii's Ashes*, pp. 185–9.
67. Nicholas Daly, 'The Volcanic Disaster Narrative: From Pleasure Garden to Canvas, Page and Stage', *Victorian Studies* 53, 2 (2011), p. 263.
68. Donald Rosenthal, 'Joseph Franque's "The Scene during the Eruption of Vesuvius"', *Philadelphia Museum of Art Bulletin* 75, 324 (1979), pp. 2–15; Coates, Lapatin and Seydl (eds), *The Last Days of Pompeii*, pp. 138–9.
69. Galina Leontyeva, *Karl Briullov: Artist of Russian Romanticism*, Bournemouth, 1996, pp. 7–24; Rosalind P. Gray, *Russian Genre Painting in the Nineteenth Century*, Oxford, 2000, pp. 104–5; [Karl Briullov], *Karl Briullov: Paintings, Watercolours, Drawings*, Leningrad, 1990, pp. 13–27.
70. Lucio Fino, *Il Vesuvio nel Grand Tour. Vedute e scritti di tre secoli*, Naples, 2012, pp. 177–80.

71. *Giornale delle Due Sicilie* (21 November 1825) on the performance in Naples: 'Poi in modo straordinario l'ultima scena presentante un quadro per quanto grandioso altrettanto desolante e terribile, la distruzione della città sotto la pioggia di cenere e lapilli in mezzo all'inondamento delle fiumane di fuoco che tra boccavano dal Vesuvio.'
72. https://yarmarkt.ru/en/zhivopisec-s-kartinoi-poslednii-den-pompei-opisanie-kartiny-poslednii.html.
73. Leontyeva, *Karl Briullov*, pp. 30–7; Gray, *Russian Genre Painting*, p. 101.
74. Margaret Samu, 'The Reception of Karl Briullov's *Last Day of Pompeii* at the Salon of 1834', *Art Bulletin* 103, 2 (2021), pp. 77–103, explains the complex story of the reception of Briullov's picture in France and the politics that surrounded it.
75. The essay, 'The Last Day of Pompeii (Briullov's Painting) 1834', is available at: vads.ac.uk/digital/collection/RVA/id/844/rec/2.
76. Ingrid D. Rowland, *From Pompeii: The Afterlife of a Roman Town*, Cambridge MA, 2014, pp. 133–4: Coates, Lapatin and Seydl (eds), *The Last Days of Pompeii*, pp. 140–3. A review of the painting in the periodical *Biblioteca Italiana* cited references to Raphael, Guido Reni, Domenichino and the Carracci brothers: Gray, *Russian Genre Painting*, p. 102.
77. Bulwer-Lytton's response is discussed in Curtis Dahl, 'Bulwer-Lytton and the School of Catastrophe', *Philological Quarterly* 32 (1953), p. 434.
78. Baum, 'Ruined Waking Thoughts', pp. 44–5.
79. Quoted in https://ermakvagus.com/Europe/Italy/Pompeii/bryulov.html.
80. Sumner Lincoln Fairfield, *The Last Night of Pompeii, a poem, and Lays and Legends*, New York, 1832, p. ix.
81. Bulwer-Lytton, *Last Days*, p. 289.
82. Moormann, *Pompeii's Ashes*, has the fullest discussion of Christians (and Jews) in representations of Pompeii. See Chapter 4, 'Jews and Christians in Pompeii Novels', pp. 215–56.
83. 'The Image in Lava': http://digital.library.upenn.edu/women/hemans/records/lava.html.
84. Blix, *From Paris to Pompeii*, p. 144.
85. Blix, *From Paris to Pompeii*, p. 6.
86. Kerstin Barndt, 'Working Through Ruins: Berlin's Neues Museum', *Germanic Review* 86 (2011), pp. 296–9.
87. [Edward Gibbon], *The Autobiographies of Edward Gibbon*, ed. John Murray, 2nd edn, London, 1897, p. 302. Scholars have been sceptical about Gibbon's memory.
88. Lord Byron, *Childe Harold's Pilgrimage*, Canto IV, 146.

Chapter 13. Vesuvius: The Spectacle of the Sublime in 'the Age of Contrivances'

1. Quoted in John Black, 'The Eruption of Vesuvius in Pacini's *L'Ultimo Giorno di Pompei*', *Donizetti Society Journal* 6 (1988), pp. 98–9.
2. Tom Gunning, 'An Aesthetic of Astonishment: Early Film and the (In)Credulous Spectator', *Art and Text* 34 (1989), pp. 114–24.
3. Bodleian Library, John Johnson Collection, Entertainments Folder 7 (46).
4. *Morning Chronicle* (17 February 1776).
5. The literature on oramas is now vast but see, inter alia, Dolf Sternberger, 'Panorama of the 19th Century', *October* 4 (1977), pp. 3–20; Bernard Comment, *The Painted Panorama*, trans. Anne-Marie Glasheen, New York, 2000; Stephen Oettermann, *Panorama: History of a Mass Medium*, trans. Deborah L. Schneider, New York, 1996; Robert Altick, *The Shows of London*, Cambridge MA, 1978; Erkki Huhtamo,

Illusions in Motion: Media Archaeology of the Moving Panorama and Related Spectacles, Cambridge MA, 2013; Ann Bermingham, 'Landscape-O-Rama: The Exhibition Landscape at Somerset House and the Rise of Popular Landscape Entertainments', in *Art on the Line: The Royal Academy Exhibitions at Somerset House, 1780–1836*, ed. David H. Solkin, New Haven and London, 2001, pp. 127–43; Ralph Hyde, *Panoramania! The Art and Entertainment of the 'All-Embracing' View*, London, 1988; S. Wilcox, 'The Panorama and Related Exhibitions in London', PhD thesis, University of Edinburgh, 1976; John Brewer, 'Sensibility and the Urban Panorama', *Huntington Library Quarterly* 70 (2007), pp. 229–49.

6. Tony Bennett, 'The Exhibitionary Complex', *New Formations* 4 (1988), pp. 73–102.
7. R.-C. Guilbert de Pixérécourt, *La Tête de mort; ou, Les Ruines de Pompeïa: Mélodrame en trois actes*, Paris, 1828, p. 94.
8. For transparencies see 'Romantic Transparencies', in Andreas Bluhm and Louise Lipincott, *Light: The Industrial Age 1750–1900: Art, Science, Technology and Society*, Amsterdam and Pittsburgh, 2000, pp. 96–7.
9. *Philosophical Transactions of the Royal Society* (1768), pp. 58, 12.
10. For the Dessau volcano see Maiken Umbach, 'Visual Culture, Scientific Images and German Small-state Politics in the Late Enlightenment', *Past and Present* 158 (1998), pp. 110–45, especially pp. 125–6 for the 1775 London visit.
11. British Library, Add MS 42069, Hamilton and Greville Papers, f.61, Pringle to Hamilton, 1768.
12. For Danson and his sons see 'Tales from a Scenic Artist and Scholar. Part 391 – The Danson Family of Scenic Artists', http://drypigment.net/2018/04/20/tales-from-a-scenic-artist-and-scholar-part-391-the-danson-family-of-scenic-artists/.
13. Huhtamo, *Illusions in Motion*, p. 169.
14. Alexander von Humboldt, *Cosmos: A Sketch of a Physical Description of the Universe*, trans. O.C. Otté, New York, 1850, vol. 2, pp. 97–8.
15. Oettermann, *Panorama*, pp. 12–13.
16. Cited in Huhtamo, *Illusions in Motion*, p. 75.
17. Sorensen, 'Sir William Hamilton's Vesuvian Apparatus'.
18. A connection made by David McCallam; see *Volcanoes*, p. 113.
19. Iain McCalman, 'The Art of de Loutherbourg's Eidophusikon', in *Sensation and Sensibility: Viewing Gainsborough's Cottage Door*, ed. Ann Bermingham, New Haven and London, 2005, pp. 181–97.
20. Ann Bermingham, 'Technologies of Illusion: De Loutherbourg's Eidophusikon in Eighteenth-century London', *Art History* 39 (2016), pp. 376–99 at p. 396.
21. P.J. van de Merwe, 'The Life and Theatrical Career of Clarkson Stanfield (1793–1867)', PhD thesis, Bristol University, 1979, pp. 111–15.
22. Christopher Baugh, *Garrick and Loutherbourg*, Cambridge, 1990; Baugh, 'Philippe de Loutherbourg: Technology-driven Entertainment and Spectacle in the Late Eighteenth Century', *Huntington Library Quarterly* 70, 2 (2007), pp. 251–68.
23. *Morning Chronicle* (17 February 1776).
24. Richard Carl Wickman, 'An Evaluation of the Employment of Panoramic Scenery in the Nineteenth-century Theatre', PhD thesis, Ohio State University, 1961, p. 170.
25. Quoted in Rebecca Hilliker, 'Karl Friedrich Schinkel's Diorama and Panorama Art for *Einfache Menschen*: A Classical-Romantic's Search for the Sublime', *Theatre History Studies* 8 (1988), p. 107.
26. For Daguerre see Stephen Pinson, *Speculating Daguerre: Art and Enterprise in the Work of L.J.M. Daguerre*, Chicago, 2012.
27. Lady Morgan, 'The Diorama', *Athenaeum* (July 1836), pp. 570–2.

28. Naguère Daguerre #1, 'Installation lumineuse sur toile peinte biface du 19e siècle'. https://jeanpaulfavand.wordpress.com/portfolio/naguere-daguerre-1/.
29. Oettermann, *Panorama*, pp. 213–15; *August Kopisch: Maler*, pp. 186–9.
30. Oettermann, *Panorama*, pp. 209, 211.
31. C.F. Langhans, *Pleorama, erfunden und aufgestellt*, Breslau, 1831.
32. Oettermann, *Panorama*, p. 214.
33. Oettermann, *Panorama*, p. 214.
34. Beinecke Library, Osborn D408, John Hincks, *Journal of a Tour on the Continent of Europe Made in 1823*, 10 May 1823.
35. Gillen D'Arcy Wood, *The Shock of the Real: Romanticism and Visual Culture, 1760–1860*, New York, 2001, especially pp. 1–22, 107–20.
36. Pinson, *Speculating Daguerre*, p. 89.
37. John Ruskin, *Praeterita*, Edinburgh, 2019, pp. 89–90.
38. Pinson, *Speculating Daguerre*, p. 33.
39. Quoted in Huhtamo, *Illusions in Motion*, p. 80.
40. Huhtamo, *Illusions in Motion*, pp. 77–8, 151–2 for examples.
41. Quoted in Huhtamo, *Illusions in Motion*, p. 192. See also Bodleian Library, John Johnson Collection, Dioramas 2 (116), 3 (75).
42. *Blackwood's Edinburgh Magazine* 15 (1824), p. 472; *The Times* (22 April 1830).
43. See the classic study of Jonathan Crary, *Techniques of the Observer: On Visions and Modernity in the Nineteenth Century*, Cambridge MA, 1990.
44. [Charles Dickens], 'Some Account of an Extraordinary Traveller', *Household Words* (April 1850), p. 519.
45. *The Times* (22 April 1830).
46. *Blackwood's Edinburgh Magazine* 15 (1824), p. 47.
47. *The Art Journal* 7 (1861), p. 331.

Conclusion

1. I take the term from Ingold, *The Perception of the Environment*, p. 274.

BIBLIOGRAPHY

Manuscript Sources

Archivio di Stato Napoli
1809 catasto provvisorio, secondo versamento, fascicolo 933

Beinecke Library, Yale University
Osborn D293, William Gell, Journal 9 August 1814–31 May 1815
Osborn D358, Travel Journal of Harriet Dennison, 1815–16
Osborn D408, John Hincks, 'Journal of a Tour on the Continent of Europe Made in
    1823'
Osborn D469, Travel Diary Anon, 1826–7
Osborn 12794, Samuel Rogers Correspondence

Biblioteca Nazionale, Naples
Teodoro Monticelli Ms

Bodleian Library, Oxford
John Johnson Collection

British Library
Add MS 64101, Louis Jérôme de Goujon de Thuisy narrative
Add MS 41536, Heytesbury Papers
Add MS 61937, Fazakerley Papers
Add MS 40714, Hamilton and Greville Papers
Add MS 42069, Hamilton and Greville Papers

Cambridge University Library
Add Ms 8908, Crackenthorpe Papers
Add Ms 3550, Colt Hoare

Houghton Library, Harvard University
MS Ital 139, Visitors' Book to Vesuvius
MS Fr 178, 'Lettres sur L'Italie'

Huntington Library, San Marino California
Stowe Mss ST88, Private Diary of Richard Duke of Buckingham and Chandos

Manchester Metropolitan University Archives
Sir Harry Page Collection

Massachusetts Historical Society, Boston
Ms SBd-40, Anon Travel Diary Naples 1796–7

National Library of Scotland
Mss 1541 and 1542, Journal of Sir William Forbes 1792–3
Hall Ms 6327

Northumberland Archives
ZMI B 52/3/1, Sir Charles Miles Lambert Monck, 'Journal of a tour through France, part of Switzerland, Italy and Sicily, in company with Lord Wallace and my son, but in Sicily alone'
324/12, William Ord Diary 1814–15

Paul Mellon Centre, London
Brinsley Ford Archive, Wedderburn Papers

Royal Academy Archives, London
Sir Thomas Lawrence Mss

Royal Geological Society, London
LDGSL/36, Italian tracts on Sicily and Etna

Royal Institution, London
Davy Letters Project, www.davy-letters.org.uk (DLP)

Royal Society Archives, London
HS2, John Herschel Correspondence

Tyne and Wear Archives
DX 985/1, Sir William Hutt of Gateshead, 'Journal of travels through Italy, Istria, Germany and Belgium', no foliation [1824]

University of St Andrews Archives
Forbes Mss Dep7, Box 14, Journal 2, Forbes Journal

Printed Sources

[Astore, Francesco A.], *Dialoghi sul Vesuvio in occasione dell'eruzione della sera de' 15 Giugno 1794*, Naples, 1794.
Atti della Quinta Unione degli Scienziati Italiani tenuta in Lucca nel settembre 1843, Lucca, 1844.

Auldjo, John, *Sketches of Vesuvius with a short account of its principal eruptions, from the commencement of the Christian era to the present time*, Naples, 1832.

Babbage, Charles, *Observations on the Temple of Serapis, at Pozzuoli, near Naples, with an attempt to explain the causes of the frequent elevation and depression of large portions of the earth's surface in remote periods. And to prove that those causes continue in action at the present time. With a Supplement. Conjectures on the Physical condition of the surface of the Moon*, privately printed, London, 1847.

——, *Passages from the Life of a Philosopher*, ed. Martin Campbell-Kelly, New Brunswick NJ, 1994.

——, *Reflections on the Decline of Science in England, and on some of its causes*, London, 1830.

[Banks, Joseph], *The Scientific Correspondence of Sir Joseph Banks*, ed. Neil Chambers, 6 vols, London, 2007.

[Bartholdy, Felix Mendelssohn], *Letters of Felix Mendelssohn Bartholdy from Italy and Switzerland*, trans. Lady Wallace, New York and Boston, 1866.

Batty, Elizabeth Frances, *Italian Scenery from Drawings Made in 1817*, London, 1820.

Beckford, William, *Dreams, Waking Thoughts and Incidents*, ed. Robert J. Gemmett, East Brunswick NJ, 1971.

Bergeret de Grancourt, Pierre Jacques Onésyme, *Journal inédit d'un voyage en Italie: 1773–1774 / Bergeret et Fragonard (par Bergeret de Grancourt)*, Paris, 1895.

Berrian, William, *Travels in France and Italy in 1817 and 1818*, New York, 1821.

[Bewick, William], *Life and Letters of William Bewick (artist)*, ed. Thomas Landseer, 2 vols, London, 1871.

Blair, Hugh, *Lectures on Rhetoric and Belles Lettres*, 2 vols, London, 1783.

Blessington, Countess, *The Idler in Italy*, 2 vols, 2nd edn, London, 1839.

——, *The Literary Life and Correspondence of the Countess of Blessington*, ed. R.R. Madden, 3 vols, London, 1855.

[Bonucci, Charles], *Pompéi décrite par Charles Bonucci; un précis historique des excavations depuis l'année 1748 jusqu'à nos jours. Traduction de la troisième édition italienne par C.S.*, Naples, 1828.

[Borel, J.M.L.], *Lettres écrites d'Italie à quelques amis; Par J.M.L. Bor***, Paris, 1825.

Boué, Ami, *Bulletin de la Société Géologique de la France: Résumé des Progrès des Sciences Géologiques*, Paris, 1834.

[Bournonville, August], Helene Darling, 'August Bournonville's Letters from France and Italy, 1841 Part Three', *Dance Chronicle* 25, 3 (2002), pp. 355–6.

Breislak, Scipione and Winspeare, Antonio, *Memoria sull'Eruzione del Vesuvio accaduta la sera de' 15 Giugno 1794*, Naples, 1794.

Briand, P.C., *Les Jeunes Voyageurs en Europe, ou Description Raisonée des divers pays compris dans cette Partie du Monde*, 5 vols, Paris, 1827.

[Briullov, Karl], *Karl Briullov: Paintings, Watercolours, Drawings*, Leningrad, 1990.

Brockedon, William, *Travellers Guide to Italy or, Road-book from London to Naples*, Paris, 1835.

Brongniart, Alexandre, *Elémentaire de Mineralogie, avec des applications aux arts; ouvrage destiné à l'enseignement dans les lycées nationaux*, Paris, 1807.

Brosses, Charles de, *Lettres familières écrits d'Italie en 1739 et 1740*, 2 vols, Paris, 1885.

Bruun-Neergaard, T.C., *Journal du dernier Voyage du Cen. Dolomieu dans les Alpes*, Paris, 1802.

Brydone, Patrick, *A Tour Through Sicily and Malta. In a Series of Letters to William Beckford, Esq. of Somerly in Suffolk*, 2 vols, Dublin, 1780.

[Buckingham and Chandos, Richard, 1st Duke of], *The Private Diary of Richard, Duke of Buckingham and Chandos, KG*, 3 vols, London, 1862.

Bulwer-Lytton, Edward, *The Last Days of Pompeii*, London, 1850.

Bunbury, Selina, *A Visit to the Catacombs, or First Christian Cemeteries of Rome: and a Midnight Visit to Mount Vesuvius*, London, 1849.

[Burke, Edmund], *The Correspondence of Edmund Burke*, 10 vols, Cambridge and Chicago, 1958–78.

——, *The Writings and Speeches of Edmund Burke*, vol. 1, *The Early Writings*, ed. T.O. McLoughlin, James T. Boulton and William B. Todd, Oxford, 1997.

Bylandt Palsterkamp, A., *Resumé préliminaire d'ouvrage sur le Vesuve*, Naples, 1833.

Caneva, Salvatore, *Lettera dell'eremita del S. Salvatore sito alle falde del Vesuvio per dare ad un amico suo un succinto ragguaglio dell'accaduta Eruzione la sera de' 15 Giugno*, Naples, 1794.

Castellan, Antoine-Larent, *Lettres sur l'Italie, faisant suite aux lettres sur La Morée, l'Hellespont et Constantinople*, Paris, 1819.

[Catel, Franz Ludwig], *Franz Ludwig Catel: Italienbilder der Romantik*, Hamburg, n.d.

Chevalier, Abbé C., *Naples Le Vésuve et Pompéi*, 4th edn, Tours, 1887.

[Christian VIII], *Konig Christian VIII.s Dagbøger og Optegnelser. II 1. halvbind 1815–1821*, ed. Albert Fabritius, Finn Friis and Else Kornerup, Copenhagen, 1973.

[Clarke, Edward Daniel], William Otter, *The Life and Remains of Edward Daniel Clarke, Professor of Mineralogy in the University of Cambridge*, 2 vols, London, 1825.

[Colomb, Romain], M.R.C., *Journal d'un voyage en Italie et en Suisse pendant l'année 1828*, Paris, 1833.

Cooper, James Fenimore, *Gleanings in Europe: Italy*, Albany NY, 1981.

Covelli, Nicola and Monticelli, Teodoro, *Storia de' Fenomeni del Vesuvio avvenuti negli anni 1821, 1822 e parte del 1823*, Naples, 1823, repr. [Monticelli], *Opere dell'abate Teodoro Monticelli*, vol. 2, pp. 167–330.

Coxe, Henry, *Picture of Italy; being a Guide to the Antiquities and Curiosities of that Classical and Interesting Country; containing sketches of Manners, Society and Customs, and an itinerary of Distances in Posts and English Miles, best Inns &c with a Minute Description of Rome, Florence, Naples, & Venice, and their Environs. In which are prefixed Directions to Travellers, and Dialogues in English, French and Italian*, London, 1815.

Coxe, William, *Travels in Switzerland. In a Series of Letters to William Melmouth, Esq.*, 3 vols, London, 1789.

[Creuzé de Lesser, Auguste], *Voyage en Italie et en Sicile, fait en MDCCCI et MDCCCII, par M. Creuzé de Lesser, Membre du Corps Legislatif*, Paris, 1806.

[Crombet, Paul], *Les Souvenirs d'Italie de Paul Crombet, officer belge de la marine royale des Pays-Bas (1817–26)*, ed. Vicomte Charles de Terlinden, Brussels, 1941.

Cuoco, Vincenzo, *Historical Essay on the Neapolitan Revolution of 1799*, trans. David Gibbons, ed. Bruce Haddock and Filippo Sabetti, Toronto, 2014.

[Dahl, Johan Christian], *Johan Christian Dahl 1788–1857: Life and Works*, ed. Marie Lodrup Bang, 3 vols, Oslo, [1987].

Damas, Adélaide-Louise-Zéphirine de, *Voyage en Italie, par la comtesse de Chastellux née de Damas*, Paris, 1834.

Daubeny, Charles, *A Description of Active and Extinct Volcanos; with remarks on their origin, their chemical phaenomena, and the character of their products*, London, 1826.

Davy, Humphry, *Collected Works*, ed. John Davy, 9 vols, London, 1839–40.

——, *Discourse Introductory to a Course of Chemistry*, London, 1802.

——, *Humphry Davy on Geology: The 1805 Lectures for the General Audience*, ed. and intro. Robert Siegfried and Robert H. Dott Jr, Madison WI, 1980.

De Renzi, Salvatore, *Della Vita e delle opere di O.G. Costa*, Napoli, 1868.

——, *Osservazioni sulla topografia-medica del Regno di Napoli: Cenni sulla topografia-medica della città di Napoli, e delle provincie di Napoli, di terra di Lavoro, ed di principato ultra*, 3 vols, Naples, 1828–30.

Degérando, J.M., *The Observation of Savage People*, trans. F.C.T. Moore, London, 1969.

[Demont, Louise], *Voyages and Travels of her Majesty, Caroline, Queen of Great Britain, by one of Her Majesty's Suite*, London, 1821.

[Dickens, Charles], 'Some Account of an Extraordinary Traveller', *Household Words* (April 1850).

[Dolomieu, Déodat], Alfred Lacroix, *Déodat Dolomieu (1750–1801). Sa Correspondance, sa vie aventureuse, sa captivité, ses œuvres*, 2 vols, Paris, 1921.

——, 'Discors sur l'étude de la Géologie, prononcé par Déodat Dolomieu, Membre del'Institut National, à l'ouverture de son cours sur les gissement des Minéraux, commence en Ventôse de l'an 5', *Journal de Physique, de Chimie* 2, 45 (1794), pp. 256–72.

——, *Mémoire sur les Tremblements de Terre de la Calabre pendant l'année 1783*, Rome, 1784.

——, Fortunée B. Briquet, *Ode sur la Mort de Dolomieu, précédée d'une notice sur ce Naturaliste*, Paris, An X.

D'Onofri, Pietro, *Elogio estemperaneo per la gloriosa memoria di Carlo III. Monarca delle Spagne e delle Indie*, Naples, 1789.

D'Onofrio, Michele Arcangelo, *Dettaglio istorico della peste di Noja in provincia di Bari*, Naples, 1817.

——, *Lettera ad un amico in provincia sul tremuoto accadduto a 26 Guglio*, Naples, 1805.

——, *Lettera del professore di medicina Michele Arcangelo in cui di da la descrizione del telegrafo*, [Naples], 1794.

——, *Nuove riflessioni sul Vesuvio con un breve dettaglio de' Paraterremoti*, Naples, 1794.

——, *Relazione ragionata della eruzione del nostro Vesuvio*, Naples, 1794.

Driou, Alfred, *Naples, les magnificences de son golfe et les curiosités de ses rivages*, Limoges, 1862.

Duclos, Louis, *Voyage en Italie, ou Considérations sur l'Italie*, Paris, 1791.

Dumas, Alexandre, *Le Corricolo*, Paris, 1846.

[Dupaty, Charles Mercier], *Lettres sur l'Italie en 1785*, 2 vols, Paris and Rome, 1788.

——, *Travels through Italy, in a Series of Letters written in the year 1785, by President Dupaty. Translated from the French. By an Englishman*, London, 1788.

Ebel, J.G., *Manuel du Voyageur en Suisse*, 3rd edn, 3 vols, Zurich, 1817.

The Edinburgh Encyclopedia conducted by David Brewster LLD, FRS with the assistance of gentlemen eminent in science and literature, 18 vols, Philadelphia, 1832.

[Edwards, Henri Milnes], *Notice Historique sur Henri Milnes Edwards, member de l'académie des sciences, par M. Bertelot*, Paris, 1891.

[Engelbach, Gottlieb Lewis], *Naples and the Campagna Felice in a Series of Letters Addressed to a Friend in England, in 1802*, London, 1815.

Fairfield, Sumner Lincoln, *The Last Night of Pompeii, a poem, and Lays and Legends*, New York, 1832.

[Ferraro, J.B.], *A New Guide of Naples, its Environs, Procida, Ischia and Capri. Compiled from Vasi's Guide, several more recent publications, and a personal visit of the compiler to the Churches, Monuments, Antiquities etc. by J.B. Ferarro, Professor of Languages*, 1st edn, Naples, 1826.

[Filomarino, Ascanio and Clemente], 'L'Uccisione di Ascanio e Clemente Filomarino', *Archivio storico per le province napoletane* XXV, 1 (1900), pp. 74–5.

[Flandin, C.], *Etudes et Souvenirs de Voyages en Italie et en Suisse par C. Flandin*, Paris, 1838.

[Forbes, James D.], *Life and Letters of James David Forbes*, ed. John Campbell Shairp, Anthony Adams-Reilly and Peter Guthrie Tait, London, 1873.

——, 'Remarks on Mount Vesuvius', *Edinburgh Journal of Science* 7, 1 (1827), pp. 11–18.

——, *Travels through the Alps of Savoy and other parts of the Pennine Chain with observations on the phenomena of Glaciers*, Edinburgh, 1845.

Forsyth, Joseph, *Remarks on Antiquities, Arts, and Letters, during an excursion in Italy in the years 1802 and 1803*, London, 1813.

Fougasse, Scipione, *Chez une Femme Illustre suivi de quelques souvenirs de l'Auteur*, Paris, 1866.

[Fremantle, Elizabeth Wynne], *Travels in the Two Sicilies 1817–1820*, ed. Nigel Foxell, London, 2007.

Fucini, Renato, *Napoli a Occhio Nudo. Lettere ad un Amico*, Florence, 1878.

Galiffe, James Augustin, *Italy and its Inhabitants: An account of a tour through that country in 1816 and 1817*, 2 vols, London, 1820.

Galignani's Traveller's Guide Through Italy, 7th edn, Paris, 1824.

Gasparin, Valérie Boissier de, *Voyage d'une ignorante dans le midi de la France et l'Italie*, 2 vols, Paris, 1835.

[Gaskell, James Milnes], *An Eton Boy: Being the Letters of James Milnes Gaskell from Eton and Oxford, 1820–1830*, ed. Charles Milnes Gaskell, London, 1939.

[Gibbon, Edward], *The Autobiographies of Edward Gibbon*, ed. John Murray, 2nd edn, London, 1897.

[Gimbernat, Carlos], Lluis Solé Sabarís, 'Diario inedito del geologo Catalan Carlos de Gimbernat (1768–1834)', *Llull* 5, 8–9 (1982), pp. 111–31.

——, 'Respecting a French traveller who perished in the crater of Vesuvius', *European Magazine* 80 (1821), p. 361.

Giros, Simone, *Veridica Relazione di Simone Giros giardiniere della Real Villa Favorita, circa l'ultima eruzione del Vesuvio accaduta al 15 Giugno per tutto Luglio dell'anno 1794*, Naples, 1794.

[Greville, Charles C.F.], *The Greville Memoirs: A Journal of the Reigns of King George IV and William IV by the late Charles C.F. Greville*, ed. Henry Reeve, 3 vols, Longman and Green, London, 1874.

Hall, Basil, *Patchwork*, 3 vols, 2nd edn, London, 1841.

[Hallam, Arthur Henry], *The Letters of Arthur Henry Hallam*, ed. Jack Kolb, Columbus OH, 1981.

[Hamilton, Sir William], *Account of the Discoveries at Pompeii communicated to the Society of Antiquaries of London by Sir William Hamilton*, London, 1777.

——, 'An Account of the Latest Eruption of Mount Vesuvius', *Philosophical Transactions* 85 (1795), pp. 92–3.

——, *Campi Phlegraei. Observations on the Volcanos of the Two Sicilies as they have been communicated to the Royal Society of London by Sir William Hamilton*, 2 vols, Naples, 1776.

——, *Oeuvres Complètes de M. le Chevalier Hamilton … Commentée par M. L'Abbé Giraud-Soulavie*, Paris, 1781.

——, *Supplement to the Campi Phlegraei, being an account of the great eruption of Mount Vesuvius in the month of August 1779*, Naples, 1779.

Hazlitt, William, *Criticisms on Art. 2nd Series, edited by his son*, London, 1844.

Hazlitt, William, Jnr, *The Classical Gazetteer*, London, 1851.

Hogg, Thomas Jefferson, *Two Hundred and Nine Days; or, the Journal of a Traveller on the Continent*, 2 vols, London, 1827.

[Hope, James], *Memoir of the late James Hope, M.D. by Mrs Hope*, London, 1843.

Humboldt, Alexander von, *Cosmos: A Sketch of a Physical Description of the Universe*, trans. O.C. Otté, 2 vols, New York, 1850.

Hutton, James, 'Theory of the Earth', *Transactions of the Royal Society of Edinburgh* I (1788), pp. 209–304.

——, *Theory of the Earth, with Proofs and Illustrations. In Four Parts*, London and Edinburgh, 1795.

[Jackson, Abraham Reeves], 'Newspaper Letters of another "Innocent Abroad": Dr. Abraham Reeves Jackson', *Mark Twain Journal* 33 (1995), pp. 6–53.

Jameson, Mrs [Anna], *The Diary of an Ennuyée*, Boston, 1860.

[Jones, Thomas], 'Thomas Jones, Memoirs, 1742–1803', *Walpole Society*, 32 (1951).

Jousiffe, Captain, *A Road-book for Travellers in Italy*, 2nd edn, Brussels, Paris and London, 1840.

[Jouy, Etienne de], *L'Hermite de la Chausée d'Antin, ou Observations sur les mœurs et les usages parisiens au commencement du XIX siècle*, 2 vols, 2nd edn, Paris, 1813.

Kant, Immanuel, *Critique of Judgment*, trans. James Creed Meredith, rev. Nicholas Walker, Oxford, 2007.

Kopisch, August, 'Seiner Königlichen Hoheit dem Kronprizen von Preussen. Auf dem Vesuv am 13. November 1828', in Kopisch, *Gesammelte Werke*, 4 vols, Berlin, 1856, vol. 2, pp. 3–7.

Kotzebue, August von, *Travels through Italy in the Years 1804 and 1805*, 4 vols, London, 1806.

Lemaistre, J.G., *Travels after the Peace of Amiens, through France and Switzerland, Italy and Germany*, 3 vols, London, 1806.

Lippi, Carmine Antonio, *Fu il fuoco o l'acqua che sotterò Pompei ed Ercolano?*, Naples, 1816.

Longfellow, Ernest Wadsworth, *Random Memories*, Boston, 1922.

[Longfellow, Henry Wadsworth], *Letters of Henry Wadsworth Longfellow*, vol. 1, *1814–1836*, ed. Andrew Hilen, Cambridge MA, 1966.

Lowry, Delvalle, *Conversations in Mineralogy*, London, 1822.

Lyell, Charles, *Principles of Geology; or the modern changes of the earth and its inhabitants*, 9th edn, New York, 1853.

——, '[Review of] *Memoir of the geology of central France . . . by G.P. Scrope*', *Quarterly Review* 36 (1827), pp. 437–83.

[Macaulay, Thomas Babington], *The Miscellaneous Writings of Lord Macaulay*, 2 vols, London, 1860.

——, *Pompeii. A Poem which obtained the Chancellor's Medal at the Cambridge Commencement July 1819 by Thomas Babington Macaulay of Trinity College*, Cambridge, 1819.

[Maceroni, Francis], *Memoirs of the Life and Adventures of Colonel Maceroni*, 2 vols, London, 1838.

[Maclure, William], *The European Journals of William Maclure*, Philadelphia, 1988.

Magne, Mattieu, '"Mon Dieu que ce Vésuve est beau!" Le récit de l'ascension dans le journal d'un aristocrate de Bohême au cours de son voyage de 1816', *Cahiers de la Mediterranée* 89 (December 2014), pp. 265–94.

Manni, P. Pasquale, *Saggio fisico-chemico della cagione de' baleni e delle pioggie che osservansi nelle grandi eruzioni vulcaniche. In occasione dell'eruzione del Vesuvio a Giugno 1794*, Naples, 1794.

Maréchal, P. Sylvain, *Le jugement dernier des rois, prophétie en un acte, en prose*, Paris [1793/4].

Matthews, Henry, *The Diary of an Invalid, being the Journal of a Tour in Pursuit of Health in Portugal, Italy, Switzerland and France in the years 1817, 1818, 1819*, 2nd edn, London, 1820.

Maximilian (Emperor of Mexico), *Recollections of My Life by Maximilian I, Emperor of Mexico*, London, 1868.

[Melograni, Giuseppe], *Manuale Geologico di Giuseppe Melograni*, Naples, 1806.

[Metternich, Klemens Wenzel Lothar von], *Memoirs of Prince Metternich, 1815–1829*, ed. R. Metternich, trans. A. Napier, Bentley and Son, London, 1881.

Michelet, Jules, *The Mountain, from the French of Michelet, by the translator of 'The Bird'* [W.H.D. Davenport-Adams], London, 1872.

Minervini, Ciro Saverio, 'Due Lettere al M. Rosini, 17 e 21 Giugno, 1794', *Giornale Letterario di Napoli* XI (1794), pp. 86–97.

[Monticelli, Teodoro], Amilcare Mazzarella, 'Della Vita e delle Opere di Teodoro Monticelli', *Giornale Euganeo di Scienze, Lettere ed Arti* 2, 3 (1846), p. 495.

——, *Notizia di una escursione al Vesuvio, e dell'avvenimento che vi ebbe luogo il giorno 16 Gennajo; in cui il francese Coutrel si precipitò in una di quelle nuove bocche*, Naples, 1821.

——, *Opere dell'abate Teodoro Monticelli*, 3 vols, Naples, 1841–3.

Monticelli, Teodoro and Covelli, Nicola, *Prodromo della mineralogia vesuviana*, Naples, 1825.

Moore, John, *A View of Society and Manners in Italy*, 2 vols, 2nd edn, London, 1779.

Morgan, Sydney, Lady, 'The Diorama', *Athenaeum* (July 1836), pp. 570–2.

——, *Italy by Lady Morgan*, 3 vols, London, 1831.

[Morgenstern, Johann Karl Simon], 'Visit to Mount Vesuvius of Professor Morgenstern [1809]', *New Monthly Magazine and Universal Register* (June 1818), pp. 387–9.

Morton, Harriet, *Protestant Vigils; or, Evening Records of a Journey in Italy, in the years 1826 and 1827*, 2 vols, London, 1829.

Murray, John, *A Handbook for Travellers in Southern Italy Being a Guide for the Continental Portion of the Kingdom of the Two Sicilies*, 2nd edn, London, 1855.

——, *Handbook for Travellers in Southern Italy*, 3rd edn, London, 1858.

Napier, Lord, *Notes on Modern Painting at Naples*, London, 1855.

Napoli e i Luoghi Celebri delle sue Vicinanze, 2 vols, Naples, 1845.

Notes on Naples and its Environs: and on the road to it from Rome by a Traveller, London, 1838.

Odier, Amélie, *Mon Voyage en Italie 1811–1812*, ed. Daniela Vaj, Geneva, 1993.

Ordinaire, Claude Nicolas, *Histoire Naturelle des Volcans*, Paris, 1802.

Owen, John, *Travels into different parts of Europe in the years 1791 and 1792 with familiar remarks on Places-Men-and Manners*, 2 vols, London, 1796.

[Pentland, Joseph], William Anthony S. Sarjeant and Justin B. Delair, 'An Irish Naturalist in Cuvier's Laboratory: The Letters of Joseph Pentland, 1820–1822', *Bulletin of the British Museum (Natural History)* 6 (1980), pp. 245–319.

Phillips, John, *Vesuvius*, Oxford, 1869.

[Piaggio], Carlo Knight, 'Un inedito di Padre Piaggio: Il diario Vesuviano 1779–1795', *Rendiconti della Accademia di archeologia, lettere e belle arti* 62 (1989–90), pp. 59–132.

Pictet, Marc-Auguste, *Correspondance: sciences et techniques*, ed. Jean Cassaigneau, Jean-Michel Pictet and Jean-Claude Pont, 4 vols, Geneva, 1996–2004.

Pilla, Leopoldo, 'Cenno Storico sui progressi della Orittognosia e della Geognosia in Italia', *Il Progresso delle Scienze, delle Lettere e delle Arti*, vol. 2 (1832), pp. 37–81, vol. 3 (1832), pp. 165–234, vol. 5 (1833), pp. 5–41.

——, *Notizie storiche della mia vita quotidiana a cominciare dal 1mo gennaio 1830 in poi*, ed. Massimo Discenza, Venafro, 1996.

[Piozzi, Hester Lynch], *Glimpses of Italian Society in the 18th Century, from the Journal of Mrs Piozzi*, London, 1892.

——, *Observations and Reflections Made in the Course of a Journey through France, Italy and Germany*, Dublin, 1789.

Pixérécourt, R.-C. Guilbert de, *La Tête de mort; ou, Les Ruines de Pompeïa: Mélodrame en trois actes*, Paris, 1828.

Platière, Roland de la, *Lettres écrites de Suisse, d'Italie, de Sicile et de Malthe*, Amsterdam, 1780.

[Playfair, John], *The Works of John Playfair Esq., with a Memoir of the Author*, 4 vols, Edinburgh, 1822.

Poggendorff, J.C., *Poggendorffs biographisch-literarisches Handwörterbuch für Mathematik, Astronomie, Physik mit Geophysik, Chemie, Kristallographie und verwandte Wissensgebiete*, Leipzig, 1863.

[Ricciardi, Francesco, Count Camaldoli], 'Discorso letto dal Presidente Conte Ricciardi nella tornata dell'Accademia alle Scienze del 14 Febbraio 1832', *Scritti e Documenti Varii di Francesco Ricciardi Conte di Camaldoli*, Naples, 1873, pp. 425–35.

Ricciardi, Giuseppe, *The Autobiography of an Italian Rebel*, London, 1860.

Richard, Abbé Jérôme, *Description historique et critique de l'Italie, ou Nouveaux mémoires sur l'état actuel de son gouvernement, des sciences, des arts, du commerce, de la population et de l'histoire naturelle*, 6 vols, Paris, 1766.

[Robert, Leopold], *Leopold Robert – Marcotte d'Argenteuil Correspondance 1824–1835 Publiée par Pierre Gassier avec la collaboration de Maryse Schmidt-Surdez*, Neuchatel, n.d.

[Rochefoucauld-d'Enville], E. Jovy, 'La Correspondance du Duc de Rochefoucauld-d'Enville et de George Louis Le Sage Conservée à la Bibliothèque de Genève', *Bulletin du Bibliophile* (1917), pp. 461–90; (1918), pp. 35–55, 135–51.

[Roscoe, Thomas], *The Tourist in Italy, by Thomas Roscoe, Illustrated from drawings by J.D. Harding*, London, 1832.

Ruskin, John, *Praeterita*, Edinburgh, 2019.

Sade, Marquis de, *Journey to Italy*, ed. and trans. James A. Steintrager, Toronto, 2020.

Saint-Non, Jean-Claude Richard de, *Voyage Pittoresque, ou Description des royaumes de Naples et de Sicile*, 5 vols, Paris, 1781–6.

Sass, Henry, *A Journey to Rome and Naples, giving an account of the present state of society in Italy, and containing observations on the fine arts*, London, 1818.

Scott, John, *Sketches of France, Switzerland and Italy*, London, 1821.

Scrope, George Poulett, *Considerations on Volcanos, the probable causes of their phenomena, the laws which determine their march, the disposition of their products, and the connection with the present and past history of the globe*, London, 1825.

——, 'Review of *Principles of Geology* . . . by Charles Lyell, 3rd edition. In 4 vols, 1835', *Quarterly Review* 53 (1835), pp. 406–48.

Seconda Lettera di un Legista Napolitano ad un suo fratello in provincia, Naples, 1794.

[Severn, Joseph], *Joseph Severn: Letters and Memoirs*, ed. Grant F. Scott, Aldershot, 2005.

Shelley, Percy Bysshe, *The Letters of Percy Bysshe Shelley*, vol. 2, *Shelley in Italy*, ed. Frederick L. Jones, Oxford, 1964.

[Sherlock, Martin], *Letters from an English Traveller Martin Sherlock Esq. translated from the French original printed at Genqva,* London, 1780.

[Shortt, W.T.P.], *A Visit to Milan, Florence and Rome. The Subterranean Cities Herculaneum and Pompeii, and the crater of Vesuvius in 1821. By W.T.P. Shortt, A.B. of Worcester College Oxford*, London, 1823.

Simond, Louis, *A Tour in Italy and Sicily*, London, 1828.

[Smith, Charlotte], *The Collected Letters of Charlotte Smith*, ed. Judith Phillips Stanton, Bloomington, 2003.

Smith, James Edward, *Sketches of a Tour on the Continent*, 3 vols, London, 1807.

Sotis, Biagio, *Dissertazione fisico-chimica dell'ultima eruzione vesuviana*, Naples, 1804.

Staël, Madame de, *Corinne, or Italy*, trans. Sylvia Raphael, Oxford, 2008.

——, *Les Carnets de Voyage de Madame de Staël, contribution à la genèse de ses œuvres*, ed. Simone Balayé, Geneva, 1971.

Starke, Mariana, *Information and Directions for Travellers on the Continent*, 5th edn, Paris, 1826.

Stendhal, *Oeuvres intimes*, 2 vols, Paris, 1982.

——, *Rome, Naples et Florence*, Paris, 1987.

Sutherland, David, *A Tour up the Straits, from Gibraltar to Constantinople: with the leading events in the present war between the Austrians, the Russians and the Turks, to the commencement of the year 1789*, London, 1790.

Swinburne, Henry, *Travels in the Two Sicilies by Henry Swinburne, Esq. in the years 1777, 1778, 1779, and 1780*, 4 vols, 2nd edn, London, 1790.

Talbot, Marianne, *Life in the South: The Naples Journal of Marianne Talbot, 1829–32*, ed. Michael Heafford, Cambridge, 2012.

[Uwins, Thomas], *A Memoir of Thomas Uwins, R.A. late Keeper of the Royal Galleries by Mrs Uwins with letters to his brothers during his seven years spent in Italy*, 2 vols, London, 1858.

Valenciennes, Pierre-Henri de, *Elements de perspective practique a l'usage des artistes*, Paris, 1799.

Vigée-Lebrun, Élisabeth, *Souvenirs 1755–1842*, ed. Geneviève Haroche-Buzinac, Paris, 2008.

Viscardi, Ferdinando, *Breve Riposta alla lettera del Signor Abate Tata de' 21 Agosto 1794. Di Ferdinando Viscardi, regio operatore di fisica sperimentale*, Naples, 1794.

Waldie, Jane, *Sketches descriptive of Italy in the years 1816 and 1817: with a brief account of travels in various parts of France and Switzerland*, 3 vols, London, 1820.

Webb, William, *Minutes of Remarks on subjects picturesque, moral and miscellaneous, made in the course along the Rhine, and during a residence in Swisserland [sic] and Italy, in the years 1822 and 1823*, 2 vols, London, 1827.

Westphal, Jean Henry, *Guide pour accompagner la carte des environs de Naples*, Rome, 1828.

[Whewell, William], '[Review of] *Principles of Geology* . . . by Charles Lyell', *British Critic* 9 (1830), pp. 180–206.

[Wilkie, David], *The Life of Sir David Wilkie with his Journals, Tours, and Critical Remarks on Works of Art; and a Selection of his Correspondence*, ed. Allan Cunningham, 3 vols, London, 1843.

Willis, Nathaniel Parker, *Pencillings by the Way, written during some years of residence and travel in Europe*, Auburn, 1854.

[Wilmot, Catherine], *An Irish Peer on the Continent (1801–1803), Being the Narrative of the Tour of Stephen, 2nd Earl Mount Cashell, Through France, Italy etc. as related by Catherine Wilmot*, ed. Thomas U. Sadleir, London, 1920.

Secondary Literature

Alisio, Giancarlo, Andrea De Rosa, Pier and Trastulli, Paolo Emilio, *Napoli Com'Era nelle gouaches del Sette e Ottocento*, 5th edn, Rome, 2004.

Altick, Richard D., *The Shows of London*, Cambridge MA, 1978.

Appel, Toby, *The Cuvier-Geoffrey Debate: French Biology in the Decades before Darwin*, Oxford, 1987.

Ashfield, Andrew and de Bolla, Peter (eds), *The Sublime: A Reader in British Eighteenth-century Aesthetic Theory*, Cambridge, 1996.

August Kopisch: Maler, Dichter, Entdecker, Erfinder, Berlin, [2016].

Bann, Steven, 'Leopold Robert and the Afterlife of Antiquity', in *Regarding Romantic Rome*, ed. Richard Wrigley, Oxford and Berne, n.d., pp. 69–90.

Barbagallo, Francesco, 'The Rothschilds in Naples', *Journal of Modern Italian Studies* 5 (2000), pp. 294–309.

Barca, Stefania, *Enclosing Water: Nature and Political Economy in a Mediterranean Valley, 1796–1916*, Cambridge, 2010.

Barndt, Kerstin, 'Working Through Ruins: Berlin's Neues Museum', *Germanic Review* 86 (2011), pp. 296–9.

Baugh, Christopher, *Garrick and Loutherbourg*, Cambridge, 1990.

——, 'Philippe de Loutherbourg: Technology-driven Entertainment and Spectacle in the Late Eighteenth Century', *Huntington Library Quarterly* 70, 2 (2007), pp. 251–68.

Baum, Constanze, 'Ruined Waking Thoughts: William Beckford as a visitor to Pompeii', in *Pompeii in the Public Imagination*, ed. Hales and Paul, pp. 36–47.

Beard, Mary, 'Taste and the Antique: Visiting Pompeii in the Nineteenth Century', in *Rediscovering the Ancient World on the Bay of Naples, 1710–1890*, ed. Carol Mattusch, pp. 205–28.

Beck-Saiello, Emilie, *Le Chevalier Volaire: Un peintre français à Naples au XVIIIe siècle*, Naples, 2004.

——, *Pierre Jacques Volaire 1729–1799 dit le Chevalier Volaire*, Paris, 2010.

Behlman, Lee, 'The Sentinel at Pompeii: An Exemplum for the Nineteenth Century', in Coates and Seydl, *Antiquity Recovered*, pp. 157–70.

Bell, David, *The First Total War: Napoleon's Europe and the Birth of Warfare as We Know It*, Boston, 2007.

Bennett, Tony, 'The Exhibitionary Complex', *New Formations* 4 (1988), pp. 73–102.

Bermingham, Ann, 'Landscape-O-Rama: The Exhibition Landscape at Somerset House and the Rise of Popular Landscape Entertainments', in *Art on the Line: The Royal Academy Exhibitions at Somerset House, 1780–1836*, ed. David H. Solkin, New Haven and London, 2001, pp. 127–43.

——, 'Technologies of Illusion: De Loutherbourg's Eidophusikon in Eighteenth-century London', *Art History* 39 (2016), pp. 376–99.

Bertrand, Dominique, 'Ce volcan en éruption de livres: Dumas face au Vésuve', in *Le Vésuve en éruption*, ed. Emilie Beck Saiello and Dominique Bertrand, pp. 179–89.

Bertrand, Gilles, *Le Grand Tour Revisité. Pour une archéologie du tourisme: Le Voyage des Français en Italie (milieu XVIIIe siècle–début XIXe siècle)*, Rome, 2008.

Black, Jeremy, *Italy and the Grand Tour*, New Haven and London, 2003.

Black, John, 'The Eruption of Vesuvius in Pacini's *L'Ultimo Giorno di Pompei*', *Donizetti Society Journal* 6 (1988), p. 95.

Blanckaert, Claude, 'On the Origins of French Ethnography: William Edwards and the Doctrine of Race', in *Bones, Bodies and Behavior: Essays in Behavioral Anthropology*, ed. George Stocking, Wisconsin, 1990, pp. 18–55.

Blix, Goran, *From Paris to Pompeii: French Romanticism and the Cultural Politics of Archaeology*, Philadelphia, 2009.

Blocksidge, Martin, *A Life Lived Quickly: Tennyson's Friend Arthur Hallam and his Legend*, Brighton, 2011.

Bluhm, Andreas and Lippincott, Louise, *Light: The Industrial Age 1750–1900: Art, Science, Technology and Society*, Amsterdam and Pittsburgh, 2000.

Braun, Theodore E.D. and Radner, John B. (eds), *The Lisbon Earthquake of 1755: Representations and Reactions*, Oxford, 2005.

Brewer, John, 'Between Distance and Sympathy: Dr John Moore's Philosophical Travel Writing', *Modern Intellectual History* 11, 3 (2014), pp. 655–75.

—— 'Sensibility and the Urban Panorama', *Huntington Library Quarterly* 70 (2007), pp. 229–49.

—— 'Visiting Vesuvius: guides, local knowledge, sublime tourism and science, 1760–1890', *Journal of Modern History* 93 (March 2021), 1–33.

——, 'Visitors' Books and Travel Narratives: The Case of Romantic Vesuvius', *Studies in Travel Writing* 25, 3 (2023), pp. 350–75.

——, 'Whose Grand Tour?', in *The English Prize: The Capture of the Westmorland, An Episode of the Grand Tour*, ed. Maria Dolores Sanchez-Jauequi Alpanes and Scott Wilcox, New Haven, 2012, pp. 45–62.

Buckland, Adelene, *Novel Science: Fiction and the Invention of Nineteenth-century Geology*, Chicago, 2013.

Buzard, James, *The Beaten Track: European Tourism, Literature, and the Ways to 'Culture', 1800–1918*, Oxford, 1993.

Calaresu, Melissa, 'Collecting Neapolitans: The Representation of Street Life in Late Eighteenth-century Naples', in Calaresu and Hills, *New Approaches to Naples*, pp. 175–202.

——, 'Constructing an Intellectual Identity: Autobiography and Biography in Eighteenth-century Naples', *Journal of Modern Italian Studies* 6, 2 (2001), pp. 157–77.

——, 'From the Street to the Stereotype: Urban Space, Travel and the Picturesque in Late Eighteenth-century Naples', *Italian Studies* 62 (2007), pp. 189–203.

Calaresu, Melissa and Hills, Helen, *New Approaches to Naples, c.1500–c.1800: The Power of Place*, Farnham, 2013.

Candela, Andrea, 'On the Earth's Revolutions: Floods and Extinct Volcanoes in Northern Italy at the End of the Eighteenth Century', in *Geology and Religion: A History of Harmony and Hostility*, ed. M. Kölbl-Ebert, London, 2009, pp. 89–93.

Castiglione, Ruggiero di, *La Massoneria nelle due Sicilie e i 'fratelli' meridionali del '700*, 2nd edn, 6 vols, Rome, 2008–14.

Cavaliero, Roderick, *The Last of the Crusaders: The Knights of St John and Malta in the Eighteenth Century*, Valletta, 2001.

Ceglie, Rosella De, *'L'anello mancante': L'opera di O.G. Costa nella biologia italiana del primo Ottocento*, Bari, 1999.

Ceserani, Giovanna, 'Antiquarian Transformations in Eighteenth-century Europe', in *World Antiquarianism: Comparative Perspectives*, ed. Alain Schnapp, Los Angeles, 2013, pp. 317–42.

Chard, Chloe, *Tristes Plaisirs: A Critical Reader of the Romantic Grand Tour*, Manchester, 2014.

Charles-Vallin, Thérèse, *Les aventures du chevalier géologue Déodat de Dolomieu*, Grenoble, 2003.

Ciancio, Luca, *Le Colonne del Tempo: il 'Tempio di Sarapide' a Pozzuoli nella storia della geologia, dell'archeologia e dell'arte (1750–1900)*, Florence, 2009.

Clifford, James, *Routes: Travel and Translation in the Late Twentieth Century*, Cambridge MA, 1997.

Coates, Victoria C. Gardner, Lapatin, Kenneth and Seydl, Jon L. (eds), *The Last Days of Pompeii: Decadence, Apocalypse, Resurrection*, Los Angeles, 2012.

Coates, Victoria C. Gardner and Seydl, Jon L., *Antiquity Recovered: The Legacy of Pompeii and Herculaneum*, Malibu, 2007.

Cocco, Sean, *Watching Vesuvius: A History of Science and Culture in Early Modern Italy*, Chicago, 2013.

Comment, Bernard, *The Painted Panorama*, trans. Anne-Marie Glasheen, New York, 2000.

Conisbee, Philip, Faunce, Sarah, Strick, Jeremy and Galassi, Peter, *In the Light of Italy: Corot and Early Open-air Painting*, New Haven and London, 1996.

Constantine, David, *Fields of Fire: A Life of Sir William Hamilton*, London, 2001.

Cooper, Alix, 'From the Alps to Egypt (and Back Again): Dolomieu, Scientific Voyaging, and the Construction of the Field in Eighteenth-century Natural History', in *Making Space for Science: Territorial Themes in the Shaping of Knowledge*, ed. Crosbie Smith and John Agar, Basingstoke, 1998, pp. 39–63.

Crary, Jonathan, *Techniques of the Observer: On Visions and Modernity in the Nineteenth Century*, Cambridge MA, 1990.

Cunningham, Frank F., *James Forbes: Pioneer Scottish Glaciologist*, Edinburgh, 1990.

Dahl, Curtis, 'Bulwer-Lytton and the School of Catastrophe', *Philological Quarterly* 32 (1953), pp. 428–42.

Daly, Nicholas, 'The Volcanic Disaster Narrative: From Pleasure Garden to Canvas, Page and Stage', *Victorian Studies* 53, 2 (2011), pp. 255–85.

D'Angelo, Fabio, *Dal Regno di Napoli alla Francia. Viaggi ed esilio tra Sette e Ottocento*, Naples, 2018.

——, 'Les hommes de science napolitains en exil en France, des passeurs scientifiques et politiques (1799–1820)', *Revue d'Histoire du XIXème Siècle* (2016), pp. 39–57.

——, 'Les Institutions scientifiques à l'heure francaise', in *Le royaume de Naples à l'heure francaise. Revisiter l'histoire du decennio francese (1806–1815)*, ed. Pierre-Marie Delpu, Igor Moullier and Melanie Traversier, Villeneuve-d'Ascq, 2018, pp. 245–57.

D'Arcy Wood, Gillen, *The Shock of the Real: Romanticism and Visual Culture, 1760–1860*, New York, 2001.

——, *Tambora: The Eruption That Changed the World*, Princeton NJ, 2014.

D'Argenio, Bruno, 'Leopoldo Pilla (1805–1848): A Young Combatant Who Lived for Geology and Died for his Country', *Geographical Society of America* 411 (2006), pp. 211–23.

Daston, Lorraine, 'Observation and Enlightenment', in *Scholars in Action: The Practice of Knowledge and the Figure of the Savant in the 18th Century*, ed. Andre Holenstein, Hubert Steinke and Martin Huber, 2 vols, Leiden, 2013, vol. 2, pp. 657–77.

Davis, John A., 'Casting off the "Southern Problem": or the Peculiarities of the South Reconsidered', in *Italy's 'Southern Question': Orientalism in One Country*, ed. Jane Schneider, Oxford, 1998, pp. 205–24.

——, 'Italy', in *The War for the Public Mind: Political Censorship in Nineteenth-century Europe*, ed. Robert Justin Goldstein, Westport CN, 2000, pp. 81–124.

——, *Naples and Napoleon: Southern Italy and the European Revolutions 1780–1860*, Oxford, 2006.

Dawes, Barbara, *La comunità inglese a Napoli*, Naples, 1988.

De Lucia, Maddalena and Russo, Massimo, 'One Hundred and Twenty Years of Italian and Vesuvian History in the Lava Medals Collection of the Observatorio Vesuvino', *Epitome* 4 (2011), p. 144.

Delli Quadri, Rosa Maria, *Nel Sud Romantico. Diplomatiche e Viaggiatori Inglesi alla Scoperta del Mezzogiorno Borbonico*, Naples, 2012.

Dolan, Brian, 'Governing Matters: The Values of English Education in the Earth Sciences, 1790–1830', PhD thesis, Cambridge University, 1995.

——, 'Representing Novelty: Charles Babbage, Charles Lyell, and Experiments in Early Victorian Geology', *History of Science* 36 (1998), pp. 299–327.

Duffy, Cian, *The Landscapes of the Sublime, 1700–1830: Classic Ground*, Basingstoke and New York, 2013.

Dwyer, Eugene, 'Science or Morbid Curiosity? The Castes of Giuseppe Fiorelli and the Last Days of Romantic Pompeii', in *Antiquity Recovered*, ed. Coates and Seydl, pp. 171–88.

Dwyer, Philip G., '"It Still Makes Me Shudder": Memories of Massacres and Atrocities during the Revolutionary and Napoleonic Wars', *War in History* 16, 4 (2009), pp. 381–405.

Echlin, Alexander, 'Dynasty, Archaeology and Conservation: The Bourbon Display of Pompeii and Herculaneum in Eighteenth-century Naples', *Journal of the History of Collections* 26 (2014), pp. 145–59.

Edwards, Catharine, 'The Roads to Rome', in *Imagining Rome: British Artists and Rome in the Nineteenth Century*, ed. Michael Liversidge and Catharine Edwards, London, [1996].

Fabian, Johannes, *Time and the Other: How Anthropology Makes its Object*, New York, 1983.

Ferraro, Giovanni, 'Manuali di geometria elementare nella Napoli preunita', *History of Education and Children's Literature* 3, 2 (2008), pp. 103–39.

Ferri, Sabrina, *Ruins Past: Modernity in Italy, 1744–1836*, Oxford, 2015.

Fineman, Joel, 'The History of the Anecdote: Fiction and Fiction 1', in *The New Historicism*, ed. H. Arram Veeser, New York, 1989, pp. 49–76.

Finley, Milton, *The Most Monstrous of Wars: The Napoleonic Guerrilla War in Southern Italy, 1806–1811*, Chapel Hill NC, 1994.

Fino, Lucio, *Ercolano e Pompei tra'700 e'800. Acquerelli, disegni, stampe e ricordi di viaggio*, Naples, 2005.

——, *Gouaches napoletane nelle collezioni private*, Naples, 1998.

——, *Il Vesuvio del Grand Tour. Vedute e scritti di tre secoli*, Naples, 2012.

Fittipaldi, Arturo, 'Museums and Safeguarding an Artistic Heritage in Naples in the Eighteenth Century: Some Reflections', *Journal of the History of Collections* 19, 11 (2007), pp. 191–202.

Ford, Rebecca, 'Images of the Earth, Images of Man: The Mineralogical Plates of the *Encyclopédie*', in *Histoires de la Terre*, ed. Lyle and McCallam, pp. 57–73.

Foscari, Giuseppe, *Teodoro Monticelli e l'Economia delle acque nel Mezzogiorno moderno*, Salerno, 2009.

Franklin, Adrian and Crang, Mike, 'The Trouble with Tourism and Travel Theory?', *Tourist Studies* 1, 1 (2001), pp. 5–22.

Freshman, Douglas W., *Life of Horace Benedict de Saussure*, London, 1920.

Friedrich, Silke, *Johann Moritz Rugendas: Reisebilder zwichen Empirie und Empfindung*, Frankfurt, 2017.

Fritzche, Peter, *Stranded in the Present: Modern Time and the Melancholy of History*, Cambridge MA, 2004.

Furchheim, Federigo (ed.), *Bibliografia del Vesuvio. Compilata e corredata di note critiche estratte dai più autorevoli scrittori vesuviani*, Cambridge, 2011.

Gallagher, Catherine and Greenblatt, Stephen, *Practicing New Historicism*, Chicago, 2000.

Galliani, R., 'Le duc de la Rochefoucauld et Thomas Paine', *Annales Historiques de la Révolution Française* 52 (1980), pp. 425–36.

Ganter, Henri, *Histoire du service militaire des regiments suisses à la solde de l'Angleterre, de Naples et de Rome*, Geneva, n.d.

Gasperini, Paolo and Musella, Silvana, *Un Viaggio al Vesuvio: Il Vesuvio visto attraverso diari, lettere e resoconti di viaggiatori*, Naples, 1991.

Gassier, Pierre, *Leopold Robert*, Neuchatel, 1983.

Ginzburg, Carlo and Poni, Carlo, ' "The Name and the Game": Unequal Exchange and the Historiographic Marketplace', in *Microhistory and the Lost Peoples of Europe*, ed. Edward Muir and Guido Ruggiero, Baltimore, 1991, pp. 1–10.

Gordon, Alden R., 'Subverting the Secret of Herculaneum: Archaeological Espionage in the Kingdom of Naples', in *Antiquity Recovered: The Legacy of Pompeii and Herculaneum*, ed. Victoria C. Gardner Coates and Jon L. Seydl, Los Angeles, 2007, pp. 37–57.

Granovetter, Mark S., 'The Strength of Weak Ties', *American Journal of Sociology* 78 (1973), pp. 1360–80.

——, 'The Strength of Weak Ties: A Network Theory Revisited', *Sociological Theory* 1 (1983), pp. 201–33.

Gray, Rosalind P., *Russian Genre Painting in the Nineteenth Century*, Oxford, 2000.

Grell, Chantal, *Herculanum et Pompéi dans les récits des voyageurs français du XVIIIe siècle*, Naples, 1982.

Guerra, Corinna, 'If You Don't Have a Good Laboratory, Find a Good Volcano: Mount Vesuvius as a Natural Chemical Laboratory in Eighteenth-century Italy', *Ambix* 62, 3 (2015), pp. 245–65.

Gunning, Tom, 'An Aesthetic of Astonishment: Early Film and the (In)Credulous Spectator', *Art and Text* 34 (1989), pp. 114–24.

Hales, Shelley and Paul, Joanna (eds), *Pompeii in the Public Imagination from its Re-discovery to Today*, Oxford, 2011.

Hansen, Peter, *The Summits of Modern Man: Mountaineering after the Enlightenment*, Cambridge MA, 2013.

Heringman, Noah, *Romantic Rocks, Aesthetic Geology*, Ithaca NY, 2004.

——, *Sciences of Antiquity: Romantic Antiquarianism, Natural History, and Knowledge Work*, Oxford, 2013.

Hilliker, Rebecca, 'Karl Friedrich Schinkel's Diorama and Panorama Art for *Einfache Menschen*: A Classical-Romantic's Search for the Sublime', *Theatre History Studies* 8 (1988), pp. 99–115.

Holland, Robert, *Blue-Water Empire: The British in the Mediterranean since 1800*, London, 2012.

Holmes, Richard, *The Age of Wonder: How the Romantic Generation Discovered the Beauty and Terror of Science*, London, 2008.

Huhtamo, Erkki, *Illusions in Motion: Media Archaeology of the Moving Panorama and Related Spectacles*, Cambridge MA, 2013.

Hyde, Ralph, *Panoramania! The Art and Entertainment of the 'All-Embracing' View*, London, 1988.

Ingamells, John, *A Dictionary of British and Irish Travellers in Italy, 1701–1800*, New Haven and London, 1999.

Ingold, Tim, *The Perception of the Environment: Essays on Livelihood, Dwelling and Skill*, London, 2022.

Jacobelli, Luciana, *Pompei. La Costruzione di un mito. Arte, letteratura, aneddotica di un'icona turistica*, Rome, 2008.

James, Kevin J., 'The Album of the Fathers and the Father of all Albums: Inscribing Wonder and Loss in the Grande Chartreuse', in *Continental Tourism, Travel Writing and the Consumption of Culture*, ed. Bryan Colbert and Lucy Morrison, London, 2020, pp. 41–61.

James, Kevin J. and Vincent, Patrick, 'The Guestbook as Historical Source', *Journal of Tourism History* 8, 2 (2016), pp. 147–66.

Jenkins, Ian and Sloan, Kim (eds), *Vases and Volcanoes: Sir William Hamilton and his Collections*, London, 1996.

Johns, Alessa, *Bluestocking Feminism and British-German Cultural Transfer, 1750–1837*, Ann Arbor MI, 2014.

Kalla-Bishop, P.M., *Italian Railways*, Newton Abbot, 1971.

Kerr, D.G.G., *Sir Edmund Head: A Scholarly Governor*, Toronto, 1954.

Laudan, Rachel, *From Mineralogy to Geology: The Foundations of a Science, 1650–1830*, Chicago, 1987.

Lazer, Estelle, *Resurrecting Pompeii*, Abingdon, 2009.

Leask, Nigel, 'Mont Blanc's Mysterious Voice: Shelley and Huttonian Earth Science', in *The Third Culture: Literature and Science*, ed. Elinor S. Shaffer, Berlin, 1998, pp. 182–203.

Leontyeva, Galina, *Karl Briullov: Artist of Russian Romanticism*, Bournemouth, 1996.

Lilti, Antoine, *Le Monde des salons: sociabilité et mondanité à Paris au 18e siècle*, Paris, 2005.

Lyle, Louise and McCallam, David (eds), *Histoires de la Terre: Earth Sciences and French Culture 1740–1940*, Amsterdam, 2008.

Maag, Albert, *Geschichte der Schweizertruppen in neapolitanischen Diensten 1825–1861*, Zurich, 1909.

Matthews, G.M., 'A Volcano's Voice in Shelley', *English Literary History* 24, 3 (1957), pp. 191–228.

Mattusch, Carol (ed.), *Rediscovering the Ancient World on the Bay of Naples, 1710–1890*, Washington DC, 2013.

McCallam, David, 'Exploring Volcanoes in the Late French Enlightenment: The Savant and the Sublime', *Journal of Eighteenth-century Studies* 29 (2006), pp. 47–59.

——, *Volcanoes in Eighteenth-century Europe: An Essay in Environmental Humanities*, Oxford, 2019.

McCalman, Iain, 'The Art of de Loutherbourg's Eidophusikon', in *Sensation and Sensibility: Viewing Gainsborough's Cottage Door*, ed. Ann Bermingham, New Haven and London, 2005, pp. 181–97.

MacCartney, P.J., 'Charles Lyell and G.B. Brocchi: A Study in Comparative Historiography', *British Journal for the History of Science* 9 (1976), pp. 177–89.

Mangoni, Adriana Pignatelli and Cabianca, Vincenzo, *Viaggio tra i vulcani d'Italia e di Francia tra Illuminismo e Romanticismo*, Naples, n.d.

Mercier-Faivre, Anne-Marie, 'Eruptions dans la presse: l'image du vesuve dans la presses europenne francophone du XVIIIe siecle', in *Le Vésuve en eruption: Savoir, representations, practiques*, ed. Émilie Beck Saiello and Dominique Bertrand, Clemont-Ferrand, 2013, pp. 83–98.

Merwe, P.J. van de, 'The Life and Theatrical Career of Clarkson Stanfield (1793–1867)', PhD thesis, Bristol University, 1979.

Miller, Mary Ashburn, *A Natural History of Revolution: Violence and Nature in the French Revolutionary Imagination 1789–1794*, Ithaca NY, 2011.

Moe, Nelson, *The View from Vesuvius: Italian Culture and the Southern Question*, Berkeley and Los Angeles, 2006.

Molesky, Mark, *This Gulf of Fire: The Great Lisbon Earthquake or Apocalypse in the Age of Science and Reason*, New York, 2015.

Montègre, Gilles, *La Rome des Français au temps des Lumières*, Rome, 2011.

Moormann, Erik, *Pompeii's Ashes: The Reception of the Cities Buried by Vesuvius in Literature, Music and Drama*, Boston, 2015.

Morrell, Jack and Thackray, Arnold, *Gentlemen of Science: Early Years of the British Association for the Advancement of Science*, Oxford, 1981.

Morus, Iwan Rhys, 'Invisible Technicians, Instrument Makers, Artisans', in *A Companion to the History of Science*, ed. Bernard Lightman, Chichester, 2016, pp. 97–110.

Nazzaro, Antonio, *Il Vesuvio: Storia eruttiva e teorie vulcanologiche*, Napoli, 1997.

Nazzaro, Antonio and di Gregorio, Angela, 'The Contribution of the Neapolitan Geologist, Teodoro Monticelli (1759–1845) to the Development of Geology', in *Volcanoes and History, Proceedings of the 20th INHIGEO Symposium, 19–25 September 1995*, ed. Nicoletta Morello Genoa, 1998, pp. 415–39.

Nolta, David, 'The Body of the Collector and the Collected Body in William Hamilton's Naples', *Eighteenth-Century Studies* 31, 1 (1997), pp. 108–14.

O'Connor, Ralph, *The Earth on Show: Fossils and the Poetics of Popular Science, 1802–1856*, Chicago, 2007.

Oettermann, Stephen, *Panorama: History of a Mass Medium*, trans. Deborah L. Schneider, New York, 1996.

Oliver, Andrew, *American Travelers on the Nile: Early US Visitors to Egypt*, Cairo, 2014.

Ortner, Sherry, *Life and Death on Mount Everest: Sherpas and Himalayan Mountaineering*, Princeton NJ, 1999.

Outram, Dorinda, *Georges Cuvier: Vocation, Science and Authority in Post-Revolutionary France*, Manchester, 1984.

Parslow, Christopher Charles, *Rediscovering Antiquity: Karl Weber and the Excavation of Herculaneum, Pompeii, and Stabiae*, Cambridge, 1998.

Perkins, John, 'Creating Chemistry in Provincial France before the Revolution: The Examples of Nancy and Metz. Part 2. Metz', *Ambix* 51, 1 (2004), pp. 43–75.

Perovic, Sanja, *The Calendar in Revolutionary France: Perceptions of Time in Literature, Culture, Politics*, Cambridge, 2012.

Petitti, Carlo Ilarione, *Delle strade ferrate italiane e del migliore ordinamento di esse. Cinque discorsi*, Capolago, 1845.

Petrusewicz, Marta, 'Before the Southern Question: "Native" ideas of backwardness and remedies in the Kingdom of Two Sicilies, 1815–49', in *Italy's 'Southern Question': Orientalism in One Country*, ed. Jane Schneider, pp. 27–46.

Pinson, Stephen, *Speculating Daguerre: Art and Enterprise in the Work of L.J.M. Daguerre*, Chicago, 2012.

Posey, W.B., *Frontier Mission: A History of Religion West of the Southern Appalachians*, Lexington KY, 1966.

Quenet, Grégory, 'When Geology Encounters a Real Catastrophe: From Theoretical Earthquakes to the Lisbon Disaster', in *Histoires de la Terre: Earth Sciences and French Culture 1740–1940*, ed. Louise Lyle and David McCallam, Amsterdam, 2008, pp. 37–56.

Raj, Kapil, 'Go-Betweens, Travelers, and Cultural Translators', in *A Companion to the History of Science*, ed. Bernard Lightman, Chichester, 2016, pp. 39–57.

——, 'Mapping Knowledge Go-Betweens in Calcutta, 1770–1820', in *The Brokered World: Go-Betweens and Global Intelligence 1770–1820*, ed. Simon Schaffer, Lissa Roberts, Kapil Raj and James Delbourgo, Sagmore Beach, 2009, pp. 105–50.

Rao, Anna Maria, 'Esercito e società a Napoli nelle riforme del secondo Settecento', *Studi Storici* 28 (1978), pp. 623–77.

Rapport, Rhoda, 'Dangerous Words: Diluvialism, Neptunism, Catastrophism', in *The Advancements of Learning: Essays in Honour of Paolo Rossi*, ed. John Heilbron, Florence, 2007, pp. 101–31.

Reiss, Tom, *The Black Count: Glory, Revolution, Betrayal, and the Real Count of Monte Cristo*, New York, 2012.

Richter, Dieter, *Napoli Cosmopolita: Viaggiatori e communità straniere nell'Ottocento*, Naples, 2002.

Roberts, Charlotte, 'Living with the Ancient Romans: Past and Present in Eighteenth-century Encounters with Herculaneum and Pompeii', *Huntington Library Quarterly* 78, 1 (2015), pp. 61–85.

Roberts, Geraldine, *The Angel and the Cad: Love, Loss and Scandal in Regency England*, London, 2015.

Robertson, John, 'Enlightenment and Revolution: Naples 1799', *Transactions of the Royal Historical Society* 10 (2000), pp. 17–44.

Rogers, Shef, 'Enlarging the Prospects of Happiness: Travel Reading and Writing', in *The Cambridge History of the Book in Britain*, vol. 5, *1695–1830*, ed. Michael F. Suarez and Michael L. Turner, Cambridge, 2010, pp. 781–90.

Rojek, Chris and Urry, John, *Touring Cultures: Transformations of Travel and Theory*, London and New York, 1997.

Romano, R., *Prezzi, salari e servizi a Napoli nel secolo XVIII (1734–1806)*, Milan, 1965.

Rosenthal, Donald, 'Joseph Franque's "The Scene during the Eruption of Vesuvius"', *Philadelphia Museum of Art Bulletin* 75, 324 (1979), pp. 2–15.

Rosso, Filippo and Formicola, Francesco, *L'Eruzione del Vesuvio del 1794. Inquadramento geo-vulcanologico*. Vesuvioweb. At http://www.vesuvioweb.com/it/wp-content/uploads/Filippo-RUsso-e-Francesco-Formicola-Laruzione-del-Vesuvio-del-1794-vesuvioweb-2012.pdf.

Rovinello, Marco, 'Un grande banchiere in una piccola piazza: Carl Mayer Rothschild e il credito commerciale nel Regno delle Due Sicilie', *Società e Storia* 110 (2005), pp. 705–39.

Rowland, Ingrid D., *From Pompeii: The Afterlife of a Roman Town*, Cambridge MA, 2014.

Rudwick, Martin J.S., *Bursting the Limits of Time: The Reconstruction of Geohistory in the Age of Revolution*, Chicago, 2005.

——, 'Charles Lyell F.R.S. (1797–1875) and his London Lectures on Geology 1832–33', *Notes and Records of the Royal Society of London* 20 (1975), pp. 231–63.

——, *Worlds before Adam: The Reconstruction of Geohistory in the Age of Reform*, Chicago, 2008.

Salvadè, Anna Maria, 'Fra satira e scienza: Ferdinando Galiani il vulcanologo', in *Geographie e Storie Letterarie*, ed. Stefania Baragetti, Rosa Necchi and Anna Maria Salvadè, Milan, 2019, pp. 141–6.

Salvemini, Biagio, *Economia politica e arretratezza meridionale nell'età del Risorgimento. Luca de Samuele Cagnazzi e la diffusione dello smithianesimo nel regno di Napoli*, Lecce, 1981.

Samaran, C., 'Alexandre Dumas Napolitain', *Europe* 48, 490 (1970), pp. 125–30.

Samu, Margaret, 'The Reception of Karl Briullov's *Last Day of Pompeii* at the Salon of 1834', *Art Bulletin* 103, 2 (2021), pp. 77–103.

Scarth, Alwyn, *Vesuvius: A Biography*, Princeton NJ, 2009.

Schaffer, Simon, 'Natural Philosophy and Public Spectacle in the Eighteenth Century', *History of Science* 21, 1 (1983), pp. 1–43.

Schama, Simon, *Dead Certainties: Unwarranted Speculations*, New York, 1991.

Schnapp, Alain, 'The Antiquarian Culture of Eighteenth-century Naples as a Laboratory for New Ideas', in *Rediscovering the Ancient World on the Bay of Naples, 1710–1860*, ed. Carol Mattusch, Washington DC, 2013.

Schneider, Jane (ed.), *Italy's 'Southern Question': Orientalism in One Country*, Oxford, 1998.

Shapin, Steven, 'The Invisible Technician', *American Scientist* 77 (1989), pp. 554–63.

Sigurdsson, Haraldur, *Melting the Earth: The History of Ideas of Volcanic Eruptions*, Oxford, 1999.

Sivard, Susan M., 'Upheaval and Transformation: The Volcano in American and European Art, 1765–1865', PhD thesis, Columbia University, 2011.

Sleep, Mark, 'Sir William Hamilton (1730–1803): His Works and Influence on Geology', *Annals of Science* 25, 4 (1969), pp. 67–96.

Sloan, Kim, *Alexander and John Robert Cozens: The Poetry of Landscape*, New Haven and London, 1986.

Smith, Paul, 'Thomas Cook & Sons' Vesuvian Railway', *Japan Railway and Transport Review* (March 1998), pp. 10–11.

Sorensen, Bent, 'Sir William Hamilton's Vesuvian Apparatus', *Apollo* 159 (2004), pp. 50–8.

Spary, Emma, *Utopia's Garden: French Natural History from the Old Regime to Revolution*, Chicago, 2000.

Staum, Martin S., *Labeling People: French Scholars on Society, Race and Empire*, Montreal, 2003.

Sternberger, Dolf, 'Panorama of the 19th Century', *October* 4 (1977), pp. 3–20.

Stites, Richard, *The Four Horsemen: Riding to Liberty in Post-Napoleonic Europe*, Oxford, 2014.

Tanguy, J.-C., Ribière, Ch., Scarth, A. and Tjetjep, W.S., 'Victims from Volcanic Eruptions: A Revised Database', *Bulletin of Vulcanology* 60 (1998), pp. 137–44.

Taylor, Kenneth L., 'Dolomieu', in *The Complete Dictionary of Scientific Biography*, vol. 4, Princeton NJ, 1971, pp. 149–53.

Todd, R. Larry, *Fanny Hensel: The Other Mendelssohn*, Oxford, 2009.

Toscano, Maria, 'The Figure of the Naturalist-Antiquary in the Kingdom of Naples: Giuseppe Giovene (1753–1837) and His Contemporaries', *Journal of the History of Collections* 19, 11 (2007), pp. 225–37.

Towner, John, 'The Grand Tour: A Key Phase in the History of Tourism', *Annals of Tourist Research* 112, 3 (1985), pp. 297–333.

Trisco, R.F., *The Holy See and the Nascent Church in the Middle Western United States, 1826–1850*, Rome, 1962.

Umbach, Maiken, 'Visual Culture, Scientific Images and German Small-state Politics in the Late Enlightenment', *Past and Present* 158 (1998), pp. 110–45.

Urry, John, 'Social Networks, Travel and Talk', *British Journal of Sociology* 54, 3 (2003), pp. 155–75.

——, *Sociology Beyond Societies: Mobilities in the Twenty-first Century*, London, 2000.

Vaccari, Ezio, 'Wernerian Geonosy and Italian Vulcanists', in *Abraham Gottlob Werner and the Foundation of the Geological Sciences: Selected Papers of the International Werner Symposium*, ed. Helmuth Albrecht, Freiberg, 2002, pp. 26–36.

Vai, Gian Battista, 'Light and Shadow: The Status of Italian Geology around 1807', in *The Making of the Geological Society of London*, ed. C.L.E. Lewis and S.J. Knell, Geological Society, London, Special Publications 317 (2009), pp. 179–202.

Vallière, P. de, *Honneur et Fidelité. Histoire des Suisses au Service Étranger*, Lausanne, n.d.

Il Vesuvio e le citta vesuviane 1730–1860. In ricordo di George Vallet, intro. Francesco M. De Sanctis, Naples, 1998.

Vidler, Anthony, 'The Architecture of the Uncanny: The Unhomely Houses of the Romantic Sublime', *Assemblage* 3 (1987), pp. 7–29.

Voltaire, *Oeuvres Complètes*, ed. T. Besterman et al., 147 vols, Geneva, 1968–2022.

Wallace-Hadrill, Andrew, 'Ruins and Forgetfulness: The Case of Herculaneum', in *Pompeii in the Public Imagination*, ed. Hales and Paul, pp. 367–78.

Webley, Derrick Pritchard, *Casting to the Winds: The Life and Work of Penry Williams (1802–1885)*, Aberystwyth, 1995.

Wickman, Richard Carl, 'An Evaluation of the Employment of Panoramic Scenery in the Nineteenth-century Theatre', PhD thesis, Ohio State University, 1961.

William, Elizabeth, *The Physical and the Moral: Anthropology, Physiology, and Philosophical Medicine in France, 1750–1850*, Cambridge, 1994.

Wilson, Leonard G., *Charles Lyell, the Years to 1841: The Revolution in Geology*, New Haven and London, 1972.

Wilson, Wendell E., 'The History of Mineral Collecting 1530–1799: With Notes on Twelve Hundred Early Mineral Collectors', *The Mineralogical Record* 25, 6 (1994).

Wood, Karen, 'Making and Circulating Knowledge through Sir William Hamilton's *Campi Phlegraei*', *British Journal for the History of Science* 39, 1 (2006), pp. 67–96.

Wrigley, Richard, *Roman Fever: Influence, Infection, and the Image of Rome, 1700–1870*, New Haven and London, 2013.

Young, Davis A., *Mind over Magma: The Story of Igneous Petrology*, Princeton NJ, 2003.

INDEX

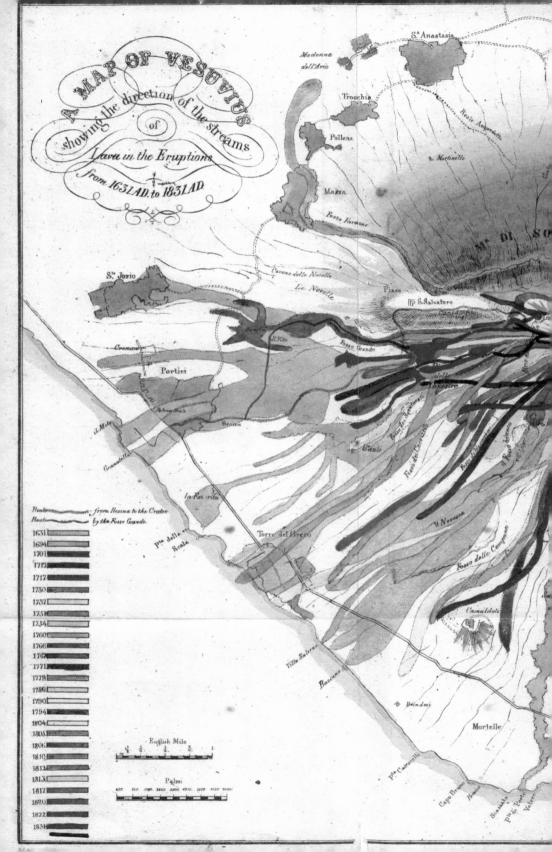

A MAP OF VESUVIUS

showing the direction of the streams

of

Lava in the Eruptions

from 1631 AD. to 1831 AD.

S.ᵗᵃ Anastasia

Madonna dell'Arco

Trocchia

Reale Acquedotto

Pollena

S. Martinelli

Massa

M.ᵗᵉ DI SO

Fosso Faraone

Cavone delle Novelle

Le Novelle

Piazo

S.ᵗᵃ Jorio

S. S. Salvatore

Cromare

Portici

S. Vito

Fosso Grande

dell'
Inventore

il Molo

Palazzitesi

Resina

Favorita

Gragnatella

la Favorita

Ercoli

Fosso del Cavallo

S.ᵗ Neccara

il Fosso Acherusa

Fosso delle Campane

P.ᵗᵃ della
Scala

Torre del Greco

Canaldoli

Villa Salerno

Basciano

S. Brindisi

Mortelle

Routes — from Resina to the Crater
Routes — by the Fosso Grande.

Year	
1631	
1694	
1701	
1712	
1717	
1730	
1737	
1751	
1754	
1760	
1766	
1767	
1771	
1779	
1786	
1790	
1794	
1804	
1805	
1806	
1810	
1812	
1813	
1817	
1820	
1822	
1834	

English Mile

Palmi

P.ᵗᵃ Catarelli

Capo Bruno

Stabia
P.gi Porto
Vetra